D1604076

The
Collected Plays
of
Gwen Pharis Ringwood

For *Megan, Mark* and *all the children*

E.D.R.

The
Collected Plays
of
Gwen Pharis Ringwood

edited by

Enid Delgatty Rutland

with

Biographical Note by *Marion Wilson*,
and Prefaces by
Margaret Laurence and *George Ryga*

Borealis Press
Ottawa, Canada
1982

The Publishers gratefully acknowledge the support of the Ontario Arts Council and the Canada Council.

Canadian Cataloguing in Publication Data
Ringwood, Gwen Pharis, 1910-
  The collected plays of Gwen Ringwood

Bibliography: p.
ISBN 0-88887-958-X (bound).   ISBN 0-88887-956-3 (pbk.)

I. Title.

PS8535.153A19 1982   C812'.54   C82-090012-5
PR9199.3.R56A19 1982

9 Ashburn Drive
Ottawa, Canada K2E 6N4

Printed and bound in Canada

3 7, 3 ⊦5

Contents

Acknowledgements

This book began, as so many things do, in a chance encounter. While at the InterAmerican Women Writers' Conference in Ottawa in 1978, I met Mrs. Ringwood, whom I had not seen for twenty years. Subsequently, in conversation with Margaret Laurence, we together thought of collecting Mrs. Ringwood's plays, and the project was born.

This edition brings together all the adult plays in the version preferred by the author, with the exception of the long musical plays *Look Behind You, Neighbour*, and *The Road Runs North*—omitted because much of their content consists of musical lyrics.

Though no bibliography is ever complete, the bibliography attempts to list all items by Mrs. Ringwood, including those of a slighter nature, and all critical material available at the time of completion of the book.

Mrs. Ringwood was ever helpful in the task of retrieving copies of the plays, and assisting in the editing process. Margaret Laurence read and evaluated the plays in the initial stages in preparation for her introduction, and Marion Wilson provided bibliographic editorial support as well as preparing the biographical introduction. My thanks also to George Ryga for his prefatory remarks.

I would like to express thanks to all those who collaborated in the production of this book, particularly Anton Wagner of the Playwright's Co-op, for his help in proof-reading and bibliography, to the staff of the National Library Reference and Circulation Division, to the Ontario Arts Council for financial assistance, and to Glenn Clever of Borealis Press, whose support in this project was constant.

Lastly, I would like to express gratitude to our families without whose patience this work could never have been completed.

Ottawa, 1982   Enid Delgatty Rutland

Biographical Note

Gwen Pharis Ringwood was born on August 13, 1910, in Anatone, Washington, the daughter of Leslie and Mary (Bowersock) Pharis, both teachers, both from farm backgrounds. Leslie Pharis combined farming and teaching during Gwen's childhood.

There were three boys in the family, the youngest, Robert, not born until 1925. The other two, Blaine and George, were both commissioned in the RCAF during the Second World War and both were killed in action.

Attracted by the availability of moderately-priced large land holdings in Alberta, Leslie Pharis moved his family to Barons, in the south of the province, in 1913, moving on to Magrath, near Lethbridge, in 1916. Taught first by her father, Gwen received most of her elementary and secondary schooling in Magrath, where Leslie Pharis was the only non-Mormon high school teacher. Part of her high school years were passed at Crescent Heights High School in Calgary, where one of her teachers was William ("Bible Bill") Aberhart, the father of the Alberta Social Credit Party.

In 1926 Leslie Pharis decided to try his hand at raising purebred cattle and the family moved to Valier, Montana. At Valier High School in her last year, Gwen acted in two plays. She worked for a time as bookkeeper for a store, Browning Mercantile, on the Blackfoot Indian Reservation at Browning, Montana and enrolled as a freshman at the University of Montana in 1927. Cattle farming was not a great success and the family returned to Alberta in 1929. Gwen transferred to the University of Alberta and graduated in 1934 with a Bachelor of Arts.

While still a student, she went to work as secretary to Elizabeth Sterling Haynes, Director of Drama in the Department of Extension.

The Banff School of Fine Arts, originally the Banff School of the Theatre, was established in the early thirties. Gwen was its first secretary, and the school produced her first stage play "The Dragons of Kent" in 1935. She wrote ten plays for the university radio station, CKUA, in the series "New Lamps for Old," and other plays for the Edmonton station CFRN. (The scripts of these radio plays have not been preserved by the author.) In 1937 a Rockefeller Foundation Fellowship enabled her to attend the University of North Carolina, Chapel Hill, Carolina Playmakers School where she wrote and the school produced the plays "Chris Axelson, Blacksmith," "Still Stands the House," "Pasque Flower," "Dark Harvest" and "One Man's House." She was awarded the Roland Holt Cup for outstanding work in drama and graduated with a Master of Arts in Drama. "Still Stands the House" won first prize at the Dominion Drama Festival in 1939.

Returning to Alberta in 1939 as Director of Dramatics for the Department of Extension she married Dr. John Brian ("Barney") Ringwood on September 16. In the fall of 1940 they moved to Goldfields, a frontier mining town in northern Saskatchewan, where Dr. Ringwood was the company doctor. Their first child, Stephen, was born in 1941 and in the same year Gwen won the Canadian Drama Award for outstanding service in the development of Canadian drama. A second child, Susan, was born in 1942. She wrote "The Courting of Marie Jenvrin" in that year; it was produced at the Banff School of Fine Arts and published in *Best One Act Plays of 1942* (Dodd, Mead, 1943). When her husband joined the Royal Army Medical Corps in 1942 Gwen returned to Edmonton. Under commission to the Alberta Folklore and Local History Project, which awarded her a playwriting grant, she wrote three plays: "The Jack and the Joker," "Hatfield, the Rainmaker," and "Stampede," all produced at the anff School of Fine Arts. Radio scripts from this period include "The Fight for the Invisible," produced by CBC radio, and "Niobe House." In 1946 her husband returned from the war and they moved to Lamont where their third child, Carol was born.

From 1948 to 1953, the Ringwoods lived in Edmonton. "A Fine Colored Easter Egg, or, The Drowning of Wasyl Nemitchuk" was produced in Banff and on CBC radio. A fourth child, Patrick, was born in 1949. "Widger's Way" was produced at the University of Alberta. Plays for CBC radio written at this time included "Right On Our Doorstep," "Health Scripts for Children," "Frontier to Farmland," "The Bells of England" and the political musical "The Wall" (composer, Bruce Haak).

In 1953 Gwen moved with her husband and family to Williams Lake, B.C., where she helped to revive the Players Club and initiated her Coffeehouses, evenings of short sketches. Here she wrote her only published novel *Younger Brother* (New York, Longmans, 1959).

In 1959 a new play "Maya, or, Lament for Harmonica" won first prize in the Ottawa Little Theatre Competition. In the same year she adopted "Heidi" for CBC radio, Toronto. She wrote the book and lyrics for the musical "Look Behind You Neighbor" (composer, Chet Lambertson) for Edson, Alberta's fiftieth anniversary, in 1961. In the early sixties she was a volunteer teacher of dramatics and creative writing at the Cariboo Indian School. Two compilations of the "writings and legends" of Grade 7 and 8 students, called *My Heart is Glad*, were issued by the school, in 1964 and 1965.

In 1967 she was awarded a Certificate of Merit for her outstanding contributions to Canada's centennial celebrations, and in 1971 the community of Williams Lake dedicated the new Gwen Pharis Ringwood Theatre in her honour. She wrote "The Deep has Many Voices, or, the Edge of the Forest" for the opening of this theatre. "Jana, or, The Stranger," was written to celebrate the opening of Centennial Park in the same year. She had earlier written the book and lyrics for "The Road Runs North," a play with music, for the centennial celebrations in Williams Lake. She gave courses in modern drama, playwriting, and acting at Cariboo College from 1967-1975, and wrote another novel "Pascal" (unpublished). She also wrote a series of short plays, "Encounters," for her Coffeehouses. In the same period she gave writing workshops and adjudicated numerous play festivals in British Columbia and Alberta. In 1973 the British Columbia Drama Association awarded her the Eric Hambert trophy for her continuing commitment to theatre. Also in 1973 she adapted "The Golden Goose" for classroom use.

The British Columbia Drama Association made Gwen Ringwood Honorary President in 1975 and in that year her play "The Lodge" won second place in the New Play Centre Women's Playwriting Competition, and was produced in 1976 by the Vancouver Little Theatre. "Widger's Way" was revived for the 1976 Kawartha Festival and her children's play "The Magic Carpets of Antonio Angelini" won first prize in the Ontario Multicultural Theatre Association's competition.

In 1978 a new radio play "A Remembrance of Miracles" was produced by the CBC. The CBC also recorded "Maya, or, Lament for Harmonica" and broadcast two of her short stories, "Restez Michelle, Don't Go," and "Some People's Grandfathers." A new full-length play "Mirage" was produced at the Greystone Theatre, Saskatoon, during the 1979 meeting of the Canadian Learned Societies; a stage version of "A Remembrance of Miracles" was completed in early 1980. Recent works include two plays: "The Furies," an Indian tragedy, and "Prisoners," "a play about women and war." She is now working on some autobiographical sketches tentatively titled "Scenes From A Country Life."

The Ringwoods, their children grown-up and gone, now live deep in the country, on the shores of Chimney Lake. The nearest town, Williams Lake, is twenty-five miles away.

Marion Wilson

Foreword

In January, 1945, when I was at college in Winnipeg, I attended a play produced by the University of Manitoba Dramatic Society. It was the first Canadian play I had ever seen, and furthermore, it was set in the prairies during the drought and depression, my own land and the time of my own growing up. It made a deep and lasting impression on me. The play was "Dark Harvest" by Gwen Pharis Ringwood, and that was its first production. In a foreword to the printed text, published by Thos. Nelson & Sons in 1945, George Brodersen—who had both directed and acted in that production—spoke of ". . .a general Renaissance of Canadian literature which seems, from all evidence, to be on the way." He was, as we can now see, quite right. Gwen Pharis Ringwood was one of the writers who helped to shape that whole new movement.

Born in Washington, she moved with her family to Magrath, Alberta, when she was three, and it was out of her prairie years that much of her writing was to come. From 1937 to 1939 she studied on a Rockefeller Foundation scholarship at Carolina Playmakers' School at the University of North Carolina. It was there that she was encouraged to write "regional" plays. These days, when it has long been accepted that a strength of Canadian writing is that very quality of regionalism, of being firmly rooted in some specific soil, it is well to remember that when Gwen Pharis began writing, our models were still largely British and our writing was still colonialist in outlook. It is interesting—and perhaps a bit ironic—to realize that it was in America that the young playwright was first encouraged to find the true voices of her own land.

"Still Stands The House," one of her early and still one of her best-known plays, was written and first performed in 1938. It was one of the first to explore the Canadian prairie farm experience of those years. The obsessive love-hate that Bruce feels towards his unfruitful land, his half-mad sister's equally obsessive determination that their dead father's house shall not be sold, and his wife Ruth's terrible loneliness and feeling of isolation, all these still exert tremendous force and strength, some forty years after the play was written.

With "Pasque Flower," written and produced in 1939 at the University of North Carolina, we have the beginnings of "Dark Harvest." The earlier version is much more naive and derivative than the later. Essentially the same themes and same three major characters are here, but in "Pasque Flower" we can see the influence of Eugene O'Neill and perhaps Robinson Jeffers, 1930s American, out of ancient Greece. The play is written in high-flown oratorical free verse, and plain prairie people talk not in their own idiom but in grandiose language. This play represents a young writer learning her craft, impressed by the giants of American drama, wanting to deal with her own land and people not yet able fully to trust their native speech and her own knowledge.

By the time that "Dark Harvest" appeared in 1945, all this had changed. The borrowed style is abandoned; the characters and feelings are now genuinely those of the people she was writing about. Thereafter her writing was to change and develop throughout the years, but she has never faltered in her ability to portray authentically the people and places she has known so well.

"Dark Harvest" is a timeless play, even though it is so firmly set in the prairies in the 1930s. As in some of the writing of Frederick Philip Grove, Sinclair Ross, and Martha Ostenso, we have in the character of Gerth Hansen one of those prairie men who worshipped their land, felt bonds of communication with their horses, and starved their wives of affection and love. Unlike Jake Hansen in "Pasque Flower," however, Gerth Hansen is no brute. He is a complex man who finds it impossible to express his love for Lisa, his wife, and his need for her love. It is not surprising that Lisa finally turns to Gerth's brother, David, a doctor newly returned to the area. The relationship between the two brothers, and the relationship of each of them with Lisa, is beautifully and subtly portrayed. This is, as well, in some ways a deeply religious play. Gerth sees God as an adversary, and Gerth's own sin is of course that of spiritual pride. But the tragedy at the end is in fact both a triumph of the human spirit and a recognition that no one can live unto himself. Also, in Gerth's words, "Maybe He doesn't want things to die" after all.

In the few years between "Pasque Flower" and "Dark Harvest" the complexity of the characters has grown enormously, as has the playwright's confident handling of her material. The acknowledgement and portrayal of a strong intelligent woman character has also grown impressively. Remember that for Gwen Pharis Ringwood, it must have been initially difficult—as it was for all women writers at that time—to portray women as she *knew* they were, not as they had been presented by generations of male writers. Lisa in "Pasque Flower" is a suffering but essentially passive woman. Lisa in "Dark Harvest" is a strong, intelligent, sexual being who knows she is offering her love to a husband who cannot accept it even though he needs it, and she is not willing to live all her life in that kind of limbo. She also recognizes as morally unjustifiable Gerth's refusal to adopt a child, after their own infant died at birth—"I'll leave no stranger's son the land I've worked for."

Gwen Pharis Ringwood's themes are frequently those of social injustice, the hurts that human individuals give to one another, the love and courage that continues to be a part of the human psyche despite all the terrors. Her people are prairie farmers, the ranch hands of Alberta, the immigrants facing a frightening life in a new land, the native peoples of British Columbia who have been robbed of their land and dignity by the whiteman's culture but who still acknowledge and hear the ancestral voices.

Some of the plays are based on actual events, such as "The Jack And The Joker," which concerns Bob Edwards of the famous *Calgary Eye-Opener*, or "The Rainmaker," based on the hiring of a so-called rainmaker in Medicine Hat during a drought in 1921, or "Stampede," based on the story of "Nigger John" Ware and some of Alberta's legendary cowboys. These plays, as with some of the comedies such as "The Courting Of Marie Jenvrin" seem to me to be good workable dramas but not really in the same class as the plays that are unequivocal tragedies and that come out of Ringwood's own imagination and deep perceptions.

After the late 1940s there is a gap of some years in the plays. During these years, Gwen Pharis Ringwood was bringing up her own children but was also holding discussion and writing groups in her home in Williams Lake, B.C.

Reading Ringwood's latest plays has been a voyage of discovery for me. "The Deep Has Many Voices," written in 1970, indicates very powerfully the playwright's growth, her more intricate sense of staging, her use of poetic and mythic forms to convey the inner truths, but without any of the borrowed styles that marked some of her very early work. In this play, she deals with contemporary society—the violence, the alienation, the materialism, the odd cults that some people cling to out of a feeling of helplessness.

"The Lodge," written in the early 70s, reflects the concerns of our times, too, without being in any way didactic. The pollution and destruction of land and forest, the immorality of hunting for sport— these themes occur. Allan and his wife Shelley have bought a rundown lodge in B.C. The family reunion with parents and aunt and uncle, is a disaster. But Shelley's grandmother, the old woman Jasmine, an artist, redeems the situation in her own highly original ways. In this character, Ringwood has created a very memorable old woman. She's no-nonsense, and she isn't about to let her children stick her away in an old folks' home. With her old-time friend, Jimmy, the Band Chief of the local B.C. tribe, she outwits her middleaged children and reassures her grandchildren. It is a play written with anger and with wisdom.

In Gwen Pharis Ringwood's 1971 play, "The Stranger," there is a coming together of many of the themes and techniques she has used in the past—the chorus, the drumming, the chanting, the mythic quality, the sense of the inevitability of the tragedy. Most of the characters are Shuswap Indians of the Okanagan. The Stranger is the "Chilcotin woman," Jana. As in Ringwood's early plays, there is an echo of the Greek tragedies, but now she has assimilated all such patterns into something that is truly of *this* land. Jana has been dreadfully wronged by her white commonlaw husband, Jason. He wants to take their son away from her, when he is about to marry, with an eye to the main chance, Barbara the white boss woman of the ranch. Ringwood has the bravery to bring the play to its terrible ending. Jana, in her sorrow and grandeur and rage for vengeance, is almost a Medea.

With "Mirage" (1979-80), the tone of the writing is in a lower key, and the speech of the people is the plain idiom of prairie people, as the story traces the lives and sufferings of two Saskatchewan families, one white and one Indian, against the backdrop of history from 1910 to the present. This is a more overtly political play than most of Ringwood's later work, but it is saved from didacticism by its moving portrayal of the fierce devotion of some of these people to a frequently harsh land, and by the presence of the Dowser, a prophet-like figure whose compassion extends to three generations and whose vision recognizes and acknowledges the ancient spirits of the land. "A Remembrance Of Miracles" (1980) is both extremely contemporary and timeless in its treatment of a young high school teacher's dilemma in the face of puritanical and fearful parents who seek to have Merrill's reading list for her senior students in English literature censored, the books banned even from the library, and Merrill herself fired. The title expresses what the teacher has hoped to convey to her students, and has indeed conveyed at least to some of them. I find this play almost unbearably poignant, as I happen to know only too well what the teacher is forced to go through.

For some forty years, Gwen Pharis Ringwood has been writing plays of a very high calibre. She saw, early on, the need to write out of our own people, our own land, and she has remained true to that vision. It is more than time that these collected plays were published together, rather than here and there in anthologies. It is also very satisfying to have a chance now to pay tribute to her and to her work.

Lakefield, Ontario   *Margaret Laurence*

Preface

A published collection of the dramatic writings of Gwen Pharis Ringwood has been long overdue. This oversight has been disturbing to those of us who have known and respected her as friend, peer, and colleague in the difficult evolution of Canadian theatre. Her contribution to our theatre heritage is fundamental to the very understanding of the qualities and origins of our theatrical experience. Neglect of her works, both critically and through active productions by our theatre establishment, is little short of tragic. Only one example need suffice for the moment as to how neglected a major dramatist can be at the hands of these illiterate theatrical apparatchicks when one is confronted with realization that her latest work *Garage Sale* was produced by a Vancouver theatre organization dedicated to developing *new writers with new plays*. It was under these auspices the last work by the author of *Still Stands the House* and *Rainmaker* was staged before an audience. It may be argued that production of a play under any auspices is in itself enough. In most cases, this would be so. But when a major talent, who has pioneered much in shaping the nature of Canadian theatre is involved, theatre owes a deeper obligation to such an artist. Neglect in showcasing such a work in the best of possible conditions is eventually a loss to the theatre. It also damages the author, if limited rehearsal time and frozen budgeting does not permit those final explorations of cadence, metaphor and pace which perfects a work through production.

This is not to decry the effort, respect and concern the Vancouver Play Centre invested in bringing a new work by this artist to public attention. But it would be short-sighted and too forgiving to not reflect on the implications of this event—the dereliction of responsibility by our large regional theatres is not displaying a concern equivalent to the Play Centre in preserving our heritage and the foundations of our national theatrical development.

It is in this area that some works contained in this collection reveal flaws. I mention this only in considering these as the *dramatic* writings and sketches of Ms. Ringwood. It in no way affects the literary value of the works included.

In over forty-five years of professional writing, Gwen Ringwood reflects as no other theatre personality I know that sense of what it means to be of this country. Raised in an Alberta rural community, she realized from childhood both the bonds and the divisions which characterized newly settled communities. That heritage was evasive and not readily recognized. And the challenge of locating roots and building a tradition on them was indeed complex and exasperating.

Her early years on the prairies were shaped in much the same way as the lives and sensitivities of most people were fashioned in that period of time. She learned Shakespeare's dramatic works as literature, not as drama in her high school. Other literary influences were colonial and accidental—bits and snippets of poetry by Poe, Milton, Keats, Shelley—with hefty dustings of Tarzan and pulps—bookended by Thomas Hardy and Charles G.D. Roberts. At seventeen years of age came her first courtship with theatre when she tried for a role in Synge's *Riders to the Sea.* She did not get the role she desired, but the play enveloped her in the turbulent landscape of the Irish Renaissance, peopled by Yeats, Synge, Lady Gregory and O'Casey.

"All of them spoke to me in tones that reverberate to this day," she writes many years later, "exciting, important, challenging work that somehow related to my prairie experience."

This is a telling self-insight. In truth, she was not alone—there were others, some arriving much later in the prairie experience, who also looked into the Irish Renaissance instinctively as one window in the dominant culture that somehow felt more comforting and natural as a thread into our own, hidden culture. Few of us then were analytical enough to recognize that the church hymns on Sunday, and cowboy songs the rest of the week, also had close links with Irish heritage. Labor songs on both sides of the border, and the fusion of continental folk music forms with the rough and tumble defiance of Woody Guthrie, also owe much to the same origins. These were the first steps Gwen Ringwood took towards elements already within the colonial culture, which were to lead her to profound discoveries in years to come.

"The Irish theatres' depiction of the fisherfolk, the farmers, the myth and history and political conflict of a non-urban and non-industrial people had a relevance to my own experience and life that was not apparent in the London and Broadway plays that I read," she was to note much later.

After studies at the University of Alberta and an unsuccessful first attempt at professional writing, Gwen Ringwood became a secretary to Elizabeth Sterling Hayes—director of drama under Carnegie Grant support to assist amateur theatre groups in Alberta. Haynes was an impressive and challenging personality who stimulated strong interest and lasting influence in the region where she worked. Gwen Ringwood probably completed her theatrical preparedness in reality, if not in fact, under the tutelage of Haynes. From the Greek classics to O'Neill, Haynes shared her enthusiasm with the community of theatre interest, and with her friend. One is left wondering if Elizabeth Sterling Haynes might also have left something of formalism in interpretation of design and structure of drama, which reveals itself consistently in the writings of Gwen Ringwood in years following.

In recent notes, Ringwood writes of Picasso complaining to Gilot that history had cut him loose. "The painter no longer lives within a tradition," he wrote. "So each one of us must recreate an entire language from A to Z. In a certain sense, that's a liberation but at the same time it's an enormous limitation. Because. . . what the artist gains in the way of liberty, he loses in the way of order." Ringwood adds her own comment on Picasso's note—"Today, the playwright can exercise liberty to choose his form. He may find he must strive hard to obtain order."

There is an unhappy sense in both her earlier and later works for theatre that in some of her plays she never resolved the inherent contradictions of formalism and the demands of character, situation and time arising out of new dynamics of regionalism and an exciting new mythology ill at ease with choruses and frozen postures.

Ringwood's physical introduction to the larger world occurred in 1937, when she went to Chapel Hill on a Rockefeller fellowship, and began writing for theatre. Here she was thrust headlong into a rapidly-changing, politically volatile world of new explorations in language, form, and musical fusion values. She was able to observe the processes of theatrical-musical interchange by Paul Green and Kurt Weill. Through Green, she was introduced into theatrical and poetic possibilities to present "the sweep of history" and the dialectics of social change in relation to theatre. The works of Odets, Stanislavsky, and John Howard Lawson brought the young prairie girl into contact with theatre beyond reflection of social reality—into the possibility of theatre as an instrument of class struggle through Marxist or Social Democratic interpretation of history. All these experiences left an impression on her and in her work, particularly the more ambitious dramas dealing directly with the relationship of person to earth.

The Chapel Hill interlude left her with a creative restlessness. She wrote: "At Chapel Hill I consciously and unconsciously searched my own background for dramatic material. I found myself leaning heavily on people whose initial language was not English, who had come to the prairies bringing with them tattered remnants of European culture, trailing small clouds of glory from other times, other places, and settling down uncomfortably in the flat, sunlit, extreme western climate, surrounded by people of Anglo-Saxon stock, some American, some English. The Europeans were strangers to these English-speaking, hard-bitten, well meaning, suspicious pioneers who dismissed the strangers as the wops, the bohunks, the Swedes, the Redskins and their squaws, the frogs, the chinks, the japs, the niggers. I heard these terms often as I grew up. The English speaking Canadians were walking a teetery bridge between the bulldog and the eagle, fawning on the patronizing English, bobbing obeisance to the bustling Americans."

And thus began the fixing of focus by Gwen Ringwood on the historical underpinnings of national cultural liberation from two overlapping colonizations. She was one of our earliest writers in theatre to recognize and explore the validity of intensely regional sources of story, language, and setting, as opposed to the "consciously national"—a centralized concept which equates the production of motor cars with the production of a culture—both from a centralist origin. Ringwood moved to the opposite end of the spectrum. Her characters and stories took on the qualities of the climate and landscape in which they were placed. And as she enriched her dramas with sound, music, and a new definition of space, she began painting in ever deepening colors the mythology which had always been there for the finding.

The myths of the native peoples in her dramas are a presence as rich and mystifying as those of ancient cultures of Europe. The eyes and ears first excited by writers and singers in Ireland served her well in selections she made from the myths of the Canadian earth.

The dark fear of the unpredictable climate and the vagaries of wind and ice haunt her settlers. In *Dark Harvest* she defines God as a presence in our landscape—a force lurking below the earth to taunt and test the will of people working the soil. Nothing is as it should be—the myths heave and roll to their own rhythms, and the strongest men hurt themselves and those they love in their ceaseless struggle against forces which defy comprehension. The people can and do mobilize to change governments and social order. But these are uneasy victories. In the end, mythology must change the man into a new harmony of people and earth.

This is the artistic territory Gwen Ringwood had painfully walked through decades ago. She walked virtually alone. Other dramatists now pace and examine the same territory. They do so with the aid of assured theatrical productions and technology. She has had little of such assurance. Yet she survives as an artist and woman of our time—leaving us with fascinating fragments of a rich talent, as well as full major dramatic works.

Her friends and admirers look forward to further works from her in defining the places we came from, and the places we approach.

January 1982   *George Ryga*

One Man's House:
A play of a Canadian Reformer

Foreword

This play is derived from the life of a Polish farmer whom I knew slightly in Alberta and who couldn't keep from making speeches against the economic order upon which he was dependent for a living. He lost several positions that might have held advancement, he spent some months in jail, his family were often hungry because he involved himself in labour agitation. His wife was never able to understand how he could sacrifice his family for something so remote and intangible. Yet he continued working, speaking, suffering for the thing he believed in. When he tried to forget it, he failed. He was, if you like, a wishful thinker, an impractical idealist, but in his own way he was trying to make a new world. He will go on trying until the day he dies.

Synopsis of Plot

Jan Lodeska has worked steadily on the railroad for six months, after several years of uncertain employment. The Railway Company has warned him, however, that if he becomes involved in labour agitation he will be fired. It is Christmas Eve and the Lodeska family are preparing to go to the Polish Christmas concert where the youngest daughter, Nina, is to dance. Josie, the eldest daughter is not going to the concert but to a cheap dance-hall with a friend who is considered wild. Stas Lodeska, Jan's married son is on strike and has been picketing at Scott's Packing Plant. His father is interested in the strike but has taken no public stand about it. As Jan Lodeska and his family are about ready to leave for the concert, Stas comes by on his way to a meeting of the strikers. He tells his father that he and several other strikers are tired of being off work and are going back. Lodeska feels that if they go back without gaining what they wanted it will all have been useless. He quarrels with Stas, and when Stas starts to leave orders him to remain. Then Jan Lodeska tells his family that he is not going to the concert but to the meeting to try to persuade the workers to hold out. His wife pleads with him not to go, because she knows he will lose his job. Josie says she refuses to be responsible for supporting the family and intends to move into an apartment with her friend. Lodeska is deeply sorry

1

that he must hurt them, but he feels it is his duty to go and despite their pleading, he goes out the door, leaving them worried and disconsolate.

Characters

NINA LODESKA, *a young girl*
JOSIE LODESKA, *her older sister*
MARTHA LODESKA, *the mother*
JAN LODESKA, *the father*
EUGENE LODESKA, *the youngest son*
STAS LODESKA, *the eldest son*

List of Properties

Furniture
Desk
Coal Heater and shaker
Chest of Drawers
Table
Three or four kitchen chairs
Arm Chairs
Winnipeg Couch
Backless kitchen chair

Stage Properties
Evergreen Tree
Two Polish Holy pictures
Two candles in holders—Matches.
Linen table cloth with Polish embroidery
Old violin
Cups
Books and Papers
Coat hooks
Decorations for Tree
Oil Lamp

Hand Properties
Mirror and Make-up box
Jug of cider
Woolen scarf wrapped in brown paper

SCENE: *The living room of* JAN LODESKA's *home in a Western Canadian city.*
TIME: *Christmas Eve. About 7 o'clock in the evening.*

A poorly furnished living room of a laborer's home. In the back a door leading out to the street and a window covered with frost. In the left-hand wall a door leading into the kitchen. It is well up stage. Along the left wall up stage is a Winnipeg couch. In the right-hand corner there is a coal heater and down stage on the right wall a desk covered with books and papers. Against the back wall at left is a battered chest of drawers with two unlighted candles on it. Left of the door at the back wall is a small evergreen tree mounted on a wooden chair that has long since lost its back. A round table, down-stage left is covered with a white linen cloth bordered by fine Polish embroidery. There are several wooden kitchen chairs about the table and another more comfortable chair beside the stove. There is also a chair in front of the desk. Above the couch is a large and brightly coloured Polish holy picture and there is another on the back wall above the chest of drawers.

When the curtain rises we find NINA LODESKA *trimming the evergreen tree with some bright ornaments and odd bits of tinsel. She is not more than sixteen, pretty and vivacious. At this time she is wearing a Polish peasant costume, richly embroidered in red and green. She is humming a song as she decorates the tree.*

At the desk JOSIE LODESKA *is applying make-up by the light of an oil lamp.* JOSIE *is nineteen or twenty, dark and rather handsome. She wears too much make-up and has an abrupt, rather harsh manner. Her dress, despite its rich, red colour, looks a little cheap and flimsy but it is new.* NINA *works for a moment, then steps back to survey the tree.*

NINA: Look, Josie! Isn't it beautiful!
JOSIE: (*Over her shoulder*) Yah. It's a little lop-sided maybe. But it looks all right.
NINA: (*On her knees before the tree*) I'm so excited! I wish you were coming to the concert, Josie.
JOSIE: Gosh, kid, I couldn't have no fun there . . . I don't know anybody in that crowd any more. Me'n Mae Goresky are going to the Tivoli.
NINA: I met Mae coming home last night. She said for you to bring me with you to see her some time, Josie.
JOSIE: Well, I'm not going to. Mae's all right but you're a lot better off with kids your own age and she oughtn't to be asking you. And I'll tell her I said so, too . . .
  (MARTHA LODESKA *enters. She is a woman of 48 but looks older; her shoulders are stooped and her sight is rather poor for she has spent many nights sewing for her family and for outsiders. She speaks with some accent, although she has been in Canada some thirty years.* MARTHA *wears a shapeless*

3

Gwen Pharis Ringwood

*dark woolen dress, her shoes are old and serviceable.
Tonight over her dress she is wearing a very attractive
white apron, embroidered with many fine stiches. She has a
woolen shawl over her head and comes in from outside, taking
off heavy mittens. Her children bewilder her somewhat with
their Canadian ways, their easy use of the language. But she
accepts them and is proud of them, nor does she try to
understand or question too much of their busy lives.)*

MARTHA: See, children, the cider Mrs. Wilcinsky gives us. (MARTHA
puts the jug on the table.) She is a good woman, Mrs. Wilcinsky.

JOSIE: Yah. She talks about us like hell the minute your back's turned.

MARTHA: Josie, you do not talk that way, you hear! Those bad words.
Get cups, Nina. Your father like some when he come home.
(NINA *goes to the kitchen and returns with some cups*). Where
your father go, Josie?
(MARTHA *takes off her shawl and hangs it behind the door.*)

JOSIE: He didn't say. He changed his clothes and ate and is out again
like a wind-storm. Maybe he went over to see Stas.

MARTHA: Nah! I come by there. Kazia say Stas is on the picket line.
You don't think your father mix himself in this strike, Josie?

JOSIE: Nah. Don't you worry, Ma. He'll be home.

NINA: (*who has finished decorating the tree*) Isn't the tree pretty,
Mother?

MARTHA: (*going over to it and touching some of the bright baubles*).
Yah, Nina. It is nice, I tell you. You know how to do things.

JOSIE: Don't give her a swelled head, Mom.

MARTHA: Hah. My children will no be swelled head! Now Nina look
like real Polish girl, eh Josie?

JOSIE: Yah. I tell her she'll be taken for an immigrant—a little
greenhorn that's just come over.

NINA: Did you wear this dress in Poland, Mother?

MARTHA: Yah. I wear it here too. (*A little shyly.*) I wear it when I meet
Jan Lodeska.

NINA: It seems funny . . . . You and Dad . . . before Stas or Josie were
ever born . . . or me or Eugene . . . And you just over from the
old country.

JOSIE: (*Putting her make-up articles in a box and taking them over to the
chest of drawers.*) Well, that's done! How do I look, Mom?

MARTHA: Nice, Josie . . . But that dress, it is too tight, I think. You
look tough that way.

JOSIE: Aw, Ma . . . it's the latest! (*Pounding at the heel of her slipper
with the stove shaker.*) I got to fix this shoe. Only decent pair I got
and the heel's wobbly.

NINA: Oh, I wish Dad and Eugene would come . . . Think of it, Mom
. . . I'll dance in front of all those people.
(*She whirls from the window to the table.*)

MARTHA: I think you be prettiest girl to dance, Nina.

4

NINA: And Sergei whirls me so fast — like this!
> (*She whirls Martha around.*)

MARTHA: (*Laughing and embarrassed*) Nina, you forget I'm old woman. No more. (*She stops a little breathless and pleased.*) But I dance like you once.

NINA: (*Stopping in front of the red candles.*) Mom, Let's light the candles.

MARTHA: Candle cost money, Nina. Maybe people come here tomorrow—tonight we go to concert anyway.

NINA: I know. But it looks so gay to come in a house with candles burning. Just till Dad comes home.

JOSIE: Sure. Let her light them Ma. Christmas only comes once a year.

MARTHA: Light them till he comes, then. (NINA *lights the candles.*) It is a better Christmas for us this year. Your Dad work steady six months. Josie work. Your Dad don't get in trouble with the bosses. I tell our Mother Mary thank you many times.

JOSIE: Kind of hard on Stas though—being on strike at Christmas.

MARTHA: Yah. I pray this strike will be over. Kazia, she cry tonight when I go there. A strike is hard on the woman.

NINA: (*Picking up a brown paper parcel on the table.*) What's this, Mom?

MARTHA: It is a scarf—I make your Dad fine wool one to wear on his neck to work. I take it to show Mrs. Wilcinsky.

JOSIE: That's swell, Ma. (*They look at the scarf.*) I got him some mitts. An old guy that eats at the joint give me a big tip today. God, I nearly fell over!

MARTHA: Josie, you do not talk so. (*There is a sound of stamping feet outside.* MARTHA *hides the scarf quickly*) Sh . . . . here he comes!

NINA: I'm going to hide.
> (*She slips between the tree and the chest. (The door opens and* JAN LODESKA *and his son* EUGENE *come in, brushing the snow off their coats and clapping their hands together to warm them.* LODESKA *is a tall, gaunt man with a mass of dark hair sprinkled with gray. He has long beautiful hands and a haggard, weather beaten face. His eyes hold more of the world's sorrow and compassion in them than is good for one man. He is about fifty. His old overcoat and dark suit are worn and shabby.* EUGENE *is the youngest of his children, ten years old, dark, eager and excitable*)

JAN: Mighty cold night, Martha. It's good to come in to a warm fire.

MARTHA: Jan, we hope you come soon.

EUGENE: Sold all my papers, Ma . . . And I got a present for you!

MARTHA: That is good, Gene. Jan, you do not forget? tonight we go see Nina dance.

JAN: Sure, I don't forget, Martha. (*He takes off his overcoat and stands by the fire.*) What you think? (*Noticing the tree*) Ho! We've got a Christmas tree even!
> (*There is a rustle behind the tree and* NINA *runs to him.*)

5

NINA: Look at me, Dad! How do you like it?

JAN: Nina! (*He looks at her proudly*) You look like your mother now, Nina. When I first saw her it was like that she looked.

MARTHA: (*Very pleased*) Yah, Jan.

JAN: The years they crowd us, Martha? Like sheep at a narrow gate. Already we grow old.

MARTHA: Yah. But the heart don't get so old, Jan. That is hard thing. Just now even I almost dance like young girl and forget I'm old woman.

JOSIE: Aw, you ain't so old, Ma. You work too darn hard—that's the trouble.

MARTHA: It is by work we live, Josie—not by talk. Nina, you help Gene to get ready now.

NINA: Come on, Gene.

JAN: Did Stas come by today, Martha?

MARTHA: No. Kazia say he pickets by the Plant.

JAN: Five weeks now they hold out. That is good.

MARTHA: (*going to the kitchen*) I tell Stas and Kazia bring the kids here for dinner tomorrow.

JAN: Yah. It is hard to be on strike now. I told them maybe they better wait till spring, but they thought now. Maybe they're right. I hear they got Scotts worried.

MARTHA: (*turning quickly, a note of fear in her voice*) Jan, you don't get mixed up in the strike, do you?

JAN: No, Martha . . . It is all right. I keep out this time.

MARTHA: (*Relieved, but still a little disturbed*) Six months now you work steady by the railroad. We go off relief. We have house to live in—not one room like last year.

JAN: Yah, I keep quiet Martha.

(*He gets up rather wearily and goes over to the desk, picking up some papers and looking at them*)

MARTHA: You do right, Jan. Already the railroad warn you you can't keep job and make trouble. They only keep you if you don't holler on the bosses.

JOSIE: Yah. And all that speakin' you done all your life ain't got you nowhere, Dad, except out of work. In jail once even. One man can't change nothin'. He loses every time.

JAN: (*intensely*) Not one man alone, Josie—but many men—they can change things. I hear today the owners of the Packing Plant are worried. If the workers stay on strike two weeks more, they get good settlement by God.

JOSIE: Well, I'd hate to be picketing in this weather.

JAN: Do you go to the concert with us, Josie?

JOSIE: Nah, Pa. I got a date at the Tivoli tonight.

JAN: Is it a nice place you go, Josie?

JOSIE: Yah, Swell music.

JAN: You go with Carl Wilcinsky maybe?

JOSIE: Nah, Pa. Oh, Carl—he's all right, but he dances like an ox.

MARTHA: (*From the kitchen*) Dancing don't make good husband Josie. Carl is hard worker.

JOSIE: Who wants him can have him. I got better ways to spend my time.

JAN: Josie, bring your young man home some time. We haven't fine house, but if he's the right kind, he won't mind that.

JOSIE: (*Embarrassed*) Yah, I been thinkin' I would. Seems like we're always with a crowd, Pa . . .

JAN: (*Gently*) I don't like you meeting fellows out, Josie. It is better to bring him home. (*He gets up, feeling he has said enough*) Are you ready Martha?

MARTHA: Soon, Jan. I get my cakes ready to take.

JAN: (*Picking up an old violin at the back of the desk*) It is a long time since I play—
> (*He plays a melody at first sad, then goes into a rollicking Polish dance.*).
> (EUGENE *and* NINA *come in.* EUGENE *is dressed in a boy's Polish peasant costume with a bright scarf around his waist.* NINA *catches his hand.*)

NINA: Faster, Dad. . . . Come on Eugene.
> (*She and* EUGENE *dance with vigour and laughter.* MARTHA *and* JOSIE *look on very pleased. As they are dancing, there is a knock and then the door opens.* STAS LODESKA *comes in. He is about 25, short and rather stocky. He has a rather sullen look and is dressed in working clothes.*)

NINA: (*Without stopping*) Merry Christmas Stas. Come and dance with us.

JAN: (*Putting down his violin.*) Come in, Stas. How is it with you, Son?

STAS: (*Shortly*) We do all right. Some dressin' up you do, Josie! Who's it for, Carl Wilcinsky?
> (*There is a bite in his joking*)

JOSIE: Nah. I got a real date tonight.

STAS: (*Moving over to the fire*) Yah. I know. You and Mae Goresky. Lay off that crowd, Josie. Or are you looking for a sugar-daddy too?

JOSIE: (*Angrily*) What's it to you, old Grouchy-mug? You weren't so particular 'till you got married and settled down.
> (MARTHA *comes in from the kitchen*)

STAS: Hello, Mother.

MARTHA: Give me your coat, Son. I put it up.

STAS: I can't stay. I'm on my way to a meeting across the street.

JAN: I didn't know there was a meeting tonight. The strike is standing up fine, Stas. I tell you in two weeks you got Scotts where you want them. Did you picket today?

STAS: (*Sullenly*) Nah. I just stand around eatin' chicken pie all day.

JAN: I was down to see the Labour News people tonight. Booth tells me they can't get any more men to scab at the Plant. Two—maybe three weeks more and . . . .

STAS: Sure! In the meantime we live on shoe leather and keep our hands warm sittin' on them.

JAN: But you win, By Golly . . . You win what you should have . . .

STAS: Yah. You don't need to tell me that again. You think I can't read.

JAN: What is wrong, Stas?

STAS: *(Angrily)* Plenty, if you want to know. No toys for the kids at Christmas. Kazia, she hollers on me all day about no warm clothes for kids—no good food. Always talkin' about oranges, like I could go pick them off a tree. I think I go back to work.

JAN: Stas! You must not. You talk foolish!

STAS: I'm not the only one . . . There's a lot of us.

JAN: But you almost win . . . if you hold out . . .

STAS: Ah, That' what you say . . . . Who keeps this strike goin'? You do, don't you? I'm not as smart as you, but I'm smart enough to know that. You don't speak — not right out so's you lose your job. But you work through the others. . . . You write to the paper, . . . You collect money. . . But you better be careful about that. The railroad wouldn't have much trouble to find out that you're mixed in this. . .

MARTHA: Jan! You mix yourself in this strike. You tell me No.

JAN: I said I don't speak, Martha. Sure I mix myself in this strike. I fight every way I can. And I keep this job too long now, Martha. Now my own boy says he'll go back to work without gaining anything for the workers.

STAS: You better keep out, Pa. You got a family to support—just like I have.

JAN: Stas, you must not do this thing. If you go back now, all is lost . . . Not to you only, but for years it is lost. It is all to do over.

STAS: Try to see it my way. I got a family to keep and I want to keep them better than you did yours. All my life I went hungry because you couldn't keep your mouth shut. Ask Ma. She'll tell you. You kept a job a few months, then we go on relief—or try to get on—or do without, because you have to talk—talk—talk. I stop school and go to work. So does Josie. We ain't never had nothin' because you thought you could change the world. Well you can't change it, and I'm going to get what I can out of it.

JAN: *(Low and angry)* So you sell out—you and a half dozen yellow cowards turn strike-breaker. All my life I work in this city for one thing—to make things better for the worker—to give him a chance to live and be glad he lived. And you come here and say your belly's empty. Do you think your belly matters?

STAS: It matters enough I'm going to be at work on Monday . . . raise or no raise . . . and I won't be the only one, I tell you. Good night.

(He starts to go.)

8

JAN: (*In loud anger*) Stay where you are! (*A pause*). (JAN *goes over and takes down his coat.*) I'm going with you.

MARTHA: (*Sharply—with fear in her voice*) No! No! You must not. You lose your job, Jan . . . you know it!

JAN: (*Disappointed*) You aren't going to see me dance, Dad?

JAN: No, Nina. My place is there—at the meeting.

STAS: You might as well save your breath, Pa. We'll go back whatever you say.

JAN: Still I will speak.

MARTHA: Jan, we almost buy this little house. You say you want Nina in the school—and Gene—Now you speak—we go on relief again —pretty soon they stop school, you see.

JAN: What is one family, Martha? One man's house? Beside the thing he knows is right.

JOSIE: But it ain't right, Pa. I can't support this family on my nine a week and I'm not going to. I'm going to have some fun—

JAN: We have managed before, Josie, without your help.

(*He goes to the desk and picks up his papers*)

MARTHA: Always you want us different—me and Stas and Josie—all of us—Always you think of the workers . . . never of your family. It is not right.

JAN: (*Awkwardly, sorrowfully*) If I love no farther than the walls my own lamp lights, Martha, then it is better I die. If a man stops caring what happens to other men, it is no good to live. Don't you see?

MARTHA: (*shrilly*) I see you don't care what happens to your children —to me. I see you never care.

NINA: Don't, Mother . . .

MARTHA: Yah. You stand up for him. But when he comes home fired from his job — sits all day staring at the snow, tapping his fingers on the table — then you see I'm right! When you stop school . . . .

STAS: Ah, it's no use, Mother . . . You go on to the concert with the kids.

JAN: A man must follow his road, Stas. This is mine.

JOSIE: Well, it's not mine, Dad. You can count me out from now on. I'm going to move in with Mae Goresky. If you don't feel responsible for this family, I'm not going to . . .

JAN: I'm sorry, Josie. You must choose. But we will always want you here.

MARTHA: You see, —you drive the children from us with your talking. . . . You have no heart, Jan Lodeska. (*She is weeping*)

JAN: I give you everything I can, Martha, but I can give you no longer silence. Six months now I keep quiet, feeling like a sneak thief in the night, working underneath but not come out and say it to the world. Now it is over—whether they listen or they do not listen, still I must speak to them and say out loud what I believe.

(*He has now gathered up his papers and put on his coat*)

STAS: Goodnight, Mother.

(He puts his hand on her shoulder. JAN *goes over to her)*

JAN: I'm sorry, Martha. Always I take you down the same road I go. Only it is harder for you—because you can't see where it leads.

MARTHA: Then you speak tonight, Jan Lodeska?

JAN: Yah. Maybe I can make them see they must not go back. I go now.

(It is as if there were a light on his face. He goes out the door. For a moment there is a silence. Then slowly MARTHA *lifts her head.)*

MARTHA: *(In a tired, resigned voice.)* Blow out the candles, Nina. We must not waste them now.

(NINA *blows out the candles as the curtain falls.*)

The End

Chris Axelson, Blacksmith

Characters

SANDY, *Chris's nephew*
CHRIS AXELSON
CARL SVENSON, *a Swedish farmhand*
WILLIAM BENNETT, *his employer*
BILLY, *a small boy*

TIME: *About 1925*
PLACE: *Chris Axelson's Smithy in a Small Western Town*

A sign says Chris Axelson — Blacksmith. CHRIS AXELSON *is working at a forge, singing his own variation of a lusty sea shanty as he works.*
CHRIS *is a powerful man of about 65 years. His laugh is a trumpet, his rage is heroic, his gentleness unexpected and full of humility.*
After a few minutes of pounding and singing, CHRIS *suddenly breaks off and turning from the forge, goes to the door. He speaks with a Swedish accent.*

Gwen Pharis Ringwood

CHRIS: Sandy! Sandy!

SANDY: (*From outside*) Yeah, I'm here.

CHRIS: Sandy Alexson, how many times do I tell you I won't have Model T's outside my shop? Come out from under that thing, you hear me.

SANDY: (*With a loud sigh*) O.K. I'm coming.

CHRIS: This is no hospital for broke-down cars.
  (*He turns to forge*)

SANDY: (*Appearing in doorway. He is about 16, with an alert, impudent face, now smudged with grease*) I could make that thing run if I had some spark plugs. (*He wipes hands on cloth*) You got any round here?

CHRIS: What do I want with spark plugs when my job is welding? You better get yourself ready.

SANDY: Say, Chris, Mason's got a good used truck up the street for $700.00. I looked at it yesterday. What do you say we. . .

CHRIS: You shut up on that truck business, Sandy. Half an hour till you go to Minneapolis and you still talk about trucks. Why the bus, she goes in just half an hour.

SANDY: I know. (*Indicating his overalls*) I got my good pants on under these.

CHRIS: What? You been fooling with that dirty engine in your good clothes? I don't know why I have to keep a kid like you around. I get so tired hollering at you I think I jump in the lake some times.

SANDY: (*Grinning*) It'd take more than a lake to make you stop hollering. (*He starts towards rear door, and then pauses with a monkey wrench in his hand which he throws at* CHRIS) Here, catch!

CHRIS: (*Sputtering as he catches it from long practice*) Looks like you show some manners just once before you go.

SANDY: (*Pleading*) Chris, I don't want to go to Minneapolis.

CHRIS: What will you do while I am in Sweden then? Be a bum on the streets?

SANDY: I could keep the shop running.

CHRIS: You stand near the top in school, Sandy. You take first prize for drawing pictures.

SANDY: I'm not interested in drawing, Chris.

CHRIS: After you learn this commercial drawing, you got good chance to be like your Dad was. Every day he draw the pictures of what they got to sell in a big store for the newspaper. Your Dad made good money and don't get dirty.

SANDY: The only thing I can draw is cars and engines.

CHRIS: Maybe you draw them fool engines then. What's the matter with you? No more ambition than working in a dirty shop. What kind of nephew do I bring up? You go get ready.

SANDY: If we bought that truck, I could put this place on its feet while you're away. There's not a good trucking service in the country.

CHRIS: Yah. Pretty soon we go broke puttin' tires on the dam-fool truck

12

or you get yourself and the truck mixed up in the ditch like you was stirred with an egg beater. I know.

SANDY: That's just a crazy idea of yours.

CHRIS: I'm sick of this talk on trucks, Sandy. You take the bus to Minneapolis tonight and I'm going to Sweden with Carl Svenson on Wednesday, whether you like it or not.

SANDY: I suppose you think you'll have a business left if you close up for six months.

CHRIS: (*Angry*) So, I got to have a kid sixteen tell me how I run my business. Now I got to take the orders. Why you think your Dad left that money for you? To go to school on, I tell you.

SANDY: (*Giving up*) Ah, I ain't listening even. Always grouching. I never did anything to please you yet.

CHRIS: I don't see you try much.

SANDY: If you weren't so stubborn — (CHRIS *turns and glares at him*) O.K. I'm going. But you know how I feel about it. (*He starts out the rear door of the shop but pauses to take up a can of solder which he throws toward* CHRIS) Catch!

CHRIS: (*Forced to drop his tool to catch it*) You get out of here.

(SANDY *goes out the rear door.* CHRIS *works a moment, then* WILLIAM BENNETT, *a busy farmer of middle age, careworn and not prosperous comes in the side door. He is followed by* CARL SWENSON, *a big lumbering youth of about twenty-six*)

BENNETT: Hello, Chris.

CHRIS: Hello, Bill. I got your chain saw all ready — so sharp it cuts right through the sidewalk. (*He sees* CARL) Why, hello, Carl.

CARL: Hello.

(*He sits down*)

BENNETT: I brought Carl in to talk over plans for your trip, Chris. We may not get to town again before Wednesday.

CHRIS: That's fine. How you feel now, Carl?

CARL: Good. (CARL *has a strong Swedish accent too. He is a bit dumb in his head but the most willing and good-natured fellow in the world. He is very conscious of his new suit, new shoes and a straw hat that is very bright and shiny.*) But those shoes was wrong size that feller sell me. They don't feel so good.

CHRIS: Too bad. You should take them back.

(*Wrapping chain saw in sack*)

CARL: (*Sadly*) It is too late. I write my name in them all ready.

CHRIS: Here you are, Bill.

(*Gives him chain saw*)

BENNETT: Fine. How much do I owe you?

CHRIS: All together it's three-eighty.

BENNETT: I'll pay up after threshing, Chris, if that's all right with you.

CHRIS: Sure, sure. No hurry.

BENNETT: You're looking hearty these days.

CHRIS: Yah, I feel fine. Ever since I quit drinking I'm strong as a horse.

13

BENNETT: You sure laid off sudden.

CHRIS: I make some big fool of myself, I think. Probably I'd be dead four—five years ago, if I kept on like crazy wild Indian.

BENNETT: Takes will power to stop all of a sudden.

CHRIS: Well, when I take nine year old kid to raise, I figure it's time I stop. What kind of life for a kid with an old boozer around? So when Sandy's Dad died I just quit. I sure look at that kid sometimes the first year and think maybe I send him to my sister.

BENNETT: You never touch the stuff now, eh?

CHRIS: I get pretty drunk two times a year now. On the first day of July and the seventeenth of November.

BENNETT: What's the seventeenth of November, your birthday?

CHRIS: Nah. That's the day I quit drinking. I get drunk to celebrate.
       (*He laughs at his own joke*)

BENNETT: Sandy's a fine boy, Chris.

CHRIS: Today he goes to Minneapolis to the drawing school. (*Anxiously*) You figure $800.00 is enough to take care of his school if he stay with my sister?

BENNETT: Should be, Chris. You'll miss him.

CHRIS: Yah. I miss him but he better get some education. This picture he drew was the best in his class for the school fair.
       (*He gets the picture down from above the work table*)

BENNETT: He's got the knack all right.

CARL: Looks just like ol' Ford, eh?

CHRIS: (*Putting it back*) He says the tree ain't no good but I like that tree.

BENNETT: (*Getting up*) Well, I'll leave you and Carl to talk over your trip, Chris. You come up to the bus at 7, Carl. I'll wait for you there.

CARL: I be there all right, Mr. Bennett.

BENNETT: (*At door*) Say, Chris, you don't know who I could get to haul my pigs to Lethbridge, do you?

CHRIS: I guess you have to get John Roebuck. He's got a truck if he ain't too busy. My kid is always wanting one of those hauling trucks.

BENNETT: Be a good investment.

CHRIS: I don't want him tipping over in no truck some night in the snow.

BENNETT: Now, Chris, you know Sandy can handle anything on wheels.

CHRIS: (*Soberly*) I lost my son on one of those trucks.

BENNETT: (*Awkwardly*) I forgot that, Chris.

CHRIS: Maybe it's foolish blaming the truck for fifteen year, but I want to keep Sandy out of this machine business.

BENNETT: I see. Well, I'll get along. See you later, Carl.

CARL: O.K. Mr. Bennett. (BENNETT *goes out.* CHRIS *starts to work*) Where's Sandy, Chris?

CHRIS: He went to change his clothes.
       (*There is a silence*)

14

CARL: Well, two days we go, eh?

CHRIS: What's that? What's that?

CARL: We go to Sweden, Wednesday.

CHRIS: (*Carefully putting down his tools, with some hesitancy he approaches* CARL) Carl, I got something to tell you.

CARL: (*Apprehensively*) Me?

CHRIS: I was going to tell you this after Sandy is gone. But Mr. Bennett says you won't be in town again until Wednesday.

CARL: Yah, Wednesday when we go.

CHRIS: Carl, I been lyin' to you. I don't go to Sweden at all with you. You got to get there by yourself.

CARL: What do you mean, Chris?

CHRIS: I just tell Sandy I go to Sweden so he quit bothering me about trucks and go to school.

CARL: You don't go?

CHRIS: No.

CARL: Why don't you go?

CHRIS: I don't have the money, Carl. I just make it all up about Sweden and I tell Sandy his Dad left him the money to go to drawing school. I take all my savings for him. I got to stay here and work to live.

CARL: (*Wrestling with the problem*) So you don't go, eh?

CHRIS: No. Now Carl, I got something more to tell you. Do you listen?

CARL: Yah, I listen. So you don't go to Sweden like you said?

CHRIS: (*Exasperated he shouts*) How many times I have to tell you I don't go?

CARL: (*Stubbornly*) Well, I don't see it.

CHRIS: (*Going to the shelf where he unlocks a box and takes some addressed letters from it*) Look, Carl, I got these letters I want you to mail for me.

CARL: Sure I go now.

(He starts to get up)

CHRIS: (*Pushing him down*) Not, now Carl. (*Pleading*) Carl, you try to put all your brain once on one thing. Try hard, Carl.

CARL: Yah. I'm trying.

(He is a picture of agonized concentration)

CHRIS: You see these letters. Well, I write them to Sandy to make him think I go to Sweden.

(He surveys them proudly)

CARL: Why you write all these letters at once?

CHRIS: (*Controlling his temper*) I tell you it's so that kid think I go with you. And don't know I'm lying. See, they each got one number on it, Carl, in pencil. One, two, three, four, five, six, seven, eight.

CARL: (*Observing him closely*) Yah, there's eight all right.

CHRIS: Now on this paper I write down: "Mail number one on 26 of September from Lethbridge." That's Wednesday when you go. In it I say we have left. And everything is fine.

CARL: But you say you don't go.

CHRIS: Carl, don't try to understand the why of things. You just put all your mind on what I say.

CARL: (*Agreeably*) I think I can.

CHRIS: Now when you go to Lethbridge Wednesday you mail this number one. But first you erase off the one. You see, I already write it down on paper for you.

CARL: Yah, I see that easy. You want me to mail one on Wednesday.

CHRIS: That's right, Carl. You smart feller. Your sweetheart think you good husband. Now here is the money for the stamps. You put those in your good suit and every morning on your trip you look to see if you got to mail a letter that day.
(*He puts the letters in* CARL's *pocket*)

CARL: (*Poring over the paper*) Yah, I understand good, you bet. One in Lethbridge. Two in. . .

CHRIS: Halifax.

CARL: Sure Halifax. The rest in Sweden in Stockholm where I'm going.

CHRIS: (*Relieved and delighted*) That is fine, Carl.

CARL: Well I do it, Chris. (*He folds the paper carefully and puts it in his pocket*) I mail them sure.
(SANDY *is heard whistling in the back room*)

CHRIS: Don't say one thing about Sweden to Sandy, Carl. If he asks you about our trip you just don't tell him nothing.

CARL: O.K. I keep my mouth shut outside my face.
(SANDY *returns through the back door. He is very clean and scrubbed and is feeling somewhat subdued and shaken.*)

SANDY: Hi, Carl.
(*He puts down his suitcase*)

CARL: Hello, Sandy.
(*He admires Sandy tremendously*)

CHRIS: (*Proudly*) You look pretty good now, Sandy. You get everything packed?

SANDY: Yeah. That's some new suit you got, Carl.

CARL: Yah. Thirty bucks.

SANDY: All ready for the big trip eh? (CARL *looks steadfastly in front of him*) Chris, you promise me to get that overcoat in Wilson's. I don't want you going home looking like a tramp.

CHRIS: Sure, I get a lot of clothes. Some of those shirts like you wear, make a feller feel he ain't got nothing on, maybe, eh Carl?

SANDY: Pretty ritzy hat too, Carl.

CARL: (*Taking it off with loving hands*) Four bucks.

SANDY: Bet your girl will be proud of you. You're going to see your girl in Sweden aren't you?

CARL: (*Looking straight ahead*) I don't tell you whether I see her or not. (*To* CHRIS) You see, Chris, I won't talk.
(SANDY *looks puzzled.* CHRIS *realizes the conversation is getting dangerous*)

CHRIS: Say, Carl, how would you like to go by the store and get me one can of axle grease? I got to finish this job I'm on.
CARL: Sure.
CHRIS: (*Taking money from his apron pocket*) There's 60 cents.
CARL: One can. 60 cents. (*He puts his hat carefully on his head and starts out painfully*) One can of grease.
(*He goes*)
SANDY: (*Smiling after him*) It's good thing you're going to Sweden too, Chris. He'd never be able to get there in one piece alone.
CHRIS: Well, he got himself over here by himself. But I hate to think how it must have been for him.
SANDY: Still Bill Bennett says he's the best man with cattle he ever had.
CHRIS: Yah. (*Pause*) Well, Sandy, I guess you was through with this dirty shop now.
SANDY: Looks like it.
CHRIS: (*Very busy to conceal his emotion*) You tell your Aunt Annie I won't be writing to her. I'll write to you and you can tell her how I'm getting along. And you send your letters to this post office. When I get there I let them know where to send my mail.
SANDY: (*Unhappily*) All right, Chris.
CHRIS: (*Unlocking his box and taking some money and a cheque from it*) Here's 80 dollars to buy your ticket.
SANDY: Gosh, it won't be that much will it?
CHRIS: You need some money in your pocket. And you eat something besides those hot dogs, you hear me? You go into the big hotel in Winnipeg and buy yourself a dinner for one dollar and have it served on a tray by a waiter.
SANDY: All right.
CHRIS: And Sandy, I make out this cheque to do all year for the school and books and a show once a week. I make it to you and not Annie so you won't have to be asking no wimmen for money.
SANDY: (*Looking at the cheque*) Seven hundred and fifty bucks! Gee, that's too much, Chris. I didn't know Dad left me all that.
CHRIS: (*Gruffly*) Well, he did. You watch out for pickpockets, Son. Keep your pocket book in your vest. And don't walk too far from the bus station when they stop or you miss it.
(*He is relieved that this is over, starts work*)
SANDY: (*Very interested in the drill he holds in his hands*) Chris—
CHRIS: Yah.
SANDY: I was. . . . I was just thinking how much.. . . I been living here with you 7 years and bothering you around the shop and you've. . . . (*He is afraid of his own emotion and casts wildly about for something to save his face. He notices what CHRIS is doing*) Say, you're not getting that put together right. Can't you see you've got to fit it in that groove?
CHRIS: (*Indignant*) Don't be crazy. You couldn't fit it there in a week.
SANDY: You'll break it square in the middle. Let me show you.
(*He takes the rod and begins to demonstrate*)

17

CHRIS: (*In a rage*) Hell and damnation, Sandy, have you got no brain? I take it apart, don't I? Now I have to be told how to put it back.

SANDY: Now just a minute. You see it's got to go right through. . . .

CHRIS: I can fix it. Without nobody telling me. I fixed thousands of these before you were born even. You give it back, I tell you. (*He yanks it away from* SANDY) You put it in like this, see. (*As he demonstrates the rod breaks in two*)

SANDY: (*Delighted*) Told you you'd break it.

CHRIS: (*Roaring*) All right, you're so smart and know every damn thing there is. You just try fixing it yourself.

SANDY: All right, I will. (*He starts to do so*)

CHRIS: Sure. Ruin your new suit like you got two million dollars in the bank every day. Why I have to have such a kid, I don't know. I just don't know. (CARL *reappears at the big door.*)

CARL: Well, here's the grease.

CHRIS: (*Still angry*) Why don't you set it down then?

CARL: One can. 60 cents.

CHRIS: (*Looking at the can*) What kind of can is that? (*He stares at it unbelieving*) Saints in Heaven, Carl, you bring me cooking grease.

CARL: (*Looking at the can in great distress*) I make a mistake, I guess.

CHRIS: Can't you read?

CARL: I go back now.

SANDY: (*Laughing*) What did he bring you, Chris?

CHRIS: He brings me lard, Sandy, to grease a binder. (*Seeing that* CARL *feels bad*) That's all right, Carl. We can take it back.

CARL: (*Sadly*) I just told him grease. I should look at the can I guess.

CHRIS: You just sit down here till time for Sandy to go. (*He pats him*)

CARL: (*Sitting disconsolately*) Next time I don't make a mistake, I hope. (*After a pause he suddenly has an idea that he hopes may place him in good standing*) You want one drink, Chris? I got this for my cold.

CHRIS: No thanks, Carl. I quit drinking, don't you remember. But you better leave this bottle here so your boss don't see it. (*He takes the bottle from* CARL *and puts it in a drawer*)

CARL: (*Puzzled*) But he don't see it. Chris.

CHRIS: You don't know. I just put it where it's safe. Sometimes when I don't sleep I take a little drink like the doctor told me. That was before I quit of course.

CARL: Yah, I see.

CHRIS: I don't think I sleep so good tonight, Carl. (*A silence*) Why don't Sam come to drive you to the station, Sandy?

SANDY: He'll be along. (*He is still working on the broken rod*)

CARL: (*Worried*) I forgot all about telling you. He said he come in ten minutes.

CHRIS: I don't like this waiting. I think I just go down and get that grease and come back when I see Sam drive up.
SANDY: Good idea. No use just sitting around.
CHRIS: I just say be a good boy like you were with me, Sandy. That's enough. And this little horseshoe wear for luck—I want you to take it.
SANDY: Thanks, Chris. (*He takes it, unable to speak*)
CHRIS: I be right back. You won't feel blue after you get on the bus, Son. (*He bustles out quickly, taking the can of lard with him. After silence* CARL *speaks*)
CARL: I sure hope you have one good time in Minneapolis, Sandy.
SANDY: (*Absently*) Yeah. I'd a lot rather stay here. If Chris should get sick on your trip, Carl, you'll write me a letter won't you?
CARL: Sure. I got to remember to mail lots of letters. (*Worried*) I hope I don't forget just like I forgot about the grease and Sam.
SANDY: Don't worry about that. It didn't matter, Carl.
CARL: No, I don't worry about the grease. But what if I forget about those letters—after I promise.
SANDY: Well you don't need to write to your sweetheart any more cause you'll be able to tell her what's on your mind.
CARL: I don't talk about Sweden to you, Sandy.
SANDY: O.K. I wish Sam would come. If I have to go I may as. . . .
CARL: (*Excitedly*) Sandy, I know how to fix it so I don't forget and so Chris don't get mad at me.
SANDY: What are you talking about, Carl? Chris isn't mad at you. He thinks you're swell.
CARL: Not if I forget to mail that number one letter. Sandy, you see I was going to mail this letter in Lethbridge on Wednesday but I might forget like I did about the grease. So if you would mail it for me when you get there it would be better, then I be sure you get it when he said.
SANDY: (*Shaking his head*) I don't get it, but I'll mail your letter. (*He goes over to get the letter and sees the whole pile which* CARL *is fumbling through*) What are you doing with all those letters?
CARL: (*Hiding them from* SANDY) I don't talk. You just take number one. The rest I got to mail out of my head. (*He hands* SANDY *the letter*) Don't you forget to mail it in Lethbridge, Sandy.
SANDY: I don't see why Chris don't mail his own letters. (*He thinks a minute and then suddenly begins to glimpse the truth*) Are all those letters addressed to me, Carl?
CARL: Yah. I mail them sure, I hope.
SANDY:I'm going to find out. (*He tears open the letter*) "Dear Sandy. . . . On our way and everything is fine. . . So everything is fine is it? (*He reads through to the end carefully*)
CARL: (*Upset*) Sandy, you shouldn't open it. I just asked you to mail it.
SANDY: Carl, this means Chris don't go to Sweden at all, doesn't it?
CARL: I won't tell you.

SANDY: Why isn't he going? (*Shaking* CARL) Does he want to get rid of me? You got to tell me, Carl. Why isn't he going?

CARL: Don't shake me so hard, Sandy. I don't know why he don't go except nobody can go without money. It takes all the money for the school.

SANDY: (*It all becomes clear*) So, Dad didn't leave me the money at all—Chris is sending me to Minneapolis.

CARL: You seal up that letter, Sandy. And here's the money for the stamp.

SANDY: O.K. Carl.

> (*He is thinking hard. The sound of an automobile and then the horn is heard outside. Immediately* CHRIS's *voice, very excited, tops it*)

CHRIS: (*Outside*) Sandy be right out, Sam. I'll tell him you're here.

> (SANDY *quickly conceals the letter*)

CHRIS: (*Coming in, flustered, still carrying the lard*) I just got down the street and meet Sam. You better hurry, Sandy. Where's your suitcase?

CARL: I'll take it out, Chris. (*He takes the suitcase. In a low tone as he passes* CHRIS.) I don't say nothing about Sweden like you told me.

CHRIS: That's right. You can ride up with them to the bus station. (CARL *goes. To* SANDY) I won't go to the bus, Son. It's better I don't keep saying goodbye every place.

SANDY: I know.

CHRIS: (*Taking him to the door*) You watch you don't have to sit over the wheel. She bump like hell.

SANDY: I will, Chris.

CHRIS: You'll have three hours in Lethbridge till you change the bus. You just go to the library and read a book or walk around the park. Then you get something to eat maybe but don't miss your bus. Now do you know what you are going to do?

SANDY: Yes, Chris. (*His voice trembles a little*) I think I know what I'm going to do. So long.

> (*They shake hands.* CHRIS *tries to cover up his emotion by blustering.* SANDY *is quiet, shaken by an inner excitement*)

CHRIS: Then you better get out there. Goodbye, Son.

> (*He puts his hand on* SANDY's *shoulder and ushers him to the door. Outside* SAM's *voice is heard: "Hi Sandy, we better get going."*)

CARL: (*Off stage*) Hurry up Sandy, she goes right now.

CHRIS: (*Calling from the door*) Goodbye. Goodbye, Sandy.

> (*The car can be heard leaving as* CHRIS *stands in the big door watching. When it has gone* CHRIS *slowly turns from the doorway. He moves aimlessly about the shop, takes up Sandy's old work gloves and holds them a minute before putting them on the shelf. Then he stands in thought before the picture of the Ford car which took the prize. He takes it*

over to the bench and sits looking at it gloomily. He is lost in memories when he hears a step outside the door of the shop. Turning, he sees a litttle boy standing at the big door)

BILLY: Mr. Chris—

CHRIS: Well, well! Hello, little boy. Will you come in?

BILLY: *(Staying in the doorway)* Is Sandy here?

CHRIS: No. Sandy, he's gone to Minneapolis. A long way off.

BILLY: *(Disappointed)* Oh. . . . Well, goodbye.
(He turns to go)

CHRIS: Can I do anything for you?

BILLY: No, thank you. Sandy said he'd mend this car if I brought it. *(He produces a toy truck)* I was racing it down the hill and it hit a rock and now it won't run right.

CHRIS: Let me see. Maybe I can fix it.

BILLY: *(Approaching)* I think the spring broke. That's what I think happened.
(He gives CHRIS the truck)

CHRIS: Well, you just let me see it. Old Chris fix that up fine in two minutes. You sit right down there.

BILLY: I didn't know you could fix it.

CHRIS: Sure, I fix it better than Sandy even. You see.
(He starts to work)

BILLY: Thank you, Mr. Chris.
(The blast of the bus horn comes through the open door)

CHRIS: You hear that bus blowin' like a ship in the fog?

BILLY: That means the bus is leaving. He blows like that at our corner.

CHRIS: Sandy's on that bus. He's going nearly three thousand miles riding over the country. Then in two days he gets to Minneapolis.

BILLY: Three thousand miles. I guess he'll see the ocean, Mr. Chris. I never saw the ocean.

CHRIS: No, he don't see the ocean but sees a big lake and a river that runs swift as this truck going down hill. And when he gets there he sees high buildings with eighteen stories in him—maybe twenty.

BILLY: Gee, that's awful high.
(There is a silence)

CHRIS: I saw them buildings when I was coming out here from Sweden. I was a young man then, just come from being a sailor on a ship. I was bigger than Sandy but not so smart. He's like his Dad. His Dad was the smartest one in all my family.

BILLY: Aren't you Sandy's Dad, Mr. Chris?

CHRIS: No, Son. I'm his uncle.

BILLY: I've got an uncle. Uncle Jack.

CHRIS: You be good to him then. Sometimes uncles like little boys just like their Dad.

BILLY: Uncle Jack lost his shirt at the races. He told Daddy.

CHRIS: That's too bad. *(Turning with the truck)* Well, son, there you are. I fix this truck up so it's good like new. You try now and see if old Chris don't fix it.

21

BILLY: (*Taking the truck*) I have to wind it first. (*He tries the car out*) Oh, that's swell, Mr. Chris.

CHRIS: You better go home quick now. It's gettin' dark and your mama be wondering where you are.

BILLY: (*At the door*) I guess you'll miss Sandy, Mr. Chris.

CHRIS: Yah, I miss him all right. But you young people got to get some education, don't you? Goodbye, Sonny.

BILLY: (*At the door*) Thank you for fixing my truck.

CHRIS: Just a minute. Can you catch, little boy? (BILLY *looks doubtful*) Here is a little magnet that picks up the pins, Catch! (*He throws the magnet towards* BILLY *who catches it*). That is good. I teach Sandy that trick a long time ago. You keep the magnet.

BILLY: Thanks Mr. Chris. Well, I better go now. Goodbye.

CHRIS: (*Coming to the door*) Goodbye.

> (BILLY *goes out.* CHRIS *stands at the door watching him go, then slowly closes the large doors, leaving the room lit by the little windows through which the evening sun casts gloomy shades. The forge still glows faintly. The old man sits down dejectedly. After a moment he goes over to the shelf and takes down the bottle he confiscated from* CARL. *He starts to take a drink from it, puts it down, and once more takes up the pictures of the old Ford. His power is gone from him and he is a lost and lonesome old man. He sits for a few moments in this attitude of despondency when the sudden loud roar of a motor outside breaks the silence.* CHRIS *turns. The noise increases. There is a sound of voices and after a moment some of them become clear: "Back up a little. That's it. Now we've got it. Good motor eh?" Then someone tries to push open the big doors which are fastened on the inside.* CHRIS, *angry and mystified, jumps up and puts on the light*)

CHRIS: Say, what is this anyway? Who do you think you are, breaking into other people's shops?

> (*Muttering imprecations, he throws the door open.* SANDY *stands in it, a little dishevelled, a little nervous, but grinning cheerfully*)

SANDY: Hi, Chris.

CHRIS: (*Staring*) Sandy! What are you doing here?

SANDY: (*Very shamefaced and a little frightened*) I,—I came back, Chris.

CHRIS: What'd you do, Son? Miss the bus?

SANDY: No, I didn't exactly. . . .

> (CARL *appears behind* SANDY. *His hat is gone. his eyes are round with excitement and he is very upset*)

CARL: He don't go, Chris. Just like you, he don't go.

CHRIS: Did you lose your ticket, Sandy?

SANDY: No, I. . . .

CHRIS: Then you must have left your suitcase. (*Bellowing*) Saints in Heaven, ain't you got no more sense than that? Now I got to get you ready all over again for tomorrow. Well, why in hell don't you say something?

SANDY: Well, I. . . .

(He can't help smiling)

CHRIS: *(Rearing)* Just stand there. Just stand there, grinning like a wild tiger. Well, you can go right back. You can just turn right round and go back with your suitcase tied to you.

SANDY: I can't go back, Chris.

CHRIS: What you mean you can't? What you done now, you blundering busterling limb of the devil? I think. . . .

(He looks past SANDY and becomes very quiet at the sight he sees through the door)

SANDY: *(Uncomfortably)* What?

CHRIS: *(Low and menacing)* Out there. What is it, I tell you?

SANDY: Oh, that. . . . yes. Well, that's a truck

CHRIS: *(A tiger in pain)* What kind of thing is this?

SANDY: It's a V8.

CHRIS: Well, whose is it? Tell them to get it out of here right away.

SANDY: I can't. It's yours.

CHRIS: Mine? What's happened to you, Sandy? First you don't take the bus, then you tell me I own some damn truck I never saw before. You gone crazy?

CARL: *(Excitedly)* I think so. I just think so. He make me miss the bus. He won't go to the station. He was crazy all right.

SANDY: Chris, that's the truck I was telling you about. They took off forty bucks. So I thought we'd buy ten barrels of gas and. . . . Now, don't get mad!

CHRIS: Mad! I bust you into the middle of next week. I put you in the cellar and lock you up. How the hell did you buy it? What you use for money? *(He comprehends. His voice is a little broken and bewildered)* You used that money I gave you for the school. Sandy, that's what you did.

(He sinks down on the bench)

SANDY: Now let me do some talking, Chris. I know I'm only sixteen but I know what I want. Honest I do. And it isn't drawing pictures for a newspaper. I just draw for fun. I don't want to go to the drawing school. I don't want to live anywhere but in this town or work any place but in this shop of yours. You can use me here and you know it. . . .

CHRIS: But Sandy. . . .

SANDY: You've been losing a lot of business, Chris, because you don't sell parts to machinery. With this truck we'll make enough money to have an up-to-date machine shop in two years. Aw, Chris, don't be mad.

CHRIS: Sandy, you was to get yourself educated.

SANDY: I can read books here, can't I? You've got to let me stay with you, Chris. You've got to.

CHRIS: (*Sad and uncertain*) Well, I don't know. I just don't know. (*Almost timidly as he looks out at the truck*) She's a pretty colour, Sandy.

CARL: You mean Sandy don't go to Minneapolis, Chris?

CHRIS: He don't go.

CARL: Why not?

SANDY: You figure it out, Carl.
 (*He grins*)

CARL: (*Agitated*) But you told me you send him off. I hear you say good-bye.

CHRIS: Well we change our mind. (*Irritably*) Can't we change it if we want?

SANDY: I'll be right back, Chris. I just want to tune up this engine a little. (*Over his shoulder*) You may be wanting to drive it to Sweden.

CHRIS: Sweden! How can I go anywhere with a crazy kid to worry about?

SANDY: (*As he goes out the big door*) I sure hate to see you give up that trip.
 (*He leaves*)

CARL: Well, Chris, I don't know what happen to you. First you don't go to Sweden, now Sandy don't go to Minneapolis.

CHRIS: Well, everything gets different sometimes.

CARL: Yah.

CHRIS: (*Regaining his old strength*) You think your boss find you here?

CARL: I don't know what he'll do. Sandy won't let me go to the bus station. Just put me in that truck and come back.

CHRIS: (*A sudden suspicion*) What you tell him to make him come back, Carl?

CARL: I don't say nothing, honest, I don't Chris. I just give him number one letter and. . . .

CHRIS: What! What you give him? Tell me!

CARL: Telling you is what I'm doing. When you was gone to the store I sit here with Sandy and he says he hopes we have a good time in Sweden and I don't say nothing like you told me.

CHRIS: Well?

CARL: Then I think about those letters. And I remember how I always forget everything. So I say! "Sandy, Chris asked me to mail number one letter in Lethbridge but I forget somethings sometimes and so if you would mail it for me today it would be better then I be sure you get it when he said."

CHRIS: So, that's it. You give him that letter. Then he knows everything.

CARL: Now don't you get mad, Chris. I give him the right one. See. . . . 2, 3, 4, 5, 6, 7, 8. (*He displays the letters*) I fix it all right.

CHRIS: Yah. You fix it. You fix every damn thing.

CARL: When Sandy read the letter he just make Sam stop at Masons

and buy a truck and puts me in it all at once. I don't know what happened to him.
(*He is very distressed*)
CHRIS: (*Slowly smiling and patting the disconsolate* CARL) Maybe you fix it the best way there is, Carl. Maybe you're the smart feller, not me. Here, you give me those letters. I tear them up.
CARL: Don't you want me to mail them for you in Stockholm when I get there?
CHRIS: (*Shouting*) He don't go, I tell you, he don't go. Nobody goes anywhere.
CARL: Well, I can't see why you always don't make up your mind.
(SANDY *enters and sees the letters. He starts toward them*)
SANDY: (*There is a grease spot on his cheek*) What's that, Chris? More mail for me? Or have I got another legacy coming?
CHRIS: (*Seizing the letters from* SANDY) Shut up, you laughing hyena. Keep yourself out of other people's business. (*Looking for something on which to vent his discomfiture*) Well, if we're going to sell that damn gas, why don't you fix some place to load it from? And for the last time I tell you why don't you get those clothes off? I think I go drown myself when I see what kind of kid I raise up—never do a piece of work in his life.
SANDY: (*Pleased at being back to the old status*) Hah, I can do more work with one hand tied in my sleeve than you can any day.
CHRIS: Get out of here, I tell you. (SANDY *disappears through the back door,* CHRIS *turns cheerfully to* CARL) You cheer up, Carl. We can take you home in the truck. Then Sandy can see Mr. Bennett about hauling those pigs of his. (*Proudly*) She looks like damn good engine.
CARL: She's good truck all right.
SANDY: (*From ouside the door at back*) Hey, Chris!!!
CHRIS: Get out of here, you. . . . you. . . .
(*He turns to roar at* SANDY, *who appears around the door. The boy's line form soundlessly the word"Catch" and* CHRIS *catches a flying monkey wrench as his roar dies away. He looks at it and at* SANDY *who begins to laugh.* CHRIS *takes up the laugh. It becomes a delighted bellow as the curtain falls.*)

The End

25

Still Stands The House

Copyright © 1939 in *American Folk Plays*,
D. Appleton-Century Co., Inc.

Still Stands The House
A drama of the Canadian Frontier

Characters

BRUCE WARREN
RUTH WARREN, *his wife*
HESTER WARREN, *his sister*
ARTHUR MANNING, *a real estate agent*

SCENE: *Western Canada. The living-room of the Warren farmhouse in Alberta.*
TIME: *The present. Seven o'clock on a January night.*

The icy wind of a northern blizzard sweeps across the prairie, lashes about the old Warren farmhouse, and howls insistently at the door and windows. But the Warren house was built to withstand the menace of the Canadian winter and scornfully suffers the storm to shriek about the chimney corner, to knock at the door and rattle the windows in a wild attempt to force an entrance.

The living room of this house has about it a faded austerity, a decayed elegance that is as remote and cheerless as a hearth in which no fire is ever laid. The room has made a stern and solemn pact with the past. Once it held the warm surge of life; but as the years have gone by, it has settled in a rigid pattern of neat, uncompromising severity.

As if in defiance of the room, the frost has covered the window in the rear wall with a wild and exotic design. Beside the window is an imposing leather armchair, turned toward the handsome coal stove in the right corner. A footstool is near the chair. A door at the center of the rear wall leads to the snow-sheeted world outside. Along the left wall, between a closed door to a bedroom (now unused) and an open door to the kitchen, is a mahogany sideboard. Above it is a portrait of old Martin Warren who

27

Gwen Pharis Ringwood

built this house and lived in it until his death. The portrait is of a stern and handsome man in his early fifties, and in the expression of the eyes the artist has caught something of his unconquerable will.

An open staircase, winding to the bedrooms upstairs, extends into the room at right. There is a rocking chair by the stove with a small stand-table beside it. A mahogany dining-table and two matching chairs are placed at a convenient distance from the sideboard and the kitchen door. The figured wall paper is cracked and faded. The dark rug, the heavy curtains, and the tablecloth show signs of much wear; but there is nothing of cheapness about them.

Two coal oil lanterns have been left beside the kitchen door. Blooming bravely on the table, in contrast to its surroundings, is a pot of lavender hyacinths.

RUTH WARREN is standing near the outside door, talking to ARTHUR MANNING, who is about to leave. RUTH is small, fair-haired, and pretty, twenty-five or twenty-six years of age. There is more strength in her than her rather delicate appearance would indicate. She wears a soft blue house-dress, with a light wool cardigan over it. MANNING is a middle-aged man of prosperous appearance. He wears a heavy overcoat over a dark business suit. His hat, gloves, and scarf are on the armchair.)

RUTH: Do you think you'd better try to go back to town to-night, Mr. Mannning? The roads may be drifted.

MANNING: It's a bad blizzard, all right, but I don't think I'll have any trouble. There's a heater in the car, and I've just had the engine checked over.

RUTH: You'll be welcome if you care to spend the night.

MANNING: Thank you, but I'm afraid I've got to get back to town. I'd hate to try it in an old car, but this one of mine can pull through anything.

RUTH: I've never seen a storm come up so quickly.

MANNING: These prairie blizzards are no joke. One of my sheep herders got lost in one last year, just half a mile from the house. He froze to death out there trying to find his way.

RUTH: How frightful!

MANNING: One of the ranch hands found him the next morning. Poor old fellow—he'd herded for me for twenty years. I never knew how he came to be out in a storm like that.

RUTH: They say when a person gets lost he begins to go round in a circle, although it seems to him he's going straight ahead.

MANNING: Yes, I've always heard that. The winters are the one thing I've got against this country.

RUTH: (*wistfully*). I used to like them in town. We went skating on the river and tobogganing. But out here it's different.

MANNING: If Bruce sells the farm and takes this irrigated place near town, you won't notice the winter so much, Mrs. Warren.

RUTH: No. I hope he does take your offer, Mr. Manning. I want him to.

MANNING: He'll never get a better. Five thousand dollars and an irrigated quarter is a good price for a dry-land farm these days.

RUTH: If only we didn't have to decide so soon.

MANNING: I talked it all over with Bruce in town a couple of weeks ago, and I think he's pretty well made up his mind. All he needs to do is sign the papers.

RUTH: I thought he'd have until spring to decide.

MANNING: I've got orders to close the deal before I go South next week. You tell Bruce I'll come by to-morrow or the next day, and we can get it all settled.

RUTH: I'll tell him. I hope he does take it, Mr. Manning.

MANNING: I know you do and you're right. I think all he needs is a little persuading. He's had a hard time here these dry years.

RUTH: I don't know what Hester will say.

MANNING: I understand she's very much attached to the place. Is it true that she never leaves the farm?

RUTH: Not often.

MANNING: She'd be better off where she could get out more.

RUTH: I don't know.

MANNING: I suppose all those years out here, keeping house for Bruce and her father, were pretty hard on her.

RUTH: The house has come to mean so much to her. But maybe she won't mind. (*Smiling hopefully.*) We'll see.

(*The door to the bedroom, left, is opened quietly, and* HESTER WARREN *enters the room. She closes and locks the door behind her and stands looking at the two in the room with cold surmise.* HESTER *is forty years old. She is tall, dark, and unsmiling. The stern rigidity of her body, the bitter austerity of her mouth, and the almost arrogant dignity of her carriage seem to make her a part of the room she enters. There is bitter resentment in her dark eyes as she confronts* RUTH *and* MANNING: *She holds a leather-bound Bible close to her breast.*)

RUTH: (*startled*) Why, Hester! I thought you never unlocked that door.

HESTER: (*quietly*) No. I keep Father's room as it was.

RUTH: Then why were you—

HESTER: I was reading in Father's room. I heard a stranger.

RUTH: You know Mr. Manning, Hester.

MANNING (*with forced friendliness*) I don't suppose you remember me, Miss Warren.

HESTER: (*without moving*) How do you do?

MANNING: (*embarrassed at her coldness and anxious to get away*). Well, I'll be getting on home. I'll leave these papers for Bruce to sign, Mrs. Warren. Tell him I'll come by to-morrow. He'll find it's all there, just as we talked about it.

(*He lays the document on the table.*)

RUTH: Thank you, Mr. Manning.

MANNING: (*turning to go*) Take care of yourselves. Good night. (*To* HESTER:) Good night, Miss Warren.
> (HESTER *barely nods.*)

RUTH: You're sure you ought to try it in the storm?

MANNING: Sure. There's no danger if I go right away.
> (*He goes out.*)

RUTH: (*calling after him as she shuts the door*) Good night.
> (HESTER *watches* MANNING *out and as* RUTH *returns, she looks at her suspiciously. There is a silence which* HESTER *finally breaks.*)

HESTER: What did he want here?

RUTH: (*uncomfortable under* HESTER's *scrutiny*) He just left some papers for Bruce to look over, Hester. He was in a hurry so he didn't wait to see Bruce.

HESTER: I see. What has Arthur Manning got to do with Bruce?

RUTH: It's something to do with the farm, Hester. I'll put these away.
> (*She starts to take up the document on the table, but* HESTER *is before her.*)

HESTER: (*after a long look at the document*) A deed of sale. (*Turning angrily upon* RUTH) So this is what you've been hiding from me.

RUTH: (*quickly*) Oh, no! Nothing's settled, Hester. Mr. Manning made an offer, and Bruce wants to think it over. That's all.

HESTER: (*her eyes betraying her intense agitation*) Bruce isn't going to sell this place!

RUTH: It's just an offer. Nothing has been decided.

HESTER: Your hand's in this! You've been after him to leave here.

RUTH: (*trying to conciliate her*) Let's not quarrel. You can talk to Bruce about it, Hester.

HESTER: You hate this house, I know that.

RUTH: No. (*Facing* HESTER *firmly.*) But I think Bruce ought to sell.

HESTER: You married him. You made your choice.

RUTH: (*quietly*) I've not regretted that. It's just that we're so cut off and lonely here, and this is the best offer we could get. But let me put these away. (*Indicating the deed of sale*) We'll talk about it later, the three of us.

HESTER: (*allowing* RUTH *to take the papers*) You may as well burn them. He isn't going to sell.

RUTH: Please, Hester. . . we'll discuss it when Bruce comes. (*She places the document on the sideboard, then crosses to the stove.*) I'll build up the fire.
> (HESTER *takes the Bible to the sideboard and places it under her father's portrait. She stands looking up at the portrait.*)

HESTER: This house will not be sold. I won't allow it.
> (RUTH *puts some coal on the fire.*)

RUTH: (*shivering*) It's so cold it almost frightens me. The thermometer has dropped ten degrees within the hour.

HESTER: I hope Bruce knows enough to get the stock in. They'll freeze

where they stand if they're left out tonight.
> (*She moves to the window and takes her knitting from the ledge.*)

RUTH: He'll have them in. (*Crossing to the table*) Look Hester, how the hyacinths have bloomed. I could smell them when I came in the room just now.

HESTER: Hyacinths always seem like death to me.

RUTH: (*her voice is young and vibrant*) Oh, no. They're birth, they're spring! They say in Greece you find them growing wild in April.
> (*She takes an old Wedgewood bowl from the sideboard, preparing to set the pot of hyacinths in it.*)

HESTER: (*in a dry, unfriendly tone*) I've asked you not to use that Wedgewood bowl. It was my grandmother's. I don't want it broken.

RUTH: I'm sorry. (*Replacing the bowl, she gets a plain one from inside the sideboard.*) I thought the hyacinths would look so pretty in it, but I'll use the plain one.

HESTER: You've gone to as much trouble for that plant as if it were a child.
> (HESTER *sits in the rocking chair by the stove.*)

RUTH: (*placing the hyacinths in the bowl*) They're so sweet. I like to touch them.

HESTER: They'll freeze to-night, I'm thinking.

RUTH: Not in here. We'll have to keep the fire up anyway. (*Leaving the bowl of hyacinths on the table,* RUTH *returns to the sideboard, taking some bright chintz from the drawer. She holds it up for* HESTER *to see.*) I've almost finished the curtains, Hester.

HESTER: (*tonelessly*) You have?

RUTH: Don't you think they'll make this room more cheerful?

HESTER: The ones we have seem good enough to me.

RUTH: But they're so old.

HESTER: (*coldly*) Old things have beauty when you've eyes to see it. That velvet has a richness that you can't buy now.

RUTH: (*moving to the window*) I want to make the room gay and happy for the spring. You'll see how much difference these will make.

HESTER: I've no doubt.
> (HESTER *rises and goes to the table to avoid looking at the curtains.*)

RUTH: (*measuring the chintz with the curtains at the window*) I wonder if I have them wide enough. (*The wind rises. As if the sound had quelled her pleasure in the bright curtains,* RUTH *turns slowly away from the window. A touch of hysteria creeps into her voice.*) The wind swirls and shrieks and raises such queer echoes in this old house! It seems to laugh at us in here, thinking we're safe, hugging the stove! As if it knew it could blow out the light and the fire and. . . (*Getting hold of herself.*) I've never seen a blizzard when it was as cold as this. Have you, Hester?

HESTER: (*knitting*) Bruce was born on a night like this.

(*Throughout this scene* HESTER *seldom looks at* RUTH *but gives all her attention to her knitting. She seems reluctant to talk and yet impelled to do so.*)

RUTH: I didn't know.

HESTER: Father had to ride for the doctor while I stayed here with Mother.

RUTH: Alone?

HESTER: Yes. I was rubbing Father's hand with snow when we heard the baby crying. Then we helped the doctor bathe him.

RUTH: You were such a little girl to do so much.

HESTER: After Mother died I did it all.

RUTH: I know, but it was too hard for a child. I don't see how you managed.

HESTER: Father always helped me with the washing.

RUTH: Not many men would stay in from the field to do that.

HESTER: No. (*Her knitting drops to her lap, and for a moment she is lost in the past.*) "We'll have to lean on one another now, Daughter." . . . Those were his words. . . And that's the way it was. I was beside him until—I never left him.

RUTH: (*at* HESTER's *side*) You've never talked of him like this before.

HESTER: (*unconscious of* RUTH) He always liked the snow. (*Her eyes are on the portrait of her father.*) He called it a moving shroud, a winding-sheet that the wind lifts and raises and lets fall again.

RUTH: It is like that.

HESTER: He'd come in and say, "The snow lies deep on the summer fallow, Hester. That means a good crop next year."

RUTH: I know. It's glorious in the fall with the wheat like gold on the hills. No wonder he loved it.

HESTER: (*called out of her dream, she abruptly resumes her knitting*) There hasn't been much wheat out there these last years.

RUTH: That isn't Bruce's fault, Hester.

HESTER: You have to love a place to make things grow. The land knows when you don't care about it, and Bruce doesn't care about it any more. Not like Father did.

RUTH: (*her hands raised to touch the portrait above the sideboard*) I wish I'd known your father.

HESTER: (*rising and facing* RUTH *with a sudden and terrible anger*) Don't touch that picture. It's mine.

RUTH: (*startled, she faces* HESTER) Why, Hester—

HESTER: Can't I have anything of my own? Must you put your fingers on everything I have?

RUTH: (*moving to* HESTER) Hester, you know I didn't mean— What is the matter with you?

HESTER: I won't have you touch it.

RUTH: (*gently*) Do you hate my being here so much?

HESTER: (*turning away*) You've more right here than I have now, I suppose.

RUTH: (*crossing over to the stove*) You make me feel that I've no right at all.

HESTER: (*a martyr now*) I'm sorry if you don't approve my ways. I can go, if that's what you want.

RUTH: (*pleading*) Please. . . I've never had a sister, and when Bruce told me he had one, I thought we'd be such friends. . .

HESTER: (*sitting in the chair by the stove*) We're not a family to put words to everything we feel.

(*She resumes her knitting.*)

RUTH: (*trying to bridge the gulf between them*) I get too excited over things; I know it. Bruce tells me I sound affected when I say too much about the way I feel, the way I like people. . . or the sky in the evening. I—

HESTER: (*without looking up*) Did you get the separator put up? Or shall I do it?

(*Discouraged,* RUTH *turns away, and going to the table, sits down with her sewing.*)

RUTH: It's ready for the milk when Bruce brings it. I put it together this morning.

HESTER: The lanterns are empty.

RUTH: I'll fill them in a minute.

HESTER: When I managed this house, I always filled the lanterns right after supper. Then they were ready.

RUTH: (*impatiently*) I said I'd fill them, Hester, and I will. They're both there in the corner.

(*She indicates the lanterns at the end of the sideboard.*)

HESTER: Bruce didn't take one then?

RUTH: No.

HESTER: You'd better put a lamp in the window.

(RUTH *lights a small lamp on the sideboard and takes it to the window.*)

RUTH: I wish he'd come. It's strange how women feel safer when their men are near, close enough to touch, isn't it? No matter how strong you think you are.

(*As she speaks,* RUTH *drapes some of the chintz over the armchair.*)

HESTER: I can't say that I need any strength from Bruce, or could get it if I needed it.

RUTH: That's because he's still a little boy to you. (*A pause, then* RUTH *speaks hesitantly.*) Hester. . .

HESTER: Yes?

RUTH: Will you mind the baby in the house?

HESTER: (*after a silence, constrainedly*) No. I won't mind. I'll keep out of the way.

RUTH: (*warmly, commanding a response*) I don't want you to. You'll love him, Hester.

HESTER: (*harshly*) I loved Bruce, but I got no thanks for it. He feels I stand in his way now.

Gwen Pharis Ringwood

RUTH: (*suddenly aware that* HESTER *has needed and wanted love*) You mustn't say that. It isn't true.

HESTER: When he was little, after Mother died, he'd come tugging at my hand. . . . He'd get hold of my little finger and say "Come, Hettie. . . come and look." Everything was "Hettie" then.

RUTH: (*eagerly, moving to* HESTER) It will be like that again. This baby will be almost like your own.

HESTER: (*as if* RUTH'*s words were an implied reproach*) I could have married, and married well if I'd had a mind to.

RUTH: I know that. I've wondered why you didn't, Hester.

HESTER: The young men used to ride over here on Sunday, but I stopped that. (*A pause*) I never saw a man I'd sleep beside, or let him touch me. And that's all they want.

RUTH: (*involuntarily; it is a cry*) No!

HESTER: Maybe you don't mind that kind of thing. I do.

RUTH: (*attempting to put her arms around* HESTER) What hurts you?

HESTER: (*rising*) Don't try your soft ways on me. (*She moves behind the armchair, her hand falls caressingly on the back of the chair.*) I couldn't leave Bruce and Father here alone. My duty was here in this house. So I stayed. (HESTER *notices the chintz material draped over the chair, and taking it up, turns to* RUTH: *angrily.*) What do you intend to do with this?

RUTH: I thought. . . there's enough left to make covers for the chair to match the curtains—

HESTER: (*throwing the chintz down*) This is Father's chair. I won't have it changed.

RUTH: I'm sorry, Hester. (*With spirit*) Must we keep everything the same forever?

HESTER: There's nothing in this house that isn't good, that wasn't bought with care and pride by one of us who loved it. This stuff is cheap and gaudy.

RUTH: It isn't dull and falling apart with age.

HESTER: Before my father died, when he was ill, he sat here in this chair where he could see them threshing from the window. It was the first time since he came here that he'd not been in the fields at harvest. Now you come—you who never knew him, who never saw him—and you won't rest until—

RUTH: Hester!

HESTER: You've got no right to touch it!

(*Her hands grip the back of the old chair as she stands rigid, her eyes blazing.* BRUCE WARREN *enters from outside, carrying a pail of milk. He is tall and dark, about thirty years old, sensitive and bitter. His vain struggle to make the farm pay since his father's death has left him with an oppressive sense of failure. He is proud and quick to resent an imagined reproach. He has dark hair, his shoulders are a little stooped, and he moves restlessly and abruptly. Despite his moodiness,*

34

he is extremely likeable. He is dressed warmly in dark trousers, a sweater under his heavy leather coat; he wears gloves, cap, and high boots. He brushes the snow from his coat as he enters.)

BRUCE: (*carrying the milk into the kitchen*) Is the separator up, Ruth?

RUTH: Yes, it's all ready, Bruce. Wait, I'll help you.

(She follows him into the kitchen. HESTER *stands at the chair a moment after they have gone; her eyes fall on the plant on the table. Slowly she goes toward it, as if drawn by something she hated. She looks down at the lavender blooms for a moment. Then with a quick, angry gesture, she crushes one of the stalks. She turns away and is winding up her wool when* BRUCE *and* RUTH *return.*)

RUTH: You must be frozen.

BRUCE: (*taking off his coat and gloves*) I'm cold, all right. God, it's a blizzard: 38 below, and a high wind.

(He throws his coat over a chair at the table.)

RUTH: (*with pride*) Did you see the hyacinths? They've bloomed since yesterday.

BRUCE: (*smiling*) Yes, they're pretty. (*Touching them, he notices the broken stalk.*) Looks like one of them's broken.

RUTH: Where? (*She sees it.*) Oh, it is! And that one hadn't bloomed yet! I wonder. . . . It wasn't broken when I—(RUTH *turns accusingly to* HESTER) Hester!

*(HESTER *returns* RUTH's *look calmly.*)

HESTER: (*coldly*) Yes?

RUTH: Hester, did you. . .

BRUCE: (*going over to the fire*) Oh, Ruth , don't make such a fuss about it. It can't be helped.

HESTER: I'll take care of the milk.

(She takes the small lamp from the window.)

RUTH: I'll do it.

HESTER: (*moving toward the kitchen*) You turn the separator so slow the cream's as thin as water.

RUTH: (*stung to reply*) That's not true. You never give me a chance to—

BRUCE: (*irritably*) For God's sake don't quarrel about it.

(He sits in the chair by the stove.)

HESTER: I don't intend to quarrel.

(She goes into the kitchen. RUTH *follows* HESTER *to the door. The sound of the separator comes from the kitchen.* RUTH *turns wearily, takes up the pot of hyacinths, and places them on the stand near the stove. Then sits on the footstool.*)

RUTH: It's always that way.

BRUCE: (*gazing moodily at the stove*) Why don't you two try to get along?

(A silence)

RUTH: Did you put the stock in?

Gwen Pharis Ringwood

(*The question is merely something to fill the empty space of silence between them.*)

BRUCE: Yes. That black mare may foal to-night. I'll have to look at her later on.

RUTH: It's bitter weather for a little colt to be born.

BRUCE: Yes.

(*Another silence. Finally* RUTH, *to throw off the tension between them, gets up and moves her footstool over to his chair.*)

RUTH: I'm glad you're here. I've been lonesome for you.

BRUCE: (*putting his hand on hers*) I'm glad to be here.

RUTH: I thought of you out at the barn, trying to work in this cold.

BRUCE: I was all right. I'd hate to walk far to-night though. You can't see your hand before your face.

RUTH: (*after a look at the kitchen*) Hester's been so strange again these last few days, Bruce.

BRUCE: I know it's hard, Ruth.

RUTH: It's like it was when I first came here. At everything I touch, she cries out like I'd hurt her somehow.

BRUCE: Hester has to do things her own way. She's always been like that.

RUTH: If only she could like me a little. I think she almost does sometimes, but then—

BRUCE: You think too much about her.

RUTH: Maybe it's because we've been shut in so close. I'm almost afraid of her lately.

BRUCE: She's not had an easy life, Ruth.

RUTH: I know that. She's talked about your father almost constantly to-day.

BRUCE: His death hit us both hard. Dad ran the farm, decided everything.

RUTH: It's been six years, Bruce.

BRUCE: There are things you don't count out by years.

RUTH: He wouldn't want you to go on remembering forever.

BRUCE: (*looking at the floor*) No.

RUTH: You should get free of this house. It's not good for you to stay here. It's not good for Hester. (*Getting up, she crosses to the sideboard and returns with the deed of sale, which she hands to* BRUCE.) Mr. Manning left this for you. He's coming back to-morrow for it, when you've signed it.

(*He takes the papers.*)

BRUCE: (*annoyed by her assurance*) He doesn't need to get so excited. I haven't decided to sign it yet. He said he wouldn't need to know till spring.

(*He goes over to the lamps at the table and studies the document.*)

RUTH: His company gave him orders to close the deal this week or let it go.

BRUCE: This week?

RUTH: That's what he said.

BRUCE: Well, I'll think about it.

RUTH: You'll have to decide to-night, Bruce. No one else will offer you as much. Five thousand dollars and an irrigated farm a mile from town seems a good price.

BRUCE: I'm not complaining about the deal. It's fair.

RUTH: (*urgently*) You're going to take it, aren't you, Bruce?

BRUCE: I don't know. God, I don't know. (*He throws the document on the table.*) I don't want to sell, Ruth. I think I'll try it another year.

RUTH: Bruce, you've struggled here too long now. You haven't had a crop, a good crop in five years.

BRUCE: I need to be told that.

RUTH: It's not your fault. But you've told me you ought to give it up, that it's too dry here.

BRUCE: We may get a crop this year. We're due for one.

RUTH: If you take this offer, we'll be nearer town. We'll have water on the place. We can have a garden, and trees growing.

BRUCE: That's about what those irrigated farms are—gardens.

RUTH: And Bruce, it wouldn't be so lonely there, so cruelly lonely.

BRUCE: I told you how it was before you came.

RUTH: (*resenting his tone*) You didn't tell me you worshipped a house. That you made a god of a house and a section of land. You didn't tell me that!

BRUCE: (*angrily*) You didn't tell me that you'd moon at a window for your old friends, either.

(*He stands up and throws the deed of sale on the table.*)

RUTH: How could I help it here?

BRUCE: And you didn't tell me you'd be afraid of having a child. What kind of a woman are you that you don't want your child?

RUTH: That's not true.

BRUCE: No? You cried when you knew, didn't you?

RUTH: Bruce!

BRUCE: (*going blindly on*) What makes you feel the way you do then? Other women have children without so much fuss. Other women are glad.

RUTH: (*intensely angry*) Don't speak to me like that. Keep your land. Eat and sleep and dream land, I don't care!

BRUCE: (*turning to the portrait of his father*) My father came out here and took a homestead. He broke the prairie with one plow and a team of horses. He built a house to live in out of the sod. You didn't know that, did you? He and Mother lived here in a sod shanty and struggled to make things grow. Then they built a one-roomed shack; and when the good years came, they built this house. The finest in the country! I thought my son would have it.

RUTH: (*moving to him*) What is there left to give a son? A house that stirs with ghosts! A piece of worn-out land where the rain never comes.

37

BRUCE: That's not all. I don't suppose you can understand.

RUTH: (*turning away from him, deeply hurt*) No. I don't suppose I can. You give me little chance to know how you feel about things.

BRUCE: (*his anger gone*) Ruth, I didn't mean that. But you've always lived in town. (*He goes to the window and stands looking out for a moment, then turns.*) Those rocks along the fence out there, I picked up every one of them with my own hands and carried them there. I've plowed that southern slope along the coulee every year since I was twelve. (*His voice is torn with a kind of shame for his emotion.*) I feel about the land like Hester does about the house, I guess. I don't want to leave it. I don't want to give it up.

RUTH: (*gently*) But it's poor land, Bruce.

> (BRUCE *sits down, gazing gloomily at the fire.* HESTER *comes in from the kitchen with the small lamp and places it on the sideboard. Then she sits at the table, taking up her knitting. As* BRUCE *speaks, she watches him intently.*)

BRUCE: Yes, it's strange that in a soil that won't grow trees a man can put roots down, but he can.

RUTH: (*at his side*) You'd feel the same about another place after a little while.

BRUCE: I don't know. When I saw the wind last spring blowing the dirt away, the dirt I'd plowed and harrowed and sowed to grain, I felt as though a part of myself was blowing away in the dust. Even now with the land three feet under snow I can look out and feel it waiting for the seed I've saved for it.

RUTH: But if we go, we'll be nearer other people, not cut off from everything that lives.

BRUCE: You need people, don't you?

HESTER: Yes. She needs them. I've seen her at the window, looking toward the town. Day after day she stands there.

> (BRUCE *and* RUTH, *absorbed in the conflict between them, had forgotten* HESTER's *presence. At* HESTER's *words,* RUTH *turns on them both, flaming with anger.*)

RUTH: You two. You're so *perfect!*

HESTER: (*knitting*) We could always stand alone, the three of us. We didn't need to turn to every stranger who held his hand out.

RUTH: No! You'd sit here in this husk of a house, living like shadows, until these four walls closed in on you, buried you.

HESTER: I never stood at a window, looking down the road that leads to town.

RUTH: (*the pent-up hysteria of the day and the longing of months breaks through, tumbling out in her words*) It's not for myself I look down that road, Hester. It's for the child I'm going to have. You're right, Bruce, I am afraid. It's not what you think though, not for myself. You two and your father lived so long in this dark house that you forgot there's a world beating outside, forgot that

people laugh and play sometimes. And you've shut me out!
(*There is a catch in her voice.*) I never would have trampled on
your thoughts if you'd given them to me. But as it is, I might as
well not be a person. You'd like a shadow better that wouldn't
touch your house. A child would die here. A child can't live with
shadows.

(*Much disturbed,* BRUCE *rises and goes to her.*)

BRUCE: Ruth! I didn't know you hated it so much.

RUTH: I thought it would change. I thought I could change it. You
know now.

BRUCE: (*quietly*) Yes.

RUTH: (*pleading*) If we go, I'll *want* this child, Bruce. Don't you see?
But I'm not happy here. What kind of a life will our child have?
He'll be old before he's out of school. (*She looks at the hyacinth on
the stand.*) He'll be like this hyacinth bud that's broken before it
bloomed.

(BRUCE *goes to the table and stands looking down at the deed
of sale. His voice is tired and flat, but resolved.*)

BRUCE: All right. I'll tell Manning I'll let him have the place.

HESTER: (*turning quickly to* BRUCE) What do you mean?

BRUCE: I'm going to sell the farm to Manning. He was here
to-day.

HESTER: (*standing up, her eyes blazing*) You can't sell this house.

BRUCE: (*looking at the deed of sale*) Oh, Ruth's right. We can't make a
living on the place. (*He sits down, leafing through the document.*)
It's too dry. And too far from the school.

HESTER: It wasn't too far for you to go, or me.

BRUCE: (*irritably*) Do you think I want to sell?

HESTER: *She* does. But she can't do it. (*Her voice is low.*) This house
belongs to me.

BRUCE: Hester, don't start that again! I wish to God the land had been
divided differently, but it wasn't.

HESTER: Father meant for us to stay here and keep things as they were
when he was with us.

BRUCE: The soil wasn't blowing away when he was farming it.

HESTER: He meant for me to have the house.

RUTH: You'll go with us where we go, Hester.

HESTER: (*to* RUTH) You came here. You plotted with him to take this
house from me. But it's mine!

BRUCE: (*his voice cracks through the room*) Stop that, Hester! I love this
place as much as you do, but I'm selling it, I tell you.

(*As he speaks, he gets up abruptly and, taking up his coat,
puts it on.* HESTER *sinks slowly into the chair, staring.* RUTH
tries to put her hand on BRUCE's *arm.*)

RUTH: Bruce! Not that way! Not for me. If it's that way, I don't care
enough.

BRUCE: (*shaking himself free*) Oh, leave me alone!

RUTH: Bruce!
BRUCE: (*going to the door*) I'll be glad when it's over, I suppose.
RUTH: Where are you going?
BRUCE: (*taking his cap and gloves*) To look at that mare.
RUTH: Bruce! (*But he has gone.*)
HESTER: (*getting up, she goes to her father's chair and stands behind it, facing RUTH; she moves and speaks as if she were in a dream*). This is my house. I won't have strangers in it.
RUTH: (*at the table, without looking at HESTER*) Oh, Hester! I didn't want it to be this way. I tried—
HESTER: (*as if she were speaking to a stranger*) Why did you come here?
RUTH: I've hurt you. But I'm right about this. I know I'm right.
HESTER: There isn't any room for you.
RUTH: Can't you see? It's for all of us.
       (HESTER *comes toward* RUTH *with a strange, blazing anger in her face.*)
HESTER: I know your kind. In the night you tempted him with your bright hair.
RUTH: Hester!
HESTER: Your body anointed with jasmine for his pleasure.
RUTH: Hester, don't say such things.
HESTER: Oh, I know what you are! You and women like you. You put a dream around him with your arms, a sinful dream.
RUTH: (*drawing back*) Hester!
HESTER: You lift your white face to every stranger like you offered him a cup to drink from. That's sin! That's lust after the forbidden fruit. (*Turning from* RUTH, *as if she had forgotten her presence,* HESTER *looks fondly at the room.*) I'll never leave this house.
       (BRUCE *opens the door and comes in quickly and stormily. He goes into the kitchen as he speaks.*)
BRUCE: That mare's got out. She jumped the corral. I'll have to go after her.
RUTH: (*concerned*) Bruce, where will she be?
BRUCE: (*returning with an old blanket*) She'll be in the snowshed by the coulee. She always goes there when she's about to foal.
       (HESTER *sits in the chair by the stove, her knitting in her hand. She pays no attention to the others.*)
RUTH: But you can't go after her in this storm.
BRUCE: I'll take this old blanket to cover the colt, if it's born yet. Where's the lantern?
       (*He sees the two lanterns by the kitchen door, and taking one of them to the table lights it.*)
RUTH: It's three miles, Bruce. You mustn't go on foot. It's dangerous.
BRUCE: I'll have to. She'd never live through the night, or the colt either. (*He turns to go.*) You'd better go to bed. Good night, Hester.
RUTH: Let me come with you.

BRUCE: No. (*Then as he looks at her, all resentment leaves him. He puts down the lantern, goes to her, and takes her in his arms.*) Ruth, forget what I said. You know I didn't mean—
RUTH: (*softly*) I said things I didn't mean, too—
BRUCE: I love you, Ruth. You know it, don't you?
RUTH: Bruce!
> (*He kisses her, and for a moment their love is a flame in the room.*)
BRUCE: Don't worry. I won't be long.
RUTH: I'll wait.
> (BRUCE *goes out.* RUTH *follows him to the door and, as it closes, she stands against it for a moment. There is a silence.* HESTER *is slowly unraveling her knitting but is unaware of it. The black wool falls in spirals about her chair.*)
HESTER: (*suddenly*) It's an old house. I was born here. (*Then in a strange, calm voice that seems to come from a long distance.*) You shouldn't let Bruce be so much alone. You lose him that way. He comes back to *us* then. He'll see you don't belong here unless you keep your hand on him all the time. (RUTH *looks curiously at* HESTER *but does not give her all her attention.* HESTER *suddenly becomes harsh.*) This is my house. You can't change it. (RUTH *starts to say something but remains silent.*) Father gave it to me. There isn't any room for you. (*In a high, childlike tone, like the sound of a violin string breaking.*) No room.
> (*She shakes her head gravely.*)
RUTH: (*aware that something is wrong*) Hester—
HESTER: (*as if she were telling an often-recited story to a stranger*) I stayed home when Mother died and kept house for my little brother and Father. (*Her voice grows stronger.*) I was very beautiful, they said. My hair fell to my knees, and it was black as a furrow turned in spring. (*Proudly.*) I can have a husband any time I want, but my duty is here with Father. You see how it is. I can't leave him.
> (RUTH *goes quickly to* HESTER.)
RUTH: (*with anxiety and gentleness*) Hester, what are you talking about?
HESTER:. That's Father's chair. I'll put his Bible out.
> (*She starts from her chair.*)
RUTH: (*preventing her*) Hester, your father's not here—not for six years. You speak of him as if you thought. . . Hester—
HESTER: (*ignoring* RUTH *but remaining seated*) When I was a girl I always filled the lanterns after supper. Then I was ready for his coming.
RUTH: (*in terror*) Hester, I didn't fill them! I didn't fill the lanterns!
> (*She runs to the kitchen door and takes up the remaining lantern.*)
HESTER: (*calmly*) Father called me the wise virgin then.
RUTH: Hester, Bruce took one! He thought I'd filled them. It will burn out and he'll be lost in the blizzard.

41

HESTER: I always filled them.

RUTH: (*setting the lantern on the table*) I've got to go out after Bruce. If he gets down to the coulee and the lantern goes out, he'll never find the way back. I'll have to hurry! Where's the coal oil?
> (RUTH *goes to the kitchen and returns with a can of coal oil and a pair of galoshes.* HESTER *watches her closely. As* RUTH *comes in with the oil,* HESTER *slowly rises and goes to her.*)

HESTER: I'll fill the lantern for you, Ruth.

RUTH: (*trying to remove the top of the can*) I can't get the top off. My hands are shaking so.

HESTER: (*taking the oil can from* RUTH) I'll fill it for you.

RUTH: Please, Hester. While I get my things on! (*Giving* HESTER *the oil can,* RUTH *runs to the footstool and hurriedly puts on her galoshes.*) I'm afraid that lantern will last just long enough to get him out there. He'll be across the field before I even get outside.
> (*She runs up the stairs.*)

HESTER: (*standing motionless, the oil can in her hand*) You're going now. That's right. I told you you should go.
> (RUTH *disappears up the stairs.* HESTER *moves a step toward the lantern, taking off the top of the coal oil can. She hesitates and looks for a long moment after* RUTH. *With the strange lucidity of madness, slowly, deliberately, she place the top back again on the can and moving behind the table, sets it on the floor without filling the lantern.* RUTH *hurries down the stairs excited and alarmed. She has on heavy clothes and is putting on her gloves.*)

RUTH: Is it ready? (HESTER *nods.*) Will you light it for me, Hester? Please.
> (HESTER *lights the lantern.*)

RUTH: I'll put the light at the window. (*She crosses with the small lamp and places it at the window.*) Hurry, Hester! (*With a sob.*) Oh,if only I can find him!
> (HESTER *crosses to* RUTH *and gives her the lantern.* RUTH *takes the lantern and goes out. A gust of wind carries the snow into the room and blows shut the door after her.* HESTER *goes to the window.*)

HESTER: (*her voice is like an echo*) The snow lies deep on the summer fallow. . . The snow is a moving shroud. . .a winding sheet that the wind lifts and raises and lets fall again. (*Turning from the window.*) They've gone! They won't be back now. (*With an intense excitement,* HESTER *blows out the lamp at the window and pulls down the shades. Her eyes fall on the bowl of hyacinths in the corner. Slowly she goes to it, takes it up, and holding it away from her, carries it to the door. Opening the door, she sets the flowers outside. She closes the door and locks it. Her eyes blazing with excitement, she stands with her arms across the door as if shutting the world out. Then softly she moves to the door of her father's bedroom, unlocks it, and goes in, returning at once with a pair of men's bedroom slippers. Leaving the bedroom door open, she crosses to the sideboard, takes up the Bible, and going to her father's chair, places the slippers beside it. She speaks very softly.*) I put your slippers out. (*She draws the footstool up to the chair.*) Everything will be the same now, Father. (*She opens the Bible.*) I'll read to you, Father. I'll read the one you like. (*She reads with quiet contentment.*) "And the winds blew, and beat upon that house; and it fell not: for it was founded upon a rock."

(*The wind moans through the old house as the curtain falls.*)

The End

Pasque Flower
A play of the Canadian Prairie

Characters

JAKE HANSEN, *a farmer*
LISA, *his wife.* LISA *is pronounced with the "i" as in Rita.*
DAVID, *his brother*

SCENE: *The living room of the Hansen farmhouse, Alberta.*
TIME: *The present. An evening in March.*

The amber light of the setting sun and the soft glow from the fireplace illuminate faintly the room upon which the curtain rises. It is an attractive room, furnished with simplicity and taste. Two comfortable chairs, one on either side of the fireplace in the right wall, and a floor lamp beside the upstage chair, are shadowy in the twilight. Above the fireplace is a print of Millet's "The Sower." In the rear wall, at the right, is a door leading outside; at the left, a window. Between them is a small table with a bright pottery bowl of ivy on it.

Downstage, left, near the door leading into the kitchen is a gate-leg table, attractively laid for one person. Other good prints, soft rose curtains, and hooked rugs lend warmth and charm to the room.

LISA HANSEN is sitting by the fire. Her sewing has fallen unnoticed on the arm of her chair and she is watching the flickering embers dully. She is about thirty, beautiful in a quiet way; but there is a patient hunger in her face. She has been crying.

After a moment in which nothing but the tick of the clock is heard, JAKE HANSEN opens the door and comes in. He is dark and stockily built, nearing forty. There is a touch of gray in his hair.

JAKE is carrying several parcels and, awkwardly, a bunch of purple pasque flowers, harbingers of spring on the northern prairies. As he enters, LISA tries to compose herself to meet him with a smile. JAKE, not

45

Gwen Pharis Ringwood

seeing her, starts toward the kitchen to find her, holding the flowers carefully. But he becomes aware of a presence in the room and turns to see LISA sitting with her back to him, drying her eyes. He goes to give her the flowers but at the sight of the drooping figure of his wife, he changes his mind and turns away, throwing the flowers down on the little table beside the door. Without turning to look at her, he speaks, his words betraying a baffled irritation.

JAKE: (*Taking off his jacket*) Sitting in the dark again, eh? Why can't you turn on the light?
> (*He snaps on the light at the switch*)

LISA: (*Rising and turning on the floor lamp*) It's only just got dark, Jake. The days are getting longer.
> (*She turns and smiles a little*)

JAKE: (*Looking down at the hat he holds in his hands, speaks in a low tone*) A man finds little comfort in a woman who moons by the fire at night, like a sick ewe.

LISA: (*Patiently*) I'm sorry, Jake.

JAKE: (*Without looking at her, places the newspaper on the dining table*) I thought David might be here by now.

LISA: Perhaps he isn't coming after all.

JAKE: (*Distantly*) That would be bad, after all the work you've done too, getting ready.

LISA: He's been away so long, he may decide it's better not to come.

JAKE: He can stay away for all of me.

LISA: I hoped you'd welcome him this time. He's your brother, and there were hard words between you when he left.

JAKE: He maybe won't come; it's getting late.

LISA: No. He maybe won't come now.

JAKE: Is that what's set you grieving?

LISA: (*Ignoring him*) I'll get your supper, Jake.
> (*She starts toward the kitchen*)

JAKE: (*Moving to the fireplace*) Sometimes you're a fool, Liz, sometimes I think. . . .

LISA: (*Turning*) Did you bring the mail?

JAKE: (*Going to her*) So you think to put me off! What are you crying for? By heaven, I'm sick of coming in to see that patient face of yours turning away, as if you'd had a sentence to a life in prison. Here, look at me!
> (*He takes her by the wrist*)

LISA: (*Quietly*) Don't, Jake, let me go.

JAKE: Then why do you sit mewling by the fire? What are you thinking of?

LISA: Please, Jake. . .

JAKE: (*Releasing her*) God is my witness, Liz, I don't know what you want. Well, get the meal.

LISA: (*Taking a step away from him, then turning*) I'm sorry.

JAKE: (*Moving to the fireplace*) Ah, let it go. You women have to have your woe whatever comes. If it isn't real, you'll find a shadow that will set you weeping.

(LISA *goes into the kitchen.* JAKE *starts to fill his pipe. Then, with a glance after his wife, he goes to take up the pasque flowers. But at her step he puts them down, turns away, and lights his pipe.* LISA *returns with a plate of food and the coffee pot. She places them on the table without looking at* JAKE. *After a moment she breaks the silence with forced lightness*)

LISA: The fire takes off the chill. I think March nights promise more warmth than they can ever give, don't you?

JAKE: (*Going to the table*) Yes, I suppose. But it's warm enough for weeds to grow all right. Did the men finish ploughing the north field today?

LISA: They said they'd take another day at least.

JAKE: (*Sitting down and beginning to eat*) They work like snails! It seems to me they'd know I'd like to plant a crop before September.

LISA: Jake, they've been working night and day. You know that.

JAKE: Where's Williams now?

LISA: Across the coulee. He said he'd see about the sheep before he left.

JAKE: Did he fix those pens? They've got to be built higher.

LISA: He didn't get it done. He wanted to finish up and go to town.

JAKE: He's been to town four nights in five this spring. I'll have to board them up myself tonight. If a dog got in, the whole flock would jump the pens.

LISA: Did you get flour and salt in town?

JAKE: I did. And thread and knitting needles. I wish you'd do your buying from now on. A man feels like a fool trying to match thread.

LISA: (*Taking up the newspaper from the table*) I know; it was good of you to get them.

JAKE: I made a big deal today. Took over that section that old Roebuck farms.

LISA: You took Roebuck's farm?

JAKE: He never paid the interest on his debt, and never could, and so today I took the land.

LISA: (*Turning on him*) But Jake, you don't need land! You've got more now than you can farm.

JAKE: I've got six sections. By getting Roebuck's place they're all in one block now. I've hoped for that a long time.

LISA: (*Smiling, but there is an irony in her tone which escapes* JAKE) Four thousand acres lying in one piece. . . .

JAKE: (*With enthusiasm*) Next fall will see me with the biggest wheat field in the country.

LISA: (*Without looking at him*) Did Roebuck take it hard?

JAKE: I don't suppose he liked it.

LISA: He's been a good neighbour to us, Jake.

JAKE: (*Resentfully*) He's a poor farmer for all that. You'd think I'd murdered him to hear you talk.

LISA: I'm not sure but it will be a kind of death for him. Think how you'd feel.

JAKE: I don't farm like he does. But if you had your way I'd have no land to lose.

LISA: (*Putting down the paper*) I didn't mean that. I'll pour your coffee. (*Going to the table*)

JAKE: (*Glancing at her and then away*) You can't bear to eat with me, I take it?

LISA: I thought when it got late you'd eat in town, so I went on. (*She pours coffee and takes it to him*)

JAKE: David will be surprised to see this farm. It was in bad shape when he left—not that he ever cared about the land.

LISA: (*Earnestly*) Will you be glad to see him, Jake?

JAKE: (*A little taken aback by her question*) Why, I suppose. Though I've some notion why he comes. And it's not love for me that brings him.

LISA: (*Withdrawing*) What brings him then?

JAKE: (*Pushing back his chair and getting up*) Crying for money, I suppose. Well, I'll not let him have it. I've worked to wring a living from this land for nineteen years; what's mine, I've earned. It's not for me to judge, but if he'd stayed on here, after Dad died, instead of selling me his share for half its worth, he'd have a living now.

LISA: You never rested till you got his land.

JAKE: (*Going to the fireplace to get his pipe*) The more fool he, reaching to the moon. The rest of us could be content to farm. Not David! He must be a doctor.

LISA: That's what he should be, Jake. He's worked hard.

JAKE: You could always see things his way, couldn't you? Never mine.

LISA: (*After a pause*) You don't want me to share things with you, Jake. (*She turns to clear the table*)

JAKE: You needn't tell him of the deal I made. If he thinks I've got something laid away he'll try to get a loan.

LISA: (*Facing him*) I hardly think you have a cause to worry. It's been five years since David asked your help.

JAKE: It'll be longer, before I give him any.

LISA: Jake, what's come over you? He's your brother, born of the same stock as you. Does blood mean nothing to you?

JAKE: I've got to buy machinery for that new place. It's my job to see that land out there is clean and sown with wheat; that takes money.

LISA: Oh, it's not only money. When David wrote that time, a friendly letter just asking how we were, you wouldn't answer.

JAKE: You answered, didn't you? That was enough.

LISA: He wanted to hear from you.

JAKE: (*Moving restlessly away from her*) He always tried to make me look a fool. Now that I've got somewhere, I'll not have him come whining to me to get him started—buy some broken-down practice for him to butcher people.

LISA: I thought perhaps you'd let the old scores die, I thought. . . .

JAKE: You thought I'd forget the things he's done to me—Well, I haven't.

LISA: David didn't hurt you.

JAKE: I didn't say he hurt me. If he wants to think himself better than I am he can go ahead. I've done all right.

(*He sits by the table*)

LISA: You never came half way for him, or me.

JAKE: Maybe I didn't. I was no use to him. He got along.

LISA: But Jake, the things you've got against him are so little, a stupid quarrel or two. The rest is in your mind.

JAKE: I'm not given to fancies.

LISA: (*Turning away*) He told me how you felt about the dog. . . .

JAKE: Sure he told you. That's only one thing though! (*He gets up angrily*) But suppose I'd done that to him? Suppose I'd gone to where he stood in a group of men. Gone, blazing with anger, called him a beast, a red-eyed brute—those were the words he used—because I'd shot a dog that killed five sheep of mine the night before.

LISA: He didn't know about the sheep, Jake, he was only a child then. He didn't know you did it because you had to.

JAKE: (*Turning fiercely on her*) No, he thought I liked to do it! Thought, because I look to my own safety, that I've no feeling to compare with his. Well, maybe I haven't. (*He turns away from her*) Maybe you and he and white-faced dreamers like you have a corner on all the feelings in the world, and we poor clod-shufflers, who have to dig the ground, or slit a hog's throat, or stick a bloated cow,— have to do this, I tell you, to survive—we've got no feelings!

LISA: Jake, I didn't know. . . .

JAKE: (*His voice low*) Ah, let it go, you feel the same. I've seen it in your eyes. I've felt you stiffen when I touch you and grow quiet, like a bird with a broken wing, when you put your hand on it. And then submit, in patient duty.

LISA: That wasn't always true.

JAKE: No? I see things. (*He moves to the fireplace, speaking in an almost matter-of-fact tone*) If I were half the brute you think me I'd have killed you for that long ago.

LISA: Jake, when I came here eight years ago I thought we'd made a home, I thought you needed me. If the baby'd lived, things would be different, I know that. He'd be three years old tonight. But since he died, you've grown to care for nothing but your land and the power you wring from it.

JAKE: A man can get more warmth from an unploughed field that welcomes his hand than from a woman who shuts herself away, peers at him out of the corners of her eyes, expecting the worst from him.

LISA: I didn't shut myself away till you—

JAKE: Don't lie, Liz!

LISA: Maybe we can try again, as if there'd never been these dreary years; begin all over. I'm older, wiser, now.

JAKE: (*Sitting now, and attempting to throw off the tension between them*) We'll go along the way we have, I guess. We're no worse off than many.

LISA: (*Turning away from him*) Or we could call it all a mistake and go our ways.

JAKE: (*Quietly*) That's what you want, isn't it? But I won't give you that.

LISA: (*Sitting near him*) Jake, if we took a child to raise—a boy. . . . I've thought of it through these long winter nights when we've sat alone, so far apart as to be nameless to each other. A child would fill the house with laughter, perhaps the love a child would bring could stay this thing that's eating at our lives.

JAKE: I'll leave to no stranger's son, the land I've worked for.

LISA: He wouldn't be a stranger's child for long, we'd have so much love to spend it wouldn't matter that he wasn't ours.

JAKE: I'll take no bastard here to bear my name, that's my last word.

LISA: (*Getting up, her voice low and cold*) Sometimes I wonder if you're human, Jake, and if you care for anything on earth besides your land!

JAKE: You've said enough, Liz. Enough, I say! I can stand so much and then no more.

LISA: (*Facing him, firmly*) I'll have my say. If we're to live here in this house together it's better that we know just how we stand. For every acre of ground you've bought, Jake Hansen, you've lost a little of your soul. The hand of every man with whom you deal is raised against you. You drive a hard bargain, Jake, that's your boast. Fate drives a hard one too. You've traded all the good in you for land, more land. You'll never have enough!

(*She starts away*)

JAKE: (*Seizing her angrily*) I've had enough of this! Stop it, I tell you! You think to drive me mad so I'll let you go, then you'll be free of me, that's what you want! But I won't let you go, even though you've come to fear and hate me, though you hide from me behind your eyes, I'll never let you go!

LISA: Jake!

JAKE: (*Lifting her face to him*) Your eyes are blue as a field of flax with the dew on it, but in an hour the flowers fall as if they'd never been. And that's the way it is with you; when I come near you, you hide from me, you take the light out of your eyes, and hide. It sets me mad!

LISA: Jake! Jake!

JAKE: (*Releasing her*) I didn't mean that, Liz don't leave me; you're safe with me, I didn't mean to hurt you.
(*There is a knock at the door*)
LISA: (*Her voice unsteady*) That's David, Jake! You let him in. I'd rather he'd not see me just yet, Jake.
JAKE: (*Quietly*) I'll let him in. (LISA *goes into the kitchen*. JAKE *goes slowly to the door and opens it*) Come in.
(DAVID *enters. He is about thirty, handsome and rather boyish, purposeful, with an easy, likable manner. He, like* JAKE, *seems embarrassed at the meeting.*)
DAVID: Well, Jake! I'm home again! How are you brother?
JAKE: (*As they shake hands*) I'm well, how is it with you?
DAVID: Fine. I'm a bit muddy from that hole down by the gate. I had to push the car a little way. Where's Lisa?
JAKE: Upstairs. She'll be here in a moment.
DAVID: (*Taking off his coat*) It's good to see you Jake. You grow no fatter, but none of us have ever run to flesh.
JAKE: Sit down. How far did you come today?
DAVID: (*Sitting by the fire*) Four hundred miles. It wasn't bad, but still I'm glad to be here. Lisa's done a lot for this old house.
JAKE: It serves its purpose.
DAVID: Remember, when we were kids, how bare it got? We broke up all the chairs doing acrobatics, and after Mother died, nobody cared as long as we'd a place to sleep and eat—Lisa's made it warm and home-like.
JAKE: Yes.
DAVID: (*Taking out a cigarette*) Well, Jake, how are things going?
JAKE: (*Holding a match for him*) Oh, a farm is much the same from day to day, little to talk of, always work to do.
DAVID: They say in town you've so much land that you could ride from sun to sun and not get round it.
JAKE: (*Drily*) That's hardly true. I bought up worn-out farms they'd let run down, more work than profit from them up till now.
DAVID: (*Chuckling*) You've got Dad's eye for business, I see that. I wish I had.
JAKE: (*Slowly*) What did you come for—money?
DAVID: Why, no. . . . I. . . . (*with quick anger*) But don't you want me here?
JAKE: You came a long way to make a social call.
DAVID: (*Getting up and throwing away his cigarette*) So it's that way. You never forget old grudges, do you, Jake? You never did when we were kids. Before I go, I'd like to tell you this—I came because I'm leaving for the Yukon Saturday, I wanted to see my home before I left. I wanted to see you and Lisa. We're the only two left now, Jake, and, strange as it may seem to you, I thought I'd like to visit you and Lisa before going North. I'll go now.
(*He takes his coat and goes to the door.*)

51

JAKE: (*With difficulty*) No, no, stay. . . . I. . . . say things. . . . Things are not always what they seem in words. Lisa would like to see you, she's been shut in close—and I. . . . I'd be ready to forget old scores if it's as you say, you come. . . . Well, we are brothers. We didn't always find it hard to talk. I'd like it if you stayed. . . .

>(DAVID *puts his hand affectionately on* JAKE's *shoulder and puts down his coat.* JAKE *follows him, speaking almost timidly*)

JAKE: And if you need money, I could help you some.

DAVID: Thanks. I don't need money, Jake, but thanks.

JAKE: Then you'll stay?

DAVID: I can't stay long. I've much to do tomorrow and—

>(*He breaks off and looks toward the door at* LISA, *who comes in flushed with pleasure*)

LISA: (*Going to him*) David! It's good to see you here!

DAVID: It's good to be here, Lisa.

LISA: How changed you are, I like you this way!

DAVID: Changed? You mean I'm older?

LISA: Yes, but something else. Don't you see it, Jake?

JAKE: He's not so long and lanky as he was, he's filled out some I guess, and older. . . . Five years will leave its mark on all of us.

DAVID: (*Looking at* LISA) Yes.

LISA: You must be starving, David.

DAVID: (*Sitting by the fire*) No, I ate in town.

LISA: How long it seems since you've been here with us. Have you come home to stay?

DAVID: No, Lisa, I've been telling Jake about my plans. I'm heading for the Yukon on Saturday. I wanted to see you before I go.

LISA: The Yukon? That's so far! (*She sits opposite him*) They say up there the Northern lights shoot clear across the heavens. I read that just the other day—you go on Saturday?

DAVID: I start my first practice there.

JAKE: (*Sitting*) Won't it be hard in winter, getting round?

DAVID: They use dogs in that country, I'll get used to that.

JAKE: If you'd rather stay and start up here—they need more doctors— I could help you some.

LISA: Why, Jake, how wonderful! But could you, David?

DAVID: No, it's good of you, but this other beckons. It's a chance to try it in a hard country. If you make good, well, there's no money in it, but you'd feel—Oh, I don't know. . . .

LISA: (*Softly*) I know.

DAVID: Jake feels that way about the land, he always has. It's something to master, and if you fail it breaks you.

JAKE: Yes.

DAVID: (*Crossing to the window, putting his hand on* JAKE's *shoulder*) But you haven't failed Jake. I never saw a cleaner farm than this.

JAKE: (*Rising*) It's some different than it was all right. I'll show you round tomorrow.

LISA: Where are you going, Jake?

JAKE: I'd better see what I can do about those pens. It won't take long. (*He takes up his tobacco pouch and begins to fill it*)

DAVID: Old Roebuck's place has run to weeds. I saw it coming out.

JAKE: It's bad.

DAVID: Does he still tell tall stories, and dream dreams of the big crop he's going to have next year?

LISA: He's looking older.

DAVID: He used to pull his hat down over his eyes and drive along, cursing his horses with a kind of tender chant.

JAKE: He'd never see you can't farm that much land with horses. He wouldn't buy a tractor, he let the place run down.

DAVID: Maybe he doesn't toil much, but he'll always get along.

JAKE: He borrowed more than his land was worth.

DAVID: We followed that man like pups when we were kids, remember, Jake? He'd take us fishing every sunny day. I'll try to get over to see him before I go.

LISA: You'll find him changed. . . . All of us have changed, David. There have been hard years.

JAKE: (*Putting on his jacket*) He's a poor farmer, no excuse! That section is the best soil in the country. But he couldn't keep it up.

DAVID: You mean he sold it?

JAKE: (*Harshly*) No, he borrowed on it, till he lost it. I own it now.

DAVID: You own it! (*A pause*) But he's still farming it?

JAKE: I'm putting Johnson on it, Roebuck's working there. He gets his room and board and some to spend.

DAVID: (*Quietly and coldly*) You shouldn't have done that, Jake.

JAKE: I renewed his note once, he couldn't pay. The weeds were spreading from his farm to mine. If I hadn't taken it, some other would.

DAVID: Jake, he helped Dad to buy this place; you can't put him to work as a hired man on his own farm.

JAKE: Dad paid him off with interest.

DAVID: You don't need that land.

JAKE: You said if you fail to conquer the land it breaks you. Well, he failed.

DAVID: You're a hard man, Jake.

JAKE: And if I am?

DAVID: You'd feel a lot better if you'd helped him instead of taking all he had away.

JAKE: Did you come here to tell me how to do?

DAVID: No, but I'll say what I think.

JAKE: It will do you no good. I needed that section, now I've got it.

LISA: David—Jake—don't talk of it any more, you know it's not in you to agree.

DAVID: I'm sorry, Lisa, but if Jake thinks I'll stand by and praise him for this rotten deal, he's wrong.

53

Gwen Pharis Ringwood

JAKE: I never asked for any praise from you.
DAVID: No, and praise or blame won't move you from the path to what you want.
JAKE: (*Sarcastically*) David, the harp-singer! The gentle shepherd boy!
LISA: Don't, Jake!
JAKE: You stay out of this. (*Turning to* DAVID) And you, if you're so broken up about John Roebuck why don't you buy the farm and give it back to him?
DAVID: I'd do it if I could. You'll get no good out of it. It will be barren soil for you. The seed you plant won't ripen, and I hope there'll come a time you'll curse the day you took it over.
JAKE: When that day comes you're welcome in this house, and when I want advice from you, I'll ask for it.
> (JAKE *leaves the house. There is a silence.* DAVID *and* LISA *do not look at one another.*)
DAVID: I'm sorry I made him angry, Lisa. I should have known.
LISA: He's not himself these days.
DAVID: We never got along. He always thought I held him in contempt. It wasn't true.
LISA: No, he. . . . he tortures himself, David. It's as if he wanted everyone to think the worst of him.
DAVID: (*Looking at her and away*) I shouldn't have come.
LISA: (*Quietly*) Don't say that, David.
DAVID: (*After a moment*) I've seen this picture somewhere before. . . . I don't remember where. . . .
LISA: I found it in a magazine; I had it framed.
DAVID: (*Studying the picture*) "The Sower."—He's like Jake.
LISA: Yes. . . . Alone. . . .
DAVID: (*With forced naturalness*) Well, I'm glad you've had good crops here these last years.
LISA: Yes, it's meant a lot to us, after the drought. I'd better get your room ready. . . .
DAVID: (*Looking at the picture*) Jake saved my life once. . . . We were swimming in the river, after school. He cried after he got me out, then swore at me for being so much trouble.
> (*He moves toward her, smiling*)
LISA: (*To him*) He never told me.
> (*They look at one another.* DAVID *goes to take her in his arms, but lets his hands fall.*)
DAVID: (*Turning toward the door*) I'm afraid I left the car blocking the road, I'd better go and see.
LISA: (*Going toward the kitchen*) And I'll fix your room.
DAVID: Lisa!
LISA: Don't, David.
DAVID: (*Going to her*) I tried to believe I came to see the old place, and Jake; I came on your account, I know it now.
LISA: No!

DAVID: It was on your account I went away.

LISA: (*Pleading*) David. . .!

DAVID: You've changed, you're not happy like you were. It's in your face.

LISA: I'm not sure that happiness is the thing to look for—I'll clear the table now. . . .

DAVID: Don't shut me out with words.

LISA: David, you mustn't; I'll wish you hadn't come.

DAVID: I had to come; I thought when I went away before I'd never see your face again. It's haunted me day and night since I left you. Has it been that way with you?

LISA: No. . . .

DAVID: Look at me.

LISA: David, I'm tired.

DAVID: Has it been so with you?

LISA: (*Looking at him steadily*) You've been in my thoughts more than I wished for.

DAVID: I can't bear to see you look like this, these years have done something to you; Jake has hurt you.

LISA: Don't blame him, he loves me better far than I deserve. Oh, it's something in myself, some restlessness that won't be satisfied. I thought a child might bring me peace, but then our child died, mine and Jake's and there wasn't any more. . . . That did something to us both. Don't ask me for love, David, I haven't any love to give.

DAVID: I've come, asking. I've wandered half across the world hoping that space or time would put a veil between me and my memory of you. Now I've come back, asking.

LISA: There might have been a time—had things been otherwise—we might have found together something to live by. Not now.

DAVID: But it's wrong for you to stay chained here; in the end it will destroy you, Lisa.

LISA: Sometimes, in summer, when the wind raises the dust like smoke, I've traced your name there on the ledge. Tried to hold on to some remembered beauty, something you gave me in your voice and smile, when you were here before. Then I'd see the dust blot out the name I'd written. I took it as a sign it was a dream I'd had, having no meaning.

DAVID: Come with me, Lisa.

LISA: No. . . .

DAVID: Let me take care of you, I'll give you faith again. This is the only answer for us, Lisa.

LISA: I couldn't go, and leave Jake here alone.

DAVID: He has his land, that's where his heart is, Lisa.

LISA: He doesn't want it that way. Something put scars on him— something long ago.

Gwen Pharis Ringwood

DAVID: It's too late to take away his hurt, come with me, Lisa, before you're hurt too.
(*He takes her in his arms*)
LISA: Oh, David, it's been so long. . . . You've been under my thoughts, and I. . . . without you, I've not been myself but something lost in darkness, a cry flung on the wind, asking no recognition.
DAVID: You said together we could find something to live by. Will you come?
LISA: (*Moving away from him to the table by the window*) David. . . . I don't know. . . .
DAVID: Oh, I'll be good to you and keep you safe, I'd make you glad you came. I'd build a house with windows toward the sun and make you glad you came.
(LISA *sees the pasque flowers. She takes them up and turns joyously to* DAVID)
LISA: David, where did you find them? Pasque flowers! They mean it's spring! Most years they don't come out till Easter —I love them so.
DAVID: The hill below the schoolhouse. . . . They always come there first. . . .
LISA: And I've let them wilt, because you didn't tell me.
DAVID: (*Quietly*) I didn't bring them, Lisa.
LISA: It wasn't you—but it must be! Tell me you brought them, David.
DAVID: I didn't bring them.
LISA: Oh. . . .
(*She turns away, slowly*)
DAVID: Lisa!
LISA: No, it was a dream. I'm sorry, David, but he brought them, he remembered, and he brought them. . . .
DAVID: Lisa, you love me; say it.
LISA: No. . . . For a moment a flame mounted in this room; but it has nothing to feed on, David, and it dies. . . I've lived with Jake through drought and wind and rain, I held our child in my arms three years ago tonight, and he brought me flowers. . . . like these. . . . He'd picked them on the hill—the first ones out. He looked so strange and blundering in that little room with its white walls. I'm held here not by duty, David, as I thought, but something else; by some blind need Jake has for me and I for him. I thought to break that tie, but years don't go down before a moment's bidding, David. All the years we've lived crowd round us always and hold us on the path that we must go; and mine lies here. . . . Forgive me.
DAVID: Then, it's finished?
LISA: Yes.
DAVID: When I'm old, I'll remember your hands, holding these flowers. . . .

LISA: (*Through her tears*) Call it a dream, David. That was all it was. (*She turns away.* JAKE *enters and stands for a moment looking at them.* DAVID *and* LISA *are aware of his presence but do not move.* JAKE *goes to the fireplace, speaking to cover the silence*)

JAKE: (*Removing his jacket*) Well, that's done! I saw a coyote slinking across the coulee. I'll see if I can get a shot at him tomorrow, he's been around here twice this week.

LISA: I heard one howling in the night.

DAVID: I'll go now, Lisa.
(*He takes up his coat*)

JAKE: You're leaving?

DAVID: I'd better go, I've much to do and. . . .
(*He makes no attempt to finish*)

JAKE: (*With difficulty*) I didn't mean to get so riled over old Roebuck. I've thought it over. You and Liz are right. I'll let him keep his land.

LISA: Why, Jake!

DAVID: You won't be sorry, Jake.

JAKE: So, if you're going because of what I said. . . .

DAVID: It isn't that, Jake.

JAKE: When you came back tonight, I didn't want you here; but out there, outside of walls, I. . . . I think better, things look clearer somehow. For what it's worth to you, I don't hate you, David. . . . You're my brother.

DAVID: (*To him*) Thanks, Jake. That's worth a lot to me. (*With forced lightness*) I'll think of you both; and write. Goodbye.
(*They shake hands*)

JAKE: Goodbye.

DAVID: (*Turning to* LISA) Goodbye.

LISA: (*Softly*) Goodbye.
(DAVID *leaves. A silence*)

JAKE: Liz, there's something you have together, you and David; I'm outside. A man can fail at other things besides his land, at bigger things. Did you send David away because you pitied me?

LISA: Then you knew?

JAKE: I'm not all rock or clay. And when things happen to you, it's in your face.

LISA: (*Smiling*) It wasn't pity, Jake.

JAKE: I'm glad.

LISA: Thank you for bringing the flowers, Jake; you didn't tell me.

JAKE: Oh, I forgot the things. They were growing there on the big hill, they always come there first.

LISA: You brought them to me when the baby came. Thank you for remembering, Jake.

JAKE: I should have given them to you when I came, they look wilted now; you'd better throw them out.

Gwen Pharis Ringwood

LISA: No. I want to keep them. Pasque flowers! Now I know that
spring has come again.
(*The curtain falls.*)

The End

Dark Harvest
A tragedy of the Canadian Prairie

ACT I: The farmyard of Gerth Hansen's farm. An April evening, 1936.

ACT II: The same as act one. An evening in early August, 1938.

ACT III: A corner of a wheat field on the Hansen farm. A late afternoon in September, 1938.

Characters

GERTH HANSEN, *a farmer*
LISA HANSEN, *his wife*
DAVID HANSEN, *Gerth's brother*
JULIA MACDONALD, *the housekeeper*
BERT MACDONALD, *Julia's son*
CHARLIE, *Gerth's hired man*
AL MORROW, *a farmer*

ACT ONE

SCENE: *The farmyard of Gerth Hansen's farm.*
TIME: *An April evening, 1936.*

The curtain rises on the front yard of the Hansen farm-house. At the left, a corner of the veranda with steps leading up to it and one white column are all that can be seen of the house itself. The branches of two large poplar trees at back and at the right are beginning to be tipped with green. Under the tree at right are a green table and two home-made benches. A path to the road runs downstage of the table and through the hedge that borders the lawn along the right. A path to the barn cuts through the shrubbery at the rear of the stage, left of centre. A garden rake has been left lying across the path to the road, and two bright cushions are lying at the foot of the steps. The evening sun slants across the lawn, and in its light a few patches of new grass show bright green in contrast to the dull brown of most of the lawn.

When the curtain rises LISA HANSEN *is sitting on the steps of the veranda. She is a graceful, blue-eyed woman in her late twenties, with a quiet beauty and a low, appealing voice. She has a quick, warm smile, but there is often a brooding sadness in her face, and sometimes her voice and movement betray the smouldering restlessness that holds her in toil. On the veranda beside her are two hand-made window boxes, filled with earth, and some baskets containing young pansy and snapdragon plants. In one of the baskets too are some lilac roots which* LISA *is busy unwrapping and placing in a pail beside her.*

Sitting on the bench at right is JULIA MACDONALD, *a woman of about forty-five, who is busy sprinkling some newly-washed clothes, rolling them up, and placing them in the basket beside her.* JULIA *is a cheerful, talkative soul, capable and straightforward. The sharpness of her tongue is belied by her tolerant smile, and her face is that of a contented, slightly stout and rather commonplace woman who likes to keep a good house and set a good table. She has helped with the housework at the Hansen farm for many years and is completely at ease with* GERTH *and* LISA.

LISA: (*unwrapping one of the lilac plants*) If Gerth will get the water down here, we'll set these out tomorrow, Julia.

JULIA: (*with a brief glance at* LISA) Lilacs take a long time to grow, seven years blooming time they say.

LISA: Seven years! (*For a moment she stops her work, looking down at the plant thoughtfully.*) I've lived here that long.

JULIA: (*sprinkling the white clothes with quick, deft movements*) A lot of water has run under the mill since then.

LISA: For both of us, Julia. . . and by the time these bloom, there's no telling what we'll be, or where.

JULIA: We'll probably be right here sitting in the cool of the evening. You'll be getting ready to plant a garden and Gerth will own more land, and work like the devil was behind him, cracking a whip, just like he does now.

LISA: (*resuming her work*) Has he always worked like this. . . I mean before he married me?

JULIA: Maybe he gets worse as the years go by, I don't know, but his Dad called him a working fool even when he was a kid. In harvest Gerth and David used to drive their bundle wagons up at the same time and start pitching. They'd never say a word but it was a fight to the finish. The other men would stand around and bet on who would win. Gerth usually finished a little ahead but there wasn't a man in the country who could pitch bundles with either of them.

LISA: I can't imagine David farming.

JULIA: He never cared about it like Gerth does. When I first came here to work, he was only a little fellow but he had his mind made up to be a doctor.

LISA: (*wistfully*) It must be wonderful, helping people. . . making them well!

JULIA: (*drily*) There's good doctors and poor ones; mostly we've had the poor ones around here lately, or none at all.

LISA: (*bitterly*) Yes, if there'd been a doctor here, I'd have a baby to look after instead of lilacs. He'd be three years old tonight. (*She puts her head down on the step.*)

JULIA: (*going over to pick up the plant that* LISA *has dropped, puts her hand on* LISA's *shoulder.*) Don't, child. We have to forget those things. You'll only upset yourself talking about it.

LISA: (*getting up and taking the plant from* JULIA) No, I mustn't talk about it or think about it. I must do like Gerth and grow things, plant them in the ground. (*An old hurt breaks through her words.*) The things you grow in the ground are quiet; they don't cry and kick the air like newborn babies.

JULIA: (*with a touch of severity*) Hush, Lisa, for all you know it's as hard for a piece of grass to grow as for a baby.

LISA: (*her bitterness gone*) I thought the baby would give us something to live for besides land; I counted on him for that. And then I had him for one day. I think something inside me died too, Julia.

JULIA: (*returning to her basket*) You've got much to be thankful for, Lisa. You've a nice home and Gerth's a good husband to you. I only hope Bert will be as good a farmer as Gerth is.

LISA: (*smiling a little*) Bert's a good boy, Julia. He was so excited today about running the new tractor.

JULIA: (*with pride and disapproval mingling in her voice*) Put Bert on anything that makes a noise and he's happy. He's wild to go careening around in an aeroplane. Well, Mac was like that—

LISA: Poor Julia, you've had it hard.

JULIA: No more than anybody. I always think Mac will come back some day, throw in his hat and act as if he'd left the day before. And I suppose I'd set to cooking the things he likes, the same as I always did. It's funny how a good-for nothing husband can stick in your thoughts.

(CHARLIE *comes around the corner of the house, carrying a milk pail. He is a man of fifty years, small and slight. There is something about his slight figure that suggests a boy rather than an old man, a boy that has worked too hard. His overalls are large on him and his face is weathered and patient.* GERTH *is his idol and when he discusses crops with* GERTH *he becomes animated and excited, but with other people he is quiet and a little timid.*)

LISA: Hello, Charlie.

CHARLIE: Evening, Mrs. Hansen. Hello, Julia. Is the boss around?

LISA: He's gone to town, Charlie, but he should be home soon. Did you want something?

CHARLIE: We were going to set the water in the North field, but I'll go ahead and milk. (*He starts to go, then hesitates.*) Those men from Raley, they've finished ploughing. They want to go home for Sunday I think.

LISA: (*smiling*) I'll tell him, Charlie.

JULIA: (*finishing her task and moving with the basket to the veranda*) Will Gerth be wanting supper?

LISA: He'll probably eat in town but put some coffee on, Julia. He always wants that.

JULIA: I'll take these in. (*Turning as she starts into the house*) Are you going to set those window boxes tonight?

LISA: Yes, it won't take long. (JULIA *goes into the house.*) This looks like good rich soil you brought down for me, Charlie.

CHARLIE: (*proudly*) It grows good wheat for the boss, Mrs. Hansen.

LISA: Then it should grow flowers for me shouldn't it? I'm going to set the lilac plants over there, after Gerth's irrigated down here.
(*She indicates the corner near the path to the road.*)

CHARLIE: (*looking at the plants*) They'll grow all right in this weather. That winter wheat shows green today.
(JULIA *comes out of the house.*)

JULIA: Mind you gather the eggs now, Charlie. You always get more than anybody else.

CHARLIE: Yeah, I'll get them.
(*He takes his pail and goes out toward the barn.*)

JULIA: (*looking after him*) He walks slower than he used to. But he's a different man from the skeleton Gerth brought home from the East fifteen years ago. you should have seen him then. . . he'd been sick a year.

LISA: (*thoughtfully*) Julia, when Gerth was a boy, did you expect he'd be the man he is?

JULIA: Why, I don't know, Lisa. (*She sits down and begins helping* LISA *with the plants.*) I never thought he'd be as good a provider as he is, if that's what you mean. He was always hot-tempered, and kept to himself a lot. Now David was always on the go when he was here. People always made a fuss over David.

LISA: I wrote to David that Dr. Gray may be going away. If he came back here—we need a doctor so badly—don't you think he'd do well?

JULIA: David would never come back here. . . after that row he and Gerth had before he went away.

LISA: That was just three weeks after Gerth brought me here. I remem-

ber waking up to hear them shouting at one another. But that
was so long ago it ought to be forgotten now.
(*An automobile can be heard outside, coming to a stop.*)
JULIA: The Hansens don't forget so easy. That must be Gerth.
LISA: Don't let me forget to ask him about getting the water on the
garden.
JULIA: You'll need it before you set these out.
(GERTH HANSEN *enters from the road. He is a tall, lean man
of about thirty-five with a dark, lined face. His eyes are
arresting in their blueness under heavy dark brows. He does
not smile easily and is quickly on the defensive. As he comes in
he picks up a garden hoe that has been left across the path and
flings it away. He carries a box of groceries which he puts on
the table.*)
GERTH: Who left the gate open up there? I had to run Milton's cows
out of the winter wheat. He hasn't got sense enough to keep
them home where they belong.
LISA: No one's been here, Gerth.
GERTH: (*giving* LISA *a small parcel*) There's your thread. After this
I wish you'd do your own buying, a man feels like a fool trying
to match thread.
LISA: It was good of you to get it. Have you eaten?
GERTH: Yes. I'd drink a cup of coffee if you have it.
(GERTH *takes out of the box of groceries a one pound package
that is heavily sealed and starts to open it.*)
JULIA: I've got it on the stove, Gerth. I'll take these in.
(*She takes up the groceries.*)
GERTH: Has Al Morrow been over here?
LISA: No.
GERTH: (*annoyed*) I sent Bert over to remind him I wanted to see him
today.
LISA: He'll probably come.
JULIA: (*starting to the house*) Do you want coffee, Lisa?
LISA: Please, Julia. (JULIA *goes into the house. There is a brief silence.*)
Did you see Dr. Gray?
GERTH: (*continuing to open the package*) No. I didn't. I've been at the
bank all day.
LISA: (*disturbed*) But Gerth, you said—
GERTH: Gray wants to sell his practice all right, Parker told me. There
have been several doctors down here to see him this week.
LISA: Then you wired David?
GERTH: No. It was a fool idea of yours, writing David in the first place.
He specialized in children's diseases, didn't he? What could he do
in a small country town? He's better off down East.
LISA: But he said he wanted to know; he wrote asking us to wire him if
Dr. Gray is leaving. I only wrote because we need a good doctor
here so badly, it's too far to Lethbridge.

Gwen Pharis Ringwood

GERTH: People run to doctors too much as it is.

LISA: (*quietly*) Sometimes they leave it till too late, Gerth. Sometimes they can't take the time from ploughing to make the trip. It seems to me this is a bad night for you to say that.

GERTH: (*after a moment, looking at her*) You never said that before. Has it been in your thoughts all the time?

LISA: (*turning away*) No—

GERTH: I'd never have gone to the field that day, if I'd known, if you'd asked me to stay. (*With some anger.*) Could I help it that the roads were like they were and I couldn't get through?

LISA: No, you couldn't help that, but you could see that it wouldn't be like that again. (*Pleading*) David would stay here, if he came—it's his home—everybody likes him.

GERTH: (*drily*) What David does is not my look-out, Lisa.

LISA: There were hard words between you when he left; it's in your hands now to set that right. You'd be doing something for him as well as for the district, but why couldn't you take time to send a telegram?

GERTH: (*resentfully*) You forget that there's more to it than sending a telegram. From what I gather from his letter, David hasn't the money to buy a practice. Those months in Europe cost him plenty. I don't imagine he's made much since then.

LISA: You could see your way to helping him if you wanted to. He's your brother, Gerth.

GERTH: You could always see things his way, couldn't you? Never mine.

LISA: You don't want me to share things with you.

GERTH: (*harshly*) That fall after Dad died there wasn't much crop, but as poor as it was, David wouldn't wait a few years to start learning to doctor people. He wanted to sell his share. I had to buy it or see someone else get hold of it so I bought it. He left me here with four head of horses, a broken-down plough, and a seed-drill that sowed the wheat as ragged as my overalls. Now he comes to me for help. I told him he'd have to!

(JULIA *comes out of the house carrying a tray with the coffee and small cakes.*)

JULIA: You had better luck with these cookies than I ever do, Lisa. I thought you'd like this out here, since it's so nice.

LISA: Thank you, Julia, You have some too.

JULIA: (*setting the tray on the table*) I believe I will. Bert ought to be home by now. I hope he didn't leave the gate open, Gerth. He rode over to Milton's.

GERTH: He's pretty careful.

(*Taking a cup of coffee from* JULIA)

LISA: Charlie said the men from Raley wanted to go home tonight, if you could take them.

GERTH: Bert can take them over in the car. I've got to set the water up there, but I want to see Morrow first.

64

LISA: He's had a bad time over there on the hill with that sick wife of his and all those children.

GERTH: There's no excuse for the way that Morrow farms. He never gets on his land till June, never rotates his crops and lets the weeds get a start on him. Of course he can't make anything! I'm through with him.

JULIA: I don't see how she keeps those children looking as well as they do, and that's bad enough, God knows. I've seen her out hoeing beets with a baby in a basket beside her, and he lets her do it.

GERTH: Yes, his wife's worn out with bearing children and his land with bearing wheat. If he can't pay a thousand on that note of his tonight, I'm going to take over his farm. If it's farmed right, you can grow anything on that hill land.

LISA: Gerth, you don't need land.

GERTH: (*lost in his plans*) I've wanted that section for a long time. I'd like to try some apple trees on the side of the hill. The wind wouldn't hit them and I could pipe a stream of water from the dam. I believe they'd grow there.

JULIA: The season's too short for apples, Gerth.

GERTH: I don't think so. I've always hoped I'd own the land from the hill up there down to where the river cuts off my place from Burns'. If I had Morrow's place, it would be that way.

LISA: (*quietly*) Four thousand acres lying in one piece!

GERTH: Next year would see me with the biggest wheat field in the country.

LISA: You've got more acres now than you can farm. It's as if you'd got a fever to buy land.

GERTH: If you had your way, I'd be where Morrow is.

LISA: There's a place to stop. Where will Morrow go?

GERTH: That's not up to me, Lisa.

LISA: You drive a hard bargain.

GERTH: And if I do? I've never asked for quarter from the world, and never found it playing Santa Claus. You'd think I'd murdered him to hear you talk.

LISA: I'm not sure but losing that farm will be a kind of death for him. It's all he's got.

GERTH: He's never tried to make anything out of it. I've worked here day in and day out since I was old enough to drive a team. I've given this place everything I've got except my bones—(*with a touch of irony*)—and there'll be time for that. If Morrow had tried, I'd have some sympathy for him.

LISA: Not everyone can work the way you do. Some people need a little time to live.

GERTH: There's plenty of women who'd be glad to have things as easy for them as you do.

(MORROW *enters from the road. He is a shifty, hang-dog individual with an arrogance that can quickly fade into*

65

Gwen Pharis Ringwood

whining humility. His clothes are untidy, and he walks with an exagerated swagger.)

MORROW: Hello, Gerth. How are you, Mrs. Hansen?

GERTH: Hello, Al.

MORROW: Julia, you're looking hale and hearty.

LISA: Won't you sit down?

MORROW: (*sitting on one of the benches*) I'd have been over before, Gerth, but I started up a coyote in your pasture. I thought I'd get to take a shot at him, but he sneaked off.

LISA: Give Mr. Morrow a cup of coffee, Julia.

JULIA: (*as she pours the coffee*) You'd be better staying at home, helping your wife wash, Al Morrow, than chasing coyotes across the stubble.

MORROW: I thought the hide might bring us something. God knows we need it.

GERTH: I told Milton you'd probably be interested in helping on that south road they're grading.

MORROW: My horses won't stand up under road work, Gerth. Prince has a bad leg. Thanks, Julia.

(*He takes a cup of coffee from* JULIA.)

GERTH: I told you if you'd take him to a vet, I'd see to it.

(*He gets up angrily.*)

MORROW: Now, Gerth, I couldn't spare him just then. Anyway I don't think he's worth spending a lot of money on.

GERTH: It's up to you.

MORROW: I don't know as I'd be able to take that road work anyway. I've got a lot of seeding to do; I thought I'd get at that this week.

GERTH: I was in the bank today; Gurney tells me that he's not advancing you any more to put a crop in.

MORROW: (*sullenly*) Yes, he's got it in for me, just because I don't trade at his damn store.

GERTH: (*taking some papers from his pocket*) I've got your note here, Al, and a deed to your farm. A month ago I gave you till today to pay something on it. Unless you can raise a thousand dollars I'm going to take over your place.

MORROW: (*startled*) You didn't mean that, Gerth. Why, I thought you were joking when you said that a month ago. You wouldn't take my farm. I've got a family to support.

GERTH: I've waited for five years for you to show some sign of paying. You can't put a crop in this year,. . . I can. That's the end of it.

MORROW: (*whining*) I've had bad luck these last years—hailed out a year ago—you know I was.

GERTH: You'd do better working at some steady job. I'll help you get settled some place else if I can.

MORROW: Who do you think you are to take away my land? I'm as good a man as you are. I'll fight you in the courts on this.

GERTH: If I hadn't let you have the money in the first place, where would you be now? You'd have lost the farm in any case. I thought when I helped you, you might settle down and try to make a living. Don't blame me because you'd rather spend your time in the pool room.

MORROW: Give me till fall, Gerth. I'll pay you in the fall, I swear I will!

GERTH: No, I'm not waiting any longer. You'd better sign the papers now.

MORROW: (*wildly*) You've always wanted my land, I know that. You always wanted to own that hill so you could look down on your fields and feel big!

GERTH: Take it easy, Al. You've had plenty of warning that I meant to settle this this year. You can stay on in the house until you find some place else to go.

MORROW: You'll let me stay in my own house will you? I suppose I can use the public road if I ask you first.

GERTH: You'd better read this over.

MORROW: Don't go so fast, Hansen. Maybe I've got the money for you—maybe you won't get my land after all. You didn't know I had an interest in that pool hall, did you? You didn't know Leffler's a good friend of mine. He's got more cash than you ever saw, and he don't get a man in the corner and then take away everything he's got. Keep your paper. (*He throws it down*) I'm not aiming to sign it. Leffler will help me out.
(*He starts out to the road.*)

GERTH: If he does, so much the better for you. But I want this settled tonight, Morrow.

MORROW: (*sarcastically*) I got that idea, Mr. Hansen. I'll be back.
(*He goes out and the sound of a car driving away can be heard.*)

LISA: Gerth, that's not much time—

GERTH: I've listened to excuses for five years. I want to get on that land this spring and get the weeds killed off. They've been spreading over this way ever since he tried to farm that place. (*As he takes up the paper*) He'd be better working by the day, his family too.

LISA: Maybe he'll get the money—

GERTH: Leffler's a fool if he lends it to him. I'll get the men ploughing over there this week; I'm going to put in clover till the land gets its strength back, and I'll break that hillside and put my apple trees in as soon as it's warm enough. You'll like them, Lisa, they look nice in bloom.

LISA: (*curiously*) You really love things that grow, don't you, Gerth?

GERTH: (*awkwardly*) Why, yes, I like to raise a crop.
(BERT MACDONALD, *a nice-looking youngster of sixteen comes in from the barn. He is active and restless, with unruly red hair and a cheerful, alert face. His engaging grin gets him out of a lot of trouble.*)

BERT: Hello, Gerth. Mrs. Milton sent back the book you took her, Mrs. Hansen.

(*He gives a book to* LISA.)

LISA: Thank you, Bert. Did you have supper?

BERT: Yes, but I could eat something. Where's Mom?

LISA: She's in the house. Go in this way if you like.

BERT: I'm kind of dusty. I'll go 'round.

GERTH: Bert, I want you to take those men over to Raley as soon as you've eaten, and don't scare them to death trying to beat a record either.

(*The telephone rings inside.*)

BERT: (*pleased*) Gee, I won't. I can take them right away. I'll just ask Mom for some cookies or something.

GERTH: There's not that much rush. Put the car in when you get back.

JULIA: (*coming out of the house*) You're wanted on the telephone, Gerth.

GERTH: (*starting to the door.*) Who is it?

JULIA: I don't know. I thought for a minute it was—

(GERTH *does not wait for an answer but goes on in.*)

BERT: Mom, can you get me something to eat right away? (*Importantly*) I've got to take those men to Raley; Gerth told me to.

JULIA: I thought you ate at Milton's.

BERT: Gosh, that was an hour ago; anyway I didn't eat much. We were planning about getting to the air show next week, Jimmy and I.

JULIA: (*good naturedly*) Air show! I'm sick and tired of hearing about air shows! All day and all night, that's all you talk about.

BERT: (*impatiently*) I better hurry, Mom.

JULIA: Go on with you, I'm coming.

(BERT *goes around the corner of the house to the back.* JULIA *pauses a moment, then turns to* LISA.)

Lisa, I thought—I thought that was David Hansen on the line.

LISA: (*startled*) David! But it couldn't be, Julia. It wasn't long distance?

JULIA: No—

LISA: He'd have known your voice, Julia.

JULIA: (*doubtfully*) I suppose, but it sounded like David. I swear it did. Oh, it was probably somebody else. We'd been talking about David—

(GERTH *comes out in time to hear the last of* JULIA'*s remark. He is angry and disturbed.*)

GERTH: Yes, it was David all right. He's in town. (*To* LISA.) So you see, you didn't need to get so concerned over my neglect.

LISA: But, Gerth, how did he get here?

GERTH: He flew to Lethbridge and took the bus out. He left this morning.

LISA: Did he come to see about—

GERTH: I don't know what he came to see about. He said he got in touch with Gray after he got your letter. Gray wired him yesterday that he'd have to know at once, so David caught the morning plane.

JULIA: You mean to tell me David Hansen's going to settle here, after all that schooling?

GERTH: That's what he thinks.

BERT: (*calling from the back of the house*) Mom! Come here a minute. I can't find the butter.

JULIA: There he goes, not even looking.

BERT: Hey, Mom!

JULIA: I'm coming, son, stop shouting at me!
(*She goes into the house.*)

LISA: (*after a brief pause*) Are you going after David?

GERTH: (*coldly*) That's what he wanted. He hadn't seen anyone he knew who lived out this way.

LISA: I'll get his old room ready while you're gone.
(*She gets up.*)

GERTH: There's no hurry; I can't spare the car until Bert gets back from Raley. I told him that.

LISA: (*turning, surprised*) But Gerth, it won't take half an hour. You must go.

GERTH: I'm running a farm, Lisa, not a taxi stand. I've got more to do than wait on David.

LISA: You can't let him sit in town until Bert gets back. It'll take two hours to go to Raley.

GERTH: (*impatiently*) If David comes back here without a word of warning, it's not my fault. (*He goes to the corner of the veranda and calls*) Bert!

BERT: (*from the kitchen*) I'm ready, Gerth. Good-bye Mom!
(*He comes running around the house.*)

GERTH: Here's the key to the car. Those men are waiting. I'll want the car after you get back, so don't fool around.

LISA: Gerth, please ask them to wait a little while.

GERTH: I've kept them waiting now. (BERT *stands indecisively, not sure whether to go or stay.*) It's Saturday night, and they're anxious to get home. I told them when I hired them they'd get home for Sunday. (*To* BERT *impatiently.*) Go on!
(BERT *goes out to the road.*)

LISA: (*going back to her window box*) I wonder that David comes out at all.

GERTH: (*going over to the table*) He chose his way. I told him when he left not to come back to me crying for money. If he'd stayed on here, after Dad died, instead of selling me his land for half its worth, he'd have a living now.

LISA: (*fiercely*) Land! Everything goes back to land with you. David's life is his own to do what he wants with—

GERTH: If David wants to set himself up as better than I, he can go ahead, I've done all right.

Gwen Pharis Ringwood

LISA: (*wearily*) Yes, you've done all right.

GERTH: I'll do better this year too. These are those samples of prize wheat I got. I'm going to stake it out in rows. I may try a cross with that early-ripening Marquis I raised last year.

(*He opens the boxes of wheat and looks at it carefully.*)

LISA: (*turning on him, bitterly*) There's no trouble too great for you to take for that field out there. Your wife, your brother, they don't count, as long as you can walk the fields and say, "I own this land—it's mine"—that's all that matters.

GERTH: Look here, Lisa, I've had enough of this. Just because you wrote David about Gray's practice, doesn't mean that I've got to play nursemaid to him. You may enjoy wearing yourself out for this district, running all over the country for every youngster with a scratched finger, getting dental clinics and baby clinics for people that don't thank you for interfering, and if you've nothing else to do, you can spend your time at it, for all I care. But I'm a farmer with a crop to put it, and it's time your understood that.

LISA: It's time we stopped and looked at each other and realized that we're as far apart as strangers, that we walk from room to room in an empty house and never touch each other at all.

GERTH: (*turning away*) I don't think talking like that will help, Lisa.

LISA: (*in a low voice*) What will help then? I've asked you to adopt a child.

GERTH: If you cared anything about this place or me, you wouldn't need an outsider to take up your mind.

LISA: Gerth, something to love together—perhaps that's all we need.

GERTH: I'll leave to no stranger's son the land I've worked for.

LISA: He wouldn't be a stranger's son for long. One of those ragged children I saw yesterday—in a little while he'd be like our own.

GERTH: Haven't you enough to do here without trying to play angel of mercy to the whole community?

LISA: (*suddenly angry*) Maybe I don't do it for them! Maybe I do it for myself, to keep myself from thinking or feeling or wanting anything more than a good car and a good house and a good farm. To keep myself from remembering what you forgot today—that we had a child once, that I planned for it and loved it and held it in my arms—and that I lost it—but the ploughing got done that year.

GERTH: (*getting up, his voice shaking. His hand sweeps the wheat to the ground where it spills out, unnoticed*) For God's sake, stop it, Lisa! (*His voice is full of pain.*) If you think that—there isn't anything more for me to say. If you think that, this is no time for us to adopt a child. You see that, don't you? There are burdens you can't ask a child to bear.

(*He turns away.*)

LISA: (*a little fear in her voice*) Where are you going?

GERTH: (*shortly*) Up to the barn.

LISA: (*going to him quickly, pleading with him*) Gerth, don't look like that. I shouldn't have said what I did. I—I wanted to hurt you. You did all you knew.

GERTH: Let go! (*He frees himself roughly.*) There's no use crying, Lisa. (CHARLIE *comes in from the barn. He pauses a moment in embarrassment.*)

GERTH: Hello, Charlie.

CHARLIE: Gerth, I wish you'd take a look at Cap. He's acting funny. He won't eat his oats.

GERTH: I saw him at noon. He acts like he had sleeping sickness.

CHARLIE: He'll never hold up in the field.

GERTH: You'd better get in Jerry. You can use him with Mick on the harrow.

CHARLIE: It's too bad; Cap's the best horse you've got.

GERTH: I'll try giving him some of that stuff Milton used. If he isn't better tomorrow, we'll have to get a doctor over here. You go on ahead; I'll go right up. (*He dismisses* CHARLIE *with a nod.*) Do you know where you put that bottle I brought from Milton's?

LISA: It's on the top shelf in the pantry. I'll get it.

GERTH: Don't bother, Julia's in there.

(*He goes in without looking at her.* LISA *goes over to the bench and sinks down on it forlornly. After a moment her eyes fall on the wheat that has spilled over on the ground. She kneels down and carefully begins to scoop up the wheat and put it in the box. The tears come to her eyes and there is a child-like intensity in her effort to recover the scattered kernels.* GERTH *comes out of the house with the medicine and stands for a moment watching her. His face softens and when he speaks there is some gentleness in his tone.*)

GERTH: You don't need to do that, Lisa.

LISA: (*looking up startled*) I want to. (*With difficulty.*) I—I do care about it, Gerth. I want to care about it. (*Trying to be matter-of-fact.*) It's good wheat, isn't it?

GERTH: (*putting on his gloves*) It's good, but no better than some I've raised. It ought to be run through a sieve. There's some chaff in it.

LISA: I'll do that.

GERTH: You've got enough to do with these. (*He indicates the window boxes. He starts toward the barn, then turns awkwardly.*) Lisa, if I've not paid as much attention to you lately as I should, it's because I've had things on my mind. A man gets an idea, and something—something outside himself pushes him on. I've planned to make this farm look like no farm I've ever seen. In a way, that's for you.

LISA: I know it, Gerth—I think I know that.

GERTH: There's times when everybody gets to feeling he's lost something along the way. We're happy together, happy as most.

LISA: Yes—

GERTH: That land of Morrows, I think I can make you proud of what I do with it. But if you think I'm wrong, if you think I've got too much, I'll let it go.

LISA: You mustn't do that, Gerth.

GERTH: That isn't what you want?

LISA: Not if it seems right to you to take it.

GERTH: I'd thought of putting it in your name, Lisa. Maybe if it was yours, if you owned it, you'd come to see why I've wanted it.

LISA: (*gently*) You don't need to put land in my name, Gerth. What we have, we should have together. Names shouldn't matter.

GERTH: I hoped you'd say that.

(JULIA *comes out of the house.*)

JULIA: I can help you with those window boxes, Lisa, if you want me to.

LISA: Perhaps you'd better get David's old room ready, Julia.

JULIA: What time is he coming, Gerth?

GERTH: (*shortly*) When I go after him.

JULIA: It will be like old times with David here again.

GERTH: I've no doubt. I'll be up at the barn, Lisa. (*He starts out.*)

LISA: (*calling after him and stopping him*) Gerth, I wanted to get these lilac plants out tomorrow. Could you irrigate down here in the morning?

GERTH: (*with irritation*) No, I couldn't, I've not enough water on that flax now.

LISA: (*withdrawing into herself, hurt by his tone*) I see. I'm afraid they won't grow if I wait too long to set them out.

GERTH: I'll get a larger stream running next week; I can't do anything for you till then.

JULIA: These shrubs will be dead by next week.

GERTH: Now, Julia, you know as well as I do, there's not that much hurry.

JULIA: I've no patience with you, Gerth Hansen. Lisa's planned to set these lilacs out every day this week. It wouldn't take two hours to soak this ground.

GERTH: (*angrily to* LISA) I haven't time to stand here and argue. I need the water for the flax. If you've got to set those things out, you'll have to carry water for them. You've more time than I have.

(*He goes out.*)

JULIA: He gets more like a bear every day.

LISA: (*wearily*) It doesn't matter, Julia.

JULIA: Let's put a few of them out tomorrow any way. David can help if he's here.

LISA: If only he and Gerth will keep from quarrelling.

JULIA: (*as they set the plants into the window box*) Whatever makes David want to come back here?

LISA: It's his home, Julia. And then he doesn't want to work for other people any longer. I hope he can stay. He's specialized in children's work and could do so much here. Some of those children at the clinic yesterday need care so badly. It made me feel guilty at having all this—when a little money means so much to them.

JULIA: What Gerth has, he's earned, Lisa.

LISA: But it's all wasted unless it goes to nourish something that's alive.

JULIA: There's plenty of people depend on Gerth. Where would I be? He's paid me more than I'd get anywhere else, ever since Mac left.

LISA: You're like one of the family, Julia. Don't ever think you owe us anything.

(*A voice from the right startles them both. Turning, they see* DAVID HANSEN *coming towards them. He carries a leather bag which he puts down as he sees them.* DAVID *is thirty, tall, well-built and attractive. There is something boyish about him, but his mouth is purposeful and his eyes, though warmer than Gerth's and happier, are of the same intense blue. He is excited and exuberant at seeing* LISA *and* JULIA).

DAVID: Hello! Is anybody home?

LISA: David! (*She runs toward him.*) I didn't hear you coming.

DAVID: Lisa! It's good to see you. (*He takes her hands.*) And Julia Mac. Here, let me look at you. (*He hugs* JULIA.) You haven't changed a bit.

JULIA: (*excited and flustered*) Go on with you. You've the same blarneying tongue you always had. But you've changed, David. I'm not sure it's you.

LISA: How did you get here, David?

DAVID: I walked up from the corner. Say, it's good to be back. Where's Gerth?

LISA: (*hesitating*) He's up at the barn, David. He couldn't meet you— Bert had to take the car—We were planning to come and then—

DAVID: It didn't matter. I got a ride with old John Roebuck. He didn't know me at first, he kept saying, "Well, I'll be damned—Mark Hansen's youngest. I never recognized you." I'll bet he said that fifteen times.

LISA: You look so well, David. Here, let me take your coat. (*She takes his overcoat from him and puts it across the side-railing on the veranda.*) We were so surprised when you telephoned.

DAVID: I should have let you know. I only decided to come last night. After I got your letter I got to thinking about coming back here. I couldn't get it off my mind, so yesterday I called Gray. He told me several doctors wanted the practice and that if I was interested I'd have to let him know at once. I got a week off from the hospital and took the plane this morning. And here I am.

LISA: I'm glad you came.

DAVID: You've done wonders for the place, Lisa.

LISA: Your room's just the same, except the walls. I had them done over.

JULIA: I'll bet you're hungry, boy, now, aren't you?

DAVID: (*smiling*) For once the answer's "No" Julia. I ate after I saw Gray. I went straight there.

Gwen Pharis Ringwood

JULIA: Where are your things? Do you mean these are all the clothes you've got?

DAVID: Almost. But I do have a bag.

(*He motions to the bag at right.*)

JULIA: You'll look fine in those pitching hay.

DAVID: Gerth's overalls won't be much too big for me.

JULIA: I'll go up and see about your room. It's been a long time since you set foot in it.

DAVID: How's Mac, Julia?

JULIA: (*flushing*) Mac—Well, you know how Mac was, David—he always had an itching heel. He got the wanderlust the year after you went away. He said he'd come back when he'd made a fortune, in the note he wrote. But he's not come back.

DAVID: (*contritely*) I'm sorry, Jule.

JULIA: (*brightening*) I still think he'll come back, and the only fortune that man will ever have will be in his mind. And half the time I'll bet he didn't half see things, he was that hungry.

DAVID: He'll get hungry to see this country, Jule, like I have.

JULIA: And I'll be a fool and take him back. That's the way I am, David—soft.

(*She goes into the house.*)

DAVID: (*after a moment*) You're as pretty as you ever were, Lisa.

LISA: That's nice of you, David; I feel much older.

DAVID: Well, we are—you were just a youngster when I left.

LISA: (*smiling*) I was nineteen.

DAVID: I used to wonder how you could be so competent, sure of things. There was I, four years older and not sure of anything.

LISA: I'm not so sure about things now, David. And you were always sure about what you wanted to do.

DAVID: Yes. (*Getting up restlessly.*) Oh, I've learned a lot. I found that medicine could be a graft as well as anything else, if that's what you want to make it. I've lost some of the high-sounding phrases that used to come so easy. But it's still the greatest thing in the world for me.

LISA: Do you really think about staying here? (*Hesitating*) When I wrote I thought you'd think it a foolish idea. Gerth thought so.

DAVID: I've thought a lot about coming back, Lisa.

LISA: We've needed someone here so badly, someone who'd stay and care about the people here, and not use it just as a stepping stone to something else.

DAVID: I was glad you wrote. Some general practice would be good for me now. And there'll be plenty of openings to specialize here if I look for them. Besides, it's home, Lisa! I'm tired of cities. I felt better as soon as I saw that hill up there and the Rockies sixty miles away.

LISA: (*enthusiastically*) Oh, David, there's so much for you to do. Gerth's made money in spite of bad years, but most of the people

74

won't farm like Gerth, and so many of the children haven't had a fair chance. (*Apologetically*) I guess I care more about the children.

DAVID: I know. You can look on and see grown people die because of carelessness or ignorance or poverty and get sort of hardened to it. But some of the cases they brought into that children's hospital down east would break your heart. If the parents can't take care of those youngsters, the government should. (*Grinning boyishly.*) I got pretty unpopular with some of the men in the hospital when we got to talking state medicine.

LISA: If only you can stay, David!

DAVID: (*soberly*) I hope Gerth will be glad to see me. He's never written.

LISA: We've been so busy.

DAVID: Roebuck says this farm's the biggest in the country.

LISA: (*smiling*) We've got more land than we know what to do with. Do you want to take your things upstairs?

DAVID: I'd like to look around out here a little, if you don't mind. I could go up and see what Gerth's doing—

(GERTH *enters from the barn. He throws the bottle down as he comes in. He doesn't see* DAVID *at first.*)

GERTH: That's not worth a damn. I don't know what to do—(*He sees* DAVID.) Hello, David.

(*He stops; he is constrained in voice and manner.*)

DAVID: How are you, Gerth?

(*He too is embarrassed. They shake hands stiffly.*)

GERTH: How did you get out?

DAVID: Roebuck was coming out this way.

GERTH: I couldn't spare the car. If we'd known before—

DAVID: I didn't know I was coming until last night.

GERTH: Things probably look different to you here; seven years is a long time.

DAVID: You've certainly made this farm something to be proud of.

GERTH: Considering how I started, it's not bad.

LISA: Sit down, David.

(DAVID, *however, remains standing.*)

GERTH: So you think you want to do your doctoring here?

DAVID: That's what I came about. But Gray wants $10,000 for his practice. I can't raise more than five.

GERTH: I see.

DAVID: (*angered at* GERTH's *manner*) Gerth, we had a row before I left. You wouldn't listen to what I had to say. If that's still between us, I'd better go.

GERTH: So you need five thousand dollars?

DAVID: (*curtly*) If I stay here, yes.

GERTH: I needed less than that the fall you left.

DAVID: (*hotly*) If I hadn't taken my share of the crop that year, I'd have had to stay out of medical school. I only had three years to go. I know it left you without much to run on, but it was mine, and I'd do it again, Gerth.

GERTH: I managed without any help. (*His voice is expressionless.*) I sold everything I had except two head of horses because I didn't have enough to buy feed. One of the horses died, and I caught a stray and worked him. That's a criminal offence, you know. But I did it, and I got a crop in. And I didn't ask for help.

DAVID: Suppose I'd stayed here, let you have my share of the crop, I'd already sold you my share of the land. Where would I be now?

LISA: David's right, Gerth.

GERTH: I think I told you you'd be glad to come back here.

DAVID: (*angrily*) All right, Gerth, let it go. I wanted your help, but it wasn't easy to ask for it. I made a mistake; forget it.

GERTH: You called me a brute once. You can't expect much of a brute, you know.

DAVID: What are you talking about?

GERTH: You don't remember? Well, I do.

DAVID: You mean that time at the sale?

GERTH: Perhaps I do.

DAVID: (*turning on him*) Well, you shot the dog, didn't you? Maybe he wasn't worth much, but a no-good dog can mean a lot to a kid of sixteen.

GERTH: He'd killed five sheep at Milton's place the night before. You didn't know that, did you?

DAVID: No I didn't. Nobody told me.

GERTH: You couldn't wait to find that out. You came raging over to where I stood in a group of men and had your say.

DAVID: You never opened your mouth. It's a little late to tell me now.

GERTH: Words don't come as easy to me as to some people.

DAVID: (*turning away, a little ashamed of the quarrel*) I didn't know you shot him because you had to.

GERTH: (*blazing*) No, you thought I did it because I liked to, I suppose. You think I've got no feelings to compare with yours. Well, maybe I haven't. Maybe people like you and Lisa here have a corner on all the feelings in the world. And those of us who have to dig the ground, or slit a hog's throat, or stick a bloated cow, we've got no feelings!

LISA: (*pleading*) Gerth, can't you see it doesn't matter now?

DAVID: It never mattered really.

GERTH: What matters now is that you want something of me. I'm somebody now because I can give you a chance to do what you want.

DAVID: Look here, Gerth, I didn't come back here because I thought I could make money—there're plenty of places that offer more than here. I came because I thought, I hoped, I belong here. When I got away, the things we'd quarrelled about seemed pretty small beside the fact that we're brothers. It didn't seem strange to me to hope you'd want me here. I see now I was a fool—

LISA: You're both fools, two grown men standing here, quarrelling about things that happened years ago! I thought you'd let the old scores die. I thought you'd see by now there isn't time for remembering all the things that put scars on you. Just because somebody shot a dog fifteen years ago is no reason for you to forget you grew up together. David saved your life in the river down there once, Gerth—you told me so. Why don't you remember that?

GERTH: (*turning to* LISA) All right, if Morrow can raise that thousand, I'll hand it over to David. Will that suit you?

DAVID: I don't want your help, Gerth, with things as they are.

GERTH: You can't expect me to dance with joy at the thought of tying up my farm to raise $5,000 to buy some broken-down practice for you to butcher people.

DAVID: I wouldn't take your money on a platter, Gerth. Let the matter drop.

(MORROW *comes in from the road.*)

GERTH: You made a quick trip.

LISA: Do you know Dr. Hansen, Mr. Morrow?

DAVID: How do you do.

(MORROW *nods at* DAVID, *then turns to* GERTH.)

MORROW: You win, Gerth. Leffler wasn't able to let me have the thousand. You'll have to give me more time.

GERTH: It's no use, Al.

MORROW: What have you got against me, Hansen?

GERTH: You're no farmer. I saved the land for you once. I'm going to put it to some use. Read this over.

(*He gives* MORROW *the papers he takes from the table.*)

MORROW: (*sullenly*) It's the same as those you left with me last month, ain't it?

GERTH: Yes.

MORROW: I should have known you let me have the money for a reason, you weren't saving the land for me—it was for yourself all the time, wasn't it? You had it all figured out. If you hadn't paid for it, somebody else might have got hold of it. Well, where do I sign?

GERTH: (*indicating*) Here. Lisa, tell Julia to come out and witness this.

(MORROW *puts his name on the paper.* LISA *goes into the house.* MORROW *reads over the paper.* CHARLIE *comes in from the barn looking worried. He goes straight to* GERTH.)

CHARLIE: Gerth, I think you'll have to get a vet for Cap if you want to save him. He's suffering bad now.

GERTH: I'll go after McLean, but I'll have to ride to Milton's and borrow his car.

DAVID: What's the matter with him, Charlie?

CHARLIE: Pardon me, David, I didn't see you. I don't know what it is, a lot of the horses have been sick this spring.

DAVID: I don't know much about horses, Gerth, but if you like, I'll see what I can do.

CHARLIE: (*eagerly*) Sure, Gerth, he's a doctor. Maybe he can—

GERTH: I didn't think you'd care to mess with horses.

DAVID: Don't be a fool. Come on, Charlie, I'll do what I can.

GERTH: Go ahead, Charlie. I'll be up in a minute. (*As* DAVID *and* CHARLIE *start to leave*) David, do you mind putting your signature on this?

DAVID: (*turning and coming back to the paper*) Where?

GERTH: Just under Al's here. (DAVID *writes his name.*) Thanks. (JULIA *and* LISA *come out of the house.*)

JULIA: What do you want me to do, Gerth?

DAVID: We'll go on up to the barn.
> (*He goes out.*)

GERTH: You sign here, Julia. It's a deed to the Morrow farm. (JULIA *signs.*) Everything's in order.

MORROW: (*getting up*) Everythings's in order, in perfect order! You've got what you want and it don't matter a tinker's damn what happens to me. I hope it never grows a blade of grass for you. I hope that patch of alkali spreads till it blights your whole god-damned four thousand acres! I'd like to see you standing on that hill and looking down with not a green thing anywhere! I'd like—

GERTH: (*sternly*) Get hold of yourself, Al. If you were so fond of your farm, why didn't you get out there and work on it when you had a chance? Put these in the desk, Lisa. (*He gives the papers to* LISA.) If you want a team to start on that road work, I can let you have one, but I won't have you treating my horses like you do yours.
> (LISA *gathers up the papers.*)

MORROW: Keep your team. I'll make you sorry for this, Hansen! I'll make you wish you'd never seen that farm.
> (MORROW *goes out and after a moment the sound of his car is heard as he drives away.*)

GERTH: (*a little regretfully*) He took it hard—

LISA: (*doubtfully*) I suppose it was fair but—

JULIA: Of course it's fair, Lisa. Morrow's no good, and his family couldn't be worse off than they are now. (*She takes the papers from* LISA) I'll take these in. David's room is ready.

LISA: Thank you, Julia. (JULIA *goes into the house.*) Gerth, since Morrow couldn't pay the thousand, does that mean you can't help David?

GERTH: I can raise the money, Lisa, but I've got lots of other things to do with it. I'll need machinery for that new place.

LISA: (*wistfully*) I wonder why we never see the same way about things.

GERTH: I'd better go and see what he can do for that horse.

LISA: He's anxious to make it up to you for any wrong he did you, Gerth. He's sorry for humiliating you in front of those men.

GERTH: I don't need David's pity.

LISA: Sometimes I think you don't need anything from anyone. I wonder why you ever thought you needed me.
(*There is a sob in her voice.*)

GERTH: Lisa! (*He is startled by her emotion. After a pause*) I'll see what I can do, Lisa.
(DAVID *comes in quickly.*)

DAVID: Have you any hot water, Lisa? And some mustard?

LISA: Of course. I'll get it. (*She goes into the house.*)

DAVID: I think he's eaten some of that death camis. I didn't know it grew around here. I may be able to do something for him.

GERTH: Look here, I've talked to Lisa about your staying here. She thinks I ought to help you. I'll see my way to raise two thousand if that's enough—

DAVID: That's enough, but it's how you feel about this that matters, Gerth. I could pay you in a year or so if things go well, but I don't want to take from you unless we're going to forget what's past. I'd much rather go—

GERTH: No, no, stay. I—I say things. Things aren't always what they seem in words. I'd like it if you stayed, and I can go your note.
(LISA *returns in time to hear* GERTH's *words.*)

LISA: Gerth, I'm so glad. You'll let us help you, David?
(*She puts her arm in* GERTH's.)

DAVID: I don't know what to answer.

GERTH: It's as you say, we're brothers. We didn't always find it hard to talk, and what's happened is done with. I can see my way to help you.

DAVID: Then I'll stay, and thanks, Gerth.

GERTH: We'll settle with Gray tomorrow.

DAVID: Fine. I'd better get up to that horse. I've got some stuff in here that may help him. I don't believe I ever prescribed it for a horse before.
(*He smiles at them, gets a small bottle out of a kit in the bag, takes up the kettle of water from the step, and goes.*)

LISA: (*shyly*) I'm glad you did that, Gerth. Not only for David but for yourself—

GERTH: It was your doing, not mine. (*But he smiles at her.*)

LISA: Anyway I'm glad. Oh, I almost forgot to put these in water.
(*She takes up the shrubs and starts in to the house.*)

GERTH: (*starting toward the barn*) I'll try to get water down and help you set them out tomorrow.

LISA: (*touched by his offer*) You're so busy, Gerth, you don't need to stay in from the field. Julia and David can help. He won't have much to do and Julia says he always did the gardening for your mother.

GERTH: I'd forgotten that.
(LISA *turns to go into the house.* GERTH's *voice is expressionless.*)

Now that David's here, there won't be any need for me to stay. (*The door closes behind* LISA. GERTH *looks at it as the curtain falls.*)

ACT TWO

SCENE: *The same as act one.*
TIME: *August, 1938. Early evening.*

Two years have made only a few changes in the scene. A bright lawn chair and footstool replace one of the benches. The table and the other bench have been repainted and some of the shrubbery has grown taller. The trees are no longer bare but in full leaf, with a few touches of yellow. The lawn is green and well-kept, and beside the wall at the right some bright gladioli are beginning to bloom.
CHARLIE *and* GERTH *enter from the barn, carrying wheat-sheaves that are ripe and yellow in the evening sun. They lay the wheat on the table and* GERTH *begins to arrange it, choosing the larger heads.*

CHARLIE: (*as they come in*) This will thresh out fifty bushels to the acre, Gerth.
GERTH: I think you're right.
CHARLIE: When does that big fair in Toronto open?
GERTH: Next week. I ought to get this off tomorrow if I'm going to show it.
CHARLIE: Sure, you get it off. There's no wheat I've ever seen that can touch it. It'll take first prize all right.
GERTH: (*putting his hand on* CHARLIE's *shoulder*) You believe farming's the greatest thing in the world, don't you Charlie?
CHARLIE: Sure. (*He is embarrassed and pleased.*) This big farm, you run it right, Gerth. You don't make mistakes.
GERTH: (*as he begins to sort and arrange the sheaf*) Lisa must have gone to town with David. The car's here.
CHARLIE: I saw him drive in this afternoon.
GERTH: David's making good around here. They've asked him to operate in the city a good bit lately.

CHARLIE: Yeah, they say he's the best doctor in the south.

GERTH: He's done fine in these two years. Lisa says he has a way with children—

CHARLIE: (*diffidently*) Mrs. Hansen likes them too. I've seen her with those kids of Milton's.

GERTH: (*quietly*) Yes, she likes them.

> (JULIA *comes out of the house with a tray and some glasses of lemonade.*)

JULIA: Gerth Hansen, if you two don't look worn out, I never saw two men that did; you haven't stopped since June.

GERTH: We won't be stopping till this crop gets threshed.

JULIA: Here's a cold drink; the dog days are here all right.

GERTH: (*taking the glass from her*) Thanks.

JULIA: I saw Al Morrow riding this way from the window.

GERTH: I got Olson to give him a job on the section. I hope he sticks to it—he's been fired five times this year.

CHARLIE: Olsen will fire him the first time he comes to work drunk, I heard him say so.

GERTH: I wonder what Morrow wants with me. He's never spoken to me since I took over that land. (*With a rueful smile.*) I guess I can't blame him much.

CHARLIE: You wouldn't know it was the same land you took from him two years ago.

GERTH: (*without interest*) It's in good shape all right.

JULIA: How are your apple trees doing, Gerth?

GERTH: I only lost half a dozen over the winter. I'll let them bear next year.

JULIA: I'll never believe you can grow apples here till I see them.

GERTH: (*annoyed*) You'll see them. (*He turns impatiently.*) Lisa ought to be home. I'm starting to cut tomorrow, and there'll be a big crew here. Is she off at one of her mother's meetings?

JULIA: I don't know.

GERTH: I take it she went to town with David?

JULIA: Yes.

> (AL MORROW *enters from the road. He is untidier and more shiftless looking than before. He is uncertain as to his welcome and puts on a jaunty cheerfulness.*)

MORROW: Howdy, Mrs. Mac. Hi, Gerth. You stopped early.

GERTH: (*continuing his work*) I don't work my men past six. I never have.

MORROW: (*ingratiatingly*) That's more than most farmers can say around here. You've got a good crop there, Gerth.

> (*He rolls and lights a cigarette.*)

GERTH: Not bad. How are you getting along?

MORROW: (*sitting down*) Oh, so, so—

GERTH: If you've got any sense you'll keep away from that joint of Birks. They've been watching it pretty close lately. They figure they know where the youngsters are getting liquor.

81

Gwen Pharis Ringwood

MORROW: (*whining*) What's a man to do Gerth, I ask you? I've got to make a little somehow. Sure they watch it; the cops haven't got any more to do.
GERTH: Well, that's a warning. You've got a job on the section. Stick to that.
MORROW: (*uneasily*) I'm not working there, Gerth. No white man could work for Olson; he sits back and lets the other fellow do the work. I quit.
GERTH: You must think jobs are easy.
MORROW: (*looking at* CHARLIE) I'd like a word with you in private, Gerth. There's some things I wanted to talk over with you—
JULIA: I guess that means us, Charlie.
GERTH: (*drily*) I don't think Al has anything to say to me he couldn't say before you. What is it you want, Al?
MORROW: (*attempting to be light*) You don't need to be worried about me, Gerth. I said a lot of things I didn't mean that night you took my place, but I ain't one to hold a grudge. (*With a laugh.*) And I don't carry a gun.
GERTH: (*without looking up*) I'm not worried Al.
CHARLIE: (*putting down his glass*) I'll go up and milk, Gerth. Bert ought to have the cows in by now.
GERTH: (*as* CHARLIE *starts to go*) If you have time, you can grease and tighten up the big binder, Charlie.
CHARLIE: Sure.
JULIA: I'll walk along with you and feed the chickens.
    (CHARLIE *and* JULIA *go out to the barn.*)
GERTH: All right, Al, what's on your mind?
MORROW: (*in a conciliatory tone*) I just ain't one to want my affairs broadcast, Gerth.
GERTH: I see.
MORROW: I—I've been feeling like I owe you an apology for some of the things I said about you taking over my land. It's been pretty hard on me, these last two years, but I've got to admit you were fair.
GERTH: (*impatiently*) Don't grovel to me, Al. What do you want?
MORROW: Well, I've been thinking, with harvest coming on, you'll need someone to run your threshing machine for you. Charlie's not so active as he was—I figured you'd want a younger man.
    (*He stops and looks inquiringly at* GERTH.)
GERTH: Go on.
MORROW: I figured you might give me a job on the separator.
GERTH: Charlie's the best separator man in this country, Al. I don't see my way to changing.
MORROW: He creaks when he walks, Gerth. Even you can see that.
GERTH: He suits me.
MORROW: You couldn't use me in the field?

GERTH: I've got my outfit hired. They start tomorrow.

MORROW: (*with a touch of surliness*) You mean you don't want me, is that it?

GERTH: That's it, Al.

MORROW: (*sullenly, as he gets up*) You've got it in for me, haven't you, Hansen? You've fixed it so I can't get a job in the country.

GERTH: If you see it that way, Al.

MORROW: No wonder they say you haven't an ounce of feeling in you.

GERTH: (*looking at* MORROW *steadily*) A man that beats his horses and drinks on the job has no place on my outfit.

MORROW: (*sneering*) Holy as Jesus, aren't you? Well, Hansen, you've got things coming your way this time. You're the Lord's own chosen. Gerth, the wheat king! Other men can go hungry but you'll go on squeezing us poor devils out of the last acre we've got. But it won't get you far. Who're you going to leave it to, this farm you're so proud of? When you're gone, who's going to care a damn about it? It'll go back to dust, just like you do!

GERTH: (*quietly*) If you want to make a speech, Al, I'll call the boys in.

MORROW: (*his voice rising*) Sure, you call and they come. Everybody comes. But I'll tell you something just to think about at night, that sad-eyed wife of yours ain't coming. She's not so sad in Lethbridge with your brother. She can play the grand lady and give to the poor with tears in her eyes, when she's around here, but she's got a smile for the doctor. I saw them dining in state in the city today. There's a place your land doesn't help you! (GERTH *catches hold of* MORROW's *arm with a grip that forces him to his knees.*) Stop it, Gerth, for the love of God! You'll break my arm off. (*Whining.*) I take it back, honest I do!

(GERTH *releases* MORROW *as* JULIA *comes in from the barn.*)

JULIA: What's going on down here? I could hear you up at the barn.

GERTH: It's all right, Julia. (*To* MORROW) Clear out.

(MORROW *starts to speak but thinks better of it and leaves quickly.*)

JULIA: (*looking after him*) He's pitiful in the sight of God, that one. What did he want, a job?

GERTH: (*absently*) Yes, but I don't hire a man like that. He'd start trouble and disrupt the whole outfit.

JULIA: I don't see why his wife doesn't leave him. My Mac was a ne'er-do-well if ever I saw one, but he had a smile to break your heart, and he was as proud as you are, Gerth Hansen.

GERTH: (*going back to his wheat, but showing no interest in it*) Pride's a sin in your Bible, isn't it, Julia?

JULIA: That's what it says, but it seems to me the good Lord would rather see a man shaking his fist at heaven than wearing out the knees of his pants on the ground.

Gwen Pharis Ringwood

GERTH: (*turning restlessly*) I told Lisa to get some screens for the combine. I wanted to put them on tonight.

JULIA: (*sitting down, she speaks thoughtfully and with some hesitation*) Gerth, Lisa ought to have young ones around her. She needs them. Why don't you take a child to raise?

GERTH: (*distantly*) We've talked about it. But with things as they are—

JULIA: It would give you something to work for.

GERTH: (*angrily*) I've got enough to work for. (*To stop further discussion.*) You see these heads of wheat? They're full and hard; you can't find another farm in the country with wheat like that this early.

JULIA: Sometimes something inside a house can mean more than a full granary outside.

(*She gets up and begins collecting the glasses.* BERT *comes in from the barn; he is exuberant.*)

BERT: Hello, Mom. Hi, Gerth, I was looking for you. Can I run the big combine tomorrow?

GERTH: We'll see. (*Gruffly*) But don't let me see you jumping around that fan belt again, do you understand?

BERT: Gosh, Gerth, I—

GERTH: (*sharply*) You heard me. You know better than to take a risk like that.

JULIA: Go round to the kitchen and bring me that kettle of corn, Son. I'll sit here in the shade and get it ready for tomorrow.

BERT: O.K. (*He goes out.*)

JULIA: Gerth, did Bert tell you he wants to apply for the Air Force?

GERTH: He said something about it, Julia.

JULIA: I hoped maybe you'd talk him out of it. If war breaks out—

GERTH: It will.

JULIA: He's only a child, Gerth—seventeen and he thinks he knows everything there is to know.

(BERT *returns in time to hear* JULIA's *remark.*)

BERT: Who, me?

JULIA: That's right.

(*She takes the kettle of corn from* BERT *and starts to prepare it for cooking.*)

GERTH: Your mother says you're still determined to fly.

BERT: A fellow's got to be doing something. You can't sit home and wait for the world to come. Gee, it must be a swell feeling, looking down on sky-scrapers and men as small as beetles!

GERTH: What makes you think the Air Force is the place to learn?

BERT: If I got in the Air Force right away, before war breaks out, I'd get my start. I'd be right up at the top.

JULIA: Call it a start if you want to. Flying around with gun fire breaking your ear drums seems a poor start to me.

BERT: I'd be drafted any way, Mom.

GERTH: What about learning over here on the field at Lethbridge?

BERT: It costs too much.

GERTH: (*impatiently*) I could take care of that.

BERT: Thanks, Gerth, but—

JULIA: (*excited*) Would you, Gerth?

BERT: Wait a minute, Mom. Gerth, I don't want you to think I'm not grateful, but I couldn't take the money from you. I don't want to take it from anybody. I want to do like you did, start on my own and go places without being beholden. Don't you see? I just wouldn't feel right—

GERTH: (*gently*) Yes, I see, Bert, but think it over before you decide.

BERT: I will, only I don't think I'll change my mind.

GERTH: (*restlessly throwing down the half-finished sheaf*) When Lisa comes tell her I went over to the Morrow place. I want to take a look at those apple trees.

JULIA: I'll tell her.

(*She looks after him as he goes out towards the road.*)

BERT: It was swell of Gerth to offer to give me flying lessons.

JULIA: (*turning back to her work*) You think a lot of him, don't you?

BERT: He's all right. He knows what he wants and gets it; that's what counts in this world.

JULIA: (*pleading*) Let him give you the money if you're bound to fly, Son.

BERT: I want to stand on my own feet, Mom. You ought to know me well enough to see that. Anyway, you have a swell life in the forces. Honest, you do. I'll get my application in this month.

(JULIA *starts to protest but gives up when* CHARLIE *comes in.*)

CHARLIE: Where's the boss, Julia?

JULIA: He just went out to see those trees of his.

CHARLIE: I don't know where he put that twine (*Worried*) I asked him once, but he didn't seem to hear me. I can't figure him out these days.

(*He shakes his head bewildered.*)

JULIA: He's tired, I guess.

CHARLIE: (*sits down wearily*) No, he doesn't get tired. He's got something on his mind, but I don't know what it is. When we were picking that wheat there, I showed him some heads. I found the biggest ones I ever saw, and Gerth just looked at them and hardly said a word. Then he walked off over to those apple trees and stood staring at them like he could make them grow by thinking about it. That ain't like Gerth.

BERT: (*who has wandered over towards the road.*) Here comes the doctor.

JULIA: Bert, you let him look at that cut on your hand.

BERT: (*coming back and sitting down to help* JULIA *with the corn*) Oh, it's all right.

JULIA: Sure, it would be a nice thing if blood poison set in. A one-handed pilot is just what they need.

85

Gwen Pharis Ringwood

BERT: O.K. I didn't say I wouldn't ask him.
   (DAVID *and* LISA *come in from the road. They seem happy and companionable together, and* DAVID *is more mature and sure of himself than before.*)
DAVID: (*smiling*) Hello, Julia. How are you, Charlie—Bert? (*Turning to* LISA) Here, Lisa, let me take that.
   (*He takes a parcel out of her arms.*)
LISA: It's heaven to come home to such a nice cool place. Look, David, these gladioli are going to be pink. (*She stops to look at some plants at the edge of the yard.*) I thought they were white.
DAVID: (*stopping beside her*) That one will be out tomorrow.
LISA: (*smiling at him*) Those are the ones we set out in June, remember?
DAVID: Rather! You made such a fuss about getting them a foot apart.
   (*He smiles down at her, then turns and puts the parcel on the table.*) How are things going with you, Bert? (*Noticing the bandage on* BERT'*s hand.*) What are you wearing that bandage for?
BERT: (*nonchalantly*) Oh, I cut my hand sharpening the sickle. It's not much.
DAVID: Let's have a look at it. (*He removes the bandage quickly.*) Bring me some iodine, Lisa.
JULIA: Let me get it, Lisa.
LISA: (*smiling*) Thank you, Julia.
   (JULIA *goes into the house.*)
LISA: I'm tired, it's been so hot.
   (*She sits down and watches* DAVID *as he bandages the hand.*)
DAVID: (*glancing at her*) You look as fresh as if you'd just got. . . (*To* BERT) You want to be careful of sharp edges, Bert. You took quite a slice out of this thumb. Did you do it yesterday?
BERT: Yes.
DAVID: (*to* JULIA *who returns with the iodine and gives it to him*) Thanks, Jule. You'll find a kit in the back of the car. I'll put a bandage on this. (JULIA *goes out to the road.*) Was the sickle clean, Bert? Had it been in the dirt?
BERT: I don't know; I don't think so, David.
DAVID: (*as he pours the iodine on the cut*) I don't think there's any danger of infection, but I'll look at it tomorrow.
BERT: (*withdrawing his hand quickly*) Gosh, David!
DAVID: (*laughing at him*) It stings, doesn't it?
   (JULIA *returns with the kit and David takes some gauze out of it, bandaging the hand.*)
CHARLIE: I heard you took old man Milton to the hospital, Doctor.
DAVID: Yes, he finally gave in. I practically had to hogtie him to get him there.
JULIA: Is it a bad cut, David?
DAVID: No, not bad.
CHARLIE: What was the matter with Milton, Doctor?
DAVID: (*bandaging the hand swiftly*) Stomach.

86

BERT: (*admiringly*) Say, David, you can sure put them on fast, can't you?
DAVID: All it takes is practice. . . (*To* CHARLIE) Milton will be out in a couple of days.
LISA: Where's Gerth, Julia?
JULIA: Out with his trees.
LISA: He's starting to cut tomorrow?
JULIA: He said the outfit would be here early in the morning.
DAVID: (*to* BERT) Now, how's that?
BERT: Swell, thanks a lot, David.
CHARLIE: (*getting up*) I came to ask Gerth about some twine. I guess I'll go out and find him.
LISA: Tell him I'm home, Charlie, please.
CHARLIE: I will, Mrs. Hansen.
> (*He goes out toward the road.*)
JULIA: I'd better get in and mix the bread if we want to bake tomorrow. Don't you go off anywhere, Bert.
> (*She starts into the house.*)
BERT: I'm just going down to the river. Will you come, David?
DAVID: No thanks, Bert. I've got to get back to town in a little while. I've still some calls to make.
JULIA: (*at the door*) I hear Mamie Stinson's child is doing real well, David. Mamie thinks the sun rises and sets in you.
DAVID: (*sitting down*) She had a close call with that young one.
LISA: I'll come in and help you, Julia.
JULIA: There isn't much to do. You stay out here where it's cool. We'll have enough to do in the next few weeks.
> (*She goes into the house.*)
BERT: (*as he starts out to the road*) You're sure you won't come along, David?
DAVID: Sure. Keep that hand covered for a few days, eh?
BERT: Yeah, thanks.
> (*He leaves.*)
DAVID: (*looking after him*) He's a nice kid.
LISA: He's grown up a lot in the last two years.
DAVID: (*with enthusiasm*) Lord, Lisa, if Gerth will sell that piece of land, we could have a children's hospital here that would beat anything in the Dominion. We could make dozens of kids as healthy as that one.
LISA: If Gerth won't sell, don't you think they'll put it here any way?
DAVID: I'm afraid not. Those people in Red Deer are after it tooth and nail. If Wilson hadn't given them the quarter that adjoins the hill land over there, I don't believe they'd have considered putting it here at all.
LISA: Weren't you surprised at him giving it to them?
DAVID: He's getting old and says he hasn't anybody to leave it to. But Hodges wants the building on the hill, so that leaves it up to Gerth.
LISA: (*doubtfully*) Gerth only put his apple trees up there last year.

Gwen Pharis Ringwood

DAVID: I know.

LISA: I don't know how he'll feel about it. It would mean a lot to the community.

DAVID: (*looking at the wheat on the table*) I want to see it here. I'd rather work here than anywhere else.

LISA: I'm so proud that they gave you the chance to direct it, David.

DAVID: I had a conference with Hodges about the plans yesterday. Swimming pool, play rooms, work shops—he's promised me them all, and enough room to take care of all the undernourished, tubercular, crippled kids in the province, whether they can pay or not. It's a big thing, Lisa.

LISA: (*her eyes shining*) You've talked about it so much, David, but I never really believed you'd get the Government interested.

DAVID: I'll be able to try out my way of curing them. God, I hope Gerth will sell.

LISA: But David, if he doesn't, you still have this chance, wherever it is.

DAVID: If we get it here—they asked me to think about someone to supervise the playrooms, Lisa—and I thought of you, if you'd like to—

(*He hesitates.*)

LISA: David! Oh, I'd rather do it than anything in the world.

DAVID: I know how good you'd be with them, and you'd give them something more than just cold-blooded efficient care. I watched you with that crowd you had out here last week. Why, you'd do them as much good as the sunshine and the food and a place to play and work. They'd get well just looking at you.

LISA: (*laughing*) David, you're out of your head with excitement, lad.

DAVID: (*turning abruptly*) You're right. Perhaps I am.

LISA: (*contritely*) I didn't mean to laugh. Oh, David, I'm as anxious as you are for the hospital to be here, especially now that you say there'd be a place for me. (*Doubtfully*) But Gerth has always wanted that piece of land—long before Morrow had it—and now that he's got it, he's made plans—you see how it is.

DAVID: I tried to get Hodges to come down and ask him but Hodges thought I'd have more influence. Influence! I didn't tell him Gerth and I can't see eye to eye on anything.

LISA: It's been much better since you settled here, David.

DAVID: Yes, it's better, and I'll pay off my note this fall, I think, or most of it. After that, he won't need to stand as my security. But sometimes I wish I'd never come back at all.

LISA: You mean that?

DAVID: (*after a pause*) No.

LISA: Gerth wants you here. We've talked about how well you're doing. He's proud of you, David, and I am too.

DAVID: You can't tell what a man's going to do in a couple of years. I've been lucky.

LISA: I know I'd be able to help with the children, David. And it would be the answer to everything for me. That little boy today—I wish you could have seen him. I'd made up my mind to bring him home for a few weeks; I'm sure Gerth would change his mind if we had him here a little while. I was so disappointed when they told me they'd already found a home for him.

DAVID: There'd be plenty of them needing love up there.

(GERTH *and* CHARLIE *enter from the road.* GERTH *barely glances at* DAVID *and* LISA.)

GERTH: (*to* CHARLIE) Tell Bert to fill the tractors tonight. He'll have to get gasoline tomorrow.

CHARLIE: He went swimming. I'll do it.

GERTH: You've got enough to do.

LISA: Hello, Gerth—You look tired.

(*She smiles at him.*)

GERTH: It's time you were home. The outfit will move out here tomorrow. Benson's wife is coming along to help. There'll be nineteen men.

LISA: (*quietly*) We've got things ready, Gerth.

DAVID: (*looking up cheerfully*) Sounds good, Gerth. If the price stays up, you'll make a fortune this year. I was looking at this.

(*He indicates the wheat on the table.*)

GERTH: (*without warmth*) You couldn't tell a good head of wheat if you saw one.

DAVID: (*coldly*) Probably not; it takes genius I gather.

GERTH: (*to* CHARLIE) Jerry's got a shoulder sore. You'd better look at him.

CHARLIE: I'm going right up.

(*He goes off to the barn.*)

GERTH: (*as* CHARLIE *leaves*) I'll be along later.

DAVID: How's Cap these days, Gerth? He's a special patient of mine.

GERTH: (*drily*) He's probably in better health than most of your patients.

LISA: (*trying again to get some response from* GERTH) I bought you some new gloves, Gerth.

(*She gives them to him.*)

GERTH: (*barely glancing at them.*) Did you get them in town?

LISA: Of course, where else would I get them?

GERTH: (*with an undertone of suspicion and anger*) I imagine they're to be found in other places. You were in Lethbridge today, weren't you?

LISA: (*without feeling any necessity to deny it*) Why, yes, Gerth. . .

(GERTH *throws the gloves on the table.* LISA *is hurt.*) Aren't you even going to try them on?

GERTH: They're all right. My hands don't require delicate fitting. Did you bring those screens for the combine?

Gwen Pharis Ringwood

LISA: (*worried and contrite*) The shop was closed when we got back to town. I'm sorry.

GERTH: (*resentfully*) That means I'll have to make a trip to town tomorrow.

LISA: (*distressed*) I—I don't usually forget things, Gerth.

GERTH: You couldn't be expected to remember a little thing like the fact that I'm harvesting.

DAVID: (*angrily*) What's the matter with you, Gerth? If you object to Lisa's going to Lethbridge with me, why don't you say so?

GERTH: (*to* LISA) Does it never occur to you I might be interested in knowing where you are?

LISA: David had a call to operate in the city. I wanted to go in to the nursing mission so I went along. I didn't think you'd mind.

GERTH: You didn't think about it at all.

DAVID: (*indignantly*) I'll bring the screens out in the morning, if you need them.

GERTH: I'll manage without help, thanks.

LISA: I went in to see a little boy whose mother died two weeks ago. I'd thought about bringing him here, but they'd already found a place for him.

GERTH: You can waste a lot of sentiment on every bastard in the country.

LISA: (*deeply hurt*) Gerth!

DAVID: (*angrily*) You'd do well to waste a little yourself, Gerth. If Lisa wants to adopt a child, I don't see what in hell keeps you from it. You can afford it.

GERTH: (*with slow hostility*) What I do with my money is no concern of yours. You're hardly in a position to dictate to me.

DAVID: (*stung to bitterness*) I'm sorry if I've overstepped a debtor's privilege. I'd forgotten my position for the moment. I expect to pay you this fall.

GERTH: (*turning away wearily, his anger subsiding*) Oh, let it go. I don't need your money.

DAVID: You'll get it in any case. I'll try not to trouble you after this. (*He starts to go.*)

LISA: David, Gerth—you're saying a lot of horrible things you don't mean. . . (*To* GERTH.) David's had a wonderful opportunity offered him, Gerth. Don't let him go away without even telling you about it. Surely—surely you didn't mind about my going to Lethbridge? (*A pause.*) Did you?

GERTH: (*after a moment*) No, I didn't mind. (*He picks up a head of the wheat on the table and looks at it carefully.*) Sit down, David. If something good's come your way, I'm glad.

DAVID: (*remaining standing*) Thanks.

GERTH: You're not thinking of leaving, are you?

DAVID: That's up to you, Gerth.

GERTH: Up to me? (*Harshly.*) I told you the money could wait.

DAVID: It isn't the money. I've been appointed director of a children's hospital the Government's going to build. They've set aside $350,000 for it.

GERTH: (*getting up*) That's fine, David. That's fine for a young man.

DAVID: Wilson's ready to give them that hundred acres of his for a site.

GERTH: So that's why Hodges was out here the other day!

DAVID: He represents the Department of Public Health. He told me today if you'd take seventy-five dollars an acre for that hundred with the hill on it, he'd recommend the hospital be put here. Red Deer is out to get it there if possible.

LISA: It would be wonderful for this district Gerth.

GERTH: What do they want with a hospital out here, miles from nowhere?

DAVID: It's a beautiful site for one thing. They'd put the building on the hill. Then the climate is especially good for lung cases.

GERTH: Two hundred acres seems like a lot of land for a hospital.

DAVID: They want that much. They plan to make the grounds pretty elaborate. (*Enthusiastically*) You see, our idea isn't only to get youngsters here who are so sick they've got to be under a doctor's care. We want to take all those who don't come up to standard health requirements and build them up. There'll be a lot of youngsters with more energy than they know what to do with who'd like a chance at learning a little about farming or raising a garden while they're here under supervision.

LISA: (*also excited*) And David says I could be in charge of the play-rooms, Gerth.

GERTH: I've got plans of my own for that land. I only set those trees out last spring.

DAVID: I know that.

GERTH: If they take it north, will you go there?

DAVID: I'll go with it.

LISA: They offer a good price, Gerth. The assessment value can't be more than $35.00 an acre.

GERTH: They must want it badly to offer that much.

DAVID: They can afford to because Wilson's donating his half of it.

LISA: At the price they offer, you could buy two sections down below.

GERTH: So that's how I strike you? Any kind of land is good enough for me.

DAVID: (*without rancour*) You'll never make any money off that hill, with a few apple trees and a couple of granaries—that's all you've got there. But I told Hodges you might not sell. He left it up to me to talk you into it—I'd rather he hadn't.

GERTH: I don't see what a hospital has to do with me, except more taxes. If it's like most of the government schemes, you'd be better out of it. You'd make a lot more on your own.

DAVID: (*with conviction*) That's for me to judge, Gerth. It's the Government's duty to take care of these youngsters—they're its security for the future. It's my duty to put what I know where it will do the most good.

GERTH: If I rip those young trees out of the dirt and set them somewhere else, they'll die.

LISA: The land would do a lot more good if used for a hospital than for growing apples, Gerth.

GERTH: (*suddenly angry*) You have it all figured out, haven't you?

DAVID: (*resenting his tone to* LISA) Leave Lisa out of this. If you won't consider it, all you have to do is say so.

GERTH: Lisa doesn't seem to be exactly disinterested.

DAVID: (*disgusted*) You never could sit down and talk a thing out. You always had to get into a row over it.

GERTH: Well, there isn't much talking needed. I can't see my way to selling, David. It seems to me I've done enough for you.

DAVID: What's the matter with you? You're not doing it for me.

GERTH: You two expect me to fall in line with any fool plan that comes up.

DAVID: I didn't ask you to do this as a favour—I asked you because Hodges left it up to me.

GERTH: You can tell him I'm not selling that land to him or anybody else; I've got other plans for it.

LISA: Wait until tomorrow to say no, Gerth. Let me talk to you about it.

GERTH: If you can stay home long enough to run your house you seem to do well these days.

LISA: I do everything there is in this house that needs to be done. I've never neglected it. I'd still have time to be of some use up there. It wouldn't make any difference to the house.

GERTH: (*going over to* LISA) That land might mean as much to me as it does to you; you don't think of that. I've put young trees in there. If we could get orchards in this irrigated country, there'd be a living for a lot more people than there is now. The time has come before when wheat was worth less than so much gravel, and it'll come again. We've got to be ready to farm something besides wheat.

DAVID: I can't see you contented with a quarter of a section of apple trees and hay. You have to have a thousand acres in wheat every year, or you don't think you're farming.

GERTH: (*turning on him*) And if I do? My land doesn't suffer for it. It won't blow away in the first dry year like the rest of the dirt around here. You want to save bodies. I want to save the ground that feeds them. In the end the ground is more important, to my way of thinking.

LISA: Yes, in the end the ground you walk on is the only thing you care about, the only thing you'd lift your hand to save.

DAVID: Lisa, Gerth has a right to refuse to sell that land. It's his.

LISA: But it would have meant so much to you to stay on here—and to the district. And when you told me I could help—oh, I—I don't

care. It doesn't matter. Let's not talk about it any more.
(BERT *comes in from the barn.*)

BERT: Gerth, they're breaking horses over at Wilson's. I could see them from the hill. Can I ride over?

GERTH: (*angrily*) No, you can't. If you're going to earn a man's wages, you'll have to get up when the rest start. You've got those tractors to fill tonight, and then you'd better get to bed. I'll go up with you.

(*He turns impatiently away from* DAVID *and* LISA *and goes to the barn.* BERT *looks disappointed but says nothing, as he follows* GERTH. *After they have gone,* LISA *and* DAVID *are silent for a few moments. Finally* LISA *takes up the gloves that* GERTH *has let fall on the ground and places them on the table.*)

LISA: Well, that's the way it is. I'm sorry, David.

DAVID: I can see it his way. Hodges might have talked him into it. I always made him angry, even when we were little. He seems to feel I hold him in contempt. It isn't true.

LISA: He's not himself these days.

DAVID: Maybe it's better that I'm going away.

LISA: You'll have the work you like, that means a lot. The place doesn't mean so much.

DAVID: No, the place doesn't make so much difference.

LISA: (*wistfully*) But there for a moment I saw myself a part of it. I saw myself taking care of those babies that didn't get a fair start, helping to do what we've talked about, leaving a better generation than ours in charge of things. . . squandering some of the love that's stored up inside me. Out here where there's nothing but wheat around me, nothing to listen for but the tractors all day and the wind at night, and nothing to look for but how near it is time for the men to come in to dinner. . . out here, there isn't any place for me to put the love I've got. Nobody needs it.

DAVID: (*a new note in his voice*) Lisa.

LISA: (*getting up quickly*) I'm tired, David. I'd better go in and see what's to be done.

DAVID: No, I've got something to say. You and Gerth have been good to me in these two years. In his way Gerth's tried to make it smooth for me and that was hard because he's never wanted me here.

LISA: I don't know, David—sometimes I think he's glad you're here.

DAVID: I wish you were happier, Lisa.

LISA: That's not Gerth's fault, David. It's my own, something in myself, some restlessness that won't be satisfied. I thought a child might bring me peace, but then our child died and there haven't been any more. (*With genuine feeling.*) Oh, I don't even know what I'm looking for, David. I don't think I ever have known. I just let things happen to me, just wait and let them happen.

Gwen Pharis Ringwood

DAVID: I remember the first time I saw you, the night Gerth and I had the row about my going back to school. You had on a blue dress.
LISA: (*smiling*) I was frightened. I wasn't used to meeting people, and it had been lonely teaching out on the lease. When Gerth first started coming to see me, the people I stayed with teased me and told me nobody could get along with the Hansens. They said you worked your women in the fields and hated each other. I expected you and Gerth to start shooting when you met.
DAVID: It never got quite that bad.
LISA: You were kind to me, kinder than anybody else, and so much younger.
DAVID: (*quietly*) Lisa, I'll be going north soon. I was almost glad when Gerth said he wouldn't sell.
LISA: Why, David?
DAVID: You're Gerth's wife. He'd say that was the reason I love you.
LISA: David!
DAVID: Didn't you know?
LISA: (*distressed*) No, I—Oh, David, why did you tell me this?
DAVID: I don't know, something in your face when you talked about the hospital and helping me. I'd never have told you if I'd been staying here. You know that, don't you? But when I go this time, I won't come back.
LISA: It would have been better if you'd gone and never told me.
DAVID: I hadn't meant to. I thought if we could work together, for something we both believed in, up there on the hill, I wouldn't ask for any more.
LISA: Yes, that would have been enough.
DAVID: Look at me. If ever you need me, if ever you could see your way to leave Gerth and come, I'd ask you to do it. I'd demand it of you. I know I could make you happy, Lisa.
LISA: I'm not sure that happiness is the thing to look for. I'm going in.
(*She moves to the door.*)
DAVID: Wherever you are, however far away, you're in my thoughts.
LISA: David, we're caught for a moment into believing this, that's all.
DAVID: (*slowly*) No, that's not all. Good night.
(*He turns to go.*)
LISA: (*involuntarily*) David, don't go. Oh, I can't let you go.
(*She starts to go to him.*)
DAVID: You mean you'll come?
LISA: (*after a long look at him she shakes her head and turns back to the door*) No.
DAVID: I'm sorry I told you. I'm sorry for us both.
LISA: (*her emotion breaking through*) Sometimes I'm sorry for everybody. Sometimes I feel like I could put my arms around the whole ragged, God-forsaken world. When I see all the lonely people walking down the lonely streets, trying to touch one another—wanting to be sure of something, I want to cry out,

"I know how it is with you, we're a part of each other; I could help!" but instead I can't even reach out to touch you whom I love, because it's too late. And I can't touch Gerth because we're on different paths. And there's nothing ahead or behind for any of us but just one person walking alone in darkness.

DAVID: (*going to her*) Lisa, don't talk like that. Believe me, it isn't like that.

LISA: (*all emotion drained from her*) It doesn't matter, David. Go now.

(JULIA *comes out of the house somewhat excited.*)

JULIA: David, they telephoned from Wilson's. They want you there. Jack Lee's horse threw him and he's unconscious.

DAVID: (*quickly*) Tell them I'll be right over. And Julia, ask them to have water heating.

JULIA: I will.

(*She goes back into the house.*)

LISA: Is there anything I could do?

DAVID: No, he'll probably come around before I get there. He's always getting thrown.

(*He starts out and almost collides with* GERTH *who comes from the barn.*)

GERTH: I beg your pardon. You seem to be in a hurry.

DAVID: Jack Lee got thrown again. They just phoned and I'm on my way there.

GERTH: He'll never learn. I'll bet it was that black he tried to ride last week. Come by after you get through, and let me know if he's all right. Tell him he doesn't need to come to work tomorrow.

DAVID: All right.

(*He leaves and after a moment his car is heard starting.*)

GERTH: (*noticing* LISA's *stillness*) What's the matter with you?

LISA: Nothing, Gerth.

GERTH: (*going over to the wheat and beginning to sort it*) You look like you'd lost your last friend. If I'd turned the whole place into a baby clinic, would that make you any happier?

LISA: Please, Gerth, I was disappointed, that's all. (*After a pause*) Is that the wheat you're sending to Toronto?

GERTH: (*perfunctorily*) Some of it.

LISA: Shall I help you to sort it?

(*She starts to take some of it.*)

GERTH: I'll do it. It doesn't mean anything to you. It buys the car you drive and the clothes you wear, that's all.

LISA: Gerth, that's cruel. What do you want of me?

GERTH: Nothing that's given in duty, Lisa.

LISA: Let's go away from here, after this crop is threshed. To the ocean, maybe; we used to talk about that—just for the winter.

GERTH: You're mighty anxious to get away all of a sudden.

LISA: I'm frightened of what's happening to us, Gerth, of what's happening to me—we're getting so far apart that we can't talk about anything any more.

95

GERTH: When you came here, I thought you'd like it. I was proud of this farm and I hoped you'd be.

LISA: I am, but there's something more to look for than things to be proud of. If we had children—

GERTH: (*cutting her off abruptly*) Well, we haven't, and I fail to see what difference it makes now.

LISA: You have the land, it gives you all you need. (*Pleading.*) You're happy in the fields, happier than I can make you. If I had something to work for like that—

GERTH: (*quietly*) Look here, Lisa, I've talked a lot about the land, the plans I've made. A man's got to believe in something if he's going to live. I never found any God except what I found out there, the one that lies in the earth and lets things die. And he's blind! He laughs at you; he makes a man slave for him and laughs!

LISA: God isn't like that, Gerth!

GERTH: The one I know is like that. When I brought you here, I thought I wouldn't need to be a slave to him any more. I thought there'd be something outside, something he couldn't touch. But it wasn't that way. You sent me back to him.

LISA: I didn't send you. Your heart was always there.

GERTH: But I didn't go back as a slave. I went back to beat him at his own game. I went back to make the land grow wheat in spite of him, in spite of hail, and dust and drought, in spite of anything he could do. I swore I'd find a way to beat him and I did. I've won! David couldn't have done that!

LISA: David—what has David to do with this, Gerth?

GERTH: It's easy enough for you to plan for David. Maybe you're right, maybe what he's doing is bigger than anything I could do, I don't know. It's always been that way, I've never known. But I don't care now. I don't care, I tell you. I don't need you or anybody else now. I've won alone! Whatever you've done to me, I've won alone!

LISA: Gerth, look at me. You know I haven't stood in your way—I haven't done anything to you. Tell me I've been some help. You've got to tell me.

GERTH: You ask me why I work out there. I'll tell you why—because out there I'm beating God. Out there I've learned to forget you with your patient smile that pities me and is afraid. You don't need to worry now. I won't bother you. I won't come prying into your thoughts or asking you for anything. I don't want anything from you now but to be left alone. You're wise to look for something outside to waste your tears on. Tears are cheap and come easy to you. But I don't need them, and I don't need you.

LISA: Then I was trying to find something that was never there. (*Pleading.*) Gerth, if you've no need of me, I've no place here. I've got to feel I count for something somewhere.

GERTH: You count with the people you carry baskets to, as long as there's food in the baskets. Isn't that enough?

LISA: Maybe you've got the only answer; maybe work is the only answer there is for people like us, lost people. I thought it was love. I'll go away.

(*She tries to conceal the sob in her voice.*)

GERTH: Yes, you'd be glad to get away, wouldn't you? You count enough with David—maybe you'll go away with David.

LISA: (*facing him quietly*) I'd be of some use there.

GERTH: That's what you think. (*He comes to her fiercely.*) He's made you think you're wasted here, hasn't he? That you're too good for this place and me.

LISA: Stop it, Gerth. That isn't true.

GERTH: But whatever David does, that's not for you. It's for himself. You know that, don't you? I'm of more worth to you than David. You think he needs your help—David doesn't need anything from you. Go away with him if that's what you want.

LISA: (*getting control of herself*) I'll go, Gerth, but not with David. I never meant to hinder you, but I can't stay with you any longer. I'll go in now.

(*She turns to go but* GERTH *turns slowly and comes to her. He speaks brokenly.*)

GERTH: I lied, Lisa. Everything I do is tied up with you. Don't leave me. All I wanted was your love. I didn't need anything else, but it's not that way with you, is it?

LISA: (*wonderingly*) We don't know each other at all, do we—after nine years?

GERTH: I—I've wanted to destroy you and everything outside that took you away from me. Don't leave me, Lisa. I've been jealous because you see David's work as greater than mine. I wanted to bind you here. With you gone, this place won't mean anything to me. With you gone, I've nothing more to work for. Will you stay?

LISA: I'll never leave you, Gerth.

GERTH: You and David have something together, a way of looking at things, of getting along with people—I don't have that. That's all there is between you, isn't it?

LISA: (*after a pause*) That's all.

GERTH: Those apple trees—I thought they'd show you I could care about something besides wheat. But they'd grow somewhere else. There's room for them and for the building up there. If you were free to work up there, you'd be happy here, wouldn't you, Lisa?

LISA: My life's tied up with yours, Gerth. I want to stay.

GERTH: (*awkwardly*) I'm glad you said that Lisa: Lisa, if Wilson can spare his land for the hospital, I can spare mine. I'll give it to him.

LISA: No, not now!

GERTH: I want to show you it wasn't just talk—that I don't care about that land except for you.

LISA: Don't decide yet, Gerth. Maybe—maybe it would be better for them to build in Red Deer.

Gwen Pharis Ringwood

GERTH: You and David want it here. And now—now I want you to have that work up there. I'll go in and telephone Hodges.

LISA: I'm not sure David would want you to. He said—

GERTH: He said he didn't want to take from me. Well he's not taking from me. I'm giving it to the Government. I'll get it over with now.

(*He goes into the house.* LISA, *disturbed, starts to follow him, then turns back.* JULIA *comes out of the house.*)

JULIA: (*taking up the kettle*) Gerth's scattered his prize wheat all over the lawn.

LISA: Leave it, Julia. He isn't finished yet.

JULIA: Bert's in there writing a letter trying to get in the Air Force. I've done everything I know to argue him out of it.

LISA: He can't get in this year, Julia. He's too young.

JULIA: I just hope he's not as healthy as he looks. Maybe they'll find he's short-sighted or something and not pass him.

(DAVID *comes in from the road. He looks weary and drawn.*)

LISA: What's the matter, David?

DAVID: I couldn't do anything for Lee. He died right after I got there.

LISA: Oh, David!

JULIA: That's terrible.

DAVID: Have you any coffee, Julia?

JULIA: I'll get you some right away, David.

(*She goes into the house.*)

DAVID: An operation might have saved him, if there'd been time, but it was too late when I got there.

LISA: It wasn't your fault, David.

DAVID: We went to school together. I hadn't expected him to be so bad.

(GERTH *comes out of the house.*)

GERTH: Julia told me about Jack Lee. That's too bad.

DAVID: You were right, it was the black that threw him. It was a concussion; I couldn't do a thing.

GERTH: Is there anything I can do?

DAVID: I think you might go over there. I've got to go to town. I'll go back tonight.

GERTH: I'll go over, David. (*A pause*) I've just phoned Hodges. I'm giving that hundred to them for the hospital. He said that settles it, they'll put it here.

DAVID: (*startled*) You've changed your mind? (*Slowly*) I wish you hadn't done that, Gerth.

GERTH: I thought you'd be relieved.

DAVID: (*looking down at the ground*) You've done enough for me.

GERTH: Well, for God's sake, make up your mind. You come here asking for the land. I gave it to you. Now you don't think you want it. Don't you know what you want?

DAVID: (*disconcerted*) I might do better away. I wouldn't have time to keep up the practice I've started here, and people would expect it—

GERTH: (*distantly*) Lisa understood you needed her.

98

LISA: That doesn't matter.

DAVID: You should have waited to decide until we'd talked about it.

GERTH: You're just discouraged because of what happened to Lee. There's no use blaming yourself. He took his own chances, David. You did all you could.

DAVID: (*getting up impatiently*) Oh, that's not it. It's not the first case I've lost, and it won't be the last, but this is no place for me. You and Lisa have your life here, you belong. I don't. I want to get away.

GERTH: (*with difficulty and embarrassment*) It's my fault you feel that way. I've not made you as welcome as I could have. It's hard to say, but I thought—Lisa's told me what a fool I was—but there for a while I thought there was a feeling between you—(*He breaks off.*) Forget it, David. Lisa wants this chance to do something she can do with her whole heart and I want her to have it. There's no good reason for you to change your mind unless it's something I don't know about. (*A pause.*) Is there?

DAVID: (*after a look at* LISA *who returns it for a moment, then looks away*) I—I guess not, Gerth.

GERTH: Then that settles it.

DAVID: Thanks. (*He turns to go.*) I'd better go on. I'll meet you at Lee's.
(*He goes over to* LISA *and stands before her, about to speak; then changes his mind.* LISA *speaks with understanding and affection, trying to make him understand.*)

LISA: David, it will be all right. You'll find a place here. We—Gerth and I—talked it over. Things that seem important to us tonight will be something to laugh at tomorrow. It's always that way.
(*He turns and goes without a word.* LISA *makes an involuntary gesture and moves after him, then turns.* GERTH *watches her closely.*)

GERTH: You'd better tell Julia not to bother about the coffee. I'll go on to Lee's.

LISA: (*piteously*) Gerth, everything will be all right now, won't it?

GERTH: (*gently*) Yes, everything's going to be all right. And if you want to bring a child here, Lisa—I—it'll be fine with me.

LISA: (*doubtfully*) I don't know. I think I could do more up there—if David wants me to help—

GERTH: (*turning away*) Yes, if David wants your help, your heart would be up there.
(*He speaks tonelessly, almost to himself. He is a lonely, aimless figure, the power gone from him for a moment.* CHARLIE *comes trudging in from the barn, carrying some blades of wheat.*)

CHARLIE: It gets dark earlier these nights. I saw these by the ditch and picked them out. You might want to put them in that sheaf. (*He gives the wheat to* GERTH *proudly. As he looks at him, his voice changes.*) What's the matter, Gerth? You look like you'd seen a ghost. What's happened?

Gwen Pharis Ringwood

GERTH: Nothing. Nothings's happened. (*He moves away from* CHARLIE, *letting his hand rest briefly on the old man's shoulder. He speaks more to himself than* CHARLIE.) I thought I could beat him at his own game, Charlie. But he wins in the end. He may be blind but he knows what a man loves best and where to strike. And he wins in the end. He makes what you've done seem useless.
(*With a sudden hurt gesture,* GERTH *crushes the wheat in his hand and lets it fall as the curtain falls.*)

ACT THREE

SCENE: *A corner of a wheat field on the Hansen farm.*
TIME: *A late afternoon in September, 1938.*

It is after supper late in September. The scene is a corner of GERTH HANSEN'S *wheat field. At the left is a water barrel on a small sledge and near it a rough bench with a wash basin on it. Below the barrel is a path leading to the cook-car off-stage. The path to the road is at the rear, left of centre, and another footpath to the hospital goes up the rise at the back of the stage. A straw stack is banked at the right with a path into the field below it. Some sacks of wheat at right and a stook of unthreshed grain at left are evidence of the harvest season. There is straw scattered upon the ground and in the distance the rolling fields of stubble may be seen.*
JULIA comes in at the left from the cook-car with a dish-pan. She fills it with water from the water wagon. As she is doing so, CHARLIE *comes in from the same direction. He sits down on the bench near the wagon.*

JULIA: I guess I'm not the only one that's glad this six weeks is almost over.
CHARLIE: Heaviest harvest I've ever seen.
JULIA: I'd as soon cook for the gang that's working on that hospital up there as this crowd. I can't bake enough bread to last a day. Lisa had to go to town for flour. I thought we had enough bread to last but by the time I got through baking those pies tonight, it was down to a cupful.

100

CHARLIE: Gerth didn't eat much. He was out before the rest got started.
JULIA: He looks bad. This threshing has taken it out of him.
CHARLIE: He usually feels better in harvest than any other time.
JULIA: He works all day and half the night. Nobody can stand up under that.

(*She starts to peel potatoes, sitting on the bench near* CHARLIE.)

CHARLIE: I can't figure him out. Yesterday when I went up to tell him about that wheat of his taking first prize at Toronto, I thought sure that would get his interest, but I had to tell him twice before he knew what I was saying. And then he just sort of smiled and said, "Well, we can say we grew good wheat once anyway, can't we?". I can't figure him out.
JULIA: I think he felt badly about moving those trees of his. He sure wanted to see them grow.
CHARLIE: A lot of them are dying. It was a bad time to move them I guess.
JULIA: It's a shame, Gerth feeling like he does when he's got such a good crop. And Lisa's happier than I've ever seen her. She's like a child with a new toy, she's that excited over the plans for the hospital. She's been reading books about play-rooms, and play-grounds, and writing letters all over the country. I never saw her so excited about anything.
CHARLIE: I don't like having the hospital up there. It's all you can see, no matter where you look. Gerth oughtn't to have given them that land.
JULIA: I guess he won't be sorry, if it makes Lisa so much happier.
CHARLIE: (*getting up*) Where did Gerth go, do you know?
JULIA: Now sit down and rest yourself, Charlie. You don't need to go following Gerth all over the place when you're dead on your feet. He's up on the hill, paying off some of the haulers. He'll be back down.
CHARLIE: (*sitting again*) They couldn't take any more wheat in town. I don't know what he's going to do with what they threshed this afternoon.

(BERT *comes in from the hospital.*)

BERT: Gosh, Gerth's having them dump two loads of wheat on the ground by the hospital. He hasn't got any place to put it.
CHARLIE: (*concerned*) That's no good. It might rain tonight.
JULIA: Doesn't look any more like rain than this potato looks like a tea pot, Charlie. Gerth knows what he's doing.
BERT: Mrs. Hansen's coming up the road. I hope she brings the mail. Say, Mom, what's the matter with Gerth these days? He's either in a rage or he won't say a word to anybody.
JULIA: He's tired, Bert, just like Charlie here and your mother.
BERT: Well, he doesn't need to take it out on me. I only asked him how it felt to have the best wheat in the province. He about snapped my head off.

JULIA: Maybe you were in his way, son. Where are you going?

BERT: Just down the road a little way. I might scare up a prairie chicken.

JULIA: You go by and put a kettle of water on the stove in the cook-car. I'm waiting to do the dishes till it gets a little cooler in there.

BERT: O.K., Mom, I'll do it, seeing it's you.

(*He makes a face at her as he goes off.*)

JULIA: David hasn't been out here in two weeks. I thought he'd want to see that hospital every day.

CHARLIE: It's a funny looking building to me.

JULIA: They've only got one wing up, Charlie. It won't look like that when they get it finished.

(GERTH *enters down the hill from the hospital. He comes down the hill slowly, his eyes are tired and he hardly seems to notice* JULIA *and* CHARLIE *as he comes in. He throws a stray bundle that has fallen across the path over to the side.* CHARLIE *gets up anxiously as he sees* GERTH, *who tosses some gunny sacks down by the sacks of wheat.*)

CHARLIE: I don't think you ought to run that wheat on the ground, Gerth. If it rained—

GERTH: Where the hell will I put it then? They can't take any more in town. They filled the two granaries up there this afternoon.

CHARLIE: They might let you run some of it in the building there for a few days. They haven't got the floors down yet.

GERTH: I don't see the Government turning its hospital over to me for a granary.

CHARLIE: The grain won't hurt their hospital.

GERTH: It's pretty close. The government won't be responsible for anything that happens to that wheat. And there's a lot of men working there.

JULIA: Another couple of days and you're finished, Gerth.

GERTH: (*sitting down*) Yes, and another six weeks and they'll be through building at the rate they're going.

CHARLIE: It wouldn't worry me none if they never finished. I suppose that building's going to look fine high up on the hill like that, but the field of wheat you cut down looked a lot better.

GERTH: I thought so once, Charlie. But you and I—we get out of the stream of things out here. We get to thinking it's only wheat that counts.

CHARLIE: Next year you should be able to put wheat in the south half.

GERTH: I don't figure on farming so big another year, Charlie.

JULIA: It's the fall of the year. If you say that in the spring, I'll believe you.

GERTH: (*wearily*) I guess you're right, Jule. When spring doesn't mean anything to a farmer, he's finished. Hello, Lisa.

(LISA *comes in from the road. She is flushed with excitement and pleasure, and her eyes are shining.*)

LISA: Gerth, the plans for the play-rooms came. They're just what we wanted. Let me show them to you.

GERTH: Sure.

(LISA *unrolls the bundle of prints she is carrying.*)

LISA: I'm so excited about them. This is the boys' workshop. We designed this end so that the crippled children can work in their wheel chairs. And the room for the tiny ones is perfect. They'll have three long tables in it and each child will have a little cupboard to keep his things in. Oh, and here's where we'll have the moving pictures. I mustn't get them all mixed up. David hasn't seen them yet.

GERTH: They look fine, Lisa. I'm glad they've given you what you want.

LISA: I can hardly wait to see them finished. They've got the East wing nearly done, haven't they?

GERTH: (*smiling at her excitement*) Almost.

LISA: I was looking at some books today in the library. Big print and beautiful bright illustrations. I'm going to get some of them.

JULIA: You've forgotten all about supper, haven't you?

LISA: Well, yes, I did, Julia, but I got the things I went for. Oh, there's a letter for Bert.

JULIA: You come in and let me get you something to eat.

LISA: I hurried back to help you with the dishes, Julia.

JULIA: I'd have had them done, but it's been so warm.

(*She takes the potatoes and goes out to the cook-car.*)

LISA: (*as* GERTH *gets up*) You and Charlie look so tired, Gerth. Can't you stop for tonight?

GERTH: I want to check those loads before the haulers go back.

(LISA *starts to go to the cook-car when* MORROW *comes in from the road. He has been drinking.*)

MORROW: Wheat-king Gerth taking his ease, eh? Howdy, Mrs. Hansen.

GERTH: What are you doing here?

MORROW: (*belligerently*) I'm hauling gas for the Government if it's anything to you.

GERTH: You ought to know better than to come around my place, Morrow. Go on, Lisa.

(*With a questioning look at* GERTH, LISA *goes out to the cook-car.*)

MORROW: (*smiling knowingly*) You forget something, Mr. Hansen— this ain't your land any more. You had to part with some of your precious land, didn't you? You had to make a place for the doctor. That's funny, that is.

(GERTH *starts toward* MORROW *but* CHARLIE *interposes.*)

CHARLIE: Don't let him rile you, Gerth. He's drunk.

GERTH: You'd better get out, Morrow. If they catch you driving a government truck in the state you're in, you'll find yourself in trouble.

MORROW: They can't do anything to me. I'm through driving their truck tonight, see? You want a drink, Charlie? We'll drink to the hospital—Hansen's hospital.

(*He produces a bottle and offers it to* GERTH *who knocks it out of his hand.*)

GERTH: Get back to the road, Al.

MORROW: (*angrily*) You've got your wheat on the ground right up against the hospital. I'm supposed to haul that tank of gasoline up there. What are you going to do about it?

GERTH: (*turning away in disgust*) Oh, show him where to go, Charlie, if you think he can drive up there. If not drop him in the river.

(*Without looking at* MORROW, GERTH *goes out at right.*)

CHARLIE: (*moving up on the rise and pointing out toward the road*) Drive round to the end between the two granaries and in to the door. That's where they probably want the gas. You ought to have got here before they knocked off. You're a fool to carry a bottle on you, Morrow.

MORROW: What are you trying to play? God Almighty like your boss? You don't need to pull that on me. I'm not the dust under his feet no more. I'll show him. He can't talk to me like he would to a hunkie and get away with it. I'm not afraid of Gerth Hansen with all his money and his elevators choking with wheat. You can follow him around like a dog the rest of your days, but I'm not going to. I'll show him how much I think of him.

CHARLIE: Get in your truck, Al, and get started.

(JULIA *comes in at left to get a pail of water.*)

JULIA: I thought it was you when I heard that commotion out here. You'd better not let Gerth see you here. He's got an idea how that smutty wheat got into that load Ellison hauled.

MORROW: If he can't grow clean wheat, it's my fault I suppose. I've got time to fool with his wheat, haven't I, trying to keep six kids from starving because he put me off my farm and fixed it so I lose every job I get?

JULIA: Get out of my sight, Al Morrow. I haven't time to listen to you.

MORROW: Don't worry, Julia, I can do without your company. Hansen's hospital—that's good, that is!

(*He goes to the road by the path at back.*)

JULIA: (*looking after him*) He's gone crazy, I think.

CHARLIE: I don't like him fooling around here. It's not all talk. He hates Gerth.

JULIA: He can't hurt Gerth. He's too afraid of him.

CHARLIE: It's being afraid that makes a man mean.

(BERT *comes in from the road.*)

BERT: Morrow's certainly on a tear, isn't he? He backed his truck into the ditch up there.

CHARLIE: What's he going to do now, leave that tank of gas on the side of the road?

104

BERT: No, he'll get it out. It's not bad. I offered to drive it out for him and he told me where I could go.
JULIA: Lisa has a letter for you, Bert. She's in the cook-car.
BERT: Boy, I'd better get it.
(*He goes quickly off at left.*)
JULIA: I don't want to know what it is. If they've accepted him—
CHARLIE: He's got to go his own way, Julia. You can't live his life for him.
JULIA: But he's not ready to go on his own way. He's just seizing the first thing that comes along.
CHARLIE: That's what you do when you're young Julia. And that's the way it's got to be. If you waited for signs to tell you what to do, you'd get left by the road. You can help the young, Julia, but you can't hinder them.
BERT: (*running in very excited*) It's come, Mom! I got the letter; they're going to take me.
JULIA: Bert!
BERT: See, here it is. They're going to take me! (DAVID *comes in from the road.* BERT *turns to him in elation.*) Hi, David, I've been accepted in the Air Force. I've got to be in Winnipeg by October 15th.
DAVID: That's fine, Bert. I hope—you're pretty young to start in the Air Force. (*To* JULIA.) Don't look like that, Jule.
JULIA: I asked you not to pass him, David. You could have found something to keep him out.
DAVID: I couldn't do that, Julia.
JULIA: You can't go, Bert. You can't go.
BERT: Mom, don't take on so, please. You shouldn't have asked David to do that. You might have spoiled my chances altogether.
JULIA: It's a fine chance you're getting. Gerth would have helped you.
BERT: Mom what have I got here? I've never seen anything. I've never been any place. Sure, Gerth would help me. But I want to do like he did—go my own way—I want to fly a plane over the Rocky Mountains and look down on the sky itself and know I'm heading some place.
CHARLIE: It's no good to head towards war, Bert.
BERT: I'm headed there anyway. Isn't that right, David?
DAVID: (*soberly*) It looks that way.
BERT: And when it comes, I want to be in the sky—I want to be up where I don't have to see it too close, where I can feel like I'm master of something. You know how I feel, David.
DAVID: (*soberly*) Yes, I know.
LISA: (*coming out at left*) Why, David, I didn't know you were here. (*To* JULIA.) Bert told me, Julia. Don't take it so hard. He may never have to go to war at all.
JULIA: (*dully*) I never asked for much.
BERT: I'm not gone yet, Mom. You're spoiling everything. You ought

to be glad. They don't take everybody. I'll be all right, honest
I will.

JULIA: No, they don't take everybody. They just take the best, like they
took my brother and Lisa's father. They don't take everybody.

BERT: I wouldn't have told you if I'd known you'd take it this way. I'd
have gone off in the night feeling just awful. Come on and get me
something to eat, Mom. I didn't eat much supper. I don't feel like
arguing. Come on, Mother.

LISA: Go with him, Julia. (JULIA *gets up and allows* BERT *to pull her
out. Looking after them,* LISA *says thoughtfully.*) Nothing would
have stopped him, David. He thinks he'll be free in the air—free
to put his little mark on the world. Maybe he will be.

DAVID: It's hard on Julia.
      (*There is a pause.*)

LISA: David, the prints for the play-rooms came tonight. I'm so happy
about them. They're going to be just like we imagined them.

DAVID: That's fine, Lisa.
      (*He turns away.*)

LISA: Don't you want to see them? I was hoping you'd come by—you
haven't been out for days.

DAVID: I've been busy.

LISA: You look almost as tired as Gerth.

DAVID: He looks bad. I saw him in town last week.

LISA: He stays out in the fields irrigating all night. After the men get
through, he goes out and walks from one corner of the place to
another. I can't get him to rest.

CHARLIE: (*awkwardly*) He's worried, Mrs. Hansen. I guess—I guess
I'm not the only one that's noticed. And it ain't the crop. It's
been the best year he's had.

DAVID: I wanted to see him. Where is he, Charlie?

CHARLIE: He's up checking the loads, Doctor.

DAVID: I'll go up.
      (DAVID *starts to go.*)

CHARLIE: (*getting up*) I've got to take these sacks up there anyway. I'll
tell him you're here.

DAVID: (*starting out*) No, I could just as well—(*He changes his mind.*)
All right, if you don't mind.

CHARLIE: They're sure getting your hospital up fast, Doctor. It makes
these granaries look like match boxes.
      (*He goes out right.*)

LISA: (*quietly*) What's the matter, David?

DAVID: A lot of things, Lisa. I've stayed away.

LISA: I know.

DAVID: Lisa, I can't go through with this up here. It will have to be
somebody else. I should never have let Gerth give up his land.
But I thought then I could stay—that we could go on as we
were—that it would be enough to work with you, and forget the

things I said that night. But it's no use. If I stay here, Gerth must know how I feel about you. Maybe he knows now. I've tried to stay clear of you both, but it's no use.

LISA: Your work's here, David. It's your job. You can't leave it.

DAVID: I'm going.

LISA: You can forget about me. You've got to! You've planned for this hospital; it's the biggest thing in your life. I—I don't have to help, David. I'd stay out of the way. It wouldn't matter to me if I didn't work up there. (*There are tears in her eyes.*) I was thinking about going away for the winter anyway. Gerth needs a change. You wouldn't need to see me even. But you've got to stay. It's where you belong. It's yours.

DAVID: I can tell myself that too. But what if I know it's an excuse to be where you are? What if I can look back and know that's why I came back here in the first place? When I thought you weren't happy with Gerth, I was glad—glad, I tell you! And I've taken from him. I've let him help me.

LISA: Oh, David, if you'll stay, I'll keep out of the way. I'll do anything.

DAVID: If I stay, I'll have to tell Gerth I love you. It's for you to say.

LISA: No, you can't do that, David. You're right. Beside Gerth, we're little people. We don't count. If only I could have loved him like he asked me to, instead of going through all the years needing you.

DAVID: Lisa!

(*He goes to her.*)

LISA: When you love somebody, it's an ache inside you, isn't it? I found the only peace I ever had with you. The work we planned—it was like a door opening into a new world.

DAVID: You'll still have that.

LISA: You mean the work—it's outside us.

DAVID: It's bigger than we are. You know that.

LISA: Yes.

DAVID: Don't cry. Please, Lisa, don't cry.

LISA: (*with a little shake of her head*) I won't cry. (*After a moment.*) David, have I given you anything?

DAVID: You made me believe in myself, Lisa. You made me able to fight for the things I believe in. You gave me that to keep.

LISA: We can go on without each other then.

(GERTH *comes in from the right. he glances at them and then speaks impatiently as he starts tying up the sacks of wheat.*)

GERTH: Charlie said you wanted to see me.

DAVID: Yes. I brought the note you signed for me. I paid it off today.

(*He takes it out of the wallet and gives it to* GERTH.)

GERTH: (*glancing at it briefly and putting it in his pocket*) Well, do you want another signed?

DAVID: No, that's all. I'm selling the practice Gerth.

GERTH: You don't think you can keep it up and run the hospital?

DAVID: I'm not running the hospital. I'm getting out.

GERTH: (*his attention on the sacks*) You're not taking this on up here?

DAVID: No, I don't want it after all. I don't want to settle down in one place I guess. You were right. Working for the Government is no good for me.

GERTH: I see. (*As he whips the twine around the sack.*) What's your real reason?

DAVID: A lot of things have come up. It wasn't what I expected. And I'm not one to be tied down.

GERTH: (*to* LISA) How do you feel about this sudden change of heart?

LISA: David knows what's best for him, Gerth.

GERTH: When are you going?

DAVID: Next week.

GERTH: That doesn't leave much time.

DAVID: It's all I need.

GERTH: What about Lisa? Does that mean she's through too?

DAVID: They'll still want her.

GERTH: (*harshly*) Six weeks ago you wanted that hospital more than anything. You've helped draw up the plans. You don't change about the thing you want the most, you know. And when you've lost that, you've nothing left to keep you going. You'd better go up and look at it.

LISA: Gerth, don't make this harder.

GERTH: (*there is a bite to his words*) It's a fine building, David. One wing of it is bigger than those granaries of wheat. It's worth more, isn't it?

DAVID: (*angrily*) Listen, Gerth, I didn't come here to quarrel with you. I came to give you that note and tell you I'm going.

GERTH: Are you afraid of the job?

DAVID: Call it that if you like.

GERTH: If you've got any guts you'll stay here and do your job.

LISA: Gerth, you're saying things you've got no business saying.

GERTH: (*his voice rising*) I've got a right to know why David's giving this up. I split my farm in half to hand over that land.

DAVID: You didn't have to give it away. They offered you a good price for it.

GERTH: They couldn't have paid me enough for that land. Even I don't count everything in money.

DAVID: Maybe you don't. It's a fine time to say that now after you've given it away. Well, I'm counting the money now. I got a better offer than this one here. I'm taking it. Now are you satisfied?

GERTH: (*His voice drops. He turns back to his work and speaks quietly, searching for words.*) I see. It's funny. I'd begun to see that building through your eyes. You called it the country's security for the future. If it's that, it's the most important thing in the world.

DAVID: (*curtly, baffled by* GERTH's *change*) It could be that.

GERTH: I've watched them while they've been building it up there. In a way I got sort of proud of it. Anybody can raise wheat—anybody —that's not hard. But to keep people from suffering—that's different, isn't it? It's harder trying to save your own kind, making them happier. Seems like that's harder all right. I thought I'd done more than you, but when I'm gone the land will go back to dust—things will die. It isn't that way with what you're doing, is it? You and Lisa here—you planned to make those kids strong so they'd go on—finding out things, finding out how things grow, what makes the weather change. Maybe they'd find out why things have to die—you know that's always been one of the hardest things for me. Like that dog of Bert's scared up a rabbit today—for a minute or two the rabbit ran ahead like it could beat the wind—then it got caught. The dog wasn't hungry even. If you could teach those kids to accept that—understand it, you'd be doing something big, wouldn't you? You might bring up a crop of youngsters that weren't afraid. (*He turns to* LISA.) That's something bigger than growing wheat for yourself—isn't it, Lisa? (*His whole hope hangs on the question, but* LISA *is caught up in the dream he has given back to them.*)

LISA: (*her eyes shining*) Yes, that's it, David. That's the way we used to talk about it. It's bigger than any of us. That's what we could do up there.

GERTH: (*after a long look at* LISA, *he turns back to the sacks of wheat*) You can see a long way from that hill. You'd better go up and look at it again. Maybe up there you'll know whether to go or stay.

DAVID: (*going slowly up the hill*) It's a good plan. I know how every room will look when it's finished, and I won't see it. I'll go up, Gerth. (*He hardly realizes that he speaks to* LISA.) Are you coming?

LISA: (*following him, but as they are almost out of sight, she turns.* DAVID *goes on*) What about you, Gerth? Would you come?

GERTH: (*without looking at her*) I've got to tie these sacks. Go on if you want to.

LISA: (*turning to go*) I didn't know you cared anything about the hospital, Gerth. Why, you feel almost the same as we do. I thought —I thought you hated it.

GERTH: There's no hate left in me. I'm finished—hating. (*His hand grips the sack of wheat a little tighter.* LISA *is unaware of the defeat in his voice. She goes out up the hill. After she has gone,* GERTH *turns and walks slowly up the rise. He watches them for a moment. He comes back down, going blindly over to the sacks of wheat, the grain trickles idly through his fingers.* CHARLIE *comes in at right, carrying a pair of rubber boots.*)

CHARLIE: (*throwing the boots down by the sacks*) You left your irrigating boots up by the ditch, Gerth. (*Trying to get* GERTH's *interest.*)

Morrow got his gasoline up there at last. He's hanging around trying to get a ride back to town with one of the haulers. From where I was, I thought he was going to knock either the granary or the hospital down, trying to get in. He's pretty drunk.

(GERTH *does not answer. After a pause* CHARLIE *speaks uncomfortably.*)

CHARLIE: That's good wheat, Gerth. No wonder it won a prize for you.

GERTH: Yes, it's good wheat. I had a dream once, Charlie—a dream of a great wheat field, yellow in the sun. It grew tall and filled out early. I could see it going out in box cars across the ocean to places in Spain and England, some of it ending up in China even. And I grew it. It was mine—mine! Gerth Hansen furnishing bread for the world, in spite of drought or grasshoppers, in spite of God! And Lisa was in my dream, standing there, her eyes as blue as flax in the morning, and the wheat around her. But a hail storm came up. I saw it smashing the wheat back into the earth, breaking it off at the roots, leaving it only fit to feed the birds. And I ran to where she was, because I didn't want the hail to hurt her. I wanted to keep it away from her, but when I got there, she wasn't there any more. She'd gone.

CHARLIE: What's the matter with you, Gerth? Don't look like that.

GERTH: I stood there and there was nothing left but the ground stretching out as far as I could see. And it didn't matter to the ground whether I raised a crop or not. It would go on waiting for the next year and the next. And it didn't matter to the sky either. And I stood there between the ground and the sky and I cursed them both, but that didn't matter.

CHARLIE: Gerth, you talk like that dream had really happened. Sitting here in your own field with the biggest crop you ever raised, you talk like that hail storm had really happened.

GERTH: Things can happen in a man's life, Charlie—a kind of storm— something outside he can't control, can't get his hands on. And it takes what he's wanted most. And then he's useless. He's like that straw there waving in the wind. Finished.

CHARLIE: Things can't stay the same, Gerth. They can't stay the same.

GERTH: And God's down in the earth there making things die. Blindly, just to show a man how small he is.

CHARLIE: (*confused*) It ain't like that, Gerth. I know it ain't.

GERTH: Well, if he isn't blind, if he's got to do it, got to take one thing away so there'll be room for something bigger, that means he's been behind me all the time. When I thought I was holding him back, beating him out of something, I wasn't doing it by myself at all. (*There is anguish in his tone.*) I can't do anything alone! I'm not anybody.

CHARLIE: You can't farm by yourself, Gerth. Nobody can. You got to have horses and rain and seed to put in. You don't farm alone. Why, I—I've helped you for fifteen years, Gerth.

GERTH: Yes. Fifteen years. And I didn't want anything to hurt you, but I couldn't help it when you got your hand hurt. Maybe he doesn't want things to die. Maybe it's like you say, one thing's got to go so there'll be room for something better.

CHARLIE: You talk funny, Gerth. I don't understand.

GERTH: It's all right, Charlie. Next year this straw will be at the root of something else, one of those apple trees—you can't tell. That's what it's for now. When you're finished, you step aside. That up there—it's just beginning, isn't it? Just beginning.

(*His eyes look up the hill to where the hospital stands.* BERT *runs in from the hospital. He is breathless and agitated.*)

BERT: Gerth, that truck of Morrow's. It's on fire! I think he set it on purpose. He's not there.

(*In an instant* GERTH *is beside him.*)

CHARLIE: If it explodes that gas, it'll take the wheat, Gerth.

GERTH: (*taking hold of* BERT) Where's Lisa?

BERT: She's on her way down here. She was coming for the plans. When I saw it, I started running and passed her.

(GERTH *starts to run out when* LISA *comes in.*)

LISA: Gerth, David's in there. He'll come out that door and he can't see it, if it explodes—(*She turns calling*) David! David!

GERTH: (*pulling her back*) Shut up. Charlie don't let her go. You hear me. (*As he leaves,* BERT *follows.* GERTH *hurls him back down the hill.*) Get back there.

(GERTH *runs out.* JULIA *comes out from the left.*)

JULIA: What's the matter? What's happened?

BERT: Morrow's truck's on fire up there. It may explode that gas.

LISA: What's Gerth going to do?

CHARLIE: I don't know.

LISA: Let me go, Charlie—please. David!

(CHARLIE *covers her mouth.*)

CHARLIE: Don't call him out, Mrs. Hansen. That's the worst thing you could do. Maybe he'll see it from inside.

LISA: No, you can't see out. It's just a hall. Where's Gerth?

BERT: I'm going up there. Maybe I can help.

(*He starts out.*)

LISA: Don't go, Bert. Gerth told you not to go. Please, Charlie.

(*She tries to free herself from* CHARLIE.)

CHARLIE: He left you with me, Mrs. Hansen. I told him I'd keep you here.

JULIA: Morrow did that. He wanted to get Gerth's wheat.

BERT: There's Gerth. He's up there.

CHARLIE: He's going to try driving it out.

BERT: It won't start. It's all in flames, Charlie.

(MORROW *runs down the hill.* BERT *stops him.*)

BERT: Wait a minute here. You're not going any further.

111

MORROW: Let me go. Where's Gerth? I didn't know what I was doing. I was crazy. Tell him I didn't know what I was doing. I went kind of crazy when I saw that wheat of his up there on what used to be my place. I wouldn't have done it if I'd been in my right mind. Don't let him send me to jail, Mrs. Hansen.

BERT: Shut up.

CHARLIE: He's got it started! He's got it started towards the river. (*There is a faint roar of the motor.*)

MORROW: Don't let him send me to jail, Mrs Hansen. I don't know what came over me. I went crazy when I saw that wheat.

BERT: He's got it clear—he's rolling to the river bank.

CHARLIE: He's all right now. He can jump.

LISA: Let me go, Charlie.
(*She frees herself from* CHARLIE *and runs out.*)

JULIA: (*running after* LISA, *calling*) Lisa, stay back.

MORROW: (*pushing* BERT *out of his way*) I won't go to jail. I won't go.
(*He runs down the hill and out to the road.*)

CHARLIE: Gerth, for God's sake, jump. He's going over the bank! Jump, you fool. (CHARLIE *is sobbing and shouting at the same time.*) Gerth!
(*There is a muffled explosion off stage.* CHARLIE *listens in stunned silence.*)

BERT: He got out, didn't he? He got out? (*He shakes Charlie*). Charlie, answer me.
(*He looks at Charlie's face and then sinks on the ground crying.*)

CHARLIE: (*coming slowly down, seeing nothing*). He could have jumped. He had time. He could have jumped, I tell you.

BERT: He must have got excited. I should have gone—He must have got excited.

CHARLIE: (*shaking his head*). No—I don't know—He had something in his mind about—about God. He was the only man worth dying for I ever knew—and I was too old.
(*The long golden straw stirs faintly in the wind. Unconsciously* CHARLIE's *hand goes to it as the curtain falls.*)

The End

Red Flag at Evening
A Sketch

Characters

MRS. ANDREW MILLINGTON (SUSAN)
MISS BESSIE HARRISON
ELMER ENGELTREE

SCENE: *Miss Bessie's tiny living room in a small-town cottage.*
TIME: *The present: 5 o'clock on a May evening. (The action may be set in the 19th century if costumes can be found.)*

The curtain rises on a charming little room. Down right is a door leading outside. In the right corner a small, graceful table. About centre in the brick wall is a large window; in front of it an old-fashioned settee. In the left wall is a fireplace with a comfortable arm-chair left. Another chair may be placed at right if needed. In the centre of the room is a low footstool.

MISS BESSIE has just finished fitting a skirt for SUSAN. She is kneeling on a small cushion, taking out pins from the hem of the skirt, while SUSAN stands militantly on the footstool, looking down at her.

BESSIE: I think that's a nice length, Cousin Susan. Dignified without being dowdy.
SUSAN: You're sure it's even, Bessie? I can't bear an uneven hem-line.
BESSIE: (*Soothingly*) It's straight as that row of tulips out there, Susan.
SUSAN: (*Turning on foot-stool*) What's that green thing on the settee, Bessie?
BESSIE: The fancy bed-spread I'm working. It's taken me nearly two years but I'm almost finished. You can step down now.
SUSAN: (*Stepping down from the footstool and going over to look at the*

113

Gwen Pharis Ringwood

spread) You ought to have about everything you need in that hope chest of yours, Bessie.

BESSIE: (*Shyly and embarrassed, as she moves the footstool back to the fireplace*) Oh, I do have most everything. That's why I started the spread, I wanted something that would take a long time to finish.

SUSAN: (*Folding the spread*) You're thirty-five, aren't you, Bessie? It seems to me you ought to be using some of these things. Not making more.

BESSIE: (*As she replaces the cushion in the chair*) Thirty-five isn't exactly old, Cousin Susan.

SUSAN: (*Sitting on the settee*) No, but it's getting on. I said to Andrew yesterday: "I can't understand why Bessie and Elmer Engletree don't get married. He's been calling regularly for nigh on thirteen years."

BESSIE: (*As she replaces her things in the sewing basket*) It's only been in the last seven years that he's been coming *regularly*, Cousin Susan.

SUSAN: (*Taking up her fancy work*) Well, it's high time you made up your minds. Andrew thinks so too. Why, Andrew and I had only known each other five years when we were engaged.

BESSIE: But you know Andrew's different from Elmer, Cousin Susan. He's of a more impetuous nature. (*Innocently*) Andrew would jump in where angels fear to tread, as the saying is.

SUSAN: (*Complacently*) Yes, he swept me off my feet. Once he asked me, it didn't take me five minutes to decide. Why, I was even ready to give up my employment in the Dry Goods, but Andrew wouldn't hear of that.

BESSIE: (*With never a thought of malice*) It's fortunate you stayed on, Cousin Susan (*She places the basket on the table at right*) since Andrew hasn't had any luck with his automatic shoe polisher.

SUSAN: I've done my best for you, Bessie. I made a special point this afternoon of showing Elmer the new cook stoves we got in the store.

BESSIE: (*Turning*) Was he. . . interested, Susan?
(*Her voice is very tiny.*)

SUSAN: I don't know that I'd call him exactly interested. (*Grimly*) But he looked at them.

BESSIE: What did he say, Susan? (*Apologizing for her boldness*) I don't think that's prying, since we do have an. . . an understanding.

SUSAN: He said "I reckon they're all right for anyone that's needing a stove, if he wants to pay that much."

BESSIE: (*Anxiously*) Well, that's not exactly disinterested, would you say, Susan?

SUSAN: It's not wild enthusiasm either. This is Elmer's night to come to supper, isn't it, Bessie?

114

BESSIE: Yes, he'll be along any time now.
        (*She crosses to the window in front of* SUSAN *and looks out.*)
SUSAN: (*As she sweeps majestically to the table for the scissors.*) Bessie
        Harrison, it's time somebody took a hand in your affairs. You'd
        let that selfish fussbudget eat you out of house and home before
        you'd say a word. Tonight when Elmer comes you're going to ask
        him point-blank about his intentions.
BESSIE: (*Very distressed.*) Why, Susan, the idea! How can you think of
        such a thing.
        (*She turns away, her cheeks burning.*)
SUSAN: Haven't you and Elmer an understanding, as you call it? You
        said you had.
BESSIE: (*Too shy to face* SUSAN, *she turns toward the fire-place.*) Well,
        of course, Elmer never really asked me to be his wife—not in
        those words—but he's been coming to supper three times a
        week and for special dinner on Sundays and holidays,. . . for
        seven years that is. Before that he just came twice a week.
SUSAN: (*Eloquently*) Hmmm!
BESSIE: (*Sitting down. Pride gives her more firmness.*) And he brought
        me a beautiful begonia plant the time I hurt my ankle shoveling
        snow off the walk. I think he's just been kind of shy about asking
        me.
SUSAN: Time he got over it, or you gave him up. Your aunt Lillian
        told me in Red Deer on Saturday that Mr. Hagedorn asks about
        you very kindly every time she sees him. She said he paid you a
        lot of attention when you were visiting up there four years ago.
BESSIE: (*Shyly*) He was very kind, Cousin Susan. Such a nice, joking
        sort of man. He brought me a pair of gloves and a cameo pin
        once, Susan, but of course I couldn't accept them because of
        Elmer and I having an understanding. It wouldn't be fair.
SUSAN: (*Getting up and preparing to leave. She puts her work in her bag
        and gets her hat from the table.*) Bessie, if you don't promise me to
        bring matters to a crisis this very evening, I'll speak to Elmer
        myself. I'll stay right here and speak to him.
BESSIE: (*On her feet. In terror at the idea.*) Oh, no, Susan. You mustn't.
        Promise me you won't.
SUSAN: Will you ask him to name the day?
BESSIE: Oh, Susan, I couldn't. I'd be a. . . a huzzy.
SUSAN: Then I'll ask him!
        (*She sits on the settee.*)
BESSIE: Oh, no! I couldn't bear that. Oh, there he comes up Main
        Street now.
        (*She sees him through the window.*)
SUSAN: Bessie, Andrew's going to Red Deer tomorrow to a sale. I've
        decided that unless you and Elmer get something settled tonight,
        you're going on a visit to your Aunt Lillian.
BESSIE: (*In a flutter*) But I'd see Mr. Hagedorn there. That wouldn't
        be fair to Elmer after thirteen years, would it, Susan?

SUSAN: Mr. Hagedorn sounds a lot more suitable to you than Elmer Engletree but I suppose you've got used to Elmer.

BESSIE: I just wouldn't want to hurt his feelings.

SUSAN: Bessie, you see this red flag you hang out the door when you want me to save milk for you.

(She takes up a red flag from the table.)

BESSIE: Of course I see it, Susan. How could I help it? Oh, dear, I must get this spread away before Elmer comes. I wouldn't want to embarrass him.

(She puts it under the cushion of the chair.)

SUSAN: Hmm! It would do him good. Now, Bessie, if you and Elmer get things settled, I won't be interfering. But if you don't decide tonight, I want you to have this red flag out the back door as a sign that Andrew's to come for you in the morning. You can surprise your Aunt Lillian. . .

BESSIE: But it's brazen, Susan. It's downright brazen.

SUSAN: Then I'll stay and have a talk with Elmer.

BESSIE: No! *(There is a pause. Finally her eyes drop before the determination in Susan's.)* I'll ask him, Cousin Susan. I'd die if you did.

SUSAN: Now you're talking like your father's daughter.

(There is a knock at the door. BESSIE hurriedly tidies her hair. SUSAN draws the settee before the fire. As BESSIE goes to the door, SUSAN gets a picture of a wedding party from the table and puts it in a conspicuous place on the mantle.)

SUSAN: *(At the door)* Come in, Elmer. *(Flustered.)* We were—I was—I was expecting you.

(ELMER ENGLETREE is a fussy, hard-bitten little man of over forty. He takes off his scarf, his overcoat and his mittens and gives them to BESSIE, then removes his rubbers.)

ELMER: Can't say I'm surprised at that, Bessie. It's Wednesday night, isn't it? Hello, Susan.

BESSIE: Yes, but it's sort of a. . . a special Wednesday night, isn't it?

ELMER: Can't say I'd noticed anything special about the night. Except shoe sales fall off on Wednesday.

SUSAN: *(Meaningfully)* Bessie and I were just saying that you ought to do pretty well in the shoe-store, Elmer.

ELMER: Not bad, Susan, not bad. I don't spare the shoe leather.

SUSAN: Well, I'll run along, Bessie. You'll be wanting to talk to Elmer.

BESSIE: *(Dropping Elmer's things on the chair at right)* Oh, no, I don't! *(Flustered)* I mean, don't hurry away, Susan. Oh please sit down Elmer. I hadn't noticed. . .

SUSAN: Well, if you'd rather, I'll sit down and have a chat with Elmer.

BESSIE: No!

ELMER: Don't worry about me. I don't aim to talk much.

(He sits on the settee.)

SUSAN: I aimed to do the talking, Elmer.

BESSIE: You'd better go—right away—Susan. Andrew will be worrying. (*She edges* SUSAN *toward the door.*) Well, goodbye,— so glad you came—I know your dress will be all right—Say "hello" to Andrew for me. . .

SUSAN: (*Not to be hurried*) Good-bye, Elmer. (*At the door.*) Remember, Bessie—the red flag means Aunt Lillian! I'll watch for an hour and if it isn't out, I'll come back.

(SUSAN *goes.*)

ELMER: (*crossly.*) What's she got in her bonnet? Red flag? You haven't gone Communist have you?

BESSIE: Oh, it's just a signal, Elmer—about saving the milk—Susan runs on so, doesn't she?

ELMER: Stubbornest woman in the province. What have you got a fire in May for?

BESSIE: (*Coming towards him.*) Well, it's. . . it's what I told you. . . about it being a special kind of Wednesday today. . . I mean the trees are getting green next month and already there's a. . . a sort of a. . . a hum in the air. . .

ELMER: (*Sharply*) What's that? Hum? If you mean mosquitoes are out, Bessie, why don't you say so?

BESSIE: (*Hurt. She sits down left of fireplace primly.*) Things can hum without being mosquitoes, Mr. Engeltree.

ELMER: (*Ignores this entirely. He sneezes and shows much concern. Shaking his head.*) This is bad weather for colds. I'd not be surprised if I hadn't got a chill just walking from the boarding house up here.

BESSIE: Sit nearer the fire, Elmer, and get good and warm.

ELMER: Evening paper here yet?

BESSIE: I'll get it. But there's no news in it, hardly.

(BESSIE *gets the paper from the table.*)

ELMER: (*Adjusting his reading glasses.*) Sitting in this kind of light is mighty hard on a man's eyes.

BESSIE: (*Giving him the paper and returning to her chair.*) Oh, but the firelight's so cosy and. . . homelike, isn't it, Elmer?

ELMER: (*Looking at the paper*) Can't see a blame thing.

BESSIE: The only news is that Matilda Brown and Jimmy Dawson where married yesterday. A very pretty ceremony—double ring.

ELMER: Yeah, I sold Jimmy his shoes. Had to order a special size for him.

BESSIE: (*Struggling to get his attention from the paper*) How is the shoe business, Elmer?

ELMER: Same as it ever was. (*Perusing paper*) A man makes a living in a shoe store even if he doesn't get a new car every spring.

BESSIE: (*Taking the cushion over to put behind* ELMER.) The idea of a small family needing a car is just useless extravagance. Don't you think so, Elmer?

ELMER: Lots of things I want before I buy me a car.

BESSIE: (*Tenderly*) What. . . sort of things, Elmer? (*Over the settee*)
ELMER: (*Oblivious of her tenderness*) I figure on getting me a new radio, with ear phones.
BESSIE: I see. (*A pause*) Elmer, I never mentioned it before in all these years but. . . (*He looks inquiringly at her over his glasses. She can't go on.*) Elmer. . . (*She sees the bedspread in all its pinkness on the chair from which she took the cushion. She edges over to it and conceals it behind her back.*) Elmer, if you want to smoke a pipe in this room, I'd be quite agreeable.
ELMER: (*Outraged.*) A pipe! With my weak chest. Bessie, what on earth has come over you? I never smoked tobacco in any form and I hope I never start.
BESSIE: (*Sitting down on the settee and stuffing the bedspread down under the end.*) Of course not, Elmer. I think you're wise. Mr. Hagedorn smokes a pipe. . . I guess I just forgot. . .
ELMER: Well, whoever Mr. Hagedorn is, he can have his pipe, if he wants to ruin his constitution. (*Looks at her closely.*) Say, Bessie, you're looking a bit feverish. You better light the lamp and get supper on. I wouldn't be surprised but you're getting anaemic from hugging the fire too much.
BESSIE: (*Her spirit roused. She gets up.*) Why, Elmer Engeltree, I'm as hard working a woman as you'll find in this town.
ELMER: Still, with only yourself to do for. . .
BESSIE: (*Prompting him. Gently.*) Yes, Elmer?
ELMER: Well, the busy woman's the happy woman. That's what I always say. You better get the table set before it's too dark.
BESSIE: (*Going to the table and pulling it into the middle of the room.*) Yes, I was just going to put the cloth on. (*She stops, her hands on the table.*) Elmer. . .
ELMER: (*Back to his paper*) Shoes are going up. I told the manager they would. Told him two weeks ago.
BESSIE: (*At last she knows she's got to face it. She stands very straight, a brave little figure.*) Elmer, you've been calling on me for nearly thirteen years.
ELMER: Fourteen, Bessie. Started the last year I was riding my bicycle. We're not so young as we once were. I used to be able to ride a bicycle straight up Main Street Hill.
BESSIE: But you're not old, Elmer. Forty-three. Why, you're just seven years older than I am. . .
ELMER: I figure on selling shoes a long time yet. I don't ruin my constitution with tobacco and strong coffee like most men.
BESSIE: Elmer, we've reached an age where I think we should be able to talk frankly with one another, don't you?
ELMER: I always speak my mind. Mother used to say "You can always depend on Elmer to speak his mind". And she was right.
BESSIE: Elmer, I'm going to speak my mind too. I know you'll respect me for it. Elmer, you've been coming to see me four evenings a week for thirteen years. . .

ELMER: (*Annoyed at her inaccuracy*) Fourteen, Bessie. I remember the date perfectly. First time I ate your mince pie.

BESSIE: (*Approaching him shyly*) Elmer, don't you think it's about time we thought of getting married?

ELMER: (*Looking at her over his paper*) You're right, Bessie, you're right. There's only one trouble about that. We're getting on, you know. (*He turns back to his paper.*) Who is there in town would have us now?

BESSIE: (*Staring at him in astonishment. She whispers as if she couldn't believe her ears.*) "Who is there would have us?" Why, Elmer Engeltree. . .

(*He is oblivious of her astonishment which suddenly changes into anger. She goes over and opens the door wide and stands beside it.*)

BESSIE: I'm a patient woman, Elmer Engeltree. . .

ELMER: (*Without hearing or seeing her.*) Shut the door, Bessie. . . I have to be mighty careful about drafts.

BESSIE: (*Without realizing what she has in her hand, she takes up the red flag and advances on him menacingly.*) Elmer Engeltree you take your bad temper and your bad health and your weak chest right out of my house. Susan was right. You're a selfish fussbudget and I've taken a long time to find it out. Who is there would have us? Mr. Hagedorn courted me at Aunt Lillians and I was distant to him because I didn't want to be unfair to you. You go right home and get your radio with ear phones and sit there and listen by yourself. And don't you come back here. . . You're right. . . nobody would have you. . . nobody but me would have been so blind.

ELMER: Why Bessie! I told you I thought you were feverish. What if you've got something catching? I better get out of here all right. I'm very susceptible to things. . .

(*He gathers up his coat and his mittens and his scarf and his rubbers.*)

BESSIE: You'd better get out all right, Elmer. I believe I've got something awful. . . I believe I've got hydrophobia and I'm feeling awfully like biting something. . .

ELMER: Goodbye, Bessie. I'll send the doctor right up. . . Watch out . . . don't hit me with that red flag. . .

(*He makes a humiliating retreat.* BESSIE *watches him for a moment. Then her eyes fall on the red flag she is holding in her hand. She doesn't recognize its significance for a moment. Then slowly in a kind of dazed astonishment, she waves it out the back door, as a signal to* SUSAN. *She is still waving it as the curtain falls.*)

The End

119

The Days May Be Long

Characters

JEAN MORRISON
MRS. MORRISON, *her mother*
SUE WALTERS, *her friend*
KENNETH MORRISON, *her brother*

SCENE: *The comfortable living room of* MRS. MORRISON'*s home in a Western city.*
TIME: *Late afternoon in September.*

The curtain rises on a comfortable and rather charming living room in which warm brown and rust shades predominate. A fire is glowing in the fireplace in the left wall. Down stage from the fireplace is a door leading outside. There is a large window in the rear wall. In front of it is a divan and an end table. Up stage in the right wall is a door leading to the kitchen. A handsome arm chair is placed down stage right. A long low bench stands in front of the fireplace. Pictures and rugs and the bookshelves on either side of the fireplace give an impression of conventional middle class comfort.

MRS. MORRISON, *a handsome woman in her early fifties is discovered sitting before the fire, contentedly knitting. Her white hair is beautifully waved and her dark silk dress is extremely becoming. Her face is serene. It is only occasionally that one glimpses the strong stubbornness of purpose which lies behind her gentle manner. A clock on the mantel chimes the half hour.* MRS. MORRISON *glances at it and resumes her knitting. At a step in the hall outside she calls cheerfully.*

MRS. MORRISON: Is that you, Jean?

Gwen Pharis Ringwood

JEAN: (*From the hall*) Yes, Mother, dear.
> (JEAN MORRISON *enters. She is slender, not very tall and would be rather lovely, if it were not for a certain nervous intensity in her voice and movement. Her dark suit and white blouse are immaculate. She takes off her hat and gloves as she comes in and drops them a little wearily on the divan, then crosses to her mother's chair and kisses her on the forehead.*)
How's your headache?

MRS. MORRISON: (*Smiling*) Better, thank you, darling. It was just Mrs. Saunders' talk of your brother being engaged to that girl that upset me.

JEAN: (*Turning to the divan*) She's a cat. As if Ken wouldn't tell us.

MRS. MORRISON: He might not, Jean. Ken hasn't been the same since. . . (*Breaking off*) But don't let's talk about it or I'll be ill again. (*Brightly*) Anyway it's my little girl's birthday.

JEAN: Yes, and it's been a terrible day. You'd think those girls in the office would realize that when Mr. Lord's away, I'm supposed to be in charge. After all I've been there longest.

MRS. MORRISON: It seems like yesterday when you started off to your first job. That was a big day for me too.

JEAN: Well, it wasn't yesterday, Mother. It was ten years ago.

MRS. MORRISON: I know it was, Darling. You needn't be so sharp about it.

JEAN: (*Getting up and moving restlessly to the fireplace*) I'm sorry. But I hate today. I hate being twenty-nine years old with nothing to look back on but carbon copies of the letters I've written.

MRS. MORRISON: Jean, you've done so well! You have the most responsible position in the office. You're just tired.

JEAN: Sue didn't 'phone?

MRS. MORRISON: (*Vaguely*) Sue?

JEAN: (*Impatiently*) Sue Walters.

MRS. MORRISON: Why, no. I was thinking today that Sue doesn't drop in as often lately.

JEAN: She's been busy. But she said she'd come today. We've got some plans to talk over.

MRS. MORRISON: (*A little hurt, but smiling bravely*) You're very mysterious, darling. Of course if it's something I shouldn't know. . . .

JEAN: Don't be silly, Mother dear. Of course you're to know. I'm not in the habit of keeping secrets from you.

MRS. MORRISON: No. I always feel we have such a complete understanding. (*Wistfully*) Kenneth used to tell me everything too.

JEAN: He'll get over this nonsense.

MRS. MORRISON: If he'd only confide in me.

JEAN: (*Facing her mother. She is a little on the defensive*) Mother, I did something today without consulting you. I felt it was a matter I must decide for myself.

MRS. MORRISON: Why, child, I hope I'm not the kind of mother that expects her children to run to her with every little decision.

122

JEAN: This isn't a little decision. I asked Mr. Taylor to give me a year's leave of absence from the office today.

MRS. MORRISON: Leave of absence? Why, Jean, whatever for. . . .

JEAN: It wasn't just a silly impulse, Mother. I've been thinking about it for several weeks. Sue and I. . . .

(*A gay voice from the hall*)

SUE: What's this about Sue? Speak of the devil. . . Here I am.

(*A laughing handsome girl of about twenty-five appears in the doorway. She is vital, completely without affectation, and attractive*)

Hello, Mrs. Morrison.

MRS. MORRISON: (*Getting up*) Come in, Sue. (*She kisses* SUE *lightly*) We were just saying that we'd missed you.

SUE: I've been so busy, Mrs. Morrison. (*Dropping a parcel in* JEAN'*s lap*) Happy birthday, Jean, darling. Brought you something.

JEAN: Thank you, Sue. You shouldn't have bothered.

SUE: It's to give you courage.

JEAN: I'm going to open it right now.

(*She opens it*)

SUE: I got myself one just like it.

JEAN: Why, Sue—a travelling kit. Oh, it's beautiful. Look, Mother.

MRS. MORRISON: Isn't it nice? Sue must think you're planning a trip, Jean.

SUE: Why, hasn't Jean told you, Mrs Morrison? Jean Morrison, you said you'd ask your boss this week.

JEAN: (*Embarrassed*) I haven't told Mother yet. I was just telling her when you came in.

SUE: But you did ask him?

JEAN: Yes, today.

SUE: What did he say?

JEAN: He said there was no reason why I couldn't go.

MRS. MORRISON: Why you couldn't go where, Jean? I'm afraid you're making me feel very left out.

JEAN: (*Very contrite*) Forgive me, Mother. The only reason I didn't tell you before was because I wasn't sure myself. You see, Sue is going down East to work on her Master's in Sociology. And she wants me. . . . that is, I thought I ought to. . . .

SUE: Jean's been wanting to get out of that stuffy office all year, Mrs. Morrison and I've persuaded her to come to Toronto with me. We're going to take an apartment and share expenses.

MRS. MORRISON: (*Shocked into dropping all dramatization of the situation for a moment*) But Jean! you wouldn't like that, would you? What about me? (*Recovering her poise*) You'd have no one to take care of you.

JEAN: Oh, Mother, it isn't that I'm not happy here. But I feel I need a change. I've got in such a rut lately. I never go anywhere except to the office, never see anybody but the other girls in the office. I want more out of life than that.

Gwen Pharis Ringwood

SUE: Our idea is to start over, Mrs. Morrison. Forget we're fast becoming spinsters and be very gay in a new setting.

MRS. MORRISON: I can understand your going, Sue. Your fiance is there, is he not?

SUE: That's what makes it nice. We'll have someone to show us around and I'll get Ronald back into my clutches. Honestly, Mrs. Morrison, I think Jean needs a change.

MRS. MORRISON: Were you planning to go to the University too, Jean?

JEAN: I thought I'd take special courses in French and Spanish, Mother. Then maybe I could get transferred to the foreign office of our company. My French is pretty good now.

SUE: And she can always come back at the end of the year if she wants to. Oh, everything is working out perfectly.

MRS. MORRISON: Well, it all sounds extremely interesting. I just wonder if. . . .

JEAN: It's a sort of an adventure, Mother. It's deciding not to let life run me but to go out and meet it. . . . Do you see?

MRS. MORRISON: Of course I do. . . . Only I'm afraid you'll get tired of meeting it in an apartment, darling. You know, Sue, Jean has never taken to housekeeping.

JEAN: You always have it all done, Mother dear. That's why.

MRS. MORRISON: Well, I haven't much reason for living except to make you comfortable, now that Kenneth is away. . . .

SUE: I didn't know Ken was away, Mrs. Morrison.

MRS. MORRISON: That's just my little way of speaking, Sue. He moved down town so that he could be nearer work. Of course we don't see so much of him now.

JEAN: I thought maybe you could get Mrs. Lawrence to come and live with you if I go, Mother. She's always wanted to.

MRS. MORRISON: I'd go mad with her around. She's one of those complaining women.

JEAN: You wouldn't need to see much of her, Mother. She works all day.

MRS. MORRISON: No, Jean. I'd be much better alone. Of course Kenneth probably wouldn't hear of it. But if he felt that way he'd come home and I'd be able to see that he was getting good meals instead of that terrible restaurant food.

JEAN: If only he would come home!

MRS. MORRISON: However if he and that girl are really planning to get married. . .

JEAN: Do you know Marian Parker, Sue?

SUE: Why, yes. Not very well, but I've met her at dances. She seems like a nice person.

MRS. MORRISON: (*Getting up and putting her knitting down on the mantel*) No doubt she is. But Kenneth brought her home for dinner a few times and Jean and I just didn't take to her very much.

SUE: I think she's rather reserved.

MRS. MORRISON: (*Turning and speaking with disarming frankness, even smiling at herself*) And I'm prejudiced of course. I'm afraid I'm one of these adoring mothers who think there aren't many girls good enough for her son. But I guess we mothers don't have much to say about our children's lives.

JEAN: Would you mind me going very much, Mother?

MRS. MORRISON: My dear, I didn't mean that. If it would make you happy, it would make me happy too.

JEAN: It's only for a year.

MRS. MORRISON: Of course it is. We'll have to talk it all over carefully. But I'm going to get tea now. Kenneth may come since it's your birthday.

SUE: Could I help you, Mrs. Morrison?

MRS. MORRISON: Not a bit. You girls have worked all day and I've done nothing but make some little cakes—the ones you like so much, Jean.

JEAN: That's grand, Mother.

MRS. MORRISON: (*As she goes into the kitchen*) I won't be long with tea, dear.

JEAN: I'm afraid Mother was awfully hurt that I didn't tell her before. But somehow I just couldn't, Sue. I thought I to decide this alone.

SUE: Don't you let her talk you out of going, Jean. Promise me.

JEAN: You heard her say yourself that she didn't mind.

SUE: (*Smiling as she lights a cigarette*) She may feel you wouldn't get enough to eat on our cooking. You know how mothers are.

JEAN: Well, you see, Sue I was never strong when I was in school, and Mother worries about me.

SUE: You're perfectly well, now, aren't you?

JEAN: Oh, yes, I think so. Though I get tired easily.

SUE: That's because you're low in your mind.

JEAN: It seems like I've not done anything but go to the office and come home and go to bed for years. It was different for a little while last winter while Ross was here.

SUE: He's a nice boy. I saw him just the other day.

JEAN: You saw Ross Hanson? But he's not in town.

SUE: He said he'd just got back.

JEAN: (*In a strained voice, trying hard to be casual*) Oh, I see. It's strange he didn't telephone or anything. You're sure you saw him?

SUE: (*Glancing at a magazine on the end table*) I ought to be. He bought me a soda.

(*She does not notice that* JEAN *is very quiet.*)

JEAN: (*Slowly*) I didn't think Ross would come to town without letting me know. I thought he'd at least let me know.

SUE: (*Startled as she realizes that* JEAN *is deeply hurt*) Why, Jean, I'm terribly sorry. I didn't know. . . . I shouldn't have told you

like that, but I didn't know you cared anything about him.
(*She goes over to the bench where* JEAN *is sitting and puts her arm around her*)

JEAN: (*Her tears break through*) I'm being awfully silly.

SUE: Honey, you mustn't feel like that. He's probably been busy getting settled.

JEAN: No. (*A pause*) When did you see him?

SUE: Monday.

JEAN: And this is Friday. Oh, I wish to God I could get out of this trap I'm in. I thought I wouldn't care if I never saw him again. I thought I'd quit feeling anything.

SUE: You're going to get away, Jean. It will be different when you get in new surroundings, meet new people. . .

JEAN: I don't know. I thought it was going to be different when Ross started coming to see me and taking me out sometimes. I had so much love to give, Sue. . . . I wanted someone to be tender to me and care what happened to me. . . . I wanted to pour out all my thoughts about everything—and Ross seemed to understand and like me. But after a while he stopped coming.

SUE: Maybe you were too frightened to let him know you liked him, Jean.

JEAN: Mother said I showed it too plainly.

SUE: Did your mother like him?

JEAN: No. That worried me too. Mother said she couldn't trust him. She thought he was very cold to her and that if he had cared anything about me, he would have been nicer to her.

SUE: But he's shy. Jean.

JEAN: I told Mother that. But there was something in what she said. Ross said several little things that made me feel he didn't like Mother very well. And he always seemed uncomfortable with her.

SUE: Maybe your mother made him feel unwelcome, Jean.

JEAN: Why Sue, you know Mother is always kind to my friends.

SUE: (*Rising and throwing her cigarette in the fire*) Jean, I've got something on my mind and I'm going to say it. Please don't hate me.

JEAN: I think I know what you're going to say.

SUE: One of the reasons I want you to go East with me, is because I think you'll never have a life of your own where your mother is. You've never been away from her. You've never been allowed to decide things for yourself. You're still playing at being a little girl and as long as you're home you'll keep on being one. Don't you feel you ought to be free?

JEAN: Yes. (*A pause*) But I don't think you should blame Mother, Sue. She'd do anything for us.

SUE: I know that.

JEAN: If Father had lived it would have been different.

SUE: Yes.

JEAN: But I do want to go—just for a little while. Sometimes at night I lie and think how it's going to be in all the years that are coming. . . . when I'm growing old and getting irritable and fussy. . . . and the same thing day after day—pretending that I'm satisfied with being a business girl. . . . they never get past the girl stage. . . . pretending that I'd rather be my own master. . . . and all the time wanting something else. And when I see it ahead like that, I think I'd rather die, Sue. But you can't blame Mother for that.

SUE: She chooses your friends, Jean. She influences you too much whether either of you know it or not.

JEAN: (*With some anger*) I had no idea you disliked my mother so much.

SUE: That's not fair—I don't dislike her. She is always charming to me.

JEAN: Mother would do anything for me. She's always said it would kill her to see me married to the wrong person—someone who wasn't kind to me.

SUE: Your mother doesn't like the thought of you being married at all. Or Kenneth.

JEAN: You're wrong there. I'll admit when I was in High School Mother used to tell me she hoped I wouldn't marry. But lately she's said she thought every girl should marry.

SUE: Well, you never will, if you don't make a break.

JEAN: I seem to have got smaller lately.

SUE: More afraid.

(*The kitchen door opens and* MRS. MORRISON *comes in with a tea wagon, attractively laid. There are some golden chrysanthemums in the centre.* SUE *starts to rise*)

MRS. MORRISON: Don't get up Sue. Everything's ready. (*As she sits down*) I always miss Kenneth at tea time. But things never stay the same, do they?

SUE: Think how awful it would be if they did!

MRS. MORRISON: Perhaps as we get older we get more suspicious of change. How do you like your tea, Sue?

SUE: Cream, please.

MRS. MORRISON: (*Pouring the tea*) I didn't make you a large birthday cake, Jean. You like the little ones so much better.

(*She hands the tea to* SUE)

JEAN: It would take a large one to hold the candles, Mother.

MRS. MORRISON: Does it seem possible that child is 29, Sue?

SUE: (*Smiling*) No. Except that I'm beginning to keep close track of my friends' ages, Mrs. Morrison. That's a bad sign.

MRS. MORRISON: Jean is much more immature than I was at her age. Why I had both my children when I was twenty-five.

JEAN: (*Laughing a little*) I don't think it's a question of immaturity, Mother.

MRS. MORRISON: Jean has bad luck with her young men, Sue. I tell her she's much too difficult to please. Do have a cake. Is your tea all right?

SUE: Just right, thank you. We'll have to learn to make these before September, Jean.

JEAN: Won't it be fun, Mother? We'll have people in to tea and. . . .

MRS. MORRISON: I've always wanted Jean to entertain more here, but she's never been interested. I'm surprised at this sudden enthusiasm.

KENNETH: (*Calling off-stage*) Hello, everybody. (KENNETH *comes into the room. He is a tall, good-humoured young man of thirty-one. Very boyish and at the moment quite excited.*) How are you, Sue? You look like a million.

SUE: You're looking very handsome yourself, Ken.

KENNETH: (*Kissing* MRS. MORRISON) How's my mother?

MRS. MORRISON: (*Very charming*) We were so afraid you wouldn't come, Kenneth. Here, let me look at you.

KENNETH: Get on with you. You'll be telling me I'm looking thin. Happy birthday, Jeannie, my girl. There's a pair of gloves for you.

JEAN: Oh, thank you, Ken.

KENNETH: I was going to get you something else but I thought I'd better stick to something where I was sure of the size.

JEAN: Aren't they nice, Sue? They just fit.

SUE: They're lovely.

MRS. MORRISON: Here's tea for you, Son. Do sit down now and don't walk about like a caged tiger.

KENNETH: I can't stay long.

MRS. MORRISON: Jean has news for you, Kenneth. She's threatening to run away from us all.

KENNETH: What do you mean?

JEAN: Only for a year, Ken. I've got a year's leave of absence from the office and I'm going to Toronto with Sue—next month.

SUE: Isn't it exciting?

KENNETH: Say, you girls decide things fast when you get started. Toronto eh? Good for you, Jean.

JEAN: (*Hesitantly*) I've thought about it for a long time, Kenneth. We were wondering if you could come home while I'm gone, so Mother wouldn't be alone.

KENNETH: Gosh, I'd like to. Only I've got a bunch of news myself, Mother. I came to tell you.

MRS. MORRISON: (*Concerned*) What is it, Kenneth? Something serious?

KENNETH: Serious—it's great. You see before you the new consulting engineer of the Cadogan Mining Corporation. I'm leaving Tuesday.

MRS. MORRISON: (*Again a note of shrill fear creeps into her voice*) Kenneth! Not way out there. You mustn't, son. I couldn't let you. . . .

KENNETH: I guess you'll have to, Mums. I've been trying to get that job for two years. I was pretty sure I had it last week, but the final word only came through today.

MRS. MORRISON: Kenneth, you mustn't decide so quickly. It's your whole future. That's a horrible, rough town a thousand miles from anywhere.

KENNETH: Now, Mother, not quite that! (*With sudden boyish disappointment.*) I thought you'd be glad. I want you to be glad. Now come on, say you are.

MRS. MORRISON: (*Pleadingly*) But what about me , Kenneth? My whole life is wrapped up in you and now you're planning to go away like this. I can't let you go.

KENNETH: (*Stiffening. He has steeled himself for this.*) I wish you didn't feel that way, Mother. (*His voices is quiet and impersonal*) It makes it rather hard to tell you. But Marian and I are going to be married before I go.

MRS. MORRISON: Kenneth!

KENNETH: I'm sorry it's so sudden, but we've only been able to decide since there was a hope of my getting this job.

MRS. MORRISON: (*Withdrawing from him as she realizes that he has made up his mind*) Oh. That makes it different doesn't it? I hope you'll be very happy, Kenneth.

KENNETH: Now, Mother—no heroics. You'll love Marian when you get to know her. I think I'll go and get her now. She's a swell girl, isn't she, Sue?

MRS. MORRISON: (*Going to him. There is a dramatic pathos about her as she says bravely*) No. Not just yet, Son. Do you mind not bringing her here yet? Give me a little while, Kenneth, to get used to all this. Give me a little while.

KENNETH: (*Uncomfortable*) Why, of course, Mother. . . . if you'd rather.

MRS. MORRISON: I know Sue thinks I'm cowardly and sentimental. But it's hard to lose your children, Sue. You'll know when you have some of your own.

SUE: You couldn't lose your son to a nicer girl, Mrs. Morrison.

KENNETH: (*Gratefully*) Thanks, Sue. You'd think I was dying instead of getting married.

MRS. MORRISON: It's all decided then, Son?

KENNETH: (*Firmly*) Yes, Mother.

MRS. MORRISON: (*Summoning her strength*) Then you must tell Marian I'm very happy. She won't mind my calling her Marian will she? And tell her that I hope she'll come to see us soon. Tomorrow if you like. . . .

KENNETH: That's the way to talk, Mother. I'd better run along now.

JEAN: I think you might have told Mother before, Kenneth. After all. . . .

KENNETH: (*Unreasonably irritated*) After all I'm thirty-one years old and I've spent thirty of them at home. What do you want me to do, wear rompers?

MRS. MORRISON: Kenneth! (*There is a pause*) Jean doesn't mean to be unkind. You'd better go. . . .

KENNETH: (*Relieved that he can go*) We'll be over tomorrow. Bye Jean. So long, Sue.

MRS. MORRISON: (*Following him to the door*) You'll forgive me, Son? You'll forgive your mother for everything, won't you?

Gwen Pharis Ringwood

KENNETH: Don't you worry, Mother. Everything will work out fine.
MRS. MORRISON: (*Taking a locket from around her neck*) Give this to her, Kenneth. Your father gave it to me.
KENNETH: Say, that's good of you, Mother. She'll be awfully pleased.
MRS. MORRISON: And now, goodbye. (*She places her hands on his shoulders*) I hope this girl is worthy of you, my dear, dear son.
(*She kisses him on the forehead,* KENNETH *pats her awkwardly and goes*)
MRS. MORRISON: (*Sitting down listlessly*) Jean, perhaps Sue would like more tea.
SUE: No, thank you. I really must go. I've stayed too long already.
MRS. MORRISON: We love to have you, Sue. I'm sorry things were. . . . a little upset today.
SUE: (*Rising and preparing to leave*) I hope my being here wasn't embarrassing. I mean when Kenneth was telling you about him and Marian.
MRS. MORRISON: My dear, embarrassing is hardly the word to describe a mother's feelings when she learns she's to lose her first-born.
SUE: I suppose not. It's been awfully nice, Mrs. Morrison and I'm glad you want Jean to go to Toronto. The change will be good for her.
MRS. MORRISON: Run in again, real soon, Sue. Jean loves to have you and I'm not much company for her, I'm afraid.
JEAN: You're grand company, Mother. Do you have to go, Sue?
SUE: I really must. Come over tomorrow.
JEAN: I will.
SUE: We'll make lists of what we're taking with us. I love making lists. Goodbye Mrs. Morrison. Bye Jean.
(SUE *goes*)
JEAN: (*Turning from the door*) You look all in, Mother.
MRS. MORRISON: (*Smiling pitifully*) Just the headache, darling. And then I was so startled when Kenneth told me about going away and marrying that girl.
JEAN: He might have given you some warning.
MRS. MORRISON: We don't matter so much to him now, Jean. I hope you won't get like that—after you've been away.
JEAN: I should have told you about my plans before. I feel terribly selfish. But they were so vague, until today.
MRS. MORRISON: Of course they were.
JEAN: You do see that I'm right in going, don't you Mother?
MRS. MORRISON: I—I'll try. But what is it you want, Jean? You have a nice home. I do everything I can for you. You don't know how it hurts me to think I've failed to make you happy.
JEAN: It's not you, Mother. It's myself. I want life. I want to be taken along in the current—not thrown aside like a dead leaf. Please try to understand.
MRS. MORRISON: (*Softly*) My dear, I do. I do. And you must go if you think you'll find something away from here that I can't give you.

130

It's only that my love for you makes me afraid. If it were anyone but Sue. . . .

JEAN: Sue's about the only real friend I have, Mother.

MRS. MORRISON: One needs to be so sure of friendship. Sue isn't sensitive like you—her tastes are different. She goes to dances and parties and you know you've never cared for that sort of thing. You've said yourself she's selfish and only interested in clothes and Ronald. Won't it be lonely for you?

JEAN: (*Desperately*) Sue says I'll meet people and go out places too.

MRS. MORRISON: Sue's never gone to much trouble to have you meet her friends here,—now has she?

JEAN: It will be different—I'm sure it will be different.

MRS. MORRISON: And you're so helpless when you're tired. You're my baby, Jean. I don't want you to be hurt—hurt like I was. I married your father when I was very young, Jean. I've never told you. . . . (*bravely*) but my children were the only thing in my marriage that brought me happiness. I don't want that to happen to you.

JEAN: (*Deeply moved*) Oh, Mother.

MRS. MORRISON: (*Smiling*) It's all right, dear. You children make up for everything. And I mustn't say any more. Don't tell Sue what an old fraidy-cat your mother is. She's never liked me and I'd hate her to know I even hesitated about your going with her—it would only make things awkward.

JEAN: (*Uncomfortably*) Why, I think Sue likes you, Mother.

MRS. MORRISON: (*Getting up and beginning to clear up the tea things*) No. Why, she even told Mrs. Allen that I had discouraged every boy who showed any interest in you. Imagine that!

JEAN: There haven't been many, mother. Ross Hanson is the only man who's taken me out for three years.

MRS. MORRISON: (*Going over and putting her hands on* JEAN's *shoulders*) Darling, please tell me the truth. Don't be afraid to hurt me. Do you feel that your mother has failed you?

JEAN: (*Hysterically*) No, Mother. No. For God's sake don't keep saying that over and over. I'm tired and I want a change that's all.

MRS. MORRISON: And you shall have it. (*The doorbell rings*) That must be the postman. (*As she starts to the door*) I wonder if he sees the changes that come over the houses he visits every day.

JEAN: (*Forlornly*) No. He wouldn't see. He changes and gets old too.

MRS. MORRISON: I'll see what he left. I can't understand what Kenneth sees in Marian. Still we'll have to make the best of it now. Let him find out. (*From the hall*) Why here's a parcel for you, Jean—it looks like candy.

(*She brings it back to* JEAN)

JEAN: (*Looking at the writing*) Why, it's from Ross.

MRS. MORRISON: Really. It's strange he hasn't called to see you if he's in town.

JEAN: He's been awfully busy. (*Excited and nervous*) Well, I'd better see what this is.

MRS. MORRISON: It's nice of him to think of your birthday, anyway.

JEAN: (*Opening it*) Yes, I didn't know he knew when it was. . . .

MRS. MORRISON: A book! How nice. Let me see it dear.

JEAN: (*Slowly. Trying not to show her disappointment*) No. It's just one I lent him, Mother.

MRS. MORRISON: What a let down, Darling. I was sure it was something exciting.

JEAN: There may be a note in it.

> (*She looks but does not find one. Slowly she gets up and puts the book on the mantel and stands looking into the fire. Her mother comes over to her and a real sympathy comes into her voice.*)

MRS. MORRISON: Don't you worry over it dear. He's only a youngster with his funny stand-up hair and you really wouldn't want him.

> (JEAN *doesn't answer*)

MRS. MORRISON: (*Sensing that* JEAN *would like to be alone*) I'll run up and run your bath for you, dear. That will rest you—then we can have a nice quiet dinner before the fire, and you'll feel better. (JEAN *doesn't answer*) Things are going to look brighter, darling. (*Patting* JEAN, MRS. MORRISON *starts with the tea wagon into the kitchen. When she gets to the door she stops and turns in excitement to* JEAN. *She is radiant with her great plan*) Jean!

JEAN: (*Dully*) Yes.

MRS. MORRISON: I don't know why I didn't think of it before. I've got just the answer. With Ken getting married and leaving there's no reason on earth why I should stay here. I could go to Toronto with you. Then I'd be there to see that you were well and you'd have your year away. . . .

JEAN: But Mother. . . .

MRS. MORRISON: I wouldn't mind leaving this old house at all—I could rent it—And you're right when you say we both need a change. I've been feeling blue myself. We'd get a little apartment near Varsity. Wouldn't you like that? Then we'd have each other and your poor old mother wouldn't wear her heart out worrying and grieving over you. That's the solution, isn't it?

JEAN: (*Giving up*) We'll see, Mother. . . . maybe I'd better not leave the office this year. . . .

MRS. MORRISON: Indeed you will. I'll just tell them you have doctor's orders. Oh, I'm quite excited about it. (*She looks young and girlish. With a rush of affection she leans over* JEAN *putting her head down beside* JEAN'*s*) I'll still have my little girl.

JEAN: I don't know, Mother. I'm not sure Sue would want. . . .

MRS. MORRISON: Jean, dear, Sue has her young man. She doesn't need you.

JEAN: (*Desperately*) But I need. . . .

MRS. MORRISON: Don't you worry, we'll work it all out. If Sue wants to come in with us. . . .

132

JEAN: But she won't.

MRS. MORRISON: Well then we'll find our own little nest. Oh, dear, I was going to run your bath. Come on now, cheer up. Everything's going to be wonderful.

> (MRS. MORRISON *goes out.* JEAN *slowly looks through the book once more to see if there is a note. Examines the wrapping paper and finally drops the paper in the fire. She puts her head down on the arm of a chair and cries silently and hopelessly*)

MRS. MORRISON: (*From upstairs*) I've started your bath, dear. Hurry.

> (JEAN *shrinks into herself and doesn't answer.*)

MRS. MORRISON: Are you coming, Jean?. . . . Jean.

> (JEAN *raises her head and gets up wearily*)

JEAN: Coming, Mother, coming.

> (*She goes slowly upstairs as the curtain falls.*)

The End

Saturday Night

Characters

MRS. WILSON
MR. WILSON
MARY ALICE (16)
ROBERT (19)
ALLAN (18)
BUDDY (13)
CHARLIE, *the hired man*

SCENE: *The large kitchen living room of the Wilson farm house.*

Down right is a good sized rocking chair and a footstool just in front of the window. Up right a cupboard and in the corner a high stool. The door outside is right of centre in the rear wall with a window left of centre. Between them is a washstand with a mirror above it.

Upstage in the left wall is the door into the hallway and the rest of the house. Down stage right is another chair. The table is left of centre and there are two chairs under it. At right and down stage are stools or backless chairs partly hidden under table cloth.

The room is simple and comfortable but shows the signs of wear and tear.

MRS. WILSON *is mending some shirts, sitting left of table. Kneeling on the footstool at right and gazing into the mirror which she has propped on the rocking chair is* MARY ALICE, *putting her hair in curlers.*

MRS. WILSON: Is Buddy out with Dad, Mary Alice?
MARY ALICE: He went to get the eggs.
ROBERT: (*appearing in bedroom door*) Say, Mom, where's my blue tie?
MRS. WILSON: I expect it's in your drawer, son.

ROBERT: No, I looked there. I bet you anything Allan has taken my
   blue tie, Mom. You've got to make him leave my things alone!
MRS. WILSON: I don't think he's had it, Robert. Look again.
ROBERT: A fellow can't have a thing he can call his own around here.
MARY ALICE: Who you dressing up for? That snippy Caroline Carter?
ROBERT: Wouldn't you like to know? Did you see my tie?
MARY ALICE: I put it in your drawer the last time you left it on the
   floor.
   (ROBERT *goes out*)
MARY ALICE: Mother, I need the car terribly tonight. I promised to
   take some girls out skating after we get in town.
MRS. WILSON: Your father may want the car himself, Mary Alice.
   You're a little young to be driving alone anyway.
ALLAN: (*Entering with pail of water which he takes to wash stand*)
   Speaking of driving, I'm about due for a little practice tonight,
   Mom. . .
MARY ALICE: Why, Allan Wilson, you had the car on Monday night.
MRS. WILSON: I will not argue about the car tonight. You'll just have
   to settle this with your father. Every Saturday night it's the
   same. . .
ALLAN: (*Washing*) Why doesn't she get somebody to drive her around?
   It's a funny thing when the girl of the family gets the car when-
   ever she wants. A funny thing!
ROBERT: (*Entering tying the blue tie*) Where's Dad, Mother?
MRS. WILSON: Probably finishing up the chores, Robert. Things have
   to be done on Saturday night as well as any other, you know.
ALLAN: (*Interrupting his washing*) Say, whose socks are you wearing?
ROBERT: (*Waving shoe polishing gear*) Step aside, small change.
ALLAN: (*Kneeling and catching Robert's leg*) I thought so. Those are the
   socks Aunt Lillian gave me for my birthday. Brand new. Mom,
   look at that big ape stretching my socks from here to the North
   Pole so I can't wear them. My new socks!
MRS. WILSON: Are those Allan's socks, Robert?
ROBERT: How can I tell his socks? These look like the ones I got at
   Christmas.
ALLAN: (*Going round to face Robert*) They're not! You can just take
   them off.
MRS. WILSON: Oh, let him wear them now, Allan. Here's a pair I just
   mended.
MARY ALICE: What are you doing tonight, Allan?
ALLAN: Oh, things. . . just fooling around. (*He glowers at socks, then
   returns to ablutions.*) A fine thing that I have to wear the old
   mended socks. A fine thing!
MARY ALICE: Joyce won't be home, you know. She's coming skating
   with us.
ALLAN: If you get the car.
ROBERT: (*Polishing shoes*) I hope you small fry aren't planning on
   running Daddy's limousine tonight. I've got other plans. . .

ALLAN: (*Face soaped for shaving*) You've got other plans! Who had the car all day Sunday till midnight? Who had the car Tuesday afternoon till midnight? Who had. . .

ROBERT: I had to get Dad's tractor parts Tuesday.

ALLAN: Nine miles and you took six hours. No, my fine brother, tonight you bay the moon.

MARY ALICE: Mom, you said you'd speak to Dad for me. . .

ROBERT: Mother, I'm the oldest, and if Dad lets Allan have the car on Saturday night I'll. . . I'll just have to move out, that's all.

MRS. WILSON: Children, don't be so selfish. Why don't all three of you go into town together and pick up your friends?

ALLAN: Mom!

MARY ALICE: I can see myself talking sweet to Caroline Carter — affected little peroxide-blonde.

ROBERT: Caroline's hair is natural. And she doesn't have to twist it up in tin curlers like some people I know. . .

MARY ALICE: If she's so sweet and natural, why are you scared to ask her to go for a nice walk?

ROBERT: Because I'm going to have the car, that's why!

ALLAN: (*Coming between them, shaving brush waving*) Over my dead body!

MARY ALICE: Mom, you promised. Just because I'm a girl. . .

ROBERT: (*Hands over ears, shouting*) Stop yelling! You give me a headache.

MRS. WILSON: None of you will go anywhere in a minute. Quiet down. Here come your father and Buddy. Some example for Buddy.
(ALLAN *at table.* MARY ALICE *continues doing her nails.* ROBERT *turns his back to the others.*)

ALLAN: It's a wonder Buddy doesn't think he ought to have the car.
(MR. WILSON *enters with milk pail followed by* BUDDY.)

MR. WILSON: Do you want to go to town, Mother? I ought to order that harness. . .

ROBERT: I'll order it for you, Dad. I have to go in anyway and I. . .
(BUDDY *interrupts.*)

BUDDY: Daddy, if you go, can I drive? Mugs Baker drives all the time and he's not 13 yet. It's time I learned. You might need me to drive the car some time, Dad. . .

ALLAN: Dad, it's terribly important that I have the car this one night of my life. Put yourself in my place. I ask a girl to go to the show. Do I arrive on horseback?
(ALLAN *turns his father to face him.*)

MARY ALICE: You could for once, Allan Wilson. Daddy, I promised the girls to take them skating.
(MARY ALICE *turns her father to face her.*)

MR. WILSON: Well, Mother. . .

MRS. WILSON: I give up. They won't hear of all going together. You settle it.
(*She goes out.*)

137

MR. WILSON: Your mother's right. . . you should all go together.

ROBERT: Dad, I asked Caroline to go for a drive, not a family huddle. At my age I shouldn't even have to ask for the car.

ALLAN: It's my turn, Robert. You know it. Socks borrower!

MARY ALICE: Please, Daddy. . .

MR. WILSON: Just how many cars have we got? One. You'd think one car would be enough for any ordinary family. You'd think we'd count ourselves lucky to have it. But oh no! How many cars do you think we need anyway?

ROBERT: (*Promptly*) Two.

ALLAN: Three. I could get a Ford cheap.

MARY ALICE: Susan's got her own car.

BUDDY: I bet I never get a chance to drive till I'm an old man. . .

MR. WILSON: (*Calling*) Do you want to go to town, Sarah?

MRS. WILSON: (*Calling back*) No thank you. There's a radio program I want to hear.

MR. WILSON: Very well. You'll have to come to some decision among yourselves.

ALLAN: (*Rushing to door*) First come! First Serve! It's mine!

MARY ALICE: (*at door also*) Mine!

ALLAN: Let go, scratch cat!

MARY ALICE: I won't! Mom. . .

ALLAN: Look, you can play gooseberry with me and Joyce, baby. . .

MRS. WILSON: Allan. Mary Alice. Sit down! Right now! (*They do so*) Now I suppose the only thing to do is draw lots.

MR. WILSON: Good idea, Sarah.

ROBERT: Mother, I'm packing my things! I will not face Caroline on foot. As hard as I work around here, it looks to me like. . .
    (CHARLIE *enters*. ROBERT *breaks off*.)

CHARLIE: Evening.

MR. WILSON: Got the fence fixed, Charlie?

CHARLIE: Yep. I fixed it three places. Hey, I hope none of you figured on using the car tonight. . .

MR. WILSON: I believe someone did mention it, Charlie. Why?

CHARLIE: Somebody left the lights on last night. The battery's run down. It'll take 12 hours to charge it up.

ROBERT: Bad management. Just plain bad management. Who left the lights on? Buddy, you were fooling around in that car last night.

BUDDY: I don't think I. . . Mom, make him stop. . . he's punching me. . .

MR. WILSON: Well, looks like we'll all be home tonight. How about a game of hearts, mother?

MRS. WILSON: Yes, dear.

ROBERT: What am I going to do? I've got a date.

MR. WILSON: Who's playing?

ALLAN: Come on, Charlie. Nothing else to do around here.

ROBERT: Kid's game. Some Saturday!

MARY ALICE: Can I play?
> (*She gets music on the radio*).

ALLAN: Sure. Come on, Buddy.

ROBERT: Oh, you might as well count me in, but next Saturday — I tell you I'm —

BUDDY: Saturday night. No homework. I just love Saturday night don't you, Mom?

The End

The Courting of Marie Jenvrin

Characters

MR. WERNECKE
MRS. WERNECKE
MARIE JENVRIN
LOUIS HÉBERT
FATHER LeBEAU
MR. DINSMORE
MICHAEL LORRIGAN

SCENE: *The combined lunch room and sitting-room of the Beaverlodge Hotel in Yellowknife, Northwest Territories.*
TIME: *The present. A late afternoon in February.*

The curtain rises on the combined lunch room and sitting-room of the Beaverlodge Hotel in Yellowknife, Northwest Territories. A bear rug on the floor, a mounted caribou head, some heavily beaded mukluks of Indian fashion and a man's parka with heavily furred hood—this last hanging near the door—are some tangible evidence of the northern setting. Less colourful but essential furniture in the room includes a good-sized wood or oil heater at the left, two old leather armchairs, a small stand-table for magazines and papers, a table with three painted chairs grouped round it, and a narrow counter at the right with three or four wooden stools in front of it. In the rear wall two windows and a door look out on the main street of the mining town. Up left is a door leading to the rooms upstairs and down right is a door that leads outside through the kitchen.

Our first glimpse of life in the Beaverlodge Hotel comes at about three-thirty on a February afternoon. Darkness comes early in the North

Gwen Pharis Ringwood

and the shadows are deepening in the room. It is a slack time since the miners do not come off shift until after four o'clock.

We discover a rather apologetic-looking little man seated on the floor in front of the large chair right of the stove, surrounded by three pulp magazines and a strange assortment of screws, coils, and machinery, the largest piece looking much like a food-chopper. In the armchair left of the stove a large, placid-looking woman with the gaudy beauty of a great sunflower is dozing peacefully, a box of chocolates beside her. These good people are MR. *and* MRS. WERNECKE, *proprietors of the Inn. Behind the counter, folding paper napkins and tidying the cigarette and gum boxes on the shelf is* MARIE JENVRIN.

MARIE JENVRIN *is perhaps twenty with a vivid, little face, framed by dark, curly hair. She wears a flared skirt, a blouse graced with a demure, little collar and tiny bowtie. Around her waist is a flared apron as gay as fancy can conceive.*

MR. WERNECKE *is muttering to himself as he ecstatically assembles his machinery.*

WERNECKE: She won't fit. His directions is wrong. (*He refers to one of his magazines.*) He says it fits but I make it and it don't fit. (*He takes up the paper and addresses it politely.*) Your directions are just plain damn wrong, Mr. Beasley. You don't ought to publish such directions.

MARIE: You work at a new invention, monsieur?

WERNECKE: Yes, Marie, but that Beasley makes a mistake. (*The light dawns.*) Wait! No, he don't! She fits. I have the wrong side. See, now she fits perfect.

(*He holds up a coil which fits inside a circle of steel.*)

MARIE: What is this—invention, monsieur?

WERNECKE: Ah, a surprise! You will know tomorrow. I have one more part to come in by the 'plane.

MARIE: I think the 'plane does not get in after all. It is three-thirty and getting dark. The storm has kept him.

WERNECKE: If it is BQQ it will not come. If it is BVY it will come—you see. That BQQ is a bad 'plane. She looks good but she won't go. I don't like that BQQ—twice I have been held up on an invention, waiting for that 'plane.

ANNABELLA: (MRS. WERNECKE, *stirring drowsily*) Fiddlesticks. I have gone outside in both. BQQ is better. I don't get sick in BQQ.

WERNECKE: Women don't know about aeroplanes. She looks nice so you think she is nice. I tell you BQQ is no good. (*To himself.*) She's a *bidget!*

ANNABELLA: (*sharply*) What's that you say, Wernecke?

WERNECKE: (*slightly belligerent*) I said, Mrs. Wernecke, that BQQ is a *bidget.* That's a word I invented.

ANNABELLA: (*taking a chocolate*) Well, I don't like it.

WERNECKE: (*going back to work*) That is too bad. I like it.

(ANNABELLA *is too sleepy to continue the argument.*)

142

MARIE: (*taking a glass of paper napkins over to the table*) Father LeBeau was to come in today. I hope the storm has not forced them down and they have lost themselves.

WERNECKE: No need to worry about the Father, Marie. He knows the North from McMurray to Aklavik. He has gone down to Aklavik alone with three dogs.

MARIE: (*at the window*) Louis Hébert stands on the aeroplane dock. How foolish to stand shivering in such cold!

WERNECKE: Perhaps while Father LeBeau is here you will marry with Louis, Marie.

MARIE: (*turning from the window and beginning to light the lamp on the table*) And perhaps I will not, monsieur. I have no mind to marry Louis Hébert.

WERNECKE: Then what of Ed McArthy or William Shumlett or Michael Lorrigan?

MARIE: Michael Lorrigan! Such a man! Non, Monsieur Wernecke, I prefer to work in your hotel, please.

ANNABELLA: We will give Father LeBeau the green room. It is warmer.

WERNECKE: He can have his choice of rooms—if he comes.

ANNABELLA: Well, he must come some time. If not today, tomorrow.

WERNECKE: If it is BQQ I shall not be surprised if he never comes.
(*The droning of a 'plane is heard quite close.*)

MARIE: (*excitedly*) Ecoutez! The 'plane! I hear it.
(*They all listen. Their faces light up. Now the engine of the 'plane can be heard distinctly. All three are excited and hurry toward the window.* MR. WERNECKE *takes time to thrust his invention into a box which he pushes under the table. Their voices rise with pleasure.*)

WERNECKE: (*gathering up his invention*) It is a 'plane! BVY has come through the storm.

MARIE: There it is! See, madame. He circles above the bay.

ANNABELLA: It is dark to land.

WERNECKE: Hah! That BVY can land any place.

MARIE: Michael Lorrigan says the ice is not safe by the Hudson's Bay dock. There is a current there.

WERNECKE: It is time a 'plane got in. Now I can finish my invention.
(*He comes to the window where the women are watching.*)

ANNABELLA: My new silk dress will be on it—and slippers for Wernecke.

MARIE: Oui, et une lettre de ma mère.

WERNECKE: He brings her down fast. No nonsense. I like to see a good 'plane brought down fast.

MARIE: Attention! He is about to land.

ANNABELLA: That is BQQ or I am not Annabella.

MARIE: I think you are right, madame. Voilà—he is on the ice. That is a good landing. He is on the ice and no bumps.

ANNABELLA: (*triumphantly*) And it is BQQ. I can see from here. So, Wernecke, BQQ cannot come in a storm?

143

WERNECKE: There is some mistake. I could swear it was the other.

ANNABELLA: Now what have you to say?

WERNECKE: (*with dignity as he dons his parka*) I say nothing. I go to meet the guests. If it is BQQ, I expect no guests—they have probably fallen out the bottom.

ANNABELLA: What stubbornness! Soon you must invent an aeroplane, I suppose.

WERNECKE: I have thought of it.

ANNABELLA: Now, hurry, Wernecke. They will be getting out in a minute.

WERNECKE: They can get out without me, Mrs. Wernecke.
     (*With offended dignity, he leaves.*)

MARIE: Father LeBeau has come. I see him. And there is Madame Barnett. Her husband and little girl are kissing her.

ANNABELLA: Marie, isn't that Mr. Dinsmore—getting off now?

MARIE: Ma foi, he only went outside last week.

ANNABELLA: He's a queer one. I wonder where he makes his money. Certainly not in that jewelry store of his.

MARIE: It takes much money to fly back and forth so often.

ANNABELLA: Michael Lorrigan says he's a crook.

MARIE: There is someone else. Oh, it is only Louis talking to the pilot. Now he is running up here. (*Giggles a little.*) Wherever he goes, Louis must run like a scared rabbit.

ANNABELLA: I'd better go up and make sure the green room is ready.

MARIE: And I must finish my pie.
     (*They turn from the window.* ANNABELLA *takes a chocolate as she starts upstairs.*)

ANNABELLA: Why don't you eat a chocolate, Marie? Michael left them for you.

MARIE: I do not eat chocolate. Besides, how do I know he leaves them for me?

ANNABELLA: I suppose a handsome young miner leaves chocolates about for Mrs. Wernecke?

MARIE: Michael Lorrigan speaks only insults. No man can speak insults to Marie Jenvrin.

ANNABELLA: (*placidly, as she lumbers upstairs*) Pride falls, Marie, pride falls. I was like you once. Now, as you see, I am a slave to Wernecke.
     (*She goes off.*)

MARIE: (*patting the caribou head affectionately*) Such foolishness they talk, mon petit. As if Marie must marry tomorrow or be forever left.
     (MARIE *moves behind the counter. As she begins rolling out a pie crust which is already mixed,* LOUIS HÉBERT *pokes his head in cautiously through the door at back.* LOUIS HÉBERT *is a dapper young man, not very tall, dark and rather good-looking. He is excitable and far from level-headed. The romance of the North is in his soul only as far as clothes are*

concerned. He wears a heavily furred parka, elaborately embroidered mitts and mukluks with huge red tassels and is indeed a colourful sight.)

LOUIS: Marie! Are you there? I bring you something.

MARIE: Of course I am here, Louis Hébert. Don't you see me?

LOUIS: *(coming into the room)* Marie, do you know what day this is?

MARIE: Tuesday, mon petit chou!

LOUIS: Ah, but is something else, also. February the fourteenth—that is St. Valentine's. And I have sent to Edmonton for a valentine for Marie Jenvrin. It comes by the aeroplane. *(He presents her with a large red envelope.)*

MARIE: You should not spend your money on me, Louis.

LOUIS: Aren't you going to open it?

MARIE: *(as she opens it)* It is a very big valentine. So much lace and ribbon!

LOUIS: *(unable to wait for her to open it, takes it from her)* Look, this is best of all. When you open this little red heart—there is my picture. Voilà! *(He demonstrates.)*

MARIE: *(with a little throaty giggle)* Oui, it is you all right and looking very solemn.

LOUIS: You like it, Marie?

MARIE: Mais oui, c'est belle. But Louis, you should not give it to me. I am not your valentine.

LOUIS: Marie, could you not love me a little bit? Louis Hébert would serve you like a slave. Even when you are angry you are beautiful, Marie. In my mind I call you la belle du nord.

MARIE: Your tongue says fine things, Louis. No wonder Cecile Rideau lies awake weeping for love of you.

LOUIS: Cecile Rideau!

MARIE: Go to her, Louis. Have I not said a hundred times—four hundred times—I will not marry you?

LOUIS: If I fall down the mine shaft or get eaten up by huskies, you will be sorry then.

MARIE: *(returning to her pie)* No man gets eaten up by huskies for love, Louis Hébert. Only for lack of brains.

LOUIS: Two years I stay in this wild country of rock only because of you, Marie. Two years I work in the mine. Two years I set myself down on the shore of a lake, one thousand miles from any place. And no way to get out except by those aeroplane which make me so sick. And still you do not love me!

MARIE: When the ice melts there will be a boat. You can go outside then.

LOUIS: What is outside to me if you are not there? Non, if you must stay by this frozen lake beside the North Pole, then Louis Hébert stays too.

MARIE: Louis, Louis, it is no use. I will never love you—not for all the gold in Yellowknife.

LOUIS: I know—I am what they call—a dope. But I stay.

Gwen Pharis Ringwood

MARIE: Très bien. If you must stay, you stay. But what if I tell you there is a whisper of love—just a small stirring—in my heart for someone else?

LOUIS: I will fight him.

MARIE: C'est impossible. Besides, he does not love me.

LOUIS: Then he is a fool with no eyes. I can fight him.

MARIE: He is twice as big as you. Anyway, perhaps I do not love him. Perhaps I hate him. Mais, j'ai mal au cœur, Louis.

LOUIS: (*solemnly*) Moi, aussi. We French suffer, Marie.

MARIE: (*with a big sigh*) Oui, nous souffrons. (*For a brief period these very young people suffer. Then* MARIE *turns briskly back to her pie.*) There, it is ready for the oven. See how beautiful, Louis.

LOUIS: You are wonderful.

MARIE: (*complacently*) I make good pies. Outside where I have cream to pile on top, I take prizes for my pie. But enough talk. Be a good boy and go down to the lake and bring me two pails of water.

LOUIS: Every day I cut holes in the ice to bring you water.

MARIE: I know, Louis. (*She smiles at him.*) You are very good, mon cher. (*She hands him the pails but before he leaves,* MR. WERNECKE *enters with* FATHER LEBEAU. FATHER LEBEAU *is a rosy little priest with twinkling eyes.*)

MARIE: Père LeBeau! Vous êtes ici. (*She runs to him and gives him both her hands.*)

FATHER LEBEAU: Marie—Louis. Comment allez-vous, mes enfants? Marie grows prettier each week, n'est-ce pas, Louis? (*He pats her cheek and shakes hands with* LOUIS.)

MARIE: (*her eyes shining*) C'est vous à la fin, mon père. We are so glad to see you.

LOUIS: Oui, it is good to have you here, Père LeBeau.

FATHER LEBEAU: Your welcome warms the heart, my children. Now I will take my things upstairs, but I will be down again soon to eat one of your fine pies, Marie.

WERNECKE: I will lead the way, Father.

FATHER LEBEAU: Thank you, Mr. Wernecke. This hotel always seems like home to me.

WERNECKE: I am honoured, Father.

FATHER LEBEAU: Have you been inventing lately?

WERNECKE: A new one—a surprise. See, the last part came in with you. (*He displays the treasured parcel.*)

FATHER LEBEAU: I shall be glad to see it. (*They go upstairs.*)

LOUIS: (*once more taking up his water pails*) Père LeBeau is here. There are rings at Dinsmore's. If you loved me, Marie, we could marry. As it is I am as lonely as (*He searches for a simile*)—as one rabbit's track in the snow.

*(He adjusts his parka hood, pulls on his fine mitts, and is
about to leave when R.S. DINSMORE enters from the street.
R.S. DINSMORE, jeweller, is a stocky gentleman with an
unctuous manner and sharp, suspicious eyes. He wears a large
fur coat.)*

DINSMORE: Well, well, get two Frenchies together and the talk flies like
crows in a cornfield. How are you behaving yourself, Miss Jenvrin?

MARIE: *(coldly)* Did you wish something, monsieur?

DINSMORE: Only to see old Wernecke. No hurry.

(He shakes the snow off his coat carelessly.)

LOUIS: *(without warmth)* You were not long in Edmonton.

DINSMORE: Just a little business trip, my boy. Some of us have to keep
a foot on the ladder, you know.

LOUIS: *(as he goes out the door)* You should take care you make no false
steps, monsieur.

DINSMORE: *(after LOUIS has shut the door)* I see you've got your boy-
friend working.

MARIE: *(ignoring the remark)* Monsieur Wernecke should be down very
soon.

DINSMORE: I can wait. Would you care to take a little walk after you're
through tonight?

MARIE: A walk? What for?

DINSMORE: Why—just a walk—over to my shop maybe. To get out.

MARIE: I have been out. When I walk in twenty below zero, I have
a purpose.

DINSMORE: Perhaps you'd like to see the moving picture?

MARIE: Thank you, monsieur, you will excuse me but I do not care to go.

DINSMORE: As you like. You know, Miss Jenvrin, I've been thinking of
opening a restaurant here. With your help the restaurant would
become a very paying proposition.

MARIE: I have no wish to change jobs, monsieur.

DINSMORE: You don't understand. You see I'm a man of some means.
I realize my position may seem rather out of reach to you but I've
been keeping my eye on you these last three months and—

*(MICHAEL LORRIGAN enters from outside. He is a tall,
homely and thoroughly attractive young man of great
vitality.)*

MICHAEL: Well, Marie Jenvrin, have you a kiss for Michael Lorrigan,
the hardest-working hard-rock miner in the town of Yellowknife?
On second thought I'll not kiss you. You've painted your mouth
like a signboard. I'll have a cup of coffee instead.

MARIE: You'll have no kiss from me, Michael Lorrigan, and you pay
for your coffee.

MICHAEL: Ten cents for cold coffee. No wonder I must go around in a
ragged shirt.

DINSMORE: *(turning)* Look here, my good man, you're interrupting—

MICHAEL: The name's Lorrigan, Mr. Dinsmore, and I'm nobody's
man but my own. You'll remember that.

147

DINSMORE: Prickly, today, aren't you?

MICHAEL: I've been waiting for you to get back.

DINSMORE: Really?

MICHAEL: I understand you lent old Carl Swanson money to pay his poker debts, after getting him that drunk he didn't know what he was doing. He's been drunk ever since but I got that much out of him.

DINSMORE: I lent him the money. Poor old codger! He shouldn't have sat in on a game with that bunch down at Joe's. They cleaned him.

MICHAEL: Did you take any security?

DINSMORE: Don't be funny. What security has Swanson got to give?

MICHAEL: I wouldn't know, Mr. Dinsmore, but I think you might. Carl keeps jabbering about some paper he signed.

DINSMORE: Oh, that, it's nothing. Tell him to come in and see me. I'll explain it to him in words of one syllable.

MICHAEL: He's soberin' up in my room now.

DINSMORE: Pleasant friends he has, eh, Miss Jenvrin?

MICHAEL: I wouldn't like to see old Carl cheated, Mr. Dinsmore.

DINSMORE: Tell him to keep away from the crowd that hang around Joe's, then.

MICHAEL: I'll tell him that—from you.

DINSMORE: Look here, Lorrigan, I felt sorry for the old soak. I lent him some money. What's the matter with that?

MICHAEL: If you did it out of kindness, I'll beg your pardon, Mr. Dinsmore. If not. . . (*He breaks off, puts a coin on the table and speaks to* MARIE, *turning away from* DINSMORE.) I did your coffee an injustice, Colleen. It's lukewarm. You're doin' better.

MARIE: There is your change. You are welcome to go now.

(MICHAEL *lights a cigarette and gazes nonchalantly at the smoke rings which he blows at the ceiling.*)

MICHAEL: I was just thinking—

MARIE: There is small use digging for gold where no gold is, monsieur.

MICHAEL: You'd be almost a pretty girl, Marie, if you controlled your tongue. Your nose is snub, of course, and there's too much red stuff on your lips, but you'd get by, if you didn't talk. Too bad. (*He shakes his head.*)

(MR. *and* MRS. WERNECKE *come downstairs and into the room, arguing vociferously.* ANNABELLA *carries a tall, rangy plant.*)

ANNABELLA: I tell you, Wernecke, it is the B_1 tablets that have made this begonia grow.

WERNECKE: B_1! The plant was withering away to a shadow until I invented my plant food. All its growing is because of my plant food.

ANNABELLA: Nonsense! Your plant food didn't help the geraniums. They died. B_1 is necessary to plant life.

WERNECKE: (*irritated*) B_1 be damned, Mrs. Wernecke. My plant food has made the begonia blossom like the pines of Lebanon. Am I right, Marie?

MARIE: Perhaps it is the soil Louis brings me for my garden that makes the begonia grow so tall.

ANNABELLA: Michael, I appeal to you. I read about B_1 and try it. Immediately this plant shoots up two feet. Now Wernecke claims all the glory for his plant food. It is unreasonable!

WERNECKE: Every time I invent an invention around here somebody makes slams. Give me that begonia. I'll throw it out the window.

ANNABELLA: So, indeed! I will put it in my own sitting-room where you can't ruin it with your plant food. Credit-taker!

(*She glares at him, then takes a chocolate.*)

MICHAEL: (*getting up*) Plant food alone cannot account for this wonderful plant, Mrs. Wernecke. B_1 alone might account for half of it. It is the combination. I am going upstairs. I'll leave it in your sitting-room.

(*With a courtly smile,* MICHAEL *relieves* MRS. WERNECKE *of the begonia plant; goes upstairs.*)

ANNABELLA: (*noticing that* WERNECKE *is grimly starting upstairs with his box*) Where are you taking that?

WERNECKE: To the green room. Intelligent people, like Father LeBeau, are interested—very interested in the things I invent.

(ANNABELLA *gives an elaborate sniff.*)

DINSMORE: I don't suppose you could spare a minute from plant foods and such junk to rent me a room, Wernecke. No time for business, I guess.

ANNABELLA: (*between chocolates*) The yellow room is ready, Wernecke.

WERNECKE: (*pausing at the foot of the stairs*) I'm sorry. I have no rooms.

ANNABELLA: Why, Wernecke!

WERNECKE: (*firmly, though it is an effort*) I have no room for Mr. Dinsmore.

ANNABELLA: Wernecke, the yellow room—

WERNECKE: (*politely*) I'm sorry. You will have to go elsewhere.

DINSMORE: Look here, everybody knows you are not full. That priest and I were the only—

WERNECKE: I own this hotel. Perhaps everybody does not know that.

DINSMORE: Why won't you give me a room?

WERNECKE: (*advancing and speaking in a very gentle voice*) Well, I will tell you. I just don't like you, Mr. Dinsmore. I never have liked you. I never will like you. So, when you ask me for a room, I suddenly decide I have no rooms. Now you know as much about it as I do.

ANNABELLA: Why, Wernecke, you've never acted like this before.

WERNECKE: I know. It surprises me too.

DINSMORE: (*belligerently*) I suppose I can't eat in your lunch room?

WERNECKE: (*considering*) Yes, you may have your supper here.

149

Gwen Pharis Ringwood

ANNABELLA: Wernecke, are you quite well?
WERNECKE: Quite well, Annabella, thank you. You will excuse me,
Mr. Dinsmore.
(*With a little bow he goes through the door leading upstairs.*)
ANNABELLA: (*solemnly*) You shouldn't have called his invention junk,
Mr. Dinsmore. He will be a great man some day. Inventing is a
passion with him, a pure passion.
DINSMORE: What a hotel! What a way to run a business! I'll take away
every customer. . .
(MICHAEL *reappears from upstairs.*)
MICHAEL: Well, the begonia plant is safe in your sitting-room, Mrs.
Wernecke. I put it in the window.
ANNABELLA: Ah! There is a draft in that window. It will freeze. Excuse
me, sir. (*She brushes past* DINSMORE *and hurries out.*)
MICHAEL: Are you fond of begonias, Marie? (*He gets in her way.*)
MARIE: (*moving to the table with two glasses of water*) Of course. But
I am not fond of people who waste my time. Allez!
(*She places the water on the table.*)
MICHAEL: (*in a startled tone*) Marie, let me see the backs of your
hands—quick!
(*Obediently* MARIE *extends her hands, palms down, lifting
startled eyes to his. With a flourish,* MICHAEL *places a glass
of water on each hand and walks off whistling "They're hang-
ing Danny Deever".*)
MARIE: Vous êtes un diable! Take them off, you hear. Take them off
at once.
MICHAEL: Never act without thinking, my pet. You can take my advice
as that of an uncle.
MARIE: Better I have advice from that stuffed caribou! Take them off,
I tell you. . .
DINSMORE: Permit me, Miss Jenvrin. (*He removes the glasses.*) A poor
joke, sir.
MARIE: Thank you. Go now, Michael Lorrigan, or I will throw the
kettle at you.
MICHAEL: 'Twould do less damage than one of your pies, my sweet.
MARIE: You dare! I win prizes for my pie—many times.
MICHAEL: Still, if I want good pie I go to the Chinaman's down the
street.
MARIE: Mon Dieu, listen to him! If I had beautiful, fresh cream from
the cow, monsieur, I could make a pie that would set you dream-
ing of heaven. And a dream is as near as you will get.
MICHAEL: Cream! Listen to her! You're lucky to have cream in tin cans.
MARIE: That! It tastes like gasoline.
MICHAEL: Perhaps you think they should fly a cow in here for you, my
grand lady. That's one thing even you can't have while you stay
in the North, little Buttercup.
MARIE: So, you know everything. I could have a cow next week.

MICHAEL: Indeed! Could you now? (LOUIS HÉBERT *enters with his pails of water.*) Hear that, Louis. Marie Jenvrin can have a cow flown in!

LOUIS: You are only talking, Marie.

MARIE: Fermez la bouche, Louis Hébert.

LOUIS: If you would marry me, we would go outside and Louis Hébert would buy you a cow.

MICHAEL: A grand idea. Marry Louis and go outside!

MARIE: (*goaded beyond all reason*) Marry, marry, marry! I am sick of this talk about marriage. I will marry the man who brings me a cow on the noose to that door there, and no other. I swear it! Now, there is your answer. Get out, all of you!

LOUIS: Do you mean it, Marie—truly? About the cow?

MARIE: I have said it, haven't I?

DINSMORE: Foolishness. What would you feed a cow here?

MARIE: Carrots, monsieur, that I raise in my garden.

DINSMORE: So, you have a garden? Very enterprising.

LOUIS: You bet. Marie is the true French Canadienne. Even in this God-forsaken rock she must have a garden. Seven of us carried dirt in pails from three miles to make a garden for Marie.

MICHAEL: I'm the only free man left in camp.

LOUIS: I will get the cow, Marie, and then we will marry and—

MICHAEL: You take the first 'plane out, Louis. Get yourself to a duck pond. The quacking would be restful after the clacking of her tongue.

LOUIS: You do not insult Marie! We will settle now.

MARIE: You do not, Louis. He would break you in two.

MICHAEL: Hold your whist, Marie Jenvrin. This is men's talk. (*To* LOUIS) Forget it, Louis. I feel no malice toward you.

LOUIS: So, you will not fight. Very well. My honour is satisfied.

MARIE: I die of boredom with all this talk, talk, talk.

LOUIS: I am going now to the Canadian Airways, Marie, to see about the cow.

MARIE: Louis, I didn't mean—

LOUIS: (*exuberantly*) A cow—you will see, it is nothing to Louis Hébert.

MARIE: But Louis—attendez! Vous ne comprenez—

MICHAEL: She's trying to tell you she didn't mean it, Louis. She talks only to fill silence.

MARIE: Who are you to know what I mean? Of course I mean it.

MICHAEL: I suppose then you'd put it in writing?

MARIE: Perhaps I would.

MICHAEL: And sign your name to it? Oh, no my sweet, you are not that foolish!

MARIE: Foolish, is it? You think I could not have a cow. You think no man would care enough to buy a cow for Marie Jenvrin.

Gwen Pharis Ringwood

MICHAEL: Not even enough to buy a teeny weeny little calf.
   (*He measures a calf as big as a mouse.*)
LOUIS: I would, Marie.
MICHAEL: She was only joking, Louis. She knows you can't fly cows
   for nothing.
MARIE: Joking, was I? I will show you (*To* DINSMORE) Give me your
   pencil, monsieur. (*He does so.*) Now, Michael Lorrigan, look with
   your eyes at this. (*She writes on the back of the valentine.*) "I,
   Marie Jenvrin, promise to marry the man who brings a cow to
   Yellowknife to me. Signed, Marie Jenvrin." What do you say now?
MICHAEL: You must have witnesses.
MARIE: (*doubtfully*) And what are those?
DINSMORE: It makes it legal, Miss Jenvrin. See—I write "Witnessed by
   R.S. Dinsmore".
   (*He does so.*)
MICHAEL: (*enjoying himself*) One is not enough.
MARIE: Write your name, Louis. (LOUIS *does so*) So, I do not mean it,
   Monsieur Lorrigan? (*Triumphantly*) Now it is—what you say?
   (*She turns to* DINSMORE.)
DINSMORE: Legal.
MARIE: That's it—legal. I will put it up here. (*She places it in a prominent
   place on the counter. To* MICHAEL.) I expect you feel very small
   now. (*She smiles contentedly, then with a sudden burst of anger,
   leans toward him, measuring with her fingers.*) Like a teeny weeny
   calf, you feel small, I hope.
MICHAEL: (*bursting into a roar of laughter*) Ah, Marie Jenvrin, you
   should listen to your Uncle Michael's advice. All the camp will
   hear of this.
   (*He goes over, gets a newspaper, and sits down to read.*)
LOUIS: I will order a Jersey cow, Marie. They have a very kind face.
   And a Jersey would fly best. They have good digestion.
MARIE: (*crossly*) Always you talk too much, Louis.
LOUIS: Do not argue, chérie. (*He puts on his fine mitts.*) I know many
   brands of cow and the Jersey, it is the kindest. Au'voir, mes amis.
   (*He goes out in high spirits.*)
DINSMORE: What a fool! No wonder he wearies you, Marie.
MARIE: Speak no ill of Louis, monsieur. He is my greatest friend.
DINSMORE: Excuse me. You know, this business of the cow—it isn't so
   foolish as it first appears. There are children in this camp. Parents
   would pay fifty cents a quart for milk for their children. Some
   cows might be a good investment.
MICHAEL: (*looking up from his paper*) You smell money like a rat smells
   cheese, Mr. Dinsmore. Milk for babes seems a little out of your
   line.
DINSMORE: (*getting up*) Look here, Lorrigan, a man can express an
   opinion. You will excuse me, Marie. I'll be back later.
   (*He puts on his coat.*)

MARIE: Very well.

DINSMORE: Perhaps you will reconsider my invitation to the moving picture?

MARIE: Perhaps—in one hundred thousand leap years!

DINSMORE: These young girls must have their jokes, eh, Lorrigan?

MICHAEL: Be on your way, sir. Miss Jenvrin is busy.

DINSMORE: She is happiest when busy, I see that. And it is charming, Marie, charming.

(He goes out, highly pleased with his compliment.)

MICHAEL: *(muttering to himself)* Blatherskite! A havering blatherskite.

(There is a moment's silence while MARIE continues setting the table and MICHAEL reads his paper. MARIE takes up a heavy coal bucket and starts to put some in the stove.)

MICHAEL: *(angrily)* Here you, put that down. *(He gets up and takes the heavy bucket from her.)* Have you no more sense than a daft mud-hen?

(He puts the coal in the stove as MARIE moves out of the way.)

MARIE: To whom do you speak, monsieur?

MICHAEL: To a lass who will sell herself for a cow on a noose—and all because a poor Irish hard-rocker says her pie is not so good as the Chinaman's down the street.

MARIE: Keep your tongue to yourself, Michael Lorrigan. You are no more to me than—than a mouse in a field!

MICHAEL: Never mind, little bird. Perhaps old Dinsmore will have a fine cow flown in for you.

MARIE: *(startled)* Oh, no!

MICHAEL: *(returning to his chair)* Why not? He's pinched his ill-gotten pennies till he's squeezed dollars out of them.

MARIE: But Michael, he's old. And there is greed in his face.

MICHAEL: Then I'll lend the money to Louis Hébert. You shall have your cow.

MARIE: *(stung by his indifference)* To hear you boast of lending money is to hear wind in an empty chimney. Have I not heard how Michael Lorrigan gets drunk on a Saturday and gives his money to the Indians?

MICHAEL: Better an Indian papoose should have it than a French vixen!

MARIE: How dare you call names at me, Marie Jenvrin!

MICHAEL: *(genuinely angry)* Who are you to say whether I can lend two hundred dollars or not? So, you think I'm a no-good wanderer with no thought for day after tomorrow? I'll show you. I'll lend the money to Black Oscar. Then you'll have to marry him and live in that dirty shack with eighteen huskies.

MARIE: I will marry whom I choose.

MICHAEL: Did you or did you not promise to marry the man who brings you a cow?

MARIE: *(close to tears)* You drove me to it, by your insults.

Gwen Pharis Ringwood

MICHAEL: I thought it time you were taught a lesson. The world is not
   your oyster, my pretty goose.
MARIE: (*shouting*) Take yourself out of the door! For a million dollars
   every day in golden money I wouldn't have you around for an
   hour. You and your two hundred dollars! Two hundred cents is
   more like it—and that is more than you are worth!
MICHAEL: (*at the door*) If I had two hundred dollars and I have, I tell
   you, I wouldn't marry you if I got a gold brick for a premium.
MARIE: Or I you for *two* gold bricks.
   (FATHER LEBEAU *comes in. He looks at the two reproachfully.*)
FATHER LEBEAU: Children, children!
MARIE: He could do penance for twenty years, Father, and not receive
   forgiveness for the wickedness of his tongue.
MICHAEL: Have I or have I not two hundred dollars Father? Am I one
   to scatter money to the waves? Answer me that!
FATHER LEBEAU: Marie! Michael! This is no way. . . Control your—
MICHAEL: Control! I have not lost my temper in ten years—but
   this—this—
MARIE: Make him go away, Father. How can you stand up for him?
   He falls asleep at mass, I've seen him.
MICHAEL: Don't worry, I'm going, and if I never come back it is too
   soon—I mean soon enough. You hear me—never!
   (*He takes up his cap and miner's lamp and goes out.*)
MARIE: (*following him*) Go, go, go! I would rather see the back of your
   heels than the face of a blessed angel!
FATHER LEBEAU: (*as* MICHAEL *closes the door*) Marie, it is not good
   to get so angry.
MARIE: I am sorry, Father, if I blasphemed.
   (*She is very meek.*)
FATHER LEBEAU: (*who has been looking at the document*) What is this?
   "I, Marie Jenvrin, promise to marry. . ." (*He reads the rest in
   silence.*) Marie!
MARIE: (*a little frightened at his disapproval*) That Michael, Père LeBeau,
   he jokes about my pie, and I make a polite wish for cream and—
FATHER LEBEAU: It is not seemly to joke about marriage, Marie.
MARIE: (*anxious to agree*) I know. You should talk gravely to that
   Michael, Father. He causes all this trouble. (*Almost ready to
   weep.*) Now I am in so much of a mix-up and all the camp will
   laugh at Marie Jenvrin. C'est horrible! Already Louis goes to get
   a cow. I wish to die.
FATHER LEBEAU: (*smiling in spite of himself*) Louis would make a good
   husband.
MARIE: But I do not love him.
FATHER LEBEAU: What of Michael Lorrigan? He is a good man.
MARIE: To you, maybe. To me he is a werewolf in a sheepskin.
FATHER LEBEAU: (*patting her shoulder*) Things may arrange themselves,
   my child. It costs much money to bring a cow by 'plane.

MARIE: (*restored to cheerfulness*) Then you are not angry, mon père?

FATHER LeBEAU: No, Marie, but you must guard your tongue more carefully.

(LOUIS HÉBERT *comes in, breathless and disconsolate.*)

LOUIS: Marie, you do not mean it about the cow. It costs two hundred dollars to fly one cow to this place. I have seventeen dollars, Marie.

MARIE: (*smiling radiantly*) I would be a bad wife, Louis. I would throw things and lie in bed in the mornings.

LOUIS: What is it about a cow that you want so much?

MARIE: Cream, mon petit chou, cream. Do not feel bad Louis. Cecile—why, I forgot to tell you—Cecile sends you a scarf. Madame Wernecke has it.

LOUIS: (*stubbornly*) I do not wear it.

MARIE: What are you saying? Cecile has been knitting that scarf for two months. (*Smugly.*) Cecile is a very bad knitter, of course.

LOUIS: (*mumbling*) Always you push, push, push me at Cecile Rideau. Sometime I will allow myself to be pushed. A man can't be strong of mind forever.

(*He is about to go upstairs as* MR. DINSMORE *comes in.*)

DINSMORE: Well, Louis, I hear you had some difficulty with your Jersey.

LOUIS: (*crossly*) Your ears are too long, monsieur.

DINSMORE: Better long ears than a short pocketbook, eh, Father LeBeau?

(*He is very much pleased with himself.*)

LOUIS: (*going out*) Scarves. I hate scarves!

DINSMORE: Marie, my girl, everything has been arranged for your satisfaction.

MARIE: I do not understand you, monsieur.

DINSMORE: No need to be coy with me, young lady. You'll be in charge of the restaurant.

MARIE: You must be mad. I work in nobody's restaurant unless it pleases me.

DINSMORE: Of course not, until we are married.

MARIE: Married? I—marry you?

DINSMORE: I have paid the money and you are to have your cow. I wired for it to come on Monday. We will sell milk at fifty cents—

MARIE: (*stricken*) You—you have bought a cow?

DINSMORE: To be flown in on the next 'plane. Two hundred dollars, it cost me, above the price of the cow, but we will soon make it up.

MARIE: Oh, no! Father—

DINSMORE: Two hundred dollars is a lot of money, but I am not worried.

MARIE: Monsieur, you did not understand. I was joking. I—

DINSMORE: I believe in striking while the iron's hot.

MARIE: Monsieur, you make a big mistake. I have no wish to marry—

FATHER LeBEAU: Surely you are not serious, Mr. Dinsmore. After all—

155

DINSMORE: Marie swore to marry the man who brings a cow to Yellowknife. I am doing this. We can be married on Tuesday.

MARIE: (*frightened and pleading*) Please, monsieur, it was a foolish vow. You would not want me for a wife. My temper—it is very bad—

DINSMORE: So was the first Mrs. Dinsmore's. Temper never bothers me. Perhaps you'd like to come in on Sunday to clean up our rooms a bit.

MARIE: Never.

DINSMORE: I've got an idea. I'll just run over to my shop and get you a ring—to wear until Tuesday.

MARIE: I won't have your ring.

DINSMORE: Now, now, no need to be foolish. We'll make our fortune, my girl, our fortune.

(*He turns to go.* MRS. WERNECKE *comes downstairs.*)

ANNABELLA: I'll give you a hand with supper, Marie.

DINSMORE: I've just done the Beaverlodge Hotel out of a good cook, Mrs. Wernecke. But to the victor the spoils, eh, Father?

(*He goes out the door at the rear.*)

MARIE: (*sinking down in a disconsolate heap*) Oh, I am so much a fool! Qu'est-ce que je vais faire? Qu'est-ce que je vais faire?

ANNABELLA: Marie, you are crying. What has happened?

MARIE: Oh, je suis désolée. Je veux mourir.

FATHER LeBEAU: (*worried*) Come, Marie, you mustn't cry. We must think. You see, Mrs Wernecke, Marie made a foolish vow to marry the man who brings her a cow.

(*He hands* ANNABELLA *the document.*)

ANNABELLA: A cow? Here?

MARIE: And that Dinsmore has bought one. Oh, I wish to die, somewhere in the snow—alone!

FATHER LeBEAU: If only you hadn't signed a paper!

ANNABELLA: Don't cry, Marie, Wernecke is clever. He will help us.

MARIE: Nobody can help. I have nobody, nothing. I will be a prisoner in those awful rooms of Dinsmore.

ANNABELLA: You shall not, Marie. Wernecke will—

MARIE: There is no time. Even now he brings me a ring. My heart is broken, broken.

FATHER LeBEAU: You might get into a rage, Marie, and throw things until he is frightened to marry you. (*Apologetically.*) It is only a suggestion.

MARIE: The vow is—what they call—legal. Oh, mon cœur, mon cœur!

(LOUIS *comes rushing in in great excitement, followed by* MR. WERNECKE.)

LOUIS: Marie! Monsieur Wernecke has invented the most beautiful, the most wonderful machinery. It is machinery to make cream. He gives it to me for you!

WERNECKE: That is the surprise, Marie.

LOUIS: Give me some canned milk and some butter. I will show you. Now we can be married, Marie.

(*He waves the cream-maker aloft.*)

WERNECKE: (*as excited as* LOUIS) I make it from Mr. Beasley's directions.

LOUIS: He says you can't tell the cream from a cow's.

MARIE: (*wailing*) Never say "cow" to me again. I hate cows. I wish they would never let any cow grow up to have horns.

WERNECKE: Marie—

LOUIS: Ma belle, you have tears—

ANNABELLA: Wernecke, read this.

(*She hands him the paper.*)

LOUIS: Don't you want to see this machinery make cream, Marie?

MARIE: He talks of cream machinery, when my heart breaks. That is friendship.

WERNECKE: (*puzzling over the document*) But I don't—

ANNABELLA: Dinsmore, Wernecke, Dinsmore is having a cow flown in. He wants to marry Marie.

LOUIS: Dinsmore! (*He looks tragically at* MARIE.) Oh, ma petite!

WERNECKE: Now I know why I don't like that man. We must stop this.

ANNABELLA: What can we do?

WERNECKE: I could dig a deep pit and cover it with snow. Then he would come along, just walking, and—

ANNABELLA: You can't dig pits in rock.

MARIE: I will take one dog and a sled and run away to the barren lands. I will not stop till I get to the Northern lights.

LOUIS: You would freeze to death, Marie. That would be suicide. Nobody likes to commit suicide.

ANNABELLA: Are you sure this is legal?

MARIE: Two witnesses makes it legal.

ANNABELLA: Maybe it doesn't. Louis, go upstairs and look in the Encyclopedia. Find out what makes a thing legal.

LOUIS: I will. (*He runs over and kisses* MARIE'S *hand.*) I will save you, Marie. (*As he goes.*) Louis Hébert will save you.

(DINSMORE *comes in from outside.*)

DINSMORE: Well, Marie, I have brought the ring. Come, my dear, give me your hand.

MARIE: No, no, I won't!

DINSMORE: It is a real diamond. Not one of the imitations.

MARIE: Monsieur, let kindness melt the rock of your heart. I do not want a ring or a cow or to get married. I want only to be left alone.

DINSMORE: I spend two hundred and fifty dollars on you and you refuse your part of the bargain. It is too late, my girl.

MARIE: You cannot force me to keep such a bargain.

DINSMORE: Can't I? I have bought the cow. That makes me your affianced husband.

MARIE: I will enter a convent.

DINSMORE: You will keep your promise or I will have a lawsuit.

MARIE: Go away. I—I hate you!

WERNECKE: I warn you, I am inventing a way to stop this.

DINSMORE: You and your inventions! I don't move a step from here unless this woman keeps her bargain, or pays me the two hundred and fifty dollars I have spent.

(MICHAEL LORRIGAN *comes in in a shining white shirt, holding a magazine in his hand.*)

MARIE: Michael—

DINSMORE: Pay me the two hundred and fifty dollars or marry me. That is your choice.

MARIE: But I never saw so much money.

DINSMORE: Then we will be married on Tuesday.

MICHAEL: (*sternly*) What's this, Mr. Dinsmore? What is your trouble?

DINSMORE: Trouble? I have no trouble. I bought this woman a cow. Now she refuses to keep her bargain. I'll take it to the law, I tell you.

MICHAEL: Just a minute, Mr. Dinsmore. I wouldn't be so sure.

DINSMORE: You keep out of things that aren't your business. She marries me or pays me the money.

MARIE: Help me, Michael; don't make me marry him.

MICHAEL: But I thought you wanted to marry a man who would buy you a cow, Marie.

MARIE: It was my temper, Michael. Help me, please, Michael.

MICHAEL: You signed the paper, Marie.

MARIE: I didn't mean—

MICHAEL: And there were witnesses. To make it legal.

MARIE: I was only a foolish girl. I am suffering now. See, how I suffer!

MICHAEL: Still, this paper—

DINSMORE: I warn you, Miss Jenvrin, as he says—it is legal. You can't cheat me. Either you pay me the money or—

MICHAEL: Pay you nothing Mr. Dinsmore. (*He tears up the document.*) That's enough!

DINSMORE: I'll take this to the law, I tell you.

MICHAEL: Listen, you black-hearted, tight-fisted, penny-pinching blackguard, you'll take nothing to the law. I've had my eye on you since you hit this camp. (*He puts his hand on* DINSMORE'S *arm.*) You paid Carl Swanson seventy-five dollars for a claim that may be worth thousands, and he so drunk he didn't know what he was signing. You'd be wise to hand over that paper to me now.

DINSMORE: What paper?—I don't know what you're talking about.

MICHAEL: (*tightening his grip*) No? Hand it over, Dinsmore. I'm not fooling.

DINSMORE: You've no right—(*He winces.*) All right, let go of me. (MICHAEL *releases him.*) There it is—for what it's worth. There's no gold on that claim.

MICHAEL: That's his business. Now you get out.

DINSMORE: I warn you, I'll have the law on you all. I'll see you in jail for this—

MICHAEL: You won't bother us again. You'll take the next 'plane out of here and stay out or you'll answer to me. And I'm the champion boxer in Great Bear Camp, Mr. Dinsmore.

DINSMORE: You can't do this. I'm a citizen of this—

MICHAEL: (*suddenly picking him up and taking him to the door at the rear*) We can do with one less citizen like you. (*He tosses him out the door. Closing it, he returns nonchalantly.*) He made a big hole in the snowbank. Now, maybe I can read my paper in peace. (*He settles down comfortably by the fire.*)

MARIE: Merci, mille fois, monsieur. You were very quick and very kind.

MICHAEL: Don't get ideas in your head. I threw him out on general principles and to save the claim of my friend, Carl Swanson, who when drunk has less brains even than Marie Jenvrin. Now, don't bother me, I'm reading.

FATHER LEBEAU: (*sitting*) Well, I am quite exhausted. I'll soon be ready for some of your pie, Marie.

MICHAEL: (*as if the subject had never come up before*) Say, Father, if you want good pie you ought to try Long Jim's. Best pie I ever ate.

MARIE: Mon Dieu, listen to him! I can't think. I cannot put on my lip rouge. I cannot speak English. I cannot cook. Nothing I do is good.

MICHAEL: (*calmly*) That's right. You're a bad-tempered, wilful, brat with no mind of what you want. Crying for a cow like a baby for the moon. There's three hundred dollars. Now don't say Michael Lorrigan never saves any money. You buy your cow and live alone in your garden and frighten the children with your sputtering.

(*He places a roll of bills on the counter before her.*)

MARIE: Three hundred dollars! You insult me with your money.

MICHAEL: I give it to you, with no strings attached—except peace from your havering.

MARIE: Oh, you are a—a devil! I call all the saints in heaven to see how I treat your money! (*She throws it at him.*) Take it—and take that, too, you—you—blatherskite!

(*She takes up a dipper of water and throws it over him.*)

ANNABELLA: Marie!

FATHER LEBEAU: Child, you mustn't—

MICHAEL: (*very quietly*) So, you threw water on me. You spoiled my clean shirt that I ironed myself. All right, Marie Jenvrin.—Now none of you interfere, you understand.

MARIE: What are you going to do? I—I didn't mean—

MICHAEL: I'm going to give you something you've needed for a long time. I'm lucky to find a weapon at hand.

(*He rolls up a magazine.*)

MARIE: Father!

Gwen Pharis Ringwood

FATHER LEBEAU: Michael, this is not—
MICHAEL: I said there's to be no interfering, Father. (*He takes up*
    MARIE *as if she were a flour sack and puts her over his knee.*) I'll
    give you twenty. One for each year. You can count them in
    French if you like. One!
        (*There is a resounding smack.*)
MARIE: Ouch! You let me go, Michael Lorrigan. Let me go!
        (*She kicks vigorously.*)
MICHAEL: Two, three, four, five—
MARIE: Ow! Diable! Father, he's hurting me. I'll bite your hand off—
MICHAEL: Six, seven, eight—
MARIE: Mon Dieu, he's killing me. You let him kill me!
MICHAEL: Nine, ten, eleven—Ouch, you vixen, would you take a piece
    out of my knee? Twelve, thirteen, fourteen—
MARIE: Enough, enough! I will never be angry again. I will—(*She beats
    on him.*) Fiend, devil, put me down, I tell you! I tell you!
MICHAEL: Fifteen, sixteen—
        (LOUIS HÉBERT *comes in carrying a very large book.*)
LOUIS: The Encyclopedia says—(*He stops short.*) Marie!
        (*He starts towards* MARIE *but* ANNABELLA *stops him.*)
ANNABELLA: No, Louis. Stay there.
        (LOUIS *starts to go on, but* FATHER LEBEAU *lays his hand on
        his shoulder.*)
FATHER LEBEAU: She is right, Louis. It is better so.
MICHAEL: Eighteen, nineteen, twenty. There! (*He sets* MARIE *on her
    feet.*) Now pick up that money and put it in a tidy roll.
MARIE: (*in a small voice*) I won't.
MICHAEL: What's that you say?
MARIE: Yes, Michael.
        (*She kneels to take up the bills. There is a pause.*)
ANNABELLA: (*suddenly decisive*) Wernecke, go and get the mail.
WERNECKE: Yes, Annabella. (*He goes quietly.*)
ANNABELLA: And, Father, you and Louis must come up to see the
    begonia plant. It has grown so you wouldn't know it.
FATHER LEBEAU: Yes. It's amazing how the begonia plant grows, Mrs.
    Wernecke.
        (*He follows her toward the door.*)
ANNABELLA: Come, Louis.
LOUIS: Marie, do you want me to look at the begonia plant?
MARIE: (*gently*) It is better so, Louis.
LOUIS: Très bien, Marie. I am—sorry—
        (LOUIS, *as he turns, starts winding a scarf around his neck*).
MARIE: What is that on your neck, Louis?
LOUIS: It is the scarf that Cecile knit for me.
MARIE: (*sadly*) C'est bon. You look very handsome. Cecile will
    be—proud.

160

LOUIS: Father—Mrs. Wernecke—wait for me. I come to look at the begonia.
> (*He follows the procession out sadly. There is a painful pause. MARIE puts the money into a neat roll and tidies herself a little. MICHAEL continues to read.*)

MARIE: (*in a very little voice*) I have picked up the money, Michael.

MICHAEL: Good.

MARIE: I feel very small.
> (*She measures.*)

MICHAEL: (*without looking up*) Good.

MARIE: Michael,—that spanking you gave me. It hurt me very bad.

MICHAEL: (*still reading*) Very good.

MARIE: (*drawing a little nearer, shyly*) Michael, was that—would you say that was the spanking of an—uncle?

MICHAEL: (*looking at her doubtfully*) What else? What other kind of spanking would it be?

MARIE: (*very small*) It is strange. I only thought—It reminds me so much of the spanking my sister Rose receives from her—husband.

MICHAEL: Indeed.

MARIE: (*daring a quivering little smile*) It wouldn't be that kind, would it, Michael?

MICHAEL: And if it were? What would you have to say? (*He gets up and puts down his newspaper.*) Come here and tell me.

MARIE: (*approaching a few steps*) I am here, Michael.

MICHAEL: Well! You're a small thing to cause a man's heart to flutter. But Michael Lorrigan is no coward. Look at me, Marie Jenvrin. (*He smiles at her as he tilts her chin up.*) Will we be getting married before the lenten season?

MARIE: (*burying her head in his shoulder*) Michael, Michael, I'm crying—

MICHAEL: You've had a hard day. (*He dries her eyes with his handkerchief.*) Come, now. Shall we buy a cow with the money there?

MARIE: Non, non. I never want to see a cow! But Mr. Wernecke will make us a cream machine, and we will buy a little house with the money.

MICHAEL: 'Tis settled, then. We'll tell Father tonight. One more thing: I'm to be boss in the household, Marie Jenvrin. There'll be no doubt of that. You understand. None of this "Michael this, and Michael that."

MARIE: Oui, I understand.

MICHAEL: Good.
> (*He kisses her lightly. Her hand goes up to trace his kiss as she looks at him.*)

MARIE: (*with a sigh*) Michael—

MICHAEL: You're happy, Marie Jenvrin?

MARIE: I'm so happy—I could—(*She searches for words.*) I could eat up the sky! (*Breaking away.*) But it is near supper time. I must hurry.

161

Gwen Pharis Ringwood

MICHAEL: I'll get a fresh shirt.
> (*He turns to go.*)

MARIE: Michael, if it would not be—if you don't mind—you see, the wood box—it is entirely empty. And it is so late, I thought—

MICHAE:L (*unaware of the web into which he has fallen*) Sure, I'll fill it for you, Marie. No trouble at all.
> (FATHER LeBEAU *appears in the doorway. They do not see him.* MARIE *runs to* MICHAEL *with the box. As she gives it to him she lays her head against his shoulder for a moment.*)

MARIE: You will be a wonderful husband, Michael. (*Her eyes are shining as she looks into the future.*) I know it!
> (FATHER LeBEAU *smiles benignly.*)

The End

The Jack And The Joker
A play about Bob Edwards

Characters

BOB EDWARDS
CLARIBELLE GUDGEON
DORINDA FOGGIN
DUDLEY B. CARP
FLORENCE WIZE
JAMES FOGGIN

SCENE: *The office of the Sheep Creek Eye Opener.*
TIME: *A June morning, 1904.*

The office of the Sheep Creek Eye Opener is far from richly appointed. The furniture consists of a large desk, a swivel chair, one or two other chairs, and a coat rack and sofa of the period, all torn and mended. There are cartoons, calendars, etc. on the walls. In the rear wall, left of centre, is a door leading into the press room and down right is a door leading outside. There is a window on the right wall.

At the beginning of the play BOB EDWARDS *is seated at his desk, writing and trying over his sentences to himself.*

EDWARDS: "Let me frolic with the Jack and the Joker and still win the game. Let me. . . .

    (MRS. GUDGEON *enters. She is an old lady, her joints are stiffened with rheumatism. She wears rusty black clothes and an outlandish hat. She comes in and immediately begins "doing up" the room.*)

MRS. GUDGEON: Good morning, Mr. Edwards.

Gwen Pharis Ringwood

EDWARDS: Morning, Mrs. Gudgeon.
MRS. GUDGEON: Have you got the paper out?
EDWARDS: It will be out by noon.
MRS. GUDGEON: Is the press working?
EDWARDS: Fine. I'm going to pay for it one of these days.
MRS. GUDGEON: I know that, sir. Mr. Edwards, the ladies are very
 upset about your paper.
EDWARDS: What ladies?
MRS. GUDGEON: The Lotus Club.
EDWARDS: Don't they think my jokes are funny, Mrs. Gudgeon?
MRS. GUDGEON: The jokes are funny, lad, but the ladies feel they're
 immoral and unrefined. They're coming to see you this morning,
 sir.
EDWARDS: You keep an eye on the street and we'll hide.
MRS. GUDGEON: Mrs. Carp in particular, she's very angry. You didn't
 ought to make fun of Dudley Carp, Mr. Edwards, he's considered
 a very upright man.
EDWARDS: He's fleeced people right and left for years.
MRS. GUDGEON: Mr. Carp's been most kind to me, Sir. Got me the job
 of doing for the church and this place after Mr. Gudgeon died.
 And he helped me invest my insurance money.
EDWARDS: What did you invest in, Mrs. Gudgeon?
MRS. GUDGEON: (Proudly) City lots. I've got three. Very high priced
 they'll be too in a year or so.
EDWARDS: You bought them from Mr. Carp?
MRS. GUDGEON: I paid a hundred dollars each. Mr. Carp sold them to
 me cheap—as a token of esteem, he said.
EDWARDS: I see.
MRS. GUDGEON: So of course it hurts me, lad, to see you using my
 poor dead husband's printing press to make fun of Mr. Carp—
 especially when he's going to run for parliament and all.
EDWARDS: Mrs. Gudgeon, could I see the deeds to your property?
MRS. GUDGEON: Why, yes. I'll get them.
 (Puts down broom.)
EDWARDS: I don't think the bank's open yet.
MRS. GUDGEON: Oh, I wouldn't keep them in the bank. I don't trust
 banks. I just keep them in my—in my stocking. If you'll excuse
 me—
 (She goes behind coat rack.)
EDWARDS: Do you really want to see Mr. Carp in the legislature, Mrs.
 Gudgeon?
MRS. GUDGEON: Oh, yes. He makes such fine speeches. A golden
 tongue, he has. A real golden tongue. (She returns with the deeds.)
 There they are, sir.
EDWARDS: A 21367, 68 and 69. (He scans deed) Have you ever seen this
 property?
MRS. GUDGEON: Oh, no! I never get to the city, but I'm going to sell

the lots next year and retire from charring. My rheumatism's
pretty bad lately.

EDWARDS: How can you retire, Mrs. Gudgeon? I need you to help me
establish a real Western paper here in Sheep Creek.

MRS. GUDGEON: That's kind of you. The late Mr. Gudgeon had just
such a notion. We tried eleven towns before Mr. Gudgeon decided
the times just weren't ripe for it. So then he opened a livery.

EDWARDS: (*Writing down the numbers*) A 21367, 68 and 69. I
wonder. . . . (*Getting up*) Mrs. Gudgeon, I'll leave you to the
cobwebs. I'm going to send a telegram.

MRS. GUDGEON: About my lots, sir?

EDWARDS: Yes. . . . just to make sure where they are. I may buy some
myself.

MRS. GUDGEON: But what about the paper?

EDWARDS: (*Getting hat*) The paper will have to wait. Perhaps I'll have
a real story for the ladies.

MRS. GUDGEON: (*At door*) Heaven help us, Mr. Edwards, here they
come now!

EDWARDS: Who?

MRS. GUDGEON: Mrs. Carp and Mrs. Foggin. Looking very determined.

EDWARDS: We're trapped, Mrs. Gudgeon. We'll have to shoot it out.

MRS. GUDGEON: Now, Mr. Edwards, don't let them browbeat you.
(MRS. CARP and MRS. FOGGIN *enter.* DORINDA CARP *is an
arrogant, somewhat affected woman who has always been
able to have her own way. She talks down to everyone unless
it suits her to cajole.* MRS. FOGGIN *is a milder person with a
penchant for ribbons and laces and a heart that thirsts for
romance. She is afraid of Mrs. Carp.*)

DORINDA: I presume you are Mr. Edwards. We've come here on
behalf of the Sheep Creek Lotus Club.

EDWARDS: (*With a touch of exaggeration in his courtesy*) Ladies, come
in. I too enjoy my Tennyson.

"Your looks are strange
And do you come like ghosts to trouble joy?"

MRS. FOGGIN: Mr. Edwards, you've been drinking!

EDWARDS: Mrs. Foggin, I never drink before ten o'clock.
(*Looking at watch.*)

DORINDA: We've come to tell you what we think of you and your Eye
Opener. We intend to have your paper stopped, Mr. Edwards.

EDWARDS: Why, thank you, Mrs. Carp. Please sit down.

DORINDA: At a special meeting of the Club at my house. . . .

EDWARDS: Ladies, forgive me. I just remembered—I have to send a
telegram. Please make yourselves comfortable until I come back.
(*At the door*) Sorry, I can't offer you tea, but you might find a wee
nip of Scotch in the desk.
(*He goes out right.*)

DORINDA: Well, really—so that's how he receives us.

BERTHA: I told you we should lead up to it gradually, Dorinda.

DORINDA: Oh, you're so spineless, Bertha. Mrs. Gudgeon!

MRS. GUDGEON: (*Jumps startled—she has been dusting around the hat rack.*) Yes, Ma'am.

DORINDA: Come here.

MRS. GUDGEON: (*Straightening her hat and apron to a worse angle than before.*) Yes, Mrs. Carp.

DORINDA: Do you think the church board would approve of your working for a wine-bibber?

MRS. GUDGEON: Mr. Edwards is a nice gentleman, Ma'am.

DORINDA: Gentleman, indeed! Do you know anything about the company he keeps?

MRS. GUDGEON: I don't really, Ma'am. Of course he and Mr. Foggin are good friends. . . .

DORINDA: What did I tell you, Bertha? Did you say James was out until two o'clock last night?

BERTHA: I'm sure Jimmy could explain. . . .

DORINDA: Of course. They always can! (MRS. GUDGEON *turns to go back to her work.*) Just a minute, Mrs. Gudgeon. Does Mr. Edwards know any women?

MRS. GUDGEON: Well, he knows me.

DORINDA: I meant younger women.

MRS. GUDGEON: He's a great friend of that nice, stylish Mrs. Wize. . . . He calls her Florence.

DORINDA: Does he go there often?

MRS. GUDGEON: Oh, no, just now and then.

DORINDA: You may go, Mrs. Gudgeon.

MRS. GUDGEON: Yes, Ma'am.

(*She goes out door at back*)

DORINDA: You see, Bertha—he brought that woman to Sheep Creek.

BERTHA: Mrs. Wize? Why, she's selling hats, Dorinda.

DORINDA: Hmmmm? She'll sell no hats to me.

BERTHA: (*Her voice lowered*) You don't think she's a. . . . bad woman?

DORINDA: I do. Did you ever see a respectable married woman wearing silk stockings?

BERTHA: Perhaps her husband is rich. . . .

DORINDA: Mrs. Wize has been here ten days and there's been no sign of a husband, day or night. I think she's an adventuress, working with Edwards.

BERTHA: Really. I read a story about an adventuress once. . . . (*There is a touch of wistfulness in her voice.*) A widow in France.

DORINDA: (*Sniffing*) France!

BERTHA: Everyone spurned her but she had a loving heart.

DORINDA: There may be room in those foreign countries for widows with loving hearts. There is no room in Sheep Creek.

BERTHA: Sometimes I think a little adventure adds spice to life. That's why I didn't mind the Eye Opener. . . .

DORINDA: You read it, Bertha?

BERTHA: Well, Jimmy says Mr. Edwards has a lot of good sense. . . . and that most of the stories he prints are true. . . .

DORINDA: (*Coldly*) I suppose you believe his attacks on Dudley.

BERTHA: Oh no, I'm sure Mr. Carp wouldn't. . . .

DORINDA: (*Closing in*) While Bob Edwards stays here, Dudley will not get into parliament. You want my husband to sit in parliament, don't you, Bertha?

BERTHA: (*Weakly*) Oh yes, of course. I think it would be lovely. (*With a touch of hope*) You'd be leaving then, wouldn't you, Dorinda?

DORINDA: We'd move on. . . . to wider fields, greener pastures. . . . certainly. Dudley and I have planned that you shall visit us, Bertha, on Parliament Hill.

BERTHA: You're very kind. (*At the window*) Dorinda, come here! There's Mr. Carp talking to Mrs. Wize. He knows her, Dorinda. So she can't be a bad. . . .

DORINDA: What's that? (*Going to the window*) Dudley. . . . So he is. Probably trying to collect her rent.

BERTHA: (*With a little squeal of excitement*) Dorinda, he kissed her hand. (*Enviously*) She does have a way with the men.

DORINDA: Kissed her hand. (*Going to the door*) Dudley! Dudley! Please come here. . . . at once!

BERTHA: (*Round eyed*) What are you going to do, Dorinda?

DORINDA: I'm going to have Bob Edwards and that woman out of this town if it's the last thing I do.

BERTHA: I don't blame you, kissing her hand and all. But that's hardly Mr. Edward's fault.

DORINDA: He brought her here. Introduced her hat shop in his paper. He's demoralizing this town. . . . and I won't have it!

BERTHA: (*At table, noticing a piece of writing on desk*) Here's something about Mr. Carp. . . . (*starting to read*) "Dudley Carp has just returned from Ottawa where we presume he successfully bartered the interests of the West for the interests of Dudley B. Carp. In our opinion. . . ."

DORINDA: (*Snatching the paper from her*) I'll take care of that.

(DUDLEY CARP *enters. He is a rather handsome, well-dressed and pompous man of forty odd. . . . very sure of himself and completely insensitive to other people.*)

DUDLEY: Dorinda, what are you doing in this place?

DORINDA: I'm doing more than you are, Dudley. I'm looking after your interests.

DUDLEY: Now, Dorinda. . . .

DORINDA: Did you or did you not kiss that woman's hand?

DUDLEY: I kiss the hands of all fair ladies, Dorinda. It's a matter of policy. Allow me, Mrs. Foggin. . . .

(*He kisses her hand.*)

BERTHA: (*Giggling*) Oh Mr. Carp, I feel quite continental.

167

Gwen Pharis Ringwood

DORINDA: Dudley is merely electioneering, Bertha. There won't be an election for you, Dudley, if we don't get this paper stopped!

DUDLEY: One must be subtle about these things, Dorinda. Where is Edwards, anyway?

DORINDA: He sneaked away, afraid to face us. Probably drunk by now. Listen to this: "In our opinion the voters of this constituency would be better advised to elect Jed the Horsethief than Dudley B. Carp. At least they would be prepared for Jed's particular brand of dishonesty". That's to come out today.

BERTHA: Mr. Carp, perhaps if you reasoned with Mr. Edwards, enlightened him. . . .

DUDLEY: You can't reason with a man like Edwards. We must take action.

DORINDA: At once!

DUDLEY: It's not for myself I object to the man. It's for Sheep Creek and for this great country, soon to become a province, soon to blaze as another jewel in the crown of the Dominion.

DORINDA: You said last night you'd like to see him tarred and feathered and ridden out of town on a rail. Why don't you do it?

DUDLEY: My dear, I could stamp out this man, single handed. But if I do, the voters may believe his lies about me. No, it is not for me. . . . you must do it. You. . . . the women, the guardians of virtue and purity.

DORINDA: How?

DUDLEY: Edwards uses a printing press that belongs to old Gudgeon.

DORINDA: Well?

DUDLEY: I happen to know he hasn't paid a cent on the press.

DORINDA: Naturally.

DUDLEY: You ladies get hold of Mrs. Gudgeon and talk her into selling the press to the Lotus Club for cash. I'll pay $200.00 for it but I want my name kept out of it.

BERTHA: Won't Mr. Edwards just buy another?

DUDLEY: He hasn't ten cents in his pocket. He invested everything he had in starting up the paper. If the press goes, Edwards goes. . . .

DORINDA: Dudley that's just splendid!

BERTHA: Mrs Gudgeon wouldn't sell the press—if she's promised Mr. Edwards. . . .

DUDLEY: Doesn't she live in a shack owned by the Club?

DORINDA: Of course she does. Very well Dudley. You can leave this to me.

DUDLEY: Here's the money. . . . my gift to the fair ladies of Sheep Creek.

DORINDA: Clubs like ours must take a firm stand on moral issues, Bertha. (*She takes the money*) Without us where would morality be?

BERTHA: (*Weakly but doubtfully*) I suppose there wouldn't be any.

DORINDA: I'd better see Mrs. Gudgeon at the church. He might come back. Well, when we get the press out of here I'll be very happy.

Very happy. We have great plans for Alberta, haven't we Dudley?

DUDLEY: Great plans. I want to see this country blossom and bear fruit. I want to see our new virginal province rise unsullied and unstained. When Alberta receives its charter, it must be without such papers as the Eye Opener, without alcohol, and without Bob Edwards.

EDWARDS: (*Entering from the street*) Show me the province without alcohol, Mr. Carp, and I promise you it will be without Edwards. Well, well, quite a gathering—is it lambs to the slaughter or vultures to the kill?

DUDLEY: Has it occurred to you, Edwards, that I might sue you for libel for stuff like this?
(*He holds up the paper read earlier.*)

EDWARDS: Charmed, any time, I'm sure. You see, Dudley, I don't want to see you representing us in government.

DUDLEY: I suppose you have ambitions. . . .

EDWARDS: None. I'm a nobody. The gadfly of Sheep Creek, that's all.

DUDLEY: Do the ranchers pay you for opposing me?

EDWARDS: I can't be bought. You ought to know that, Dudley. You tried.

DUDLEY: Nobody believes your stuff. Why, you're nothing but a one-horse publisher who's drunk most of the time.

EDWARDS: It's all right, Dudley. You go right ahead trying to bow yourself into parliament and I'll go on with my paper. But God help you, Dudley, if I stay in Sheep Creek, you won't make the legislature.

DUDLEY: When a two-bit editor can stop me, I'll let you know. . . . if I can find the gutter you're lying in.
(FLORENCE WIZE *enters. She is about twenty-five, gotten up in the extreme of fashion with a few extra touches here and there. Her figure is excellent. Her appearance is lush but she is as ingenuous and trusting as a child.*)

FLORENCE: Good morning Mr. . . . Oh, I beg your pardon. I didn't mean to interrupt anything.

EDWARDS: Come in, Florence.

FLORENCE: (*Talking to cover embarrassment*) We meet again, Mr. Carp. It's a lovely day, isn't it?

DUDLEY: Indeed it is, Mrs. Wize.
(*He is about to kiss her hand in its long lace glove.*)

DORINDA: Dudley!

DUDLEY: Well, I must be running along. You'll attend to that little matter, Dorinda?

DORINDA: I certainly will.
(DUDLEY *goes out to the street*)

EDWARDS: Mrs. Wize, may I present. . . .

DORINDA: (*Icily*) Please don't bother, Mr. Edwards.

169

Gwen Pharis Ringwood

FLORENCE: (*Apologetically*) I shouldn't have broken up your session. You see, I've been in the Klondike and I forget about being formal and all that social swirl.

EDWARDS: No need to be formal, Florence. How's your hat shop going?

FLORENCE: I haven't sold any, Mr. Edwards, but I have some beauties. I hope you ladies are interested in hats, but then I guess every lady is. . . . hats and men. I know I am.

DORINDA: That's obvious. Come, Bertha.

FLORENCE: Don't you folks go. I'll go along myself. I just came here to meet Mr. Foggin.

DORINDA: Mr. Foggin!

FLORENCE: Yes. Little guy—wears glasses.

BERTHA: Well, really. . . .

DORINDA: My poor Bertha. Perhaps you'll believe me now.

BERTHA: Mr. Edwards, tell me the truth. Has Mr. Foggin been here?

EDWARDS: I haven't seen him.

DORINDA: Of course he's here. . . . hiding.

FLORENCE: (*Without malice*) Where would he be, under the sofa?

DORINDA: You'd better look, Bertha.

BERTHA: I won't demean myself. James Foggin come out from under that sofa if you know what's good for you.

FLORENCE: Jumping Juno, I've lost them. . . .

EDWARDS: What is it, Florence?

FLORENCE: I'd forget my head if it. . . . (*gathering up herself to go*) If Mr. Foggin comes before I get back, you tell him I must have left his trousers in the store. . . .

DORINDA: You left his what, Mrs. Wize?

FLORENCE: (*At the door*) Trousers. You know. . . . a pair of pants
          (*She goes*)

BERTHA: Trousers! Oh, Jimmy. . . .
          (*She swoons*)

EDWARDS: (*Catching her*) Here, here, Mrs. Foggin. . . . easy now. . . . Have you any smelling salts, Mrs. Carp.
          (*He places her on the sofa*)

DORINDA: Of course not. I'm not given to swooning.

EDWARDS: I'll send Mrs. Gudgeon in with some water. Cold towels on her head should help.
          (*He goes out back*)

DORINDA: (*Shaking* MRS. FOGGIN *roughly*) Bertha, Bertha, now don't be foolish. Wake up.
          (*She leaves* BERTHA *and gets down on her hands and knees in front of the sofa.*)

DORINDA: Come out, James Foggin. (*With her parcels she pokes under the sofa*) I don't believe he's there. Isn't that just like a man?
          (MRS. GUDGEON *enters from back*)

MRS. GUDGEON: Why, Mrs. Carp, what are you looking for?

DORINDA: A man. But he got away. Oh, it's you.

MRS. GUDGEON: Here's some water. Mr. Edwards said to keep her head down and her feet up.

DORINDA: *(Flipping water on* MRS. FOGGIN*)* Bertha! Bertha! *(to* MRS. GUDGEON*)* Where is Mr. Edwards?

MRS. GUDGEON: He went for Mr. Foggin. Poor lady. . . . whatever happened?

DORINDA: The heat. Stop fussing.

MRS. GUDGEON: Yes, ma'am.

DORINDA: Mrs. Gudgeon, I understand you own a printing press.

MRS. GUDGEON: I do.

(MRS. CARP *starts to sit on sofa and sits on* MRS. FOGGIN)

MRS. GUDGEON: Be careful, ma'am.

DORINDA: *(Ignoring her and pushing* MRS. FOGGIN *over a little)* Now Mrs. Gudgeon, I want to give you two hundred dollars of your very own for the press.

MRS. GUDGEON: I'm selling it to Mr. Edwards, ma'am. I only asked $125.00.

DORINDA: The Lotus Club want that press.

MRS. GUDGEON: I'm sorry, Ma'am.

DORINDA: Edwards doesn't intend to pay you. We won't have him cheating an old woman so we're taking it off your hands.

MRS. GUDGEON: But how would Mr. Edwards print his paper?

DORINDA: That is not your concern. Now I'm just writing out a bill of sale. . . . what is your first name?

MRS. GUDGEON: Claribelle.

DORINDA: You just sign here. Claribelle Gudgeon.

MRS. GUDGEON: Mrs. Carp, I couldn't do that. . . . it wouldn't be right.

DORINDA: Be careful, Mrs. Gudgeon. Remember, we're only trying to help you.

MRS. GUDGEON: I respect agreements.

DORINDA: Are you aware that the Lotus Club owns the shack in which you live?

MRS. GUDGEON: Why no, I. . . . I. . . . I didn't know. . . .

BERTHA: *(Faintly)* Oh. . . . trousers. . . . oh. . . .

DORINDA: Bertha, get hold of yourself. *(With a faint moan* BERTHA *subsides)* Now Mrs. Gudgeon, you've never paid any rent for the house. Seven years rent is not to be sneezed at. If you refuse to sell the press, we'll seize it for back rent.

MRS. GUDGEON: Oh no. . . .

DORINDA: What's more, we'll be forced to put you out.

MRS. GUDGEON: But I haven't any place to go. . . .

DORINDA: You'll be placed in an old ladies' home.

MRS. GUDGEON: Oh no, I couldn't. They wouldn't let me take Timmy. . . . that's my cat. . . . Oh Ma'am you wouldn't do that.

DORINDA: Do you know how much rent you owe us?

MRS. GUDGEON: Nobody ever said anything about rent. It's just a shack.

171

Gwen Pharis Ringwood

DORINDA: Probably a thousand dollars.

MRS. GUDGEON: If I could sell my lots. I'll go ask Mr. Edwards. . . .
(*She starts toward door*)

DORINDA: There's no time for that. Now make up your mind. (*A pause*)
Well, Mrs. Gudgeon?

MRS. GUDGEON: I'll sign whatever it is. I couldn't go to an Old Ladies'
Home. . . . without Timmy.

DORINDA: That's something like.
(MRS. GUDGEON *signs*)

BERTHA: (*Moaning*) Oh, I'm so miserable.

DORINDA: Be quiet, Bertha. There you are, Mrs. Gudgeon, and here's
two hundred dollars all for you. Isn't that wonderful?

MRS. GUDGEON: Would you sell me the shack for two hundred dollars,
Mrs. Carp?

DORINDA: No, no, we just won't say anything more about it.

MRS. GUDGEON: I want to be sure I've got a place of my own. . . . in my
last years. . . .

BERTHA: (*Rallying somewhat*) Dorinda, I didn't know the Lotus Club
owned. . . .

DORINDA: Really, Bertha, how could you? You're not one of our
chartered members. You just go back to your cleaning now Mrs.
Gudgeon.

MRS. GUDGEON: (*Somewhat dazed*) Yes, Ma'am (*She goes out back*)

DORINDA: Well, that's done. Now to dismantle the press. . . . smash it
up if necessary. . . .

BERTHA: (*Woefully*) Oh, I must go and pack. I'm going home to my
mother. . . . after fourteen years.

DORINDA: Don't be a fool, Bertha. You'd just leave him free for his
intrigues. . . . Fight, my dear, fight for the right.

BERTHA: I thought I was a good fighter, but I'm not. . . . I don't
like fighting.
(JAMES FOGGIN *enters. He is a nice ordinary little man who
is both faithful and unimaginative*)

DORINDA: I think you'd be ashamed of yourself. We know why you
came here. We know whom you expected to find.

BERTHA: Jimmy, haven't I been everything to you a wife should be?

JIMMY: Bertha. . . .
(*He is completely at sea*)

BERTHA: Haven't I nursed you through measles. . . .

JIMMY: Mumps, Bertha.

BERTHA: Haven't I helped you cover the cabbages in a hail storm and
mended your socks? Haven't I shared your pillow and baked
your bread. . . .

JIMMY: Bertha, what's come over you?

DORINDA: As if you didn't know. . . . having intrigues under your
poor wife's very eyes. . . .

JIMMY: Bertha, what's happening here? What are you talking about?

172

BERTHA: Jimmy, has this been going on ever since she came to town?

JIMMY: Who came to town?

BERTHA: I'm leaving, Jimmy. I'm going home to mother.

DORINDA: I suppose you asked Edwards to bring her here.

JIMMY: (*Savagely*) Damn it, will you keep quiet and let me talk to my wife.

DORINDA: You dare!

BERTHA: (*Aghast but thrilled*) Jimmy, you swore! You swore at Dorinda Carp!

JIMMY: (*To* BERTHA) Now, Bertha, what's all this about going home to your mother? Bob came to tell me you'd fainted and I rushed on ahead. . . .

BERTHA: (*Sobbing quietly*) To think you'd cast aside fourteen years with me for a woman with silk stockings and ostrich feathers on her hat.

JIMMY: Ostrich feathers! Whose ostrich feathers?

DORINDA: You planned to meet her here this morning.

JIMMY: Meet who?

BERTHA: Florence Wize.

JIMMY: Mrs. Wize. Heavens, I forgot all about that!

BERTHA: See, you admit it.

> (BOB EDWARDS *has entered and is standing quietly in the door smiling*)

EDWARDS: Looks like you're in the soup, Jimmy.

JIMMY: I don't admit anything. Do you think there's something between me and Mrs. Wize? Bertha, you're mad.

BERTHA: With grief, Jimmy.

JIMMY: Ask Bob here. Ask anybody. Why I was only coming here to get my trousers. . . . Mrs. Wize. . . .

BERTHA: Trousers! Oh, Jimmy!

> (*She swoons again. He catches her*)

DORINDA: (*Annoyed as* BERTHA *falls*) There she goes again.

JIMMY: Bertha, Bertha. . . . well do something, somebody. Wait, it's her stays. She always makes me lace them too tight.

> (*He starts unlacing her*)

EDWARDS: Now take it easy, Jimmy. . . . Give her a nip of this. . . .

DORINDA: It's all your fault for bringing that woman here.

EDWARDS: Come now, Mrs. Foggin, just take a little swallow. . . . that's it. . . . Not so bad, is it. Now. . . . just lie back.

BERTHA: (*Fluttering*) Where am I? Jimmy, don't leave me.

JIMMY: I'm not leaving you, Bertha. Now all of you people that are so interested, listen. . . . My trousers were in Mrs. Wize's house. . . . yes. . . . but I wasn't in them.

DORINDA: (*Acidly*) That's quite obvious.

JIMMY: (*Shouting*) I mean I wasn't in her house.

EDWARDS: Let me explain, Jimmy. Mrs Foggin, last night I met Jimmy and talked him into coming into the Blind Pig with me.

173

JIMMY: Bob told a story, Bertha, and I got laughing and I spilled a glass of beer all over my trousers.

EDWARDS: Jimmy was afraid you'd know he'd been drinking beer. . . .

JIMMY: I know you don't like alcohol, Bertha.

EDWARDS: We went outside.

JIMMY: I walked around eating sen sen. I was worried sick. . . .

EDWARDS: For fear you'd smell the beer on his suit.

JIMMY: We saw Mrs. Wize bringing in her clothes off the line.

EDWARDS: I've known Florence since she was a youngster, and I told her our troubles. Florence said she had a pair of trousers that would just fit Jimmy and she'd take his and clean them.

JIMMY: So I went into the Blind Pig and changed.

EDWARDS: And I handed Jimmy's pants over the fence to Florence.

JIMMY: I arranged to pick up the trousers here.

EDWARDS: And that's how it all happened. I swear, Mrs. Foggin.

JIMMY: If you don't believe me, Bertha, I'll. . . . I'll go home to my mother.

DORINDA: A likely story.

BERTHA: Jimmy, that's all there was to it?

JIMMY: Honest, Bertha, that's all.

BERTHA: Oh, Jimmy, next time don't be afraid to come home. Even if you smell of beer. . . . even if you smell of rum, Jimmy, just come home.

(He pats her awkwardly as she melts in his arms. FLORENCE *enters at right)*

FLORENCE: Oh, there you are, Mr. Foggin. I finally found your. . . . oh, she's Mrs. Foggin.

EDWARDS: That's right, Florence.

FLORENCE: Well, *(awkwardly)* well, you see, Mrs. Foggin. . . . this is a. . . . It's a tent I was going to. . . .

EDWARDS: Never mind, Florence. She knows.

FLORENCE: I was trying to help. He must think the world of you to be so upset about a little beer. . . . Here they are.

(Offers the trousers)

BERTHA: Thank you, Mrs. Wize.

DORINDA: Really, Bertha, are you going to forget what you've been through because of this woman? I'm not. Mrs. Wize. . . . we know what you are. . . . you. . . . you husband snatcher!

FLORENCE: You be careful what you call me. I'll tell Bertie. . . .

DORINDA: And who is Bertie?

FLORENCE: Bertie's my husband. He's beat up on a lot of mashers that thought they could get fresh with me and if you've got a husband I bet he could beat him up with one hand. I bet a dame like you hasn't even got a husband.

DORINDA: I do so have one.

FLORENCE: I pity him then. I bet he sleeps under the kitchen stove.

DORINDA: Why, he does not. The idea!

FLORENCE: Mr. Edwards, you told me Sheep Creek was a nice, quiet town where I could settle down and Bertie could come home week-ends. I thought I'd go to church and visit back and forth and belong to things and raise a family. And here you are, a den of suspicious-minded old dames. I'm not even sure I want to raise a family here. . . . (*to* DORINDA) and I think your hat is just awful, so there.

(FLORENCE *turns and goes out in tears.*)

DORINDA: Why this hat cost twenty dollars.

BERTHA: I don't blame her, Dorinda. Of course you were so sure.

DORINDA: I suppose she thinks her hat is stylish.

BERTHA: I'm going to ask her to join the Lotus Club.

DORINDA: You'll do nothing of the kind.

EDWARDS: Now, Mrs. Carp, if Florence wants to belong to the Lotus Club, I think she ought to have the chance.

DORINDA: You're telling me what to do?

EDWARDS: Just suggesting.

DORINDA: Hmmmmm!

EDWARDS: I suppose I could write a story about how exclusive the Lotus Club has become under your presidency. . . .

DORINDA: I don't think you will, Mr. Edwards, it happens that the Lotus Club has just purchased the press you've been using. There'll be no more Eye Openers run off that press!

EDWARDS: (*Quietly*) I see. (*He goes to the back*) Mrs. Gudgeon. . . . could you step in here a moment?

MRS. GUDGEON: Oh, Mr. Edwards, believe me. I didn't want to sell. They made me.

EDWARDS: It's true then.

MRS. GUDGEON: If I hadn't sold it, they'd have got it anyway.

EDWARDS: Never mind, Mrs. Gudgeon.

MRS. GUDGEON: (*Tearfully*) I never dreamed they could take my house, lad. Please understand. I had to do it.

EDWARDS: (*Patting her shoulder*) Here, now, don't feel so bad. Sheep Creek's no place for a smart, upstanding sober newspaper man anyway. I'll do better somewhere else. I'll flag the old C.P.R. and. . . .

JIMMY: C.P.R.? Bob, I've got a telegram for you. Forgot all about it with all the. . . . (*Finds it in his pocket*) I told Pinky I'd see you got it right away. . . .

EDWARDS: Thanks, Jimmy.

(*He tears it open and reads it quickly*)

JIMMY: I hope it isn't bad news.

EDWARDS: Bad news? No, I don't believe it is. Jimmy, would you step across and ask Mr. Carp to come over here for a few minutes. Tell him there's a fairly large sum of money involved.

DORINDA: Tell him I want him to dismantle that press. At once.

JIMMY: All right, Bob. Then I'll go on to the store.

BERTHA: Wait, Jimmy, I'll come with you.

EDWARDS: The trousers, Mrs. Foggin. You'd better hang on to them after this, Jimmy.

JIMMY: Believe me, I will.

BERTHA: I'll take them home. Do you know I don't think a woman knows how valuable her husband is until she almost loses him? I'm going right home and bake Jimmy a blueberry pie.

(*They go*)

MRS. GUDGEON: I better get on to my work, sir.

EDWARDS: No, Mrs. Gudgeon. I want you and Mrs. Carp to stay.

DORINDA: I'll stay. I want to see that press removed, personally.

MRS. GUDGEON: Mrs. Carp, ma'am please sell me my house. All my life I've wanted to be independent in my last days. . . . and I thought I'd retire and learn to paint china.

DORINDA: Paint china! Mrs. Gudgeon, that takes a certain artistic instinct.

MRS. GUDGEON: I know ma'am. It was just an idea.

DORINDA: A very foolish one.

EDWARDS: Has it never occurred to you, Mrs. Carp, that everyone. . . . even the waitresses and ditch-diggers of this world. . . . even the drunken bum. . . . has some kind of idea about himself. Nothing to do with making money. . . . some idea of a way he could pull his weight and be the person God meant him to be. That's the immortal spark. . . . the drive. . . . that's what pulled man out of the slime. . . . and out of the tree. . . . and out of the joyless, fenced-in world of the money-changer. Of course some people have a bit longer pull than others. . . .

DORINDA: Evolution! I might have known. . . . you and that Darwin.

EDWARDS: (*Quietly*) No. It never occurred to you, Mrs. Carp. You have no doubts.

(DUDLEY CARP *enters*)

DUDLEY: What's all this, Edwards? If you want to see me, I've got an office.

EDWARDS: Sit down, Dudley.

DUDLEY: I can't spare much time.

EDWARDS: This won't take long.

DORINDA: We've got the press, Dudley. The Lotus Club own it.

EDWARDS: Yes, it looks like the Eye Opener and Sheep Creek are about to sever connections. You wouldn't have anything to do with that?

DUDLEY: I don't belong to the Lotus Club.

EDWARDS: That's right isn't it? Well, I liked this town, but it seems it was you or me and you moved fastest. But before I go there's one little matter I'd like cleared up.

DUDLEY: Yes?

EDWARDS: Mrs. Gudgeon, who sold you the three city lots we were talking about today?

MRS. GUDGEON: Why, Mr. Carp, of course.

EDWARDS: They're no good, Mrs. Gudgeon. . . . never will be any good. They're four miles up the river on a gravel patch.

MRS. GUDGEON: Oh no, Mr. Edwards. . . . oh they can't be. . . .

EDWARDS: You might as well have thrown your money away.

MRS. GUDGEON: It was all I had. . . . all Carl left me. Are you sure, lad?

EDWARDS: I had Paddy Nolan check them. This is his answer.

MRS. GUDGEON: Mr. Carp. . . .

DUDLEY: There's just some mistake, Mrs. Gudgeon.

EDWARDS: No, there's no mistake. Well, Dudley, I win here anyway. This is the first clear-cut case of fraud I've been able to catch you in. . . . I've had to hint at the rest.

DUDLEY: Mrs. Gudgeon, you don't believe him before me do you? My old friend, do you think I'd. . . .

EDWARDS: We don't need golden words, Dudley. You sold the lots to Mrs. Gudgeon for three hundred dollars. You knew they were no good. If you don't return her money here and now I'll publish 20,000 copies of a story exposing the whole dirty business. Then what will your electors say?

DUDLEY: That's blackmail, Edwards.

EDWARDS: An ugly word but this is an ugly business. I've never used my paper, here or anywhere else for any motive but the public good. . . . as I see it. I never will. And I'll stoop to blackmail unless you. . . .

DORINDA: Pooh! You can't publish anything without a press.

DUDLEY: You forgot that, didn't you?

EDWARDS: I've got plenty of time. I can write the story by hand. . . . or borrow a child's printing set. . . . Don't worry. . . . I don't need a printing press to rock Alberta with this story. . . . a special edition devoted all to you.

DUDLEY: I'll have you in jail for this.

EDWARDS: That's fine. Good-day, Mr. and Mrs. Carp.

DUDLEY: What do you want, Edwards?

EDWARDS: I want Mrs. Gudgeon's money returned. . . . with interest. . . . and I want her to have clear title to the house she occupies. Oh yes, I want Mrs. Wize invited to join the Lotus Club too. That's all.

DORINDA: Dudley, are you going to let this man. . . .

DUDLEY: Of course I'm going to settle this matter, Dorinda. (*Suavely*) You might be a little less belligerent, Bob. Mrs. Gudgeon, I'm so sorry that I failed to check those lots. . . . some mistake in the office of course. I wouldn't see you lose out for the world, Mrs. Gudgeon. Here's my cheque for three hundred and twenty-five dollars.

(*He writes cheque*)

MRS. GUDGEON: Oh thank you, Mr. Carp. I knew there was some mistake.

DUDLEY: These things will happen to a busy man, you know. Inefficient office help.

EDWARDS: Return the deeds to him, Mrs. Gudgeon.

MRS. GUDGEON: Oh yes, of course.

> (*She retires behind coat rack*)

EDWARDS: How much did you pay for the press, Mrs. Carp?

DORINDA: Two hundred dollars.

EDWARDS: I suggest that sum be payment in full for the house.

DORINDA: I can't very well do that. You'll have to ask the church board.

EDWARDS: Then it doesn't belong to the Lotus Club?

DORINDA: I'm not sure. . . . I don't believe. . . . oh, I'm all upset.

MRS. GUDGEON: But Mrs. Carp, you told me. . . .

DUDLEY: Now, now, Mrs. Gudgeon. Mr. Edwards and I will approach the church board. I'm sure everything can be. . . .

MRS. GUDGEON: That's a wicked thing, Mrs. Carp, telling me you could put me out. (*with spirit*) Here's your two hundred dollars. I'm not selling you my press at all. I'll thank you kindly for that paper I signed.

DUDLEY: Give it to her, Dorinda.

DORINDA: (*Tossing it at her*) I'm going home, Dudley. I'm leaving this town. There is not room in it for this man and me. . . .

EDWARDS: About Mrs. Wize, and the Lotus Club, Mrs. Carp. . . .

DORINDA: Never.

DUDLEY: This story would kill my chances, Dorinda. . . . you must agree.

DORINDA: Very well, but I'll resign. Do you mean to say you trust this man not to spread the whole story across his rag of a paper?

EDWARDS: Dudley knows I keep my word, Mrs. Carp. Now that you've met my terms, the matter can drop. That doesn't mean that I won't continue to oppose your husband's campaign.

DUDLEY: Here's your cheque.

MRS. GUDGEON: Thank you, Sir.

EDWARDS: Well, it's been an interesting morning. Perhaps you'll drop in again. . . . Good-day Mrs. Carp. . . . Mr. Carp. I must get back to the Eye Opener.

> (*He seats himself at his desk*)

DORINDA: (*Shaking with anger*) You trickster!

> (*She leaves behind* DUDLEY, *slamming the door after her.*)

MRS. GUDGEON: Thank you, Mr. Edwards. . . . you're a good man and a smart one too.

EDWARDS: We newspaper people must stick together, Mrs. Gudgeon.

MRS. GUDGEON: What are you writing, lad?

EDWARDS: It's a kind of prayer, Mrs. Gudgeon. . . . I was going to publish it this week. . . .

MRS. GUDGEON: A prayer? In the Eye Opener?

EDWARDS: Why not? Even clowns. . . . and rogues occasionally look beyond the stars, Mrs. Gudgeon.

MRS. GUDGEON: Would you read it to me, sir?

EDWARDS: All right, now let's see. . . . (*He hunts for two or three slips of paper*)

(*Reading*) "Lord, let me keep a straight way in the path of honour. . . . and a straight face in the presence of solemn asses. . . . Let me not truckle to the high, nor bulldoze the low; let me frolic with the jack and the joker and win the game. . . . Lead me into Truth and Beauty. . . . and tell me her name. Keep me sane, but not too sane. Let me not take the world or myself too seriously, and grant more people to laugh with and fewer to laugh at. Let me condemn no man because of his grammar and no woman on account of her morals, neither being responsible for either. Preserve my sense of humour and of values and proportions. Let me be helpful while I live, but not live too long. Which is about all today, Lord. Amen."

MRS. GUDGEON: Thank you, sir. (*Quietly*) Goodbye, lad. I'll be going home now.

EDWARDS: (*Smiling*) Goodbye, Mrs. Gudgeon.

(MRS. GUDGEON *goes out quickly and EDWARDS picks up his pencil thoughtfully as the curtain falls.*)

The End

The Rainmaker

for Robert and Maryo Gard

Characters

TOM, *a farmer*
MARG, *Tom's wife*
SAM, *a man past middle-age*
JOE, *a barker*
MIRANDA, *a fortune-teller*
ED, *a farmer*
SARAH, *his wife*
TIM, *a farmer*
WALT, *a farmer*
BENNY, *a boy of 11*
DAVID, *a boy of 12 or 13*
CHRIS, *a boy of 14 or 15*
BERT, *a farmer*
JODY, *a Negro lad*
CISSY, *a girl of 16*
JIMMY, *a young man*
HATFIELD, *a rotund little man past middle-age*
MAYOR BURGESS, *the town mayor*
WILLIE, *the Lamplighter*
CAROLINE, *a middle-aged woman*
TOWNSPEOPLE, FARMERS, BANDSMEN

SCENE: *A street corner in Medicine Hat, Alberta*
TIME: *The main action of the play takes place on May 22, 1921. The epilogue and prologue take place in May, 1945.*

Gwen Pharis Ringwood

Production notes based on the original performance of the play will be found at the end of this copy.

As the curtain rises, TOM *is found seated on a bench down right. He is a man of between 45 and 50 years. The street lamp throws a light on* TOM *but the rest of the stage is in deep shadow.* SARAH, *a middle-aged, neatly-dressed woman, comes hurrying down the street towards home. As she crosses the stage she sees* TOM *and pauses.*

SARAH: Why, Tom Arnold!

TOM: Hello, Sarah.

SARAH: What are you doing in town at this hour?

TOM: Just sitting here, Sarah, till train time. I've got some tractor parts coming from Calgary.

SARAH: You come right along home with me and visit with Ed awhile. It looks like rain.

TOM: Thanks, Sarah, I'll wait. Rain never hurt a farmer any.

SARAH: We've been meaning to get out to see you, Tom, but the car's broke down.

TOM: I'll always be glad to see you. The place don't look the same though—without Marg.

SARAH: I know, Tom.

TOM: Twenty-four years ago, Sarah, Marg and I were waiting for the night train, right here.

SARAH: Twenty-four years. That's a while ago, isn't it? (*A trace of wonder at the swift passing of the years*) Why, we were young then, Tom.

TOM: Yes. We were young. And Marg and I were waiting on the train and the rest of the folks were waiting on Hatfield. Do you remember Hatfield, Sarah?

SARAH: I should. Ed and I put up a hundred dollars to bring him here.

TOM: I was looking through some of Marg's things today. Found a clipping about Hatfield. (*He shows* SARAH *an envelope*) Just this clipping and a black button. Medicine Hat, May 22nd, 1921. That's Marg's writing. Don't know what she'd want with a button.

SARAH: (*Gently*) Likely one of yours, or the children's, Tom. It's little things a woman stores away in boxes and in her heart. Sure you won't come over to the house?

(*She starts to move off*)

TOM: No thank you, Sarah. You've a pretty place there now.

SARAH: Yes, it's pretty. And Ed can't work so hard in town. Well, good night, Tom.

(*She moves off left*)

TOM: Good night, Sarah. (*He sits looking at the envelope and speaks softly*) I always wanted Marg to have a pretty place before she died, but she never got it.

(*Then* MARG *is a soft voice and a dim, quiet figure behind him. He does not know she is there but her love for him is a warm and living thing.*)

MARG: Why, Tom Arnold, our place was beautiful those last years; wild cucumber vines all around the porch and my geraniums at the window—I loved every corner of it.

TOM: (*Looking at the clipping*) May 22nd, 1921.

MARG: I thought I could leave you, Tom. I must have been awfully young and foolish.

(*There is a lilt of laughter behind the words*)

TOM: (*Reading*) "A banquet in honour of Mr. Charles Hatfield, our distinguished guest from California, was held last evening in the Moose Hall".

MARG: Who was Hatfield, Tom? I remember about the button and the train, but the rest of it isn't quite clear anymore. Who was Hatfield?

TOM: (*Musing over the clipping*) Charles Hatfield. Hatfield, the Rainmaker.

(*The light above* TOM *dims and light begins to come up at the back of the stage. A crowd busy and noisy comes in from the entrance at back and as they enter* TOM *and* MARG *slip back unnoticed off the stage. The sound of a merry-go-round is heard off stage right. The lights reveal a corner of a village street. The bench remains downstage right. Backstage a picket fence runs from the right corner to near centre. In front of the fence is a rude stall or counter. About centre back is a platform or set of steps that might be the front of a simple public building. A path leads off towards the town at back left. Upstage left is a small tent decorated with the signs of the Zodiac and in front of the tent a chair and stand on which is a crystal ball. Downstage from the tent is a fairly high platform which gives a view of the "towers" off left. The path to the towers is downstage left. The women are wearing the fashions of 1921 but are not well-dressed. The scene has an air of strained gaiety based on an attempt to rise above despair. As the lights come up* JOE *is at his platform, down left, with a small megaphone.* MIRANDA *is seated in front of the fortune-telling tent.* CHRIS, *a boy of 14 or 15, is arranging a portable lemonade stand near the path up right.* SAM, *a man past middle-age, seats himself on the bench down right. He has an accordion, banjo or mouth organ, and plays softly as the scene goes on.* TIM *and* WALT *come in from the fairground*)

JOE: Come on, gentlemen, place your bets. Hatfield versus the elements. Will it rain before midnight? Ten cents a ticket. Step right up.

TIM: Hatfield! I wouldn't bet on that guy if I had a nickel.

WALT: I've got a nickel but I'm not risking it.

JOE: He made it rain in California, folks. He'll make it rain in Medicine Hat.

TIM: You think so, brother, that's fine!

Gwen Pharis Ringwood

WALT: (*Kicking at the dust*) Better take off your shoes, boy, you may
get them muddy.
JOE: That's right, sir. Bet on Hatfield. By midnight you'll be in mud up
to your ankles.
TIM: I remember it raining in this country once. Water come right
down out of the sky.
WALT: You got to show me.
TIM: My brother plumb swooned away with the shock of that rain.
Took us four hours to bring him to.
WALT: You don't say. Four hours.
TIM: We tried everything. Glass of water. Glass of wine. Whiskey.
(*To* JOE) You know what finally revived him?
JOE: Couldn't guess.
TIM: Glass full of dust. Brought him right to. That was the stuff he was
used to—only thing that could save him.
JOE: Thanks, I'll remember that one.
(SAM *plays softly a few measures of "It Ain't Gonna Rain No
More"*. ED *and* SARAH *come in with some cases of eggs and a
few boxes of seedlings*)
MIRANDA: (*As* ED *passes her to go towards the stall, down right*) Tell
your fortune, sir. Twenty-five cents to know the future.
ED: (*Shaking his head and smiling*) Lady, if I had two bits I'd buy a pair
of socks.
SARAH: (*Rather shy and apologetic*) We're going to set up a little stall
ourselves. (*To* BENNY, *a boy of about 11 who is behind her*) Now,
Benny, don't you get in anybody's way.
BENNY: (*Fascinated by* JOE *and* MIRANDA) No, Aunt Sarah.
(TIM *and* WALTER *seat themselves on the steps, back centre.
They nod to* ED *and* SARAH. SAM *stops playing*)
SAM: How you doing, Ed?
ED: (*Arranging the seedlings*) Two more days without rain and I'm
burnt out.
SARAH: Same as last year.
ED: Me too.
SARAH: Looks like Hatfield can't do nothing. After all our hoping.
TIM: He's done one thing, Sarah. Made us look like a bunch of fools.
WALT: And how they're laughing! The whole Dominion is busting
its sides.
TIM: Headlines from Vancouver to Halifax—"Medicine Hat hires a
Rainmaker".
SARAH: Well, it was a chance and we took it.
WALT: Hatfield took us, you mean.
ED: He won't get paid unless it rains tonight.
WALT: He gets expenses. (*Bitterly*) Railway, hotel, fried chicken and
strawberries.
SARAH: Tenth day ain't quite over, Walter. It could rain yet.

JOE: That's right, lady, and it will rain. Those thirty-foot towers will disturb the sky. (*To* SAM) Come on, sir. Three for a quarter. Bet on Hatfield.

SAM: Sorry, brother, the sky ain't disturbed enough. From where I'm sitting the sky ain't even impressed.

> (*More people come in from the back. The younger ones are gay but the older ones have a strained, tired look. The sight of the crowd moves* JOE *to renewed fervour.* CHRIS *tries to shout his wares in the manner of a tried barker*)

CHRIS: Lemonade. Ice cold. How about it?

> (*The Merry-go-round is heard again offstage*)

JOE: Place your money on the Rainmaker, folks. Name your time. You stand to win a hundred dollars. Step right up. (*One or two men pause to buy tickets*) That's right, Mister. Have faith in Hatfield and win a hundred dollars. Take a chance. Ten cents a ticket.

MIRANDA: Twenty-five cents for a private reading with Madame Miranda. Foretold the sinking of the Titanic. Foretold the Halifax fire.

> (BENNY *sees another boy of his own age who has just come in*)

BENNY: Hi, Davie.

DAVID: Hi.

BENNY: (*Moving over to* DAVID) What you doing?

DAVID: Just looking.

BENNY: Me too.

DAVID: 'Taint much. Figured there'd be a snake charmer.

BENNY: Say, you ought to been to the station.

DAVID: Why?

BENNY: I saw his trunk. (*He indicates* JOE) All covered with stickers. Know what they said?

DAVID: No.

BENNY: Saskatoon, Chicago, Nashville and New Orleans. Honest.

DAVID: Boy. (*Looking at* JOE) Been all over, eh?

BENNY: I bet he's seen the ocean.

DAVID: Dare you to ask him.

BENNY: Come on, then.

> (*They move towards* JOE)

JOE: Ten cents, folks. Will it rain before midnight? Ten cents a ticket.

BENNY: Excuse me, Mister.

JOE: Yes, son, what is it?

BENNY: We wanted to ask—we was wondering—say, Mister, have you ever seen the ocean?

JOE: Ocean? Which ocean?

DAVID: Any ocean?

JOE: (*Chewing at a match and studying*) I seen the Atlantic once.

BENNY: What was it like?

JOE: Well, I'll tell you. There's a lot of water there. Big.

BENNY: (*Nodding*) Yeah, I thought so.

Gwen Pharis Ringwood

JOE: Then I seen the Pacific a couple of times.
BENNY: What's it like?
JOE: Real big.
BENNY: Waves coming in?
JOE: All the time. High. High as them towers sometimes.
DAVID: Golly!
BENNY: Tides?
JOE: Tides, regular. In and out. In and out. (*His hand unconsciously describes the motion*) Never missed in ten thousand years.
BENNY: (*With deep satisfaction*) Yeah, that's the way it is, all right. I thought so.
DAVID: Many people get drowned when the tide comes in?
JOE: All the time. Wait too long and the tide sweeps over them. Can't seem to learn.
BENNY: Thanks, Mister.
DAVID: Yeah, thanks.
JOE: Glad to oblige. Ten cents, folks. Bet on Hatfield. Ten cents a. . .
(BENNY *and* DAVID *moving towards right*)
BENNY: Can you beat it? Us guys meeting up with a man like that. Been everywhere, seen everything. Ain't life amazing?
DAVID: Sure is. We better go tell Lee Wong. Come on.
(*They go out*)
CHRIS: (*Moving among the crowd who are going out right*) Ice cold. Home made. How about it? Glass of lemonade, Mr. Sprague?
BERT: How much, son?
CHRIS: Ten cents.
BERT: (*Embarrassed*) Give me half a glass, Chris.
CHRIS: Thanks. It's not very sweet, Mr. Sprague.
BERT: (*Draining the glass*) It's fine, son. Most water I've seen in ten years.
(*He moves on out with the crowd*)
MIRANDA: Know the future, folks. Miranda has travelled in Hindustan, Rangoon, Vienna and Arabia. All the secrets of the ancient East. Will you get your wish? Will you find your heart's desire?
(*Most of the crowd has gone out*)
SARAH: Guess we're all wishing for just one thing, ain't we—rain?
WALT: (*Savagely at the sky*) Yeah, rain.
(*Like a sigh the word is repeated over the little group, half to themselves and half to the heavens. The sigh blends into the voice of* JODY, *a slight Negro lad who has come in from the back and is standing with his face lifted to the sky*)
JODY: Oh, Lordy, Lordy, if we could have one good steady rain.
(*The silence is broken by the sound of a band offstage right*)
CHRIS: (*Taking up his stand*) Think I'll see what I can do over there.
WALT: Come on, Tim. We can listen to the band free.
ED: You go on, Sarah.
SAM: Both of you go. I'll keep an eye on your stuff.

ED: Thanks, Sam. Don't look like there'll be much buying tonight.

SARAH: Maybe they should have cancelled the carnival.

ED: Now who's losing faith in Hatfield?

SARAH: I don't really think he can make it rain, Ed, but I just keep on wishing he could.

ED: Yeah, I know.

(*They go out*)

MIRANDA: (*Turning angrily to* JOE) Some ideas, you have!

JOE: Now Randy. . .

MIRANDA: Dragging us here from Winnipeg to muscle in on Hatfield's racket.

JOE: Hatfield hasn't got a racket.

MIRANDA: Not after tonight, he hasn't. Joe do you honestly believe Hatfield can make it rain?

JOE: I seen him do it twice, that's all.

MIRANDA: You poor long-eared fool. (*With anger and affection*) You've played small-time stands for twenty years and still believe in the dog-headed man.

JOE: Hatfield's a scientist.

MIRANDA: If I was Hatfield I'd get out of town before midnight. These folks may want to celebrate the rain they didn't have, the rain they've got to have that don't come. Half a glass of lemonade! Oh my God!

(*There is a touch of hysteria in her voice. She sits down and gazes moodily into the crystal.* CISSY, *a pretty girl of about sixteen, shabbily dressed, enters. She carries a basket of paper souvenirs and a few coloured balloons*)

CISSY: Souvenirs of Hatfield. Hand-made miniature umbrellas. (*She sees there are only three people there*) Guess I may as well save my breath.

(*She sits on the corner of the steps*)

SAM: (*Taking one of the umbrellas*) Make these, Cissy? (CISSY *nods*) Well, aren't they pretty?

CISSY: I thought they were.

SAM: Not selling eh?

CISSY: Everybody laughs. If we'd had a shower even. . .

SAM: How much?

CISSY: Ten cents.

SAM: I'll take them all.

CISSY: (*Getting up quickly*) Oh no, you're just feeling sorry for me.

SAM: Hell's Bells, Cissy, I never felt sorry for anybody. Haven't time. I'm having a birthday party next week and can use these for decorations.

CISSY: Honest?

SAM: Honest Injun.

CISSY: (*Doubtfully*) There's forty-three.

187

SAM: (*Counting his money*) Let's see. I need thirty-seven. Three seventy
—that's right. You take out six.

CISSY: You're sure?

SAM: Sure. Now you run on and have a good time.

CISSY: Oh, thank you, Mr. Bruce. You see dad broke his pipe so he quit
smoking to save the money. He's smoked for twenty years and. . .

SAM: Go on, then. Buy your dad some tobacco.

(CISSY *runs out*)

MIRANDA: (*With irritable tenderness*) Now what you going to do with
them? Make yourself a paper skirt?

SAM: (*Standing several of the bright little umbrellas up in the cracks of
the counter*) Might at that.

MIRANDA: (*Ironically and softly without intonation*) Will you get your
wish? Will you find the golden apple of the sun?

(SAM *begins to strum softly.* CHARLES HATFIELD *enters. He
is dressed in new and good clothes—rather flashy—and a top
or bowler hat. He is a rotund little man, past middle-age*)

HATFIELD: Good evening, friends, good evening.

MIRANDA: Maybe you can answer that one, Mr. Rainmaker.

HATFIELD: I beg your pardon, Madame. Answer what?

JOE: Don't mind her, Mr. Hatfield.

MIRANDA: Will they get their wish? Is it going to rain? That's all.

HATFIELD: Rain? Of course it will rain. My solution has been a little
static, but everything's all right I tell you.

JOE: Just what I said.

HATFIELD: All we need is patience, a little patience.

SAM: That blue sky can make a man feel mighty powerless, can't it,
Hatfield?

HATFIELD: Not me. I refuse to feel powerless. I walk in the van of
progress. It's people like you—and you, madame—doubters, that
hold up the march.

MIRANDA: I only asked you if it was going to rain.

HATFIELD: It's bound to rain, Madame. Sooner or later it's bound
to rain.

MIRANDA: I see.

JOE: (*As* BENNY *asked for corroboration about the ocean so* JOE *turns to*
HATFIELD) You believe in yourself, don't you, Hatfield?

HATFIELD: Eh, what's that?

JOE: You can do it, can't you? You can make it rain? You think you
can?

HATFIELD: Believe in myself? My dear fellow, as Ben Franklin-
harnessed the lightning so Charles Hatfield can harness the
rainfall. Science, dear fellow, pure science.

MIRANDA: P.T. Barnum was a wise old man.

JOE: Randy.

(SAM *has been playing "It Ain't Gonna Rain No More"*)

HATFIELD: Look here, sir, don't you know any other song?

SAM: (*Gently*) Know some. What's wrong with this one?

HATFIELD: It gets on my nerves that's all. I don't like it. Never have liked it.

SAM: Starts raining, I'll sure change my song.

HATFIELD: Songs like that discourage folks, undermine their morale.

MIRANDA: Folks here don't need a song to discourage them. Folks here are about to hit bottom.You're their last straw, Mr. Rainmaker, and they're clinging to you. But they're losing their faith—in you, themselves, everything. It's slipping away from them, out of their faces and their hearts and their bones. It's drying up, like their crops, like dust.

HATFIELD: (*For a moment shorn of all pretense and bravado*) I know it. That's why I can't fail. I've tested the solutions twenty times—by now we should have had three inches of moisture.

JOE: (*Excited*) Look, Mr. Hatfield, there's a little cloud over by the towers right now.

HATFIELD: (*Turning*) You're right, my good man, you're right. (*He leaps on* JOE'S *platform*) See that cloud. I brought that cloud. See it! (*Desperately*) There's time. There's still time, I tell you.

(WILLIE *the* LAMPLIGHTER *comes in on this last speech. He is an old man with the eyes of a fanatic*)

WILLIE: Yes, there's still time, Charles Hatfield, time to repent.

HATFIELD: (*Startled*) Who are you?

WILLIE: I'm a gleaner in the granary of the Lord, a saver of lost souls. Pluck your limbs from the burning, Charles Hatfield. Repent before it is too late.

HATFIELD: My dear fellow. . .

WILLIE: You have dared to tamper with the elements. No man, no man, Charles Hatfield, shall make the tempest rage or the rain to fall. You are lost, lost in the bottomless.

(*He lights the gas lamp*)

HATFIELD: Now, now, my man, don't go on that way. Get your facts right. Science is my mistress.

WILLIE: Science! Satan's handmaiden. Be warned for your hour is at hand and the day of judgment. Hell's mouth gapes, Charles Hatfield, Hell's mouth gapes.

(WILLIE *goes out*)

HATFIELD: (*Condescendingly*) The town character, I suppose?

SAM: Oh no, just old Willie Sims trying to get to heaven on a narrow road. Got bogged down at the first turn.

MIRANDA: There's a lot of us like that, ain't there—crying in the wilderness.

(*The* MAYOR *enters. He is a self-important man, a bit excited. He has a gold chain draped across his front. His dress may be 'outlandishly' formal if desired. He goes at once to* HATFIELD *and stands looking up at him*)

MAYOR: Mr. Hatfield. Mr. Hatfield.

HATFIELD: Mayor Burgess.

MAYOR: I've been looking all over for you. I want you to lead the procession.

HATFIELD: I thought you cancelled it.

MAYOR: I did. But folks seem restless. A little fanfare may be a good thing, brighten things up.

HATFIELD: Very well. I am your servant.

MAYOR: Right this way. Right this way. (*He guides* HATFIELD *towards the right*) I'll expect you to make a speech.

JOE: Tell them about you and Ben Franklin, Hatfield.

MIRANDA: (*Softly*) Half wolf, half alligator.

JOE: Atheist.

> (SAM *and* MIRANDA *chuckle quietly as* SAM *resumes a few measures of his theme song*)

HATFIELD: (*Grimly to the* MAYOR *as they pass* SAM) The only song he knows.

MAYOR: Come on, Sam, be a booster, not a knocker.

SAM: All right, Mayor, I'll stop. (*The* MAYOR *and* HATFIELD *go out.* SAM *turns to* JOE *and* MIRANDA) Let's walk over and join the procession. This stuff will be all right.

MIRANDA: (*Taking up her crystal*) Mustn't forget the future.

SAM: No? Most people too burdened down with the past to remember it. (*They go out right. As they leave* TOM *and* MARG *enter from the back.* TOM *is carrying a suitcase which he places on the bench*)

TOM: (*Awkwardly*) I guess everybody's gone to see the parade.

MARG: Yes.

TOM: You want to go over.

MARG: Not now.

TOM: There's a cloud out East. Might shower out that way.

MARG: It might. (*A pause*)

TOM: I'll water your geraniums, Marg.

MARG: (*Hesitantly*) I told Mrs. Pearson she could have them. I didn't think you'd want to bother.

TOM: You don't figure on coming back, do you, Marg?

MARG: I don't know, Tom.

TOM: I should have let you go two weeks ago.

MARG: (*Pleading*) Sell out, Tom. Don't hang on.

TOM: I couldn't. Not now. I've worked too hard, sweated, planned. Can't you see?

MARG: Not any more.

TOM: We still care about each other, Marg. That's the same?

MARG: I don't know. I think so. But nobody can go on fighting dust forever.

TOM: (*Withdrawing*) No, I guess not. Well, I'll get the cheque cashed. (*He starts towards the path at back but turns as he gets to the*

platform steps) Marg, when I asked you to stay, until tonight, I wasn't pinning my faith on Hatfield, exactly. I was believing in us, what we've had. I've been praying that something would happen, some kind of miracle, a rain, maybe, that would bring us back together the way we have been. (*He speaks with difficulty, embarrassed by the attempt to put his emotion into words*) I was so sure, I've been kind of light-hearted all week. But I guess it ain't that way. I guess if people have to depend on something outside, like a rain, to keep them together, why they just aren't worth saving. Maybe there ain't anything, anybody caring about anyway. I don't know (*He has twisted at a button on his jacket and it falls on the ground*) There goes a button.
    (*He picks it up*)
MARG: I'll sew it on.
TOM: No, keep it. (*He hands it to her*) Keep it as a souvenir of Tom, the dude rancher of Medicine Hat. (*His tone is bitter. As she takes the button he looks at her and speaks involuntarily*) Gosh, Marg, you're pretty.
MARG: Tom, I. . . (*There are tears in her eyes*)
TOM: (*Brusquely, turning away*) You wait here. I'll get the money.
    (*He starts off at back very quickly*)
MARG: Tom! Wait, Tom.
    (*But he doesn't hear.* JODY *comes in and meets* TOM)
JODY: Evening, Mr. Arnold.
TOM: Hello, Jody.
    (TOM *goes out.* JODY, *seeing* MARG, *pauses*)
JODY: I'm going down to the station, Mrs. Arnold. You want me to take your suitcase?
MARG: No, thanks, Jody. Leave it.
JODY: Here comes the Band. Maybe they can pipe a few rain clouds over.
MARG: I wish they could, Jody.
JODY: (*As he goes out left*) Me too, Mrs. Arnold. I sure do.
    (BENNY *and* DAVID *come in with some firecrackers*)
BENNY: How many you got?
DAVID: Six.
BENNY: So have I. We've got firecrackers, Mrs. Arnold.
DAVID: Lee Wong gave them to us.
BENNY: We're going to contribute them.
MARG: Contribute them?
BENNY: To the parade. They're the only firecrackers in town.
DAVID: We're going to set them all off at once—bang, bang, bang.
    (*They pause by the fence to examine their treasures.* JIMMY, *a boy of 17 or 18 enters. He looks around, then speaks to* MARG)
JIMMY: Excuse me, do you happen to know Cissy Mills?
MARG: Why no, I'm sorry, I don't.
JIMMY: I just thought you might have seen her. I was looking for her.

Gwen Pharis Ringwood

MARG: I don't think she's been through here.
JIMMY: It's all right. It's not important at all! (*As he starts off right*)
    I just thought you might happen to. . . You'd know her if you saw
    her. Brown eyes and soft hair and she's kind of—well, she's just a
    slip of a thing.
MARG: I'll look out for her.
JIMMY: Thanks. I might just happen to run into her out here. It's not
    important at all.
        (*He gets himself off stage in some embarrassment*)
BENNY: Look, they're coming this way.
DAVID: Let's get right behind Hatfield.
BENNY: You got your matches?
DAVID: Yeah.
        (*The sound of the band is louder. The* MAYOR *comes in with
        the five-piece band following*)
MAYOR: Now, now, boys. Clear the way. Clear the way. Don't give
    us any trouble here. Clear the way for the procession. Hatfield's
    coming. Hatfield's coming. (*He shoos the boys to one side. The
    band breaks off abruptly*) What's the matter with you fellows? Go
    on playing. You hear me. Play something.
BAND LEADER: Too dry. We was only hired to play if it rained.
PLAYER: Tell Hatfield when he does his job we'll play for him.
MAYOR: You're fired.
LEADER: No, we quit.
PLAYER: It's your party, Mayor. Take it away.
MAYOR: Deserters.
CROWD: Where's the rain, Mayor? Yeah, some rain. We been swindled,
    Mayor. What you going to do about it? Where's Hatfield? Let's
    see Hatfield. Bring him out. Bring out Hatfield.
MAYOR: (*To* SAM) Sam, do something. They may get out of hand.
SAM: Well, I'll try, Mayor—but like the boys said, it's your party.
CROWD: Bring out Hatfield. Bring out the Rainmaker.
SAM: Just a minute, folks. The Mayor here wants me to start off the
    meeting with a song. I reckon I can hoax up something appro-
    priate. Figure it'll put Hatfield here on his mettle. Now you folks
    just listen and then join in.
CROWD: What's the matter with the Rainmaker? Is he scared? Bring
    him out. Bring out Hatfield.
SAM: (*Playing and singing over the crowd to the tune of Oh, Susannah*)
    Rained all night the day I left,
    The weather it was fine.
    Rained so hard I choked to death.
    Now Hatfield, don't you cry.

    Come on, folks, join in:

    Oh now, Hatfield, Hatfield, don't you cry.
    Get out there to your towers and disturb the Western sky.

Never rained in forty years
Till Hatfield hit the town
The folks all came to watch him bring
The rain a pouring down.
Oh now, Hatfield, Hatfield, don't you cry.
Get out there to your towers and disturb the Western sky.
    (*Some of the crowd join in*)
Oh now, Hatfield, Hatfield, don't you cry.
Get out there to your towers and disturb the Western sky.

Once more, folks. Let's hear it.

Oh now, Hatfield, Hatfield, don't you cry.
Get out there to your towers and disturb the Western sky.

WILLIE: (*Appearing at right—confronts the crowd*) Kneel, sinners, kneel. Cast off idolatry. Flee the fiery furnace. I find you in wickedness and sloth. . .
SAM: Now, Willie, you may find us in wickedness but we ain't in sloth. Nothing I'd like better than to stretch out my toes and slosh around in a little sloth.
BENNY: What's sloth, Ma-mud?
SAM: Means the same thing in this country, son, and we don't see much of it. Now, Mr. Mayor, I believe you have a few words to say. . .
    (SAM *gives place to the* MAYOR)
MAYOR: Fellow citizens. We in Medicine Hat are doers, not talkers. We have had four years of drought, but are we discouraged? No.
VOICE: Speak for yourself, Mayor.
MAYOR: Ten days ago we hired Charles Hatfield to set up a rain precipitation and attraction tower here on our home ground. We did not hire him without investigating his reputation. In the past seventeen years Mr. Hatfield has conducted forty successful rainmaking experiments. So, we are privileged, my friends, privileged to take part in the forty-first venture of this new science.
WALT: Look out, Mayor, or you may drown.
TIM: Hatfield's brought so much rain there's frogs roosting in my chicken house.
MAN: Rains dust in this country, don't it, Mayor?
MAYOR: Gentlemen, if you please. Mr. Hatfield assures me that he cannot fail. He may be a little late, but he cannot fail. Come up, Mr. Hatfield. Speak to my fellow citizens as you have spoken to me. Mr. Charles Hatfield.
    (HATFIELD *mounts the platform*)
HATFIELD: My friends, when I came here I told you to be of good cheer. Where there is Hatfield, there is rain. I brought floods to California. . .
JOE: That's right. I saw him do it. I was there.
HATFIELD: Thank you, sir. Perhaps I should explain that the solutions with which I work are so powerful that great care is required

before the final, dynamic ingredient is added. This morning I
went out to the towers. . .

WILLIE: Your towers will crumble like the tower of Babel, Charles
Hatfield. The Lord will rend you with fire, impale you with
lightning. Your hour is at hand.

HATFIELD: Mr. Mayor. . .

WILLIE: You will be drowned in your sin, devoured in your pride—Lost,
lost! (*There is a sudden sharp explosion of the firecrackers*) Behold,
it is a sign. Oh Lord, we have been sent a sign!

CAROLINE: (*Coming grimly forward with* BENNY *and* DAVID, *holding
one by the ear and the other by the back of the neck*) I'm afraid that
weren't no sign, Willie. I reckon that was these kids. Now you
behave yourselves.

BENNY: We're sorry, sir.

WILLIE: Brethren, are you saved?

BENNY: I'm afraid not, Mr. Sims.

WILLIE: Do you believe that this man can make the rain fall? Answer
me.

DAVID: We hoped so, sir.

WILLIE: You see—even your young are sunk in sin.

BENNY: But Mr. Sims, we only. . .

WILLIE: Little black sheep, damned through eternity. Lost! Lost!

DAVID: We ain't black sheep. . .

SAM: 'Course you ain't sheep—you're all right. Now, Willie, you better
go and light up the rest of your lamps. It's getting real dark.
(WILLIE *goes*)

BENNY: We didn't do nothing, Mr. Bruce, we only climbed up the
towers.

HATFIELD: You climbed the towers!

DAVID: Only part way. We got scared.

HATFIELD: Young man, you might have been killed. You might have
destroyed all my work.

BENNY: We were only trying to help. Our wheat's dying, Mr. Hatfield.

WALT: Yeah, what about it, Hatfield? Our wheat's dying.

WOMAN I: Another two days and we're finished.

WOMAN II: You've had ten days. You promised rain in ten days.

MAN: Our wheat's dying, dying, do you hear that?

TIM: That don't matter to Hatfield. He's all right.

MAN: He's got plenty of water in his private bath.

WOMAN: Rainmaker. Some rainmaker.

A MAN: Run him out of town, boys. Let's run him out of town.

MAYOR: Friends, Ladies and Gentlemen, one minute please. . .

(*The crowd advances. Various voices speak, very low,
intensely and with an underlying menace born of despair. The
voices are not raised but the intensity increases as the crowd
nears* HATFIELD. *The director can use his own judgment
about breaking up the speeches and about using 'choral*

*speech' at the climax. It is important though that the crowd
remain grounded in reality and if the use of choral speech
destroys this effect it is better to keep all lines spoken by
individuals in the crowd with a mounting climax. The lines are
begun on a soft, almost conversational but ironic note)*

CROWD: We want rain, Hatfield. That's what you promised us.
Our wheat's dying, dying of thirst. Where's your rain Hatfield?
Look at us—these are our best clothes.
We wore them to celebrate the rain you promised us.
We don't run to top hats or tails.
We've been hungry. We've seen our kids go hungry.
We've seen our kids beg for an orange but we couldn't buy it.
Only one orange, Hatfield, but we couldn't buy it. Maybe we're
lazy, Hatfield. We only work sixteen hours a day.
Dawn to dark, dawn to dark.
Maybe we're quitters.
We've been hanging on for a lifetime, that's all. Our lifetime.
Maybe we don't deserve oranges.
Maybe the dust is our inheritance. Dust. . .
It sifts under the windows
And up from the floor
And across the fences
And over the houses
And over our hearts.
Dust. . .

MIRANDA: It buries their hopes and their dreams, blots out their faith,
weakens the will.

CROWD: Where's the rain, Hatfield? Where's the rain you promised?
We want rain—rain—rain.

(As they advance toward the platform, HATFIELD *is visibly
shaken)*

HATFIELD: Ladies and Gentlemen. *(His throat is dry)* Ladies and. . .
CROWD: Rain.

SAM: *(Aware of the taut nerves, steps easily between the crowd and the
platform on which* HATFIELD *is standing)* Take it easy, folks. Take
it easy. Don't forget how to laugh. You've always been able to
laugh before. You can do it now. Why there's Ad and Ella Jones—
remember the last good crop they had four years ago? Best crop
in the country and they were hailed out in a half hour. What'd
they do? They made ice cream out of the hail stones that had
smashed their wheat into the ground. They invited the neighbours
in and somehow they laughed. Here, Walt, have an umbrella.
Good for sunstroke. Tim, Charlie. *(He hands out the umbrellas,
giving one to* HATFIELD. *The crowd wavers, surprised)* Now folks,
we've told Hatfield our troubles. How about giving him a chance
to tell us his? He's got them all right. We all have. Neighbours,
I want you to let him finish his talk. Mr. Hatfield.

Gwen Pharis Ringwood

HATFIELD: (*Wiping his brow*) Thank you, Mr. Bruce. Thank you. I know the past ten days have been anxious days. You called me here to this great country to do you a service. I can render that service. Conditions have been adverse, very adverse. But believe me, they will be overcome. In a few days at most, the desert will flourish as the rose of Sharon. The land will blossom and the streams run swift. Save your umbrellas, friends, you will need them. Where there is Hatfield, there is. . . (*There is a low growl of thunder*) Listen!
> (*A silence. Somewhere in the crowd there is a whisper—'Thunder'*)

CROWD: Thunder.
> Did you hear it?
> I heard thunder.
> Thunder in the West.
> Thunder.

A MAN: (*Jumping up on the platform*) The clouds are banking beyond the towers.

CROWD: Clouds. Clouds beyond the towers. Clouds, out West.
> (*The thunder rolls again a little louder*)

HATFIELD: (*A new man*) Look folks, look. It's raining out West, beyond the towers. Can you see it? Those streaks on the sky. It's raining.

JOE: He's done it, folks. Hatfield's brought rain.
> (*A crash of thunder*)

CROWD: A good rain could save us. It's got to come this way. Wind's in the right direction.

TIM: That's my place, do you hear? That's my place where it's raining. It's hitting my place.

SARAH: Oh God, give us a rain—one good steady rain.

HATFIELD: (*All his confidence regained*) Ladies and Gentlemen, the time has come. I must get to the towers at once. Let no one approach. You're going to get your rain.
> (*He jumps down and runs off left*)

A MAN: Look out West. It's blacker than the Ace of Spades. Must be a cloudburst.

A MAN: Come on, let's follow him. See what happens.
> (*Some of the crowd go off*)

JOE: (*With his megaphone*) Step up, folks. Buy your tickets. Ten cents. How many inches of rainfall? Place your bets, boys. Get in on the fun. Put your money on a sure thing. All right, brother. . . how many?
> (*Several men crowd round* JOE *to purchase tickets*)

MIRANDA: Know the future. Madame Miranda reveals the past, the future. All the secrets of the Orient.

TIM: It's hitting my place. Can't help it. Do you hear that? (*He's on a rocket to the moon*) Boy oh boy. (*To* BENNY) Got any more of those firecrackers?

BENNY: Got six.

TIM: Use 'em, boy, use 'em. (*There is a roll of thunder*) Sam, do you see that? Right over my place. Bet that lightning burnt my house down. I'll build a new house seven stories high. Do something, man, do something.

SAM: What do you want me to do, Tim?

TIM: Sing. . . play. . . dance. . . Do 'em all. Anything. By God, what a country, what a country. (SAM *breaks into "Dance with the Gal with a Hole in Her Stocking" or "Turkey in the Straw", tapping his foot as he plays*) Come on, Sarah, we're only forty once. (*He starts calling the dance*) And all join hands and circle to the left. Get in here, Jimmy. Ed, Caroline. . .

JIMMY: (*Who has found* CISSY) Shall we?

(CISSY *nods. The dance is on, with* TIM *calling loud and fast. As the dance finishes,* SARAH *laughs breathlessly*)

SARAH: Stop it, Sam. I'm plumb wore out.

JOE: (*On the platform*) Hatfield's climbing the towers, folks. He's climbing the east tower. That bank of clouds is dark and high. Shows what science can do.

CHRIS: (*Coming through with his stand*) Ice cold. Home made. How about it?

ED: Here, Chris. You take a glass over to the lady in the blue hat—with my compliments.

(*He gives* CHRIS *a dime*)

SARAH: (*Twinkling at him*) Crazy.

JOE: Hatfield's up, folks. He's at the top. What are we staying for? Let's go. Let's go watch Hatfield.

(*The crowd follow him out*)

JIMMY: You want to go, Cissy?

CISSY: You go. I'll wait for you here.

JIMMY: Promise?

CISSY: Oh yes, I promise.

JIMMY: Don't go way now.

(*He goes*)

ED: Coming, Sam?

SAM: Too tired.

ED: I've got to follow the crowd. See what happens.

(*He goes out*)

CISSY: Madame, Madame Miranda?

MIRANDA: What is it, little lady?

CISSY: Would you—could you tell me. . .

MIRANDA: Your future, child. Of course. Come in. (*Pausing at the door of the tent*) You're falling in love, little lady, falling in love for the first time.

CISSY: Oh, how did you know?

MIRANDA: (*Looking at the shining face*) The stars, child. It's all there, shining in the stars.

(*They go into the tent.*)

197

SARAH: (*To* MARG *and* SAM *who are left with her onstage*) My, this tastes good. (*Drinking lemonade*) If we get a rain now, my flowers will pick up. They've been awful thirsty.

MARG: Your tulips are beautiful.

SARAH: Yes. I've been giving them well water.

MARG: They're so gay.

SARAH: I've got some more in the car. Come along, I'll give you some.

MARG: Oh no.

SARAH: Come on. (*Taking her arm*) I want you to have them.
    (*They go out right.* SAM *is left alone on the stage until* JODY *comes in from down left*)

SAM: Hi, Jody.

JODY: Evening, Sam.

SAM: You on tonight?

JODY: Yeah, man. Medicine Hat. . . Moose Jaw. . . Regina. . . Winnipeg. . . and back again. (*Jumping on the platform and looking off*) I hope those clouds mean something more than just a shower. All the way along the run, it's the same—hot and dry.

SAM: Oh Western wind, when wilt thou blow
    That the small rain down can rain?

JODY: Christ, that my love were in my arms
    And I in my bed again.
    (*Their voices are very quiet*)

SAM: You know that too?

JODY: (*Jumping down*) Learned it from you. (*He smiles*) Last year.
    (*The sky is beginning to darken and continues to do so until the end of the play.* WILLIE, *the* LAMPLIGHTER, *comes in—there is a flash of lightning and thunder.* WILLIE *hurries across the stage and pauses below the platform.* SAM *and* JODY *are sitting on the steps at back*)

WILLIE: Now the time is at hand. The towers will crumble. The blasphemer will perish. The lake of fire and the branding iron await. Now's your chance, Lord. Smite him down. Smite the sinner down.
    (*He goes out left*)

SAM: Poor old Willie sure wants to see folks suffer.

JODY: Yeah, boy.
    (SARAH *and* MARG *come back with the flowers*)

SARAH: Sam, they phoned in from out West. They're had a near cloudburst. Over an inch of rainfall, and it's settling down. They think it's going to be general.

SAM: Say, that's fine, Sarah. It's getting darker all right.

SARAH: I should have known Hatfield could do it. My corns have been hurting all day.

MARG: Oh, if it only hits our place.

SARAH: It will, you'll see (*Wrapping the flowers*) Glory be, I'd almost stopped hoping.

MARG: You too?

SARAH: (*Looking at her and with swift understanding*) Not quite. Not like when I was your age. I used to expect things to be smooth. Takes a long time to learn that struggle is the first law of life. Shall I put these here?

(*She indicates the suitcase*)

MARG: Thank you.

SARAH: That your suitcase?

MARG: Yes.

SARAH: Going visiting?

MARG: I planned on it.

SARAH: Seems a woman never can plan a holiday. When things are bad you can't leave your old man and when they're good you don't want to leave. Only thing you can do is both go fishing now and then.

(*There is a sharp roll of thunder. The two women move towards the left and stand together looking off*)

SAM: Did you feel that, Jody?

JODY: Yeah, I felt it.

SAM: (*Softly and with much emotion*) God, Jody, it's raining. Do you know that? The small rain's raining down.

TOM: (*Entering from the back, nods at* SAM *and* JODY *and sees* MARG *down left*) Marg. . .

(*He moves toward her*)

MARG: Tom. . .

TOM: (*Tight lipped*) We'd better go down and get your ticket.

MARG: Tom! It's raining.

TOM: Little late for us, isn't it? (*He glances at the sky*) Joke eh?

MARG: Tom, listen to me.

(*The thunder sounds again and on top of it the sound of the crowd cheering and singing offstage. The crowd surges in,* HATFIELD *on the shoulders of two of the men. They are singing to the tune of "John Brown's Body"*)

CROWD: Hatfield raised his towers up until they reached the sky.
Hatfield raised his towers up until they reached the sky.
Hatfield raised his towers up until they reached the sky.
And the rain came a tumbling down.
Glory, Glory, Halleluia
Glory, Glory, Halleluia
Glory, Glory, Halleluia
The rain came a tumbling down.

(*As the crowd comes in,* TOM, MARG *and* SARAH *move back.* SAM *and* JODY *move over left. The crowd bear* HATFIELD *to the centre platform. As they finish the song* JOE, *standing beside his platform at right, cries 'Speech, Hatfield! Speech'. The crowd takes it up.* CISSY *and* MIRANDA *have come out of the tent.* JIMMY *sees* CISSY, *leaves the crowd and goes over to*

her. They link arms and move near HATFIELD. MIRANDA
stands beside her tent.)

HATFIELD: (*Simply and quietly*) My friends, go home, rejoice. Put up
your cars and your wagons. The roads are going to be too muddy
to use them. Sleep in the morning. Take it easy. Mend your
harness. Clean up your machine shed. You've got a million dollar
rain on your hands. Your crops are saved (*The crowd cheers*)
Friends, I told you I'd do it. I've fulfilled my contract. Where
there is Hatfield there is. . .

CROWD: Rain.

(*Cheers. A voice in the crowd takes up the song again. The
crowd follows it.* 'The Lord sent Hatfield to us, in the hour
of our need, etc. And the rain came tumbling down'. *As they
reach the chorus, the crowd begins to move out, bearing*
HATFIELD *on their shoulders. Some stop to buy things from*
ED *and* SARAH, *who at the end of the song go out after the
crowd—the chorus of the song may be repeated if necessary.*
TOM, MARG, JOE, MIRANDA, SAM *and* JODY *are left on
the stage*)

JOE: Come on, Randy. We can move this stuff later.

MIRANDA: All right.

JOE: You see. I told you. He did it, didn't he?

MIRANDA: (*Pulling his ears*) What long ears you have, show-boy.

JOE: Always belittling.

(*He goes out ahead of her, afraid to miss anything*)

MIRANDA: (*As she passes* SAM) Would you like to know your future,
sir?

SAM: Scared to, Lady.

MIRANDA: (*Smiling*) I see a big birthday party and it's all yours.

(*She suddenly leans over and kisses him on the cheek and
then goes out*)

SAM: (*Surprised*) Why say, Lady—thanks. (*Turning to* JODY) Now
wasn't that nice?

(WILLIE *enters from left. He stops at the platform and looks
up at the sky*)

WILLIE: (*Irritated and annoyed at the Lord*) You didn't to it. You didn't
smite him down. There won't ever be another chance like
that—those towers raised up, Hatfield on top, thunder and lightning and the people cheering down below. There won't be another
chance like that in a hundred years.

SAM: Now, Willie, a hundred years ain't long in the sight of the Lord.

WILLIE: It's too long for me, though. Listen to them out there singing
in their pride—but pride falls, oh sinners, pride falls. (*He goes out*)

TOM: Here's a present for you, Marg, for the train.

(*He gives her a box of candy*)

MARG: Oh Tom, thanks.

JODY: (*Starting to take the suitcase*) Train's right on time, Mrs. Arnold.

200

MARG: Leave it, Jody, please. . .

JODY: It'll get wet, Mrs. Arnold. Gonna rain hard and long. Those little old gophers be drowned right out of their holes, they ain't careful.

MARG: I'm not going, Jody. I'm going home.

TOM: Marg!

MARG: That's right, Tom.

TOM: You won't be sorry?

MARG: No.

TOM: It's settling down, Marg, to a quiet, steady rain. (*They are close together*) May be a miracle at that. Come on, we better be starting home. (*He takes up her suitcase. They move off*) Good night, fellows.

SAM: Good night, folks.

(*Offstage the long whistle of the train*)

JODY: (*Starting down left and turning*) Sam, you reckon Hatfield's responsible?

SAM: What do you think, Jody?

JODY: Golly, I don't know. If he isn't he sure drew a lucky card.

SAM: Won't hurt to believe it was Hatfield, Jody, if you want to.

(*The whole scene is played quietly*)

JODY: You see, I've been praying, Sam, praying every night for rain.

SAM: Why, Jody? You don't farm.

JODY: So's all the people I see could stop looking up at the sky and muttering. So's they wouldn't look so broken down.

SAM: I see.

JODY: Now I got to decide whether it's Hatfield or Him. Those towers look mighty imposing, Sam.

SAM: So do the Rocky Mountains, Jody, and they've been there a lot longer.

JODY: (*After a pause*) Guess you're right.

SAM: Maybe Hatfield's just lendin' a hand. Anyway, seems like a miracle—this rain. It sure does.

(JODY *glances at the sky. The whistle of the train sounds very near*)

JODY: Medicine Hat, Moose Jaw, Regina and all points East. Good night, Sam.

SAM: Good night, Jody.

(JODY *goes out.* SAM *playing "Deep River" very softly as he leaves. There is a flash of lightning and the roll of the thunder. The stage darkens. When the lights dim again* TOM *is sitting on the bench alone*)

TOM: (*Peering at the clipping*) Medicine Hat, May 22nd, 1921. Marg must have thought a lot of Hatfield. Guess I got a lot to thank the Rainmaker for—a lot of memories.

MARG: (*Behind him*) Hatfield, the Rainmaker. Strange, I'd forget him Tom. I suppose I've too many important things to remember—things that happened to us—to remember Hatfield. (*The train whistles very near.* TOM *gets up to go off left*) Don't be lonely, Tom. I'm with you, in your heart, just like I always was. Don't be lonely.

The End

*   *   *

Production Notes

Setting

The setting for *The Rainmaker* can be described in different ways—as a corner of a street, as a vacant lot, or as an open space adjoining a street. The general playing area should seem much larger than it probably will be, carrying the imagination of the audience far beyond the physical confines of the set. Actually, it should be sufficiently large and unbroken to permit varying numbers of individual characters to move with freedom from one grouping to another. On the other hand if this general playing area is too large, the limited number of actors making up the crowd will have difficulty in filling even a part of it, and of giving an impression of many people, instead of perhaps a mere dozen.

By the use of a board fence approximately seven feet high, running diagonally across the stage, the general playing area was closed in well to the front of the stage. By angling it from downstage right to upstage left, a longer line was obtained, and this line should be continued well offstage into the wings. Also, the angling of the fence permitted greater area stage left to accommodate the platform. Instead of considering this platform as the front steps of a public building, it can be designed more as a roughly erected speaker's platform, decorated with bunting and streamers.

The fairground in the distance can be suggested by having only the top of a merry-go-round appear above the board fence. So the front part of the stage will not be too crowded, and also to extend the setting into space, the lamppost should be placed behind the fence, appearing to the audience only over the top of it.

The alley leading to the fairground can also help in extending the set without actually adding much space to it. This alley should be not more than five feet wide.

In the above setting, the entrance to Miranda's tent was placed in a break in the fence, with the backing for the tent behind.

In order to keep the scene opened up, all the entrances should be used as variously as possible.

The box for Ed and Sarah can be a large orange crate or something similar. This takes up less space and is easier to handle than a

202

more permanently erected 'stall'. Ed can carry the box in filled with many of the articles they are going to sell. As they lay their things out, Sarah can cover or decorate it with some sort of cloth.

Joe's stand need be no more than a small table, but solid enough for him to jump on when he comes to the lines about Hatfield climbing the towers.

Points of Action

At the end of the prologue, the single spot on Tom should dim to a blackout just long enough for Tom to get offstage with his chair. The lighting for the play proper should then start to come up slowly, and as it comes first one character and then another drifts onstage—first Sam coming through the alley, then Joe from down right, then Miranda with her crystal from her tent, then Tim and Walt from the fairground. By this time the lights will be fully set, and the action of the play should start.

The reverse procedure can be used just before the epilogue. As Jody is giving his final speech, the lights should start to dim; then when Jody has gone, Sam, whistling or playing his musical instrument, should drift slowly out through the alley. By the time he is gone there is the blackout, and when the single spot comes on again, Tom is in place in his chair. As Tom gives his final line, he can rise and cross slowly up to the alley; as Marg's words follow him, the spot is dimming and the curtains are slowly closing.

So that the stage be not too cluttered up, Chris need not have any permanent set-up for his lemonade stand. A tray supported by a strap around his shoulders, and on which he carries his glasses and pitcher of lemonade, will do just as well.

The Crowd

The crowd makes its entrance from the fairgrounds through the alley. It should never at any time come too far downstage, and at all times the alleyway should be well-masked and filled by the actors in the rear, thus giving the impression that there may be many more persons behind. Even when the crowd in its resentment and anger surges forward toward the platform, it should keep well upstage and never leave the alleyway open.

When Hatfield leaves after the peals of thunder to go to the Towers, perhaps half the crowd should follow him out, but a sufficient number should remain to keep the stage filled, and carry on with the dance.

Choral Speech

As the playwright suggests, the use of choral speech may be left to the discretion of the director. However, if he feels he can manage this, while still keeping the crowd 'grounded in reality', it will help tremendously in the build to the climax when the first crack of thunder is heard.

Single lines in the crowd, starting with Walt's 'Yes, what about it Hatfield, our wheat's dying' should be taken very quickly, with one line topping the other. These lines should be heard by the audience, but they should be given with an increasing volume of mutterings from the crowd.

The first three or four lines of the speech starting 'We want rain, Hatfield, that's what you promised us' may be taken individually or line by line may be picked up by two, three, four and more actors in unison, until the whole crowd is giving the final line 'Maybe the dust is our inheritance. Dust!' In other words, the indistinguishable mutterings of crowd grow into the actual words. At the word 'dust' there can be a decided drop, with the next line, 'It sifts under the windows', taken by a single light voice, with two or three further voices coming in in unison on each succeeding line, until the further climax is reached with 'And over our hearts. Dust!' Then again a second quick drop to Miranda's line with a final climactic burst from the crowd on, 'Where's the rain, Hatfield, where's the rain you promised? We want rain, rain, rain!'

Following the first crack of the thunder, there should be another sudden drop, with the whole succeeding scene building quickly into a new excitement, without the strained tension of the previous scene.

The dance has been added since the original version was produced at Banff. This has been done in order to keep the play going, as it were, after the climax has been reached. The dance should be full of wild excitement, not set in any way, but free and spontaneous in appearance and feeling.

Characters

The character of Jody is visualized by the author as a young and sincere lad, with a gay smile.

Willie should be played as rather weird, rather pathetic creature, and on no account should be treated as a comic individual.

It is not expected that a director will utilize any or all of these ideas. They are offered simply as suggestions which may help the director in devising his own production of the play.

Stampede
A Play in Three Acts
For Sydney Risk, who made *Stampede* happen.

Author's note: *I hope that those old timers who knew and loved John Ware ("Nigger John") will find in this play a tribute to a great Albertan. Part of the story has been based on fact, part of it is fiction. Certain liberties have been taken with the time of some of the events portrayed here. My desire in writing "Stampede" was to tell a story that would recall the last years of the great ranching era in this province, a story based on some of Alberta's cowboy legend.*

Characters

LONESOME
JIM, *the cook of the Bar X Y*
SLIM
LARRY
JOHN WARE *(Nigger John)*
BUD
SHARK
SHORTHORN, *foreman of the Bar X Y*
PETE, *cowboy from the Bar O 7*
MA RAYBOURNE
CELIA
WHITE CALF
BEANIE
LOLLIE
BERTIE
SUZANNE
BETSY
A MAN
A WOMAN
A CHILD
VENDOR

Gwen Pharis Ringwood

1st Girl
2nd Girl
A U.S. Marshall
A Policeman
Announcer
Other spectators at the Stampede

Scene:
Act I: *A camp site on a cattle trail leading North to Calgary.*
Act II: *The living-room of Ma Raybourne's boarding house in Calgary.*
Act III: *An enclosure behind the Chutes at the first Calgary Stampede.*
Time:
Act I: *Mid-summer, 1912. Evening.*
Act II: *A week later. Early evening.*
Act III: *The next day. The last afternoon of the Stampede.*
Music For Stampede: *Arrangements of authentic cowboy songs might be played as an overture, between the acts, and at the close of the play. If this is done the music should seem to be an integral part of the production and should be in keeping with the spirit of the play. Songs used in the script were taken from* Cowboy Songs *edited by E.J. Lomox (Published by McMillan, 1938) and were used with the editor's permission. Anyone producing the play should ask permission from Mr. Lomox to use the songs, and a programme note should acknowledge their source. Other songs could be substituted) The songs used, with their melodies, are as follows:*

1. Doney Gal
2. Gettin' Up Holler
3. The Colorado Trail
   (*Eyes like the morning star*)
4. Old Chisholm Trail
5. The Night Herd Song
6. Sweet Betsy from Pike
7. Great Granddad
8. Strawberry Roan
9. Rye Whiskey
10. Poor Lonesome Cowboy
11. Double Jawed Hyena
12. Square Dance Call
13. Oh a Man There Lives on the Western Plains.

Act I

SCENE: *A camp site on a cattle trail leading North to Calgary.*
TIME: *Mid-summer, 1912.*

A few scrub poplars, a small knoll at back, some shrubs and rocks, a camp fire, the bed rolls of several of the riders, their saddles, and the tongue and entrance or the rear entrance of the Chuck Wagon, comprise the "furnishings" of the setting.

When the curtain rises LONESOME *is discovered seated on his bed roll, up right from the camp fire. He is strumming on a banjo or guitar and singing "Doney Gal". There are no particular cowboy mannerisms in his singing, just the pleasing effect of a good though untrained voice, singing about the life he knows.*

JIM, *the cook, is busy with preparations for the evening meal.*

LONESOME: (*Singing*)
    We're alone, Doney Gal, in the rain and hail
    Got to drive these dogies down the trail.

    We'll ride the range from sun to sun
    For a cowboy's work is never done.
    He's up and gone at the break of day
    Drivin' the dogies on their weary way.

CHORUS: It's rain or shine, sleet or snow,
    Me and my Doney Gal are bound to go.
    Yes, rain or shine, sleet or snow,
    Me and my Doney Gal are bound to go.

    A cowboy's life is a weary thing,
    For its rope and brand and ride and sing;
    Yes, day or night in the rain or hail,
    He'll stay with his dogies on the trail.

JIM: (*Who has completed arrangements for the evening meal, goes up to the top of the rise and calls.*) Grub Pile! Come and get it! Come and get it! (*Turning to* LONESOME) Where are them buzzards anyway?

LONESOME: Bedding down the herd, I reckon. (*He continues singing*)

> Travelling up the Lonesome Trail,
> Where a man and his horse seldom ever fail;
> Jogging along through fog and dew,
> Wish for sunny days and you.

JIM: (*Grumbling half to himself, half to* LONESOME.) They're slower'n molasses in January. (*Calling again.*) Hey, you fellers, grub's on! Come a-runnin'.

LARRY: (*Running in, he trips on a tree root and falls at Jim's feet.*) Oh, I beg your pardon. Excuse me.

JIM: You must be hungry, youngster.

LARRY: Starved, but I can't eat now. I got to take Shorthorn his gun. We saw a coyote down in the coulee.

JIM: Wait, I'll get it for you. (*He reaches inside the chuck wagon and brings out a 30 30 carbine.*) There you are. And you tell that foreman for me that he'll have to eat coyote for supper, if he don't get in here pretty soon.

LARRY: We won't be long. Maybe Shorthorn will let me shoot him.
(LARRY *starts to run off.* JIM *shouts at him.*)

JIM: Hey you, wait a minute. Ain't there nothing but bone between your ears? Now point that gun down and don't run, you hear me.

LARRY: Right, Sir. I mean—Certainly, I sure as hell will.
(*He goes off in some confusion.*)

JIM: How's he doing, anyway?

LONESOME: Not bad, for the first week. Shorthorn gave him Daisy and he can handle her. But God, he's green, talks like a book.

JIM: Does he yell Yippee?

LONESOME: I been waiting for it. (*Looking in the pot.*) Not beans again! What a nice surprise!

JIM: Quit your beefin'. We're just out of caviar.

LONESOME: (*Breaking into the musical call.*)
> Beans in the pan. Coffee in the pot.
> Come on now and git it while it's hot.

SLIM: (*Entering*) Well, well, our little meadow lark! (*He pats* LONESOME *on the head.*) Hi, Jim. Hope you got plenty. I'm gaunt as a gutted snow bird.

JIM: There was plenty once. May be petrified by now.

SLIM: (*Arranging his bed roll and saddle.*) Did you have a nice rest, Lonesome?

LONESOME: Who has to sing to them babies all night tonight? Me.

SLIM: Saw old Chief White Calf and his family back there.

LONESOME: Going to the Stampede too, eh?

SLIM: Yeah. He tells me there's riders coming from all over, far as Mexico, to enter.

SHARK: (*Coming in in time to hear* SLIM) That's right, Slim. They'll show you prairie dogs some riding, too.

SLIM: Sure, Shark, sure. Up here we've never seen any real horse-manship. Our horses are all born halter broke. And our steers lie down and let us rope them, don't they Bud?

(BUD *has entered with his saddle.* NIGGER JOHN *is behind him*).

BUD: I didn't think that one-eyed black was ever going to lie down. I finally tied him though, didn't I, John?

NIGGER JOHN: You were good, Bud.

BUD: Good as Shorthorn?

SHARK: Better.

NIGGER JOHN: No. You're nearly as fast, boy, but you haven't got his style.

SHARK: Hah! Don't you believe it. Just because Shorthorn's foreman of this outfit, you don't need to lick his boots.

LONESOME: What are you tying up old One-Eye for?

NIGGER JOHN: He's been making the herd awful jumpy ever since we started drivin'. He can't see and he's feared of his own shadow. We staked him over the hill.

JIM: Come on, you fellows. Do you think I want to wait all night to wash the cut glass?

SLIM: (*As if saying grace.*)
Bless the bread, bless the meat,
Now by Joe, let's eat. Sit down, Shark.

NIGGER JOHN: I can move over.

(*He does so.*)

SHARK: (*Pointedly*) I'll sit over here, if you don't mind.

SLIM: (*Quietly and with antagonism.*) Nobody minds, Shark. Nobody minds.

BUD: (*Breaking a moment's tension*) You figure we'll hit Calgary before sun down tomorrow, John?

NIGGER JOHN: Should do, Bud, failing a storm or the herd stampeding.

(LARRY *enters, bending all efforts to be a part of the Western scene.*)

LARRY: Time for chuck, eh? Yippee!

(LONESOME *shudders*)

JIM: Shoot your coyote?

LARRY: No, I left him for Shorthorn. I'm not used to that gun. Say, do I hanker after that grub!

SLIM: (*With a wink at* LONESOME) You don't figure on eating tonight?

LARRY: Why not?

SLIM: Well, this is your first day's hard riding. It ain't safe to eat. You better just have a cup of coffee, drink it slow.

LARRY: But I'm hungry.

SLIM: Have you ever seen a case of Range Riders' Cramp?

LARRY: No.

209

Gwen Pharis Ringwood

LONESOME: I've been doubled up in knots.
BUD: Yeah, give me snake-bite any time.
LONESOME: You sometimes have to operate.
LARRY: Operate?
SLIM: Without instruments. Just a butcher knife and a pair of pliers.
LARRY: Gee whillikins, I didn't know—
NIGGER JOHN: Go ahead and eat your dinner Larry. Don't pay them no mind.
SLIM: All right. But if anything happens, I won't take any responsibility.
BUD: Here's Shorthorn. I'll get another plate of beans.
LONESOME: Hi, Mr. Foreman.
SLIM: Mighty fisher, mighty hunter.
LARRY: Did you get the coyote?
> (SHORTHORN *has come down the rise. He takes the rifle over to the chuck wagon, placing it inside.*)
SHORTHORN: Sure I got him. Got a hawk too.
LARRY: I shot a hawk just before I left home. It had a four foot wing spread.
SHORTHORN: That was Ontario, boy. We raise hawks in this country. Why I figure from tip to tip this critter would measure, oh about fifty feet.
LARRY: Fifty—!
SLIM: Aw, Shorthorn, you went and killed a young one.
SHORTHORN: We'll get his pappy tomorrow. (*He takes a plate of beans from* BUD *and* LONESOME *pours him a cup of coffee*) Thanks, boys. (*He turns to* SHARK *and speaks quietly without emphasis.*) Are you trying to make a killer out of that horse of yours, Shark?
SHARK: Just teaching him a few tricks. Any objections?
SHORTHORN: Yes, I have. Do your instructing when we're not driving cattle. I thought once today you were going to stampede the herd.
SHARK: Can't we speed this drive up a little?
SHORTHORN: We're getting there.
SHARK: I could make this drive in two days.
SHORTHORN: Not with my herd, you couldn't.
SHARK: Your herd? Are you rustling from Tilson on the side?
SHORTHORN: Yeah, I'm hiding them in a deep, dark cave. Going to develop a breed that can see in the dark.
LONESOME: Have some bacon, Shorthorn.
LARRY: Mr. Woolf—
SHORTHORN: Just call me Shorthorn, Larry.
LARRY: But you are Charlie Woolf, aren't you?
SHORTHORN: That's my name.
LARRY: My uncle says you can ride any horse that was ever born.
SHORTHORN: Sure, sure. I'm a rip-snortin', ring-tailed wonder, ain't I, John?
NIGGER JOHN: That's right, youngster. Why I've seen that man riding a horse that was pawing the white out of the moon every jump for a mile.

210

SHORTHORN: Wolf of the world, boys, that's me, the wolf of the world. Never met a horse could scare me yet. Mule did once though.

LARRY: A mule?

SHORTHORN: Big black mule. Down in Whiskey Gap. This mule started following me around. Every time I looked back there was that mule, just looking at me. I took to walking backwards so he wouldn't creep up behind me. You know he never did nothing; just followed me around watching me, all the time watching me. Big eyes!

NIGGER JOHN: That's bad, Shorthorn. What did you do?

SHORTHORN: Got so I couldn't stand it. I jumped a freight out of Milk River.

LARRY: What happened to the mule?

SHORTHORN: Old Mule broke his neck, trying to climb aboard.

SLIM: A mighty close shave.

SHORTHORN: I don't know. Figure now I oughtn't to have hopped that freight. Maybe that old mule wanted to tell me something. I might have been a better man if I'd listened to him.

SLIM: He probably was trying to tell you to quit cow punching and settle down to farming.

LONESOME: I don't need any old mule to tell me that. I'm quitting, soon as Tilson pays me off.

SLIM: I know, back to Iowa and raise hogs. Piggee—Pig—Pig—Pig. (*He imitates a hog caller*).

BUD: Way I figure it, the cattle man of the future has got to be part farmer whether he likes it or not.

SHORTHORN: Now Bud don't be so pessimistic. Only way to raise cattle is have good range and lots of it.

BUD: And good hay and lots of it too.

SHORTHORN: Oh, maybe have to raise a little hay all right. But these two-by-four farm sites are all right for pigs. They're not ranching.

LONESOME: I kind of like pigs.

SHORTHORN: Not me. Come spring, boys, you're going to see a new brand on the range. John and I think we can swing a place of our own.

SLIM: You got a place lined up?

SHORTHORN: We're hoping. Back in the Porcupines. Foothill country.

SLIM: Good range. And about the only place left.

SHORTHORN: Yeah. Barbed wire's creeping up on us.

NIGGER JOHN: Been the same everywhere, like a slow tide.

SHORTHORN: This big stampede they're holding—that's the writing on the wall. Next thing they'll dress us up and show us off like they do old Chief White Calf.

BUD: They've had stampedes in Texas for years. It's still cattle country.

SHORTHORN: Sure. They have them in New York too. White tie and tails.

BUD: You weren't too proud to take the money there, Shorthorn. And you been coaching me to ride in Calgary.

211

SHORTHORN: I know.
SLIM: Stampede gives a man a chance to show what he can do.
BUD: Sure it does. He's up against the best.
NIGGER JOHN: Maybe. Still it seems a waste—raking a horse from head to flank, making an outlaw out of him, so's people can yell.
SHARK: Takes guts to ride those outlaws. Guts and skill.
NIGGER JOHN: That's right. It does.
SHARK: They're just getting old, boys. You get in there and have your fun.
SHORTHORN: No man can handle a raw, fighting four-year-old better than John Ware. He breaks them gentle and when he's finished they're useful.
SHARK: (*sneering*) I suppose you talk to them?
NIGGER JOHN: Sometimes.
SHARK: Nothing shows a man's metal better than a mean, ornery horse that likes to buck.
LONESOME: You can have them. I'm going home. I'm not sold on this life.
SLIM: You been saying that every year for five years, Lonesome.
LONESOME: This time I mean it. I've saved my wages since round-up. Maybe I can pick up a little more cash in the calf roping. And I'm gone. Why, I got a girl in Iowa, did have, if she's not married.
SLIM: You planning to get hitched?
LONESOME: What if I am?
SLIM: Nothing—if you don't mind being shackled and tied, muzzled and browbeat. Not for me.
BUD: What's your girl's name, Lonesome?
LONESOME: Laura, just like in the song. You know. (*He sings softly*)
Eyes like the morning star,
Cheeks like a rose,
Laura was a pretty girl,
God Almighty knows.
NIGGER JOHN: (*Joining in*)
Weep all ye little rains,
Wail, winds, wail,
All along, along, along,
The Colorado trail.
SHORTHORN: That's pretty, Lonesome. Reckon we'll all make a fortune at the Stampede and settle down to raisin' a family. Sounds nice.
LARRY: You're going to enter the bronc-riding, aren't you, Shorthorn? Shark says you won't enter.
SHORTHORN: Shark's right. It's a young man's game.
LARRY: I bet you could still win.
SHORTHORN: Thanks, Larry.
LARRY: I been reading a story about a bronc-buster, just like you, only he was young of course. But he could rope and tie and shoot and ride like—well, just like you do, Shorthorn.

SHORTHORN: That's me all right. Bound to be. (*To* SLIM) You can touch me if you want.

LARRY: This is a true story, honest. Anyway, this fellow got in a fight in a poker dive in Texas and he killed a man.

SLIM: Them was the days. You don't like somebody, you don't fuss around.

LARRY: This man's name was Weston.

LONESOME: I read something about him once. He disappeared.

SHORTHORN: (*after a moment's pause.*) Reckon he was lucky, eh?

LARRY: He got shot in the fight too—in the right arm.

SHORTHORN: Hey, it must be you Shorthorn. You got a scar on your right arm?

SHORTHORN: Sure—half dozen.

SHARK: I've seen that scar. Bullet wound? Sure looks like it.

NIGGER JOHN: Happens it ain't though. That's where he got gored by a bull. Thought you were a goner.

SHORTHORN: So did I, John.

LARRY: Anyway I bet you could shoot as good as Weston. I saw you hit an old tree stump at. . .

NIGGER JOHN: Reckon we better get moving. Dark's creeping in.

SHORTHORN: (*Rising*) Yeah. Larry, you night herd with Lonesome until 2:00. Shark and Slim can take over then.

SHARK: You only need one night-herder for that bunch.

SHORTHORN: I'm putting on two.

SHARK: I tell you one rider's enough. You ride pretty high in the saddle, don't you, Mr. Foreman?

SHORTHORN: I'm giving the orders, Shark. Bud, you look after the horses. Rest of you get some sleep. We ought to hit the big town before supper tomorrow. We'll bed the herd down in Hull's pasture and load the next morning. After that, your time's your own. The boss wants us back at the ranch on the Monday after the Stampede.

LONESOME: Here's one little hang-over he won't see.
    (*As he gathers up his gear, he sings*)
With my knees in the saddle and my seat in the sky
Gonna quit punching cows in the sweet bye and bye
Come a ti yi youpee, youpee yea, youpee yea
Come a ti yi youpee, youpee yea
    (*Others join in as they start drifting off*)
Fare you well old Trail Boss, I don't wish you any harm
But I'm quittin' this business to go on the farm,
Come a ti yi youpee, youpee yea, youpee yea,
Come a ti yi youpee, youpee yea.
    (LONESOME *turns as he starts off stage.*)
You coming, Tenderfoot?

LARRY: Be right there, Pard.

NIGGER JOHN: I'll take care of Midnight, Bud.

BUD: Good.

(They go off together.)

SLIM: (*To* LARRY) You nervous about being out there alone?

LARRY: Why would I be nervous?

SLIM: No reason. Except maybe—grizzlies.

LARRY: Grizzlies. Bears?

SLIM: Saw some tracks. Glad you're not nervous.

LARRY: I better take a gun.

SLIM: Gun's no use with a grizzly. They sneak up from behind. Well, I'll relieve you at two bells. . . that is, if you're still around.

    (SLIM *goes off.*)

LARRY: Shorthorn, are there really. . .

SHORTHORN: No. Here, take this. . . you been trying to roll that one for an hour. (*He hands* LARRY *a cigarette.*) Now go along. Lonesome will tell you what to do.

LARRY: Thanks, Shorthorn.

    (LARRY *goes.*)

SHORTHORN: Hold on a minute, Shark. I want to talk to you.

SHARK: Certainly, Mr. Trail Boss.

SHORTHORN: MacNab rode up with me today.

SHARK: Yeah?

SHORTHORN: He said you'd spoke for the job of foreman at the Bar 0 7.

SHARK: That's right. He's looking for a foreman.

SHORTHORN: He asked me straight out whether I thought you could handle it.

SHARK: Well, I can.

SHORTHORN: (*Finding it difficult to say*) I didn't think so, Shark. I hated to do it but I told MacNab I couldn't honestly recommend you.

SHARK: (*Blazing*) Double cross eh?

SHORTHORN: No. I told MacNab you was one of the best riders I ever saw, that you'd work like two men at anything exciting. But you dodge out on the chores every time.

SHARK: He wants a foreman, not a chore boy.

SHORTHORN: MacNab's got a big outfit. He wants someone he can depend on day in, day out. Somebody that can take orders as well as give them. You can't. I'm sorry. I wish I could have said more for you.

SHARK: The hell you do. You been jealous of me ever since I signed on.

SHORTHORN: No. You've been looking for trouble though.

SHARK: Who's MacNab hiring?

SHORTHORN: John Ware—that is, if John and I can't swing our own place.

SHARK: That nigger.

SHORTHORN: Nigger John, Shark.

SHARK: Yeah, Nigger John.

SHORTHORN: That's all, Shark.

SHARK: You think so? Nobody ever double-crossed me and got away with it, Shorthorn.

SHORTHORN: I can see how you feel. But when a man asks me what I think, he gets just that.

SHARK: The rest of these boot-lickers may think you're God Almighty, Shorthorn. Not me. I'm not taking this lying down.

SHORTHORN: We know where we stand anyway.

(LARRY *comes bustling in, filled with importance*)

LARRY: Forgot my lariat. You know when I was a kid in Toronto I used to imagine myself riding out in the night with my lariat over my saddle horn. And here I am.

SHARK: Come on, kid. I'll teach you a few tricks. I'll take Midnight and give you Cinders.

LARRY: You mean it? I've been wanting some action all day.

SHORTHORN: You stay off Cinders, Larry.

LARRY: But I'd like to—

SHORTHORN: You ride Daisy in this outfit till you can buy a horse of your own. You heard me. Now go on and find Lonesome.

(LARRY *goes out.* SHORTHORN *turns to* SHARK.)

What are you trying to do, break his neck?

SHARK: Be too bad if the boss's nephew got tossed wouldn't it? He might be looking for a new foreman too.

SHORTHORN: Another thing, you leave Midnight alone, Shark. He's Nigger John's horse.

SHARK: He's Tilson's horse.

SHORTHORN: You know nobody but John can ride him. Stay away from him. I'm not having you or anybody else make an outlaw of him.

SHARK: So! Tilson didn't tell you. Midnight will be anybody's horse next week, anybody at all that wants to ride him.

SHORTHORN: What do you mean?

SHARK: Tilson entered Midnight in the bronc-riding contest.

NIGGER JOHN: (*Coming in in time to hear the last*) That ain't true.

SHARK: Don't you call me a liar, black boy. Look at this.

(*He hands* SHORTHORN *a paper.*)

SHORTHORN: (*Slowly*) That's what it says, John.

(*He hands the paper to* NIGGER JOHN).

NIGGER JOHN: Tilson's Midnight—bronc-riding contest, Event No. 3. He can't do it, Shorthorn. Tilson can't enter Midnight.

SHARK: He owns him doesn't he? I hope I draw the black devil. I'll rip him wide open.

NIGGER JOHN: You won't ever ride Midnight, Shark. Nobody is ever going to stay on Midnight's back but me.

SHARK: I thought you were the fellow who knew how to break horses?

NIGGER JOHN: I never broke Midnight, Shark. I spent seven hours getting throwed off his back, then he just decided he'd let me ride him, before I killed myself trying. That's the way it was. He likes me now and he trusts me, but he don't feel that way about anybody else. I don't know why. You won't ever ride Midnight, Shark.

SHARK: I'll be on there trying.

BUD: (*Entering*) The horses are playful as colts tonight.

SHARK: (*Starting out*) How'd you like to ride Midnight, Bud?

BUD: Midnight's John's horse. Anyway I'm saving my bones for the Stampede. Going to break them in public.

SHARK: Tilson's entered Midnight.

BUD: No?

SHORTHORN: Seems that way, Bud.

SHARK: (*As he leaves.*) You better get in there, boy. We'll see how much the great Shorthorn's taught you.

     (SHARK *goes off*)

SHORTHORN: Maybe we can talk Tilson out of it, John.

NIGGER JOHN: You know Tilson, once he's made up his mind. I tried to buy Midnight from him but he won't sell. And yet I can't help feeling that Midnight's my horse.

BUD: But people ought to have the chance to see him, John. There's not a bronc like him in the province.

NIGGER JOHN: If Midnight goes into the chutes, I won't be going back to the ranch. I collect my pay.

SHORTHORN: You won't be going back to the ranch anyway, John. You're going to have to make a choice—coming in with me, like we planned, or going in as Foreman of the Bar 0 7.

NIGGER JOHN: MacNab's outfit?

SHORTHORN: That's right. It's a big deal.

BUD: Boy, that's the best job in the South.

SHORTHORN: That's why he wants the best man in the South as foreman, Bud.

NIGGER JOHN: Reckon I can pass that up, Shorthorn—unless our deal for our own place falls through.

SHORTHORN: You better think about it, John.

NIGGER JOHN: I don't need to think about it.

SHORTHORN: I hoped you'd feel that way. (*A little pause*) You're grieving over Midnight, ain't you, John?

NIGGER JOHN: Yeah, I reckon I am. He's got a proud spirit, proud and strong. And they'll hurt him, try to break him down—

SHORTHORN: I'll do my best with Tilson. (*Off stage* LARRY's *voice is heard in an excited cry.* "Whoa, Daisy, hold still now, hold still. Whoa—Please Whoa, Daisy please whoa.") (SHORTHORN *turns*) I guess I better get out there and make sure the youngster's facing the right end of the horse.

    (*He goes out.*)

BUD: (*Getting some tobacco out of his saddle bag*) Do you think I have a chance in the bronc riding, John?

NIGGER JOHN: A good chance, Bud.

BUD: Shorthorn says I'm inclined to pull the horse a little. But I stayed on Rocket 13 seconds over at the Bar last Sunday.

NIGGER JOHN: You'll be all right. You'll be as good as Shorthorn was before you're through, Bud, if you want to be. Maybe not this year—but some time.

BUD: Honest?

NIGGER JOHN: I think so.

BUD: I suppose a big stampede like this is old stuff to you.

NIGGER JOHN: No. I've never been to many. I like the range better. A city can be a lonely place for a cow-hand, unless he's drunk.

BUD: I won't be lonely. I've got a girl to take to the dances.

NIGGER JOHN: Thought you liked a different one every night?

BUD: Not any more. This gal beats the rest of them a mile. I just met her a month ago. She's pretty and little and—oh, I don't know, I reckon Celia is just a real nice girl.

NIGGER JOHN: That's fine, Bud. (*Looking at the sky*) Let's see, next week we're due for a full moon too. A real, courtin' moon.

BUD: That's right, just what I ordered. Well, I better give Trigger a rub-down.

(*He goes off.* NIGGER JOHN *sits quietly a moment. In the distance* LONESOME *can be heard singing "We're alone, Doney Gal."* SHORTHORN *comes in.*)

SHORTHORN: I see old Chief White Calf heading north, with all his family and fourteen dogs. Like you said about Midnight, John, that Indian's got a proud spirit, proud as they make them. And he's pushed off on the sidelines too. Wonder if that's progress?

NIGGER JOHN: I don't know. Way I see it, just a few people in each generation go ahead, Shorthorn. Most of us are still runnin' behind with the pack.

(*There is a brief pause*)

SHORTHORN: Thanks for speaking up tonight, John.

NIGGER JOHN: Forget it.

SHORTHORN: Have you always known?

NIGGER JOHN: No, I never knew, until tonight. I've wondered.

SHORTHORN: Why? Do I look like a killer?

NIGGER JOHN: No. But until the last couple of years you were always waiting for something. Waiting and watchful.

SHORTHORN: Yeah. Twenty-two years of waiting. Nearly half my life-time.

NIGGER JOHN: You've seemed easier in your mind this last while.

SHORTHORN: I got to thinking I was safe John. Then this kid comes up with a story he's read in a two-bit magazine. Do you think the others—?

NIGGER JOHN: Never entered their heads. They ain't known you like I do.

SHORTHORN: Seems like it happened to somebody else now, not me at all. I've tried to be square the best I know. I didn't want to kill him, John. He was looking for trouble.

Gwen Pharis Ringwood

NIGGER JOHN: Forget about it.

SHORTHORN: (*Looking at the scar on his arm*) You do what you see to do at the time, that's all anybody can do.

NIGGER JOHN: Let it go, boy. It's way back there behind you where it don't matter no more. And you've paid for it. You're safe now. You hear me.

SHORTHORN: Yeah. You're right, I got to forget it, let it go. The only thing, I want to ask a girl to marry me, John.

NIGGER JOHN: You can still ask her.

SHORTHORN: I don't know. I wouldn't want her to see trouble. She's never had much from life but hard work. She's just a slip of a thing too.

NIGGER JOHN: You known her long?

SHORTHORN: Three months maybe. She works at Ma Raybourne's boarding house where we'll stay. Seems like I've wanted to know her, somebody like her, all my life.

NIGGER JOHN: Be nice having a woman partner for the ranch, Shorthorn.

SHORTHORN: If I'm lucky. What's Lonesome's song? "Eyes like the morning star, cheek like a rose"—sounds just like Celia.

NIGGER JOHN: Celia!

SHORTHORN: Celia Brant. You'll like her, John.

NIGGER JOHN: You better ask her, Shorthorn.

SHORTHORN: Yeah, if we get the ranch I'll get my courage up and ask her. Anyway if she says 'no' she'll say it nice. She wouldn't ever laugh at a man, I know that.

(*There is a silence. . . LONESOME'S voice comes very close off-stage. He is singing "Doney Gal"*).

Listen, John. I reckon that's my favorite song. By God, we'll keep it this way. Up there in the Porcupine we'll be free to go on the way we have been, raising cattle, herding them under our own brand, living the only way I ever want to live, close to the sky and the stars, knowing the wind and the way the herd beds down and the sound of an old bull bellowing his pain and his challenge out in the night. I'm just an old rawhide, John, and so are you. We can't change. We can't ever change.

NIGGER JOHN: No, we won't change. The tide'll keep coming though.

(*Off-stage there is a shout and muffled profanity and sounds of confusion.*)

SHORTHORN: What's happened now?

NIGGER JOHN: (*On his feet*) Sounds like Midnight. I'll take a look.

BUD: (*Entering quickly*) Midnight just tossed Shark in two jumps.

SHORTHORN: Shark's a goddamn fool. Was he hurt?

BUD: No. Shaken up. Midnight's off down the coulee like greased lightning.

NIGGER JOHN: I'll go after him.

SHORTHORN: Take my horse John. (NIGGER JOHN *goes out*) Bud, you ride out and see if the herd's nervous, be ready to give Lonesome a hand. And tell Shark I want to see him.

218

BUD: Right.
> (*He goes off*)

JIM: (*Coming out of the chuck wagon*) What's all the excitement?

SHORTHORN: Somebody got tossed.

JIM: Everybody so steamed up about this Stampede, it's a wonder they don't all break their necks. Wish they would, maybe I could get some sleep.
> (*He goes off.* SHORTHORN *rolls a cigarette and turns as* SHARK *enters*).

SHORTHORN: Two jumps eh,

SHARK: I suppose you could do better?

SHORTHORN: I don't know. I've never tried to ride Midnight. I think I could last 10 seconds though.

SHARK: No, you're through. You're a has-been, Shorthorn. But I'll ride him yet, you see.

SHORTHORN: Maybe. (*A pause*) You're fired, Shark.

SHARK: Suits me. You're firing your best rider, though.

SHORTHORN: I know that. You can collect your pay from Tilson in town.

SHARK: Tilson may have something to say.

SHORTHORN: He may. I've said mine. Get your things together and get out first thing in the morning.

SHARK: I'll go tonight, thanks.

SHORTHORN: That's up to you. (*He turns his back on* SHARK *and walks up the rise, speaking without turning.*) You better ask Jim for anything you'll need.

SHARK: I'll get along all right. Keep your mind easy. I wouldn't want you to worry about me—Charlie Weston.
> (*His voice cracks in the stillness.* SHORTHORN *stops, stands for a moment, his back to* SHARK, *his hand involuntarily reaching for his gun.* SHARK *is ready to draw. Then* SHORTHORN *relaxes and turns slowly*).

SHARK: That's all I wanted to know.

SHORTHORN: The name's Woolf, Charlie Woolf. (*Quietly*). Don't let me keep you, Shark. You've got a long ride ahead.
> (*The two men look at one another for a moment. Finally* SHARK *takes up his saddle and walks off. Off-stage* LONESOME's *voice rises in The Night Herd Song.* SHORTHORN *turns and walks up the rise and off stage. Curtain.*)

Gwen Pharis Ringwood

Act II

SCENE: *The living room of Ma Raybourne's boarding house.*
TIME: *September, 1912. Evening, one week later than Act I.*

MA RAYBOURNE'S *living room is a mixture of Victorian furniture and Western odds and ends. On the walls are some Indian bead work, pictures of range men and horses, a mounted Moose head and some large horns which serve as a hat rack.*
LONESOME *and* PETE *are sitting at the table with a bottle between them. They have been imbibing and singing for some time.*)

LONESOME: (*Chalking up on a small slate*). Seventy-seven. That makes seventy-seven songs I've sung.
PETE: I've sung seventy-five.
LONESOME: You're slowing up, though. You might as well kiss your hundred bucks goodbye.
PETE: Hah! I'm not even started yet.
LONESOME: Here's one you don't know.
  (*He begins to strum.*).
PETE: My turn!
LONESOME: Don't argue. I can't stand argument;—argument and cattle, I'm through with them.
PETE: If you don't like arguing you shouldn't get married.
LONESOME: My wife starts to argue, you know what I'll do, I'll start to sing loud, loud as I can, like this: (*Singing*)
  Did you ever hear tell of sweet Betsy from Pike
  Who crossed the wide prairie with her lover Ike,
  With two yoke of cattle and one spotted hog,
  A tall Shanghai rooster and an old yaller dog.
    (*He chalks up seventy-eight, as he sings.*)
PETE: (*Belligerently.*) You can't count that one. It's my turn.
LONESOME: (*Placing his hands over his ears, continues to sing very loudly.*).
  Sing too-ral-li-oo-ral-li-oo-rall-li-ay.
  They swam the wide rivers and crossed the tall peaks
  And camped on the prairies for weeks upon weeks.
PETE: (*Beginning to sing louder than* LONESOME)
  Great Granddad when the land was young.
  Barred the door with a wagon tongue.
LONESOME: (*Singing above him*)
  Starvation and cholera and hard work and slaughter
  They reached old Macleod spite of hell and high water.
PETE: Now I have to start over. You got me off the tune. (*Singing*)
  Great Granddad when the land was young
  Barred the door with a wagon tongue
  For the times was rough and the red skins mocked
  And he said his prayers with his shot gun cocked.

220

LONESOME: (*Joining in for the next verse.*)
Twenty-one children came to bless
The old man's home in the wilderness.
But Great Granddad didn't lose heart,
The boys hunted rabbits and they ketched right smart.

PETE: (*Chalking up.*) Makes me seventy-six. This is better than their old stampede. Trouble with stampedes is people, everywhere you look there's people.

LONESOME: Yeah, people and calves. Too many mean old calves around there. I know a song we haven't sung yet.

(*He begins on Strawberry Roan and after a moment* PETE *harmonizes.* MA RAYBOURNE *opens the outside door and stands listening for a moment. She is a big, sharp-tongued woman with red hair and a soft heart for cattlemen. She has been to the Stampede and is wearing a once-fashionable riding skirt, a man's shirt and an old felt hat.*)

MA: What in blazes is going on here? Sounds like a den of coyotes.

LONESOME: We're having a singing contest, Ma. We ain't doing nothing wrong.

MA: What's in that bottle?

LONESOME: Just a little old root beer.

MA: (*Sniffing*) Yeah, Johnny Walker's brand. You know I don't allow spirits in my parlour. You put that bottle away.

LONESOME: (*Meekly, looking at bottle*) I reckon we've already put it away, Ma.

MA: (*To* PETE) Who are you?

LONESOME: This is Pete McCartney of the Bar 0 7. My friend, my very good friend.

MA: (*Thawing*) Howdy, Pete. You boys ought to be out at the chutes.

PETE: Yes, Ma'am.

LONESOME: We got discouraged.

MA: Lonesome, I've seen a lot of calf-roping in my time, but before God, I never saw any worse roping than what you done today. Looked once there as if the calf was going to tie you up.

LONESOME: That wasn't a nice calf, Ma. He kicked me in my stomach and then he butted me, from behind. There I was, in pain, and what did everybody do, laugh like a bunch of loons.

PETE: Did we miss much this afternoon?

MA: Plenty. Midnight threw Shark in four jumps, just like he piled every other rider this week.

LONESOME: Shark was so sure he could ride Midnight.

PETE: Wish I owned that horse.

LONESOME: How did Bud do?

MA: Bud got thrown hard. Cyclone jack-knifed on him. He didn't look good when he got up, but he said he was all right.

LONESOME: Too bad, Bud had top score.

MA: He's still high for the week, with Shark running pretty close. The steer roping was coming up when I left. I bet twenty dollars on

221

Gwen Pharis Ringwood

Shorthorn. He's the only cowboy I ever saw that could out-rope my old man.

LONESOME: What about me, Ma?

MA: You! Could do better myself. Oh, Ceeley!
  (*She calls toward kitchen.*)

CELIA: (*From the kitchen*). I'm here, Ma.

MA: Bring me my slippers, will you? (*To* LONESOME *and* PETE) My feet hurt. Ed bought me these boots twenty years ago. They never did fit but I wore them so I wouldn't hurt his feelings. Ed was a very sensitive man.

CELIA: (*Coming in with the slippers. She is a pretty girl of about nineteen with a shy, friendly manner.*) Hello, Lonesome, Pete. Here you are, Ma Raybourne.

MA: Thanks, Ceeley. Did you get that side of bacon?

CELIA: I did, Ma.

MA: You missed a good day. Be your turn tomorrow. Anybody back yet?

CELIA: Just Lonesome. How did Bud do?

MA: He's still top score but Cyclone—
  (SHORTHORN and NIGGER JOHN *come in from outside.*)

SHORTHORN: Evening, folks.

MA: How did you do, Shorthorn?

SHORTHORN: Not bad, did I John?

NIGGER JOHN: He won the money, Mrs. Raybourne.

SHORTHORN: Even got a present for you, Ceeley.
  (*He gives her a pair of silver spurs*).

CELIA: For me! Oh, they're beautiful.

SHORTHORN: Roped and tied in 17 seconds. How's that, Ma?

MA: My old man did it in 15 once.

SHORTHORN: I'd have been faster too if you'd been there watching, Ma.

MA: My feet were killing me, or I'd have stayed. Well you won me twenty dollars, boy.

SHORTHORN: Is Bud here?

MA: No.

SHORTHORN: I talked to him right after he was thrown.

CELIA: Thrown?

SHORTHORN: Cyclone tossed him just under the gong. He's a riding fool, though.

CELIA: Was he hurt?

SHORTHORN: I thought so at first, but he said he was just shaken up.

NIGGER JOHN: He came down awful hard.

LONESOME: Don't anybody rub out that score. Pete and I aim to continue.

SHORTHORN: Continue what?

LONESOME: Our singing contest. We got tired of the Stampede.

SHORTHORN: I warned you, Lonesome.

LONESOME: I knowed better myself, but I was in the grip of greed. You know Shorthorn, I don't think that was a calf at all I was roping.

I think that was old Satan dressed up in a calf's hide. Calf and I get down there, nose to nose and I see blue flames spitting out of his eyes and his breath smells of sulphur. Right then I knew I'd made a mistake. Who am I to tie up old Satan? I ain't no reformer.

MA: You couldn't tie a sick sheep, cowboy.

(SLIM *enters*)

SLIM: Shorthorn, you were greased lightning this afternoon. We're mighty proud of him, aren't we, Ceeley?

CELIA: He knows we are.

SHORTHORN: Wolf of the world, boys, that's me, the wolf of the world! Shall we tell them, John?

NIGGER JOHN: (*Smiling*) Yeah, tell them.

SHORTHORN: Take a look at us, folks. You see before you the holders of the Diamond J Cattle Ranch, three hundred acres of deed land and a thousand acres under lease.

NIGGER JOHN: Mountain water and grass so high you got to wear stilts to find your way home.

SLIM: So, you swung it, boys! Congratulations!

MA: Do you mean it, Shorthorn.

SHORTHORN: There it is, all down in writing. (*He puts the lease on the table.*) Why, we may even have a couple of head of cattle, Ma.

CELIA: (*Looking at the paper*) Charlie Woolf and John Ware. Oh, that's wonderful, Shorthorn.

SLIM: Mr. Woolf, sir.

SHORTHORN: (*Entering into the game.*) Hurry it up, boys, hurry it up. Want them mavericks branded before sunset.

NIGGER JOHN: Don't push them, Shorthorn. Why we got so many cattle it'll take us all summer just to cut the babies out from their mas.

SHORTHORN: I'm leaving it in your hands, Partner. Going to hitch my cats and take a run out to our near range. Be back in two months.

LONESOME: By golly, if I wasn't going home I'd come and work for you.

NIGGER JOHN: There'll always be a place for you, Lonesome.

(LARRY *comes in from the Stampede. He is dressed from head to toe in everything the story-book cowboy might wear.*)

LARRY: Howdy, everybody.

(*He starts upstairs importantly.*)

SLIM: Boy, oh, boy, would you look at that? That man's all dressed up like a cowboy. (*He lassoos* LARRY *and pulls him over.*) Come on over, Ranger, and let us admire you.

LARRY: I'm in a hurry.

LONESOME: Now where do you reckon he got an outfit like that? (*He takes off* LARRY's *hat and puts it on.*) Yippee!

SLIM: Would you look at these gloves?

(*Takes the gloves off*)

PETE: Mighty fancy neck-piece here.

(*Off it comes*)

223

SLIM: Boots. (*With one movement* SLIM *and* PETE *tip* LARRY *into a chair and remove the boots*). Hand-tooled genuine cowhide, Ma. I always hankered for a pair of real cowboy boots.

LARRY: Whoa, you guys, whoa!

LONESOME: I'd sure admire to have a belt like that.

SLIM: Shootin' irons, eh?

    (*Off comes the belt.*)

LARRY: Hey, what you fellows going to do? Take off all my clothes?

SLIM: (*Primly*) Mind your tongue, boy, there's ladies present. You reckon that shirt's real silk, Ma?

    (*He pulls out the shirt-tail*).

MA: Now, Slim, you give that boy back his clothes.

SLIM: But I always wanted a cowboy suit, Ma. You don't mind borrowing me this stuff, do you, Larry? (*Turning from the door.*) Look at that now, he's trying to get away with my new rope. Why, you can't trust anybody any more. (*He recovers the rope swiftly*). See you all later.

    (SLIM, LONESOME *and* PETE *fade swiftly out the front door, taking* LARRY's *gear, and leaving him dishevelled and upset.*)

LARRY: Now look at me! My underwear showing! I thought you were my friend, Shorthorn.

SHORTHORN: They won't take them far, Larry.

LARRY: (*At the window*). They're putting them up on those trees all down the boulevard.

SHORTHORN: Chase them down, boy, chase them down.

LARRY: (*As he goes, valiantly*) I hope I don't have to beat up on anybody.

    (*He goes out.*)

MA: John, have you and Shorthorn had anything to eat?

NIGGER JOHN: Sure, Mrs. Raybourne. We had a little lunch up at the Stampede.

MA: Lunch! Sandwich! I'll fix you a real supper.

SHORTHORN: You're spoiling us, Ma.

MA: I ain't very beautiful and I ain't very smart. Only way I can get a rancher to smile at me any more is to set a good table. (*She starts out, then turns.*) Shorthorn, there was a man here to see you today—Charlie, Charlie Russell.

SHORTHORN: I saw him, Ma. He's coming up to paint some pictures of the spring round-up.

NIGGER JOHN: Never was a man could draw a range pony like Charlie.

SHORTHORN: Or a herd of stampeding cattle.

NIGGER JOHN: Or a bronc pawing at the stars.

MA: He didn't look like a painter. He looked like a cattle man.

NIGGER JOHN: He is, Mrs. Raybourne. Charlie's a cattle man right down to the ground. You want me to fix your fire?

MA: Thanks, John.

    (*They go into the kitchen*).

SHORTHORN: Yes, sir, most everything I ever saw or hated or loved I can find again in one of Charlie Russell's pictures—except you, Ceeley.

CELIA: Why, Shorthorn—

SHORTHORN: And you're there in a way too, the way the wind and that coolness that comes creeping over the grass at sundown is there. You can't see them, but you feel them. Why that coolness—it's like drinking the wine of God, Ceeley.

CELIA: That's beautiful, Shorthorn. Tell me some more.

SHORTHORN: Well, you're riding alone; out in front the old Rockies are there, watching things come and go, summer and winter, storm and sun. You hear a river. You listen, sometimes it sounds loud and then it dies away. You get to thinking that if you listen long enough maybe that river could tell you some of the answers. You see an old hawk wheeling high, high—half way between you and the stars.

CELIA: Go on.

SHORTHORN: Coyote howls somewhere. It's a lost sort of sound, yeah, that's it, lost. Maybe your horse shies at a porcupine jogging along like a happy old man. Pretty soon it all goes together. You catch yourself thinking that no matter how blind you're riding, living's a good thing, Ceeley, a real, good thing.

CELIA: Sometimes you seem like the wisest man in the world to me, Shorthorn.

SHORTHORN: No. What I've seen, I've noticed, that's all. A wise man knows something more than he's seen, like Nigger John.

CELIA: Will living be like that for me, like you said, not jangled or tight or little,—a real, good thing?

SHORTHORN: I want it to be, Ceeley.

CELIA: Sometimes I feel like something wonderful was going to happen, as if the whole world was trembling with it, but I don't know what it is or what I want.

SHORTHORN: You will know, Ceeley.

CELIA: When you come, Shorthorn, you talk so fine. It's like you pushed the walls back for me, so I can see beyond just working and eating and washing dishes. Ever since I've known you things have looked different to me, as if there was magic, little pools of magic that settled down on people now and then.

SHORTHORN: One settled round you right now, Ceeley.

CELIA: And there's times when everything seems so beautiful and sad, all the moments going by and we can't hold on to them—

SHORTHORN: I know.

CELIA: (*Jumping down from the table*) Imagine us talking like this! So serious. I must put these in my room. (*She takes up the spurs*). I'll keep them always, Shorthorn.

SHORTHORN: Ceeley, wait—

(CELIA *turns.* LARRY *comes in very indignant*)

Gwen Pharis Ringwood

LARRY: Do you know what they did? They sold my hat to that
black down the street. I had to pay him two dollars to get it back.
SHORTHORN: Looks like you're having trouble getting to that dance,
Larry.
LARRY: (*Going upstairs*). I was planning on getting my picture taken too.
(BUD *comes in from outside. He looks tired and shaky.*).
BUD: Hello.
CELIA: How do you feel, Bud?
SHORTHORN: I was proud of you today, boy.
BUD: I didn't ride him.
SHORTHORN: You made a good try, and you're still high man.
BUD: Yeah, thanks to Midnight. Shark's right behind me.
CELIA: You weren't hurt, Bud?
BUD: Jarred me up a little.
SHORTHORN: You look shaky.
BUD: Tired. I've drawn Midnight for tomorrow.
SHORTHORN: I think you may ride him, Bud. You've got to, its the
last day.
BUD: Can't help hoping I will, but Shark didn't—or anybody else
so far.
SHORTHORN: You're better than Shark, boy. You could be a great
rider—if you want to.
BUD: Want to!
SHORTHORN: It'd mean following the rodeos from here to Mexico, son.
BUD: What's wrong with that?
SHORTHORN: Nothing, only—John and I made a deal for our ranch
today. We hoped you'd sign on as top-rider.
BUD: Why, thanks, Shorthorn—the Diamond J, eh? That's fine! (*He
is looking at the lease.*) I could still contest the bronc-riding.
SHORTHORN: Maybe.
BUD: When do you take over?
SHORTHORN: Two months.
BUD: I'll sure think about it, Shorthorn. But this stampede game's
getting in my blood. I could make a lot of money at it, in the next
five years, if I'm lucky.
SHORTHORN: We figured you might buy in to the ranch before long.
John and I aren't as young as we once were—
BUD: Sounds all right, doesn't it, Ceeley?
CELIA: Don't turn it down, Bud.
(MA *appears in the doorway*).
MA: Come on, Shorthorn. Hello, bronc-buster. Come and eat. You
look like you need a good meal.
BUD: I ate down town, Ma. Thanks, anyway.
MA: Hmmm! Insulting me in my own home.
BUD: Now, Ma—
MA: No excuses. Hurry up, Shorthorn.
SHORTHORN: I'm right on the spot.
(*They go into the kitchen*).

226

Stampede

CELIA: Maybe you're too tired to go to the dance, Bud.
BUD: I'll feel all right after I rest awhile.
CELIA: I'm sorry you were thrown.
BUD: It happened awful fast. I thought I was better than I am, I guess.
CELIA: Do you have to ride tomorrow?
BUD: I want to ride. There's five hundred dollars in it.
CELIA: But they say nobody can ride Midnight, but Nigger John.
BUD: I can try.
CELIA: What if you get hurt?
BUD: You have to take your chances in this game.
CELIA: I wish you didn't have to ride again. There was a man killed last
    year. What does the money matter?
BUD: It could matter a lot to me, to us, Ceeley.
CELIA: To us?
BUD: That's what I said, Ceeley.
CELIA: Oh, Bud!
        (*She moves toward him.*)
BUD: I didn't mean to tell you yet, but you know now. That's how I feel.
CELIA: That's how I feel too, Bud.
BUD: Ceeley! (*He kisses her*). I'll take good care of you. I'll give you
    everything I can, the moon with a ring around it, if you want it.
CELIA: I feel like I've got the moon with a ring around it, Bud.
BUD: I meant to wait to ask you, until the Stampede was over. Then if
    I was still in one piece, we were going out to some ritzy place and
    I was going to get you some red roses and—
CELIA: I'm glad I know now.
BUD: So am I. You're awfully pretty, did you know? Prettiest thing on
    God's green earth.
CELIA: I can cook too. Ask Ma.
BUD: Good thing. Now all I have to do is teach you to ride and shoot
    rabbits and I won't ever have to work at all.
CELIA: And you won't follow the rodeos, will you, Bud? You'll stay
    and go in on the ranch—
BUD: Bossing me round already eh?
CELIA: Oh, Bud, isn't everything—
BUD: It sure is. (*He starts to kiss her again when the sound of singing and
    several loud Yippees are heard outside.*) They would come busting in.
        (LONESOME *and* PETE *enter singing. When they get inside*
        BUD *and* CELIA *have moved apart.*)
LONESOME and PETE: (*Singing*)
    Rye whiskey, rye whiskey, rye whiskey, I cry
    If I don't have rye whiskey, I surely will die.

    Oh baby, oh, baby, I've told you before,
    Do make me a pallet, I'll lie on the floor.
PETE: (*Chalking up*). Ninety-two.
LONESOME: (*Singing as he waves to* CELIA *and* BUD *and chalks up 97*).
    I'm a poor lonesome cowboy, I'm a poor lonesome cowboy,

227

I'm a poor lonesome cowboy,
And a long ways from home.

Home, Ceeley, that's where I'm going, home. Going home tomorrow as soon as Bud gets bucked off Midnight.

PETE: We don't have no home. We're just poor lonesome cowboys.

LONESOME: I have so got a home. Right in the plumb centre of Iowa, I got a little home.

CELIA: Are you boys going to the dance?

PETE: No, we're waiting for Slim. We've got a big game on at the Alberta.

LONESOME: We came home to sandpaper our fingers, Ceeley, so's nobody will cheat us.

BUD: You better leave your roll at home, Lonesome.

LONESOME: Not me. I'm covered with horseshoes. I won't get anything under a straight flush, you see.

(LONESOME *and* PETE *go upstairs.* SHARK *comes in.*)

SHARK: Evening, Bud. I was looking for you.

BUD: What do you want with me, Shark?

SHARK: You don't feel too good, do you?

BUD: Never better.

SHARK: You're crazy, trying to ride tomorrow. That horse is a killer.

BUD: He tossed you clean.

SHARK: I had a loose stirrup.

BUD: Sure.

SHARK: How about giving me another chance at him tomorrow?

BUD: I've drawn Midnight and I go in.

SHARK: Look, you broke a rib today and I know it.

BUD: How do you know?

SHARK: I talked to the doctor that fixed you up. He told you not to ride again didn't he?

BUD: It's none of your business, Shark.

SHARK: I'm making it my business. If you withdraw in my favor I get a chance at the money.

BUD: I'm not withdrawing.

SHARK: I'll make it worth your while.

BUD: Get out, Shark.

CELIA: Bud, is it true, did you break a rib?

BUD: I'm all strapped up, Ceeley. I feel fine. You stay out of this.

SHARK: Hmmm? So this is your prize package, is it, Bud? No wonder you want to win the money.

BUD: I said get out, Shark.

(*He makes a move toward* SHARK. SHARK *gives him a swift punch in his ribs and* BUD *pulls back with the pain.*)

SHARK: That hurt didn't it? How are you going to feel after the pounding that black will give you?

(SHORTHORN *and* NIGGER JOHN *come in.*)

SHORTHORN: What's going on?

SHARK: Your wonder boy isn't feeling so good.

CELIA: Bud broke a rib this afternoon. The doctor told him not to ride again.

SHORTHORN: That right, Bud?

BUD: Leave me alone. I'm riding.

CELIA: Please, Bud, withdraw. You might be killed!

SHORTHORN: Why didn't you tell us you were hurt, boy?

BUD: So you wouldn't interfere.

CELIA: Why wouldn't we interfere? Shark could go in.

SHARK: If I ride him, I'll split with you. Think it over. I want to see Lonesome, I'll be back.

(*He starts upstairs.*)

BUD: There's no use coming back. I won't withdraw.

SHARK: Suicide artist eh?

(*He goes.*)

CELIA: You could take the honors next year, Bud.

BUD: I've a chance to take them this year, Ceeley. I'm on a rocket and I can't quit now. Like I said, five hundred bucks could mean everything to us.

CELIA: I don't care about the money, I just care about you. Please withdraw, Bud, for me.

BUD: Look, Ceeley, you can't make me over. If you're not willing to let me take my chances, tomorrow, or any other time, why we better just call it a day.

(SHORTHORN *has been watching the two closely.*)

CELICA (*Hurt, she turns away*). I wasn't trying to make you over, Bud. I just don't want you to be killed, that's all. I won't say any more.

(*She goes into the kitchen*).

BUD: (*Moving toward her.*) Ceeley—

(*But she is gone.*)

SHORTHORN: (*After watching* CELIA *go out, he turns to* BUD). So that's how it is, Bud, you and Ceeley—?

BUD: Yes. I've got her to think about now. I want to give her nice things.

SHORTHORN: I see. (*He is shaken by his realization that he has no chance with* CELIA *but quickly recovers himself.*) You won't do it, by getting yourself a nice coffin tomorrow.

BUD: You said I had a chance tomorrow.

SHORTHORN: I didn't know you cracked up. You haven't a chance to stay on Midnight with a broken rib. If you're thrown, you could puncture a lung. I've seen it happen.

BUD: I'll risk it.

SHORTHORN: I've taught you everything I know.

BUD: I know what you've done for me.

SHORTHORN: When I say you're in no shape to ride, I know what I'm talking about. There'll be a lot of money bet on you tomorrow and you're hiding the fact that you cracked up. It ain't fair.

BUD: I'm strapped up tight. None of you even suspected.

SHORTHORN: Shark might stay on him tomorrow. You could give him the chance.

BUD: Shark had his chance at Midnight today. I won't give him mine. You saw how he dug in. I ride better than that and you know it.

SHORTHORN: Will you withdraw in my favour, Bud?

BUD: Yours? Why, you're too old. You said so yourself.

SHORTHORN: I've changed my mind.

BUD: I won't do it.

SHORTHORN: The doctor at the grounds never saw you today, did he?

BUD: What do you think?

SHORTHORN: If you had reported a busted rib, you'd be disqualified.

BUD: That's why I didn't report it.

SHORTHORN: I can still report it.

BUD: You wouldn't! Why, even Shark isn't that yellow.

SHORTHORN: I shouldn't have to.

BUD: All right, you don't have to go tale-telling to the doctor. I'll withdraw, in your favour, because you asked me to.

SHORTHORN: Good.

BUD: Because of what you've done for me. But that ought to about even things up, Shorthorn. We'll be quits from then on. You can find somebody else for your ranch—

SHORTHORN: If that's the way you want it, Bud.

BUD: That's the way.

SHORTHORN: Come on, let's go over and fix it up then.

(SHARK *comes downstairs*.)

SHARK: Did you make up your mind, cowboy?

SHORTHORN: Bud's withdrawing.

SHARK: Good.

SHORTHORN: I'm going in in his place.

SHARK: You! (*To Bud*) Is that right?

BUD: That's what he said. That black bounced you around enough today, Shark, let him work on Shorthorn tomorrow.

SHARK: I can bust you faster than that bronc can, Shorthorn.

SHORTHORN: Go ahead, Shark.

SHARK: I go in, or I tell what I know.

SHORTHORN: You don't know anything, Shark. Come on, Bud.

SHARK: No? I know you rode out of Dallas with Whitey McKinnon in July 1889. You were nursing a bullet wound in your left arm. Whitey was—

NIGGER JOHN: Shorthorn was in Montana in 1889.

SHARK: Not in July. And Mick Dryden was shot in July.

NIGGER JOHN: You're barking up the wrong tree, Shark. You better go sleep it off.

SHARK: Shut up, Black Boy. I don't take orders from any Jim Crow.

SHORTHORN: (*Moving quickly toward* SHARK) The only thing that ain't white about John Ware is his skin, Shark. You're going to remember that. I'm going to make you remember it.

SHARK: Twenty years ago you didn't use your fists, did you, Weston?

SHORTHORN: Fists will do this job.

NIGGER JOHN: (*Moving in.*) Stop it, Shorthorn. Stop it.

SHORTHORN: You don't have to take that, from anybody.

NIGGER JOHN: (*For the first time the full strength and power of the man's personality is indicated. Authority takes the place of gentleness.*) I'll fight my own battles. (*He pulls* SHORTHORN *back.*) You and Bud go on. You hear me. Go now. I'm asking you.

SHORTHORN: All right, John, just as you say. Come on, Bud.
    (*They go out.*)

SHARK: He'll never get a chance at that fancy horse of yours. I'll fix the double-crossing bastard—

NIGGER JOHN: You make any trouble for Shorthorn and I'll kill you, Shark.

SHARK: You haven't got the guts.

NIGGER JOHN: Don't try me, that's all. Get out.
    (MA *comes in to put away some dishes as* SHARK *leaves.*)

MA: What's the trouble, John?

NIGGER JOHN: Nothing,—nothing, Ma.

MA: Ceeley says Bud was hurt today. Bad?

NIGGER JOHN: Enough that he wouldn't have a chance tomorrow. Shorthorn's going in on Midnight.

MA: Shorthorn? Well, I'll be damned. He's too old for bronc-riding, ain't he, John?

NIGGER JOHN: I'm afraid he is. He don't care enough about making his mark now.

MA: You must be proud of Midnight, John.

NIGGER JOHN: No, Ma, I'm just sorry. Midnight trusted me and now he's been hurt, deeper than his skin, deeper than any spur can rake him.

MA: He'll be famous.

NIGGER JOHN: Yeah, he'll be famous, cause there's nothing can hurt him any more. He's got a good clean hate inside him and he don't figure there's a man living he could carry on his back without lowering himself.

MA: If you could buy him from Tilson and keep him quiet for a while—

NIGGER JOHN: Not now. From now on papers is the only part of Midnight anybody will ever own. You see he knows now what he was always afraid of, he knows that man's got a mean streak in him, a queer, twisted mean streak that likes to hurt, to turn the knife. They've made an outlaw of him and he's on his road. He'll be the greatest bucking horse that was ever born, but he won't trust anybody ever again.

SLIM: (*Entering*) Did Lonesome come back here, Ma?

MA: They're upstairs, Slim.

SLIM: I've looked in every saloon in town. Hey, Lonesome! Lonesome!

LONESOME: (*From upstairs*) Hi, Slim. We'll be right down.

231

Gwen Pharis Ringwood

MA: Shorthorn's going in on Midnight tomorrow, Slim. Bud broke
    a rib today.
SLIM: Well doggone! Still, if anybody can ride Midnight, it's Shorthorn.
NIGGER JOHN: I think you're right, Slim.
    (LONESOME *and* PETE *come down the stairs*).
SLIM: You fellows run out on me.
LONESOME: We looked around and you weren't there any more. You
    were gone—vanished.
SLIM: I was talking to a pretty girl.
LONESOME: What are you doing here then?
SLIM: She went off with a drug-store cowboy, chaps four inches deep
    and three pounds of bead work.
LONESOME: See that roll, Ma? That's my wages all saved up so I can
    take that train and ride home in style. Going to double it tonight.
MA: You better leave that roll with me.
SLIM: If Shark's playing I'm not sitting in. He's too good for me.
LONESOME: Not me. I'll take him to the cleaners.
NIGGER JOHN: Use your head, Lonesome. How do you think Shark
    got his name?
PETE: Shark? His mother never give it to him. That man was suckled
    by a she-wolf and raised by a bear.
    (LARRY *comes down, trying to be unobtrusive*)
LARRY: Well, good night everybody.
SLIM: Hey, he's going somewhere. Smell that eau de cologne.
PETE: What's your hurry, Larry?
SLIM: Here, let me fix your collar. You want to wear my red hand-
    kerchief?
LARRY: You don't think it would be too much?
SLIM: Course not, would it, Pete?
PETE: Just harmonizes. Now, boys, don't he look nice, real nice?
SLIM: Going to dance off with some little filly's heart.
LARRY: Why, thanks, fellows. Well, guess I better hit the trail.
PETE: Do you know your steps? Can you swing your lady?
SLIM: We better make sure. Come on Larry, Dosey Do. Strike up the
    band, Lonesome.
    (LONESOME *plays and calls the dance.* SLIM, PETE, *start
    with* LARRY *and pull* MA *in as they dance.*)
LONESOME: Join your hands and circle to the left,
    Circle right back, swing your pard.
    And lady on left, right to Pard and
    Grand right and Left—meet your pard and promenade away.

    First gent swing the lady
    Now the one right over there,
    Now the one with the curly hair,
    Now the belle of the ball room. (*Swing*)
    Everybody swing and Promenade all.
PETE: Yippee!

MA: No more. I'm out of breath and my feet hurt.
(*She sits down.*)

PETE: Here, Larry, let me tuck your shirt in. Too much blouse ain't fashionable. (*As he tucks in the shirt he quickly pins a lace doily or antimacassar just below* LARRY's *belt at rear.*) Isn't he handsome, Ma?

MA: Just like a Christmas tree.

SLIM: Have a good time now, and don't get in any trouble.

LARRY: Good night, Mrs. Raybourne. See you later, fellows.
(*As* LARRY *turns the lace doily flutters daintily behind*).

PETE: Goodbye, goodbye, my double-jawed hyena.

LONESOME: (*Singing*)
He's a double-jawed hyena,
He's the villain of the scene,
He can snatch a man bald-headed while he waits.

PETE: (*Basso*) While he waits.
(LARRY *goes out*).

MA: Slim that was a pole-cat thing to do.

PETE: We'll buy you another little old lace doily, Ma'am.

SLIM: We got to toughen up these lavender cowboys, Ma.

MA: (*Getting up*). I suppose so. Now don't you make a lot of racket coming in tonight. That means you too, Lonesome.

LONESOME: Why I never made much noise last night, Ma. I was a mouse, a little tiny mouse.

MA: Uh huh. That's the reason you were going up and down the hall on all fours eh?
(*She goes into the kitchen*).

SLIM: Well, let's get going. Come along, Nigger John.

NIGGER JOHN: No thanks, Slim.

LONESOME: Wait, I forgot my rabbit's foot. I can't play poker lest I have my rabbit's foot. If I've lost that—
(*He starts upstairs*)

SLIM: Help him find it, Pete, or we'll never get started.

PETE: Right. (PETE *follows* LONESOME).

LONESOME: (*On the stairs, singing*) Rye whiskey, rye whiskey, rye whiskey, I cry.

PETE: (*Joining in*). If I don't have rye whiskey, I surely will die.

LONESOME: (*Singing first line.*) Oh baby, oh baby, don't spit on the floor.

PETE: (*Responding*) What do you think that a cuspidor's for?
(*Or some other variation*)
(LONESOME *and* PETE *go off upstairs.*)

SLIM: They've got a jag on already. I'm coming home early. I want to rope tomorrow.
(SHORTHORN *and* BUD *come in*).

SHORTHORN: (*There is weariness in his voice and manner*) It's all fixed up, John,—me and Midnight at 2:45 tomorrow. I'm sorry Bud.

233

BUD: (*Sullenly*) I'm sorry, too. Looks like you were all mighty frightened I'd take the honors.

NIGGER JOHN: Take it easy, Bud.

(CELIA *comes in. She has changed to a pretty summer frock*).

CELIA: Bud—

BUD: Well, I'm out of it, Ceeley. Are you happy now?

CELIA: Oh no, Bud. You know I didn't want—

BUD: That makes two of us. Bud Walker, the boy wonder, thought he had the world by the tail, thought he could ride, thought— (*he stops*). Gosh, I—I feel kind of faint. (*He sits down*). Maybe I better—

CELIA: Bud—

SLIM: Here, Shorthorn.

(*He produces a bottle*).

SHORTHORN: Drink this, boy.

(BUD *drinks*).

BUD: I'm all right, Ceeley. I just.—

SHORTHORN: (*Sharply*) You're going to bed, boy, you hear. You were hurt and you need rest. Now quit fighting and get up there.

NIGGER JOHN: Come on, son.

BUD: I'm all right, I tell you.

(*But he allows* NIGGER JOHN *to help him upstairs.* CELIA *follows*).

LONESOME: (*Coming down, flattens himself against the wall to let them by*). Too early for that, Bud. Look at me, I'm still sober. You want to borrow my rabbit's foot?

NIGGER JOHN: Go on, Lonesome. (*They go up*).

LONESOME: (*Coming down*). Unfriendly, that's what they are, unfriendly. I'm going home and see my girl. (*He sings*)
Eyes like the morning star,
Cheeks like a rose,
Laura was a pretty girl,
God Almighty knows. (*He chalks up 98*)

Hi, Shorthorn. We're going out to raise a ruckus. Want to con

(SHORTHORN *has watched the others go upstairs and is standing quietly, his face in the shadows*).

SHORTHORN: No thanks, Lonesome.

PETE: (*Coming down*) We're going to paint the old town red. You better come. (*He sees the score*) Ninety-eight! You been cheating, Lonesome.

LONESOME: I did so sing a song, didn't I?

SLIM: He did, Pete.

PETE: What was it?

LONESOME: I forget now. Oh yes, it was about my girl. (*Singing*) Eyes like the morning star—(*He breaks off*) Shorthorn, you ain't with us. You look far off, like an outrider on a hill all by himself.

SLIM: He's thinking about that new ranch.
    (*He puts on his hat*).
LONESOME: Dreaming of his first round-up. Why, in ten years you
    fellows will have so many cattle they'll tromp down the Rocky
    Mountains in one night's grazing.
SHORTHORN: (*With an ironic little smile*) Yeah, wolf of the world,
    boys—that's me, the wolf of the world.
SLIM: Let's ramble.
LONESOME: (*As they go*). Got my roll, got my rabbit's foot, got my hat.
    Yippee!
    (SLIM, LONESOME *and* PETE *leave*.)
NIGGER JOHN: (*Coming down the stairs*) He's just worn out, that's all.
SHORTHORN: He thinks I double-crossed him.
NIGGER JOHN: I never thought about you riding.
SHORTHORN: I didn't either, John, but that was the only way he'd
    withdraw. I did it for Ceeley. You see, Ceeley and Bud—
NIGGER JOHN: I know, Shorthorn.
SHORTHORN: It's better that way, John. I reckon Shark's got my
    number. And if he's dug up the whole story, he'll use it, John.
    Can't say I blame him either.
NIGGER JOHN: Don't worry about Shark tonight, Shorthorn. You get
    some sleep. You got to ride tomorrow.
SHORTHORN: You going out?
NIGGER JOHN: Over to the stables. I want to take a look at Midnight.
SHORTHORN: I won't hurt him, John.
NIGGER JOHN: I'm not afraid of that, Shorthorn. Good night.
    (*He puts his hand on* SHORTHORN'S *arm for a moment,
    then turns.*)
SHORTHORN: Good night, John.
    (NIGGER JOHN *goes.* CELIA *comes downstairs.*)
CELIA: You haven't much light here, Shorthorn.
SHORTHORN: That's all right, Ceeley, I ain't used to much light.
CELIA: Bud will be all right, won't he?
SHORTHORN: Of course he will, all he needs is three days to rest up. You
    make a mighty handsome couple, little Ceeley.
CELIA: I told you something wonderful was going to happen, didn't I?
    I'm glad it's you that's taking his place, Shorthorn. I've heard
    them all talk about the way you used to ride.
SHORTHORN: (*It is as if he was trying to make some confession, to get rid
    of an inner burden.*) Ceeley, did you ever hear of a fellow named
    Weston—Charlie Weston—?
CELIA: No.
SHORTHORN: Way before your time, I guess. He wasn't a bad sort,
    Ceeley. He wanted to do the right thing, but he got into some
    trouble. It was like a shadow walking with him for twenty years.
    He—(*He stops, realizing that* CELIA *isn't listening.*) Oh, let it go.
CELIA: Oh, I'm sorry. I wasn't listening. I was thinking of something
    else.

Gwen Pharis Ringwood

SHORTHORN: It doesn't matter. It's just an old tale, of something that happened a long time ago. It doesn't matter any more.

CELIA: Listen, Shorthorn. (*From outside comes a whistled refrain*) That's Lonesome's song.

> CELIA *sings "Eyes like the morning star" softly*)

SHORTHORN: (*As she sings he moves away from her. Finally he turns and breaks into the song. His voice is low and tortured*). For God's sake, Ceeley, leave me alone. Go on, go on now and leave me alone. (*Curtain.*)

ACT III

SCENE: *An enclosure just off the chutes at the Stampede Grounds. A path leading towards the Grand Stand runs across the front of the stage from left to right. A high board fence angles across from down left to left of centre. A break in the fence indicates the way out to the chutes. A similar fence runs along the back with a break near the right corner, entering towards the stables. The wall of a frame building runs from down right to up right.*

TIME: *The last afternoon of the Stampede.*

At the opening of the act the music continues as if it were a band off stage playing for the opening of the Stampede.

> *There is the sound and laughter of a crowd. LONESOME is asleep on a cot near the fence at back. No one notices him.*

VOICE: (*Off Stage.*) Souvenirs of the Stampede. Last chance folks. Last chance for a souvenir of the Old West.

> (*Several people hurry on to the stage carrying pennants, balloons, noisemakers, etc.*)

A MAN: They stable the horses back there.

WOMAN: Somebody said Midnight broke out of his stall three times last night.

A MAN: I don't envy the bronc-buster who draws him.

VOICE: (*Off stage*) Get your seats for the Musical Ride, folks. Get your seats for the world's greatest musical ride.

POLICEMAN: Move along, now, move along. You aren't supposed to use this thoroughfare. Move along to the Grandstand.

CHILD: But Daddy, why can't you ride a wild steer?

MAN: Because I can't, that's all.

WOMAN: Be quiet, Gilbert. Your father doesn't want to ride a wild steer.

CHILD: But why? Why doesn't he want to?

(SLIM *enters and takes his rope down from the board fence*) I bet *he* can ride a wild steer.

SLIM: Nothing to it, son. You just get on and stay on—if you can.

CHILD: You see, I knew he could. I wish he was my Daddy.

MAN: You're going to wish it a lot more in a minute, if you don't be quiet. Come on.

(*The small family goes out.* LOLLIE *and* BERTIE *come in, burdened down with souvenirs.*)

LOLLIE: Oh Bertie, this is practically back-stage, isn't it? Such a horsey smell.

BERTIE: Watch this fellow. Some roper, eh?

(SLIM *is doing some simple rope tricks. The music continues off stage.* SAL, *a cowgirl dressed for riding, comes through*)

SAL: Hi, Slim! Giving a show?

SLIM: No, just limbering up. What time you riding, Sal?

SAL: Right away. The Grandstand's filling up now.

(*She goes off to stables.*)

PEANUT VENDOR: (*Passing through towards the Grandstand*). Peanuts! Fresh, roasted peanuts! Can't watch the Stampede without 'em, Folks. Get your fresh roasted peanuts. Can't watch the Stampede without 'em.

BERTIE: Come on Lollie. We better have some of those.

(*They follow the Vendor out*).

VOICE: (*Off stage*) Grandstand tickets! Get your seats folks for the big show. Watch the world's greatest Musical Ride.

(*There is a burst of music off stage.* NIGGER JOHN *comes in from the stables. He doesn't see* LONESOME *but moves directly over to* SLIM).

NIGGER JOHN: Have you seen Shorthorn, Slim?

SLIM: No. Ain't he here?

NIGGER JOHN: I haven't seen him today.

SLIM: You ain't worryin' John?

NIGGER JOHN: I don't know. Funny he's not here by now.

SLIM: He wasn't drinkin' last night?

NIGGER JOHN: No.

SLIM: I'll take a look around. (*He sees* LONESOME) Who's that?

NIGGER JOHN: (*Moving over to the sleeping figure*) Why, it's Lonesome—Hey, Hey, Lonesome, Wake up Boy. Come on now, wake up.

SLIM: Passed out eh? (NIGGER JOHN *nods*). He sure had a load on when I left him last night.

237

Gwen Pharis Ringwood

NIGGER JOHN: You go on, Slim. See what you can find out about Shorthorn. I'll take care of Lonesome.
SLIM: See you later, then. (*He starts off, then turns.*) How's Midnight acting, John?
NIGGER JOHN: Strung up like a thread of lightning.
SLIM: Going to be a tough ride eh?
NIGGER JOHN: Yeah, it sure is. (SLIM *goes.* NIGGER JOHN *shakes* LONESOME *gently*) Come on, Lonesome, rouse yourself. Wake up, now.
LONESOME: What is it Mom? What do you want?
NIGGER JOHN: It ain't your Ma, Lonesome. It's just me, Nigger John.
LONESOME: I'm all right, Mom. Don't you worry about me none.
NIGGER JOHN: You want some coffee, son?
LONESOME: (*Rousing*) Look, you, go away. Leave me alone. I'm going home, see. And you can't come. You got to find your own home, you hear. There's plenty of homes to go round. All I got to do is to find mine and then I won't be lonesome no more. (*He tries to sing*) I'm a poor lonesome cowboy, a poor lonesome cowboy!. . .
(*His voice trails off and he sinks back into a stupor.*)
NIGGER JOHN: You sure got a skinful of red eye, didn't you, boy? I'll bring some cold water.
LONESOME: (*Singing back*) I don't feel very good, Ma. I must have ate something.
(*As* NIGGER JOHN *turns to go out toward the stables, a U.S. Marshall comes in from the right*).
MARSHALL: Hello, John Ware.
NIGGER JOHN: How are you, Marshall?
MARSHALL: Can't complain. When you coming to visit us over in God's country?
NIGGER JOHN: May be down in the spring buying cattle, Marshall. You can't tell.
MARSHALL: John, do you know a fellow named Shark Lester?
NIGGER JOHN: (*After a tiny pause*). Yeah, I know him.
MARSHALL: Seen him around?
NIGGER JOHN: No,—no, I haven't. Not right lately. Why? Do you want Shark?
MARSHALL: No—that is, I just want a talk with him. Seems he's got some dope on an old case of ours.
NIGGER JOHN: I see.
MARSHALL: If you see him, tell him I'll be over below the judging stand.
NIGGER JOHN: I'll tell him, Marshall.
MARSHALL: Thanks.
(*He waves an acknowledgment toward* NIGGER JOHN *and goes off left.* NIGGER JOHN *watches him go thoughtfully.* LONESOME *stirs and moans*)
LONESOME: Oh. . . my head. I want a drink of water. . .

NIGGER JOHN: (*Turning*) I'm getting it, Lonesome.
> (*He goes off back.* NIGGER JOHN *goes out back stage right.*
> BEANIE *enters with* WHITE CALF *in full chief's regalia*).

BEANIE: (*A brash young man in a loud suit, bow tie and straw hat*)
Here's the angle, White Calf. We walk around in the crowd and
I do the talking. All you have to do is shake hands and look noble.
I handle the pictures and the money. Check? (WHITE CALF *nods*).
Double check. I'll get the pictures. (*He starts off, then turns, snaps
his fingers.*) Idea! Give them the old lingo, White Calf—"Heap
big chief glad to smoke pipe with Pale Face." Can you say that?

WHITE CALF: Hmm. I try.

BEANIE: (*Almost off stage*). Wait, got a better idea! We'll give them the
old Tecumseh. Can you say "How are you?" in Indian?

WHITE CALF: Canni mucki-nistis?

BEANIE: Sure, sure. That's wonderful, excellent. That's good.

WHITE CALF: (*Smiling a little*) Exsokopi.

BEANIE: Now we're hitting the——. Their quarters will fall out like
sunflower seeds. Be right back.
> (*He goes out.* WHITE CALF *sits down.* NIGGER JOHN *returns
> with a couple of towels and some water.*)

NIGGER JOHN: (*Giving* LONESOME *a drink and placing a towel on his
head*). Here you are, Lonesome. Come on, boy, rise and shine.
(*He sees* WHITE CALF) Why, hello, White Calf.

WHITE CALF: Hello, John.

NIGGER JOHN: This boy's going to have a hard day.

WHITE CALF: Sick?

NIGGER JOHN: No. Got awful drunk last night.

WHITE CALF: Maksokopi.

NIGGER JOHN: (*Leaving towel on* LONESOME's *head, he comes over to*
WHITE CALF. *They shake hands.*) How are things going?

WHITE CALF: (*With a shrug*) Sometimes good, sometimes bad.

NIGGER JOHN: Smoke? (*They roll cigarettes*) You making any money?

WHITE CALF: Few dollars. Buy new dress, coats for kids. Candy.
(*After a pause.*) My wife, she's sick. (*He taps his chest.*) Cough all
the time. Bad.

NIGGER JOHN: I'm sure sorry, White Calf.

WHITE CALF: I get some medicine over here. They say it cure my
wife, sure.

NIGGER JOHN: I hope so, White Calf. Don't let this fellow cheat
you now.

WHITE CALF: (*Smiling*) Little man, big talk. Talk, talk, talk—can't
stop. (LONESOME *groans*) He wake up eh?
> (LOLLIE *and* BERTIE *reappear.* NIGGER JOHN *returns to*
> LONESOME. LOLLIE *speaks in a shrill voice.*)

LOLLIE: Oh Bertie, Bertie, look at the Indian!

BERTIE: Say, he's really decked out, isn't he?

Gwen Pharis Ringwood

BEANIE: (*Returning, he seizes the opportunity at once*) Howdy folks.
How would you like to shake hands with a genuine chief of the
fierce Blackfoot, Chief White Calf, whose head was engraved on
the American nickel. Souvenir picture—only fifty cents. Step
right up. Shake hands with a genuine Indian warrior. Don't be
scared, shake his hand, lady, shake his hand.

BERTIE: Go ahead, Lollie, if you want to.

LOLLIE: (*Giggling*) Oh dear, I wonder—well might as well try anything once, eh Bertie? How do you do, Chief White Calf?

WHITE CALF: Canni muskinistis?

LOLLIE: And it's your head on the American nickel. Just imagine that.
That's a great honour isn't it, a very great honour. (*To* BERTIE,
giggling) As if he could understand me.

BERTIE: I'll interpret. Pale Face Lady say White Calf heap big chief eh?
(*He uses awkward signs and speaks as if to a deaf person*).

WHITE CALF: Ugh.

LOLLIE: Oh Bertie, he's smiling. You've pleased him. You are clever.

BERTIE: I can always talk to anybody with ears. You want one of
these?
(*He indicates the pictures*).

LOLLIE: I'd simply love it. It will be a souvenir—a real souvenir of a
perfect afternoon.

BEANIE: There you are, sir, only fifty cents.
(*There is a surge of music from off stage. A small crowd
hurries through with noise makers, balloons, etc. A vendor
passes through with the crowd.*)

LOLLIE: (*Looking off towards the grandstand*) Oh Bertie, Bertie the
cowgirls are riding in—we mustn't miss them. Hurry!
(BERTIE *gets his change and he and* LOLLIE *lope off*).

VENDOR: Grandstand tickets, folks. See the greatest exhibition of of
Bronc Riding ever seen on the North American continent. Wild
calf roping, saddle bronc riding, thrills and danger. Get your
tickets for this hair raising thrill-packed show of death defying
horsemanship. See Midnight in Action—the black horse that
nobody can ride. Grandstand tickets, folks.
(*He passes out toward the Grandstand*).

BEANIE: (*Interrupting the crowd as much as possible*) Step right up and
shake hands with Chief White Calf, a genuine Vanished American.
Souvenir pictures of a scalp-collecting full-blooded Blackfoot only
fifty cents.
(MA *enters with the crowd. Today she is very grand in silver
fox furs, ostrich plumed hat, diamonds and velvet. She pauses
near* WHITE CALF).

BEANIE: Come on, Ma'am. Shake hands with the fire-eating chief
of the—

MA: Hello, White Calf. How are you anyway? Long time since
I saw you.

240

WHITE CALF: Mrs. Raybourne.

MA: You haven't changed a bit, White Calf.

WHITE CALF: I remember your man. He was good rider.

MA: You bet he was—none better. Well, don't take any wooden nickels.

(*She moves on*).

BEANIE: (*Indignantly*) Look, White Calf, you got to stop recognizing everybody and shaking hands free. It ain't business like. Be more noble, get it. Come on we'll follow the crowd.

(*He pushes* WHITE CALF *out left*).

MA: (*As the rest leave*) Well, John, this is the big day. Where's Shorthorn?

NIGGER JOHN: I wish I knew. Slim's gone to look for him.

MA: He was out before breakfast. I've got to meet Bud and Ceeley. Give Shorthorn this for me, will you?

NIGGER JOHN: Sure, Mrs. Raybourne.

MA: It's my old man's luck charm. He always wore it when he rode. I never give it to anybody before.

NIGGER JOHN: I'll give it to him, Ma.

MA: Is that Lonesome?

NIGGER JOHN: Yeah, He'll be all right, Ma. He's coming round now.

MA: I'll be back after I find those young folks.

NIGGER JOHN: Good. (*He turns to* LONESOME) Hey, Lonesome.

LONESOME: Say, what is this place?

NIGGER JOHN: You're out at the grounds, boy.

LONESOME: How'd I get here?

NIGGER JOHN: Reckon you lost yourself last night, Lonesome. A while ago you thought you were back in Iowa.

LONESOME: (*With much effort*) I remember. I couldn't find Ma Raybourne's house anywhere. I kept walking into all the wrong places and then they'd throw me out. Finally I thought about that little old calf I was trying to rope yesterday. I was going to make friends with him before I bought my ticket. I got to buy my ticket right away. (*He sits up quickly, tries to get to his feet. His hand goes to his pocket. After a moment he turns to* NIGGER JOHN *in a panic.*) Nigger John, Nigger John—my money, I ain't got it any more. It's gone.

NIGGER JOHN: Look in your other pocket, boy.

LONESOME: (*Quickly emptying all his pockets*) No, no, it ain't there. It's gone. My money's gone.

NIGGER JOHN: (*Gently*) Did somebody roll you, boy?

LONESOME: They must have. No, wait. (*He slowly pieces together what happened*). I was winning and then, then I had a streak of bad luck. That was after Slim left. And Shark sat there smiling and I got mad and put down the whole roll. I must have—yeah, I lost. Oh God, I'm broke, dead broke.

NIGGER JOHN: You sure you haven't got it, Lonesome?

241

LONESOME: No, I lost the whole roll. I'm right back where I was before. (*After a pause, in a flat convinced tone*) I can't go home now. I won't ever go home again. I just know it.

NIGGER JOHN: I'll lend you the money, Lonesome. You can pay me back when you—

LONESOME: No. I ain't going home on borrowed money, John. That ain't how I planned it. Why, I was going to make a splash at home—

NIGGER JOHN: Come on, we'll find a cup of coffee. Maybe we can figure something.

(SLIM *enters*)

SLIM: I didn't run across Shorthorn, John. He was in the Alberta a couple of hours ago, though.

NIGGER JOHN: Thanks, Slim. Lonesome and I will see what we can do. He'll have to check in pretty soon. He's first up.

(NIGGER JOHN *and* LONESOME *go out left.* SLIM *takes down his saddle from a hook on the wall and begins polishing it up a bit.* PETE *comes in from the stables.*)

PETE: Hello, Slim. Where is everybody?

SLIM: Watching the cowgirls do their show, I reckon. Well, I figure to rope and tie in 17 seconds flat today. Anybody entered from your bunch?

PETE: Big Tom and Johnny Hall.

SLIM: I don't know about Johnny. I'm faster than Big Tom, though. (BUD *comes in from the grandstand*) Hi, Bud, how are you feeling?

BUD: I'm all right.

PETE: Too bad you can't ride today. You were right up in the top bracket.

BUD: I'll get over it, I guess.

SLIM: Have you seen Shorthorn?

BUD: No.

PETE: Some of the boys tell me Shark's on the tear, talking all over about how he's going to fix Shorthorn.

BUD: He's got no call to be sore.

SLIM: Guess he figured he'd be in there today if it wasn't for Shorthorn.

BUD: I'd have been in there, you mean. But Shorthorn put the pressure on. . .

SLIM: Forget it, Bud. You couldn't ride.

PETE: Sure, what's the difference? I'm glad the stampede's about over anyway. I'm broke, I got a hangover and I'm tired of people. (*Two young women cross the stage, they are dressed in the extreme of fashion and are rather heaviliy made up*)

SLIM: Hmmm. Nice eyes, eh? (*He throws a rope which settles round the girls and their feet become somewhat entangled.*) I beg your pardon, Ladies, I don't know what come over me. I'm not usually so awkward with my rope. Allow me. (*He disentangles them.*)

GIRL: You did that on purpose. I know you did.

OTHER GIRL: You might have killed us.

SLIM: Why, ma'am. . .

GIRL: Don't bother explaining. Come along, Daisy.

(The two girls start off, but DAISY *pauses to drop her handkerchief.* SLIM *picks it up and returns it with elaborate courtesy).*

SLIM: Excuse me, your handkerchief, Miss Daisy.

OTHER GIRL: Oh, how stupid. Thank you, thank you very much.

GIRL: Daisy!

(They go out)

SLIM: Well, boys, looks like my last evening may not be so dull anyway. Pardon me while I arrange a rendez-vous.

PETE: Don't forget you got a rendez-vous to rope a steer in about fifteen minutes.

SLIM: I'll be back. I may want to borrow some money.

PETE: You had a hundred dollars last night. Where's it gone?

SLIM: Well, I bought the drinks for the house at the Alberta, that was thirty dollars. Then I bought the drinks at Pete's—twenty dollars. About four a.m. I bought a round for everybody at the Palace—another twenty bucks.

PETE: Still leaves thirty dollars. What did you do with it?

SLIM: Gosh, you know I don't remember. I must have spent that other twenty bucks on something foolish. See you later, boys.

(He goes out after the young ladies).

PETE: Wonder where Lonesome is.

BUD: Haven't seen him.

PETE: Guess I'll take a gander around. You coming?

(He starts off left).

BUD: No. I'm going over to the stables.

(He leaves as two very young ladies come in wide-eyed.)

SUZANNE: Oh, Betsy, there's one now. Stop him.

BETSY: I don't dare. What would Aunt Abigail say?

SUZANNE: She won't know. Come on, let's see what's back here.

BETSY: Suzanne. That's bold.

SUZANNE: I don't care. I'm just peeking.

(She pulls BETSY *with her and they stand together looking over the board fence.* LARRY *comes in, absorbed in trying to twirl a rope. He is doing rather badly).*

BETSY: *(Turning)* Suzanne, look.

SUZANNE: He's doing rope tricks.

BETSY: Isn't he wonderful? Ask him, Suzanne.

SUZANNE: La, I never did speak to a strange man before, let alone a cowboy.

BETSY: We'll never have another chance.

SUZANNE: Stay right by me then. *(They advance toward* LARRY*)* Mr. Cowboy. . .

LARRY: Beg pardon, was there something I could do for you, Ma'am?

SUZANNE: We wondered if you'd give us your autograph. We're from the East and we've never seen a real cowboy before.

LARRY: (*Swelling*) Glad to oblige, Ma'am.

SUZANNE: Just write whatever you feel like.

LARRY: Ridin' and shootin' is a bit more my line than writin', ladies, but I'll do what I can.

BETSY: (*As* LARRY *writes*) You must have had some wonderful adventures.

LARRY: (*Modestly*) Oh, nothing outstanding. I've met up with a few tough hombres in my time, but luckily I'm pretty fast on the draw.

SUZANNE: Just imagine, Betsy.

LARRY: (*Handing back the books*) There you are, ladies. Hope that fills the bill.

SUZANNE: "All good wishes from Larry, the Kid." Oh, thank you.

BETSY: "Ever thine, Larry, the Kid". (*Transported*) Oh. . .

SUZANNE: You couldn't tell us just one of your experiences. . .

BETSY: Just a minor incident that you don't mind talking about.

LARRY: Well, I reckon my life ain't hardly been one for purty little ladies to hear about. Bad language, dives, the reek of rum, the smell of gunshot—it ain't what I'd want you to know about—then back to the range, ridin', ridin', day after day,—rattlers, Pohelia monsters, grizzlies—

BETSY: Grizzlies. Suzanne!

    (*She sways at the thought*).

LARRY: (*Gathering steam*). Mind one time I was riding along on my trusty pony, about two in the morning it was. A storm gathering and the herd restless. Suddenly there was a crash of thunder. The cattle began stampedin'. Balls of lightning flashed from their horns.

    (SLIM *and* PETE *enter. On hearing the last sentence,* SLIM *motions to* PETE *to be quiet.* LARRY *or the girls are too absorbed to notice them.*)

LARRY: They were heading for a cut-bank. I knew if I couldn't turn them, the whole herd was doomed.

SUZANNE: Oh, how terrible!

LARRY: So I galloped hell for leather towards the lead steer. If I could turn him. . .

    (*Turning he sees* PETE *and* SLIM)

PETE: Yes, sir, boy, if you could turn him—

SLIM: The gal was saved.

PETE: The mortgage lifted.

SLIM: The villain foiled.

PETE: Say you turned him, Larry Boy.

    (*He pleads*)

SLIM: Don't let your old pappy down, Son. You played a man's part didn't you?

LARRY: (*Embarrassed*) They're friends of mine,—always joking.
SUZANNE: Hmmmm. They just wish they were real cowboys. Anybody can see that.
BETSY: Some people are always butting in on other people.
LARRY: I was just telling the young ladies here—
SLIM: Don't listen to his purty talk, Gal. He's a tough hombre.
PETE: Hard as nails and twice as stubborn.
SUZANNE: (*Ignoring* PETE *and* SLIM) Can't we go someplace where we could talk?
BETSY: (*Shyly*) Maybe—maybe you'd have a glass of lemonade with us.
LARRY: Thanks, I'd like to very much.
SUZANNE: (*As they start off*). Jealousy plays a fool's part, as my grandmother says. Come, Betsy.
> (*They go out, their skirts swishing indignantly.* LARRY *follows them, wiping his brow.*)
PETE *and* SLIM: (*Singing.*)
> Oh a man there lives on the Western plains,
> With a ton of fight and an ounce of brains,
> Who herds the cows as he robs the trains,
> And goes by the name of Larry.
> (*They call the name after him.*)
SLIM: He's certainly having himself a time, isn't he?
PETE: Got those little gals practically swooning.
> (PETE *and* SLIM *are laughing as* LONESOME *and* NIGGER JOHN *come in.*)
Well! I thought you'd got yourself jailed, Lonesome. We got to finish our contest before you take the train.
LONESOME: Contest's off, Pete.
PETE: Aw, we got up to one hundred and forty-seven. We got to finish.
LONESOME: I can't. Besides, I don't feel like singing, I just want to go off and eat a few worms.
> (CELIA *and* MA *enter.*)
CELIA: Why, Lonesome, what's the matter?
SLIM: He's got a bad hangover.
LONESOME: Why didn't you lock me up last night, Ma?
NIGGER JOHN: Shark won his last cent in the game.
LONESOME: So I won't be taking the train, Pete.
MA: Oh Lonesome, Lonesome!
> (*There is a mixture of affection and impatience in her tone*).
LONESOME: (*Dolefully*) I know, I just ain't no good, that's all.
SLIM: Did you find Shorthorn, John?
NIGGER JOHN: No. He ain't been around here all morning. I wonder. . .
> (*The band rises very loud for a few seconds. Then a voice over the megaphone comes through*).
MEGAPHONE: Contestants in the Cowboys' Calf Roping Contest please report at the chutes. Contestants in the Cowboy's Calf Roping Contest please. . .

Gwen Pharis Ringwood

SLIM: I'm off, boy. I report way over to the other side.

LONESOME: Good luck, Slim.

MA: You be careful now.

NIGGER JOHN: Don't get excited and take your time. Forget all about
the people and imagine you're back at the round up, branding
calves.

SLIM: Thanks. See you later.

> (*He starts out.* BUD *returns meeting him.*)

BUD: Good roping, cowboy. (SLIM *acknowledges this with a wave and
goes off.* BUD *speaks in a low tone to* NIGGER JOHN). Shorthorn
ain't come in yet.

NIGGER JOHN: I know. Take a look over at Ma's, will you, Bud? I'd go
but I'm afraid I'll miss him.

BUD: Yeah. Ceeley, I'll meet you and Ma at the grandstand. You've got
your tickets?

CELIA: I have them, Bud. We'll wait for you there. (*Bud goes off*) Shall
we go, Ma?

> (NIGGER JOHN *moves restlessly back stage and then goes out
at the back*).

MA: Might as well. (*She looks off left toward the grandstand*) You
know, Ceeley, when I see thousands of people all bunched up like
that, so their faces are just white blurs in space, I get a queer
feeling, like nothing is real, like that's all we are, a little white
blur in a fog and one by one we're just blotted out. I do, Ceeley,
I feel that.

CELIA: Oh no, Ma. There's more meaning to it than that. I know there is.

MA: Maybe. Well, come on, we better get out where we can see. (*As
they start out* NIGGER JOHN *reappears. Ma turns to speak to him.*)
Now stop your worryin' John, Shorthorn will be here in time,
you see.

NIGGER JOHN: I hope you're right, Mrs. Raybourne.

> (CELIA *and* MA *move off left.*)

PETE: Hurry up, Lonesome, we want to be out there cheering for Slim.
They say today's calves are heavy and wild.

LONESOME: They're wild all right. Their idea of fun is to get all four
feet up in your face and kick.

> (PETE *and* LONESOME *go out.* LARRY, BETSY, *and* SUZANNE
come through toward the grandstand.)

BETSY: Aren't you roping this afternoon, Larry?

LARRY: No. You see, my horse, well, my horse he—

SUZANNE: Your horse isn't ill?

LARRY: Oh no, no. My horse is perfectly all right only he's tired, that's
all, he's just a little tired.

BETSY: You're so thoughtful, Larry.

> (*They go off.* SHORTHORN *comes in. He looks tired and
speaks quietly*)

SHORTHORN: Hello, John.

NIGGER JOHN: Shorthorn! Where have you been? You're up at 2:35.

SHORTHORN: I know. I had to—there were some things I had to do, down town.

NIGGER JOHN: You didn't see Shark?

SHORTHORN: No.

NIGGER JOHN: I've had a man keeping an eye on him, Shorthorn. I don't think he's going to make any trouble.

SHORTHORN: I don't figure on shooting Shark, if that's worrying you, John.

(*He smiles affectionately at* NIGGER JOHN).

NIGGER JOHN: You checked in?

SHORTHORN: Yeah. Jumped the fence over there. I just have to get my saddle. I'll be right back. I've got to talk to you, John.

(BUD *comes in*).

BUD: He's not over at Ma's—(*He sees* SHORTHORN) I was looking for you. John was afraid something might have happened.

(*He speaks with constraint*).

SHORTHORN: You going to wish me luck, Bud?

BUD: (*Tight lipped*) I hope you get whatever you want out of it, that's all.

SHORTHORN: (*Biting back.*) I'll get what I want, Bud.

(*He goes off back.*)

NIGGER JOHN: What's the matter with you, Bud? Can't you see—

BUD: No. I can't see nothing, except that I ought to be in there fighting it out with Midnight.

NIGGER JOHN: You couldn't ride Midnight. Look at you, you're all stiffened up. You don't have a chance. You go sit down somewhere and think things over. There's a lot of things you don't know about yet. Looks like one of them might be loyalty. You might think about that a while.

(BUD *goes off right. From a distance a voice comes over the megaphone and a cheer is heard.*)

MEGAPHONE: That was Tom Patterson, folks, who roped and tied in 24 seconds. Next contestant, Slim Randall of the Bar X Y—Slim Randall.

(SHORTHORN *returns*).

SHORTHORN: I drew first out, John.

NIGGER JOHN: If anybody can ride Midnight, you can.

SHORTHORN: I wonder.

NIGGER JOHN: Watch for a little twist he gives after the fourth or fifth jump. That's what usually piles them.

SHORTHORN: I'll watch. I never figured on trying to ride your horse, John. I always felt it'd be sort of dishonourable. He didn't want nobody but you to touch him.

NIGGER JOHN: Midnight ain't my horse now, Shorthorn. I couldn't get near him this morning. He ain't anybody's horse from here on out.

SHORTHORN: You said it'd be that way. I'm sure sorry.

NIGGER JOHN: You got something on your mind, Shorthorn.

SHORTHORN: Yeah, I want to give you this, John. It's the deed to the Diamond J. I spent the morning fixing it so's Bud can take my share. It'll be you and Bud on the Diamond J, John.

NIGGER JOHN: No.

SHORTHORN: That's the way I want it. That's the way it's got to be, John. It'll be sort of a wedding present for Bud and Ceeley.

NIGGER JOHN: What are you going to do?

SHORTHORN: I ain't figured yet, but I can't stay here. Shark's dug up my whole history and sooner or later it'll catch up with me—

NIGGER JOHN: Shorthorn, there's a U.S. Marshall here from Montana. I know him. Let's go to him and tell your story.

SHORTHORN: No. It's too late now,—twenty-two years too late. Besides I wouldn't want Ceeley to know—

NIGGER JOHN: Don't you think she'll hear it anyway?

SHORTHORN: I reckon she will. There's something else, John—I couldn't stand being locked up. I haven't got that kind of guts I guess. You see, that's what I've been running away from all the time.

(There are cheers off stage).

MEGAPHONE: That was Slim Randall who roped and tied in 17 seconds, folks. Seventeen seconds to rope and tie his calf.

SHORTHORN: Good for Slim.

*(*PETE *and* LONESOME *come running in*)*

LONESOME: Slim made good time. Hello, Shorthorn.

PETE: They're hazing the broncs into the chutes, Shorthorn. You're going to light your fag on the sun. Midnight's rarin' to go today.

LONESOME: So's Shorthorn rarin' to go. Ten seconds is all it takes. Hang on, Cowboy.

MEGAPHONE: Shorthorn Charlie Woolf on Midnight, report to Chute 1. Tom Three Persons on Cyclone, Chute 2. Johnny Barker on Challenge, Chute 3. Tim Bercuson on Gay Roan, Chute 4. Lucky Al Wilson on Aztec, Chute 5.

*(*SHORTHORN *has taken up his saddle.* LARRY *rushes in.*)*

LARRY: Mr. Woolf, Shorthorn, I—I just want to—(*He is at a loss for words and finally just shakes Shorthorn's hand and explodes*) Yippee!

SHORTHORN: Thanks, Larry.

NIGGER JOHN: Ma said to give you this, Shorthorn.

SHORTHORN: (*Looking at it*) Horseshoe Ed's silver dollar. I need it. I sure do.

*(*CELIA *enters*)*

CELIA: Good luck, Shorthorn. We'll be watching you ride him.

SHORTHORN: I got to ride him now. So long, little Ceeley.

(He touches her cheek gently. BUD *enters and goes to* SHORTHORN).*

BUD: I come to wish you luck. Good riding, Shorthorn.

(They look at one another a moment and shake hands.)

SHORTHORN: You'll ride him next year, Bud.
>   (SLIM *comes in from the chutes as* SHORTHORN *turns to go out that way*).
SHORTHORN: Say, you did fine, Slim. Puts you right up in the top bracket.
SLIM: I should have done it in sixteen seconds but I got nervous. How do you feel, boy?
SHORTHORN: (*For a moment, whether real or assumed, the old touch of heroic gay braggadocio is there*). Wolf of the world, boys—just clear the way for the wolf of the world.
SLIM: Don't let that black outlaw bust you, now.
SHORTHORN: If he busts me, just plant me where I land.
SLIM: Don't worry, we won't move you. I got to save my strength.
>   (*As* SHORTHORN *turns to go,* NIGGER JOHN *is standing near the exit to the chutes. He places his hand on* SHORTHORN'*s shoulder*).
NIGGER JOHN: You want me to belt you down?
SHORTHORN: No, you watch from here. (*Smiling*) What is it you always say to the youngsters when we're breakin' horses?
NIGGER JOHN: Sit deep in the saddle, take a far distant look, and hope to God you land soft. (*The lines somehow sum up all the friendship they have shared for a long time.*) Good luck—partner.
>   (SHORTHORN *goes out. The men crowd round the fence.* CEELEY *and* BUD *go off*).
MEGAPHONE: The broncs are in the chutes, folks, for the Saddle Bronc Riding Contest. A purse of $500.00 for this contest. Saddle Bronc Riding is probably the most dangerous event of the Stampede. Today's Broncs include the wildest horses of the week's entries.
LARRY: They're having trouble with Cyclone.
SLIM: He's a veteran at making trouble. Watch that Midnight rear.
MEGAPHONE: In this contest the rider must keep the rein in one hand, the free hand must be kept floating at least 18 inches away from the horse. Both feet must remain in the stirrups and move in a kicking motion throughout the ride.
PETE: Sounds easy, don't it?
LONESOME: I'd sooner ride a tiger than any of them broncs.
LARRY: Shorthorn can ride him. My uncle says—
MEGAPHONE: Charlie Woolf's waiting to mount Midnight, folks. That's the coal black horse in Chute One that has everybody talking. His first week in the ring and he's bucked off every rider in less than five jumps. Woolf's going to try to stay on him for ten seconds.
SLIM: Ten seconds seems like a long time when you're straddling a tornado.
MEGAPHONE: They've got the saddle on Midnight. They're tightening the the flank rope. The horse rears. Woolf waits—he's mounting, he's up!

LONESOME: Hang on, boy, hang on.
MEGAPHONE: Woolf's got the buckshank in his left hand. He pulls his hat down and gives the signal. . . They've opened the chutes, folks. They're off.
> (*A cheer goes up. The boys on the stage shout and Yippee.*)

SLIM: Stay with him, Shorthorn, stay with him.
MEGAPHONE: Midnight's jumping high, wide and handsome. Look at him twist.
PETE: That horse is a fighting devil. Ride him, Shorthorn. Ride him.
LONESOME: Hang on Cowboy, Yippee!
> (*He and* LARRY *shout together*).

MEGAPHONE: That's the fourth jump. Watch that black buck, folks, Higher every time. He's jack-knifing. The rider's taking a lot of punishment.
PETE: Four seconds to go.
SLIM: Shorthorn's sure giving him his head.
MEGAPHONE: Sixth jump and seven seconds gone. Three seconds to go—
NIGGER JOHN: Watch him, boy. He's fixing to throw you.
MEGAPHONE: Midnight's reaching for the sun now. Woolf sticks. It's some ride. Nine seconds. The horse rears—Woolf's still in the stirrups—there's the gong folks. Ten seconds. Charlie Woolf has stayed on Midnight ten seconds.
NIGGER JOHN: Watch him, Shorthorn!
MEGAPHONE: Look out, Charlie Woolf's been thrown just over the ten seconds mark. Midnight bucked him off on the ninth jump when he sunswitched. Woolf's taken a hard fall. He's still down—The Black's off down the field.
SLIM: He's hurt.
PETE: No. No. He's getting up.
MEGAPHONE: It's all right, folks. Woolf's getting to his feet. He looks shaky but he's walking off under his own steam.
MEGAPHONE: What a ride! That was Charlie Woolf riding Midnight for ten seconds—he's in the running for the purse of $500.00.
NIGGER JOHN: Feel like I'd taken the pounding myself.
LARRY: What'd I say? He's some rider isn't he?
SLIM: He's a great rider, son. And Midnight's a great horse.
PETE: Midnight likes the game now. Nothing can stop him—
NIGGER JOHN: I think that was the hardest ridin' I ever saw.
MEGAPHONE: Johnny Barker is up on Challenge folks. They've belted Barker down. He's mounted and—
> (SHORTHORN *enters.*)

LARRY: Shorthorn. Oh boy, Mr. Woolf, if I could ride like that—
LONESOME: Congratulations, old timer—are you all right?
SHORTHORN: I think so. When I get my wind. (*He sinks down on the bench at back*) I'm too old to take that though. It was some ride, John, and Midnight tossed me fair and square.

SLIM: You stayed on ten seconds, boy. That's all it takes.

NIGGER JOHN: You stayed on longer than I thought a man could stay.

SHORTHORN: No, he won, even if I stuck it out to the gong. It was him or me and he threw me. In a way I'm not sorry, John. Like you say, he's a proud horse. I don't think anybody will ever ride him in.

(SHARK *comes in from the right. He has been drinking.* NIGGER JOHN *is the first to see him.*)

SHARK: (*To* SHORTHORN). Ten seconds, eh?

SHORTHORN: That's right.

SHARK: And you rode right straight into a noose.

NIGGER JOHN: Where you going, Shark?

SHARK: Where do you think I'm going? Going to help the law close out one of its files—an old file on Charlie Weston. You rode Midnight, didn't you, Weston? Ten seconds. You think you're going to see your name in the paper? You'll see it all right. You're going to read about how Charlie Weston alias Charlie Woolf was arrested as he walked off the grounds. Charlie Weston wanted for a shooting in Texas—it'll be in the papers all right, all of them, splashed sky high!

NIGGER JOHN: (*Moving forward.*) Shut up, Shark.

SHARK: I've got the whole story and I've got it for sure this time.

(NIGGER JOHN *jumps at* SHARK *and they struggle.*)

NIGGER JOHN: I warned you, Shark.

(SHORTHORN *tries to pull* NIGGER JOHN *back*).

SHORTHORN: Stop it, John. John! Stop, I tell you. For God's sake man, you'll kill him.

(*He finally pulls* NIGGER JOHN *back*).

NIGGER JOHN: Yeah. That's just what I'm aiming to do.

SHORTHORN: No. No. Can't you see, that won't help, John. You can't help nothing that way. I ought to know.

PETE: (*Examining* SHARK) It's all right. he's still breathing but he don't know it.

SHORTHORN: (*Turning*) Look, boys. I need six hours. Will you give it to me? What Shark said is true—my name was Weston, twenty years ago. It's up to you.

(*He looks from one to the other*).

SLIM: (*After a slight pause*) Reckon we can give you six hours, Shorthorn. Time's cheap. Why don't you ask for something hard, like money?

SHORTHORN: Time's all I need, Slim. Six hours time. Keep him from talking for that long. Then let him go.

PETE: Come on, Lonesome, give me a hand here. If anybody asks, this guy's just passed out, that's all.

(SLIM, PETE *and* LONESOME *take* SHARK *out*).

LARRY: Shorthorn, was it my fault, telling that story?

SHORTHORN: No. It was just the way the cards was stacked, son, that's all. You go on and enjoy yourself now. I want to talk to John.

(LARRY *goes off left.* SHORTHORN *goes over to take up the saddle he has dropped by the fence*).

SHORTHORN: Well, John, we rode together for a long time.

NIGGER JOHN: How about going on together?

SHORTHORN: No, you're too well-known, John. It wouldn't be safe. Besides, you can look after Ceeley and Bud. Bud's pretty young yet—help him, John.

NIGGER JOHN: Take my saddle, Shorthorn.

SHORTHORN: Yours? You got the best saddle East of the Rockies—

NIGGER JOHN: Take it.

SHORTHORN: Thanks. I'll hang mine up here.

(*He goes over and begins to take down* NIGGER JOHN'S *saddle which is hanging near the rear exit. As* SHORTHORN *is standing with his back partly turned, the Marshall comes through again*).

MARSHALL: John, have you heard anything about a fellow named Weston? There's a lot of talk going round. He's wanted—

NIGGER JOHN: Yeah, Marshall, I heard the talk. Reckon it's some kid letting his imagination run wild.

MARSHALL: You don't know anything about it then? I've got to check it anyway.

NIGGER JOHN: I knew a Charlie Weston once, Marshall. Down in Montana. But he died about five years ago, maybe more. In Miles City. Pneumonia they said.

MARSHALL: Thanks. That's probably the one. I'll see what I can find out about this story anyway.

(*He goes out*).

NIGGER JOHN: (*Turning*) Reckon you ain't got much time, Boy.

SHORTHORN: No.

MEGAPHONE: Keep your seats, folks. There's been an accident. Al Wilson fell under Aztec. A stretcher is on the way out. Keep your seats, please.

SHORTHORN: (*Looking over the fence*) God, look at that. He don't move. He must be smashed up bad.

NIGGER JOHN: Waste, waste, so's a lot of folks can yell. I just can't see it, that's all.

SHORTHORN: I know. (*He moves forward with* NIGGER JOHN'*s saddle*). Look, John. I'm heading North to the Cariboo. That country's just opened up for ranching. Nobody's going to to know me there. I reckon I can ride herd for somebody for another ten years, anyway.

NIGGER JOHN: I'll sure miss you.

SHORTHORN: Yeah. I wish—I better get moving. Take care of yourself.

NIGGER JOHN: Good luck, Shorthorn.

(*They shake hands.* BEANIE *comes in with* WHITE CALF)

BEANIE: Come on, White Calf. There'll be a big crowd coming to see if Wilson's been killed or not. I'll milk them.

SHORTHORN: (*As he passes* WHITE CALF) Don't get discouraged, White Calf.

BEANIE: (*Recognizing* SHORTHORN) Say, cowboy, you're some rider ain't you?

SHORTHORN: Sure. I'm a ring-tailed wonder (*He turns and looks at* NIGGER JOHN *affectionately. With a little smile*) The wolf of the world, ain't I, John?

NIGGER JOHN: That's right, boy. You sure are.

BEANIE: Come on, White Calf. (*He moves off stage.* WHITE CALF *stands quietly at stage left.*) Step right up, folks, shake hands with a genuine vanished American.

SHORTHORN: (*Who is now at stage right speaks to* NIGGER JOHN *who is standing near the back centre*) So long—partner.

NIGGER JOHN: So long—Shorthorn.

> (*He stands very quietly watching* SHORTHORN *go. Then slowly takes up the saddle* SHORTHORN *left on the ground at centre back and hangs it up on the nail where his own has been. As he does so, a voice off stage or a whistle begins the song Doney Gal. One by one more voices join in until they reach a great swell of song which after its climax begins to get farther and farther away. The lights dim until all that can be seen is the rope, saddle and boots that hang on the fence and the dim figures of* NIGGER JOHN *and* WHITE CALF. *From afar off the song comes faintly and from a little distance we hear* BEANIE)

BEANIE: Last chance for a souvenir of the old West, folks. Last chance.

The End

A Fine Coloured Easter Egg
A Comedy

Characters

GEORGE LITOWSKY, *bachelor*
WASYL NEMITCHUK (*pronounced Waseel Nameechuk*)
OLGA NEMITCHUK

TIME: *A spring morning in the 1950s*
PLACE: *The yard and interior of George Litowsky's bachelor shack in the northern Alberta bush.*
(If desired, action may be designed to play entirely in the interior of the cabin)

Stage right is a rough board well with wash basin on it. Trees are indicated at edge of stage.
    Down centre runs the wall of the cabin, with stops leading up to the door.
    Inside the cabin is a bunk bed high on the wall, ladder to bed, a table, 2 chairs, stove and a rough screen.
    Tacked on outside wall of cabin is a bear skin with half mounted head.
    Setting should be suggested without any attempt at realism. Necessary properties (ladder, chair, etc.) should be rough and simple.
    Costumes should be bright—not of any particular style.
    The Canadian-Ukrainian speech pattern should be obtained by inflection rather than by a heavy "accent."
    The play needs speed and a great deal of vitality. The director can use spatial relationships and vocal pitch to enhance the comedy.
    As the curtain rises we see GEORGE LITOWSKY *wake in his bunk bed, sit up, draw on pants over the long underwear he wears for sleeping,*

255

descend the ladder, put a match to the fire laid in the stove and move coffee pot forward, go outside to the well where he dips water in a dipper, pours it into the wash basin and begins his morning ablutions. While he is at the well we also see WASYL NEMITCHUK *creeping on stage, looking behind him cautiously, concealing himself in the bushes stage right.*

WASYL: George. George. (*A whisper*)

GEORGE: (*Startled*) Yes? What's that? Yes?

WASYL: George Litowsky.

GEORGE: (*His face lathered with soap.*) I hear you. Who is it? (*He is nervous.*)

WASYL: Sh. . . don't shout. It's me.

GEORGE: That's no answer! (*Moving toward sound*). Come out, whoever you are. Come out I say. What do you mean, sneaking around like a beast or a savage? Ah, soap in my eye! I can't see. I'm blinded.

(*He rushes back to basin and splashes his face with water.* WASYL *emerges from the bush, an outlandish figure wrapped in a red blanket, his bare legs showing above work boots. He pauses, listening, the blanket held over his face.* GEORGE *turns and sees* WASYL.)

GEORGE: Ahhh! It is a savage! Saint Christopher, protect me!

WASYL: (*Still looking off*) Don't shout, I tell you. I may be followed.

GEORGE: (*Fearfully advancing with dipper*) Yes, sir. Of course. Whatever you say. Don't move or I'll. . .

WASYL: (*Turning suddenly*) Fool!

GEORGE: Ahh! (*He throws dipper of water at* WASYL *and retreats toward cabin, cowering.*) Accident, sir. . . accident! (*Running into cabin he hides under table or raises chair threateningly*) Police! Police!

WASYL: (*Advancing*) Quiet, I tell you.

GEORGE: (*Meekly*) Yes, sir. (*Whispering*) Police. Police.

WASYL: Idiot! It's me. . . Wasyl. . . your cousin, Wasyl Nemitchuk.

GEORGE: (*Holding chair in front of himself*) I don't believe you.

WASYL: Look at me! Isn't this my nose? My left ear? My right ear? My moustache. If not mine, whose?

GEORGE (*Tugging at* WASYL's *moustache fearfully.*) The moustache. . . it looks like yours.

WASYL: Oww! Of course it's mine. Are you crazy?

GEORGE: Crazy. I think someone is crazy all right. But who. . . that's what I'm asking. (*He is very angry*) Who's crazy? Me? Or my cousin. You're the crazy one, Wasyl Nemitchuk. You, my lordly upstanding prosperous cousin. . . that's who's crazy!

WASYL: Quiet, I tell you. Quiet!

GEORGE: (*Shouting*) I won't be quiet. This is my house!

WASYL: (*Turning away*) You are right, Cousin. It is your house. I had a house once too. . . A fine house, trees, land, wife, chickens, cattle. . . All vanity. Dust and ashes. Vanity. (*Recovering from philosophy*) Well, aren't you going to invite me in?

GEORGE: Come in, then. So, it is you, the little Wasyl. Wait, what's that in your hand? A bomb?

WASYL: Bomb? This? What does it look like?

GEORGE: An Easter Egg. A coloured Easter egg.

WASYL: Right. A fine coloured Easter egg. (*He places it carefully on the table*) Memory of past joy. Why are you staring at me, George?

GEORGE: Was I staring? Excuse. It's just that I'm not used to you. . . I mean, you look strange. . . in the blanket. . . you know, funny. . . (*He laughs nervously*) Won't you take it off?

WASYL: No!

GEORGE: Sorry, cousin. It's a very fine blanket, of course. No doubt the latest. . . the very best.

WASYL: See! As usual you just wrap everything up in words, throw it away. No ideas. No mention of breakfast. Just words.

GEORGE: (*Expansively*) My dear cousin, you shall have breakfast. Coffee (*he takes coffee pot*). An egg? Two eggs?

WASYL: What time is it?

GEORGE: (*Looking at clock*) Nearly eight o'clock.

WASYL: Four eggs.

GEORGE: Sit down. I shall fix. (WASYL *sits*. GEORGE, *breaking eggs, speaks with elaborate casualness*) Well, Wasyl, have you been joining anything lately? Lions? Elks? An Indian tribe maybe?

WASYL: Indian tribes? (*He thinks hard*) A brave people. Indians—they kept their women in their place. The Indian squaw softened the tough buffalo hides by chewing with her teeth.

GEORGE: (*Lost*) Of course. Quite. (*Turning with resolution*) Wasyl, I am a blunt man. Why did you come here?

WASYL: I was hungry.

GEORGE: Why are you wearing that blanket?

WASYL: (*Reasonably*) I was cold.

GEORGE: I see. (*Trying again*) Are you in trouble, cousin? Are you concealing something?

WASYL: Yes.

GEORGE: Ah, I understand. What are you concealing, Wasyl?

WASYL: Me. Myself.

GEORGE: Wasyl, we are blood cousins, we have hunted and fished together. I was best man at your wedding. I have dandled your six daughters—

WASYL: Seven.

GEORGE: Your seven daughters—

WASYL: Seven daughters, fourteen granddaughters, and that's all. Never a boy. Never a single, solitary boy. (*It is an old sorrow—he leaves it to turn to present things*) I like my eggs turned.

GEORGE: Wasyl, (*Turning eggs*) tell me, be honest, have you lost your mind?

Gwen Pharis Ringwood

WASYL: (*Getting up excitedly*) That's right. Exactly. Take them up, George, do you want to ruin them entirely? (*Shouting*) Take them up, I tell you.

GEORGE: (*Completely unstrung*) Oh, I see—the eggs. (*He takes them up*) There we are. (*Pushing* WASYL *into chair behind table*) Eat, Wasyl. Eat, my poor cousin. Me, I am not hungry. Me, I shall never eat again. Sugar in your eggs, cousin?

WASYL: (*About to cut bread, he points knife at* GEORGE) Are we alone here?

GEORGE: (*Pouring coffee*) Oh, yes, yes—completely alone. (*Looks up to see knife*) That is—what am I saying? Who is alone—never—never alone. (*He is backing towards window, convinced* WASYL *is mad*) Why, there is my friend, Steven Mihailovitch. (*Runs to window*) How, Stefan—I mean, Hi, Stefan. Lovely morning. See, there he goes, my good friend, Stefan.

WASYL: (*Darkly*) Is he gone?

GEORGE: Oh no, no, just feeding the rabbits. A kind man, but fierce mind you—dangerous when defending a friend.

WASYL: You lie, George. There is no Stefan. The eggs are good.

GEORGE: Have another, Wasyl? A half dozen?

WASYL: (*Waving him away*) No more. You ask me if I lost my mind? Sometimes I thought I would. (*Pointing to chair with knife.*) Sit down, George. A terrible thing has happened.

GEORGE: (*Sitting meekly*) Olga is dead?

WASYL: (*Crossly*) Olga? No. Olga is alive. Olga blooms. The worse it gets the more she flourishes. (*Back to tragic tone*) George, calamity falls on Wasyl Nemitchuk.

GEORGE: Yes? Too bad, Wasyl.

WASYL: Yes. Terrible!

GEORGE: You're a good man too. I'm sorry.

WASYL: Thank you.

(*They brood*)

GEORGE: Your house burned to the ground eh?—Tch—Tch.

WASYL: (*Indignantly*) Who said anything about my house? It stands.

GEORGE: That is one blessing then. (*Pause*) Your daughters all ruined, is that it?

WASYL: My daughters are respectable—all married!

GEORGE: Your hogs, then—stricken?

WASYL: No! Two hundred and twenty beautiful white pigs I got.

GEORGE: Well, it's too bad, that's all, whatever it is.

WASYL: Trouble, trouble, nobody knows—up—down. Crash—bang—day and night—up down bang crash. In my brain!

GEORGE: (*Thinking he understands at last*) The doctor gives no hope?

WASYL: Doctor?

GEORGE: About your brain? The noises in your head?

WASYL: (*Angry*) What the devil are you talking about, George? The noises is not in my head. The noises is on my farm. The noises is

Oil. Oil, George. Bang—crash—raise—drill—release—bore—up—down—back door—front door—behind the barn—behind the outhouse. Crash—bang—raise—drop. They're drilling for oil on my farm, George. That's what's the matter—Oil!

GEORGE: (*Jumping up*) Ah, congratulations, my little one! Congratulations. I knew you would be a great man. Brains will tell. (*Shaking* WASYL'S *hand vigorously*) Brains will out. Felicitations and all that.

WASYL: Tchkai! Tchkai! (*Pronounced Chekeye*) Do I look like a happy man? Do you congratulate a man in a blanket? A shroud? You are looking on a dead man George. Understand—dead.

GEORGE: (*Weakly sitting in Morris Chair*) I see. Dead. Well, my congratu—my commiserations, cousin. Completely dead eh?

WASYL: Quite. Deceased. (*Pause*) By my own hand.

GEORGE: Suicide eh? (WASYL *nods*) That's a sin.

WASYL: Accidental suicide. Drowned. No sin there.

GEORGE: Drowned in a muddy river?

WASYL: The mighty Saskatchewan.

GEORGE: (*Shaking his head*) Of course, it's not for me to say—there are other ways—still, it's your suicide, not mine.

WASYL: They'll find me by the spruce tree near the ferry.

GEORGE: Find you?

WASYL: All that's left. My red shirt, pants, underwear—neatly folded under the spruce. Poor Wasyl, they'll say, that good father and husband.

GEORGE: A fine farmer, they'll say—good wheat. Good pigs. Fine solid bone structure.

WASYL: And Olga,—my proud Olga—she'll weep, lie in the night beating her hands on the pillow, weeping for me.

GEORGE: The widow Olga.
     (*It is a pleasant phrase*)

WASYL: (*Changing tone entirely*) Olga—don't say her name to me. I'm finished with Olga. It is Olga who drove me to my death! Olga ruined me. Olga—and oil!

GEORGE: Always the woman.

WASYL: (*Getting up*) George, I must borrow some clothes? This blanket itches.!

GEORGE: (*With alacrity*) Of course, Wasyl. Here, behind the screen. Underwear, pants, jacket.

WASYL: Thank you.
     (*He goes behind the screen, his head is showing over.*)

GEORGE: (*Busily, as he mounts ladder to bunk*) Let me see. Socks—shirt—shoes.

WASYL: I have shoes. Do you think I'd walk out here barefoot in the dew? Why, I might catch my death.

GEORGE: A shirt then. (*Starts to mount ladder*) Take what you like, Wasyl. Anything. You will need warm clothes for your trip.

WASYL: Trip?

GEORGE: (*Starting down ladder with shirt, then pausing on ladder*) Don't worry about things here. I will comfort Olga. Just disappear, Wasyl—into the blue. You can trust me with Olga, the oil, the funeral.

WASYL: Funeral? Whose funeral?

GEORGE: Yours, but I'll act as if it were my own—everything of the best, black plush with gold handles. Wreath of lilies. Just disappear, my old one.

WASYL: (*Coming out in long underwear and reaching for shirt*) But, I'm staying here with you, George. I thought I'd hide here until—

GEORGE: Staying here? You can't.
(*He holds shirt out of reach*)

WASYL: After all, we are blood cousins. Our mutual uncle, was he not bodyguard to the Czar?
(*They salute solemnly*)

GEORGE: But this shack—not suitable—small, dirty—

WASYL: It is quiet—the blessed quiet. You've no idea what it's like at home, George. Five oil wells being drilled in the yard. In the house Olga is saying "We must give the granddaughters dancing lessons." Raise, lower—"We'll buy a Cadillac." "Shall I have a mink or squirrel, my husband?" My Olga, for 25 years has baked bread, made cabbage rolls, borne seven fine daughers. Now that same Olga nags, plans, goes shopping, is always wanting something.

GEORGE: You should put your foot down.

WASYL: I tried. Heaven knows I tried, but it goes deep. My Olga has been seduced.

GEORGE: (*Very shocked*) Oh!

WASYL: Seduced by Oil. I give you an example. (WASYL *comes out from behind screen. This time he has on a pair of trousers, loud checks, over the underwear. The trousers are too large. He is wearing one sock and shoe.*) A symbol, that's what it is, a symbol. (*He indicates the Easter egg.*) Look at this, George.

GEORGE: I see it.

WASYL: What is it?

GEORGE: You told me already—the memory of past joy.

WASYL: Yes, a fine coloured Easter egg. Such colour, such design, such patience.

GEORGE: Beautiful.

WASYL: She took hours of the careful etching through the wax, and all for me. My Olga made it for me last year.

GEORGE: (*Knowingly*) Hah! Love eh?

WASYL: Yes, last year she loved me passionately. Nothing is too much trouble. But this year—this year—

GEORGE: Well?

WASYL: Olga says: "Wasyl, I'm tired of coloring those old-fashioned Easter eggs—such work is for peasants! From now on, I'll buy chocolate Easter eggs from the store for you and the grand-daughters. They are pretty, good to eat, and no trouble."

GEORGE: Hmmmm. That seems sensible.

WASYL: Sensible? You are a bachelor, with no fine feelings. Sensible to give up something made by hand and beautiful, for something produced by thousands in a factory? No, I won't live that way. So, I take a stand.

GEORGE: In a blanket.

WASYL: Yes. Why this oil well business has changed Olga's whole nature. A good farm and happy husband mean nothing. We must get rich quick with oil. I refuse. So, I have disappeared.

GEORGE: And she will think you are drowned already?

WASYL: Exactly. They find my clothes. Olga remembers my last words "with such a woman, wanting such a life, I can no longer exist". So, of course, she'll think I'm drowned.

GEORGE: Poor Olga.

WASYL: Poor Olga, nothing! It would serve her right if I desert her for another woman.

GEORGE: You have another woman in mind?

WASYL: Hmmmm! I could find one, if I wished.

GEORGE: So? You are not exactly the young rooster, Wasyl.

WASYL: The widow Rodinsky goes out of her way to ask my advice. She admires my pigs, my farm, my personality.

GEORGE: Ha. Franca Rodinsky. But she has a good farm herself!

WASYL: And no oil on it! Still, it is Olga I love. So I think if I stay here until just before my funeral and then come forward Olga will be so glad to see me she will come to her senses.

GEORGE: Oh no, Wasyl, you mustn't stay here! Why Olga would find you at once. You must disappear; teach her a lesson.

WASYL: Disappear?

GEORGE: Completely.

WASYL: Where?

GEORGE: South America, that's the place! Peru! She'd never think of looking in Peru!

WASYL: But I only planned to stay drowned for a day or two. At my funeral, I will be alive! I can see Olga now—weeping at my grave—and then I appear—like an angel! How she will appreciate me then!

GEORGE: (*Very magisterial*) Useless. Believe me, cousin, I know women. It will take months, years perhaps.

WASYL: Women! If only there'd been a boy in the family—a son or a grandson to carry on the farm, to see my side of it. But no, seven daughters, fourteen granddaughters, and never a single, solitary boy! Wouldn't you think, George, by the law of averages—? (*His voice rises*)

GEORGE: Sh—Don't excite yourself, Wasyl. Rest, relax. Leave everything to me!

WASYL: Ah yes, the quiet—the blessed quiet.

    (*Off stage after a brief pause, comes a loud outcry*)

OLGA: (*Off stage*) Wasyl! Wasyl! Oi, oi, where are you? Wasyl?

WASYL: That's Olga!—Coming here! What do I do now?

GEORGE: Go out the window.

WASYL: But after that—?

GEORGE: Hide in the woods until she goes. Then we'll get your ticket to Peru.

WASYL: I'm not dressed for travelling.

GEORGE: I'll fix. Here, take your blanket.

WASYL: I'm tired of it.

OLGA: Wasyl, it is I, Olga.

WASYL: I'll hide in the cupboard? The bunk?

GEORGE: No. She'd find you. Go now. Hurry.

WASYL: Very well. Tell her I drowned myself from sorrow. That she lost a treasure; a great lover, and a man of ideas too. Understand.

GEORGE: Yes, yes, go on.

WASYL: (*Sadly, draping blanket over his underwear*) Di Bozsha, cousin.

GEORGE: (*Pushing him out window*) Di bozsha.

    (*He closes window and turns with great relief. Outside* OLGA *runs across the clearing and knocks on the door loudly. She is a good looking woman in her forties, wearing a bright colored head shawl and house dress.*)

OLGA: (*Knocking*) George. George, are you there?

GEORGE: Yes. Who is it?

OLGA: Olga Nemitchuk, George. Open.

GEORGE: (*Opening top half of door.*) Why, Olga. Olga, my dear woman, what brings you here? An unexpected pleasure. Wait, I'll come out.

OLGA: (*Looking up pleadingly*) Have you seen, Wasyl, George?

GEORGE: (*Coming outside*) Wasyl? Is he missing?

OLGA: Gone. Out of my bed, out of the house. I thought he might come here.

GEORGE: What clothes was he wearing?

OLGA: His red shirt, brown pants, and the old fur hat I said I was going to give to the junk man.

    (*She sobs*)

GEORGE: You quarrelled, little Olga?

OLGA: Oh yes. Yes, and now he's gone.

    (*Sinks on doorstep.*)

GEORGE: Olga, my dear, we must talk. Wait, I'll get you some wine. You need it. (*He burrows under side of wall and brings out a gallon wine jug*) Here's a whole jug. My best. Blueberry, you know.

OLGA: Wasyl! Oh, my poor husband.

GEORGE: Sh! Don't cry. Let his poor drowned spirit rest.

OLGA: Drowned? Oh no. Why do you say drowned?

GEORGE: Well, a man quarrels with his wife, slips out—

OLGA: Wasyl would never drown himself. He hates cold water.

GEORGE: Come into the house, Olga. We must talk.

OLGA: Ever since they began the drilling, Wasyl broods, cries out in the night. Argues and quarrels with me.

(GEORGE *leading her up steps.*)

GEORGE: Acts strange, eh?

OLGA: Oh yes.

GEORGE: You see, it is his mind snapping—going—going—gone. (*He ushers her inside*) Sit down, dear cousin. I will pour the wine.

OLGA: He'll come home, I'm sure he will.

GEORGE: Olga, listen to me, this morning a wandering savage wakes me up. Tells of a pile of clothes beside the river. Red shirt, pants, old fur hat—all empty.

OLGA: No, I can't believe it. Oh, I meant to be a good wife to him.

GEORGE: You were a good wife to a selfish brute. Look, little Olga, I can be a comfort to you. I'll manage everything.

OLGA: (*Drinking wine he gives her*) Drowned—Wasyl, Oh, no! I must go to the police.

GEORGE: Lean on me, little widow.

OLGA: He's not dead, I know it!

GEORGE: He wants to be dead, Olga. He is selfish. Drowns himself on purpose to make you suffer. Here, drink deep.

(WASYL *comes around the cabin outside on all fours. He crouches beside the step. The top half of the door is open.*)

OLGA: I thought if we moved to the city, the quiet,—near the daughters, but he became furious.

GEORGE: (*Patting her*) My poor widowed woman. How you have suffered! We will build a new life, Olga. You are free now. Wasyl is gone.

WASYL: (*Through clenched teeth*) Gone am I? Gone all ready?

OLGA: (*Startled*) What's that?

GEORGE: I'll see. (WASYL *slips under the bear skin that is backed on the wall.* GEORGE *looks out door.*) Strange. There is nothing.

OLGA: But I heard—

GEORGE: We were mistaken.

OLGA: Oh, I'm so tired, so nervous.

(*Leans against* GEORGE.)

GEORGE: Rest, little cabbage, rest.

OLGA: We must drag the river.

GEORGE: Why go to such expense, Olga? We'd never find him. He's too tricky, that one.

OLGA: Oh, my poor darling. Oi, oi, oi. Such a good husband.

GEORGE: Drink deep, little cousin.

Gwen Pharis Ringwood

OLGA: My poor Wasyl. You are very kind, George.
>*(She drinks. Outside,* WASYL *weeps too, partly concealed by the bear skin, but looking in the window every now and then to see what is going on.)*

GEORGE: *(Patting her.)* And to me, Olga, you are very rich and beautiful.
>(WASYL *gnashes teeth*)

OLGA: *(Rising suddenly)* George, where did you get this?

GEORGE: Get—this—that. You mean—

OLGA: My Easter egg? Where did you get it?

GEORGE: Oh yes, of course. Well, my great aunt—it's worthless and all that, you know.

OLGA: This is my Easter Egg! I'd know it anywhere.

GEORGE: Yours? Now Olga, don't be foolish.

OLGA: I made it for Wasyl last year.

GEORGE: You made one just like mine! What a coincidence.

OLGA: Tchkai! This is mine. See the break in the pattern here. That is news of the 12th granddaughter's birth. So? *(Advancing)* Wasyl is here then, George?

GEORGE: *(Frightened)* Oh no, no, Olga—Gone—Vanished—Drowned, I tell you!

OLGA: You murdered him. He brought this with him because of his great love and you murdered him.

GEORGE: Olga, little cousin, I swear.
>*(Backs over by table.)*

OLGA: *(Following)* Two cups! Four egg shells. You ate breakfast with Wasyl and then you killed him.

GEORGE: Now, Olga, put down the frying pan. I can explain—

OLGA: Where is his body? Tell me.

GEORGE: Don't hit me. Wait, Olga! Wasyl, he did come here, early, wearing only a blanket—nothing else.

OLGA: Where is he now?

GEORGE: He left suddenly. Where could a man go, wearing only a blanket? Let me think. I know!

OLGA: Where?

GEORGE: Rodinsky. That was the name! He called her his darling. Franca Rodinsky, the widow. He went to her,—just stopped by here on his way to her. He said he loves her madly.

OLGA: Franca Rodinsky! That fence post! No!

GEORGE: *(Quickly)* Yes, Olga. She's been interested in him for years. You must have noticed.

OLGA: Yes, I've seen her ogle him. So! He went to her.

GEORGE: He did, Olga.

OLGA: In a blanket, you say?

GEORGE: Nothing else. Just a blanket.

OLGA: I'll kill them. I'll kill them dead as a doornail!

GEORGE: I don't blame you.

264

OLGA: Why didn't you tell me at once? Why did you say he was drowned?

GEORGE: I wanted to spare your feelings, Olga.

OLGA: After 25 years, he deserts me for a bean pole? Oh, George, how could he?

(*She weeps loudly.*)

GEORGE: There, there—lean on me. Drink deep, little cabbage, drink deep. We will build a new life together.

OLGA: I'll put him in jail, lock him up.

GEORGE: Exactly. Nothing is too bad for him.

(*During the last scene,* WASYL *has stolen several glances at* OLGA *and* GEORGE. *Unable to bear more, he now disguises himself by putting the bear skin on, with his face hidden behind the bear's head.*)

OLGA: Do you think they ran away together? Wasyl and that Franca?

GEORGE: Of course. No doubt about it. They are probably in South America all ready. More wine, little apple?

(WASYL *appears in top half of doorway, a fearful sight.*)

WASYL: Fiend! Wife stealer. Lying, treacherous—

OLGA: (*Falling to her knees in superstitious terror.*) Oh, the devil come for us.

GEORGE: (*Climbing up ladder to bunk where he pulls blankets over him.*) Ah, It is the devil—

WASYL: (*Entering*) Come down you wife stealer—come down, or I'll strangle you with my bare hands. (*He notices the claws over his hands and laughs wildly.*) You see! Bear Hands. (GEORGE *peeks out but hastily hides again.*) Come down, you betrayer. (*He turns to* OLGA, *who is still cowering.*) And you, woman, if you could have one wish—one wish what would it be?

OLGA: Wasyl,—to see, Wasyl.

WASYL: Ha, you love him then?

OLGA: Better than life.

WASYL: Better than oil?

OLGA: Much better.

WASYL: (*Turning his back to* OLGA *to gloat over* GEORGE *who is still in the upper bunk.*) You see, Back-biter! (*As he turns to* GEORGE, OLGA *looks up to see that the bear skin only covers part of him. The truth dawns on her.*) So, woman, you want to see Wasyl again?

OLGA: (*Between clenched teeth.*) Oh, if I just had him here!

WASYL: So?

OLGA: So! (*She yanks off the bear skin.*) Look at you. Just look at you, Wasyl Nemitchuk.

WASYL: Now, Olga—

OLGA: Running around the country making public scenes. Disgracing us. In a blanket! In a bear skin! You, Wasyl Nemitchuk, pretending to be drowned.

WASYL: Wait, Olga.

GEORGE: (*Starting down the ladder.*) One can't believe a thing he says, Olga. He promised he'd hide, for instance. He's treacherous, that's all.

WASYL: (*Pulling him down.*) Treacherous. I'm treacherous? Why, I'll beat you to death with your own arm. I'll tear you apart.

GEORGE: Now, Wasyl, I only did what you said. "Tell her I'm dead" that's what you told me. And you said yourself you were going to the widow Rodinsky.

WASYL: "Lean on me, little cousin—drink deep, I will take care of everything—". You wolf in sheepskin. I'll feed you to the crows, like a yellow dog. Take that, George Litowsky. And that—too.

GEORGE: Oh—

OLGA: Wasyl, stop, you have hit him. You have knocked him senseless.

WASYL: Senseless is it? Then is no difference than before.

OLGA: What if you've killed him?

WASYL: No, he still breathes.

OLGA: Please, Wasyl, put your own clothes on and come home.

WASYL: I have no clothes.

OLGA: Your blanket then,—anything.

WASYL: Very well. Hand me my blanket.
      (*He drapes it around him again.*)

OLGA: Now, come along.

WASYL: Where?

OLGA: Home of course.

WASYL: Never! I refuse!

OLGA: You refuse?

WASYL: I'm not going home in broad daylight in a blanket. Why, that would look silly.

OLGA: Silly! Silly, he calls it, after—George, wake up. Wake up at once.
      (*She pours water on him.*)

GEORGE: Ah.—Drink deep.

OLGA: George, get up now.

GEORGE: I'm struck down. I'm killed—my head.

OLGA: George, here are the keys to the car. Go and bring Wasyl's clothes back. And hurry.

WASYL: Don't worry about things here, Cousin. I'll manage everything.

GEORGE: Now, Wasyl, not again. No more. I'm going.
      (*He runs out.*)

OLGA: (*Turning*) And now, husband, we have things to settle.

WASYL: Yes, old woman, we do.
      (*He starts up ladder, carrying jug of wine.*)

OLGA: Don't you "Old Woman" me, Wasyl Nemitchuk. Where are you going?

WASYL: Up here.

OLGA: What for?

WASYL: To sit. To drink. To sing perhaps.
      (*He breaks into a Ukrainian folk song.*)

OLGA: Stop that!

WASYL: You don't like music?

OLGA: I'll pull the ladder down.

WASYL: Touch it and I'll pour this jug of wine on you.

OLGA: Wasyl, you're acting like a mad man.

WASYL: Who wouldn't? Cadillacs, houses in the city, chocolate Easter eggs. Bang. Crash, release, drill. . .

OLGA: And is the noise my fault?

WASYL: Of course it's your fault. Who wanted to drill?

OLGA: But it means 25 hundred dollars without lifting a hand.

WASYL: My pigs grow weak, my head aches, my heart aches, my brain throbs. That is nothing.

OLGA: If they strike oil, we are rich, Wasyl.

WASYL: Hah! Who wants to be rich?

OLGA: Everybody, but you.

WASYL: Comfortable yes,—rich no. Olga, I will not go home as long as those oil people remain.

OLGA: I suppose you'll go to that Franca Rodinsky.

WASYL: She appreciates good farming.

OLGA: Oh, you've lost your mind. Look at you. A scarecrow. A drunkard. You, the owner of a big farm.

WASYL: Power in the house too. Water works.

(He leers down at her.)

OLGA: You the father of seven fine daughters, fourteen beautiful granddaughters, and a grandson.

WASYL: What difference if I had 20 granddaughters—*(He stops)* *(Very low tone)* What's that you say? Grandson? *(Shaking)* No, no, you didn't say grandson, Olga?

OLGA: Fool, of course I said grandson.

(She smiles)

WASYL: *(Leaning over bunk)* No? No? Grandson! Glory be to God— Grandson! *(Starts down)* But who, Olga? How? When?

OLGA: Katerina, last night. A boy. Here's the telegram. It came just before I left.

WASYL: *(Patting telegram)* Well, that changes everything. *(Beside himself with delight)* Congratulations, Olga. We have a grandson. A boy in the family. My dear, dear good old woman, that changes everything. Olga. I embrace you. A boy—they're sure?

OLGA: Of course they're sure.

WASYL: A very small puny child, of course—little, not strong at all?

OLGA: Nine pounds five ounces. Strong and lusty.

WASYL: My dear good grandmother, congratulations. *(He pours wine shakily)* Named Edward for his father of course?

OLGA: No.

WASYL: John, for the Prime Minister then?

OLGA: No—for his grandfather, Wasyl Nemitchuk.

WASYL: For me? A grandson named for me? To our grandson, Olga, the little Wasyl. No, they must use the Canadian—the little

Gwen Pharis Ringwood

William. (*Raising glass he pauses*) By God, to Bill, Olga. To Bill, my grandson. Di bozsha!

OLGA: Di bozsha!
    (*They drink*)

WASYL: Look at me, 15 times a grandfather and dressed like an old hay stack. Sit down, Olga. A grandson eh? That changes everything.

OLGA: (*Eagerly*) I knew you'd see it. We can buy a house in the city, near Katrina and the boy, and—

WASYL: A house in the city—for a grandson—Never!

OLGA: But—

WASYL: Never. A house in the city where two old people sit and holler on him. Don't touch the china dog, off the street, off the grass, away from the flowers. A life to drive the strongest grandson mad! No holidays, Olga. That way—no holidays!
    (*He pounds table*)

OLGA: (*Uncertainly*) No holidays?

WASYL: I tell you how it must be. He must have a horse, a tractor, pigs. He must bring in cows, help fix fence, run with the old dog barking across the pasture. He can hide in the hay stack, fish by the river.

OLGA: No, he'd drown.

WASYL: Ah, not that one. A fine swimmer, I can tell you.

OLGA: So you have decided. We don't move to the city.

WASYL: That's right.

OLGA: Suppose I move to the city myself?

WASYL: Leave me? You wouldn't, Olga.

OLGA: You left me.

WASYL: That was different. What are you going to do?

OLGA: (*Preparing to mount ladder with jug of wine.*) Go up here. Sit. Sing, perhaps.

WASYL: Olga, you're mad. What will people think?

OLGA: I may stay a week, even.
    (*She starts to sing as she mounts ladder.*)

WASYL: (*Throwing his arms around her waist, tries to pull her down the ladder.*) No, no, don't be silly. What will George say? Come down now, there's a good girl, come down. Do you hear me, Olga Nemitchuk?

OLGA: Stop, Wasyl. Oh, you've broken it already.

WASYL: Broken what?

OLGA: (*Coming down*) It was a surprise. An Easter egg. I was making for you.

WASYL: Not a chocolate one?

OLGA: Of course not. I was only talking. This was to be very beautiful, with spruce trees on it. Spruce trees are hard, Wasyl.
    (*She shows him the crushed egg and then throws it in the stove.*)

WASYL: Spruce trees? For me? Then you are not seduced, Olga?

OLGA: Seduced? How dare you, Wasyl? The idea! Seduced!

WASYL: By oil, I mean. You don't really intend to leave me—

OLGA: Well—

WASYL: Of course you don't. You dote on me—you love me passionately. Now all we have to do is—

(GEORGE *knocks on door, opens top half, looks in*)

GEORGE: Wasyl, Olga, I have news!

WASYL: Come in, George, All is forgiven. (*Rushes to door*) You see before you a grandfather with a grandson. A boy, George. (*Shakes* GEORGE'S *limp hand*) A boy, you understand. He will inherit the farm of course. A big boy, George—eleven pounds seventeen ounces. You may congratulate me. To my health, George.

(*He drinks*)

GEORGE: But I have news—

WASYL: My clothes, man. Give me my clothes.

GEORGE: There. (*He throws clothes through the window*) Bad news.

WASYL: My grandson?

OLGA: Someone is hurt?

GEORGE: No, nobody hurt.

WASYL: My pants, blockhead—where is my pants?

GEORGE: Oh yes, exactly. (*Throws pants through the window.*) I hate to tell you this but—

WASYL: Speak up, idiot, have you turned the car over?

GEORGE: No. No. You see the man at the ferry told me.

WASYL: My pigs?

GEORGE: Not the pigs. The oil, five wells.

WASYL: They've struck oil then?

GEORGE: I'm sorry, cousin. They—

WASYL: We can move away I guess, start over.

GEORGE: It is a shame.

WASYL: We can clear the land again, eh? Olga?

GEORGE: They won't drill another foot, pulling out today, like that. (*Snaps fingers*) They say it is useless.

WASYL: What's that?

GEORGE: The oil company. They have decided there is no oil on your place. They are leaving.

WASYL: Leaving! Then we don't have to move. We can stay. Hear that, Olga, there is no oil. They are going away.

GEORGE: You are happy, Wasyl? Are you mad?

WASYL: Happy, George. I live again. George, you see before you a whole man, clothed and in his right mind. George you can congratulate me. I am no longer drowned.

GEORGE: (*Entering house weakly*) I see. Congratulations, cousin. Well, it's your life, not mine.

WASYL: (*Gathering up his gear, very busy*) Come, Olga, we must get home. So many things to attend to, the grandson to visit, some pigs to sell, You will excuse us, George.

GEORGE: Of course, cousin. Exactly. Well, Di bozsha.

(WASYL *and* OLGA *start out the door*)

269

Gwen Pharis Ringwood

WASYL: Di bo—Wait, Olga.
    (*Re-enters the house*)
GEORGE: (*Exhausted*) You want something, Wasyl?
WASYL: An egg.
GEORGE: (*Waving wildly*) By all means—Take two, a dozen.
WASYL: Just one, George. My fine coloured Easter egg—(*Running off*)
    Coming, Olga—coming—Di bozsha, George, di bozsha.
GEORGE: (*Collapsing into arm chair*) Certainly. Exactly—God give
    you health—Di bozsha.

The End

The Wall
A comedy for radio

Characters

JOHN STARBORNE
MRS. CARMELODEON
FREDDY CARMELODEON, *a boy about 8*
ERNIE APPLEBY, *a boy about the same age*
MRS. DOGBA

EFFECT: STARBORNE *whistling. Clink of oil can, etc.*

STARBORNE: Good morning. You're out early. The lake's beautiful this morning, isn't it? You want a boat? Sure, I'll fix you up. Come along down to the pier.

MUSIC: *Sneak in behind.*

Starborne's my name. John Starborne. Yes, I build all the boats myself, work on them in the winter, sell a few and rent the rest out to you summer people here at Lake Carla. It's a good life— the best I could figure for a man with *two* artificial legs. That's right. Navy. We hit a mine off the coast of France. Sure, I took it hard, but that passed. Well, here we are, you pick your boat. The lake's smooth as glass this morning, isn't it?

MUSIC: *Swell briefly (Lake music)*

The big place? That belongs to Mrs. Mervin Carmelodeon. Yes, she's the one that built the wall. You haven't heard that story? Well, you see, it was this way.

MUSIC: *Sneak in music here (transition to Carmelodeon music)*

First of all, there was Mrs. Carmelodeon:

271

Gwen Pharis Ringwood

MRS. CARMELODEON: (*Speaking as if to several friends at a tea. Gushy. A little silly, bit stupid, but fairly kind. A large woman, inclined to put on airs.*) I've just bought the most divine summer place on Lake Carla. Twenty thousand dollars—that includes the boat of course. But as I told Mervin, if you're going to live in an exclusive district, you have to pay for it. The Dogba's are on the west. She was presented, you know. And on the other side of them are the Androssadies. *Oil*! Really worth while people. I don't know who owns the cottage on the East, but it's charming, perfectly charming. Some writer, I believe. The Lake will be so good for Freddy, too. After all it's important for Freddy to grow up knowing the right people. He'll take over the Sleepy Bye Mattress Company when Mervin retires. And it's so soothing to know one will spend one's summers with people of one's own sort, only more so, if you know what I mean.

MUSIC: *Punctuates.*

STARBORNE: And then there was Freddy Carmelodeon:

MUSIC: *Sneak in transition to* FREDDY's *music.*

FREDDY: (*With all a child's wonder and delight*) Boy, I like this place. I can see the lake from my window—blue as anything and there must be millions of birds singing. And the sky, it's all kind of pink and red from the sun coming up. I wonder if there'll be any kids to play with.

MUSIC: *Out here.*

STARBORNE: And then, of course, there was Ernie. Ernie Appleby. He lives in the cottage on the East.

MUSIC: *Sneak in* ERNIE's *music here.*

ERNIE: A kid about my age moved in next door yesterday. I wonder if he likes fishing. He's got a great looking bike there. Wonder what he's like. I wonder how he and I are going to get along.

MUSIC: *To end movement. Very brief.*

STARBORNE: When Mrs. Carmelodeon bought the place there wasn't any wall on the east side. There wasn't a wall anywhere, that you could see. And so on the morning of the first day, the very first day at Lake Carla, Freddy got to know Ernie.

MUSIC: *Sneak in here.*

Freddy was walking East along the Beach and Ernie was walking West along the Beach and there they were.

FREDDY: Hi.

ERNIE: Hi.

FREDDY: What you got in that pail?

ERNIE: Minnows.

FREDDY: Minnows, eh?

ERNIE: Yeah, Minnows.

FREDDY: How many minnows?

ERNIE: About a million, maybe.

FREDDY: Whewww. You live in that little white house?

ERNIE: Yep.

FREDDY: I live in that big one.

ERNIE: I know.

FREDDY: We just bought it. $80,000 bucks.

ERNIE: (*Whistles*) That's a lot of dough.

FREDDY: Counting the boat, that is.

ERNIE: Ours don't belong to us. It's a friend's, but he went to India for the government.

FREDDY: You here for the summer?

ERNIE: Reckon.

FREDDY: So am I.

ERNIE: I figure to dam up a pool for these little old minnows.

FREDDY: I could help you, if you want.

ERNIE: Don't mind.

FREDDY: I'll get my shovel.

ERNIE: O.K. You can have some of my minnows, if you want.

FREDDY: Gee, thanks.

ERNIE: My name's Ernie—Ernie Appleby.

FREDDY: Mine's Freddy Carmelodeon. My Dad has a mattress factory. Must be two hundred men workin' for him. What does your Dad do?

ERNIE: My Dad writes books—in the summer. Winters he works on a train.

FREDDY: I'm going to get my shovel. You wait here. (*Calling*) I'll be right back. You wait up eh? (*Off mike, breathlessly*) Mom! I've met a new friend and his name is Ernie and we have to make a dam to hold about a million minnows.

MRS. CARMELODEON: How nice, Freddy. Run along now and play. Mother has to get unpacked. (*Raising voice*) and Freddy—

FREDDY: Yes, Mom?

MRS. CARMELODEON: Don't fall in the lake.

FREDDY: (*Running off*) No, Mom. (*Calling*) Hey, Ernie, Wait up. Wait up, Ernie.

MUSIC: *Up to close scene and then softly behind.*

STARBORNE: All day on the first day, Freddy and Ernie played together at the end of my pier. And that night Freddy went to sleep to the sound of the lake and the summer night, and in behind was the sound of his new friend, Ernie. Oh, it was good to have a friend, Freddy thought. On the second day right after breakfast Freddy said to his mother.

FREDDY: I'll be playing with Ernie, Mom.
(*Leaving*)

MRS. CARMELODEON: Alright, Freddy. (*Calling*) And Freddy—

FREDDY: Yes, Mom?

MRS. CARMELODEON: Don't fall in the lake.

FREDDY: No, Mom.

STARBORNE: Freddy and Ernie worked very hard. They were building a tree house. It was hot work and it's not surprising they got into difficulties.

MUSIC: *Leads in quickly.*

FREDDY: I'm going to put the ladder up here.

ERNIE: That's no place. I want it over here, where the door is.

FREDDY: I already got it started.

ERNIE: You'll have to take it down.

FREDDY: I won't. It's my hammer.

ERNIE: Well, it's my tree.

FREDDY: It is not. It's the government's.

ERNIE: That's a dumb place for a ladder, you dumb kid!

FREDDY: Who's dumb? Give me that board.

ERNIE: I won't have the ladder there.

FREDDY: O.K. I'll take my hammer home.

ERNIE: Go ahead.

FREDDY: I'm not going to play with a long-eared mule!

ERNIE: If I'm a mule, you're a jack-ass. Go home.

FREDDY: (*Dropping his tone and trying scorn*) You don't know anything about building.

ERNIE: I know more than you do.

FREDDY: Bet you'd be scared to climb the ladder. Scarecrow.

ERNIE: Pig Whistle.

FREDDY: I'll sock your nose.

ERNIE: Try it. Just try it.

FREDDY: You dare me?

ERNIE: I could wrestle you down easy.

FREDDY: Nyah. Black Face!

ERNIE: Nyah. Milk Face!

FREDDY: I'll black your eyes and beat your ears off.

ERNIE: I'll pound you in the ground and stamp on your tin head.

FREDDY: Old sissy wets the pants!

ERNIE: Old root hog! Come on then.

FREDDY: O.K. Come on.

MUSIC: *They fight.*

FREDDY: (*Over music*) Mom—Mom, Ernie hit me and my nose is bleeding and he tore my shirt and I'm never going to play with him again, never.
(*Music out*)

MRS. CARMELODEON: Darling, did that rough old boy hit my Freddy? Here, Mother will wash his face. It's all stopped bleeding. There. Now—does he feel better?

FREDDY: Can I have some cookies?

MRS. CARMELODEON: Of course you can. Here, they are.

FREDDY: Thanks.

MRS. CARMELODEON: (*Changed tone*) Freddy, where are you going?

FREDDY: I'm going to take some cookies to Ernie.

MRS. CARMELODEON: But, darling, he hit you—made your nose bleed.

FREDDY: I gave him a good one, right on the chin—bet I knocked his wind out.

MRS. CARMELODEON: You aren't going to play with him again, are you?

FREDDY: Why, sure, Mom. That was just a fight. Ernie's my friend. Well, I gotta go. Thanks for the cookies. (*Calling*) Hey, Ernie, wait up (*Off*) I got an idea.

MUSIC: *A chord or two to end scene.*

STARBORNE: Oh, it was good to have a friend and the lake and the sky and a tree house. It was good to be alive, Freddy thought. On the third day Mrs. Carmelodeon met Ernie. She was talking to Mrs. Dogba, who had come to call, when it happened.

MRS. CARMELODEON: Oh yes, Mrs. Dogba, we're so delighted with the place. Freddy adores it. He's found a little friend already.

MRS. DOGBA: How nice.

MRS. CARMELODEON: Do let me get you another Baked Alaska.

MRS. DOGBA: Thank you. Never notice what I eat though.

MRS. CARMELODEON: I should be dieting, but—

FREDDY: (*Calling from kitchen*) Mother, I brought Ernie up. Can we have some buns?

MRS. CARMELODEON: Of course, darling. You and your little friend wash your hands before you come in.

MRS. DOGBA: Who is Ernie?

MRS. CARMELODEON: Next door. I haven't seen him yet.

FREDDY: (*From doorway*) We washed, Mom.

MRS. CARMELODEON: Come in, darling. This is my little boy, Freddy, Mrs. Dogba.

MRS. DOGBA: How do you do, Freddy.

MRS. CARMELODEON: (*Still very gushing*) And this is Ernie (*Complete drop in tone*) Oh. (*Very flat*) Is *this* Ernie, Freddy?

FREDDY: (*Completely unaware*) Yes, Mom, and his Dad's coming out this week-end and we're going to Loon Island. Aren't we Ernie?

ERNIE: Yes, Ma'am, that is if Freddy can—

MRS. CARMELODEON: Oh dear. Well, Freddy, we'll see. (*Very sugary and fast*) Now, Ernie, you take this nice bun and run along dear. Away you go—home to your mother. She'll be wondering where you are. Away you go now. That's right. No, Freddie, you stay here. Freddy, you'll stay here please.

SOUND: *Door closing.*

FREDDY: (*Protesting vigorously*) But Mom, Ernie and I—

MRS. CARMELODEON: (*Hard and cold*) Freddy, you go up to your room and put your toys away.

FREDDY: But, Mom—

MRS. CARMELODEON: Now, Freddy.

FREDDY: Yes, Mother.

EFFECT: *Walking upstairs.*

MRS. CARMELODEON: Oh dear, I never dreamed.

MRS. DOGBA: Have they bought the place?

MRS. CARMELODEON: I don't know. And right next door. Oh, that horrible agent. He assured me this was a choice locality.

MRS. DOGBA: Of course, it isn't that I have any prejudice, but after all the backgrounds are so different. I'd do something about it at once, if I were you. You know what it means, the value of the property will sink to nothing—just sink to nothing. It's all very well to be broadminded, but one's pocketbook is sacred to one's self.

MRS. CARMELODEON: Oh, I never dreamed. (*Wail*)

MUSIC: *Chords to end Scene.*

FREDDY: But mother, why can't I play with Ernie? He's my friend and you sent him home. Why? Why?

MRS. CARMELODEON: Darling, he's—he's different from you.

FREDDY: That's silly, he's my friend.

MRS. CARMELODEON: But he's *black*, dear. Black as the ace of spades. Why didn't you tell me? You should have told mother, Freddy.

FREDDY: I never thought about it. Can't I go out now?

MRS. CARMELODEON: No, Freddy. You can't go out. And you are not to play with that child any more. Do you understand?

MUSIC: *Out here.*

STARBORNE: But on the fourth day Freddy waited until Mrs. Carmelodeon was busy and then he was out like a streak of greased lightning. He found Ernie and they explored awhile and ended up sitting on my boats.

FREDDY: Ernie and I are going to have a club, Mr. Starborne, a Secret Society. Do you want to be an honorary member?

STARBORNE: Why, thanks, Freddy. I'd be honored.

ERNIE: I reckon your Mother's going to raise a row if you belong to a club with me, Freddy.

FREDDY: I'll talk her into it. After all, I'm her only child.

ERNIE: Grown folks don't like mixing their colors much. Except ones like you, Mr. Starborne.

FREDDY: I sometimes think grown folks are kind of crazy.

ERNIE: My Dad told me I got to expect to meet some prejudice.

FREDDY: You know, you're the only black colored kid I ever knew, personally.

STARBORNE: Did you ever know a man with two wooden legs before, Freddy?

FREDDY: No. I don't know if there's anything unusual about me. Except I got two warts on my left big toe.

STARBORNE: Reckon you'll qualify to be unusual too, Freddy boy.

MRS. CARMELODEON: (*Off*) Freddy—Freddy.

STARBORNE: There's your Ma.

FREDDY: I'm not going. I'm going to stay here with the club.

MRS. CARMELODEON: Freddy! Come here!

STARBORNE: You better go. She might think you're drowned.

FREDDY: (*Reluctantly*) O.K. Coming, Mother. (*As he goes*) You look after my tadpole for me, Ernie, I'll be back as soon as I can.

MUSIC: *Bridges up and under.*

MRS. CARMELODEON: Freddy, you're a bad boy to disobey your mother. Can't you find some suitable children to play with? You're just a naughty, unusual child.

MUSIC: *Swells slightly. Then out.*

STARBORNE: On the morning of the fifth day Mrs. Carmelodeon came to see me.

MRS. CARMELODEON: I want a wall built, Mr. Starborne. It will have to be very thick and very high, between me and the people to the East. And could you build it today, please?

STARBORNE: Sorry, Ma'am. I'm not much of a one for putting up walls.

MRS. CARMELODEON: But you will try?

STARBORNE: No, Ma'am.

MRS. CARMELODEON: Well, really! Of course if you don't want the work, I'll find someone else. I'll spare no expense, but I must have my wall. I must have my wall!

MUSIC: *Chords. Then builds as wall begins behind.*

STARBORNE: So all day on the fifth day Mrs. Carmeledeon's hired contractors worked at putting up a wall 8 feet high, 3 feet thick and running from the road right out into Lake Carla. The sky was dark and the lake was sullen. In the afternoon a big storm came up. The lake snarled and pounded against the shore, but that didn't stop the building of that wall. I watched the wall go up. Freddy watched from his window as they pounded and mixed and mortared. Ernie sat on his porch and watched them dig and pound and shovel concrete. Right before our eyes the wall went up—solid as granite; Strong as iron. Ugly as sin.

MUSIC: *Crescendoes.*

FREDDY: I hate that wall. Now I can't see Ernie's place at all. I hate that damned old wall.

ERNIE: Freddy's mother sure is determined to fence him in.

STARBORNE: I heard Mrs. Carmelodeon paying off the men.

MRS. CARMELODEON: Of course my cheque won't bounce! Whatever gave you such an idea. Mr. Carmelodeon owns the Sleepy Bye Mattress Company. We're international mattress makers. Of course my cheque is good. Can I trust that the wall won't fall down in the night? Oh yes, it looks strong. I'll take your word. I might as well tell you, I didn't expect it to be so ugly. Did you have to make it so ugly? I suppose I can plant vines to cover this side. Well, there's your money. Wait. Wait. Aren't you going to clean out the wheel barrow. . . you've left it half full of concrete. You've left my wheel barrow half full of. . . They've gone! Oh, it's impossible to get good workmen these days. But at least we're protected. I have my wall!.

STARBORNE: Yes. She had her wall. And the two little boys one on each side looked at the wall and cried.

MUSIC: *Slips in behind.*

FREDDY: I'll be seein' you, Ernie. Somehow I'll be seein' you. I'll get through the wall some way. Wait up, eh? I'll be seein' you.

ERNIE: (*Softly too*) You're my best friend, Freddy. I'll take care of your tadpole for you, till I'm an old man. I'll cherish your tadpole till my dyin' day. Word of honor, Freddy, word of honor.

MUSIC: *Out.*

STARBORNE: But Mrs. Carmelodeon didn't hear the crying. Mrs. Carmelodeon was very busy. She had invited Mrs. Dogba to tea so she made a cake which she planned to decorate with tiny flags of the United Nations. She got the idea from the radio, but the icing was sticky and the flags drooped. She was much too busy to pay any mind to Freddy. As for Freddy, he got busy too.

FREDDY: (*Calling low*) Ernie, Ernie.

STARBORNE: But there was no answer. So Freddy took a little hammer and he started going along the wall.

MUSIC: *Sneak in here.*

Tapping and tapping, and tapping, looking for a weak spot. And pretty soon on the other side came a tap. Someone else was tapping and tapping and tapping. You see, Ernie was looking for a weak spot too.

MUSIC: *Builds.*

And then, what's that? Listen—does it sound hollow? There's something wrong. The wall sounds hollow here. This is the place Freddy starts making a hole in the wall. He taps and chisels and pounds, and on the other side Ernie is chiseling too. They've started to chisel a hole right through the wall. They have—they've done it. They can see each other, talk to each other. Listen.

FREDDY: (*Very low*) Hi, Ernie.

ERNIE: Hi, Freddy.

FREDDY: We made it.

ERNIE: Now we can talk through this hole.

FREDDY: I don't aim to just talk. I aim to crawl through.

ERNIE: You couldn't; it's not big enough.

FREDDY: We got to make it bigger then. Come on.

MUSIC: *Establish briefly.*

FREDDY: Hey, Ernie. I think I can get through now.

ERNIE: You'll have to squeeze yourself.

FREDDY: I'll suck my breath in. Here I come.

MUSIC: *Bliss.*

ERNIE: Come on, boy.

FREDDY: Got my head through, but I can't seem to. . .

ERNIE: Here, I'll pull you. Make yourself small as you can.

FREDDY: I got myself shrunk to nothing.

ERNIE: Try again now. Come on, I'll pull.

FREDDY: Wait! Stop! Stop pulling, Ernie, seems like—seems like I'm stuck. I can't get through.

ERNIE: Maybe you better back up, Freddy.

FREDDY: I can't do that either. I'm stuck. What do I do now?

ERNIE: Are you still breathing alright?

FREDDY: I think so. Do you suppose I'll have to stay here until I get down to skin and bones?

ERNIE: We got to think of something.

FREDDY: I'm awful thirsty.

ERNIE: I'll get you a drink. You wait here, eh?

FREDDY: Reckon I will. Reckon I'm not going anywhere.

ERNIE: (*Going off*) Don't be worried. Don't be scared, Freddy. I'll be right back.

MUSIC: *Up briefly and out.*

MRS. CARMELODEON: Do come in Mrs. Dogba. You're puffing. Such a hot day, isn't it?

MRS. DOGBA: I see you got your wall up. Huge, isn't it?

MRS. CARMELODEON: I'm planting some flowering vines to cover it. It will look much better then.

MRS. DOGBA: I should hope so. I mean, it is. . . well, it's not a thing of beauty is it? But of course you had no choice.

MRS. CARMELODEON: Exactly. I had it put up at once. I don't stop and think, you know. I *act*. The wretched men charged me an exorbitant amount and then they didn't even clean up my wheel barrow. And it's too heavy for me to move. I'll have to wait till. . .

MRS. DOGBA: Oh dear, I've left my glasses in the car. I can't knit without them.

MRS. CARMELODEON: I'll send Freddy for them. Freddy! Freddy dear! He must have gone outside. Freddy!

MRS. DOGBA: Don't you worry about the lake?. . I mean, he could fall in.

MRS. CARMELODEON: I've warned him not to fall in. But we'd better look. Freddy! Freddy, where are you? Answer Mama.

MUSIC: *Bridge.* . .

ERNIE: Here you are Freddy. I'll hold the cup for you.

FREDDY: Tip it more. More. Watch out. Oh, it's all spilled and I didn't get a drop. I bet I'm getting dehydrated. My mouth's dry.

ERNIE: You got to have water, Freddy, or you'll die.

FREDDY: Maybe you'll have to put it in my veins.

ERNIE: I know. If I get a bottle and a straw you can suck it up. Right?

FREDDY: Sure I could. You're my best friend, Ernie.

ERNIE: Well I bet if I were stuck like you are, you'd be my best friend. You wait here, eh?

MUSIC: *Bridge*

279

MRS. CARMELODEON: Oh, I'm worried now. Freddy! Freddy!

MRS. DOGBA: Mrs. Carmelodeon—that hole in your wall. . . was it there when. . .

MRS. CARMELODEON: Oh those stupid men. One has to watch them every minute. Do you think Freddy could have. . .

MRS. DOGBA: Something's sticking out. . . some sort of person. . . I think it's Freddy—one end of Freddy.

MRS. CARMELODEON: Move, Mrs. Dogba. Let me see. It's Freddy all right. Those are his legs. Freddy Carmelodeon, are you in there?

FREDDY: *(off)* Yes, Mom.

MRS. CARMELODEON: You back out of there this minute! You've torn the seat out of your best trousers. Freddy, do you hear me?

FREDDY: *(off)* Yes, Ma.

MRS. CARMELODEON: Freddy, are you backing out yourself, or do I pull you out?

FREDDY: I can't back out. I'm stuck.

MRS. CARMELODEON: Then Mama's going to pull.

MRS. DOGBA: You take one leg and I'll take the other. Now. Heave. . . Pull. . .

FREDDY: *(off)* Stop, Ma. You're hurting me.

MRS. CARMELODEON: Stop kicking, Freddy. Relax.

FREDDY: I'm stuck, I tell you.

MRS. DOGBA: Once more. Heave. . . Oh, you little fiend. You kicked me. . .

MRS. CARMELODEON: Are you all right, Mrs. Dogba?

MRS. DOGBA: Oh yes. I *like* being kicked in the stomach. Help me up.

MRS. CARMELODEON: I'm sorry Mrs. Dogba. *(Calling)* Freddy, where exactly is your head?

FREDDY: Over here, on the other side.

MRS. DOGBA: You'd better climb up the wall. Here, I'll give you a leg up.

MRS. CARMELODEON: But it's so high.

MRS. DOGBA: Put your foot here, and then step on Freddy.

FREDDY: No!

MRS. CARMELODEON: I'll try.

MRS. DOGBA: Up you go, then. Up you go. You *are* an elephant!

MRS. CARMELODEON: I'm not. I lost three pounds in June.

MRS. DOGBA: Can't you pull yourself up now?

MRS. CARMELODEON: No, just a minute.

MRS. DOGBA: But I can't hold you—I have to let go—

MRS. CARMELODEON: Oh no,—Oh.

MUSIC: *Falling effect.*

MRS. CARMELODEON: Oh, I didn't mean to fall on you Mrs. Dogba—

MRS. DOGBA: You did fall on me though. All two hundred pounds.

MRS. CARMELODEON: A hundred and seventy four!

MRS. DOGBA: Rubbish! You mashed my hat too. I'm sorry, Mrs. Carmelodeon, but I'm going home. You'll have to get some *man* to rescue your son. I can't help you do it.

MRS. CARMELODEON: Very well, go. I'll get a step ladder.

MRS. DOGBA: Do. I wish you luck. Good-bye.

MRS. CARMELODEON: Good-bye! Freddy, Mama will get a step ladder and come over to your head. Don't be nervous now—Mama will cope.

MUSIC: *Bridge up briefly and wash out.*

ERNIE: I found some lemonade, Freddy. It's in the bottle and here's the straw.

FREDDY: Hold the bottle lower. . . There! Boy, that tastes good.

ERNIE: You better not drink too much or you'll just be stucker.

FREDDY: Seems like I'm about as wedged in as I can get. . .

ERNIE: I can get you out, Freddy. I know I can.

FREDDY: How?

ERNIE: With a secret formula. It's here. . . in this sprayer.

FREDDY: Hey, you're not going to spray poison on me, Ernie Appleby. I'm not a bug.

ERNIE: It's not poison, I promise.

FREDDY: What is it then?

ERNIE: It's warmed up goose grease.

FREDDY: Goose grease?

ERNIE: Yeah, you rub it on your chest when you got a cold.

FREDDY: But I don't have a cold.

ERNIE: I know. But if I spray this goose grease all around you. . .

FREDDY: No.

ERNIE: It won't hurt, honest. Put your head down now.

FREDDY: O.K.

ERNIE: Shut your eyes. Here goes. . .

MUSIC: *Sound of spraying.*

ERNIE: See. I said it wouldn't hurt.

FREDDY: Oh,—it's kind of hot.

ERNIE: I had to heat it so it would spray, but I put my finger in it and it didn't blister. Can you stand it?

FREDDY: I'll stand it. But, what good is goose grease?

ERNIE: (*Still spraying*) You'll see. This will make you good and slippery and then you can wiggle out easy. I used it to get a ring off my finger once.

FREDDY: Spray away then.

ERNIE: You're awful brave.

FREDDY: I know.

ERNIE: I'm going to give you my sling shot, if you get out.

FREDDY: Ernie, look! I can wiggle a little! See, Hurry, Spray some of that goose grease under me.

ERNIE: Pull in your stomach.

FREDDY: See, I'm moving. Keep spraying, boy.

281

Gwen Pharis Ringwood

ERNIE: Push yourself.
FREDDY: I'm coming—a little farther—and—
ERNIE: I'll catch you.
FREDDY: One. Two. Thr—I'm out. I made it!
ERNIE: (*Proudly*) You made it, Boy.
FREDDY: Say, being stuck like that sure tires a fellow.
ERNIE: Lots of guys would have bawled their heads off.
FREDDY: Well, I knew you'd stand by me.
ERNIE: I sure did, didn't I?
FREDDY: I reckon we'll always stand by each other, Ernie, like my
    great grandfather stood by Churchill in the Boer War. Marched
    right by him, forward into battle. Wearing his kilt. Drums
    beatin'. Bagpipes playin', Flags flying!
MUSIC: *Tiny swirl of martial music.*
ERNIE: Gee, my grandfather was a warrior too. Marched forward into
    battle just like yours. Drums beatin', gourds a rattlin', Voodoo
    men dancing.
MUSIC: *Transition to tiny African drums.*
FREDDY: Gee.
MUSIC: *Out.*
MRS. CARMELODEON: (*From above*) Freddy, here's Mama up on the
    ladder. Don't be worried. Mama will cope. Oh you're out! Why
    did you get out on that side of the wall? Here, I'm letting down a
    rope. I'll pull you up.
ERNIE: (*Low*) You'd better let her pull you up, Freddy.
FREDDY: I reckon so.
MRS. CARMELODEON: Catch hold, Freddy.
FREDDY: I've got it, Mom. I'll see you, Ernie. Thanks for saving my
    life.
ERNIE: That's alright.
MRS. CARMELODEON: Mama will pull hard now. Hold on tight.
FREDDY: O.K. Watch your balance though.
MRS. CARMELODEON: Hang on now. Mama's pulling. Up you come.
    Up you come.
FREDDY: O.K. Ma—I can—I'm on the wall. I'll follow you down.
    Watch out. The ladder. The ladder's tipping! It's tipped! Mom!
MRS. CARMELODEON: Oh . . . . . ooo . . . . .
MUSIC: *Falling crescendo.*
FREDDY: Mom. Are you all right?
MRS. CARMELODEON: No! I'm not all right. I'm stuck in this wheel
    barrow. I can't get out.
FREDDY: You're all spattered with concrete, Mom. You're all speckled
    white. Like those chickens we saw in. . .
MRS. CARMELODEON: Never mind that, Freddy. Get down off that
    wall and get help. Get someone to help me out of this wheel
    barrow.
FREDDY: Yes, Mom. Hey, Ernie. . . My mother's stuck in the wheel
    barrow. We got to get help.

ERNIE: Mr. Starborne's at the beach. I'll get him.

FREDDY: O.K. I'm going to try climbing down this wall. You get Mr. Starborne to come up this side.

ERNIE: Right.

FREDDY: O.K. Mom. You just stay put. I'm climbing down.

MRS. CARMELODEON: Hurry, Freddy. I'm hardening.

MUSIC: *Bridge.*

STARBORNE: Well, Mrs. Carmelodeon, it looks like you've got yourself in trouble.

MRS. CARMELODEON: Please help me, Mr. Starborne.

STARBORNE: Don't you worry, Ma'am. . . Now let's see. Freddy and Ernie can hold on to the handles of the wheel barrow, hold them down, while I pull. . . Ernie you push down on the left handle, Freddy you push down on the right. . . and Mrs. Carmelodeon you give me your hands. . . Ready, Ma'am? I'll give you a good hard steady pull and I think we can get you out. O.K. boys. . . let's go. . . Pull, boys, Pull. . . Yo ho Heave Ho. . . (*Volga Boat song*) There you are, Mrs. Carmelodeon.

MRS. CARMELODEON: I'm so humiliated. Thank you, Mr. Starborne. I. . .

STARBORNE: You look a little like the Statue of Liberty, Ma'am. . . before it set.

MRS. CARMELODEON: I. . . I must get myself in order. Freddy, you clean yourself up too. Look at you. You look like a greased pig. Good day Mr. Starborne. . . Thank you.

STARBORNE: Any time, Ma'am. Any time.

MUSIC: *Bridge up and over.*

STARBORNE: Well, Mrs. Carmelodeon took to her bed with a headache, after she ordered the hole in the wall to be repaired. That night Ernie Appleby dreamed that he was marching forward into battle with Freddy's grandfather—drums beating, pipes playing, flags flying. Oh, he was a bonny lad.

And Freddy Carmelodeon dreamed that he was an African Chief, armed with a spear, and marching forward into battle to the beat of native drums. Drums beating, gourds rattling voodoo men dancing. It was all there.

MUSIC: *Out.*

STARBORNE: On the morning of the seventh day, Mrs. Carmelodeon had a telephone call from Mr. Carmelodeon.

MRS. CARMELODEON: Yes, Mervin. I had to have a wall put up between us and the Applebys. Because they're different! . . . well you know, a different color! Black! What's that? Your client is the guest of the Applebys. He'll be staying with them? And he's ordered fifty. . . thousand mattresses? Mervin, who is your client? The Ethiopian Trade Commissioner! You mean, he's black too? Oh dear—you don't need to be so angry, Mervin. I'll try, yes. I'll get the wall down some way if I have to use

Gwen Pharis Ringwood

dynamite! No, there won't be any wall. I know, Mervin. I know fifty thousand mattresses is a lot of mattresses. I'm no fool.

MUSIC: *Hysterical and excited.*

MRS. CARMELODEON: (*Over music*) Freddy, your father's called. He's very angry about the wall. He wants it down. He's—he's bringing the Ethiopian Trade Commissioner to dinner and—fifty thousand mattresses—Freddy!

MUSIC: *Out.*

STARBORNE: But Freddy and Ernie had dug a tunnel under the wall and were off exploring. Poor Mrs. Carmelodeon. She tried everything.

EFFECT: *Telephone ringing.*

MRS. CARMELODEON: Send me the men who put my wall up. I want it taken down, today. They're gone. Oh dear.

MUSIC: *Sneak in. Frantic mood.*

EFFECT: *Telephone ringing.*

MRS. CARMELODEON: It's Mrs. Carmelodeon. I want some dynamite to blast down a wall. No, I don't belong to the dynamiter's union. Oh, I see—.

EFFECT: *Telephone ringing.*

MRS. CARMELODEON: (*Over music—more excited*) It's Mrs. Mervin Carmelodeon. Send me a bulldozer to bull doze my wall down today. Please. But it wouldn't take long with a bulldozer. Oh—.

EFFECT: *Telephone ringing.*

MRS. CARMELODEON: (*Over music—desperate*) It's Mrs. Mervin Carmelodeon—the mattress Carmelodeons. Would you bring a team of horses and pull down my wall? I'll pay. I'll pay well. You're ploughing? Oh. . . goodbye.

STARBORNE: She tried everything. That's how she happened to come to me.

MRS. CARMELODEON: Mr. Starborne, I want that wall down. . . at once. Today. Can you suggest anything?

STARBORNE: You want it down. You just put it up. Don't you like it?

MRS. CARMELODEON: Oh no, I hate it. It's ugly. And Mrs. Appleby sent over a lovely pie when I fell in the wheel barrow. And besides the Ethiopian Trade Commissioner is going to be visiting the Applebys and if he sees the wall, he'll cancel his order for fifty thousand Sleepy Bye mattresses. And if that happens my husband will probably leave me forever.

STARBORNE: Well, it's a mighty solid wall. I don't know.

MRS. CARMELODEON: Couldn't you use some dynamite?

STARBORNE: I don't know. Pretty dangerous. There may be a way, Mrs. Carmelodeon, but it means enlisting the aid of Freddy and Ernie. . .

MRS. CARMELODEON: That's all right.

STARBORNE: Freddy *and* Ernie. . . Ernie Appleby.

MRS. CARMELODEON: Get him here. If it will help get down that wall.

STARBORNE: Very well. (*Calling*) Freddy! Ernie!

MUSIC: *Sound of African drums behind.*

FREDDY: Hi, Mr. Starborne. Look at me! Oh. . . hello, Mom.

MRS. CARMELODEON: Freddy, what's that you're wearing?

FREDDY: It's a witch doctor's suit. . . like Ernie's great grandfather wore. . . we made it.

MUSIC: *Swirl of bagpipes in and behind.*

ERNIE: Hi, Mr. Starborne. Look at me.

STARBORNE: Great Heavens, Ernie, what's that you've got on?

ERNIE: The Royal Stuart kilt, like Freddy's great grandfather wore with Churchill. This is my sporran.

FREDDY: We didn't have a real one, so we used an old badger tail we found.

MUSIC: *Out.*

STARBORNE: Boys, our club is faced with a problem. Freddy's mother wants her wall down.

FREDDY: You want us to build a ram rod?

STARBORNE: No time. Boys, I've heard it told that when Joshua wanted a wall to fall down he marched around it seven times, sounding a bugle—and the wall crumbled.

MRS. CARMELODEON: That was a miracle!

STARBORNE: Only a miracle can get this wall down today. Now, my idea is that if you two boys could stand there together and whistle just the right notes, maybe the vibration would smash that wall.

MRS. CARMELODEON: Impossible!

STARBORNE: Come on, boys, try it. Whistle, Freddy, Ernie. Come on. No, harmonize it, kids. Together. Together you can do anything, you know. That's it. You're getting it. Now, you're getting it. That's it, boys, you're together now. Come on. Take it! Take it away!

MUSIC: *Builds together with sound of rumble. The music and whistling blend to a full exciting sound and then with a great rumble the wall disintegrates.*

STARBORNE: Well, there's your wall, Mrs. Carmelodeon. Just a pile of rubble.

MRS. CARMELODEON: Oh thank you. I was afraid I'd never get rid of it in time. . . Well, after all, one can't sneeze at 50,000 mattresses. Thank you, Mr. Starborne.

FREDDY: We did it, Ernie. We whistled down a wall. Just like that old Joshua.

ERNIE: I guess it was because there was two of us. Hey, what about the tree house?

FREDDY: We got to get to work on it. Mom, Ernie and I are going to add another room to our tree house. Can I have some cookies?

Gwen Pharis Ringwood

MRS. CARMELODEON: I. . . well yes, yes. . . you can. . . Freddy.
　　(*Calling*) You be careful. Don't fall in the lake.
FREDDY: No, Mom.
MUSIC
STARBORNE: Well, there's your boat, Sir. Hope you have a good day
　　fishing.
　　Yes, that's right. Starborne's the name. John Starborne.
MUSIC: *Up and out.*

The End

Widger's Way

For Imbert Orchard

Characters

WIDGER
PLANTER
JAKE
ROSELLE
PETER
SOKOLANDER
ANASTASIA
PROFESSOR BOND
GARROW
DOWSER
OFFICER DOCKET

Gwen Pharis Ringwood

SCENE 1

PLACE: WIDGER's *kitchen.*

TIME: *The Present. About 3:30 a.m. on a stormy June night.*

A flash of lightning illuminates the room. There is the crash of thunder, a sound of knocking and of rain. The thunder wakes WIDGER *who sits up in bed. He is a spare, small man in his sixties, wearing a nightshirt and a nightcap. He takes a flash-light from under his pillow and beams it toward the door.*

WIDGER: Yes? Who's there? *(Pause. Another crash of thunder)* Oh that's it — thunder. Too late for the crops now. We needed this a month ago. *(WIDGER covers himself again and turns off flash-light. Wind rises. There is a loud knocking at the door)* Who's there? Answer.

PLANTER: *(Outside)* Ho, inside. Open the door.

WIDGER: It's robbers. . . oh. . .
(He covers his head.)

PLANTER: Open I say. Open. *(Knocks loudly)*
(WIDGER gets out of bed. He is thin, irritable, frightened. He has an old sock tied around his throat.)

WIDGER: Stop that. You'll break my door. *(Lightning. Thunder. Wind.* WIDGER *opens the top half of the dutch door)* There's no one home. *(An unshaven face can be seen through the upper half of the door)* What do you want at this time of night?

PLANTER: Food. Shelter.

WIDGER: I've nothing for you. Now go, before I set the dog on you.

PLANTER: I'm starving.

WIDGER:Get out or I'll. . . *(He turns from the door and growls savagely)* Hear that? Down, Lance down. *(He growls again)* He's savage, mean, hates strangers. He'll tear you limb from limb.

PLANTER: For God's sake man, be merciful. I can pay.

WIDGER: *(Interested at once)* Pay? Money?

PLANTER: Gold if you like. Come, open.

WIDGER: What have I got worth buying?

PLANTER: Food, lodging.

WIDGER: Hah, You haven't two cents to rub together. Go along.

PLANTER: See this? *(He holds up leather bag)* That's gold, old man. A sack of golden nuggets.

WIDGER: You're lying!

PLANTER: Lift it.

WIDGER: *(Lifting bag while* PLANTER *keeps hold of string)* It's rocks and worthless.

PLANTER: Look! *(He holds up a nugget)* That's gold and only I knew where it came from.

WIDGER: *(Fascinated)* It looks like gold. How much will you give me if I let you in?

PLANTER: Oh, let's say — Fifty.

WIDGER: A hundred.

PLANTER: Done. Now open.

WIDGER: *(Unfastening the door)* I will. . . but don't forget. . . you made a bargain. There!

> *(Lightning. Thunder. WIDGER opens door and PLANTER comes inside. He is a stocky, grizzled fellow with gray whiskers. . .red Mackinaw, dark trousers, heavy boots and faded red wool shirt. He puts the gold bag back in a knapsack.)*

PLANTER: *(Shivering)* I think I've caught a chill. Here, shut the door.

WIDGER: Oh yes. *(He closes door)* And now my gold, my hundred dollars?

PLANTER: Where's the dog?

WIDGER: Oh, he's. . .he's hiding.

PLANTER: *(Suddenly grabbing WIDGER by the front of his nightshirt)* You lie, you old dog you!

WIDGER: Let go! You'll tear my nightshirt. I had a dog. He died. He'd have been no use anyway, his teeth were gone. Now, about the money—

PLANTER: Have you no lamp here?

WIDGER: Yes, I'll light one.

> *(He does so.)*

PLANTER: *(At stove)* I'll set a blaze to warm my aching bones. Now, what about some clothes?

WIDGER: I'll put on something.

PLANTER: For me, fool! dry clothes!

WIDGER: I haven't any—that is, I have a Sunday suit and the clothes I wear on week days—that's all.

PLANTER: I'll take the Sunday suit.

WIDGER: You want to—buy it?

PLANTER: *(He moves to back wall where suit hangs on hanger)* Is this the garment?

WIDGER: Yes, but—

PLANTER: A little threadbare—

WIDGER: I never claimed to be a man of fashion.

PLANTER: Well, while I change, you scurry with the skillet. *(He strips off Mackinaw and shirt. Goes behind a screen and as he changes clothes, talks over it)* I haven't eaten for two days.

WIDGER: What's your name, stranger?

PLANTER: Why its — Plantaganet!

WIDGER: You mean the King. . . the Lion Hearted. He's dead.

PLANTER: Dead but lives on in me—his grandson. Sic transit gloria. Do you agree, old nightcap?

WIDGER: It's Greek to me.

PLANTER: Not Greek, Latin. The tongue of kings.

Gwen Pharis Ringwood

WIDGER: Widger's my name. Milton Ephraim Widger. *(As an after-thought)* Esquire.
PLANTER: Well met, Widger.
    (Lightning and thunder.)
WIDGER: You want a sandwich?
PLANTER: Sandwich? My belly cries out for a meal, a feast.
WIDGER: Food's dear these days. An egg's worth 7 cents, a slice of bacon, five. Bread's gone up and coffee's out of sight. . .
PLANTER: Cheese, bread, meat. Let's shoot the works.
WIDGER: *(Doubtfully)* I'll rouse my daugther.
PLANTER: We're not alone?
WIDGER: My daughter sleeps above. *(At stairway)* Roselle!
PLANTER: Let her sleep, old man! *(Jumping at WIDGER)* I want no gossip.
WIDGER: Why, yes, of course.
PLANTER: *(Playing with hunting knife)* Whoever comes, you'll swear you never saw me.
WIDGER: I swear.
PLANTER: Good. Bring on the food. Have you a car, old nightcap?
WIDGER: *(Removing his cap)* I had a Ford in 1930 but it won't go now.
PLANTER: A horse then?
WIDGER: *(Brings cheese and bread)* Just old Polly—she's spavined and half blind.
PLANTER: I'll take her.
WIDGER: Oh, I couldn't sell old Polly.
PLANTER: *(Menacingly)* I'll take her, friend.
WIDGER: *(Looks at knife)* Oh. . . Yes.
PLANTER: Now bar the door.
WIDGER: Why? Are you going to. . . Are you expecting someone?
PLANTER: Bar the door.
WIDGER: *(Frightened, bars the door)* Please eat and go, Mr. Plantaganet.
PLANTER: You want to get rid of me? *(Mock surprise.)*
WIDGER: Yes, No—that is—
PLANTER: Are you afraid?
WIDGER: I'm not a man for violence, never was. If you'll go now, I'll only charge you half.
PLANTER: Half?
WIDGER: Half the hundred dollars.
PLANTER: Hah, I may hole up here until after Christmas.
WIDGER: Oh, you can't. I'll go to the police.
PLANTER: *(Turning in lamplight)* I wouldn't, if I were you.
WIDGER: *(Throat dry)* Oh no. I wouldn't either.
PLANTER: *(Playing with WIDGER, cat-like)* I think I'll stay here and be your hired man, Widger. I'll slop the hogs, make hay, fish, shoot partridge up and down the river and get drunk on Saturday on Widger's wages. A tidy life and restful.
WIDGER: *(Spilling tea)* Hired man? Oh no. . .
PLANTER: You're old, Widger. You need a man.

WIDGER: Hired man to Widger? *(He is shaken)* But of course you're joking. I'm not rich, you know. A poor farmer wrestling with poor land to get the meanest living. Cutworms and taxes, drought and early frost, hail-storms, grasshoppers, potato blight. . . Why sir, you've no idea how nature contrives to keep a man's nose hugged to the grindstone. I work from dawn to dusk. At night, I dream of dying in the poor-house. When I get up, what do I find? A hawk has killed my chickens. The old sow's devoured all her litter, bugs ravished the potatoes and the bull's been struck by lightning. That's how it goes with Widger. I couldn't afford you, sir. Besides it's very dull here. You wouldn't like it.

PLANTER: I'd rather be dull than dead, old fellow, wouldn't you?

WIDGER: Dead. Oh. . . Dead! I see. *(He freezes.)*

PLANTER: I'm being followed, Widger. Pursued by a stalking vengeance whom I left for carrion. Fancy yourself, old nightcap, poised on a mountain crag, looking down a sheer drop to nothing. You hear your partner step behind you. You turn to speak and see there, looking at you out of a familiar face—

WIDGER: What? *(Eyes round.)*

PLANTER: Murder! *(WIDGER shrinks.)*

WIDGER: Murder!

PLANTER: You slip, struggle and feel yourself being pushed to the edge of nothing. By a miracle you regain your foothold and over he goes instead. You hear a crash below you and then silence. And in that awful silence you break camp, pick up the gold and start down the mountain. You're lost in silence—for days and nights and days—until half mad you stumble on the trail that leads you out.

WIDGER: *(Like a child lost in a tale of terror trying to regain reality)* He tried to kill you, so you killed him, is that it? Well, that's only fair.

PLANTER: But I didn't kill him, Widger.

WIDGER: Eh?

PLANTER: I saw him in Barkerville, again at Wells. And every move since then I've felt him close behind. I stole a boat and drifted down the river. The storm hit. I was nearly drowned. And here I am. *(WIDGER nods dolefully)* I may have put him off. But if he comes, you've never seen me—Understand?

WIDGER: Comes here? Oh, he wouldn't come here, would he? What does he look like?

PLANTER: Strong. Black bearded. Green glittering eyes, the ace of spades tatooed on his right forearm.

WIDGER: Maybe the storm got him. Drowned him in the river.

PLANTER: I hope you're right. *(Thunder. There is a knock on the door)* What's that?

WIDGER: Someone knocking.

PLANTER: Get him away, you fool. *(He hides.)*

Gwen Pharis Ringwood

WIDGER: If I don't answer, he might go along. *(Second knock.*
WIDGER *calls out squeakily)* You've got the wrong address.
There's no one here.
JAKE: *(From outside)* I want a man named Planter. Is he here?
PLANTER: That's Jake all right. Answer!
WIDGER: Who? Whom do you want?
JAKE: PLANTER. RICHARD PLANTER. . .
WIDGER: Oh. . . Oh yes. . . Well now. . .
JAKE: He's in there?
WIDGER: Oh no. No. Not here.
JAKE: Let me in.
WIDGER: I can't.
JAKE: I'll burn you to the ground. Open, I say.
WIDGER: *(Opening the door a little but leaving bottom half bolted)* How
do you do.
JAKE: Where's Planter?
WIDGER: Is he a scrawny man, carrying a knapsack. . . with a nose. . .
on foot?
JAKE: That's him, the Lion Hearted. *(Laughs)* He's here then.
(Lightning. Thunder.)
WIDGER: Oh no, no. He was here earlier. Enquired the way to the
abandoned mine. That's where you'll find him.
JAKE: Where is this mine?
WIDGER: Seven miles south. You'll find him there for certain, dead
or alive.
JAKE: Hm! He'll be dead when I'm through with him.
(Lightning. Thunder.)
WIDGER: You're welcome. *(Starts to close top of door)* You'd better
hurry or he'll steal a car and slip across the border. Good night.
*(He watches a moment and then closes door and bars top.
Whispering to* PLANTER*)* He's going. He's taken my advice. He's
heading South.
PLANTER: I'll go North. Was he on foot?
WIDGER: Yes.
PLANTER: Good. Get me some bread and meat and matches. And I
want your razor.
WIDGER: Razor? What for?
PLANTER: To shave with, stupid. Get it.
WIDGER: Yes, sir. Potatoes, meat, bread, matches. . . you'll pay me.
You said you'd pay in gold. *(He is nervously filling a gunny sack
with food)* Cheese. There!
PLANTER: The razor.
WIDGER: Oh yes. *(He starts towards wash stand shelf.)*
PLANTER: Here. Give it to me! *(He holds the straight razor in his hand.
(There is a knock at the door)* He's back!
WIDGER: He's come to kill us!
PLANTER: Where does this door go?
WIDGER: The barn.

PLANTER: A bridle?
WIDGER: Above the stall. Here's your food. *(Knocking again)* Yes, I'm coming.
PLANTER: Hold him here as long as you can.
(Loud knocking.)
WIDGER: Coming. Just a minute.
PLANTER: *(Giving WIDGER knapsack)* And you hide this. Guard it with your life. I'll be back, Widger. If it's not here, I'll kill you.
WIDGER: Oh. . everybody's killing me. I'll hide it.
PLANTER: Good. I'm off, old nightcap.
WIDGER: Don't sell old Polly. Goodbye, Planter. *(PLANTER rushes out back)* Wait, my hundred dollars. *(The knocking comes again. WIDGER crawls under the table with knapsack)* Strong, black bearded with green glittering eyes. . . and the ace of spades. . . that's death!
ROSELLE: *(At door)* Father, Father, it's Roselle. Please let me in.
WIDGER: *(Head out)*. . . Roselle's asleep upstairs. This is some devil's trick.
ROSELLE: Father.
WIDGER: *(Coming out a little)* Is that you, Daugther?
ROSELLE: Yes, Father. Please.
WIDGER: *(Up)* What are you doing out there?
ROSELLE: I'm freezing.
WIDGER: *(Going to door)* It is Roselle. *(He opens the door)* Get in, you girl. . . What do you mean by this? *(Pulls her in)* It's four o'clock. And you, like a bedraggled kitten mewling at the door. Whose clothes are those—I never bought you those.
ROSELLE: Yvonne's. . . I borrowed them.
WIDGER: Where were you?
ROSELLE: At a dance at Lakeview.
WIDGER: How did you get there?
ROSELLE: Yvonne's friend, Walter, has a car.
WIDGER: You sneaked out after I slept, to meet them?
ROSELLE: *(Nods miserably)* I wanted to go so badly.
WIDGER: Who brought you home—this Walter with his car?
ROSELLE: No. When the dance finished I look for them everywhere but they'd gone. Oh it was awful—everyone going home, the janitor starting to sweep the dance floor.
WIDGER: So you came home alone!
ROSELLE: No, sir.
WIDGER: Who brought you?
ROSELLE: A boy named Peter. He came and asked me, just like I was —anybody.
WIDGER: Go on.
ROSELLE: First I said "No thank you" and then I said "Yes please" and then when I told him it's seven miles, he said "We'd better get started then".
WIDGER: So you got in a stranger's car like any common baggage.

Gwen Pharis Ringwood

ROSELLE: Oh no, we walked.

WIDGER: It's all true, the things your Aunt Abigail told me. You're deceitful, treacherous, you cheat, run about, and lie!

ROSELLE: No!

WIDGER: Seventeen and out all night with a stranger! Seventeen and you dance like a wanton down the primrose path.

ROSELLE: It wasn't a primrose path. It was a muddy old road with thistles on it.

WIDGER: This stranger made advances I presume?

ROSELLE: No!

WIDGER: Don't lie to me. His arm was around your waist. He kissed you?

ROSELLE: No.

WIDGER: Plied you with wine and Turkish cigarettes?

ROSELLE: He didn't.

WIDGER: What did he say to you? What promises fell from his lips like poisoned honey?

ROSELLE: He talked a lot about the Pre-Cambrian Shield. And when I said I was cold, he said "Imagine this country in the Ice Age".

WIDGER: Tell me his name.

ROSELLE: Peter. That's all I know. He goes to University.

WIDGER: He'll have to marry you.

ROSELLE: What, Father?

WIDGER: He'll marry you I say.

ROSELLE: Oh no. He hardly noticed me. I wish he had.

WIDGER: The only dowry I could give you was your good name, Roselle. And now that's gone. If your dead mother could see you now she'd weep for shame—

ROSELLE: Don't, Father, please—

WIDGER: I'll find this Peter and force him to marry you if it's the last thing I do. Now get to bed!

ROSELLE: I'm sorry. *(She moves towards stairs and sees knapsack under the table—turns)* Whose knapsack? Was someone here?

WIDGER: No. Leave it alone. It's nothing to do with you.

ROSELLE: I only—

WIDGER: I'll deal with you in the morning. Go!

ROSELLE: Good night. *(She goes upstairs.)*

WIDGER: *(Looking after her)* Talked of the Pre-Cambrian Shield— That's not likely. Why, it's nearly dawn. The thing to do is get her married straightaway—before she brings disgrace on both of us, mothers some bastard that I'll have to feed. I'll find this man and marry them at once. Tomorrow! *(He takes up knapsack)* And this—he said to hide it.—I wonder—*(Opens knapsack, takes out some clothing and then the leather poke)* He wasn't lying. *(He opens it)* It's gold all right—a sack of golden nuggets. *(He sits greedily at the table)* Well, if he comes back, it's here. If not, I'm a wealthy man. I'm rich. Suppose he comes. I'll say I never saw it. What could he do? What could the partner do? Who's to believe

294

their story? And I'll be rich, a man with money. Sokolander with his bulging granaries could curl the lip no more at old man Widger. I could buy them all—be village reeve or mayor. Be clapped on the shoulder, asked to bend an elbow. They'd call me Milt or Widge at noon-day luncheons—and all by virtue of my sack of gold. I could buy Roselle a husband. No. This gold can slip through my fingers like a greasy pig if I give way to every impulse. Not me, not Widger. I've worked too hard, grubbed for the last potato in the patch, scratched on my hands and knees for a fallen penny. I'll hide it away against a rainy day. But where? Not here. If he comes back, he'd find it. *(The storm mounts)* I have it—there's a board loose beside the wall. *(He puts an old coat or dressing gown on and takes up lantern)* You'll be safe there, my pretty. . . *(The storm rages)* That's right. . . *(Lightning)* Snarl wind, rage heaven, Lightning take your pleasure. Under the storm's cover, Widger conceals his treasure.

SCENE 2

PLACE: The yard of WIDGER's *place. A shabby fence with stile runs from downstage right to upstage right, dividing* WIDGER's *place from an old churchyard. Downstage right is a dog kennel and the stile is above centre right. The well is about left centre and the front of* WIDGER's *house (door. . .steps. . .window above) can be seen.*

TIME: Very early the same morning. Dawn.

Sound of birds. JAKE SCHOLTZ *is standing near the back window using it as a mirror as he shaves off his beard. He has almost finished shaving. When he finishes, he pockets the razor, removes his black raincoat, folds it over his hat. Putting these down he examines the yard for footprints and then very quietly tries the door. He is trying to slip the bolt with a knife and makes a slight noise.* ROSELLE's *voice comes from upstairs.*

ROSELLE: Is that you, Father? *(JAKE runs off, collecting his gear as he does so. After a moment,* ROSELLE *appears in the doorway. She wears a soft old-fashioned nightgown and is in her bare feet)* I was sure

I heard someone—I must have dreamed it. *(She steps outside)*
Oh. . . how beautiful! *(She walks out a little way)* Good morning
Sun. And Meadow Larks. And Trees. Hello, Frog. I'm Roselle!
The little girl who used to run barefoot through the wet leaves.
I'm Roselle, remember? I'm grown up now. I'm not sure I like it.
(She sits down disconsolately on the bench) Oh Peter, Peter, why
didn't you notice me? I wanted you to notice me so much. Where
have you gone, Peter? *(From the kennel comes a loud snore.
ROSELLE is startled. She runs to kennel and looks inside the partly
open door)* Peter! It's you. You didn't go. *(She reaches in and
shakes him)* Peter, wake up. You're snoring.

PETER: *(Groaning)* Oh. . . *(He peers out)* Oh. . . Where's my bone?
*(*PETER *grasps at a large bone near mouth of kennel.)*

ROSELLE: *(Shocked)* Bone?

PETER: Sh. . . it's a secret. Go away.

ROSELLE: Peter, don't you know me?

PETER: *(Examining bone with pride)* Oh, you're the girl I walked home
last night.

ROSELLE: I don't know what I'd have done without you. I was so
frightened.

PETER: What's your name?

ROSELLE: You don't remember?

PETER: Why should I?

ROSELLE: *(Offended)* No reason I guess.
(She turns.)

PETER: *(Crawling out)* Wait. It's Roselle.

ROSELLE: *(Turning, all smiles)* Oh, I'm so glad. I thought you'd lost
your mind.

PETER: That's not a nice thing to say.

ROSELLE: Well, it does look queer, sleeping in kennels, with a bone.

PETER: *(Getting the kinks out of his back)* Do you always run around in
nightgowns without shoes?

ROSELLE: *(Shocked)* Oh. *(Embarrassed)* I'll go. I hope I see you some
time. *(She is backing towards door)* Soon, I mean. . . Like today,
maybe. . .

PETER: Sure. Last night was a milestone in my life.

ROSELLE: *(Forgetting her embarrassment)* It was?

PETER: Changed my whole future.

ROSELLE: I felt the same way, Peter.

PETER: *(Marvelling)* On such a night to find something so rare, so
suddenly—

ROSELLE: *(Eyes shining)* That's how it was with me—suddenly.

PETER: Look, can you keep a secret? After I left you, I stubbed my toe
and fell—When I got up I held this clutched in my hand. I lit a
match— *(He shows her the bone.)*

ROSELLE: After you left me? Then it hadn't anything to do with me
—your secret?

PETER: *(Oblivious)* What does this look like?

ROSELLE: *(Crossly)* Like what it is. I don't have to go to University to know an old bone when I see one.

PETER: Do you know how old this bone might be?

ROSELLE: I don't care.

PETER: Six million years perhaps. This is the ankle of a great horned dinosaur. Don't touch this bone. It's against the law to bother dinosaurs.

ROSELLE: I don't intend to bother it or you. Goodbye.

PETER: I think it's a Triceratops. Stand guard till I get back.

ROSELLE: Guard your own dinosaur. I'm busy.

PETER: *(Following her)* Women always think of themselves first.

ROSELLE: That's not true Peter. . . Peter. . . What's your last name anyway?

PETER: Traptow.

ROSELLE: Peter Traptow. You're just a self-centred prig, that's what you are—Goodbye.

WIDGER: *(From inside)* Roselle!

ROSELLE: That's my father. If he finds me dressed like this he'll kill you. Hide!

PETER: Nonsense.

ROSELLE: You don't know him. He thinks the worst of everyone. Quick, lie down. *(She pushes him to kennel.)*

WIDGER: Roselle! *(ROSELLE stuffs PETER back in dog house.)*

ROSELLE: Yes, Father. . . Coming. *(She turns to well and starts to draw a pail of water.)*

WIDGER: *(At door)* Roselle, why aren't you dressed?

ROSELLE: I couldn't sleep.

WIDGER: Go and dress yourself.

ROSELLE: Yes, sir.

WIDGER: At once. *(She goes in reluctantly)* I'd best make sure. *(He kneels by well)* Oh, there's tracks—a gopher, badger. . . digger of some kind. . . *(He is kneeling by well when JAKE comes in.)*

JAKE: Could you direct me to the village please?

WIDGER: *(Without looking up)* Turn at the churchyard, down the hill, across the tracks one mile and there you are.

JAKE: Thank you.

WIDGER: *(Suddenly realizing he is not alone)* Oh. Where did you come from?

JAKE: Up river.

WIDGER: What do you want here? You're trespassing. Move along. And don't come back or I'll have to set my dog on you?

JAKE: Dog?

WIDGER: In the kennel. I'd better lock the door before he hears you. *(Runs over and locks kennel)* Now's your chance. Run!

JAKE: I'm going.

WIDGER: *(Following him)* Wait. Were you looking for someone?

JAKE: Perhaps.

297

Gwen Pharis Ringwood

WIDGER: My daughter? Oh I see it now. It was you who brought her in at dawn. Well, I won't have it. You'll not play fast and loose with Widger's duckling. You'll marry her—today!
JAKE: I beg your pardon?
WIDGER: You'll marry her I say. I'll go to law.
JAKE: Hands off, old man. I've never seen your daughter.
WIDGER: Your name's Peter?
JAKE: No.
WIDGER: What is it?
JAKE: Jacob—Foote.
WIDGER: Student?
JAKE: No—Barber.
WIDGER: Oh—barber. You. . . You're not the one?
JAKE: Unfortunately, no.
WIDGER: Oh, I beg your pardon. *(Pause)* I thought—You plan to ply your scissors in our village, Mr. Foote?
JAKE: If things work out—
WIDGER: Oh I wouldn't. Around here we mostly shave ourselves. You won't get rich in Bones. *(Knocking inside kennel. WIDGER starts)* What's that?
JAKE: Your dog?
PETER: Help! Let me out!
JAKE: Good day. *(He goes off.)*
WIDGER: *(Opening kennel carefully)* Come out. Come out.
PETER: Oh thank you.
WIDGER: What are you doing in my kennel?
PETER: I found something very precious last night. I want to claim it for the University.
WIDGER: That's not fair. I hid it. It's mine. I'll call a policeman. Docket. Mr. Docket!
PETER: To you it's just an old bone. But to me, to science, it's a signpost on our road back to the Protozoic. Let me keep it.
WIDGER: You mean you only want this bone? *(Joyfully)* Oh take the bone, boy, take it! By all means. Take it and run along.
PETER: Now if I could just dig here.
WIDGER: Oh no—No digging!
PETER: The spine of the Triceratops may lie beneath the house, the jawbone by the well.
WIDGER: No digging by the well. Be off, I tell you.
        (SOKOLANDER's voice offstage.)
SOKOLANDER: Nephew! Nephew!
PETER: Oh, that's Uncle Clifford.
SOKOLANDER: *(Entering rapidly)* So, there you are! Morning, Widger. *(To PETER)* Out all night eh boy? Why haven't you milked the cows?
PETER: I'm sorry Uncle.
SOKOLANDER: Get over there and milk.
PETER: Yes, Uncle.

SOKOLANDER: The cows are bawling. I suppose while I'm campaigning
they'll not be milked at all.
ROSELLE: *(Appearing at door. Dressed in simple cotton)* Your breakfast's
ready, Father.
PETER: Breakfast!
SOKOLANDER: You've missed it. Good morning, Miss Roselle.
ROSELLE: Good morning, Mr. Sokolander.
SOKOLANDER: This is my nephew. He arrived last week.
ROSELLE: *(Coldly)* How do you do?
PETER: I'm hungry.
SOKOLANDER: After the cows, the stables, after the stables, the hogs,
after the hogs, the turkeys.
PETER: Can't I leave the turkeys Uncle?
SOKOLANDER: Turkeys must eat like anyone else.
PETER: The old gobbler hates me.
SOKOLANDER: *(Laughing)* The day you catch that gobbler, you can
have him.
ROSELLE: I doubt you'll lose your gobbler, Mr. Sokolander.
PETER: *(Stung)* I'd like to see you catch him.
ROSELLE: I could.
PETER: Try then.
ROSELLE: You're afraid of him.
PETER: He's dangerous I tell you.
ROSELLE: Good luck, Mr. Traptow.
(They glare at one another.)
SOKOLANDER: Look sharp now, boy, before I send you packing.
PETER: *(Going out)* Muscle—just muscle is all that counts around here.
SOKOLANDER: *(Looking after him)* I don't know how he'll manage
while I'm campaigning. You get prettier every day, Roselle.
ROSELLE: *(Primly)* Thank you, Mr. Sokolander. *(She goes into the
house.)*
SOKOLANDER: I'd better make sure Peter can run the milker. *(He
moves off a little.)*
WIDGER: Peter?
SOKOLANDER: My nephew.
WIDGER: Oh. *(Pause)* This Peter, he goes to University?
SOKOLANDER: He did, last year.
WIDGER: Then he's the one.
SOKOLANDER: What's that?
WIDGER: *(Thinking himself very subtle)* As you know, Mr. Sokolander,
I have a daughter. Motherless since she was five years old, now
seventeen. In short, she's ripe for marriage. Now knowing as we
do the hot propensities of youthful blood—I speak as man to
man of course—I feel it wise not to delay her longer. You get
my meaning?
SOKOLANDER: No.
WIDGER: Roselle and your nephew Peter—

299

SOKOLANDER: You'd marry Roselle to Peter? Why the young fool hasn't two cents to rub together.

WIDGER: Still as your heir, he has prospects.

SOKOLANDER: I'm a long way from dead. Oh no, Widger.

WIDGER: He's young, educated.

SOKOLANDER: Can you make a settlement on your daughter?

WIDGER: Oh no. Hard times. Taxes. Potato blight. No dowry, except her youth and beauty and skill in the domestic arts.

SOKOLANDER: It wouldn't do at all.

WIDGER: It must—after last night.

SOKOLANDER: Why? What do you mean?

WIDGER: Oh, well you see last night. . . I had some sort of heart attack —I'm far from well and want my daughter cared for.

SOKOLANDER: *(A sudden decision)* Marry Roselle to me.

WIDGER: To you!

SOKOLANDER: I'll take her.

WIDGER: But you're old.

SOKOLANDER: I'm not so old. Look here. *(He bends a pitchfork)* Show me the young blood that can do that.

WIDGER: My pitchfork.

SOKOLANDER: Old eh? I'll. . . *(He looks around for something else to bend.)*

WIDGER: I'll take your word.

SOKOLANDER: I'm well off, I'm sure to be elected—

WIDGER: Yes.

SOKOLANDER: Before the year's out I'll be in the legislature. Portfolio perhaps. From there—

WIDGER: Prime Minister?

SOKOLANDER: Who knows?

WIDGER: A wedding is expensive.

SOKOLANDER: We'll charge it up to my campaign. A wedding's just the thing to start it off tomorrow. The whole constituency can drink my health.

WIDGER: Tomorrow!

SOKOLANDER: Votes man! I'll pay for everything—food, dance, dress, even a haircut for yourself, old fellow.

WIDGER: That's generous.

SOKOLANDER: You've no bags of gold to throw around?

WIDGER: What made you say that?

SOKOLANDER: Take my offer, Widger.

WIDGER: About that load of hay I owe you. . .

SOKOLANDER: If we marry tomorrow, I'll throw in the hay.

WIDGER: You'd treat my daughter kindly.

SOKOLANDER: I'll make a lady of her. Come, call her out.

(ANASTASIA BURROWS enters.)

ANASTASIA: Good morning, good morning, good morning. And how are we this morning?

SOKOLANDER: Mrs. Burrows.

ANASTASIA: What a dreadful storm! It broke my pump. Was it Roselle came in so late, Mr. Widger?

SOKOLANDER: Roselle?

ANASTASIA: Ah, madcap youth! It must be watched, you know.

SOKOLANDER: We're as young as we feel, dear lady.

ANASTASIA: How true! Last night when it thundered, I shivered like a child. But you, Mr. Widger—out with your lantern working at your well!

WIDGER: My well?

ANASTASIA: Oh, I saw you bobbing about. But that's what I came for—water.

WIDGER: *(Hurriedly)* I'll get it for you. *(He takes bucket from her and rushes to well.)*

ANASTASIA: Thank you. Ah, Mr. Sokolander—our own Disraeli, I'm voting for you.

SOKOLANDER: Splendid.

ANASTASIA: If I can help you, tell me.

SOKOLANDER: I need help, Mrs. Burrows. Perhaps your Ladies Club—

ANASTASIA: The Lilies! I'll see to it. There's thirty votes right there.

SOKOLANDER: And then of course, our slogan—

ANASTASIA: Sock for Sokolander!

SOKOLANDER: Whisper it! Shout it! Sing it! You can help me.

ANASTASIA: Oh Clifford, depend on me. I'll sock for Sokolander.

SOKOLANDER: Thank you, dear lady, thank you.

WIDGER: *(Returning with water)* Your water, Mrs. Burrows.

ANASTASIA: Thank you, Mr. Widger. *(As she speaks she hands water to SOKOLANDER)* Here I am a widow for six years and still forget I must do my own fetch and carrying.

SOKOLANDER: I'll be glad to carry it home for you, Mrs. Burrows.

ANASTASIA: Anastasia!

(PROFESSOR BOND enters.)

BOND: I'm looking for a Mrs. Burrows, please.

ANASTASIA: I am she!

BOND: I'm Bond, Willoughby Bond.

ANASTASIA: The professor! He's come to consider the lilies, Clifford.

BOND: Eh?

ANASTASIA: The Lily Valley Lilies. You're our entertainment.

BOND: I speak tonight. *(A little uncertain.)*

ANASTASIA: Yes. After the financial report and before the Bingo.

BOND: I see. Sic transit gloria.

WIDGER: *(Startled)* That's Latin!

BOND: Yes.

WIDGER: And you've got a beard! Then you're the partner!

BOND: I beg your pardon.

ANASTASIA: Now Mr. Bond. . . you'll want a bath of course.

BOND: Oh, it's not necessary.

ANASTASIA: All our speakers want baths. I'll have to billet you.

BOND: I see.

301

Gwen Pharis Ringwood

ANASTASIA: I had to fight to get you here, Professor. The Ladies wanted Swami, the magician.
BOND: *(Ruefully)* I could put on a turban, do card tricks, if you like.
WIDGER: Card tricks—the Ace of Spades.
ANASTASIA: Oh no. But be as amusing as you can, won't you? What's your subject.
BOND: The Pre-Cambrian Shield.
ANASTASIA: Oh. . . Oh yes. Well it will have to do. Mr. Widger, could you put the professor up?
WIDGER: Oh no. No plumbing, no baths—Impossible.
ANASTASIA: Clifford?
SOKOLANDER: The campaign committee has taken over my house, Anastasia.
ANASTASIA: I can't take you—there'd be talk. Well, the vicar will have to have you. Come along.
WIDGER: But that's just next door.
ANASTASIA: *(Moving towards stile)* This church is old, Professor.
BOND: *(Meekly)* It looks old.
ANASTASIA: *(Turning)* Mr. Widger, the Lord hates a shabby fence. Why don't you paint it?
WIDGER: Oh I will. I mean to.
ANASTASIA: Do! Are you coming, Clifford?
SOKOLANDER: Oh yes, yes. I'll be back, Widger, to arrange about —tomorrow.
> *(He hurries after* BOND. WIDGER *hurries after* MRS. BURROWS.*)*
WIDGER: Mrs. Burrows, wait—this man. He's an imposter!
ANASTASIA: Nonsense.
WIDGER: Believe me, I know something. He's dangerous.
ANASTASIA: Don't be silly. These University people aren't nearly as dangerous as they're made out. There's nothing to them but a few ideas.
WIDGER: He's after something.
ANASTASIA: No. Just wants to talk. *(She hurries off after the others)* Wait, Gentlemen. Wait for me.
WIDGER: Oh dear. He's no professor. That's Scholtz, the partner, looking for my gold. I should never have hidden it here. Everyone's taken to coming here. I'll have to move it.
> *(WIDGER gets down on hands and knees beside well. GARROW enters backing and backs into WIDGER.)*
GARROW: Hey, get out of the way, will you. I gotta get a line on this.
> *(He is laying wire)*
WIDGER: You're trespassing!
GARROW: Think nothing of it, boy.
> *(He goes right on working without looking at WIDGER.)*
WIDGER: Who are you?
GARROW: Garrow. Gulf Oil. Seismic Crew. Get off the wire.
WIDGER: What are you doing?

GARROW: We've sunk a test hole on the road allowance. I'm going to lay the recorder along here.

WIDGER: You can't. *(Pause)* Look sir, I'm a poor man, not well, my daughter's getting married. . .

GARROW: Good for her. Get off the wire.

WIDGER: Come back tomorrow.

GARROW: We'll blast in a few minutes. Nothing to be alarmed about.

WIDGER: Tomorrow I'll let you dig.

GARROW: There, that's got it.

WIDGER: Tomorrow's not too late.

GARROW: Now don't be scared when we blast. May shake you up a bit. That's all.

WIDGER: Blast. No, no, I won't have it.

GARROW: Keep your shirt on, old man, eh? You want to stay on the good side of me. Gulf's a big company. Don't kill the goose that lays the golden egg, Old Rooster.

(GARROW runs off the same way he came.)

WIDGER: Goose—Egg—Gold? Oh, he knows something. I've got to hide my gold somewhere else—at once.

(ROSELLE comes out.)

ROSELLE: Father, your breakfast's cold. Please come.

WIDGER: No, I can't. I mustn't leave the well.

ROSELLE: You act sick, Father.

WIDGER: Worry.

ROSELLE: You needn't worry about me.

WIDGER: You? Oh you, of course—It's all settled, Roselle,. You're going to marry Mr. Sokolander. Isn't that lucky? Be Prime Minister.

ROSELLE: Oh, I couldn't.

WIDGER: He's rich, remember.

ROSELLE: I wouldn't.

WIDGER: Then back you go to Abigail.

ROSELLE: No.

WIDGER: I'm old, Roselle. My heart stopped several times today—

ROSELLE: But, Father—

WIDGER: If I die, you'll be an orphan. The world's a wicked place, especially for orphans. Here comes Mr. Sokolander now. Say yes, Roselle, say yes.

(SOKOLANDER enters.)

SOKOLANDER: Splendid woman, Mrs. Burrows. Ah, Roselle. Your father's told you of my offer?

ROSELLE: Yes, sir.

SOKOLANDER: And I'm accepted?

ROSELLE: Oh no, I've had no time.

SOKOLANDER: Come, come, girl. I'm no bleating boy. I'll make you mistress of my house and land, buy you fine clothes and if all goes well you'll sip your tea in the nation's inner sanctums. How's that?

Gwen Pharis Ringwood

ROSELLE: I'm young, sir, I'm not ready.

SOKOLANDER: You'll settle down.

WIDGER: Roselle and I, we appreciate the honour. Only her modesty prevents her answer. She accepts with pleasure, Mr. Sokolander.

SOKOLANDER: I understand. Come now, Roselle, a kiss to seal the bargain. *(PETER runs in.)*

PETER: Help, help, I'm wounded.

SOKOLANDER: Are my cows all right?

PETER: That old gobbler, he's possessed. He chased me all around the barn, attacked me. Look. That's blood.

ROSELLE: Peter, let's see. *(He kneels and ROSELLE stops the blood with her handkerchief.)*

PETER: He stabbed me with his beak. Will it leave a scar?

ROSELLE: A little one, perhaps—but that will look distinguished.

PETER: *(Gets up)* Uncle, I'm not cut out for ranching. I resign.

SOKOLANDER: You promised to stay until my election.

PETER: Get some one else.

SOKOLANDER: There's no time. My gate! You left it open.

PETER: He was after me.

SOKOLANDER: My best cows—the railway tracks. Help, Widger, head them off.

(SOKOLANDER and WIDGER run out.)

PETER: Have I stopped bleeding?

ROSELLE: Yes. Did you mean it about—leaving, Peter?

PETER: Yes.

ROSELLE: When are you going?

PETER: I'll wrap the Triceratops and then I'm off.

ROSELLE: Then I won't see you any more, I guess.

PETER: Not likely. But I'll always remember that through you I found a fossil.

(He is polishing his bone.)

ROSELLE: Peter?

PETER: Yes?

ROSELLE: Your Uncle's asked me to marry him.

PETER: Asked you. Why that's ridiculous. Why would he ask you?

ROSELLE: Maybe he thinks I'm—

PETER: Hah. You'd never do for Uncle, much too flighty. Do you want to get married?

ROSELLE: Every girl wants to get married, Peter.

PETER: There's bigger fish than Uncle. If I were you I'd look around a bit. You're not bad looking. Some young rancher should be glad to have you.

ROSELLE: *(Turning)* Thank you very much. I guess there's nothing more to say.

PETER: Wait. Yes, there is. . .

ROSELLE: *(Turning back)* Yes, Peter?

PETER: I wonder—could you sew up some sort of bag for the Triceratops? I'd want it of some soft material—

304

ROSELLE: No, I couldn't. You go on—go on and do your Uncle's chores and hunt for fossils. I hope that gobbler eats you up, that's what I hope. *(SOKOLANDER and WIDGER return)* Mr. Sokolander, I accept with pleasure *(She is crying)* your offer of my hand in marriage. I'm very happy to be the future Mrs. Clifford Sokolander —very happy. *(She wails into the house.)*

SOKOLANDER: Ah that's settled.

PETER: Hopes that gobbler gets me! Accepts your hand! Why that girl's crazy! Uncle, I'll pack my things.

SOKOLANDER: Don't be hasty. Stay for the wedding, boy.

PETER: Hopes that gobbler gets me! She's sadistic! *(He goes out.)*

SOKOLANDER: I'll arrange the wedding tomorrow at ten then, Widger? I'll send loud speakers through the constituency tonight. Start the ball rolling.

WIDGER: Goodbye. You won't forget you're throwing in the hay? *(SOKOLANDER goes off)* Well, that's done. My poor Roselle. He's a blunt man, blunt as a sledgehammer. But he promised he'd be kind, he's rich. She couldn't have done better. And now to hide the gold some safer place. But where? *(He looks around)* The church tower—beside the bell, they never use it now. That's the place. *(He picks up gunny sack beside well and reaching down, gets out bag of gold, placing it in sack)* You'll be safe there, my treasure—safe on Peter's rock. *(He approaches stile with sack)* "The Lord hates a shabby fence," he said. I wonder if I should paint it—No, let the church board do it. They get paint wholesale. I won't paint the fence.

> *(A blast shakes the place. WIDGER falls to the ground on top of gunny sack. ROSELLE runs out.)*

ROSELLE: Father? Are you all right?

WIDGER: I'm struck down, killed.

ROSELLE: What was it?

WIDGER: Roselle, run—fly! Bring back a gallon of white fence paint, hurry.

ROSELLE: Fence paint?

WIDGER: He hates a shabby fence, Roselle.

ROSELLE: Father—

> *(GARROW runs in.)*

GARROW: Knocked you down eh? I told you it would shake you up. Here let me help you.

WIDGER: *(Clutching sack)* No, no, perfectly all right. So that was you?

GARROW: You should see what we do some times.

WIDGER: Never mind the paint, Roselle. It's only the Americans again.

ROSELLE: Are you hurt?

WIDGER: Oh no. No. Get me a cup of tea. Go.

> *(ROSELLE hurries into the house.)*

GARROW: Say, what you got there?

WIDGER: Oh, just—potatoes.

GARROW: You're all right?

WIDGER: Oh yes, fine.

GARROW: Good. For all you know, old man, you're sitting on a fortune. See you. *(GARROW runs off.)*

WIDGER: Oh, that was close. I fooled him. He thinks I've got potatoes. *(Looking up)* I'll paint the fence tomorrow. Tomorrow's not too late.

GARROW: *(Offstage)* Let her blow!

(A second blast leaves WIDGER clinging to the fence.)

WIDGER: Today, I mean. Today. Just my side, mind—my side. *(Going up stile)* Widger's the name—Milton Ephraim Widger. Bringing his treasure to your church for safety. I'll hide it by the bell. It's all I have, I pray you, guard it well.

SCENE 3

PLACE: *The same.*

TIME: *Late afternoon of the same day.*

WIDGER *is painting his side of the church yard fence. As he paints a trill of bird song comes from stage right. He turns apprehensively looking up at the tower. A moment later the sound comes from backstage—an impudent rollicking twirl. Again WIDGER tries to locate the sound, goes back to painting. Once more he is arrested by a twirl of gay whistling all around him. Then DOWSER RINGGO, a pedlar, comes in view.*

WIDGER: Dowser Ringgo. I might have known. Be on your way.

DOWSER: Your welcome warms like the sun, friend Widger.

WIDGER: I thought you'd left the country.

DOWSER: I'm a slave to the month of June. She pulls me back. And how's Roselle?

WIDGER: She needs nothing.

DOWSER: Shall I witch you a well today Widger?

WIDGER: You and your willow sticks. Be off.

DOWSER: What's a stick to you, in my hand turns to a wand. That's magic.

WIDGER: I have a well.

DOWSER: Corn pads, lemon extract, amulets of garlic to ward off weakness in the lung?

WIDGER: I want none of your salves or extracts, Dowser Ringgo.

DOWSER: Love charms of amethyst or a gold chain with the special property of increasing fertility in man or beast. All these at cut rate prices.

WIDGER: Fake charms. Lemon extract. Just you wait till Constable Docket catches you. You won't chirp like a robin then.

DOWSER: Poor Docket. He needs a charm for his wits. More brush, less paint there, Widger.

WIDGER: When I want your advice, I'll ask.

DOWSER: Oh, but for you, friend, I've got a special potion.

WIDGER: For me?

DOWSER: Brewed of young mosses and deadly water hemlock dug in November, when the evening star rides closest to the rim of the cold crescent moon.

WIDGER: Nonsense. Fiddlesticks.

DOWSER: These herbs, wrapped in a bat's wing and worn next the heart protect the wearer from night-prowling thieves and process servers, safeguard the thing he loves most. What's that, Widger?

WIDGER: Leave me alone, you Dowser. I—I've got something better than your charm. All I have to do is keep a sort of bargain. Paint this fence and all's well with Widger. I hope!

DOWSER: You hope? But you can't be sure. Why at this very moment the fates may be spinning a web to—Hello!

(JAKE comes in.)

WIDGER: Oh, Mr. Foote.

JAKE: Mr. Widger.

WIDGER: The barber.

JAKE: That's right—Barber.

WIDGER: You're just walking around eh?

JAKE: Yes.

WIDGER: No business here. I told you.

JAKE: I can wait.

(He starts to tack up a 'Sock for Sokolander' sign.)

WIDGER: No. No. You can't post bills. I won't have it.

JAKE: Sokolander said you'd not object.

WIDGER: He hired you?

JAKE: I offered.

(Posts the bill on the house.)

DOWSER: New here, aren't you? Staying long?

JAKE: I may.

(He starts to post bill on fence.)

WIDGER: No. Not there. Wet paint.

JAKE: The old bell tower then.

Gwen Pharis Ringwood

WIDGER: No! No!

JAKE: Why not?

WIDGER: You can't. It's—sacrilege. *(Running up stile to prevent* JAKE'S *crossing)* It's mixing religion and politics, that's what it is. I tell you no!

JAKE: Oh, very well. The road then.
(He goes off right.)

WIDGER: You see, no place is safe any more—Sacred, I mean. Dowser about your charm—How much were you asking? Just in case—
(ROSELLE comes out of the house.)

ROSELLE: Father, I found this knapsack underneath your mattress—whose is it?
(Whistle.)

DOWSER: Roselle!

ROSELLE: *(Running to him)* Dowser! Dowser Ringgo! I'm glad you've come. You're late this year. I've watched for you since the first ducks flew North.

WIDGER: Roselle, give me that knapsack. You'd no business touching it.

ROSELLE: I only wondered where it came from.

WIDGER: This knapsack belongs to a man I know—an oil man—I'll get rid of it at once. You go in. I'll be right back. Right back—no sack. See, a rhyme. Ha, ha.
(He goes nervously off with knapsack.)

ROSELLE: He acts so strange today.—Oh, Dowser, it's good to see you.

DOWSER: You've grown up, young lady. Here's a trinket for you.

ROSELLE: A charm bracelet. Thank you. Has it a charm to make—someone love me?

DOWSER: There's a young man then?

ROSELLE: He doesn't even know that I'm alive.

DOWSER: He will.

ROSELLE: No. And I've done such a foolish thing. I tried to make him jealous. I said I'd marry Mr. Sokolander.

DOWSER: Roselle.

ROSELLE: I didn't mean it. But now they think I mean it. And Mr. Sokolander's buying hams and ice cream for the wedding dance. And he's sent out a loud speaker to invite the whole electoral division. *(She weeps)* Oh, Dowser, Dowser.

DOWSER: Your father wouldn't let you.

ROSELLE: Oh, yes, he's anxious. He says a girl in my position can't afford to pass up prime ministers.

DOWSER: When's the wedding?

ROSELLE: Tomorrow. At ten. To start off the campaign.

DOWSER: Tonight, just after dark, you meet me at the crossroads. I'll take you to my sister. She'll look after you.

ROSELLE: Oh, Dowser, would she? But what about my father?

DOWSER: Do as I say.

ROSELLE: How will I find you?

DOWSER: When all's clear I'll whistle. *(Trill of a bird song.* WIDGER *returns from back.)*

WIDGER: Go in Roselle. You've little enough in your head without learning bird songs from pedlars.

ROSELLE: Goodbye, Dowser.

DOWSER: Remember. *(Whistle. She goes in.)*

WIDGER: Wait—I'll buy this charm you offer—just to get rid of you.

DOWSER: You've something better to safeguard the thing you love most. Would that be a daughter, Widger?

WIDGER: How much for the charm?

DOWSER: For you five dollars and a fat spring cock.

WIDGER: That's robbery. I'll give you two.

DOWSER: You've no need of charms, you said so. Four and the chicken.

WIDGER: For this amulet three fifty and a cockerel hatched in April. *(*DOWSER *starts up stile)* Your moss and dried roots, a few cents would buy them. Wait, three sixty.

DOWSER: Sold to you, Widger, for three sixty and the cock.

WIDGER: Give me the charm then.

DOWSER: I'll bring it by on Thursday.

WIDGER: I need it now, today.

DOWSER: Today's a holiday.

WIDGER: Look at the calendar! You can't do that.

DOWSER: For Dowser Ringgo there's no calendar. He can declare it holiday when the sun shines or the fish are biting or a pretty woman narrows her eyes at him. I'm free, Widger, I go where I please, sleep in a hay stack, I drink a pint of ale when I'm in pocket and when I'm not I wander from place to place selling my wares. I tell you, Widger, call off this marriage and I'll charge you nothing.

WIDGER: No.

*(*SOKOLANDER *enters with a wheelbarrow of potatoes.)*

SOKOLANDER: Widger, you'll have to peel potatoes for the dinner. One sack should be enough.

WIDGER: I can't. I'm busy.

SOKOLANDER: I'm busy too. Oh, Dowser bring your fiddle to the wedding tomorrow. I'll pay you. We'll dance right after dinner.

DOWSER: When you marry, Sokolander, I'll fiddle for the dancing.

SOKOLANDER: Good. I can cross these off—potatoes, music.—Let me see—the turkeys, baked ham, barbecued young steer, silk pyjamas *(that's for me)* and a load of hay for Widger. All looked after. That leaves the ring, the dress. I'll see about them now. Know-how! That's the secret, Widger—know-how!

*(*SOKOLANDER *hurries off left.)*

DOWSER: Don't marry Roselle to Sokolander, Widger.

WIDGER: *(Crossly)* It's nothing to me, Dowser, whether you approve this marriage.

DOWSER: Oh, but I do. There goes the very man I'd choose if I were selling daughters.

WIDGER: That's all very well to say. You have no daughter. We can't all live like you do. No rules, no morals, nothing in the bank. Where would Roselle be if I went on like that?

DOWSER: She'd be free, Widger, fearless, as the young should be.

WIDGER: Oh you can talk. Talk's cheap. If Roselle runs wild and gets herself in trouble, and it happens all the time, what's that to Ringgo? Most of us can't live like you do, hand to mouth. Most of us have to plot a course around tomorrow. We can't all sleep in haystacks, Dowser Ringgo. Not everybody can go round making bird noises.

DOWSER: More should than do, Widger, more should than do.

(ANASTASIA runs in frantically.)

ANASTASIA: Help! Help! Emergency! Help! Help!

ROSELLE; *(Coming out)* What is it, Mrs. Burrows?

ANASTASIA: Oh, Mr. Dowser, help me—

DOWSER: Yes, Ma'am.

ANASTASIA: There's a man in my potato patch. He's dead.

DOWSER: Who is it?

ANASTASIA: I don't know. Please go and see.

DOWSER: All right, I'll go along. *(He goes out quickly.)*

ANASTASIA: And your horse, Mr. Widger, your horse was tied up beside him.

WIDGER: Old Polly. Then it's—

ANASTASIA: Such a shock. I'll never be able to preside at the meeting now. A man named Foote has gone for Constable Docket.

WIDGER: Oh, the barber—

ANASTASIA: I went out to tell him not to post sign and found the—Oh—

(GARROW hurries in with transit instrument.)

GARROW: What's all the racket? Someone hurt?

ANASTASIA: More than hurt, young man—dead. Who are you?

GARROW: Garrow. Gulf. Seismic.

ANASTASIA: I think it's murder.

WIDGER: Murder. I told you that imposter was a bad one.

GARROW: Murder eh? Where is he, Ma'am?

ANASTASIA: Right by the patch in my potato fence. I mean—Oh, dear—

GARROW: Might be one of our men. I'll come with you Ma'am.

(Moves to ANASTASIA. They start out.)

ANASTASIA: And what about your horse, Mr. Widger?

WIDGER: Oh, yes, of course, Old Polly. I'll come and get her.

ANASTASIA: Nothing should be moved. Especially the horse. Mr. Docket will want fingerprints and pictures for the paper. You can imagine what a shock it was, Mr. Garrow. In fact, I still feel faint.

(He catches her as she sways.)

GARROW: Steady, lady, steady.

ANASTASIA: *(Clinging)* Oh, thank you. That's better—much, much better. *(She leans heavily on GARROW as they go out.)*

WIDGER: Wait, I'm coming. *(To ROSELLE who has moved after him)* No, Roselle. You stay here.

ROSELLE: Father, I don't want to marry Mr. Sokolander. I can't.
WIDGER: You can't back out now. He's sent the hay, already. Stop
being stubborn and peel those potatoes while I go get Old Polly.
(WIDGER goes off. ROSELLE sits down disconsolately.)
ROSELLE: I'll stay at Dowser's sister's. Potatoes! He won't even listen!
*(PETER comes in from back with the knapsack. He is very
solemn and constrained and so is ROSELLE.)*
PETER: Excuse me, is this your knapsack?
ROSELLE: Father's keeping if for someone.
PETER: I found it underneath the barn.
ROSELLE: Thank you. I'll put it where it won't get lost. *(She places
knapsack near kennel.)*
PETER: Well—Goodbye.
ROSELLE: Goodbye.
PETER: Excuse me, there's a jawbone beside the barn.
ROSELLE: It's been there for years.
PETER: Six million years. Could I have it?
ROSELLE: If you wish.
PETER: Thank you. I thought I'd label all the bones today. If it's
convenient.
ROSELLE: By all means, do.
PETER: You'll be very busy, getting married.
ROSELLE: Yes I will—that is, I would be if—
PETER: *(Earnestly)* I certainly do wish you all good things.
ROSELLE: Thank you.
PETER/ROSELLE: *(They speak together)* Well, I—Well—
PETER: I beg your pardon.
ROSELLE: You go ahead.
PETER: I probably won't see you again—alone. I'm going away after
the wedding.
ROSELLE: Where?
PETER: I'll get a job somewhere. After you're settled, I'll come back.
ROSELLE: You will?
PETER: To get my bones.
ROSELLE: Weren't you supposed to stay on with your uncle?
PETER: Married people should have the place to themselves I always
think.
ROSELLE: But, Peter, I'm not. . .Oh Peter, why are you so stupid?
SOKOLANDER: *(Rushing in and interrupting everything)* Peter! Roselle!
Telegram! Listen to this. "Mitchell just announced he will run
against you. Promising roads wholesale—bridges, bonfires!
Tribune shows picture of Mitchell with five sons—all singing
hymns. Question. Can you sing? You've got to get in there and
fight!" Your hear that. We've got a fight on our hands.
ROSELLE: Mr. Sokolander—
SOKOLANDER: Five sons! He's got me there! But I'll counter with a
rose for every lady and a miniature bride and groom to hold the
place cards. We'll get in there and—

311

Gwen Pharis Ringwood

PETER: Fight. *(Flatly)*

SOKOLANDER: That's my boy. Roselle, you come along to the village and try your dress. And Peter, I want the old church bell to ring for ten minutes after the wedding. Get a new bell rope and see to it. Right away.

PETER: Yes, Uncle.

SOKOLANDER: Come, Roselle.

ROSELLE: Goodbye, Peter.

PETER: *(Going to her)* Tomorrow you'll be Aunt Roselle. Well, I certainly wish you all—

ROSELLE: *(Gazes at him wistfully)* I do too.

SOKOLANDER: No time to waste, Roselle. Make every minute count now, nephew. Get in there and fight.

> *(He makes a great jab at the air.* SOKOLANDER *propels* ROSELLE *off by the arm.* PETER *pats his Triceratops forlornly. Makes a vicious jab at the potato with his knife.* DR. BOND *enters.)*

BOND: Oh, good evening. What's all this about a murder?

PETER: Murder? Oh, Dr. Bond, don't you remember me?

BOND: I know your face—

PETER: Traptow—Geology.

BOND: Of course!

PETER: I think your lectures are very good, sir, no matter what they say.

BOND: Thank you. One has to cover the ground, Traptow, cover the ground. Particularly in Geology, eh?

PETER: I stumbled on something this morning. I'm certain this is a fragment of Triceratops—very rare you said.

BOND: Well, well, Triceratops! Good work Traptow. I suggest you dig up the whole area.

PETER: I can't. I have to get a job.

BOND: Perhaps we can get you a job digging fossils.

PETER: Where?

BOND: Research—we'll put you on the payroll.

PETER: Thank you, Dr. Bond. But, if you don't mind, sir, how much would the payroll be?

BOND: Oh, the usual University stipend—a hundred a month and we supply the shovel. Any rare fossils you find, you might pass on to me. I'll do a paper. One should publish, you know, part of one's function really.

PETER: I thought I'd write a paper.

BOND: We'll collaborate. Under my name—to give it standing. Good luck, Traptow. *(He is about to go off when* DOCKET *comes in with* WIDGER.*)*

DOCKET: Stay where you are. Don't move. Is this the man?

WIDGER: Yes, that's him.

DOCKET: *(To* BOND*)* Now you, don't try any tricks.

BOND: Who do you think you're talking to?

DOCKET: I'll ask the questions. All right, how did you do him in?

312

BOND: Do who in?

DOCKET: The dead man. How did you do it?

BOND: Look here, Officer, are you sure there's been a murder?

DOCKET: *(Darkly)* Of course I'm sure. The man's dead and the horse was tied up, wasn't it?

BOND: I'm the speaker for the Ladies Club—the Lilies.

WIDGER: That's just an alias. He's the murderer.

BOND: This is pure fabrication.

DOCKET: Save it for the judge.

PETER: Officer, you mustn't talk to Professor Bond like that. He isn't used to it.

DOCKET: What about that, Widger?

WIDGER: Anybody can act like a professor, if he has to.

DOCKET: I'll put him in jail until the Mountie comes. *(JAKE comes in and stands, watching proceedings)* Mr. Widger saw you following him.

BOND: Following who?

WIDGER: The dead man.

JAKE: Where did you see them, Widger?

WIDGER: Oh, Mr. Foote. Yes, well, he—the dead man came by my house in the storm—to get a drink of water. I gave it to him and saw this partner after him. That's how it was.

JAKE: Did the dead man leave anything behind?

WIDGER: Oh, no, nothing. Not a smitch, not a farthing. And now he's dead—struck down. Arrest this fellow, Docket.

PETER: No!

DOCKET: Even professors can't get away with murder. Now Willie B.

BOND: Willoughby.

DOCKET: All right, Willoughby. I arrest you— *(ANASTASIA enters.)*

ANASTASIA: Oh, Professor, I've been on the wire. The meeting is postponed. You see, I found the body and I'll be giving evidence and—Why, what's the matter?

DOCKET: The Professor won't be talking to no ladies club, Mrs. Burrows.

ANASTASIA: That's what I said, but—

DOCKET: The Professor is going to jail.

ANASTASIA: Oh, how terrible. Now they'll all say "We should have got Swami, the magician." *(SOKOLANDER enters burdened down with fancy floral pieces.)*

SOKOLANDER: Look here, Widger, father-in-law or no father-in-law, I think you might help a little.

ANASTASIA: Father-in-law!

SOKOLANDER: Yes, Friends, tomorrow, Widger will give his rose away to me.

ANASTASIA: You're marrying Roselle? Oh, Clifford! *(She faints away. Crumples against SOKOLANDER.)*

SOKOLANDER: Quick, quick, she's fainting. Get something. Do something. Loosen something.

PETER: Push her head down, Uncle. *(SOKOLANDER does so, holding her around waist.)*

Gwen Pharis Ringwood

BOND: *(Moving to right corner of well)* Don't desert me Mrs. Burrows. You're my witness.

DOCKET: Wake up, Anastasia. Come to, there's a good girl, come to.

ANASTASIA: *(Rallying)* Oh Clifford, it's you. What happened?

SOKOLANDER: You had a shock, Anastasia.

ANASTASIA: Oh yes. . . Your marrying Roselle. . . Oh Clifford.

SOKOLANDER: Chin up, Anastasia. Chin up. Peter, you fix that bell. I'm taking Mrs. Burrows home. She's had a bad shock. *(They go off)* I want her in shape for the campaign tomorrow.

PETER: Dr. Bond. I'd be glad to phone the President of the University.

BOND: Oh, no, boy. I don't want the President stirred up.

DOCKET: Come along peaceful now.

WIDGER: Well, constable, you got your man—thanks to me. Keep a close eye on him, he's dangerous.

DOCKET: Docket knows his business.

WIDGER: *(Very busybody)* Good for you, Mr. Docket, good for you. *(DOCKET and the rest go off, leaving PETER and WIDGER.)*

WIDGER: Well, young man, why don't you go too?

PETER: I have to put a new rope on the church bell, so we can ring it for your daughter's wedding.

WIDGER: Bell? Oh no, that's too much trouble. No indeed.

PETER: I promised Uncle. He wants the bell to ring.

WIDGER: No need. We'll beat on pans.

PETER: But Uncle's set his mind. *(Starts to stile.)*

WIDGER: Wait. You peel potatoes. *(He dumps out some potatoes.)* I—I'll run up the tower and test the ladder. If it's safe, I'll let you fix the bell. How's that? *(He rushes off.)*

PETER: Potatoes!

WIDGER: *(Calling)* I'll be right back, boy, right back. *(JAKE comes in from barn.)*

JAKE: Can I help you?

PETER: No, thanks.

JAKE: This Widger—have you known him long?

PETER: No.

JAKE: Do you think he's hiding something?

PETER: He's queer, that's all. He doesn't like people looking for bones around his well.

JAKE: *(Looking down well)* Is it a deep well?

PETER: *(Looking down too)* It looks deep.

JAKE: *(Tossing a pebble down)* Sounds deep. I wonder.

PETER: What would he be hiding?

JAKE: Oh—evidence, treasure. Some skeleton or other. *(WIDGER returns with sack of gold.)*

WIDGER: Don't fall in Gentlemen.

JAKE: A deep well, Mr. Widger.

WIDGER: Sixty feet. You can go now, boy.

PETER: Mr. Widger, if Roselle didn't marry Uncle—

314

WIDGER: Of course she'll marry Uncle. Now get that bell in order. *(PETER goes off)* Well, Mr. Foote, isn't this a business about the murder? Docket would never have got his man without my help.
JAKE: Sit down.
WIDGER: Sit down? Why?
JAKE: I'm going to give you a haircut and shave.
WIDGER: No thank you. Never mind.
JAKE: Sokolander paid me.
WIDGER: Well, just the shave then. I've lost my razor.
JAKE: Shall we go inside?
WIDGER: No. Let's do it here.
JAKE: Hot water?
WIDGER: In the kitchen.
JAKE: Get it.
WIDGER: Oh no, you—that boy might fall—you get it.
(JAKE goes into kitchen. WIDGER starts to hide sack in well, decides against it. Starts to stile when PETER calls down.)
PETER: Hey, this ladder. It's not safe!
WIDGER: Of course it is. Up, up you go. That's right. *(JAKE returns with water and towel.)*
JAKE: Sit down.
WIDGER: *(Keeping potatoes close)* Yes. *(JAKE begins lathering WIDGER)* Seen any good ball games lately? *(Silence)* Seen any ball games lately? *(Silence)* What do you think of the government, Mr. Foote?
JAKE: Buzzards.
WIDGER: Oh yes. Mr. Sokolander knows them personally. He plans to be one. You say he paid you?
JAKE: Yes.
WIDGER: Too bad about this poor man, Planter. Dying like that, no relatives. Must have been a great shock to Old Polly—that's my horse. Do you like horses?
JAKE: Sit still.
WIDGER: Oh, of course, you don't ride, do you? Foote foots it, ha, ha—a joke!
JAKE: Hmmmph!
WIDGER: I feel hot and cold. I think I have a temperature.
JAKE: Hmmmph!
WIDGER: You don't talk much do you? You can trust me. I wouldn't hurt a fly. I'm not like that Professor. That's awful. I wouldn't think of doing a thing like that just for a sack of—
JAKE: What, Widger?
WIDGER: Oh, I'm only talking. What's the matter?
JAKE: Razor's dull.
WIDGER: Where is everybody?
JAKE: Gone.
WIDGER: It's cold for June.
JAKE: You knew Planter?

WIDGER: Just slightly. Nodding acquaintance. A bad man that partner. Black beard, glittering eyes. I knew him instantly, even without the ace of spades.

JAKE: What's that?

WIDGER: Ace of spades tattooed on his right forearm—about there.

JAKE: You saw it?

WIDGER: Oh, no, Planter told me.

JAKE: What else did he tell you, Widger?

WIDGER: He hadn't a good thing to say for that partner. I'm glad we caught him. Why, Mr. Foote—

JAKE: Yes?

WIDGER: That's my razor.

JAKE: Really?

WIDGER: I broke that little piece out—but I gave it to—how do you come to have it?

JAKE: I found it.

WIDGER: Where?

JAKE: Where would you think, Widger?

WIDGER: Beside the—Oh, I did lend the poor man my razor—he asked for it. But we could just keep that between ourselves, Mr. Foote. No need to raise a hue and cry.

JAKE: Unless—

WIDGER: Unless?

JAKE: You refuse to tell me what I want to know. Did Planter have anything valuable with him?

WIDGER: Oh, yes, that is, he took my Sunday suit, bacon and tea— Ow, Mr. Foote. You knicked my ear. No offence meant.

JAKE: Where is it?

WIDGER: Be careful—that razor's sharp.

JAKE: Where's the gold, Widger?

WIDGER: Gold? Oh, yes, yes—Gold eh? Oww—you cut me. *(Jumps and spills bag over—a few potatoes run out)* That's no way to do. These potatoes. The price they are, they're worth their weight in—you know. (DOWSER *comes in whistling.*)

WIDGER: Oh, Dowser Ringgo, how glad I am to see you! Mr. Foote here is interested in gold. I was just going to tell him the Dowser can witch wells, gold mines, everything. Well, they got the murderer all right, thanks to me. He's bad, you know.

DOWSER: What made you so sure Bond was the murderer, Widger?

WIDGER: Why, all the evidence. Speaks Latin, had a beard, prowling around early this morning.

DOWSER: You're wrong, Widger. He's Professor Bond all right, and he has an alibi. Air tight.

WIDGER: For all night?

DOWSER: Yes, a respectable alibi. The Professor spent the night in the manse at Gilpin. Fortunately he snores.

WIDGER: Then he's not the one? He is, he must be.

DOWSER: No. And now, they're saying strange things in the village about you.

WIDGER: What would they say about me, Dowser?

DOWSER: They say someone was here last night. Today he's dead and your horse was tied up beside him. They're looking for a motive. Was there a motive, Widger?

WIDGER: Oh no. You know me, Dowser. I live to myself. I don't go in for violence. They wouldn't believe that I could kill a man? You don't think that, Dowser?

DOWSER: The village thinks it. You've set them on their ears. The story's spreading like a prairie fire, close to the ground at first, with the little tongues of flame flickering malevolently here and there, until all at once you've got a conflagration. Some say "This stranger seduced old Widger's daughter. . ."

WIDGER: They lie.

DOWSER: And some: "He owed Widger money. . ."

WIDGER: Yes—No.

DOWSER: And others: "It was Widger who was in debt."

WIDGER: That's not true.

DOWSER: And still others say: "What do we know of Widger? He's lived here twenty years, done nothing for his neighbours, and kept his daughter close. What do we know of Widger?"

WIDGER: I'm a poor man. I couldn't buy her clothes like some. Say she wants fancy skates—they're twenty dollars.

DOWSER: Some say: "Widger's been acting queer of late—he consents to marry his child to Sokolander."

JAKE: I've heard a story too. The stranger stopped here carrying a treasure and Widger kills him for it. Then under cover of the storm carries the body to his neighbour's pasture. *(DOWSER looks at JAKE appraisingly.)*

WIDGER: I can explain everything, and they'll believe me. True, I've lived to myself. I don't lend things, discourage the children from tramping down my pasture, but neither have I borrowed anything or bothered anybody. They'll all remember that. That's my way. They'll say: "That's Widger's way." *(Enter* ANASTASIA, BOND, SOKOLANDER *and* GARROW. WIDGER *runs out to meet them fawningly.)*

WIDGER: Come in, my friends, my neighbours. We were talking about this poor man Planter. Why, Mrs. Burrows, to think only this morning you borrowed water from this very well. Remember? Remember?

ANASTASIA: The well? What if he's poisoned it? Oh, Clifford.

WIDGER: And see, my friends, I'm painting the fence to save the church board a little money.

ANASTASIA: The coldbloodedness of it! To leave the horse tied up there all night, after the crime. And then to paint the churchyard.

WIDGER: Oh, Professor, I'm afraid I've caused you inconvenience. But would you roll up your sleeve? The right arm, please.

317

Gwen Pharis Ringwood

BOND: He's mad. I'd better humour him. *(Rolls up sleeve.)*
WIDGER: No ace of spades? Oh, oh, I beg your pardon.
BOND: Manic-depressive type. Dangerous when annoyed.
WIDGER: And Mr. Garrow. You know me. Come in. Isn't it nice of
   Mr. Garrow, an American, to come up here and show us how to
   get out oil? Two thousand miles of borderline. Two hundred
   years of peace. That's a fine record, Mr. Garrow. I'm sure the
   Commonwealth would take you back now, if you ask.
GARROW: Gone off his base. A fellow went like that drilling for Texaco.
WIDGER: Mr. Sokolander, Clifford. My almost son-in-law. He's
   marrying my daughter. Does that sound like Mr. Sokolander
   considers me a murderer?
SOKOLANDER: The marriage is off. While scandal hovers over Widger,
   the people would not want his name linked with Sokolander.
ANASTASIA: You're so unselfish, Clifford.
WIDGER: *(Slowly)* You're not standing by me?
SOKOLANDER: No.
WIDGER: Roselle. Where is Roselle?
SOKOLANDER: In the village.
ANASTASIA: Probably looking for a lawyer who'll take your case.
WIDGER: You mean she thinks—my own daughter thinks—!
   (DOCKET comes in.)
ANASTASIA: We kept him, like you said, Officer. Do your duty.
WIDGER: But Mr. Docket, I didn't do it. You've no evidence!
DOCKET: Puttin' the blame on the Professor here, a man what's given
   his life to look for the P. Cameron shield. And all the time you
   did it.
WIDGER: No evidence.
DOCKET: No? The dead man's wearing your suit. Your horse is tied up
   beside him. You admit you saw him last night and the man's
   dead, ain't he?
BOND: You're satisfied it's murder?
DOCKET: Of course it is. A dead man don't get up and tie his horse
   up, does he?
WIDGER: Oh, Officer, you couldn't arrest me. I've lived here twenty
   years.
DOCKET: I'd arrest my own grandmother if she broke the law.
ANASTASIA: He's been unbalanced ever since yesterday. Won't let
   anyone near that well of his. He probably put the body in the well.
DOCKET: What body?
ANASTASIA: The body we found in the potato patch.
DOCKET: That's a felony, moving a body around like that. But, if it's in
   the well, how could it be in the potato patch?
BOND: It couldn't.
ANASTASIA: I didn't say it was. I said he acted like it.
DOCKET: Acted like what?
ANASTASIA: Like there was something in the well he didn't want us to
   know about, like a body.

318

DOCKET: Hmmm. . . I see. A double crime, one in the potato patch and one in the well.

WIDGER: No, no!

ANASTASIA: I didn't say it was, I said it might be. Down on all fours in the middle of the night like that.

BOND: Where's your evidence?

ANASTASIA: You don't need to bully me, Dr. Bond. It isn't my fault you can't speak.

SOKOLANDER: She's just upset, Professor.

ANASTASIA: I'm not upset at all. I'm simply trying to aid and abet the law. You'd best take him into custody, Mr. Docket. After all, even though he's lived here twenty years, what do we know of Widger?

DOCKET: That's right. What do we know about you? Nothing.

SOKOLANDER: Yes, when it comes down to it, what do we know of Widger?

WIDGER: *(Backing up towards the stile)* What do you know of Widger? Of me? But my friends, of course you know me.

ANASTASIA: What do we really know about you?

WIDGER: *(On stile)* What do we know of anyone—of anyone at all? What do you know of each other? Of anyone at all?

DOWSER: *(Diverting the mob for a moment)* There's your question. There, he's got you. A bird sings three notes in a birch tree, that's simple and requires a simple answer.

> *(*WIDGER *is on top of the stile facing mob.* DOWSER *at right, or isolated in a strong, cross position.)*

WIDGER: I'm a poor man.

DOWSER: You know his bank account.

WIDGER: Over sixty.

DOWSER: You know his age.

WIDGER: A farmer.

DOWSER: Occupation.

WIDGER: With a daughter.

DOWSER: Family status.

WIDGER: I pay my taxes.

DOWSER: Property owner.

WIDGER: Vote Liberal.

DOWSER: Politics.

WIDGER: I was baptized Episcopalian.

DOWSER: Religion. And what more?

WIDGER: Why, why that's all. That's all.

DOWSER: All—there you have it. Here's a poor man, over sixty, a farmer with a daughter, pays taxes, votes a respectable party and was baptized. That's all you know.

WIDGER: Oh, no! *(It is a cry)* There's more. There's much, much more!

DOWSER: *(Fast)* Yes, there's the fear and the malice and the envy. The pricking conscience and the greed, and the skeleton in the respectable closet. The little hurts to pride, the desire to know things, and the desire to own. The urge to get on and the fear of death. *(WIDGER looks at DOWSER)* And there's the will—the thin bright spire of a man's will thrust forth from the encircling cave. *(Gently)* There's love and a need for loving.

WIDGER: *(Whispering)* Yes, Dowser.

DOWSER: Oh, there's more to a man than flesh and bones and his name on the census. What do we know of any one at all? There's your question. Give me three spring notes twirled from a birch tree any time. That's simple. *(Slight pause.)*

WIDGER: *(His throat dry from fear)* You see, Dowser means it might be any of you. God knows I've made mistakes, but I've nothing to hide. Nothing at all to hide. *(The church bell rings. WIDGER feels it is his Maker warning him and looks up)* Wait, wait, I was about to tell them. Plantaganet was here—Planter—maybe he was Plantaganet, poor soul. He took Old Polly, a good suit of clothes, bacon, and bacon's high now, bread and tea. He was here, but I—*(The church bell rings again. WIDGER speaks apprehensively towards the church tower)* I'm confessing. I'm confessing everything.

DOCKET: That's what I want. You killed him.

WIDGER: No! No!

PETER: *(Entering from left)* The bell's fixed Uncle.

SOKOLANDER: Never mind the bell. There'll be no wedding.

PETER: No wedding?

SOKOLANDER: Take the wine and potatoes home.

WIDGER: *(His greed again takes over)* Not the potatoes. Leave the potatoes, please.

PETER: They're Uncle's.

WIDGER: But it's my sack. My sack of—

PETER: Oh, here it is Mr. Widger!

WIDGER: The knapsack. No.

PETER: I found it underneath the barn.

JAKE: Yes, the knapsack. *(He tries to examine it)*

DOCKET: Here you, I'll take that. Hah, that's a knapsack all right. Wet clothes inside. Wait. Here's a name—Richard Planter. The name in the dead man's wallet—Planter.

ANASTASIA: *(Whisper)* Planter.

SOKOLANDER: *(Louder)* Planter.

THE REST: *(Advancing towards WIDGER.)* . . . Planter.

WIDGER: He was here, yes, but I—I didn't kill him.

DOCKET: Milton Ephraim Widger, I arrest you for the murder of Richard Planter found in the potato patch of the aforesaid Mrs. Burrows.

WIDGER: Arrest me?

DOCKET: And I warn you that anything you say may be alleged against you in a court of law.

WIDGER: Not me! Not Widger!

DOCKET: Sokolander, go and call the Mounties. Tell them that Docket, Constable of Bones, has got their man.

SCENE 4

PLACE: *The same.*

TIME: *Late the same night.*

The stage is lit dimly. SOKOLANDER *comes in, looks around the place and finally gets down on hands and knees to shine a flashlight into the dog house. A moment later* ANASTASIA *comes in on tiptoe. She doesn't see* SOKOLANDER *and after examining the doorstep she goes to the well. She looks down intently when she inadvertently makes a clatter with the bucket.*

SOKOLANDER: *(Frightened)* What's that?
ANASTASIA: *(A squeak of fright)* Oh—Clifford. Is that you?
SOKOLANDER: Anastasia!
SOKOLANDER/ANASTASIA: What are you doing here?
        (Their flashlights cross to light each other.)
SOKOLANDER: Well!
ANASTASIA: You frightened me. I'm shaking. I feel faint.
SOKOLANDER: *(Over to her. Fanning her with flowers)* Oh, no. No. Not again.
ANASTASIA: Were you—looking for something?
SOKOLANDER: No—no—just a breath of air. What about you?
ANASTASIA: I couldn't sleep. I—Oh, Cifford, why pretend. The story's all around the village. You heard it.
SOKOLANDER: Yes. But where would he hide thirty thousand dollars?
ANASTASIA: A hundred thousand.
SOKOLANDER: If we found it—
ANASTASIA: Just stumbled on it—
SOKOLANDER: Exactly.
ANASTASIA: Not for myself of course. I'd give it to the Lilies. What would you do?
SOKOLANDER: Rodent control, my dear, is close to my heart. I'd free Bones of rats for ever.
ANASTASIA: Or we could share it. Half for the rats and half for the Lilies. Have you searched the barn?
SOKOLANDER: Yes. Nothing.
ANASTASIA: I think it's in the well. Could you go down the well?
SOKOLANDER: Oh, no. No. That well's deep.
ANASTASIA: What about the house?
SOKOLANDER: No harm in looking. Come along.
ANASTASIA: Wait. *(A light flashes in the upstairs window)* There's someone in there.
SOKOLANDER: Hmmmm. Who's got ahead of us?
ANASTASIA: You can't trust anyone. Wait, maybe it's the Mounted Police.
SOKOLANDER: The thing for us to do, Anastasia, is leave all this to them. Do you agree?

321

ANASTASIA: I do. After all, why should we private citizens do their work for them. We'd best go home.

SOKOLANDER: *(Picking up floral pieces)* I really came to return these to the florist.

ANASTASIA: Oh, Clifford. A wedding would have given you such an edge on Mitchell.

SOKOLANDER: One learns to take these things.

ANASTASIA: I've thought and thought. What can I do for Clifford? Of course, it would solve everything if you married someone else.

SOKOLANDER: But who?

ANASTASIA: Some woman in full flower who understands that little wheels must move the bigger wheels that turn the wheel of state.

SOKOLANDER: Yes.

ANASTASIA: Clifford, let's face it. I doubt you'll get a portfolio without a wife.

SOKOLANDER: That's unfair.

ANASTASIA: But true. So true that in my mind I finally thought: "I'll marry him myself."

SOKOLANDER: You?

ANASTASIA: Don't laugh. It's just my way to sock for Sokolander.

SOKOLANDER: *(Thinking hard)* You could, you know.

ANASTASIA: Clifford!

SOKOLANDER: It's a most practical suggestion.

ANASTASIA: You mean you're proposing—to little me?

SOKOLANDER: Why, yes, yes, I am. Marry me, Anastasia, tomorrow.

ANASTASIA: But this is so sudden.

SOKOLANDER: Once I make up my mind, I act.

ANASTASIA: I accept you, Clifford—gladly. *(She throws her arms around him and the flowers.)*

SOKOLANDER: Thank you. I'll make you very happy.

ANASTASIA: You have.

SOKOLANDER: We'll need these then, and the church bell can toll tomorrow as arranged. *(*DOCKET *suddenly pokes his head out of the door.)*

DOCKET: Who goes there?

SOKOLANDER: Good night, Docket.

DOCKET: Hurry up there, Widger. *(Over his shoulder.)*

ANASTASIA: Mr. Docket, haven't you taken that man to jail yet?

DOCKET: Jail's full. Anyway I been searching the domicile.

ANASTASIA: Did you find anything?

DOCKET: What I find's official and remains undisclosed. Just what are you two snooping around here for?

SOKOLANDER: Well, you see, officer, these flowers—

ANASTASIA: Don't be shy now, Clifford. Tell him.

SOKOLANDER: Mrs. Burrows and I will be married in the morning. We hope you'll honour us.

DOCKET: Congratulations, Ma'am. My missus says you've been after him for years.

322

ANASTASIA: Nonsense! He swept me off my feet. Come, Clifford.
SOKOLANDER: Coming, Anastasia, coming.
    (They go off arm in arm, garlanded with floral pieces.)
DOCKET: Hmmmm! It's a big price to pay for politics. *(Shouting)*
    Come along out here, Widger.
WIDGER: *(Comes out meekly)* I've got my nightshirt and a pair of
    socks. I don't have a good suit now.
DOCKET: I still don't get it. Why you changed his clothes.
WIDGER: Oh, I didn't. He did.
DOCKET: Sit down. I wish those Mounties would hurry up. My missus
    never believes I'm out in the course of duty.
WIDGER: Couldn't you put me in jail now and get it over?
DOCKET: Told you twice. The jail's full.
WIDGER: Oh, excuse me.
DOCKET: A drunk and disorderly don't relish being locked up with
    no murderers.
WIDGER: No. Roselle's not home yet, Officer. I'm worried.
DOCKET: Probably run off. The disgrace and all. Young people take
    things hard.
WIDGER: I know. She cried for the skates. *(Pause)* Is it true that
    anything I say can be used against me?
DOCKET: I told you. Yes.
WIDGER: I hope I'm careful.
DOCKET: You haven't a chance. Hiding his wet clothes and all.
WIDGER: But why would I kill Planter, Officer?
DOCKET: Most murder is done for filthy lucre, Widger.
WIDGER: You think I killed him for the—for the—
DOCKET: The root of all evil—gold.
WIDGER: Oh, but I didn't kill for it. I wouldn't.
DOCKET: Brrr. It's cold.
WIDGER: There's wine there. Mr. Sokolander brought it for the
    wedding. Why don't you have some?
DOCKET: I'm on duty. Wouldn't think of it.
WIDGER: I thought a sip might warm you.
DOCKET: What kind of wine? *(WIDGER hands jug to DOCKET)* No
    label. That means it's homemade wine. I'd better sample it.
WIDGER: Do.
DOCKET: All in the course of duty, mind. It's against the law for
    homemade wine to contain more than 2½ per cent proof spirits.
WIDGER: I see.
DOCKET: *(Drinking from the jug)* Hmmm. Hmmmmmmm!
WIDGER: Yes?
DOCKET: Suspicious, Widger, very suspicious. I'm not sure yet.
    (He drinks again) But I'm most suspicious.
WIDGER: Imagine! Unlawful, eh?
DOCKET: *(Drinking again)* It burns the gullet, warms the stomach.
    That's suspicious.

Gwen Pharis Ringwood

WIDGER: I suppose you run into unlawful things like this all the time, Officer.

DOCKET: All in the course of duty. *(Drinks again. There is a sudden flash of a torch near the stile)* Who goes there? Answer, you. In there. *(The* PROFESSOR *appears.)*

BOND: Don't shoot. It's just me, Willoughby Bond.

DOCKET: Well, Professor, stop creepin' about. Come here.

BOND: I'm not creeping about. So, you've still got your prisoner.

WIDGER: *(Apologetically)* The jail's full, Professor, otherwise, I'd be in it.

BOND: Too bad, old man. I don't believe you murdered the fellow at all.

WIDGER: Thanks, Professor. You see he came by, took my good suit.

DOCKET: No fraternizing, please!

BOND: You look cozy here.

DOCKET: See this wine? Taste it.

BOND: Why, certainly. *(He drinks.)*

DOCKET: What do you think?

BOND: Good. *(Drinks again)* Excellent.

DOCKET: Strong, isn't it?

BOND: I don't know—medium.

DOCKET: Strong. Very strong.

BOND: Perhaps you're right, Officer.

DOCKET: I find myself looking on the prisoner like a brother. That's suspicious, isn't it?

BOND: Very. Have some wine, Widger?

DOCKET: No. He mustn't! It might muddle him. Stop interfering. Here, have a drink.

BOND: To your health, Officer.

DOCKET: To your health, Professor.

BOND: To the prisoner, Officer.

DOCKET: The prisoner.

WIDGER: Why thank you very much. *(He is sitting very small between the two.)*

DOCKET: No talking, prisoner! We could play crib to pass the time, Professor. Have you a crib board, Widger?

WIDGER: I'm sorry, no.

DOCKET: What about Penny Ante or Spit in the Ocean? Got a deck of cards?

WIDGER: I'm sorry. No, I haven't.

DOCKET: Well, Professor, I'll match you for a quarter.

BOND: I'm sorry—I haven't got a quarter.

DOCKET: Say, can't you fellows play any games at all?

WIDGER: There's Mumblepeg.

DOCKET: What's that?

WIDGER: You know. You play with a jacknife.

DOCKET: Oh, no. You don't catch Docket playing knife games with a murderer.

WIDGER: I don't blame you. I wouldn't either. What about "I Spy"?

DOCKET: I spy?

WIDGER: I say: "I spy with my little eye something that is red."

DOCKET: Blood.

WIDGER: No, no. I have to spy it. Then you say: "Animal, Vegetable or Mineral?"

BOND: Vegetable.

WIDGER: No, Professor, you ask me. And I say: "Animal", meaning it belongs to the animal kingdom.

BOND: Red animal, eh?

DOCKET: Fox. Got you, Widger.

WIDGER: Oh, no, no, Officer. I have to spy it with my little eye. Now think. It's red. It belongs to something animal, like a man. It's your nose, Officer. Now it's your turn.

DOCKET: Oh, I see. All right. I spy with my little eye something that is yellow.

BOND: Vegetable, animal or mineral?

DOCKET: None.

WIDGER: But is has to be. That's the game.

DOCKET: Stop interfering! Give up, Professor? *(Drinking)* I'll have to arrest whoever made this wine. Give up Widger?

BOND: I give up, Docket.

DOCKET: It's the light in the lantern. Ha. That's not animal or vegetable or mineral now, is it? Got you, Professor, got you.

WIDGER: I wish Roselle would come. It's late.

DOCKET: *(Showing his wine)* I spy with my little eye something that is brown and that's a rope. How did you do it, Widger?

WIDGER: Do what?

DOCKET: The murder.

WIDGER: Oh, I didn't.

BOND: You see.

DOCKET: Taking up for him, are you? Murder ain't your business.

BOND: Justice is everybody's business.

DOCKET: Stop meddling.

BOND: The scientific approach is to marshall one's facts before drawing one's conclusion. Whereas the untrained mind—

DOCKET: Who's got a untrained mind?

BOND: You have.

DOCKET: That's a insult. You get out of here.

BOND: Very well, I'll go.

DOCKET: Where?

BOND: To see the coroner. To marshall facts.

DOCKET: This is my murder. *(BOND goes off a little uncertainly)* Busybody. Down with higher education. How did you do it, Widger?

WIDGER: I didn't. And yet, when I heard he was dead, I wasn't sorry. I was glad. I suppose that's almost murder.

DOCKET: Robbed him and took his clothes. That's awful.

WIDGER: It wasn't that way, and yet, you all believe it. Even Roselle. That's the awful thing, to think you all believe it.

Gwen Pharis Ringwood

DOCKET: You took the wrong path, Widger. In my capacity as a
officer, I see many a wrong path took.
WIDGER: The wrong path—but that was long ago. *(Pause)* And now,
I'm here alone, suspected by my neighbours, feared by my own
child. How can this be me? This hand that grasped so greedily
at a sack of gold. Is this my hand? How did I shrink so?
DOCKET: Shrink?
WIDGER: I wasn't always this way. There was a time when Widger
had a grasp on manhood, met the day ready to take what came.
The world was his oyster, Docket, Widger's oyster. But then
there were lean years and my youth was gone. And after that the
times moved fast, so fast that run as I might, I found myself
behind them. And the world changed. The world was a giant,
Docket, waiting to crush a man. The thing to do was hide, be
small and careful. The thing to do was shrink. And yet for all
my care, at his own time, the Giant closes his fist on Widger.
Since it's so, I'd wish myself a bigger fistful. Do you see, Officer,
how it is with me?
DOCKET: I don't believe in Giants. It's just your mind.
WIDGER: I know.
DOCKET: Oh, I'm sleepy.
WIDGER: I could make you a cup of tea if we went in.
DOCKET: *(Drinking)* Tea? Ha, who wants tea? I'll find it, Widger,
I'll follow every clue until I find it.
WIDGER: What?
DOCKET: The motive, Widger. Filthy lucre. *(He takes dog chain)* Here.
WIDGER: What are you going to do?
DOCKET: Lock you up now. With this padlock so you won't escape.
WIDGER: I'm not escaping.
DOCKET: I know the criminal mind. *(Puts chain around WIDGER's
ankle and padlock through links. Puts key in his pocket)* See. Now
you're locked up and I'm free to follow clues.
WIDGER: Officer, would it be all right if I went on painting?
DOCKET: No.
WIDGER: The chain will reach.
DOCKET: All right then. Paint. Oh, I don't feel good.
(He lies down.)
WIDGER: Thank you. *(He moves over to the fence and begins painting,
addressing the bell tower)* This is good paint. $4.95 a gallon.
I've certainly made a mess of things, haven't I? If I get out of this
alive, I think you'll find me changed. I'll buy Roselle the skates.
I'll buy new hymn books and some padded pews. That is, I
think I will.
(PETER appears very stealthily at fence.)
PETER: Mr. Widger.
WIDGER: *(Thinking he is being called from above)* Yes, yes, here I am.
PETER: It's me, Peter Traptow.
WIDGER: Oh, it's only you. Go away. I'm not supposed to talk.

PETER: I've brought you something.
WIDGER: You'll get me in more trouble. Mr. Docket, wake up, there's someone trying to fraternize.
DOCKET: Oh, lie down—shrink.
PETER: Mr. Widger. I took something of yours.
WIDGER: Oh, the bone. Take it.
PETER: No. It's valuable.
WIDGER: My daughter?
PETER: Roselle? Where is she?
WIDGER: She didn't want to marry Sokolander.
PETER: She's not home?
WIDGER: No.
PETER: She shouldn't be out so late. I'd better find her.
WIDGER: Please find her, boy. Tell her—tell her I'm not guilty, no matter how it looks.
PETER: I will.
WIDGER: And if I'm in jail, say I'm away—on business.
PETER: Don't worry, sir, I'll find her.
WIDGER: Thank you.
PETER: Oh, I forgot. I thought it was potatoes.
     (He puts down sack of potatoes.)
WIDGER: You mean—it's not—potatoes.
PETER: At the top—but at the bottom there's your sack of gold.
WIDGER: No, no, boy. It's the last thing I want found here—you take it. It might come in handy.
PETER: No, it wouldn't be right. It's yours. Goodbye, Mr. Widger.
     (PETER rushes off.)
WIDGER: Wait, wait—if they find me with the gold, they'll hang me. . .
DOCKET: Ohhh—did I hear someone talking about gold? I'll find it. I'll track it down. Here's a clue—a foot print. *(He is nosing along the ground)* Come on, old jug, we follow. Down with Mrs. Docket! *(WIDGER moves sack as DOCKET approaches it)* Wait, what's this? *(He seizes WIDGER's paper wrapped nightshirt and socks and tears it open)* Ow. . . I'm stabbed.
WIDGER: What happened, Officer?
DOCKET: I'm hurt. I'm bleeding.
WIDGER: *(Approaching)* But that's just my nightshirt—to take to jail.
DOCKET: Concealing weapons—that's a felony.
WIDGER: It's a pin—there's a note pinned on my nightshirt!
DOCKET: Hmmmmmmm. . . Dear. . . Oh, I can't read it. . .
WIDGER: Let me—
     Dear Father: I'd rather die than marry Sokolander. Forgive me. Roselle.
     She's gone to kill herself. Roselle! I've got to find her.
DOCKET: Dear Father—I'd rather die than—
     (He subsides.)
WIDGER: Officer, I've got to find my daughter. Let me go.
DOCKET: No.

Gwen Pharis Ringwood

WIDGER: The river—the abandoned mine—I've got to find her. Mr. Docket, could you release me for an hour? I'll come right back, I promise.

DOCKET: No.

WIDGER: Then I've no choice. I'll try not to hurt you. *(He hits* DOCKET *on head with bone)* Now, the key—I'll just unlock myself and put it back—There, that's better. My poor, poor child—No skates, no mother. Well, I'm off—*(He trips)* Oh—More haste, less speed. *(He gets up—hoot of an owl)* What's that? An owl! And there's a bat! I never could like bats. Somehow I'm not very fond of nature any more, it's so unnatural. Thumpy noises, bats, things eating each other up. It makes a man feel small. Well, off we go now, Widger, off we go.

> *(Manfully he takes a run towards the stile but as he reaches the top* JACOB FOOTE *suddenly steps forward.)*

WIDGER: Ahh—

DOCKET: *(Groans)* Ah. . .

JAKE: Well, Widger?

WIDGER: Sh. . . Oh, Mr. Foote, it's only you. I thought it was someone dangerous.

JAKE: Did you think you could escape, Widger?

WIDGER: Just to find Roselle—I'm afraid she's gone to the river. Let me by—I've got to hurry.

JAKE: Wait, Widger.

WIDGER: *(Trying to push by him)* I can't. Please Mr. Foote.

JAKE: You stole a poke from Planter? Where is it?

WIDGER: Poke?

JAKE: Bag—Sack of gold.

WIDGER: Oh, yes. I'd forgot—I'll tell you later.

JAKE: Now, Widger.

WIDGER: *(Pushing by)* I want to find my daughter—
> *(He starts off.)*

JAKE: *(Pushing him down)* Now, Widger. Where's that gold? I want it.

WIDGER: I won't tell you.

JAKE: No? *(He twists his arm.)*

WIDGER: No, I'm not supposed to give evidence against myself.

JAKE: Give me the gold and I'll say nothing. Where is it?

WIDGER: *(Running for the potato sack)* Here, take it then. I don't want it any more. Please take it away and go.

JAKE: Dump out the bag.

WIDGER: Yes, sir. *(He does so, but there is no gold)* Oh, it isn't there. He didn't bring it back. Well—neither of us will have it. *(A sick little laugh)* That's funny, isn't it? We've both been fooled. Your eyes, Mr. Foote—

JAKE: *(Rolling up sleeve)* Yes, Widger?

WIDGER: The ace of spades! Then you're—the partner, Jake Scholtz. You shaved your beard—I didn't kill Planter. He left the gold with me. I didn't kill him.

328

JAKE: No. I did.

WIDGER: You! How?

JAKE: Fear, Widger. A flash of lightning and he sees me at his horse's head. *(JAKE's arm goes up—there is a razor in his hand)* His weak heart stops. I didn't have to lay a hand on him, Widger, nor will I lay a hand on you.

WIDGER: Why, thank you. *(Starts to go.)*

JAKE: Your death will be called—suicide.

WIDGER: Oh!

JAKE: That's reasonable. A man, suspected of murder and sensitive to public opinion, kills himself.

WIDGER: How?

JAKE: Perhaps with your own razor—it doesn't matter how.

WIDGER: But then they'd all be sure I murdered him. I won't do it!

JAKE: You won't have to. I will.

WIDGER: You're—joking.

JAKE: No. Hand over the gold.

WIDGER: I tell you, I don't have it. It was in a potato sack—

JAKE: Stop stalling.

WIDGER: You really mean to kill me? *(JAKE just looks at him)* But that's wicked, killing people. How could you be so wicked?

JAKE: Easy. I want something, take steps to get it, and justify them after. Like you did.

WIDGER: But I didn't kill for it. I wouldn't.

JAKE: No?

WIDGER: I don't think I would.

JAKE: You kept the gold, hid all trace of Planter, lied, threw blame on others.

WIDGER: *(Ashamed)* I know. *(He looks menacingly at JAKE)* Your face— it's cruel and greedy!

JAKE: Don't tell me you've not seen cruelty or greed before.

WIDGER: I've seen them on other faces, yes—

JAKE: Where else, Widger?

WIDGER: *(Deeply ashamed)* I've seen them in the mirror—looking at me, out of my own eyes.

JAKE: You see, we're brothers, Widger. Where's the gold?

(He moves in on WIDGER *who backs towards the well.)*

WIDGER: *(Inventing fast)* It—it's in the well. I hid it there this morning. I'll help you down. Be glad to.

JAKE: Get it.

WIDGER: It's a long way down—sixty feet.

JAKE: Get it.

WIDGER: How long can a man stay under water? *(He starts to go down)*

JAKE: Indefinitely.

WIDGER: Oh. If I don't come up, you'll be sorry. I've got friends.

(JAKE laughs.)

JAKE: Who?

WIDGER: Why, there's—there's—

Gwen Pharis Ringwood

JAKE: Go down and get it, Widger.
WIDGER: But if I can't—
JAKE: You'll drown in your own well.
WIDGER: And you'd go free?
JAKE: Free and respectable. And before I'm through I'll own half the town.
WIDGER: Oh, no, you mustn't. All those people in the village, they're my friends. I won't let you loose among them.
JAKE: Go down, before I—
WIDGER: If I go, I'll take you with me. *(He jumps at* JAKE *and they grapple over the well. Sound of a bird call)* Dowser! Dowser Ringgo! Help me! Help, help, Dowser!
DOWSER: *(Offstage)* Coming. Hang on, Widger, hang on.
WIDGER: I'm hanging on, Dowser—I'm hanging on.
    *(*DOWSER *runs in, pulls* JAKE *off* WIDGER, *stops to help* WIDGER *and* JAKE *runs off quickly.)*
DOWSER: Who was it? The barber?
WIDGER: Yes. Ace of spades. *(He faints away)*
DOWSER: I'll catch him. *(As he goes past* DOCKET, DOCKET *catches him by the leg.)*
DOCKET: Help, help! Police. My head's bumped! My prisoner's escaped.
    *(*DOWSER *frees himself and runs off after* JAKE.)*
DOCKET: Stop! Stop! *(He sees* WIDGER*)* Widger, are you dead? Wake up—come alive now, man.
WIDGER: Is he gone? Oh, I didn't find Roselle and now it may be too late—
DOCKET: *(Picking up chain)* Escaping eh?
WIDGER: My neck hurts. Do you suppose it's broken?
    (He collapses again unsteadily. PROFESSOR BOND *comes in.)*
BOND: It's all right, Widger, old man, all right. The coroner says there was no murder.
DOCKET: No murder!
WIDGER: Oh, but there was, Officer. The poor man died of fright.
BOND: Coronary occlusion, brought on by—
WIDGER: Fear.
BOND: No possible charge of murder.
DOCKET: The horse was tied up, wasn't it?
WIDGER: Scholtz did that. He's bad.
DOCKET: You come with me. I want a complete statement.
WIDGER: Well, you see, Plantaganet came by—he took my Sunday suit, tea and bacon—
DOCKET: *(Hands over ears)* Not now. Come along.
BOND: Where are you taking him?
DOCKET: To jail. I'm going to let them drunks out and put him in.
BOND: But why?
DOCKET: For assault and battery on an officer.
WIDGER: But Roselle, my daughter—
    *(*PETER *rushes in.)*

PETER: Mr. Widger, I know where Roselle is. That Dowser took her to his sister. She's coming home tomorrow.
WIDGER: Thank you, young man.
PETER: And Mr. Widger, I made a mistake last night. I brought the wrong potatoes.
WIDGER: It's all right, boy.
PETER: Oh no, it isn't. It's your—your treasure.
WIDGER: Oh, no.
DOCKET: Here, what's this? Potatoes.
WIDGER: Not exactly. *(Swallows—then, smiling)* You have it, Officer. Take it for a present. *(Puts bag in* DOCKET's *hand)* See what you can do with it.
DOCKET: But what is it?
WIDGER: It's mineral, Officer.
DOCKET: Hm. . .Let me see.
   (As DOCKET *is examining the bag,* WIDGER *moves paint can over beside fence.)*
WIDGER: *(Towards bell tower)* If I get out of jail, I'll finish up the fence. Both sides, sir. Both sides.

SCENE 5

PLACE: *The same.*

TIME: *In the middle of the next morning.*

ROSELLE *enters quietly. She has more poise than before and is somehow grown up.*

ROSELLE: *(Knocking at the door of the cabin)* Father, it's Roselle. I'm home. Father—
   *(*PETER *comes in from the left and sees her.)*
PETER: Roselle!
ROSELLE: *(Softly)* Why, hello, Peter.
PETER: You might have told me where you were going. I looked everywhere for you.
ROSELLE: You looked for me?
PETER: I didn't get much sleep—worrying.

ROSELLE: *(Her eyes beginning to shine)* About—the triceratops?

PETER: About you. A hundred a month, and they supply the shovel. That's not much, is it?

ROSELLE: I don't understand.

PETER: To live on, for two. Do you eat much?

ROSELLE: Peter, you're asking me—

PETER: To marry me, Roselle. Will you?

ROSELLE: Oh, yes, I will. I'd like to.

PETER: *(With a sigh of relief)* Thanks, that's settled.

ROSELLE: Aren't you going to—kiss me?

PETER: Oh, yes. Sure. *(He kisses her awkwardly)* Certainly.
    (He kisses her again, more effectively.)

ROSELLE: I love you, Peter.

PETER: So do I. I'll try to give you a good home and be successful and be a father to your children.

ROSELLE: Professor and Mrs. Traptow! Oh—

PETER: I got this ring—

ROSELLE: How did you buy it Peter?

PETER: I stood up to him.

ROSELLE: Your uncle?

PETER: No. That gobbler. I caught him in a corner, threw a sack over his head, and sold him to the butcher. Then I bought the ring.

ROSELLE: It's beautiful.

PETER: I wish we had a house. A man's supposed to carry his bride across the threshold. I can't do that, Roselle.

ROSELLE: Oh, Peter, yes, you can. I'll draw a line on the earth anywhere, call it a threshold. You'll lift me over and where we are is home. Believe me, Peter.

PETER: *(Humbly)* I do. Come on, we'll find your father. He should be out now.

ROSELLE: Out?

PETER: Out of—out of the conference he's in.
    *(*DOWSER *comes in.)*

ROSELLE: Oh, Dowser, I didn't need the charm. He loves me.

DOWSER: A wrinkled black hag of a girl like you? I don't believe it.

ROSELLE: You'll play at our wedding, Dowser?

DOWSER: I'll start after sunset, play right into dawn, set the stars singing: "Roselle, Roselle." Will that be satisfactory?

ROSELLE: *(Solemnly)* Oh, yes, that's just what we want, isn't it, Peter?
    *(*DOCKET *comes in miserably, carrying the sack of gold.)*

DOCKET: I've been looking for you, Dowser.

ROSELLE: If Father comes, tell him we'll be right back.

DOCKET: I just let your father out, Miss.

ROSELLE: Out?

PETER: Sh. . .

DOCKET: Out of jail.

ROSELLE: Oh, Peter.

PETER: Don't feel bad, Roselle. It isn't serious.

DOCKET: Oh, no? I may still get concussion.

ROSELLE: He probably hasn't even had a cup of tea. Let's find him, Peter.

(They go off. ROSELLE *passes* DOCKET *with her head up indignantly.)*

DOWSER: Any more murders, Constable?

DOCKET: I only done my duty as I saw it.

DOWSER: I know.

DOCKET: And you didn't need to hand that barber over to the Mounties. You could have brought him back and let me do it.

DOWSER: You had no charge against him. You're well rid of him.

DOCKET: *(Gloomily)* My Missus won't let me in at home. Nobody spoke to me at the wedding. I have to carry this gold around everywhere I go.

DOWSER: I'll take it.

DOCKET: I got to restore it to the legal owner. Way people talk I should hand it out like candy.

DOWSER: Why not?

DOCKET: The question is, is this gold Widger's gold, or the barber's gold, or the dead man's heir's gold. And this map. Who does it belong to?

DOWSER: Map?

DOCKET: It was at the bottom of the sack.

(He hands it to DOWSER.*)*

DOWSER: I know this country—it's in the Park.

DOCKET: Provincial Park?

DOWSER: Federal. The boundary runs here.

DOCKET: Federal Park. Ha. That's settled then. There's a law on that. "I claim this gold and the mining property thereof for the Government of Canada for all time to come." I'll take it to the bank.

(He starts off right.)

DOWSER: Why not just hand it out like candy, Docket?

DOCKET: Oh, I couldn't do that. It's the government's. Next thing you know people might try to evade the income tax.

DOWSER: Oh, no, Docket!

DOCKET: They might, Dowser. You've no idea how bad good people are. Are you coming?

DOWSER: No. I'm going to the wedding party.

(DOCKET goes off right and DOWSER *goes off left, whistling. The music swells offstage.* WIDGER *comes in alone from the back of the stage.)*

WIDGER: *(Picking up her coat and folding it neatly)* Roselle. Roselle. You're home! *(He knocks on the door timidly)* It's Papa—your father—Milton Widger. *(Knocks again)* Roselle! *(Turning away)* I couldn't expect her to stay home—the disgrace and all. *(He takes up the coat and folds it again forlornly)* Her own father locked up in jail, taking other people's gold, assaulting officers. I couldn't

expect anyone to welcome me—the way I act. *(Burst of music offstage.* WIDGER *moves a little towards it)* Hmmm—music! *(He sees the empty potato sack and moves it tidily by the door)* Well, the gold's gone anyway. I'm poor as a church mouse, like I was before. I'm glad, I think. *(He takes up brush and paint pail and goes to fence)* I'll finish painting. *(To the Lord, subdued, lonely)* It's only me again—Widger. A nobody. I wasn't cut out to make a splash, I guess. I couldn't expect to be invited out to parties—not me—not Widger. Not the way I act.
    *(*GARROW *comes in breathlessly.)*

GARROW: Mr. Widger. Mr. Widger. At last! I've looked for you all over town.

WIDGER: *(Dolefully)* Hello, Mr. Gulf.

GARROW: Garrow. Gulf's the company.

WIDGER: Oh, I beg your pardon.

GARROW: Sign on the dotted line, please.

WIDGER: Sign?

GARROW: Hate to rush you, but it's important. Have to get you before Texaco.

WIDGER: What for? I haven't done anything. I'm no danger to the United States. A man's got a right to speak his mind, even about the United States. If he's a Canadian. We don't belong to you—not yet. Why, we're just as good as anybody almost.

GARROW: Don't waste time, Widger, they're right behind me. Sign.

WIDGER: But where—why?

GARROW: Dotted line.

WIDGER: I haven't got a—

GARROW: Use this. Just on the market. Guaranteed to write in a vacuum and pick up radioactivity a hundred years after a major blast.

WIDGER: *(Taking pen)* Oh!

GARROW: Sign.

WIDGER: Why?

GARROW: Your oil rights, Widger. We'll pay fifty thousand—no more, no less.

WIDGER: Dollars?

GARROW: That's right.

WIDGER: For me? Not the government?

GARROW: For you. Hurry.

WIDGER: *(Writing)* Milton Ephraim Widger.

GARROW: Here's the cheque. Thanks. Gotta go. Want to start drilling in an hour. Oil! Oil for the lamps of China. *(He stops aghast, looks around)* Forget it pal, will you—I wasn't thinking. It's just a phrase! You won't say anything, will you?

WIDGER: No. Oh, no, I wouldn't, Mr. Gulf. We Canadians are very reserved, you know. We're so reserved we don't know our own minds, hardly.

GARROW: Thanks. Goodbye, pal, see you—in jail. *(Shakes hand.)*
WIDGER: Goodbye. Wait, you didn't mean that about jail?
GARROW: Forget it, Buddy. See you in the funny papers.
　　(He runs off.)
WIDGER: See you in the funny papers—ha, ha—those Americans—so
　　original. Friendly too. Called me Buddy—just like I was anybody.
　　(He is aware of cheque in his hand. Awed) Fifty thousand dollars—
　　oh—I'd better hide this before they find out I'm rich. I'll get the
　　shovel—bury it—
　　　　(He hears ROSELLE *and* PETER *coming in and quickly stuffs
　　　　cheque in his pocket.)*
ROSELLE: Hello, Father.
WIDGER: *(Shyly)* Welcome home, daughter.
ROSELLE: *(Moving to him, shyly too, but with her new poise)* Welcome
　　home, Father.
WIDGER: Roselle, before I change my mind, you take a pig to town and
　　trade it for a pair of fancy skates.
ROSELLE: But Father, this is June.
WIDGER: All the better—they'll be on sale.
ROSELLE: Father, Peter has something to say to you.
WIDGER: Well?
PETER: You go on Roselle.
ROSELLE: You don't—need me?
PETER: *(Bravely)* No. You go along.
ROSELLE: Yes, Peter.
　　(She goes into the house.)
WIDGER: Well, young man, what is it?
　　(He is painting.)
PETER: Sir, with your permission, I'd like to—Warm for June, isn't it?
WIDGER: Yes, yes, of course. Well, run along now.
PETER: Mr. Widger, I'm a student at the University. I haven't
　　any prospects.
WIDGER: I don't lend money.
PETER: I don't want money, sir. I want Roselle. We'd like to be married.
WIDGER: Indeed. Can you support her?
PETER: Not exactly, but I have a summer job—I'll support her even if
　　I give up University.
WIDGER: All right, then, you can have her, if she's willing.
PETER: She is, sir.
WIDGER: But no money, mind.
PETER: Oh no, sir. Thank you. I'll go now.
　　(He starts off.)
WIDGER: Wait.
PETER: Sir?
WIDGER: You'd best not stop your studies. I doubt you'd make a
　　farmer. How much does it cost to go to University?
PETER: Over a thousand a year, sir.

WIDGER: Dollars? *(PETER nods.* WIDGER *swallows)* Oh. *(He crumples cheque nervously)* Well, I'll loan—give, that is, a thousand when you marry, That's all.

PETER: Why, thank you, Mr. Widger.

WIDGER: Children are expensive items. I won't finance children.

PETER: *(Bravely)* I'm sorry sir. I must refuse your offer.

WIDGER: You mean—you mean Roselle's going to—

PETER: I simply mean that Roselle and I expect quite a lot of children.

WIDGER: *(After a pause, hopefully)* Oh—Two, perhaps? One of each?

PETER: Six.

WIDGER: —Six—that's a lot. Hard to find names, you know.

PETER: We'll call one Peter, one Roselle, one Milton—

WIDGER: After me? *(The thought is suddenly quite pleasant)* Oh—Oh, well, I tell you I could manage to give that Milton a thousand dollars since he's my grandchild.

PETER: They'd all be your grandchildren.

WIDGER: So they would. All six. Well—a thousand a head—but no more than six.

PETER: That's generous.

WIDGER: Me? Oh, no, I'm not. I never was. You'd better go before I begin to worry.

PETER: Yes, sir.
> *(He starts off.)*

WIDGER: Six children—that's highway robbery. I'm spending money like a drunken sailor.
> *(ROSELLE returns from the party at left.)*

PETER: It's—it's all right, Roselle.
> *(They embrace lightly.)*

ROSELLE: Oh, Peter! Thank you, Father.

WIDGER: *(Sickly)* Not at all. Nothing. No more than six.

ROSELLE: They want you to come to the party, Father.

WIDGER: Me? Want me? Who?

ROSELLE: Everybody.

WIDGER: Oh, no—No Sunday suit, I have to paint this fence, too much to do. You go—Oh, I couldn't. Go along girl, go along.
> *(He paints distractedly. The music rises.* ROSELLE *stands quietly—*PETER *a little behind her.)*

BOND/SOKOLANDER: *(Offstage)* Hey, Widger. Come on over.

WIDGER: *(Painting)* Oh no, no—

DOWSER: Widger—
> *(Sound of bird whistle.)*

WIDGER: *(To the Lord)* That Dowser—he makes bird noises. You can't tell which is which.

VOICES OFF: Widger—come on over.

WIDGER: *(Putting down brush)* It's Widger. I—I think I will go over. They might think—It's more polite to go. I'll finish the fence tomorrow *(Music rises. Whistle above it)* Hear that? Sounds like your birds, doesn't it? But it's the Dowser. *(*WIDGER *is brushing* *his hair awkwardly and straightening his tie)* Well, I'll be on my way. They're waiting for me—all my friends are waiting. *(The music rises. He moves across the stage*—ROSELLE *and* PETER *wait for him.* WIDGER *calls)* One minute, just one minute—I—I might want to stand treat.

(He rushes back to doorstep where he hid the cheque.)

VOICES OFF: Widge, old fellow.

WIDGER: *(Pocketing cheque)* Coming, fellows, coming.

(Music rises and they go off gaily.)

The End

Lament for Harmonica (Maya)

Characters: In Order of Appearance

JOSEPHINA SAMUEL, *an old Shushwap woman*
MARTHA PAUL, *her friend*
MRS. ROLAND, *an agency worker*
MAYA SAMUEL *(pronounced May-ya)*
ELLEN, *Martha's niece*
WILLIAM, *an Indian*
ALLAN, *a white man*

TIME: *The present. Late evening in spring.*
PLACE: *The doorstep and clearing outside* JOSEPHINA's *cabin on the reserve.*

The reservation is set in a valley surrounded by high rhythmic hills. Back centre is indicated the shape of a high-steepled church against the darkening sky.

A section of weathered log fence (corral type) cuts across the upstage left corner. Down left another section of fence runs somewhat parallel to the upstage piece. Between may be a broken gate.

Down right is the doorway and stoop or porch of a worn log house. The porch slopes slightly. Two 2 x 4 pillars support a light roof. The porch has been swept and is not cluttered.

Center stage (downstage centre) is a low camp fire with a black pot suspended on a stick above the rock enclosure for the fire. On either side of the fire are rough wooden benches. The legs for the bench consist of two round sections of logs.

This setting may be simplified by using only the benches, fire, and indicating the porch and doorway.

Gwen Pharis Ringwood

As the play opens MARTHA *and* JOSEPHINA *on the bench at stage right. From a house off stage comes the sad thin sound of a harmonica very well played. . . the unseen player improvises a plaintive tune, slides into some cowboy folk song, then returns to his improvisation. Somewhere in another house the player, a boy of fifteen, lies on a ragged mattress, looking up at the chinks of light that filter through the roof, and plays his music. The sound recurs from time to time during the play and is never obtrusive, merely a part of the place.*

MARTHA *wears a dark cotton print dress, almost to her ankles, and heavy shoes. She has a dark shawl or jacket around her shoulders. Her hair is tied back. She is smoking a cigarette.* MARTHA *is about 60 years old.*

JOSEPHINA *is dressed in a long dark skirt, dark blouse and shapeless sweater. Heavy low black shoes and dark stockings. Her hair is in two long braids and is very black. She is older than* MARTHA. *She is broad and stocky with a strong patient face.*

When the two women speak they speak usually without much inflection, and with a slower rhythm than white people use.

JOSEPHINA *moves to the fire and, lifting a lid off the pot, stirs at the soup she is making.*

JOSEPHINA: On such a warm night, we don't need the fire.
MARTHA: It keeps off the mosquitoes, Josephina, and when the sun's gone, the fire feels good.
JOSEPHINA: And it keeps the soup hot. You want some soup, Martha?
MARTHA: (*nodding*) I want some. (*After a brief pause*) Maya went past my house.
JOSEPHINA: (*ladling soup into an enamel cup*) She did?
MARTHA: She never stops now. She goes right by.
JOSEPHINA: She's always in a hurry.
MARTHA: I suppose she was hitchhiking into town.
JOSEPHINA: (*giving* MARTHA *the soup and getting some for herself*) That's right.
MARTHA: She goes to town every day now. Does she have a job?
JOSEPHINA: She did have, but she quit.
MARTHA: You should make her work.
JOSEPHINA: She don't listen to me. Since her child died, Maya spends all her time in town. It was bad for her when he died, Martha. Now she don't care what she does.
MARTHA: It was bad for you too, Josephina, losing a great-grandson. Now you have only Maya.
JOSEPHINA: (*sitting down with her soup*) The house is empty without the child.
MARTHA: In the old days I remember many got sick as he did. At sun rise they would be well and walking about and when the sun set they would be gone.

340

JOSEPHINA: You know, Martha, on the morning Maya's boy died, a whiskey-jack flew round the fire here three times, crying as he flew. Always my grandmother said that was a sign of death.

MARTHA: (*solemnly*) The old ones were not fools.

JOSEPHINA: And the night before he died, a black lizard crossed my path and went under the old church. That too is bad sign.

MARTHA: The priest would not like to hear that. He would tell you to go down on your knees and pray.

JOSEPHINA: I pray. And on my knees. But I have not seen Maya on her knees once since the child died.

MARTHA: She is too proud, Josephina. All the young ones think so. And my niece, Ellen, says Maya drinks too much too.

JOSEPHINA: I tell her she should not run around or drink so much but she won't listen. Not to anyone. When the priest comes she leaves the house.

MARTHA: (*putting her cup down and lighting a cigarette*) Ahh ya, the young are like magpies. They go screaming from one thing to another. If they find a coloured string, they clatter with joy, as if it were the world.

JOSEPHINA: (*with a rueful smile*) Still it's better to be young than old, Martha. What's left when you're old but to remember the old days or sit together railing against the young, with envy stale in the mouth? (*Getting up to take* MARTHA'S *cup and her own back to the ledge on the porch.*) Look at us! Two old women tossing the hulls of wisdom back and forth. No one else listens to us.

MARTHA: In the old days people stayed home and there were stories told around the fire. It was a proud thing to be old and tell the stories. But not any more. Yet old as I am I can be glad of warm nights or a fresh salmon or good soup hot from the fire. (*Smiling at her friend and pointing knowingly with her finger.*) For us death is the enemy, Josephina, not age. And death takes even the young some times.

JOSEPHINA: Yes, you are right, Martha. (JOSEPHINA *stands, remembering.*) I thought she'd cry out, pray or weep for her boy but she stood there, silent as a stone. "Maya," I said, "Maya, come away." Still she stood silent with a gray face. (*She looks at* MARTHA *then.*) I never saw her weep.

MARTHA: Did the man—his father—ever come or send her money?

JOSEPHINA: (*turning away impatiently and rinsing out cups at water barrel on the stoop*) How do I know?

MARTHA: She won't say who he is?

JOSEPHINA: No. He's white, like her father was. That's all I know. (*She brings from the back of the barrel a basket containing some pieces of buckskin, a sharp knife and coloured silks down to her bench.*)

MARTHA: Does Maya give you money?

JOSEPHINA: Some.

MARTHA: She has good clothes.

JOSEPHINA: Yes.

> (*She takes out a piece of leather cut in the shape of a glove and begins working on it.*)

MARTHA: (*unwilling to drop the subject*) My niece says Maya is bad. She says Maya is a—

JOSEPHINA: (*angrily*) Your niece hates Maya. Ellen wants William for herself and William only looks at Maya. You know that. Ellen has been jealous of Maya since they were children.

MARTHA: Ellen is jealous all right. She's afraid Maya will marry William.

JOSEPHINA: I wish she would. William is a good boy. He can work hard.

MARTHA: He's a good rider.

JOSEPHINA: He can get a job on a ranch any time.

MARTHA: She would be lucky to marry William.

JOSEPHINA: I don't know about Maya, Martha. (*With controlled feeling.*) I don't know what will happen.

MARTHA: She is too clever, I guess.

JOSEPHINA: She was the brightest student from the reserve, the only one to finish High School.

MARTHA: (*without emotion*) Running with the whites always brings us trouble.

JOSEPHINA: For all her white blood, Maya wanted to be Indian. She would come home from school and ask me how they did things in the old days, how my grandmother cooked or made the clothes, what stories the old ones told. She wrote down the stories in a book she had. At night she begged me to sing the war songs or the potlatch songs, but I couldn't remember them. Or she would say, "Show me the dog dance or the chicken dance. Show me how they made the wolf mask." When I couldn't show her she looked at me as if I'd robbed her somehow.

MARTHA: (*comforting her*) None of us remember.

JOSEPHINA: (*indicating the glove*) I am making her gloves. I can do that. I know the old designs.

MARTHA: They take too long to make.

JOSEPHINA: When she was a child I thought Maya would bring great honour to me. Now she don't care what she does. She hides behind her eyes even from me who raised her. She won't listen to me.

> (MRS. ROLAND, *an efficient, pleasant woman, comes in from off stage right through the gate. She looks uncertainly at* JOSEPHINA *and* MARTHA.)

MRS. ROLAND: Hello. Is one of you Mrs. Samuel? Josephina Samuel?

JOSEPHINA: (*remaining seated*) That's my name.

MRS. ROLAND: (*approaching them*) I'm Mrs. Roland from the Agency. And this is—(*She smiles.*)

JOSEPHINA: Mrs. Paul.

MRS. ROLAND: How do you do, Mrs. Paul. (*She shakes hands with* MARTHA.) Mrs. Samuel, is your granddaughter at home?
JOSEPHINA: (*warily*) No. She's not here.
MRS. ROLAND: Where could I find her?
JOSEPHINA: I don't know.
MARTHA: She's in town.
MRS. ROLAND: I see. Will she be home soon?
JOSEPHINA: I don't know when she's coming back.
MRS. ROLAND: She'll be here tomorrow?
JOSEPHINA: I think she will.
MRS. ROLAND: I'll have to come back tomorrow then. (*She turns to go, then changes her mind.*) May I sit down, Mrs. Samuel?
JOSEPHINA: Sure.
MRS. ROLAND: I'll tell you why I want to see Maya. We want her to go back to school, to University this fall.
JOSEPHINA: (*unenthusiastic*) I don't think she would go to school any more. She finished school.
MRS. ROLAND: We want her to train for a teacher.
JOSEPHINA: Maya's too old to go to school. She's nineteen.
MRS. ROLAND: Nineteen isn't old, Mrs. Samuel.
JOSEPHINA: Besides, it costs money.
MRS. ROLAND: The Agency has the money. We've got a special grant for outstanding students. Your granddaughter is the first on the list from this reservation.
JOSEPHINA: She should get married.
MRS. ROLAND: That could come later. She could come back here and teach. We need Indian teachers.
JOSEPHINA: (*obstinately*) I need her home to help me.
MRS. ROLAND: You wouldn't stand in the way of her chance to get a good job, Mrs. Samuel?
JOSEPHINA: Maya is all I have. My son died in the war. My daughter, her mother, died at Coquilitza.
MRS. ROLAND: Mrs. Samuel, she's a brilliant student. You must give her this chance.
JOSEPHINA: I don't think she would want to go.
MRS. ROLAND: (*annoyed*) I'll talk to her tomorrow. Please realize that this is good for Maya.
JOSEPHINA: I'll tell her you came to see her.
MRS. ROLAND: And why I came.
JOSEPHINA: I'll tell her.
MRS. ROLAND: Give her these papers please. They explain the terms of the grant. We can fill out her application tomorrow. (*She gives a large envelope to* JOSEPHINA.) Goodbye, Mrs. Paul. Goodbye, Mrs. Samuel.
MARTHA: Goodbye.
MRS. ROLAND: (*at gate*) Don't hold your granddaughter here. She needs this chance.

343

JOSEPHINA: I don't know what she'll do.

> (MRS. ROLAND *goes out, disconcerted and annoyed. There is a pause.* JOSEPHINA *looks at the papers, puts them in the basket.*)

JOSEPHINA: Maya will read these, I guess.

MARTHA: She should stay home with you now and take care of you.

JOSEPHINA: I think she won't go.

MARTHA: You're getting old.

JOSEPHINA: I can still work.

MARTHA: The white people I worked for at Soda Creek sent their girl to that school. It costs much money.

JOSEPHINA: You heard her say the Agency would pay.

MARTHA: If the whites know how Maya is always drinking and running around with tramps, I don't think they'd pay money for her to go.

JOSEPHINA: (*resentfully*) They know she is bright.

MARTHA: She should be married now.

JOSEPHINA: (*turning away*) She needs something. I don't know. . .

MARTHA: You could take Maya away. She should stay with you.

JOSEPHINA: Take her where?

MARTHA: To your sister's place at Alkali. If the white woman finds you gone, she won't bother. They forget soon. In the fall you could come back here.

JOSEPHINA: She said she was coming back tomorrow.

MARTHA: Go early in the morning. William can take you.

JOSEPHINA: I think you are right, Martha. Maya should stay with me.

MARTHA: Will you show her that paper?

JOSEPHINA: No. I'll throw it in the fire. (*She throws the envelope in the fire.*) There. It will soon burn up.

> (*There is a sound of a car approaching off stage. It stops and young voices shout and laugh.*)

MARTHA: Listen!

MAYA: (*off stage*) Wait for me. Don't go without me, you promise?

VOICE (*off stage*) We'll give you five minutes.

SECOND VOICE: Taxis cost money, Maya.

MAYA: William's got money, haven't you, William? Pay him.

> (*There is more laughter, slightly ribald and drunken.*)

MAYA: Come on, William, you can help me!

MALE VOICE (*off*) Let me help you, Maya. I'll help!

MARTHA: (*getting up*) I'll be going.

JOSEPHINA: (*urgently*) No, you stay, Martha.

> (MAYA *appears in the gateway. She is a beautiful girl, quite tall, dark with a golden skin, rich full mouth, dark eyes. She is wearing a bright sheath that has been torn from the sleeve across the back. She is vivid, hard and angry under her cynical gaiety. She has been drinking. Her hair is somewhat disheveled. She is carrying a light coat and under it has concealed a small bottle of whiskey.*)

MAYA: Here I am, Grandmother! A poor thing but thine own!
JOSEPHINA: You're drunk, Maya.
MAYA: (*laughing, pretending to be shocked*) Oh no! No! Am I drunk, William?

(WILLIAM *has come in behind* MAYA. *He is very dark, all Indian, quiet. He wears blue jeans, light cowboy shirt, good boots.*)

MAYA: We brought you a present. See! (*She holds up the bottle.*) To give you nice dreams!
JOSEPHINA: Get in the house.
MAYA: No.
JOSEPHINA: Why did you let her drink so much, William?
MAYA: (*leaning lightly on* WILLIAM'S *shoulder*) Leave William alone. He wants me to marry me. Shall I marry William, Grandmother, and live like a queen in William's castle?
JOSEPHINA: (*moving to* MAYA) Look at you! Your dress is torn.
MAYA: I came home to change.
JOSEPHINA: You're not to go back in town!
MAYA: I will go back. The taxi's waiting for me. Don't you want your present?
JOSEPHINA: (*taking the bottle*) Where did you get the money to buy this?
MAYA: William has money. He took all the money in the bronc riding Sunday. He rode like a wildcat, didn't you William? He has lots of money. (*She smiles at him provocatively, then her expression changes quickly to mockery.*) But not enough to buy Maya, have you, William? Oh, I'm for sale, but the price is too high yet. That's so, Martha. Some pay for virginity. Some want experience! William just wants Maya!
JOSEPHINA: (*pushing* MAYA *on the shoulder*) Go in and change, Maya. Now!
MAYA: (*angrily shrugging her off*) Keep your hands off of me. I won't be pushed. I'll do what I like. (*To* WILLIAM.) Wait for me.

(MAYA *goes into the cabin.*)

JOSEPHINA: What happened?
WILLIAM: (*awkwardly*) Maya was in the beer parlor with some others. I wasn't there then. She started to sing some Indian song. They told her to be quiet and she swore at them. The beer slinger grabbed her and was going to push her out and he tore her dress. She bit his hand and he was yelling like a pig.
JOSEPHINA: Did he get the police on Maya?
WILLIAM: No. I brought her home then to change her dress.
JOSEPHINA: You don't let her drink any more, William. She should stay home now.
WILLIAM: It's early. We were going to the drive-in.
JOSEPHINA: Do you have to work tomorrow?
WILLIAM: I told Johnson I'd fix fences.
JOSEPHINA: I thought you'd borrow your uncle's car and take me and Maya to Alkali in the morning.

345

WILLIAM: I could do that.

JOSEPHINA: The Agency wants to send Maya away. I'll take her to my sister.

WILLIAM: What time?

JOSEPHINA: About six o'clock.

WILLIAM: I'll tell Johnson I'm not coming.

(ELLEN, *a thin, rather untidy Indian girl, comes in from left.*)

ELLEN: Come on, William. The taxi man wants to get back to town. Let's go. Hello, Aunt Martha.

MARTHA: You should stay home too, Ellen.

ELLEN: The night's young. Come on, William.

WILLIAM: Maya won't be long.

ELLEN: You'd wait for her if she took all night.

WILLIAM: It's not your business what I do.

ELLEN: Do you think she cares two cents for you except when you have money to spend?

MARTHA: Ellen—you had best leave it alone.

ELLEN: I won't. To Maya he's the dirt under her feet. How can you be such a fool?

WILLIAM: Go on back to the others.

ELLEN: You've seen him, Josephina! How on a Sunday he always looks to see if Maya's watching the chutes. He puts on his white shirt, polishes his forty-dollar boots, walks out smoking a cigarette, leans on the fence and waits for the meanest bronc they've got— all to show off for Maya!

WILLIAM: You don't know about me.

ELLEN: (*fiercely*) I know. I've watched you. I've watched you straddle the bucking horse, your knees tight to the wet flanks, and you twist as the horse twists, thinking that Maya smiles her slow smile to see you. She doesn't even notice you, William. She doesn't care whether you're thrown or broken or make a good ride to the whistle. She doesn't hold a thought for you. She uses you, that's all. Why do you risk your neck for her?

WILLIAM: Go on. Leave me alone.

ELLEN: Yes. Leave you to dream of Maya. Well, dream small, that's all she's worth.

(*She has taken hold of his sleeve.*)

WILLIAM: (*pushing her off*) Shut up, Ellen.

ELLEN: Maya's a slut, you know it. She bore one white man's bastard. Perhaps she'll get another for you to feed. She'll spend your money but she sleeps with white men!

WILLIAM: (*slaps her*) Get out!

(MAYA *appears on the step of the cabin.*)

MAYA: No, let her stay. What Ellen says is true. I am a slut. (*Her tone is disinterested and low.*) I—I thought to be something different— not that it matters. (*She picks up the enamel cup, goes to the bottle on the bench and pours a drink.*) Here's to you, Ellen. (*She drinks.*)

If William wants you he has only to say so. I've no hold on him. Take her, William. What she is, you know. You can count on it. She's a wasp—but faithful. What I am, I don't know myself. Do you know, William?

WILLIAM: I don't care.

MAYA: I care. Sometimes at school I'd read things. I learned fast, didn't I, Grandmother? I liked to learn. Sometimes I thought I'd find a book, some book somewhere to tell me some answers, show me what to look for, but there is no book. (*She looks at* WILLIAM.) What love I had, I gave. I'm no good for you. Go on, I'm not coming.

(WILLIAM *looks at her uncertainly. There is a silence. The sound of the harmonica is faint and plaintive in the distance. In sudden anger* MAYA *advances on* ELLEN *and* WILLIAM.)

MAYA: Get out! Get out! I don't want you here. I'm alone, I tell you. I'll always be alone. (*To* MARTHA.) You too. . . Go! I don't believe your books, your prayers, your songs. I don't believe them, hear me? (*To the old women.*) I hate your old faces, I hate your lips like dried leaves and your trembling hands and your eyes rimmed red with cataracts. I hate it all. We're ants crawling under the sky and the journey we take means nothing. Get out, I tell you.

(WILLIAM *and* ELLEN *go out left.* MARTHA *goes slowly out right.*)

MAYA: (*to* JOSEPHINA) And you believe the prayers they taught you. You and your Latin and your rosary. When your son died you said the mass and when my mother died. And when my son died you prayed and wept. For eighty years you've lived on a crust of bread and some white men's prayers. And that's a life, a destiny! Well, it's not enough. I hate it, I tell you, I hate it! (*More quietly and with great self-loathing.*) Look at me. Shall I bleed now or wait till after? Take my harmonica and dream at night of songs I almost heard, sing of how deep the frost lies on the golden heart while Time, the ape, sits grinning at the wheel. Do you know what that means—nothing, like your Latin, Grandma! Me, I'm an Indian. I'll show them. I'm an Indian, stretched on a plain as barren as a burnt-out star. To hell with them all, I'll show them! (*After a pause, in a broken tone.*) I wanted something. I wanted to be different. Here I am!

JOSEPHINA: Maya, tomorrow we'll go away, to Alkali or up the valley. We'll go into the woods and mountains, fish for salmon, hunt berries and trail the young deer, like in the old days. That will heal you.

MAYA: Oh Grandmother, I'm no good, for you or anyone.

JOSEPHINA: William will take us.

MAYA: It's no use.

JOSEPHINA: You'll come with me, Maya.

MAYA: No. I don't belong there. I'd get restless. I'd say things and they'd hate me and take it out on you. I won't go, Grandmother. You go.
> (*A pause. The harmonica is heard again. After a while,* JOSEPHINA *reluctantly makes up her mind to speak.*)

JOSEPHINA: Would you want to go away to school?

MAYA: Now? You talk foolish.

JOSEPHINA: A woman from the Agency was here. She said they had the money to send you.

MAYA: Where? They've got nothing on me.

JOSEPHINA: To University, she said. To be a teacher.

MAYA: Me? A teacher. Now! Don't make me laugh. (*Pause.*) I would like to teach.

JOSEPHINA: She said you were the first from this reserve. She thinks you don't belong here with these people.

MAYA: They're my people, whether I belong or not.

JOSEPHINA: She's coming tomorrow to see you. I threw the papers she brought in the fire. You're all I have now, Maya, and I'm old.

MAYA: I would come back here.

JOSEPHINA: It's hard to be old and alone, Maya. I haven't anyone but you.

MAYA: I know. I won't leave. I'm going in.
> (*Abruptly* MAYA *goes into the house, closing the door after her.* JOSEPHINA, *looking old and worried, banks the fire, then turns to move towards the porch. As she nears it her eye catches something upstage of the stoop. She raises her stick, and speaks in a low tone with awe and terror.*)

JOSEPHINA: Get out, you black lizard! Get away! I'll kill you! (*But her hand remains raised, clenching the stick, as she looks down.*) Go. . . Go away from us. Leave us alone.
> (ALLAN, *a white man, enters from the road. He is in his middle twenties, good-looking with a sensitive, rather weak face.*)

ALLAN: I beg pardon, I'm looking for someone, a girl named Maya Samuel.

JOSEPHINA: What do you want with her? (*She turns, startled.*)

ALLAN: (*resenting her tone*) I want to see her. Do you know her?

JOSEPHINA: She's my granddaughter.

ALLAN: (*taken aback*) Oh. Oh, I see. Maya lives here?

JOSEPHINA: What do you want with her?

ALLAN: (*trying to win her confidence*) I knew her one summer. I was making a trip through here and thought I'd look her up.

JOSEPHINA: She's not here.

ALLAN: Where could I find her?

JOSEPHINA: I don't know.

ALLAN: I want to see her.

JOSEPHINA: She's gone.

ALLAN: Where? Where is she? (JOSEPHINA *is silent.*) Look, is it a crime to look up a friend?

JOSEPHINA: (*slowly*) It was you she went with three years ago, when I was sick. (*Pause.*) It was you, wasn't it? (*Another pause.*) She was sixteen.

ALLAN: I didn't know that then. She said she was older.

JOSEPHINA: She just finished high school. After you left she went to learn typing and business.

ALLAN: I know.

JOSEPHINA: She was back home before Christmas. She had a child.

ALLAN: She never told me that.

JOSEPHINA: She wrote to you.

ALLAN: She didn't tell me about the child. Why didn't you write? You could have had someone write?

JOSEPHINA: She wouldn't say your name.

ALLAN: I'm sorry. I should have answered her letter but I got busy and—

JOSEPHINA: You are no good for Maya.

ALLAN: Look, I've got to see her. Tell me where she is.

JOSEPHINA: No. She's had enough of you. Leave her alone.

(MAYA *comes out, stand looking at* ALLAN. *She is smoking. There is a long silence except for the music off stage.* MAYA *flips her cigarette away, motions to* JOSEPHINA.)

MAYA: Go in, Grandmother. We'll talk here.

JOSEPHINA: Maya—

MAYA: Please.

(JOSEPHINA *moves past her into the house.* MAYA *waits quietly on the step as she goes in and closes the door.*)

ALLAN: Maya!

MAYA: Hello, Allan. How did you get here?

ALLAN: I've been up north. This is the first time I've been this way since—

MAYA: For three years.

ALLAN: I couldn't come back the next summer. There was no job. I stayed on and worked at the station.

MAYA: Yes.

ALLAN: I wanted to come back. Maya, your grandmother said you had a child, my child. Why didn't you write to me?

MAYA: I wrote.

ALLAN: Just once. I didn't answer, but if you'd told me—

MAYA: She lied. There was no child.

ALLAN: I don't think she lied. Why would she?

MAYA: Why? To get money from you, why else? She's old and greedy and has nothing.

ALLAN: She said—

MAYA: Suppose it were true. Suppose I'd written to say I'm in trouble. Would that have brought you back? Or would you send money

349

and the address for an abortion? Everything fixed up with relief, regards and no regrets. Isn't that the usual way, the white way?

ALLAN: I'd have come, Maya.

MAYA: And if you had, would you believe him yours, seeing my people's eyes look back at you? Oh no. You'd have denied him. We're lucky there was no child.

ALLAN: You swear that?

MAYA: I swear nothing. He'd have been more white than Indian, Allan. Would I have kept him here on the reserve? Or would I give him to some kind barren pair to raise as their own? Soon he'd grow tall in a suburban house, watch the wide screen, and behind his thoughts begin to wonder who he is and why. If I had borne your child, would I have kept him?

ALLAN: For God's sake, Maya, tell me.

MAYA: There was no child. (*Cruelly*) If there had been I'd have killed him, dashed him from the rock yonder to the river and rid us forever of a summer passion. If there had been a son, I'd have left him to die on a cliff somewhere. Why keep a souvenir of something that doesn't matter?

ALLAN: (*shaking her*) Stop it, Maya, stop!

MAYA: (*breaking away from him*) I have no child. Let your mind rest.
(*A pause as they look at each other.*)

ALLAN: I thought of you all the time after I left. I wanted to come back, meant to come back, and then—

MAYA: Then you got married.

ALLAN: You knew about that?

MAYA: I read it in the papers. I can read, you know. My grandmother doesn't read but I read well. That's progress.

ALLAN: I've never forgot those days in the mountains. Have you?

MAYA: No. Each morning was a promise. Each night when I put my arms around you I felt we were one flesh, one hope. I remember.

ALLAN: I had to come back. I had to see you, even for a few hours, a day.

MAYA: Maybe I put a curse on you, an Indian curse.
(*She turns away from him.*)

ALLAN: I've got two days, Maya. I drove night and day to give me time here. I've got two days and money. We can spend them.

MAYA: Sure. We can spend them both.

ALLAN: Get what you need. Let's go.

MAYA: I waited for you the next summer. I'd look at the hills and whisper "how beautiful upon the mountain are the feet of my beloved." And each evening when the trees turned black over the water I'd bargain with tomorrow to bring you back.

ALLAN: I'm here now.

MAYA: Yes.

ALLAN: Let's get out of here.

MAYA: No. It's too late, Allan.

ALLAN: Not for us. Remember.

MAYA: Don't touch me.

ALLAN: What's the matter? I'm here—after three years, Maya. We're together.

MAYA: Three years is a lifetime. You were the first. Do you think you were the last? Look at me. I'm an empty room, despoiled by any passing stranger, gutted of hope and faith and desolate of love— the refuge of the lost, the lonely and the hungry, that's Maya.

ALLAN: Maya, listen. I've come because there's no rest for me without you. You got inside of me. You belong to me.

MAYA: I can belong to any man at all. You don't believe that, do you? Hah, it's easy. Put your arms around them, enfold them, be wife, mother, child, brief respite from the world's woe and let them go. Look at me. Maya, the hill-side whore. Mistress of the toothless and the angry, concubine to the half-wit and the sot, wife to the fumbling and the fearful. I can take them all and leave them and I do! Oh, I'm a foxy doxy, Chicken Little, and the world may end tomorrow, so bestride me, little man, be my Colossus and I'll be your world. That's how it is—it's easy, believe me. Get out now. You've seen me.

ALLAN: No matter what you are, I can't go.

MAYA: Sure. When you stop caring, everything comes.

ALLAN: You haven't stopped caring. You're still waiting for me. You know it.

(*He moves towards her, pulls her to him.*)

MAYA: (*breaking away*) Let go. (*She whirls and picks up the knife from* JOSEPHINA'S *basket.*) Keep off me. You think because I'm any man's, I'm yours? Not any more, believe that.

ALLAN: I don't believe it. Play hard to get if you want to, Baby . . . I don't mind. (WILLIAM *enters from left, stands quietly watching for a moment.* ALLAN *takes* MAYA'S *wrist.*) Drop the knife. You couldn't use it if you wanted to. (*The knife falls to the ground.*) That's better.

WILLIAM: Leave her alone.

MAYA: Go on, William. I can look after myself.

ALLAN: Who's he, your husband?

MAYA: He could be.

ALLAN: You could do better.

WILLIAM: (*moving towards them*) Get out.

ALLAN: He's drunk.

WILLIAM: Sure I'm drunk—

ALLAN: Lay off.

(ALLAN *pushes at* WILLIAM, *who sways.*)

WILLIAM: I'm drunk—and I'm going to kill you.

MAYA: William, listen to me.

WILLIAM: Sure, I'll listen. It's like Ellen says. . . be nice to the whites, they're kind to us. They let us pick up their cigarettes butts, wear their cast-off clothes. You've worn them, Maya. We come to their back doors. My mother begged bones from the meat they cooked to feed us. Our women have your children and we feed and clothe your bastards. And Maya put your son to her breast—not mine—and watched him die and waited for you to come but you didn't make a sign.

ALLAN: (*to* MAYA) It's true then.

MAYA: It's true. He died last winter.

WILLIAM: Sure, he died. And she becomes a tramp and that's your doing.

MAYA: No, William. Mine.

WILLIAM: So now you've come back to claim your Indian scum—that's what you call us, scum! You'll never get her.

MAYA: William, go home. Get out of here.

WILLIAM: Oh no. Not now. I've waited for this. I think since I was born I've waited. And now my time comes. I'll show you we're not scum. Come on, I'll show you who's a man.

ALLAN: You drunken fool, get out of here. Come back when you're sober.

(*He slaps* WILLIAM.)

WILLIAM: I'm here. I don't have to come back.

(*He suddenly throws* ALLAN *off balance and pushes him to the ground.*)

ALLAN: Take it easy.

WILLIAM: They'll take scum to be soldiers, white man. How about that?

MAYA: Let him up now, William. You've proved enough. Let him up now.

WILLIAM: I hate him. I've hated him all my life. I've felt him between my hands.

MAYA: William stop. . . For God's sake, stop.

WILLIAM: They fondle us like dogs or kick us, take everything. I hate the bastards. . .

(*He is almost sobbing.*)

ALLAN: Help. . . he's. . . he's. . .

(WILLIAM *is choking him.*)

MAYA: (*trying vainly to pull* WILLIAM *away*) No, William, no. . .no. . . Look, I've got a knife, William. . . I'll. . .

WILLIAM: I'll kill him if I hang for it. . . I've got to kill him. . .

MAYA: Stop. William. No!

(*Unable to pull* WILLIAM *away, she raises the knife and stabs down hard.* WILLIAM *turns, looking at her, letting* ALLAN *go.*)

WILLIAM: Maya. . .

MAYA: I had to do it. You were choking him. (ALLAN *gets up.* MAYA *looks at him, her eyes wide with shock.*) Get out, Allan. Please. Get out of here.

ALLAN: You'd better come with me. There'll be trouble.

MAYA: No. Go on. . . Go!

(*She kneels beside* WILLIAM. ALLAN *goes out quickly.* JOSEPHINA *comes out of the house, sees* MAYA *kneeling beside* WILLIAM.)

WILLIAM: I had to get rid of him. He was no good for you. I showed
him we aren't scum, didn't I?

MAYA: Yes, you showed him. I saw you.

WILLIAM: Then why did you hurt me, Maya?

(*He slumps forward, his head on her knee.* JOSEPHINA *kneels
on the porch, saying a prayer over and over. In the silence the
sound of the harmonica drifts across the night.*)

MAYA: (*at last*) He's dead, Grandmother. He won't ride any more, he
won't jump on the black bronc, tighten his knees against the
twisting flanks or take first money in the chutes on Sunday. He's
dead, and I killed him. I killed you, William. I, Maya—I wanted
something. I don't know. I thought to be something different.

(MAYA, *staring dully in front of her, remains kneeling beside*
WILLIAM *as the plaintive song off stage slips away and the
curtains close.*)

The End

The Deep Has Many Voices

Characters

MARIA
SARAH
JUDITH
MELISSA, *a graduating student*
WINONA, *her mother*
MITTER
WILLIE THANIS (Niko)
OLLIE
Young Men Training for the Army
STEVE, *a truck driver*
MR. THANITOPOLIS
MIRIAM
The Masked Dancers and Chanters

Several playing levels are connected by risers from audience floor to a ramp at rear stage which rises rather sharply towards back stage right. The playing spaces are set against blue sky and light changes from time to time during the play.

The background should be one on which slides may be projected. A good sound system which can make sounds reverberate throughout the hall, which can surround the stage or again come from a special place, will be helpful in the production.

TIME: *1970.*
PLACE: *Any Canadian town.*

Two middle aged women, wearing skirts and sweaters or some such 'dateless' costume move from the audience to a playing level down stage right on which a simple bench is set. They are aware of the air and the valley and very used to one another.

Gwen Pharis Ringwood

MARIA: Sunrise is late this morning.
SARAH: Gray sky, gray hills. There's grayness in the air.
MARIA: The hills are not gray, they're green. Drab green with a ragged black fringe along the backbone. See.
SARAH: The hills are like sleeping bears around this valley. Winter or summer, the hills are sleeping bears around the valley.
    (SARAH *moves to a bench, sits down, busies herself with needlework.*)
MARIA: I like to remember spring. The budding poplars, spring-livened grass, pine,—tufted with piercing green—, and dandelions rioting down the hillside.
    Do you remember, Sarah?
SARAH: Of course I remember. Sun yellow as a buttercup. Sun yellow, and the lake green or blue or is it green?
MARIA: (*Sitting down beside* SARAH *and beginning to knit.*) Blue green I think, or greenish blue, no matter—sky blue or sky or bottle-green or blue. A dragon fly's the bluest thing I know. Then flax or bachelor buttons. Blue birds.
    Knit one, purl one, knit one, purl one, knit three.
    (JUDITH, *a woman of strength and decisiveness enters, carrying branches or flowers from the woods.*)
JUDITH: No sun this morning. Good morning, Maria, Sarah. I found these at the edge of the forest. Perhaps they'll entice the sun.
SARAH: You didn't go into the deep woods, Judith?
JUDITH: No. No. I wanted to. . . I heard the sound. . . I thought I heard—
MARIA: You were wise to stay at the edge of the forest. The forest swallows people.
JUDITH: Sometimes it pulls you. . . .
SARAH: I heard that if you go deep into the woods, you find a mirror. You look down and down into a deep well that is a mirror and you see yourself and all the barnacles fall from you, and you see yourself the way you could be.
    (*Pause. Her reflective mood is displaced by impatience.*)
    Who'd want that?
MARIA: Too late. Too late.
JUDITH: I suppose so. I don't know.
    (*From off stage there is a sound of wild geese honking as they go over.* JUDITH *looks up as she moves off stage.* MARIA *and* SARAH *look up too and go on with their work. The lights go down on their area and come up stage left where* MELISSA *is practising her valedictory.*)
MELISSA: (*reading.*) And so, my fellow students, we say goodbye to school days. We are grateful to our School Board, our beloved teachers, and our dear parents for this educational experience. They have given us the tools. Now we go out into the world to use them.

(*She throws down the speech.*)
And so, my fellow students, since we've been taught that money is not important except that you're a failure if you don't make a lot of it; and we've been taught to love our fellow men unless they get in our way; and we're been taught to live in peace except when forced to use the Napalm bomb. . . having been so taught, we're ready to go out and make a life.

(*The words reverberate from a whisper to loud "make a life, make a life, make a life."*)

WINONA: (*Off*) Melissa. . . Melissa. . . Melissa. . .

(*The sound vibrates as if through a microphone.*)

MELISSA: Coming, Mother. Coming.

WINONA: (*Entering with pink dress*) Good morning, dear. You've been practising your Valedictory?

MELISSA: Mother, I wanted a green dress!

WINONA: Pink is more becoming, dear. You're inclined to be sallow. Now don't slump. We can pad a little. (*As she fits dress.*) At your age I had a figure. Don't forget to say something nice about your teachers and your parents. All the sacrifices, loving care. The T.L.C.. . . that means tender loving care you know.

MELISSA: No, Mother. I mean, yes, Mother.

WINONA: Your class will all come back here after the graduation. Mr. Slater will take pictures for the paper. Stand up straight, Melissa.

MELISSA: Mother, I want to ask Willie Thanis to the dance.

WINONA: Chicken croquettes and buns with fruit punch and my baked Alaska. Whom did you say, dear?

MELISSA: Willie Thanis.

WINONA: Thanis. I don't think I remember him.

MELISSA: He isn't in school now.

WINONA: Oh, a drop-out. Thanis? The father's a sort of handy-man, isn't he? I think not, Melissa.

MELISSA: Please listen.

WINONA: Hardly fair or suitable. Not fair to him, I mean. That funny name and living a different kind of life. I'll arrange something, don't worry.

MELISSA: Mother. . . .

WINONA: But you've reminded me of the roof, Melissa. I want this Willie's father to come and mend the roof. I discovered a leak last week. The day it rained. I heard this drip, drip, drip, and sure enough I found water dripping on the wall to wall. That mean's there's a hole in the bonded roof. I couldn't believe it. Such impossible things happen to the best of us. To me. To your father.

MELISSA: Listen to me, Mother. . .

WINONA: So, you go by today and tell the handy-man, Mr. Thanis that I want him to come at once. To fix the bonded roof.

MELISSA: That's when I can ask Willie to be my escort, if he's at home. I haven't seen him lately.

WINONA: No, Melissa. No! Unsuitable! Graduation is an important ritual. The valedictorian has responsibility. You can't appear with drop-outs. Now don't forget to say something nice about the chairman of the School Board. He's one of Daddy's best customers.

MELISSA: I hate that pink dress, Mother. I hate pink!

WINONA: Don't be ungrateful, Melissa. Parents need gratitude. They can do without many things but they must have gratitude.

MELISSA: How can I be grateful for something I hate?

WINONA: You must try, dear. That's all we ask. Just try. We must have a serious talk, Melissa. . . after we get all the graduation ceremonies behind us. . . Remind me.

MELISSA: About what?

WINONA: A serious talk. About your future. Get it settled.

MELISSA: Mother, I. . . I hear things. Sometimes it frightens me.

WINONA: Hear things? Gossip? Talk?

MELISSA: No. A sound like trumpets blowing, way off, in the middle of the forest.

WINONA: Nonsense. It's in your head. There's no such sound.

MELISSA: Then why. . .?

WINONA: You get that from your father's people.

MELISSA: Did they hear trumpets?

WINONA: They said so. An excuse for self-indulgence. An excuse to sell everything they owned and go off teaching in that jungle. No responsibility, to me, to you, the family. I won't have you hearing trumpets, Melissa. They're dangerous.

MELISSA: And sometimes I hear guns. The sound of guns.

WINONA: Well, of course you hear guns. That's the war.

MELISSA: What war?

WINONA: How would I know what war, Melissa? There's always war. Always has been. Always will be.
I can't understand how a bonded roof could spring a leak. You just can't trust anyone at all. I hope you'll remain a virgin, Melissa. Mother can't be everywhere. Stand up straight. Get dressed and go now.

MELISSA: Yes, Mother.

WINONA: (*Calling after* MELISSA *who starts off left.*) Tell the handy man to bring his own ladder. Then we're not responsible if he falls.

> (MELISSA *goes. There is a strange sound of drip, drip, drip.* WINONA *tries to find the place from which it comes as she sings or recites to a frenetic rythym perhaps plucked on a guitar.*)

WINONA: My bonded roof has sprung a leak
We only built the house last week
What restitution can I seek?

Rain's dripping on the wall to wall
You can't trust anyone at all
Whom to turn to? Whom to call?

What makes this leak in bonded roof
That stains my carpets warf and woof?
Is it beak of bird or devil's hoof?

Whom to call in time of doubt
To restore the roof and mend the spout
To keep the rain and evil out?

It's raining on the wall to wall
I can't trust anyone at all
Whom to turn to? Whom to call?
Who? Who? Whom?

> (*The sound of rain dripping accelerates and is drowned by the sudden boom of guns.* MELISSA *moves on stage left now dressed to go out.*)

MELISSA: The guns! I hear guns, Mother.

WINONA: (*Impatiently*) Of course you hear them. It's just the war. It's trumpets you can't hear, Melissa. Remember that. Go now. Down to the village. (*As the lights go down on her playing area*) And stand up straight, Melissa.

MELISSA: (*Wearily*) Yes, Mother. (*She moves down stage left*) (*Speaking to the audience.*) What do you tell your children when they ask you how to make a life? (*Whispered reverberation. . . "make a life, make a life, make a life."*) Do you know the answers? Do any of you know? I want an answer. There must be something you can tell me. Is there no certain answer?

MARIA: (*As lights go up*) Knit one, purl one, knit one, purl one, knit three. . . .

> (*Sound of wind rising as* JONATHAN *as an old man crosses the stage with an imaginary dog.*)

JONATHAN: Come on, old dog, come on, that's a good dog. Yes, old dog, it's chill when the sun hides. Wind rattles the weed pods, seed pods, chill wind blowing no good. The bones ache in the casement. See my hands, crow claw, clawing at box, pine box, smells of verbena.

MELISSA: Hello, Jonathan.

JONATHAN: I don't seem to recall. . .

MELISSA: Melissa. I used to play under your big pine tree. Remember?

JONATHAN: (*Lost in memory*) Spring and the sweet pine. Oh long-drowned ecstasy and the sun-drowned flesh spilling its seed, star-bursting comet curving to ocean. It's hard to remember spring, Melissa.

MELISSA: Was it a good life, Jonathan?

JONATHAN: Hard to remember spring. (*A sound of muffled drums and the boom of guns.*) Survive. . . that's it. . . survive! Kill or be killed. We learned that early. Kill or be killed. So you killed that other to survive. Cain and Abel. That's how it was, is, has to be. . . kill or be killed.

> (*Whispered reverberation above the sound of drums and guns, "Kill, Kill, Kill. . . Kill, Kill, Kill. . ." crescendo. The drums take a special beat.* MELISSA *stands beside* JONATHAN *as two young men with knives come in circling one another and to the mounting sound play out the killing, their shadows thrown against the back wall with fearful size. One young man falls, the other stands frozen in horror for a moment. . . as the whispered sound "kill, kill, kill" and the guns and drums fade.*)

JONATHAN: Kill or be killed. Get them before they get you. That's how it is, Melissa. Cain and Abel.

Lie down, old dog, lie down. A chill wind this morning. Hard to remember spring.

The deep has many voices so they say, but it's hard to remember spring.

> (MELISSA *moves away from* JONATHAN *who slumps down.* WINONA's *voice comes through microphone calling*)

WINONA: Melissa. Melissa. Melissa.

MELISSA: (*Speaking to audience.*) I'm not going. I hope I'm not. I have to look for something.

When I draw pictures of my family they don't seem real. They turn into things and animals instead of people.

That's true. My father is a turtle chained to a bank. My mother is a pudding chained to a tea pot. My brother turns into a convertible. Our minister's a head of celery, and the teachers are all penguins with True on one side and False on the other.

> (MELISSA *has moved towards centre stage and is overheard by* SARAH)

SARAH: (*to* MARIA) Who'd draw pictures like that?

I think she's touched. . . you know, crazy!

MELISSA: (*Still speaking to audience.*) My best friends look like magpies and all the boys have "out of order" signs on their ear phones.

SARAH: (*To* MARIA) That couldn't happen to me. I have a good grasp on reality.

MELISSA: (*More to herself than anyone.*) So I thought perhaps if I could find my grandparents, they'd be real. (*Speaking to* SARAH *and* MARIA) You wouldn't be. . . . You don't happen to be. . .

SARAH: Oh no, no, no! Certainly not.

MARIA: No, indeed!

MELISSA: (*Turning away from them, looking stage left.*) I wonder what it was like in the old days. Was it easier then to make a life?

> (MITTER *comes in from stage left with two stools that he sets up as if at a coffee bar.*)

MITTER: I cut firewood on my West quarter that year. 51 below. Cold as blue blazes. Smoke, white as a swan's wing, rose straight up like a pillar. Seemed like the earth would crack apart with cold.

JONATHAN: (*No longer old but middle aged. Moves to second stool*) Branches, frost rimmed and bare, bend to the quiet snow. No bird, no rabbit, nothing anywhere.

MITTER: Horses' breath froze to their nostrils. It was cold.

JONATHAN: Cleared my land in the fall. Poplars blaze down the coulee. Which way you look is Moses burning bush. Red rose haws hang from the thorny branch like the tree of life itself.

MITTER: The black bitter fruit of the wild cherry makes good wine.

JONATHAN: Days of wine and rose, wild geese arrowing south, high, high.

SARAH: (*remaining in position*) How high the sky is, high, high, hiding the face of God from me and mine.
The Mormon missionaries came to call and they were young.

MARIA: My friend's a Mormon. She works for the dead. Three days a week she makes her visitation to the temple helping the ancient dead. But who's to help the living? Answer that, Melissa.

MELISSA: Couldn't we. . . help each other?

MARIA: We tried that once. It didn't work.

JONATHAN: Your turn to buy the coffee, Mitter.

MITTER: Sure. Come on, Melissa, I'll buy you coffee too.

MELISSA: (*Moving to them*) Why, thank you, Mitter. Thank you.

MITTER: Three mugs of Java. Cream and sugar too.
(JUDITH *enters with the coffee.*)

JUDITH: Three it is, and hot.
(*The lights are centred on down stage front as a small group of boys or young men march in to the beat of drum. Occasionally the roll of guns can be heard off.*)

SOLDIERS: Get tough, get tough, the thing to do is get tough.
Be tough, be tough, you must be tough and rough
Get tough, get tough, if you're not tough enough
You'll find the other fellow can get rough, get tough, get tough.
Get tough, get tough, you must be tough enough
Get tough, get tough, the other fellow's rough.
(*The soldiers chant this as they march to the drum beat. Chanting the soldiers march from right to left and off.* WILLIE THANIS *stops stage right and remains behind.* OLLIE *sees him stop and turns and comes back to him.*)

OLLIE: Look Willie, you want your ass kicked by old Sarge?

WILLIE: I'm sick of playing soldier. I don't want to get tough. I don't want to kill somebody.

OLLIE: You got to survive, Willie. Anyway we won't have to kill them face to face. This ain't the old days.

WILLIE: Then why do we practise with rifles and bayonets?

OLLIE: For discipline. But in a real war we can sit up in the sky and let them have it. . . let everybody have it. Boom!

361

Gwen Pharis Ringwood

WILLIE: Yeah, everybody might be my brother or a girl or some kid.
Might even be you, old Ollie. . .
(Off stage sound of drum and voice.)
SGT.: *(Off)* Company, fall in.
OLLIE: Come on, Willie. Come on.
(OLLIE runs off. WILLIE hesitates, pondering. MELISSA, standing in the cafe sees WILLIE and moves slightly towards him.)
MELISSA: Willie. . . Willie Thanis.
(WILLIE doesn't see her and he goes off thoughtfully after the other soldiers. STEVE is tall, western, a kind of gleam of adventure about him.)
STEVE: He didn't see you, honey.
MELISSA: No. He never does.
STEVE: If he'd seen you, he'd have come a running. Believe me.
MITTER: Hi, Steve. Where you driving?
STEVE: *(Moving to "cafe" MELISSA following)* Pine Pass. That road's murder. Snow, black ice, can't see the edge. I almost got it last night.
MELISSA: What happened to you?
STEVE: *(Taking a coffee from JUDITH as he passes her)* I'm on this steep downhill turn, come round it and there's this shape in front of me, no way around it. Nowhere to go.
MITTER: Another car?
STEVE: *(Shaking his head.)* Young moose. Not five feet from my headlights when I skid to a stop. That's right. Not five feet. He had slipped on the ice, and gone down to his knees. You ever seen a young moose close?
MITTER: Yeah. I've seen them. Long, slender legs like they can't bear his weight. Loose hide.
STEVE: Hide red-brown and loose. Strange looking. . . spraddled like that he looked grotesque and strange. Helpless. There in my headlights. Finally he managed to get on his feet. He looked proud then. His head bearing those antlers lifted to the light. Then he edged off the road and with one leap was up the snowbank. I could see him start up the mountain, a mountain king . . . that's what he was. . . king of the mountain. Funny thing. . . I felt lonesome after he'd gone. Real lonesome.
MELISSA: I know. Like you were empty, like you were missing something.
STEVE: Yeah, honey, like that. He was strong and sure footed once he got where he belonged.
MELISSA: Tell me, in the mountains. . . do you hear any sound?
STEVE: What kind of sound?
MELISSA: Don't laugh. Sometimes I think that from deep in the forest comes a sound of trumpets blowing. Maybe I imagine it. . .
STEVE: I think I know the sound. Yeah.

JONATHAN: Could be the wind. The wind makes strange noises.

MITTER: Elks make a strange sound. Could be an elk, you know.

STEVE: (*To* MELISSA) I've heard horns, trumpets. . . something like that I think. But don't be following them into the deep forest, honey. We don't want to lose you.

MELISSA: You didn't lose the young moose and he left. You didn't lose him. I'd better go now.

STEVE: Me too. Time I got a move on. See you Mitter, Jonathan. Judith.

> (*He is moving away*)

JUDITH: So long, Steve. Be good.

> (*Calling*)

MITTER: If you can't be good, be careful. So long, Steve.

> (*Calling. The words "So long" reverberate over and over softly and are topped by a faint sound of horns off as Steve moves away.* MELISSA *starts to move down but is frozen as the soldiers march in again this time to a wordless chant. Drums. Ah bah ah bah ah bah a dum a dah ah chee ah cho a cha a chee a cho etc.*)

SGT.: Company, Charge.

> (*The others charge as if with fixed bayonets but* WILLIE *and* OLLIE *drop back as the rest move off left.*)

WILLIE: I don't like the music. I don't like the tune.

OLLIE: Stop buttin' your head, Willie. We got no say about the tune.

WILLIE: That's a lie. I have a say.

OLLIE: You just pretend to yourself.

WILLIE: I can choose my own music. Play another tune.

OLLIE: Try it, Willie. Just try.

Don't you want to be a success, make your old man proud of you?

WILLIE: What about just living, thinking, feeling. . . that's success.

OLLIE: For the saints maybe. In this town you got to own two cars, a split-level random ranch house, and you deep-freeze your six antlered hand-shot bull elk to barbecue in the backyard. That's success. You can't fight it.

WILLIE: I'm a human being ain't I? I got a will. A human being can change things. Like Gandhi. Like Shaftesbury. Jesus.

OLLIE: We still got war, Willie. Nothing you can do will change the way things are.

WILLIE: That's a lie!

OLLIE: Lay off. I didn't make the world.

WILLIE: It's people like you are going to blow it up. . . A man can change things! What's the use of living if. . .

OLLIE: Show me, Willie. Show me.

> (*He goes off as the drum sound increases and then fades.* WILLIE *stands looking after* OLLIE, *then turns the other way and starts to go out.* MELISSA *comes down, calling after him.*)

MELISSA: Willie. Willie Thanis.

(For a moment he seems to hear her but then decides no one called and he is gone. MELISSA *sits disconsolately on the steps.* SARAH *and* MARIA *get up.)*

MARIA: Time to plant the pansies, Sarah. Where are they?

SARAH: Here. *(She unwraps them carefully from the newspaper.)* You're sure it's not too early?

MARIA: Of course I'm sure. I'll do it. You never get them straight.

SARAH: I don't like them straight. I like them crooked.

MARIA: I knew you'd say that. You were always muddled. Even as a girl. You were pretty, Sarah, but you were always muddled.

SARAH: And you were always bossy. Maria! *(She is reading the newspaper.)* Albert Einstein is dead. See, it says it here. . . in the paper. Einstein is dead. Oh. . . .

MARIA: He died a long time ago, Sarah. That's an old paper.

SARAH: I hadn't heard. *(Pause)* I feel lonely now.

MARIA: You didn't even know him.

SARAH: I knew about him. He didn't believe in clocks. He didn't believe in time either. And he wrote mathematics that changed the world altogether. I feel lonely now.

MARIA: You're putting on airs, Sarah.

SARAH: I'm not! It takes brains to be a genius.

MARIA: Yes. That Gandhi running around everywhere in a loin cloth!

*(*MELISSA *approaches.)*

MELISSA: Good morning.

MARIA: Hello, my dear.

SARAH: We were just talking about a man named Gandhi.

MELISSA: I know. He led the Salt March.

SARAH: I remember. It was like music. It started small and became bigger and bigger and more and more until your heart felt it would burst its skin. Like Jesus riding a donkey into Jerusalemn.

MARIA: *(Crossly)* I never heard of anything like a Salt March.

SARAH: Oh yes, it happened.

MARIA: But in the Depression, the unemployed were marching to Ottawa and in Regina the police fired on them. I saw that happen.

MELISSA: Fired on them with guns?

MARIA: They did.

MELISSA: But why, Maria. . . if they were only marching.

MARIA: They were marching because they were hungry. People are afraid of hungry people. You know that.

SARAH: I'm glad I didn't see that. *(Deliberately cheerful)* Nobody needs to go hungry any more. That's one thing. Why, my son makes a hundred dollars a day just feeding facts to a Unicorn.

MELISSA: A Unicorn?

SARAH: A big machine, dear. It eats facts and sorts them out.

MELISSA: Oh. I think you mean a Univac.

364

SARAH: Univac. Unicorn. What difference? Just a word somebody made up. A hundred dollars is a lot of money. I'll keep this paper about Einstein. We need great men. (*Pause*) Did you want something, dear?

MELISSA: No. . . I. . . I don't know. Sarah, in the old days did you ever go far into the forest?

MARIA: Of course not.

SARAH: That deep wood's hungry as a unicorn and swallows people.

MARIA: You said Unicorn again. It's univac. U N I V A C.

SARAH: Leave me alone, Maria.

MARIA: Words are important, Sarah.

SARAH: I hate the pansies straight. And he had a perfect right to wear a loin cloth. Anybody has. I'm going in. It might be time for lunch.

MARIA: (*Impatiently*) Oh, I'll come with you. (*To* MELISSA) She was muddled even as a girl.

(*The two little ladies start off right.*)

MELISSA: (*To the audience.*) She said "we need great men". I wonder why people never talk about great women. I should think we'd need great women too.

MARIA: (*Turning back and speaking sharply*) Our bodies weren't designed for greatness, Melissa. Our bodies were designed to bear children and to nurture them. We supply the great men. Then we can bask in their reflected glory. That's how it is. . . ask any woman here. . . (*She glances briefly at the audience*) You see.

(*And* MARIA *goes off after* SARAH)

MELISSA: (*to audience*) Why should we have to bask in reflected glory? We have minds of our own. Why should we. . . .

WINONA: (*Calling*) Melissa. Melissa. Melissa. (*Reverberation.*)

MELISSA: (*Turning away*) Oh dear, I'd better find Mr. Thanis.

(*Off stage there is a sound of* MR. THANIS *singing a Greek song.* MR. THANIS *comes in towards stage centre with his folding ladder and tool box. On the wooden tool box is pasted a post card showing the Acropolis of Athens.* MR. THANIS *places the tool box on the bench, sets up the ladder and is starting up it when* MELISSA *comes to him. He breaks off the song when he sees her.*)

THANIS: Ah, good morning, young lady.

MELISSA: You're Mr. Thanis?

THANIS: I am. Come in. What can I do?

MELISSA: I'm Melissa Andrews. Our roof has a hole in it. My mother asks would you be able to come and mend it, please.

THANIS: Of course I come. "Handyman Service, day and night. . . Your trouble is our delight." That's what my sign says.

MELISSA: And bring your own ladder, please.

THANIS: I will. After I eat something.

MELISSA: You live alone, Mr. Thanis? I thought your son lives with you.

365

Gwen Pharis Ringwood

THANIS: Yes, my son, Niko. But he is off practising to be a soldier.

MELISSA: The boy I know is *Willie* Thanis.

THANIS: That is my boy. When he first goes to school his teachers said Niko was too. . . too strange. They called him Willie.

MELISSA: Niko. That's a nice name. (*Looking at postcard.*) This is the Acropolis!

THANIS: That's right. You recognize!

MELISSA: Oh yes. I'd like to see it. To stand on the Acropolis.

THANIS: Is beautiful. My home was Athens.

MELISSA: Say something in Greek please. Say "how are you".

THANIS: Sure. It is "takarnite"

MELISSA: Takarnite. How are you.

THANIS: And if things go well you answer "Carroll."

MELISSA: Takarnite. Carroll.

THANIS: You know my name rhymes with Acropolis, until I change it.

MELISSA: Why did you change your name?

THANIS: No one could say my name here.

MELISSA: I could say it.

THANIS: Without stumbling or making jokes?

MELISSA: Yes, I can.

THANIS: (*Coming down the ladder*) My name is Thanitopolis. Thanitopolis of Athens, Precinct Nine.

MELISSA: Hi, Mr. Thanitopolis. Takarnite?

THANIS: Carroll, Melissa. Thank you very much.

MELISSA: So Willie isn't Willie Thanis. He's Niko Thanitopolis.

THANIS: I don't know who Willie is. He's looking for himself. My son is a philosopher, Melissa. He takes after his mother's side. She was a Stephanides from Mycenae, and they're deep people. Deep.

MELISSA: Oh. (*Pause. Then comfortingly.*) Well, we can't all be deep, Mr. Thanitopolis.

THANIS: That's true. That's very true. It isn't exactly that I mind not being deep, Melissa. It's only. . . well, I often wish I was deeper than I am. . . if you understand me.

MELISSA: Oh I do. I understand very well. I feel the same. It's hard to make a life.

THANIS: Work helps. Mending things. That can be important.

MELISSA: Oh yes. Very. Do you get lonely for the Acropolis?

THANIS: Sometimes.

MELISSA: Did you go up there and stand on the Acropolis?

THANIS: I did, often.

MELISSA: Did you ever hear anything. . . a sound as if. . .

THANIS: A sound?

MELISSA: Like something was calling you. Like trumpets blowing.

THANIS: Something calling. . .? I think this is so, Melissa. I was young then. I think I heard them. But its a long time since then now. (*Pause*) Well, I come in an hour, Melissa. Bring my ladder.

MELISSA: Say hello to your son Niko, please Mr. Thanitopolis.

THANIS: Thank you, I will. He says he must find out who he is. I don't know. . . does anybody find out Melissa?

MELISSA: Didn't you?

THANIS: I. . . no. . . I don't know. I don't even have the same name now. So easy to lose track. Bit by bit, moment by moment, one loses track. "Prosehe". . . that's Greek for "Take care".

MELISSA: Prosehe.

(Fairly far off there is a sound of horns. MR. THANIS takes out his ladder and tool box. MELISSA moves down stage centre. MITTER and TOMMY move in down left, followed by JONATHAN. MARIA and SARAH come in down right. JUDITH moves towards MELISSA. MIRIAM appears on the level above them. After the sound of horns there is a muffled roll of drums which becomes louder as the people above move into position. MIRIAM is a middle aged beautiful woman who moves like Martha Graham in a dance of despair.)

MIRIAM: *(A whispered plea that spreads over the audience.)* Help me. Help me.

MELISSA: *(Low voiced.)* Who is she, Judith? Who is she?

JUDITH: Her name is Miriam.

SARAH: She stands at the window, looking at the village.

MARIA: And in her mind her empty travelling bags are packed and waiting. . .

MIRIAM: All packed and waiting, underwear neatly folded, basic dress in black, hat, gloves, crinoline for the bombazine all packed for nowhere.

(Sound "nowhere" reverberates softly through the hall.)

SARAH: The morning is October the air is gray, the hills gray green like sleeping bears around the village.

MARIA: Grass gray brown and the trees are gray with one yellow leaf quivering on a poplar.

MIRIAM: How long can the leaf hold out? Will it reach November?

JUDITH: October, November, the sound is soft in an empty room. The sound is regretting, remembering and regretting.

MITTER: Soft in November comes the first snow fall when all small animals make hieroglyphs, antique hieroglyphs on new-fallen snow.

TOMMY: Made in the swift night-rushing.

JONATHAN: Dog and rabbit or a cat moving unfettered, uncommitted from crumpled weed clump to the shadowed wall.

JUDITH: Her name is Miriam.

MARIA: She stands looking at the village.

MIRIAM: Waiting for spring. Oh willow, wait. Oh willow, weep for me.

(The light changes to a golden sunlight and on the backdrop is projected flickering spring green leaf and shadow, flowers. All of the characters gradually take on a stance of youth as they watch MITTER and JUDITH play out the following small scene for MELISSA.)

Gwen Pharis Ringwood

MITTER: Ah, Judith, they were good days. . . we owned the land. We
gathered bright apples, stored them in the loft, there was the
smell of cedar, hay.
JUDITH: (*Her voice young and vibrant*) Sweet cream in the stone house,
cheese and butter.
MITTER: That white Percheron team that pulled the plough.
JUDITH: The patchwork quilt in gingham, feather-stitch. The birth
of children.
MITTER: We paid our debts, I kept books, we sent our children out
better clothed than we were
JUDITH: We gave them schooling. That was the key we thought. Learn-
ing was the key.
MITTER: I tried to live by the good book, Judith, hurt no one.
JUDITH: You weren't cross or boastful. You've nothing to regret. We
chose the good road, Mitter, it was spring, remember. Can you
remember spring?
MITTER: I remember.
(*The rest join in and all the characters become young as they
mime a tennis game or bouncing a ball, flying kites, etc.
During the following scene.*)
MARIA: Spring is a good time, Sarah. Sun rises early, windows turn
to gold.
SARAH: See how jewels hang on leaf and blade and the lake shines like
mirror under the spledid sun.
MARIA: Sun mounts the sky like a prince in a chariot.
JONATHAN: And the dew-washed grass is knife-bright, life-bright
under the splendid sun.
MITTER: Spring is a good time, fly time, my time,
Squirrels chatter and the small creeks run.
SARAH: Spring is spring green with a daffodil sun
And all down the hillside the small creeks run
JONATHAN: To the angry dark river and the caves of the sea.
MITTER: Spring is a good time, fly time, my time.
JUDITH: Spring is sweet wine and a daffodil sun.
SARAH: Squirrels chatter and the small creeks run
To the singing dark river and the caves of the sea.
JUDITH: Do you remember spring, Mitter?
MITTER: I remember.
(*Once more the sound of wild geese flying over rises, fades.
They all freeze in their young positions for a moment. Then
as the lights go down and change and as an ominous roll of
thunder is heard they assume once more their middle age or
old bodies. MIRIAM is once more the centre as she moves
forward. . . .*)
MIRIAM: Oh willow, wait. Oh willow, weep for me.
MELISSA: What does she look for, Judith?

JUDITH: She stands at the window, hunting the destination, stands idly pin-pricking at the turning globe. Journeys not taken, journeys yet to take.

MELISSA: Inside and outside. Oh my child, my husband, oh my friends, see how I run to where you stood, run with my arms out, coming, coming, this time not too late. And all you dead, all you beloved dead, listen. . . I remember how you smiled and spoke and that your words somewhere still ripple in the quivering air.

MARIA: Unfinished sentences, poems half written,—

SARAH: Words spoken long ago falling like snowflakes in a crystal ball.

MARIA: Arms linked in childhood.

MIRIAM: Nights full with love, perambulating days, meal time and bed time, work and play. . .
Domestic tasks, husband and children, community and school associations.

SARAH: Don't bite your nails in public, learn your spelling.

MARIA: That's a bad boy to make pee patterns in the rusty snow.

JUDITH: Schubert's tall symphony and Handel's Largo invigorate the air stream. Could deaf Beethoven wear a hearing aid?

MIRIAM: But there are things not thought on for a long time now, things never thought on for a long time now.

JONATHAN: Hide them beneath the carpet, sweep them under. . .
Still murder will out, murder will out and the dark stain spreads. . . .

MIRIAM: Belsen belches its stench and the long gray train stops while they shuffle out, old men and children.

MITTER: Women with stone faces and a young girl with burning eyes.

MIRIAM: A girl clutching a handbag hiding a comb and a child's toy, a pair of socks and a pin shaped like a butterfly. All gone. All murdered.

MELISSA: Oh no. No.

MIRIAM: Then there's this woman, Japanese, up early stirring the porridge, waters a flower, glances at sleeping children.

SARAH: Suckles the nuzzling infant, soft cheek on breast.

MITTER: Across the street a boy wakes, wanting a drink of water.

JONATHAN: And a man threads new laces into old boots, preparing to go fishing.

MIRIAM: The cone mushrooms in blinding beauty, does them to death, some quickly, and the stain spreads into the oncoming phalanx of the years.
(*To the drums the young trainees march through chanting ah bah ah bah. They march deliberately over the pansies* SARAH *and* MARIA *had placed and go out on their wordless chant.* WILLIE *is not with them.* MIRIAM *moves down to* MELISSA, *looks long into her face.*)

MIRIAM: You see, it is not enough to nurture a family, seek friendship, accept the minister's pronouncement on the will of God. When

Gwen Pharis Ringwood

that's all done and neatly written down and rolled up like a
parchment, then you see it's not enough. The quick and dead
still beat against the skull bone. A skull's too small for living.
(*Turns away*) You feet of Belsen shuffle some other corridor,
pilgrims of Canterbury, Sacho and Vanzetti, Robespierre, I
can't contain you. Nor the Bacchanalian Attic celebrants with
flowing hair, satyrs or saints, Nansen or Schweitzer, Lincoln,
Socrates, you Kennedys or Kings, I can't contain you. Leave me
alone. Nor brown-faced Gandhi, barefoot in the desert, nor the
Golgothan cross. Stay outside. This skull's too small for living.
No room. No room.
JUDITH: The morning is October.
SARAH: Time is an instant.
MARIA: Macbeth as real as Diefenbaker.
MITTER: And a world beats at the skull bone, the quick, the dead
beating against the skull bone.
MIRIAM: (*Moving towards* JUDITH) Could you see to the children,
Judith. . . move them on, get rid of them somehow. You see,
they're not my children. But they stand there, stand raising their
toothpick arms, gnawing at withered apples, stand, whimpering
like dogs while the black smoke spreads over the bleached and
hollow bones, over the skulking wolf and the hollow bones. My
children were not hungry, not once, not ever. Tell me they're not
my children, Judith. Tell me.
(*She looks from* JUDITH *to the others but there is no answer.
She moves back to her original playing space.*)
JONATHAN: (*As if memorizing a meaningless phrase.*)
Amo amas amat amamus amatis amant
I love you love he loves we love you love they love
Amo amare amo amas amat amamus amatis amant amo
amare.
MIRIAM: (*In a removed flat tone, drained of feeling.*)
When I was nine I dreamed of the apocalypse with fire-rimmed
saucers floating down to claim the blest and save them from the
vultures. I was chosen for the resurrection and yet I woke up
crying. I think now I would choose to stay on the riven planet,
choose to view the apocalypse from here rather than catapult to
glory. Yes, better to die on this small beloved earth than take part
in some unearthly glory. One could perhaps shelter a flower,
shelter a single seed of some small flower, salvage something. I'd
like that. (*To* MELISSA) So you see, dear child, all those half
truths, the good intentions, domestic virtues, all those singalongs
were not enough. . . statistically summed up they amount to
nothing. There must be some other road if one can find it.
(*Turning away from them all*) Oh my world, see how I run back
now, run with my arms out, coming, coming this time not too
late.

JUDITH: The morning is October. Miriam stands gazing at the window and in the hall her empty travelling bags are packed for. . .

MIRIAM: (*Looking off stage right and then going off that way*) Oh willow weep, oh willow wait for me.

MELISSA: (*Running to* JUDITH) I'm afraid now, Judith. I'm afraid. I can't find any answers. Help me.

JUDITH: Don't ask me, child. Don't ask me. I can't help you.

MELISSA: (*Turning to* MITTER) Mitter. . . .

MITTER: I can't help you, Melissa. I have to go. . . You see I've always known there was some road I should find and travel. . . but I put it off. (*To* JUDITH) Forgive me, I'm going now. Will you come?

JUDITH: Through the forest. . . into the deep woods?

MITTER: Yes.

JUDITH: (*After a pause.*) I can't, Mitter. I'm safe here. I'm afraid to go with you. I can't go.

SARAH: They say deep in the woods you find a mirror and when you look in it, the barnacles fall from you. . . what would be left then? Who'd want that?

MITTER: Goodbye now. Goodbye Melissa. Judith. Jonathan.

JONATHAN: So long, Mitter.

(*Their voices echo in waves of soft "So long, so long so long."* MITTER *goes out right not on the high ramp but on a lower incline. Far off is the sound of horns*)

JUDITH: You could have gone with Mitter, Melissa.

MELISSA: How could he leave you alone like that?

JUDITH: He's alone too, Melissa. We all are. Part of everything but separate too. He had to leave me.

MELISSA: (*Turning away*) Part of everything but separate. That's no answer. Look at these pansies. . . they're not part of anything. They're dead. (*Ruthlessly she throws away the pansy she has picked up.*) You're nothing when you're dead. So what's the use of anything?

(*The lights change and a pulsating rock rhythm engulfs the space. Dancers, some masked, some without masks, some are the young men of the marching trainees, surround* MELISSA *and cause the others to shrink back. Whispered allurements come over the music as some of the dancers approach* MELISSA.)

DANCER: Hi, baby, wanta fly. . . come on. . . we'll fly, fly, fly. . .

(*There is a mask of the wolf, the falcon, the spiked helmet and cruel mask of war, the soft appealing mask of a lotus eater. . . among the wildly dancing crowd, a discotheque peopled with* MELISSA's *contemporaries and nightmare figures.*)

DANCER: Let's live. Live. Live. Fly. Fly. Fly. Live. Fly. Come on baby. . . come on baby. . . fly. . .

(MELISSA *is surrounded, pulled into the dance, moved from*

Gwen Pharis Ringwood

one dancer to another and the dance becomes wild as something uncontrolled and nightmarish takes over. . . Suddenly MELISSA *cries out and runs from the dancers as if escaping)*

MELISSA: No. No. No.

(She sinks down crouched and afraid. As MELISSA *screams "no" the music breaks off suddenly and the dancers and other characters (on the edge of the playing spaces) freeze.* WILLIE *enters stage right opposite* MELISSA *stage left. He searches the crowd with his eyes as if impelled to look for* MELISSA *but he doesn't find her and sits down. From the mouths of the frozen dancers come the following lines thrown on top of one another.)*

YOUNG MAN: The system's rotten, rotten to the core.
Smash the system. . .

YOUNG GIRL: I can't go home. I didn't get along with them.
I can't go home again. . . not any more.

SECOND GIRL: They send me money so's I'll stay away.

2ND MAN: Smash the bitch goddess. Pull her down and down.

3RD MAN: I went back twice. I tried, but we were strangers.

YOUNG GIRL: It's boring, boring, boring. . .

YOUNG MAN: I wouldn't mind a war. A war's exciting.

YOUNG MAN: Rats running in a maze. We're trapped like rats that are running in a maze. There's no escape.

YOUNG MAN: No use. No use. No use in anything.

YOUNG GIRL: We need a water bed. We have to have it.
We have so much to buy. More every day.
So many things to buy.

YOUNG GIRL: I can't go home again. Not now. Not ever.

(The dancers regroup as a roll of drums and muffled sound of guns is heard. Some (those masked) stay frozen. . . others group into the Hare Krishna chanters, the Catholic penitents, the United Church Marching Christians, and the evangelical Jesus people. There is a sound of bells. . .)

(The Catholic penitents kneel and begin chanting the Miserere in Latin or English
Hail, Mary, mother of God, blessed be the fruit of thy womb, Jesus etc. . . .)

(From another space comes the chant and bells ring off
Hare Krishna, Hare Krishna, Hare, Hare, Hare, Krishna Hare Rama, Hare Rama, Hare Hare, Hare, Rama)

(Again the sound of bells)

(The Evangelist
Follow Follow Follow The only way to salvation is to be born again in Jesus. . . born again. . . be born, be born, be born again. . . Brother and Sister, follow, follow.)

(*During this scene slides of pagan, primitive, Egyptian, Christian, Eastern religious paintings are projected*)
(MELISSA *gets up.* . . *moves first to one group then another. Sound of bells*)
(*The Christian soldiers stand and march on the spot. Singing:*
    Onward Christian Soldiers, marching as to WAR
    With the Cross of Jesus, going on before.
    Christ, the royal banner leads against the foe.
    Onward into Battle see our armies go.*)
(*Bells*)
(*A fifth group take the half-lotus position and begin intoning*
    Ohm mane padre hum. . . Ohm mana padre hum. . .
    etc.*)
(WILLIE *looks from one group to another without moving in.* . . MELISSA *moves towards them and away*)
(*Bells ring wildly and suddenly all of the groups are competing with one another in a bedlam. The paintings overlap on the back drop.* MELISSA *screams and runs down stage centre, falling on her knees and rocking.* . .)

MELISSA: Oh, I don't know. I don't know.
    (*Softly all the people on stage disappear except* MELISSA *crouched down stage centre and* WILLIE *looking off down stage right.*)

WILLIE: I think and I think and I think. But I don't find any answers.

MELISSA: (*Almost a whisper*) Willie. . . Niko. . . Niko Thanitopolis. . .
    (*A despairing little cry.*)
    (WILLIE *pauses, looks but does not find her and sinks down as the lights go off him and* MELISSA. *The lights come up on the upper stage where* WINONA *and* MELISSA *played their first scene. Sound of* MR. THANIS *singing as he enters. Carrying tool box and ladder he turns to* WINONA *who follows him.*)

WINONA: Well, Mr. Thanis, I'm sure you've fixed the roof as good as new. What a relief.

THANIS: No ma'am.

WINONA: You haven't fixed it?

THANIS: I patched up the leak, Mrs. but there'll be others. Soon.

WINONA: But my roof's bonded. This is a good district. Floating policy. Indefeasible title. White supremacy. Capital gain.

THANIS: You've no security against. . . them, Mrs.

WINONA: Against who? whom?

THANIS: Them. The carpenter ants.

WINONA: The what?

THANIS: Carpenter ants. They explore, burrow, bore. They can reduce you to sawdust before you know it. Oh they're bad ones, Mrs.

WINONA: I'll hire an exterminator.

THANIS: You can try that.

WINONA: You sound sceptical. Don't you realize that I can't be reduced to sawdust? It's unthinkable.

THANIS: Yes, Mrs.

WINONA: Well, isn't it?

THANIS: Not for them. Carpenter ants will go to a lot of trouble to eat up your house, Mrs. In my experience you haven't got a chance against carpenter ants. There's only one way to fool them.

WINONA: What's that?

THANIS: Move. Move away. Move on. Move upward. Move out.

WINONA: Leave my house, Mr. Thanis? Is that your advice?

THANIS: Yes. Leave your shell behind, Mrs.

WINONA: You're frightening me.

THANIS: I'm sorry, Mrs.

WINONA: What kind of a handyman is that? Going around frightening people. Send me your bill.

THANIS: Yes, Mrs.

WINONA: And if I were you, I'd get rid of that old world superstition about carpenter ants. . . . (*Recovering*) Things are different here. You've come to a great new free enterprise country where everyone has a chance to win the lottery. You must adapt. You understand that I'm only trying to help you.

THANIS: I do. I do.

WINONA: Where can Melissa have gone? She should be here by now. If you see her, tell her. . . .

THANIS: Tell her?

WINONA: Oh, there were so many things I meant to tell her. Mr. Thanis. . . You're not a Pisces are you?

THANIS: Oh no, Scorpio.

WINONA: Oh that accounts for it. (*He looks puzzled.*) Your superstition about the carpenter ants. Pisces wouldn't give them the time of day. Goodbye, Mr. Thanis.

THANIS: Goodbye, Mrs.

(*He goes.* WINONA *moves distractedly towards* MELISSA)

WINONA: Melissa! Melissa?

Oh, there are so many things I meant to tell you.

MELISSA: (*From far down the world*) (*Eagerly, Importunately.*) What things, Mother? Tell me, what things?

WINONA: (*Not speaking directly to* MELISSA *who has remained down stage crouched on the step.*) Well, I meant to tell you. . . Oh, of course, I remember. . .

Watch your posture, be a lady, stand up straight.

Say nice things about your teachers, don't be late,

Eat your porridge without urging

Don't forget to stay a virgin

Be a lady, watch your posture, stand up straight.

And. . . and there was something else. . .

MELISSA: Yes, Mother. Tell me. Tell me.

WINONA: Oh, I. . . I don't know. Where is that girl?
(WINONA *goes off up stage left.* MELISSA *beats her fists on the step in despair*)
MELISSA: Oh, I hate. I hate. I hate.
(WILLIE *hears her crying and moves across from stage right towards* MELISSA).
WILLIE: Melissa.
MELISSA: Willie. . .
WILLIE: Hi.
MELISSA: Hi.
WILLIE: You're a long way from your house.
MELISSA: Yes, I am.
WILLIE: I haven't seen you for a long time.
(*He stands, looking down at her uncertainly*)
MELISSA: I haven't seen you for a long time either.
WILLIE: I've been busy. Since I left school. Trying to sort things out.
MELISSA: I know. Finding yourself. Your father told me.
WILLIE: He doesn't know about me. Nobody does.
MELISSA: I suppose that's right. I know your real name though. You're Niko Thanitopolis.
WILLIE: You can say it! That's great. (*Pause.*) I phoned you twice and left my number for you to call and then I phoned again but your mother said she thought I might as well stop phoning. I thought so too on account of you never called me. I left my number.
MELISSA: I didn't know you called. I would have called back, if I'd known you called.
WILLIE: I thought you didn't want to talk to me.
MELISSA: I did, Willie. I did.
WILLIE: I'll be leaving soon, I guess.
MELISSA: Leaving?
WILLIE: Hmm. Soon as I fix my bike. I'll be on my way.
MELISSA: Where?
WILLIE: All over. I'm going to roam the planet. I'm going to know its roads, and its swimming holes and where you can get a good cup of coffee, and where the wild flowers grow. The whole thing.
MELISSA: That sounds wonderful. What will your father say?
WILLIE: He'll say "God take care of my son, Niko. Don't let the dragons get him." And my Uncle will say "That damn fool should have stayed home and learned the business and not go running off."
MELISSA: What about your brother?
WILLIE: I don't have a brother, but if I had he'd say: "Now Niko's gone I can have his room. I'll move in tonight." That's what he'd say all right.
MELISSA: What about your girl friend? What will she say?
WILLIE: Well, I'll go round and kiss her on the mouth and pull her red hair and say "I won't be back until I've killed the dragon. It's

me or him." She'll cry, and watch me go, and then put curlers in her hair and say "I don't figure to wait around for Willie, while he's off chasing dragons."

MELISSA: (*Smiling*) No, she won't. She'll wait.

WILLIE: I don't have a girl friend. Except you. I mean maybe I could come and say goodbye to you, before I go.

MELISSA: Oh please do. Do you. . . do you have to go away?

WILLIE: (*Looking into her eyes*) I think so. I can't hang around home forever.

MELISSA: Willie, do you ever hear sounds, coming out of the deep woods?
        (*She glances off up right.*)

WILLIE: I've heard guns. But not from there.

MELISSA: Not guns. A different sound. . . like trumpets blowing. . . calling. . .

WILLIE: What do they say?

MELISSA: I don't know. Something inside me tries to tell me. . . maybe. . . maybe they say. . .

WILLIE: Survive?

MELISSA: Not just that. Change. Change things. Change the world.

WILLIE: Hah. It sure needs changing. You know Melissa, maybe we could. . . after all, we're human beings. We're not cabbages or muskrats. We have will power. We could change things. I believe that. But I don't hear the sounds. . .

MELISSA: I wish you'd hear them. You'd know what I mean. It's like they called you to go farther into the deep woods Willie. I heard an old man say "The deep has many voices." I think he must have heard. . .

WILLIE: The deep has many voices. That's for sure. (*Pause.*)
        I could walk home with you, if you want.

MELISSA: Thank you. I wanted to ask you something. Would you. . . the graduation dance is Saturday. Would you be my escort to the dance?

WILLIE: I wouldn't mind. I wouldn't mind at all. I mean I will. I'd like to.

MELISSA: I'm glad.

WILLIE: What about your mother? If I'm not suitable to telephone, I won't be suitable to take you to that dance.

MELISSA: My mother's only mixed up, Willie. She's all right.

WILLIE: I'll feel scared. But I'll lay my foot down. I'll call for you at eight.

MELISSA: Thank you.

WILLIE: I'm always saying a man has a will. That he can change things. It's time I started.
        (*Improvising.*) I'll walk up to your door and simply knock. I'll put on a tie and jacket, and I'll knock.
        (*The game takes over.*)

Should the hankie in my pocket match my sock?
When I walk up to your door and simply knock.
   (*He is miming the action.*)
MELISSA: (*Delighted with the game.*)
   Shine your shoes up like a rocket.
   Put a hankie in your pocket
   Then you walk up to my door and simply knock.
WILLIE: I'll say: "I've come to take Melissa to the dance."
   I'll be wearing my best jacket. . .
MELISSA: And some pants.
   Oh, she'll rejoice to see her daughter have the chance.
   (*She offers him her hand as in a minuet*)
WILLIE: (*Twirling her around*) To go dancing, dancing, dancing at the dance.
   (*As he brings her around they move together in a loving kiss.*)
WILLIE: (*Breathlessly.*) You're beautiful.
MELISSA: You too. (*Pause.*) I. . . I have to get home.
   I'll see you Saturday.
WILLIE: I can walk you to your gate. I've got time.
MELISSA: Come on, then.
   (*They go out stage left down stage.*)
WINONA: (*Returning to up stage space*) Melissa. Melissa!
MELISSA: (*Calling off.*) Coming, Mother. Coming.
   (*As MELISSA moves towards the upper playing space and WINONA, WILLIE comes from off stage left and crosses to down stage right whistling the happy Greek folk song that his father sang earlier. MELISSA moves as one lost in a dream of love moves. As WILLIE goes off right WINONA speaks crossly.*)
WINONA: Well, Melissa! Where were you? You've been no help at all.
MELISSA: I'm sorry, Mother. I've been. . . I've been a long way.
WINONA: The Bradley boy is coming home, Melissa. His mother is sure he'll be delighted to take you to the dance. So suitable. The Bradleys are one of your father's largest depositors.
MELISSA: I have an escort, Mother.
WINONA: What's that?
MELISSA: I asked Willie Thanis to the dance. His real name is Niko Thanitopolis. He's taking me.
WINONA: I told you, he's not suitable. I thought I made it plain. After all your father and I have planned. The loving care. You'll have to tell him you've changed your mind.
MELISSA: No, Mother. I won't change my mind.
WINONA: You must. You have to. Why do you want to upset me?
MELISSA: I don't. I just won't change my mind.
WINONA: Oh. I hope that boy appreciates the honor. With that queer name, he's probably never heard of baked Alaska. I'm very upset. Carpenter ants and then this. . . I don't feel safe. I feel like I've lost my shell.

377

Gwen Pharis Ringwood

MELISSA: Mother. . .
WINONA: Yes?
MELISSA: Did you ever dream of standing on the Acropolis?
    (*Pause.*)
WINONA: (*Uncertainly*) Why yes. Yes I did. I remember now. I used
    to think how wonderful it would be to. . . . Why?
MELISSA: No reason.
        (WINONA *bemused goes out quietly.* MELISSA *stands looking
        far off right. Clearly the triumphant sound of the horns is
        heard.* MELISSA *freezes, listening.* WILLIE *appears down
        stage right and looks up right then to* MELISSA)
WILLIE: Melissa.
MELISSA: Yes?
WILLIE: I heard them. I heard the trumpets calling. Like you said.
    Did you hear?
MELISSA: I heard them. Listen.
        (*They sound again. The other people begin to enter quietly
        into down stage positions. There is a muffled sound of guns.*)
WILLIE: I'm going, Melissa.
        (*He starts up towards centre*)
MELISSA: Wait. I'm coming. Wait for me.
        (*She comes down towards* WILLIE. *Together they start up
        the ramp as if it were a long hard climb. Music may be used
        here. The other characters stand looking at them.*)
SARAH: Wait. The deep woods are hungry as a unicorn and swallow
    people.
MARIA: Stay out of the deep woods, children. Go around. Around.
JUDITH: Those horns demand and demand and demand. . . more than
    a person can give. They ask too much. Oh, Mitter, I can't follow.
    I can't follow.
SARAH: Stay. Stay. Better not venture further.
JONATHAN: The deep has many voices, so they say.
    So long, child. So long. So long.
        (*The words "so long" reverberate.* WILLIE *and* MELISSA
        *appear high on the ramp at right as the triumphant sounds
        of Beethoven's Ninth Symphony rise for a brief time. Then
        the lights go down and the music continues. Curtain.*)

The End

Wail, Winds, Wail

Characters

MAME
ELSIE
EDGAR
JONES
WILLA
BERT
CLEM

SETTING: *The end of a dinner party. The people are sitting around with coffee and liqueurs.*

MAME: I told Jeannie I wouldn't see her caught dead in that parade.

ELSIE: I don't know why they have to protest everything. Our Jim's growing a beard!

EDGAR: If we put these kids in a labour camp and show them what it means to do a good day's work, they'd soon knuckle down. Soft. Too soft — they've had it too soft too long.

JONES: Get that hair cut, Ron, or get out of my house. That's what I told him. I'm not one to pussy-foot around.

ELSIE: What did he do, Alex?

JONES: Well, he — he got out. He — left.

WILLA: We don't know where he is.

JONES: I can't figure it out. Why would a son of mine want to look like a girl?

MAME: Jeannie said *we* ought to be out protesting the war. Imagine, Daddy and I out carrying placards in the street.

BERT: Oh, they don't really know what they're doing. God knows, I don't hold any brief for war.

EDGAR: Let's face it . . . there always have been wars. War's human nature. You can't change that. That's one thing you can't change.

ELSIE: You're right Edgar. You can't change human nature.

CLEM: It's the dope. Those awful drugs. There ought to be a law.

JONES: There is a law. There ought to be a tougher law.

MAME: I said "Jeannie, you look ridiculous, a pretty girl like you carrying that great sign." She spent all night making a sign.

JONES: I said to that kid "What are you trying to do, look like Jesus?"

BERT: Nobody's going to hire someone that looks funny.

CLEM: It's the drugs. They don't know what they're doing.

WILLA: And you know where it comes from! You can't tell me it isn't a plot to deliberately destroy our young people — our country, for that matter. *They* know what they're doing. I just don't know where it will all end. College was so different for me. We talked a lot but we didn't get out in the streets.

MAME: Remember the proms, Daddy? The football games? We had such good times.

BERT: No, I don't remember much about college, Kitten. I've been too busy making a buck or two to keep us in shoes to look back.

MAME: Oh, I remember! I even remember the dresses I wore to every prom. And Guy Lombardo. And Mark Kenny. And then the war — (*sings*) "There'll be blue birds over the white cliffs of Dover. ."

CLEM: As if any of us want war. People killing other people. It does seem dreadful when you think about it. I try not to think about it.

JONES: Comes a time you've got to draw the line. It's them or you. How would you like to have them come in and take over your house and you'd be the servant?

CLEM: Oh, I wouldn't like it.

JONES: You see.

ELSIE: You can't change human nature.

MAME: Bert put his foot down. He said to Jeannie, "If you march in that protest parade, I'm through putting out money for college." After all she's only 17. What would she know about the war?

EDGAR: The people up there know what they're doing. They've got their finger on things. Right on the button.

CLEM: I think it will all just blow over.

JONES: I said to Ron "Why can't you cut that god-damn hair and look like a man?" I said "What do you want to look like — some god-damn fairy? or some god-damn guitar-playing poet?" That's what I said to him.

MAME: Remember when we had such pretty songs, like 'Tammy' and 'Lili' and 'You Forgot to Remember'?"

EDGAR: Now they just go "Yah, Yah, Yah." Primitive! Noise! Beat!

ELSIE: The worst of all is that sometimes I wonder if they're right and we're wrong. You know, they could be right even if they're young.

JONES: You read too much. You listen to the C.B.C. all the time. You're brainwashed.

ELSIE: Well, we should try to communicate —

JONES: Look, the only way to communicate is round them up, put them to work, give them a haircut and put them to work.

MAME: Turn on the television, Bert. It's the Bob Hope special.

CLEM: No, this is Tuesday. Red Skelton. Old Red wears pretty well.

ELSIE: Not for me. That silly Kadoodlehopper. I guess I'm too young to like Red Skelton very much. But I like Bob Hope. So original.

(Television comes on)

WILLA: Oh, it's something else entirely. Some documentary.

EDGAR: C.B.C.!

JONES: It's your god-damn protest march, that's what it is. Look at that. Traffic snarled up right down to City Hall. That's the youth of our country. A fine looking bunch aren't they?

EDGAR: Must be a thousand of them.

MAME: Imagine Bert and I mixed up in that melee. We'd look fine out there carrying placards. Daddy, look — there's Jeannie. Look, that's her sign. She's wearing her white sweater.

BERT: It's not Jeannie, mother. I expressly told Jeannie to stay out of it.

MAME: It's Jeannie. I know it is.

BERT: By God, she'll whistle for the car this next month. Defying everything we've tried to teach her, everything I stand for in this town.

CLEM: Isn't that the police at the side? They're going to move in!

ELSIE: So far it's all very peaceful.

JONES: Peaceful! How would you like to have signs all over calling you names? Pigs!

CLEM: There's going to be a riot. You see. They said it would be a peaceful demonstration. It's going to be a riot.

EDGAR: I better get down to the store. I got my new stock in.

JONES: That-a-boy! Rough him up a bit. Put him in the paddy wagon. Long-haired screw-ball.

WILLA: Look, that boy's bleeding. His head's bleeding. Do they have to be so rough?

JONES: Sure they've got to be rough. Time we put our foot down.

MAME: Oh, I wish Jeannie had stayed home. Do you see her Bert?

JONES: It's a riot all right. Now they're throwing rocks. It's a riot.

MAME: Was that a shot?

JONES: Yeah. The police are protecting City Hall now. That's what we hire them for — to protect our property. You got to take a stand.

MAME: Somebody's been — Bert, it's Jeannie. It's Jeannie. She's been shot.

BERT: No, mother, no. Not Jeannie. It's not Jeannie.

MAME: There, see. It's her white sweater. Oh God, my baby, my baby.

Gwen Pharis Ringwood

BERT: I'd better go down there, Mame. I — I'd better go down there.
ELSIE: Don't watch dear, don't watch. Come away.
MAME: Jeannie. Oh no, no, no! Why — why — WHY?
    (*Blackout*)

The End

Compensation Will Be Paid

Characters

LINDA
SHARON
MOLLIE, *the Grandmother*
ANNETTE
JANICE
LENA
ABNER
YOUNG MAN
MARGOT

SCENE: A segment of a yard in the prairie village. An old fashioned pump at a well, a clothes line, a watering trough, a bench and the front stoop of a house.

LINDA *is hanging out clothes. Her* GRANDMOTHER *sits on stoop knitting.* SHARON *comes by with shopping basket.*

SHARON: Good morning. It's a lovely morning. The sun's turned the world into a jewelry shop. Diamonds on the grass.
LINDA: There's spring in the air.
GRANDMOTHER: A silent spring, I'm thinking.
LINDA: Now Grandma, don't start that again. You're forever crying doom.
SHARON: What if she's right? They made the test this morning.
LINDA: Albert drove the sheep into the hills yesterday.
SHARON: Larry too. Everything in sixty miles had to be moved. Every animal. Every person. Larry thinks they shouldn't test that gas here. He thinks its dangerous.

383

GRANDMOTHER: In the old days they fought with swords and guns. Now it's bombs and chemicals. No one's safe.

LINDA: Albert talked to those scientists. He's sure there's no chance of contamination beyond the sixty miles.

GRANDMOTHER: The wind changed an hour ago.

SHARON: She's right, Linda. The wind's in the south now.

LINDA: The government knows what's best. They don't need us to tell them.

(ANNETTE *and* JANICE *run in with a dead frog.*)

ANNETTE: Mama, look at this frog.

JANICE: This tiny green frog, it's dead, Mama.

LINDA: Then throw it away, dear. If its dead — things have to die you know.

ANNETTE: I hate it when it's dead. Throw it away.

(JANICE *reluctantly throws frog away.* JANICE *comes out of the house.*)

LENA: I feel better now, Mama. Can I go with them?

LINDA: If you're feeling better.

ANNETTE: Come on, we'll look for a live frog.

LENA: Wait for me, you kids. I'm coming.

(*She follows.* ABNER, *an old man enters.*)

ABNER: A strange thing, Mollie. (*He speaks to the Grandmother.*) A chicken is dead on her nest. I go out to feed the chickens and I find this hen. Just — dead.

LINDA: Are the others all right, Grandpa?

ABNER: They seem all right.

(*A* YOUNG MAN *in a protective suit with mask hanging around his neck enters.*)

YOUNG MAN: I beg your pardon. Could I borrow a pipe wrench?

ABNER: Sure. I'll get it. You the fellow from the testing site?

YOUNG MAN: That's right.

GRANDMOTHER: The wind changed an hour ago.

SHARON: And the children found a dead frog.

ABNER: This chicken — she is dead on her nest.

(*He goes inside for wrench.*)

SHARON: Our men are driving the stock up into the hills. You're sure there's no danger?

YOUNG MAN: Nothing to worry about. Nothing at all. As long as you keep out of that 60 mile radius.

ABNER: There you are.

GRANDMOTHER: Tell him about the chicken, Abner. A hen nesting.

YOUNG MAN: Lady, hens die. However if by chance it had anything to do with the plant, I assure you compensation will be paid. I'll bring the wrench right back.

(*He goes out.*)

LINDA: You see, he said we're safe. They know what they're doing.

SHARON: You could ask him for compensation for the hen. After all the way they spend money they can afford it.
(ANNETTE, JANICE, *and* LENA *return.*)
ANNETTE: Mama, we found two frogs.
JANICE: But we let them go. We watched them hop and then we let them go.
LINDA: That's good, dear.
ANNETTE: I'm tired of hunting frogs.
JANICE: So am I.
LENA: I'm tired too.
(*Children group together.*)
ANNETTE: We can play mumblypeg.
(YOUNG MAN *returns with wrench.*)
YOUNG MAN: That did the trick. Thank you.
(*Gives wrench to* ABNER.)
ABNER: You figure on going down to there to the site?
YOUNG MAN: Of course. Why?
ABNER: I think I'd be nervous about going down there, if it was me.
YOUNG MAN: I've got this special suit, face mask, gloves. You know.
(MARGOT *enters.*)
MARGOT: Oh Linda, my puppy. My puppy's dead. Just now. While I was coming here.
ANNETTE: We found a dead frog, Margot.
ABNER: That hen was dead on her nest. I told you, Millie, they should never put that plant here. I told you all along didn't I? Now see what's happened. Our livestock's dying. What's your plant going to do about that?
YOUNG MAN: If the plan's responsible I assure you you'll be reimbursed. Compensation will be paid.
(*There is an uproar as they all speak at once.* ANNETTE *rushes to the adults.*)
ANNETTE: Mama, Mama, Lena's sick. Lena's very sick.
LENA: Mama. Mama.
(*She dies. They turn together and look at the* YOUNG MAN *who has donned his mask.*)
YOUNG MAN: Compen—Compensation. . .
(*They freeze. Curtain.*)

The End

The Stranger

In memory of Elizabeth Haynes, a great director and teacher.

Characters:

ALPHONSE, *an old Indian man*
SERAPHINA, *an old Indian woman*
JANA
GILBERT, *a young Indian*
JASON, *a white man*
LARRY, *an Indian ranch hand*
ANDREW, *an Indian ranch hand*
JOHNNY, *an older Indian man*
LUCY, *a young Indian girl*
The last four and several women make up the chorus.

COSTUMES: *The men wear "cowboy" clothes. . . boots, shirts, jeans and neckerchief, well worn and somewhat faded.* SERAPHINA *wears a long black shirt and blouse and cardigan sweater.* LUCY *may have a light cotton dress. In the early scenes* JANA *may wear a dark skirt and a soft shirt or blouse. In the final scene she wears a fine buckskin dress or skirt and shirt and head band and moccasins.*
TIME: *The present.*

A clearing banked by looming rock, dark fir, is shrouded in mist which gradually dispels as the dawn breaks. An old man, ALPHONSE, *drums softly beside a circle of rocks enclosing the ashes of a camp fire. As he drums the voice of the* CHORUS *rises above the sound of the drum. This* CHORUS *is a group of women gathering deadfall for fire wood. They are dark shapes at the edge of the clearing.*

Stumps, a log or a rock serve as sitting places.

The play may be played on a bare stage with a few elements to break up the space. Any setting should be simple, austere, with some

387

Gwen Pharis Ringwood

*variation in levels to add interest to the grouping. A high rock or level
centre left is needed for final scene.*
  If possible, changes in light should be used.

ALPHONSE: Speak, drum, the voice of my people,
Speak of the drift of the seasons,
The change of the moon and the seasons.

CHORUS: Spring, with the wild waters rushing
over the roots of the willow

Summer, the hum and the humming, wild cherry
drips from the branches,

dry grass and sizzle of insects,
and the young buck is sprouting his antlers.

Autumn, the lonely loon crying,
sage bloom and blaze of the poplar,
while in the marshes
the beaver is chewing his way into winter.

Winter, the snow on the spruce tree,
silent and soft on the spruce tree,
Snow falling, silently, softly,
silently shrouding the meadow.

ALPHONSE: Speak, my drum, of the old days,
The days of the hunt and the fishing.

CHORUS: Speak of the great leaping salmon
Fighting the fall and the current,
Fighting the way from the sea-way
Back to the place of its spawning
Back for the birth and the dying.
(*The* CHORUS *is silent as the drum mounts in volume and
intensity then the* CHORUS *is heard again, its tone harsh and
hard.*)

ALPHONSE: Speak, drum, the voice of my people.
Speak of this day and its dying.

CHORUS: Who knows what quivers in sunlight,
sounds in the song of the river,
flashes in sun on the crow's wing?

ALPHONSE: Who knows what shivers the pine tree,
What trembles the leaf of the willow?
No man knows. No man living knows.

No man, no man can know.
(SERAPHINA *enters carrying a basket with wild berries in it. She looks shocked and afraid.*)

SERAPHINA: Alphonse! We must leave here. This place is bad for us. We must leave today.
ALPHONSE: Leave? You talk foolish, Seraphina. Jana will not leave without her man. She came here to wait for Jason.
SERAPHINA: We should go home. As I come from the river, an owl speaks to me, speaks in our language. That means death. Someone will die before the moon rises.
ALPHONSE: You heard this thing?
SERAPHINA: I heard. The last time the owl spoke was when my brother went on the trap-line at Tatlayoka. A storm came from the West. They found my brother frozen, a long time after.
ALPHONSE: I would like to go home, old woman. Ah yes, I would like to go home. Where is Jana?
SERAPHINA: Sleeping in the cabin with her child.
ALPHONSE: Her man came back last night.
SERAPHINA: Jason come back? No. He is not with Jana.
ALPHONSE: I was up in the night, and the dogs barked, and a truck drove in. I heard Jason's voice.
SERAPHINA: I will go tell Jana. She will be so happy. She has waited a long time for Jason.
ALPHONSE: Wait. Maybe he does not want to see Jana.
SERAPHINA: Why do you say such a thing?
ALPHONSE: He has not come to find her.
SERAPHINA: How would he know we are here?
ALPHONSE: The ranch woman would tell Jason she is here. (*Pause*) I think he stays with the white woman at the ranch.
SERAPHINA: You lie, old man. You lie.
ALPHONSE: I hear things. The Shuswap here on the ranch talk to me. They say Jason stays often at the ranch house when he comes back from cattle drive.
SERAPHINA: The Shuswap want to make trouble. Jana has Jason's son. He has not seen his son. He will come when he finds out she is here.
ALPHONSE: I don't know. This is a big ranch with no man to run it.
SERAPHINA: (*Angrily*) So, the white woman hires Jason to be foreman . . . that is all.
ALPHONSE: I have seen Jason look far off with the look of a man who wants land. I know that look.
SERAPHINA: Ayeh. . . Jason looks for a place to own for him and Jana.
ALPHONSE: Jason wants much land, Seraphina. No small place. And the white woman owns much land.
SERAPHINA: She owns the cabin that Jana sleeps in too. If she wants Jason, the ranch woman would not let us stay here.

ALPHONSE: Perhaps she does not know that Jana is Jason's woman.

SERAPHINA: She knows. You and I and the child were in the wagon, and Jana rode the Palomino stallion through the gate to the ranch house. "I'm Mrs. Jason Carr" she said to the ranch woman. "I come from the Chilcotin to be with my husband."

ALPHONSE: He is not Jana's husband by the law.

SERAPHINA: For five years Jason buys my niece good clothes. He gives her money. Now she has his child. He is a good white man.

ALPHONSE: It is an old story, Seraphina.

SERAPHINA: If what you say is true, I don't know how it will be for Jana. The owl spoke in our language, Alphonse. I will tell Jana we must go.

ALPHONSE: Will you tell her that Jason sleeps with the white woman at the ranch? Will you tell her that?

SERAPHINA: I don't know. I am afraid to tell her. She is proud, Alphonse. Too proud.

ALPHONSE: She is a chief's daughter. She rides the fine horse her father gave her. If she is proud, she is proud in the old way. That is no sin.

SERAPHINA: She leaves her own people to follow Jason. And we are here in a strange place, strangers. I am afraid, Alphonse. . . afraid for Jana. . . for us all.

(GILBERT *enters*)

GILBERT: Where is the woman Jana?

SERAPHINA: She sleeps in the cabin, Gilbert.

GILBERT: She must leave here. Today. If she stays, there will be trouble. The Shuswaps say the Chilcotin woman brings it. She must go.

SERAPHINA: Why do they put a bad name on Jana? She has not hurt them.

GILBERT: A man is dead. Harry Peter is dead. He was riding after the stallion she brought here. He was going to catch the Palomino and bring him in. But Harry Peter's horse fell and he was thrown down against a rock. When we came up to where he was lying we find him dead. The Shuswaps say if the stranger had not come here with her golden horse, Harry Peter would be alive.

ALPHONSE: The stallion is not hard to catch. Always we can ride up to him and catch him.

GILBERT: The stallion was wild with pain and fear. He was cut last night.

ALPHONSE: Cut? Someone cut the horse?

GILBERT: Gelded him. He is no good now as a stallion.

ALPHONSE: Why, Gilbert? For God's sake, Why?

SERAPHINA: Who could do such a thing? The horse is young. Jana counted on him for many colts. Who would do such a thing?

GILBERT: Baptiste did it. He told me.

ALPHONSE: What reason? Why?

GILBERT: He had orders from the boss woman. She told Baptiste it is the law. The stallion was running loose on her land. He was getting at her mares. So Baptiste gelded that horse. And Harry

Peter is dead. The people whisper that the stranger should leave here before more trouble comes. They don't trust her.

SERAPHINA: I am afraid to tell Jana that her horse is cut. I am afraid what she will do.

GILBERT: The people are gathering for the funeral. You should go before tonight. Tonight they play La Hel for Harry Peter. There will be drinking. You should go now.

SERAPHINA: Jana will not go until she sees Jason. I know her mind.

GILBERT: He came in last night. He brought in sixty heifers.

ALPHONSE: Does Jason know we are here?

GILBERT: I wouldn't know that. He stays always at the ranch house now. I hear he will marry with the boss woman.

SERAPHINA: I will find Jason and tell him Jana is here with his son. He will come then and take us away from here.

GILBERT: You must leave all right. I go now. I will tell the people the Chilcotin woman will be gone before tonight.

SERAPHINA: You can tell them, Gilbert, but I don't know if Jana will go. Jason is her life.

(GILBERT *goes out stage right.*)

SERAPHINA: The owl spoke true, Alphonse. (*Her voice, low and trembling.*) You see. Harry Peter is dead. And the Shuswaps speak bad of Jana. Jason must take us away.

ALPHONSE: Go find him then. Tell him. (*Pause.*) Why do you not go?

SERAPHINA: I am afraid to go.

(*She moves stage left and stands immobile.* ALPHONSE *touches the drum softly, an ominous beat. The sun is higher and the leaves make strange patterns on the clearing. Clouds change the light. The* CHORUS *speaks from each side of the stage and from the back of the stage.*)

ALPHONSE: Speak, drum, of the woman whose crying
Will shudder the shaft of the sunlight.

CHORUS: Shatter the song of the river,
Will shiver the sway of the grasses.

Speak of the moan and the crying and the
death of the day and the dying
And the fall of the darkness like thunder
over the fast-running water.

(*With increasing speed.*)

Speak of the stranger whose crying
Wails over wind and the water

Shivers the leaves on the willow
Trembles the breath of the pine tree.

ALPHONSE: Of these things no man knows the answer.
No man alive knows the knowing.
No man living knows which place he should
put down his foot
To be safe from the thing in the shadow,
The hooded, coiled thing in the shadow.
No man knows.
(*The* CHORUS *disappears*)
(JASON *enters*)

JASON: So, Alphonse.
ALPHONSE: You are back from the cattle drive, Jason.
JASON: I'm back.
SERAPHINA: I was coming to find you.
JASON: You shouldn't have come here, Seraphina. You and Jana do not belong here.
SERAPHINA: I know that, Jason. Take us away.
JASON: Where is Jana?
SERAPHINA: She is in the cabin, with your son. You could go to her.
JASON: Tell her I'm here.
SERAPHINA: You could go to her. She has made the cabin nice for you. She has waited a long time here for you.
JASON: Best I see her here, Seraphina. Tell her that. Tell her we will talk here in the clearing.
SERAPHINA: (*Maliciously*) You do not trust yourself with Jana, eh? Not like before, eh Jason?
JASON: Go on.
(*The old woman goes out left*)
JASON: (*Moving restlessly*) I heard your drum last night, old man. Do you never sleep?
ALPHONSE: When I sleep I have bad dreams. I dream someone is choking my life out. And so I sit and drum the old songs. Sometimes I think I drum myself to my own death. (*He chuckles.*)
JASON: Why did you come with Jana? Why did you let her follow me here? Why did she come?
ALPHONSE: You know why, Jason. Jana is young, and blood is high in the young.
JASON: I told her to wait in the Chilcotin, that I'd send for her when. . .
(*He stops*)
ALPHONSE: When, Jason? You had been gone since summer. You have not seen your son. Jana won't look at Indian men now. . .or any one. . . You know why she came.
JASON: Yes. Yes, I know. Things change, Alphonse. Everything changes. (*Pause*) What did she name the boy?
ALPHONSE: Jason. Jason Carr.
JASON: He is healthy?

ALPHONSE: (*Nods*) Your son and a chief's grandson. A man is proud to have a son. (*Pause*) I heard you come in from the cattle drive last night. I heard you unload the horses.

JASON: (*Angrily*) So. . . you heard me!

ALPHONSE: They say you stay often at the ranch house. The Shuswap say you will leave Jana for the boss woman. . .

JASON: What I do has nothing to do with you, or the Shuswap.

ALPHONSE: (*With ironic malice*) This is a good ranch, Jason. A big ranch in good shape with many cattle. And you want land, much land.

JASON: Shut up, old man. Get out!

(ALPHONSE *begins to move out stage right, carrying his drum. He passes* JASON, *pauses, turns back.*)

ALPHONSE: Jana is proud, Jason. Proud to be her father's daughter. Proud to be the mother of your son. I do not know how it will be for Jana if you do what your mind tells you to do.

JASON: Leave me alone, old man. Go on. Go.

(ALPHONSE *exits right.* JASON *moves towards the left, turns, walks back right.* JANA *enters. His back is towards her.* JASON *does not realize she is there until she has run to him, her face buried against his back, her arms around him.*)

JANA: Oh, Jason, Jason. Oh. . . you've come. . . you've come! I thought you'd never come.

JASON: I'm surprised to find you here, Jana. You've changed. . . You look more. . .

JANA: Grown up? A baby makes a woman grow up, I think.

JASON: You look. . . beautiful.

JANA: I feel good now. . . with you here. . .

JASON: You shouldn't have come, Jana. . .

JANA: I had to come. It was so long. I couldn't eat or sleep. I had to come, Jason. Hold me. . .

JASON: (*Moving back a little from her*) I told you to wait in the Chilcotin, with your people.

JANA: I waited. And then. I couldn't wait. I'd lie awake thinking about your touch, how it was when we were together. I couldn't wait. I wanted you, Jason. To be with you.

JASON: You don't understand. (*He turns away slightly*) If it had been convenient. . . if I'd wanted you here, I would have sent for you. You see I'm away a lot now, riding for this ranch. I'm a foreman at this ranch, Jana. In charge of a lot of the operation. . .

JANA: I knew you were too busy with your job to write. So I came with your son and Alphonse and Seraphina. We took nine days. We brought a team and the wagon with my things in it, and I rode the golden stallion.

JASON: Your father's horse. You must take him back.

JANA: My father gave him to me. His gift to us. If we find a small place to own, Jason, people will pay money to breed their mares to the

Gwen Pharis Ringwood

stallion. He is beautiful and strong and has good blood. He can serve many mares for us.

JASON: No, Jana, no. Not now.

JANA: Don't move away from me, Jason. You mustn't turn away from me. Now we're together and it will be the same as before, only better. . .

It rained when were coming from the Chilcotin and we were cold. Some dogs ate our meat and we were hungry. But I wouldn't turn back. At the river we fished for salmon and I cleaned it in the old way with my father's knife. . . like a ceremony. Now when you and I fish many salmon will come to our nets, I promise.

Oh, I am talking so much. I'm sorry. Come with me to the cabin. Now, Jason, come now.

JASON: You can't stay here. You and the boy and the old people must pack up. . . go back to the Chilcotin. You must go home tomorrow.

JANA: It's not home to me now, Jason. Home is with you. . . since that first time we were together.

JASON: You don't understand. I can't look after you here. You can't live here on the ranch.

JANA: The boss woman gave us a cabin. It was over-run with mice and pack rats and full of filth, but I cleaned it. I got poison for the rats and they're all gone. I fixed the cabin clean and good for us. I have wild flowers on the table, Jason. And I made curtains. I fixed the cabin for when you came and we could be together.

(SERAPHINA enters with a child in an Indian basket)

SERAPHINA: I bring you your son, Jason. He is a good boy.

JASON: My son. (Pause. JASON moves to SERAPHINA and takes the child out of the cradle.) My son. He's never seen me. He wonders who I am.

JANA: (Standing away from them but watching) I named him Jason. You weren't there to name him.

JASON: Little Jason.

SERAPHINA: He looks like you.

JANA: Everyone says that, Jason.

JASON: My son. Alphonse is right. A man is proud to have a son. He's a fine boy, Jana. . . you've taken good care of him. I'll buy him clothes.

JANA: I made his clothes. The moccasins too. The softest skins I could find. I made gloves and moccasins for you too, Jason. I've learned to make things in the old way since you left. Seraphina taught me.

SERAPHINA: Jana. Tell Jason to take us home today. There's a bad feeling on this ranch. Tell him we must go.

JANA: You talk foolish, Seraphina. Jason can't leave his job.

SERAPHINA: The owl spoke to me in the Chilcotin tongue this morning. Someone has died. Someone else will die before the moon rises. I feel it.

(She grips JANA'S arm. JANA speaks to her gently but indulgently.)

394

JANA: No, old woman. No owl speaks in Indian. The owl only mourns a chief's son he rescued and lost again. That's all. No owl speaks of death. Take the child now to the creek. I want to be alone with my husband. There is much we have to say. And give us time to be alone, Seraphina, in the cabin. Time to be together.

SERAPHINA: Jana, I am afraid for us. (*She moves to* JASON) I will take your son now, Jason.

JASON: You say he looks like me?

SERAPHINA: He has dark eyes of our people but he looks like you. Poor baby. This is no home for you.

    (*She takes the baby from* JASON *and moves away*)

SERAPHINA: (*Turning at the edge of stage*) I beg you, Jason, take us home. This place is no good for us. We are strangers here. Your son too.

    (*She goes out*)

JANA: The old are foolish. Afraid of everything.

    (*She is nervous, feverish because she senses that things are going wrong.*)

JASON: Seraphina is right. I will see that you get home. I can send you in a car or by the stage.

JANA: I won't go. I won't. No, Jason. Come, let me show you the Palomino. You will be proud to ride on such a horse. Remember the horse my father rode. . . this is his seed. (*She calls*) Alphonse! Alphonse!

ALPHONSE: (*Off*) I hear.

JANA: Bring in the Palomino stud. Bring him here. Jason has not seen him. Hurry!

ALPHONSE: (*Entering at side of stage*) I can't bring the stud in, Jana.

JANA: Where is he?

ALPHONSE: Gilbert put him in the corral.

JANA: Then bring him here! You have a hackamore.

ALPHONSE: He is sick. He was cut last night.

JANA: Cut? What do you mean?

ALPHONSE: Gelded. Baptiste gelded him.

JANA: Oh no. . . No. Oh no. (*Pause*) Why? Why?

    (*Sinking down. Her voice is barely audible.*)

ALPHONSE: Baptiste had orders from the boss woman. The stallion was running her mares. She said that.

JANA: Did you know this, Jason?

    (*A hardness is in her voice*)

JASON: It was done when I came home last night. I heard then. I would have stopped it, Jana. I'm sorry.

JANA: Oh I hate her. I hate her. . . with her milk face and her cold eyes and her dirty cabin that I worked so hard to clean. She's bad, bad. How could she do such a thing?

JASON: You mustn't blame Barbara. It is the law. No stud can run loose.

JANA: He was so beautiful. I was so proud to bring him to you. Next to your son, I was proudest to bring you the stallion. (*Pause*)

Give my horse some oats, Alphonse. Do what you can for him. I'll come soon.

ALPHONSE: It is too bad, Jana. I don't like to say bad news.

(ALPHONSE *goes out*)

JANA: Seraphina is right. This place is bad. Take me away.

JASON: (*Going to* JANA) Jana, we had good years together, you and I.

JANA: Five years. I was seventeen.

JASON: I was lonely in the Chilcotin and you were good to me. You took care of me when I was hurt. You were good to me.

JANA: A woman should be good to her man.

JASON: I thought then I would stay out there. . . as you say, find us a small place.

JANA: There or here. . . no matter. I only want to be with you.

JASON: Things change. A man grows older, changes. He wants different things, a different life. He wants to get somewhere with his life.

JANA: I know that. I came here ready to learn a new way. I dress different. After you left I am reading books, school books. The teacher says I learn quickly. He gave me many books to read. I do, Jason, I do learn quickly. (*Moving to him*) Jason. Hold me.

JASON: (*Moved*) Jana. . . you must try to understand. . .

JANA: I nursed you when you saved my father's life from the grizzly and the grizzly hurt you. When you were getting strong you said "Some day we'll have our own place." And you said it often after that when we are living in my sister's cabin. So I came here to tell you I am ready now. I will leave my father and my sisters, my family, the reserve and be with you and our son where you want us to be. Where you go, I will go.

JASON: Jana, listen. You must listen to me. When I left the Chilcotin I thought I'd come back to you. But here, on this ranch, my life changed. Barbara, the white woman at the ranch,. . . she and I have been together for three months. We're going to be married. . .

JANA: Oh no, Jason. No. You're only saying that. You're not speaking true.

JASON: It's over, you and me. . . it's over.

JANA: (*A whisper*) But we have a child together. . .

JASON: I'll take care of him. He'll go to good schools. I'll do everything for the boy. I promise.

JANA: He's my son too. We belong together. The three of us.

JASON: It won't work. Believe me, I know myself. Sooner or later I'd hurt you. Leave you. I've already left you, Jana. You deserve better than I gave you. . . but I've already left you. I made a new life here. I belong. And this is the place I want. Barbara. This ranch.

JANA: You're not joking? Lying? You speak true.

JASON: Forgive me. I did love you, Jana. I swear—I thought then we could make it together.

JANA: You don't dare hold me, Jason. You still want me. I'm in your blood. You don't dare hold me. You think to marry her. . . but you still want me. I know it!

JASON: Barbara and I are to be married next month. I planned to write you. I didn't know you'd follow me here.

JANA: (*Dazed*) So all the years go down. I left my father's place and lived with you. Your wife. I followed you here and made this place clean. . . a place that stank with vermin. And I got no friendly word because I was a stranger, but I didn't care because you would come and we would be together. Now I don't know what happens to me. What happens to my child.

JASON: Barbara wants us to raise him as our own. He is my son. And I want him.

JANA: And if I won't give him up? What then?

JASON: You want what's best for him.

JANA: What kind of mother will she make? A woman who spoils a fine horse out of spite. A woman who hires ranch hands to warm her bed? What kind of mother will she make?

JASON: Stop that, Jana. With me the boy would have the best. Good schools. Perhaps this ranch. I'll see that you have money too.

JANA: Sure. You will pay money so your son grows up on the edge of the world. You will buy your own son. You think to pay me off as if I were a whore. For you my name was made ugly in the mouths of my people. For you I groaned with birth pain. For you I came to this place where they spit on me as a stranger. Go now, Jason. Get out of here. Tell your white whore I'll send our child so she can look at him and know she'll never give you such a son. Tell her I curse the seed you spill from this day on. Tell her I wish your children born blind and hideous and twisted with hate as I am now. I hate you, Jason.

JASON: Stop it Jana! It would have been better if I'd never set eyes on you. Better for both of us. I wish I'd never seen you.

(*JANA now towers with rage as if the floods of hate were unleashed after being damned up for a long time.*)

JANA: You'll see me, Jason. You'll see me when you ride alone and a storm comes. You'll see me when you wake in the night and know you sold your good word for something you'll never really own. You'll see me when you see a black-haired boy and wonder if he's our son. You'll see me in your dreams, Jason, and you'll have bad dreams. You'll wake sweating and crying with bad dreams and I'll be there, just beyond touch. You'll see me, Jason. Though all the lights go out and you put out your eyes, I'll be there in your sight, just beyond touch.

(*Her voice has become a menacing whisper.*)
Go now. Get out of here. . .

Gwen Pharis Ringwood

JASON: I'll fight for the boy, Jana. Understand that. I want my son.
I can do things for him. He won't be growing up on a backwoods
reservation. Think about it. Think about him.

JANA: (*Throwing down a bracelet.*) Take this. It's yours. . . I'll see you in
hell, Jason, before I'm finished. Get out now. Go!

> (JASON *leaves. The drums sound softly off stage.* JANA *sinks
> down on the ground rocking with pain and grief. She intones a
> wordless chant ay ya ay ya. . . biting at her hands trying to
> surround her grief. After a brief interval* GILBERT *enters.*)

GILBERT: Jana?

JANA: What do you want?

GILBERT: To help you.

JANA: I need no help. I don't want your help.

GILBERT: You are going away?

JANA: Maybe.

GILBERT: Where do you go?

> (*She turns away without answering.*)
> I have worked in the fish camp up North. If you wish to come
> with me, we could go today. The boy too.

JANA: You would take a stranger, and a stranger's child?

GILBERT: I would take you.

JANA: No.

GILBERT: My wife died. I have no child. I would like children.

JANA: I do not think I go with you, Gilbert, but if I go I will give you
children.

GILBERT: I would be good to you.

JANA: And my son?

GILBERT: Your son too. We could leave today.

JANA: No. Tomorrow. Maybe I'll go with you tomorrow. Away from
this place. For bad things blow in the wind, and hate burns inside
me like a branding iron, until I don't know what I say or what I
do. If I go, we go tomorrow.

GILBERT: We must leave today, Jana. . . before the funeral.

JANA: What funeral?

GILBERT: Harry Peter died. He was thrown from his horse this morning.
He was trying to bring in your Palomino.

JANA: (*Dully*) Oh. My horse is spoiled. And a man dies because of
her. And she would have my son.

GILBERT: This place is no good for you. Come with me, now.

JANA: No. Tomorrow is time enough. Tonight I go to Harry Peter's
funeral.

GILBERT: No! You must stay away from there! The Shuswap blame
you. They say you bring bad luck. You could get your things
together. We could leave now. I have good horses for us. Come
with me, Jana.

JANA: Leave me alone now, Gilbert. I have things to do.

GILBERT: You will get ready?

JANA: I am thinking about it. Tonight. . . soon, I will tell you if I will go
with you.
GILBERT: I'll pick up my pay from Jason. We can be gone before they
come to play La Hel. I will come for you.
JANA: No! I will come to you when I am ready. Go now, Gilbert. I have
things to do.
> (GILBERT *leaves reluctantly.* JANA *stares after him. She
> bites her hand as if stifling a scream. Then slowly she gets up
> and goes out stage left.* ALPHONSE *and the* CHORUS *appear
> in the shadows. The drumming resumes. The lights change to
> a strange evening luminous light.*)

CHORUS: Speak now of the stranger whose crying
Shudders the shaft of the sunlight,
Speak of the day and the dying,
The blood at the roots of the willow
And a cry in the darkness goes screaming
Over the fast flowing water.

Speak of the deed in the making
Speak of the blood and the screaming
That trembles the breath of the pine tree
And falls to the fast flowing water.
Into what dark is she going,
This woman who came as a stranger?

> (*The sky darkens as before a storm. The* CHORUS *retires
> and* JANA *returns carrying a small woven basket containing
> wild berries, a tin cup with sugar and a package clearly
> marked Rat Poison.*)

JANA: (*Calling*) Bring me my son, Seraphina. Hurry!
> (*The drumming continues off stage. Muffled and ominous.*
> JANA *takes the berries from the large basket* SERAPHINA *has
> left and puts some in the smaller birchbark basket. She sprinkles
> the berries with the poison and then pours the sugar over
> them. She places the empty cup and the package of rat poison
> on a stump.* SERAPHINA *comes on stage, holding the baby in the
> Indian basket.*)
SERAPHINA: I bring little Jason, Jana. He is sleeping. Shall I take him
to the cabin?
JANA: No. Leave him here. Put down the basket there.
SERAPHINA: Why?
JANA: Because I say.
SERAPHINA: We should be putting our things in the wagon. I will call
Alphonse.
JANA: No. I want you to go to the ranch house.

SERAPHINA: I do not think Jason will come to you, Jana. Not now. Not any more. I think he will marry the white woman.

JANA: He may not marry the ranch woman Seraphina. Jason still burns for me.
  (*A roll of thunder*)

SERAPHINA: We should leave before the storm comes.

JANA: (*Her fingers close around* SERAPHINA's *wrist*) Listen to me, Seraphina. You must do what I say. Do you hear me?

SERAPHINA: (*Uneasy as she notes* JANA's *feverish resolution*) I hear.

JANA: You must take these berries to the ranch house. You will give them to the woman of the ranch, give them in her hand. Tell her that we are leaving and that I send her this gift. Tell her I will leave my son behind with her and Jason.

SERAPHINA: No. You don't mean that, Jana.

JANA: Tell her so. Tell her that tonight before I leave this place. I will bring my son on to live with Jason. Tell her, Seraphina, that Jana is thankful that her son shall have a fine home. Be sure to tell her so, Seraphina.

SERAPHINA: You do not mean what you say, Jana. Your face is like a stone.

JANA: Do what I say. Here, take the berries.
  (*The old woman sees the package of poison on the stump.*)

SERAPHINA: Jana. Why is this here? This poison?

JANA: Do what I tell you, Seraphina.

SERAPHINA: What do you do, Jana? Why is this poison here?

JANA: Oh that. . . The pack rats are bothering again. I smelled them in this clearing. But since we are leaving I do not care if they spoil the cabin. We will leave this place to the pack rats.
  (*She throws poison container in to the fire or away*)

SERAPHINA: What do you do, Jana?

JANA: (*Her eyes very bright, her face is a mask*) They are strange animals, pack rats. They take something and they leave something in its place. Like us, Seraphina. We send sweet wild berries and a child, and we get back old blankets and some stinking clothes. Give the berries into her hands, Seraphina. You must promise. (*She again catches* SERAPHINA's *wrist*) Trust me. I know what I'm doing. Say you will do what I ask. Swear it.

SERAPHINA: I will give them. Into her hands.

JANA: Good. Now I get ready for our journey, step by step. Go now. Quickly.
  (*The old woman starts off right. Then turns.*)

SERAPHINA: We leave tonight?

JANA: Yes. You will leave tonight.

SERAPHINA: And you?

JANA: Gilbert wants me to go north with him. The old man and you and I came to this place together, but now we take different roads. Do this thing for me before you go home. Tell that white

woman I'll leave Jason's son here on this ranch.
(SERAPHINA *goes out.* JANA *croons over the child.*)

JANA: Seen-tuh, seen-tuh, sechel (come here, come here, little brother)

Seen-tuh, seen-tuh sechel
Nee zoon Ne zoon (You're nice)

Neen-teeh, Neen-teeh, Nee zoon (Go on sleep)
Nona steen go lain. Nona steen go-lain (I love you)
Neen teeh Neen teeh Nee zoon.

What I must do, I will do.
What I will do, I must do.
Jason. Jason. My son. My son.

Shall I leave you to live here, a stranger?
Shall I leave you with no home to go to?
To hear curses on the name of your mother?
My son. My son.

Shall I leave you with no place of kindness
No voice to say Stay or Go?
No hands to rock you when the dark falls? My son! My son!

Neen teeh my son. Neen teeh
Nona steen go lain. Nona steen go lain
Neen teeh Neen teeh Nee zoon.

What I must do, I will do.
What I will do, I must do.

Neen teeh, neen teeh, my son.
Seen-tuh, Seen-tuh, sechel
Nona steen go lain. Sleep, my son. Sleep. Sleep.
(*She rocks the baby in her arms as she kneels on the stage.*
SERAPHINA *returns.*)

SERAPHINA: Now we must go, Jana.
JANA: Did you give the ranch woman the berries? In her hand?
SERAPHINA: I gave them.
JANA: And you told her she would have my son?
SERAPHINA: I told her so.
JANA: Was Jason there?
SERAPHINA: He was outside. I told him you would leave the boy. He will come here for the baby and to say goodbye. He gave me money for our journey.
JANA: You are trembling.
SERAPHINA: I am afraid. The people are coming now to play La Hel for Harry Peter. They come with lanterns to this clearing.
JANA: Let them come.

401

SERAPHINA: You must take the baby and find Gilbert. I will get my things in the wagon. The people blame you for Harry Peter's death. Go, Jana. Go!

JANA: I will go. I am not afraid of the Shuswap but I go to get ready to leave this place. You stay here, Seraphina. Tell the Shuswap we mean them no harm. Stay a little, while I do what I must do. It is my last favor from you, old woman. You have been good to me.

SERAPHINA: Take the boy and hurry, Jana. There is not much time.

> (JANA *goes out with the child. She takes the cup with her. The drums sound off and slowly the people move in with torches. They bring wood and long boards on which to play La Hel.* SERAPHINA *moves to the side, stands in the shadow watching. The boards are placed in position and several men sit in front of them. If other drummers are used they will be near the fire where they can tune the drums or perhaps only* ALPHONSE *drumming off stage will be heard. The women gather in a small group at left. During the following sequence the men throw down blankets, bridles, prized possessions which will be played for in the game. This scene may be as simple or as elaborate a ritual as the director wishes.*)

LARRY: These are Harry Peter's La Hel bones. You play the game my brother played when he was alive. La Hel was my brother's game. He played it many times, since he was a man.

JOHNNY: Many times Harry Peter won with these bones.

LARRY: And many times he put down his saddle and his bridle and his money to another winner. You play La Hel as Harry Peter played it.

JOHNNY: He was a good man.

ANDREW: He was a good rider and worker.

> (ALPHONSE *enters with his drum and moves to* SERAPHINA *sitting on a log or rock.*)

LARRY: Old Man, why do you come here? You are no Shuswap. You don't care about my brother.

LARRY: You are leaving. You and the old woman and the woman, Jana. It is her fault my brother is dead. If she had not come here with her golden horse, he would be alive now. Where is she?

ALPHONSE: I don't know.

LARRY: She brings bad luck on us. Gilbert told me she was going away.

SERAPHINA: It is true. She goes with Gilbert.

LARRY: I do not feel right playing La Hel for my brother when the woman is near. It is her fault he lies dead. I don't forget that.

SERAPHINA: No! It is the white woman's fault. The boss woman. She gave orders to geld the Palomino.

JOHNNY: I think the Chilcotin woman must leave here. I think we will set fire to the cabin, force her off this ranch. Get rid of her.

ANDREW: Is it what you say? She is the cause of your brother's death?

LARRY: It is that way.

402

ANDREW: Then before we play La Hel we should send her away. . .
We should get rid of this stranger.

JOHNNY: We have torches. We can burn down her cabin. That will get
her out.

SERAPHINA: No! Her child is there with her. Jason's son.

JOHNNY: Bring your torches. We'll fire the cabin. Then she must go.
Come on. Follow me.

(*They are a tight group ready to move towards the cabin*)

SERAPHINA: No! No!

ANDREW: (*Pushing her aside*) Out of the way, old woman. Come on,
let's go! We'll burn her out!

(JASON *enters*)

SERAPHINA: Jason, stop them! They are after Jana.

JASON: Andrew! Larry Peter! What are you doing? Johnny, come here.
What's got into you? Listen to me!

LARRY: You can't stop us, Jason. It's the Chilcotin woman,—Jana.
We want her off the place. She brings bad luck where she
comes.

JASON: She is leaving, Larry. That's why I came here. . . to see that she
goes back home and to get my son. Put down your torches. . .

ANDREW: You can't stop us Jason. That cabin is on Shuswap land.

JASON: The land your chief leased to the ranch, Andrew.

JOHNNY: That's right, Andrew. The cabin belongs to the ranch.

JASON: Stay away from it. That's an order.

LARRY: The woman was the cause of my brother dying.

JASON: No. It was an accident. Believe me, Larry.

AANDREW: We don't want to play La Hel for Harry Peter while she is
here. We think she brings bad spirits.

JASON: I'm driving her to town tonight. I swear it. Look, I brought
your wages.

LARRY: You promise she will leave the ranch tonight?

JASON: I promise.

LARRY: I will take his word. Come back.

JASON: Here are your cheques. Don't lose them at La Hel.

LARRY: You can start the drums. The people will be coming soon.

(*The drumming begins.*)

LARRY: (*To* JASON) Will you play with us for Harry Peter, my brother?

JASON: I will play later. First I must take my son to the ranch house
and then I will drive Jana to town.

(JASON *moves towards the cabin but before he is off stage a
young Indian girl runs in. She is in a hysterical state.*)

LUCY: Jason. Jason, come!

JASON: What's the matter Lucy?

LUCY: I seen her! I seen her!

JASON: What is it?

LUCY: I seen her lying on the floor.

SERAPHINA: Jana? Did you see Jana?

LUCY: She was lying there, twisted like a rope!
LARRY: The Chilcotin woman? Someone has. . .
LUCY: She was twisted like a rope.
JASON: Get hold of yourself, Lucy. What did you see?
LUCY: I didn't do nothing. I didn't do it. She was lying there. She's
    dead.
JASON: Jana?
LUCY: No. It is. . . the ranch woman. I didn't do it, Jason. She's dead.
    I know it. The boss woman lies there dead.
JASON: Barbara! It's Barbara you saw!
    (JASON *starts to move back to the ranch but is stopped when*
    JANA *appears on the rock above the clearing. She is holding*
    her child in the Indian basket. She wears a native buckskin
    skirt and jacket and her hair falls loose from a beaded band.
    She is Indian in the old proud way.)
JANA: Yes. She's dead, Jason. She died from the gift I sent her.
    Your white whore dies from the twisting pain I sent her. And you
    suffer now!
JASON: (*Low*) You. . . killed her? Murdered her. . . Jana, no!
JANA: Yes, I killed her—like a rat—
    You think you suffer now, Jason. Oh, no,—
    I will show you how to suffer.
    You will know pain and where you walk or run or cry out
    in bad dreams, your pain runs with you.
    So, you would use me and throw me down.
    No, Jason, no!
    A flower lies bruised under your feet,
    Or a wild tree, ripped from its roots,
    Will die and make no sound,
    But flesh and blood cry out!

    I will show you how to suffer, Jason.
    Here is your son, sleeping. Sleeping.
    See your son.
    (*A knife flashes in her hand above the basket and comes down*
    swiftly.)
    He sleeps forever Jason. I have killed our son.
    Now you suffer.

    Live, Jason. Live for a hundred years and remember Jana.
    Then I am paid back. Then I am satisfied.
JASON: (*Cries out*). . . (*Low to a terrible loud cry*) Oh. . .
JANA: And for the rest.
    I came to this place with the old man and the old woman.
    Gilbert will take them home.
    But this man, Jason Carr, made me and my son homeless.
    He would pay me off like a whore on the street.
    His word was a hooded snake.

There is no honor in him.
He thought to throw me down.
Suffer, Jason! Suffer!
Then I am paid back.

Now I, Jana, see you suffer! I am paid back.

Now, I am satisfied.
(*She holds the basket to her breast*)

Nona steen go lain,
Neen teeh, sechel, Nee Zoon.
Nona steen go lain.
Seen tuh. . . seen tuh. . . sechel.
(*Her voice rises from the gentle croon to a wild cry.*)
Nona steen go lain!
(*She raises the knife again and stabs her own breast. Then* JANA *sinks down, slumped across the rock holding the basket.*)

SERAPHINA: Jana! Jana!
(*There is complete silence. At last* SERAPHINA *speaks.*)
SERAPHINA: So, it is over for Jana—over!
Bring her and her child down to me, Gilbert. We will take the bodies home to the Chilcotin. She was too proud. I told her. I said "You are too proud, Jana."
(GILBERT *moves to the rock and lifts* JANA *in his arms after* SERAPHINA *takes the basket holding the child.* GILBERT *stands silently. The people freeze as old* ALPHONSE *begins his drumming. All people become the chorus and speak out of a darkening stage.*)

ALPHONSE: Speak of the stranger whose crying
Falls in the darkness like thunder
Over the fast-flowing water.

CHORUS: And speak of the drift of the season—
Spring flood on the roots of the willow.
Summer, the hum and the humming,
Autumn, the loon's cry and sage bloom.
Winter, snow falling in silence.

Speak of the old angry river,
The river that cradles our people,
The wrench of the net and the fishing,
And the salmon hung dry for the winter.

ALPHONSE: I who am old, half blind, and drunk with cheap wine,
Speak through my drum of these things and of my people.

And my drum speaks too for every man alive.
I drum for each man who is wrenched from the warm dark of nothing,

405

Gwen Pharis Ringwood

Cries out, grow tall, and walks upright.
I drum for every man who knows not where to put down
his foot
To escape the thing in the shadow,
The hooded, coiled thing in the shadow.

I am old, half blind, and like every man
I drum myself to my own death.
(*The drumming rises and then fades and the play ends.*)

The End

A Remembrance of Miracles

Characters

MERRILL ADAMS
PAUL RAE, *student*
JODY MONIHAN
CLINT MONIHAN
MR. DUBRICK, *principal*
STEVE HARDING, *editor*
OPAL PURVIS, *chair person of School Board*
VERNA GLIDDENS, *concerned citizen*
ANNOUNCER

The play employs voices, embodying MERRILL'*s doubts, fears, the attitudes of the community. . . the company may simply become a chorus and do these on stage or they may be taped.*
CLINT MONIHAN *and* MR. DUBRICK *may be played by the same actor.* JODY *and* OPAL PURVIS *may be played by the same actor. The* ANNOUNCER *can be played by someone in the eight principal characters, so the play can be done with a cast of six.*

TIME: *The mid-70s.*
PLACE: *A small Western town—Willamont.*
SETTING: *Three playing areas are visualized, Area A perhaps slightly raised above Area B and Area C might be small and quite a bit higher than the rest.*
   However the director will find the staging quite simple as actors move from one area to another. The important part of the staging is the light. . . it should be highly flexible so that one area can be dimmed and another brought into focus. . . Light may be used to give a kind of dissolving edge to scenes. A couple of desks,

some chairs, the school motto, microphones, flag or posters may be used to give substance to the playing areas and be useful but minimum furniture.

Music is employed. . . possibly guitar is most evocative for this play. . . the director should be able to orchestrate the poetry "collage" with music, to use it to bridge scenes and for the call-in nightmare scene. The poetry collage may be shortened if desired. There is no intermission.

MERRILL is sensitive, emotional, introspective, and from the beginning we should accept her spoken thoughts and her unspoken fears etc. as embodied in the "cold impersonal voices".

The stage consists of several playing areas, each of which can be lighted while the others dissolve in shadows.

MERRILL ADAMS *is standing with her back to the audience on a slightly raised playing area at stage right. She looks out the window.*

Two or three voices speak from various places around the stage sometimes separately sometimes in unison sometimes in a whisper and sometimes loudly.

VOICES: Miss Adams. Miss Adams.
What are you doing, Miss Adams?
Where are you hiding?
What about the list? The list.
What kind of a teacher are you?
Calling Miss Adams. Miss Merrill Adams.
Report to the office. Report. Report.
Calling Miss Adams.
(The telephone rings shrilly. After a moment MERRILL turns and takes it up.)

MERRILL: Hello. Hello. Oh no,. . . Hello. *(There is no answer.)* Please answer. I know you're there. *(She puts down the receiver)* Oh please, don't do this to me. Not any more.
(She sits at the little desk, head on her arms.)

VOICE: The motto of Willamont High School is "Whatsoever things are of good repute." Do you think you uphold that motto?

2ND VOICE: If you had it to do over again, would you put up that list of books, Miss Adams? Would you? Did you make a mistake?

1ST VOICE: Or do you like discussing questionable subjects with your students? Is that it?

2ND VOICE: Read the list, Miss Adams. Read the list you gave your class, Miss Adams. The list.
(MERRILL moves down to the center area and in confident and pleasant tone reads the following list of books as if to a High School class.

MERRILL:The Catcher in the Rye
King Lear

The Poetry and Songs of Leonard Cohen
The Playboy of the Western World
Tess of the D'Urbervilles
The Diviners
Songs of Innocence
Long Days Journey Into Night
Look Homeward, Angel
Arms and the Man
You'll find these books on the shelf at the back of the room, class. You may write your essay on any one of them.
> (*As* MERRILL *moves back to first platform (her room) the voices unemotional and impersonal again surround her.*)

VOICE: Where did you get this list, Miss Adam?

2ND VOICE: You feel that all of these books are quite suitable for young minds? You don't see anything offensive in the subject matter or the language?

VOICE I: No threat to innocence?

WHISPER: (*As if a childhood memory*) Bad girl. Bad girl. You mustn't say those dirty words. Bad girl.

VOICE I: Why did you choose those books for your list? Are you fit to teach our children? Are you worthy? What kind of person are you? What are you teaching, Miss Adams? What kind of teacher are you? Are you of good repute? Are you a good teacher?
> (*The school bell rings as* MERRILL *crosses down to school room area centre and speaks out toward audience as to a class.*)

MERRILL: That was a good discussion on Leaving Home. After all we don't all have to make the mistakes of Holden Caulfield. Well, class dismissed. If I were you I'd go down by the river and run through the fallen leaves. It's a golden October.

VOICES: Good night, Miss Adams. . . Good night. . .
> (*Sound of second bell.*)

MERRILL: (*As if watching the class leave*) They look so young. Vulnerable. I wanted so much to talk to someone. . . but there wasn't anyone. I suppose that's why I'm so anxious to give them something besides rules, facts, dates. I remember what it was like to be fifteen. . . so confused, so full of yearning. . .
Yes, Paul.
> (PAUL, *A boy of about sixteen moves to* MERRILL.)

PAUL: I just wanted to ask you about the books on that list, Miss Adams. Are they your favorites?

MERRILL: Some of them. But actually the books on that list nearly all explore human relationships and that's why I gave them to you.

PAUL: You mean men and women relationships?

MERRILL: Yes. Love. Marriage. Death. Family ties. Some of the books were on a list I had for Family Life instruction. . . I added others I liked.

Gwen Pharis Ringwood

PAUL: I'm going to write my essay on Leonard Cohen. If it's all right I thought I'd bring my guitar and play and sing some of his songs.
(JODY MONIHAN *moves to desk*.)
MERRILL: That would be fine, Paul. Oh Jody, I'm sorry. You waited to speak to me.
JODY: Yes.
MERRILL: Are you having trouble with your essay?
JODY: No. I didn't write an essay.
MERRILL: Maybe we can find you a subject. What book do you want to use as the basis for your essay?
JODY: I don't figure on staying in this class, Miss Adams. I want to transfer to business English.
MERRILL: Jody! Why?
JODY: I just do, that's all.
MERRILL: Something's bothering you, Jody. What is it?
JODY: I just don't like this class, Miss Adams. I looked at the books on that list. . . I read some of every one, and they aren't even decent. And some of the stuff you read aloud to us isn't decent either.
MERRILL: Not decent? Jody, some of them are classics. All of them were written by serious artists.
JODY: I don't care. I think a lot of those poems are just sick. And I think that whiny Holden has a dirty mind and shouldn't even be in a book. I don't think kids our age should be reading that stuff.
PAUL: What are we supposed to do? Hide our heads like an ostrich? What about movies and t.v. and t.v. ads! They're a lot worse than books. We've talked about some important things in this class.
JODY: We talk about things that shouldn't be talked about too. I don't notice Miss Adams reading us from the Bible.
MERRILL: Jody. There are beautiful writings in the Bible.
PAUL: Sure. The song of Solomon. . . that's love poetry.
MERRILL: Sometimes people read things into what's written that distort the whole meaning. There's a great difference between pornography and the books on that list, Jody.
JODY: That book of sculpture. . . all those women with holes in their bodies. I think they're ugly.
PAUL: They're beautiful!
JODY: That's what you think. Ever since we started all this talk about Family Life I've hated this class. That's why I want a transfer.
MERRILL: I'll talk to your parents, Jody.
JODY: They don't send me to school to learn about touching and sex and family life. They send me to learn things so I can get a job.
MERRILL: Some knowledge of literature and language might help you get a job, Jody. What's more, from some of the things written and said in class, I find a lot of you are confused about sex and love

and human relationships. At your age I was confused too and I couldn't talk about those things at home. That's why felt the books on this list might be useful—both as literature and as guides to how other peoples feel and act. You'll be grown up very soon.

PAUL: You're just hung up on sex, Jody.

JODY: I'm not the one. She is.

MERRILL: That's enough, Jody.

JODY: What about my transfer?

MERRILL: I'll discuss it with your father and mother.

JODY: If I'm grown up enough to read those books and listen to the stuff you read aloud in class, I'm grown up enough to decide about a transfer.

MERRILL: Ask your father or mother to come and see me. Go along now. You too Paul. I have work to do. And put your books back in your desk, Jody. You're still a member of this class.

JODY: You can't make me stay.

MERRILL: I know that. But let's take a little time to think about it. Perhaps I have been insensitive to your feelings. Good night, Paul, Jody.

PAUL: Good night, Miss Adams.

MERRILL: See you tomorrow.

> (PAUL *leaves.*)

JODY: You better just give me the transfer, Miss Adams. My Dad will be up in arms when I show him some of the writing in those books. My Dad's very strict. And he's not scared to say what he thinks, even if he don't count in your kind of society.

MERRILL: Don't be silly. Of course he counts. People count. That's what poets have to say. That it's people who count. . . even foolish, stubborn little girls like you. You tell your father I'll be happy to discuss how I teach English with him at any time. When you and your father have decided what books are fit for your eyes, you'd better get to work reading them. . . if you want to pass this course.

JODY: Huh. You'd fail me anyway now.

MERRILL: That's not true. I may want to spank you but I don't want to fail you. Go now, Jody.

> (JODY *leaves*)

MERRILL: Oh Jody, Jody. How can I reach you? I wanted to give you something besides facts, the rules. . . I wanted to shed light. I think that's why I read those poems in class, why I put up that list of books. . . I think that's why. . .

> (*Voice as* MERRILL *moves back to playing Area A*)

VOICE: Do you teach things outside the curriculum, Miss Adams? Are you of good repute?

2ND VOICE: "A poet is unlikely to make a good regular soldier or a conscientious member of a parliamentary committee." True, Miss

411

Adams? "The poetic imagination is not at all a desirable quality in a statesman." Comment? Plato wanted to bar poets from his republic.

VOICE: He knew they were dangerous. Didn't you?

2ND VOICE: Perhaps you should have barred some of those poets from your English class. Was Jody right? Did you go beyond the bounds, Miss Adams?

(*Sound of telephone on* MERRILL'*s table in playing Area A.* MERRILL *moves to Area A. The actor who plays the male characters in the play appears in Area C with telephone as* CLINT MONIHAN.)

MERRILL: Merrill Adams speaking.

CLINT: Hello? Miss Adams? You teach at Willamont?

MERRILL: Yes.

CLINT: Clint Monihan's my name.

MERRILL: Jody's father.

CLINT: Right. Josephine. I guess you know what this is about.

MERRILL: Jody. . . Josephine asked for a transfer.

CLINT: Yeah. Well, I'll see she gets that all right. What I want to know is why you insist she read books that are blasphemous and unmoral. She showed me some of the sex scenes and dirty obscene words you even read aloud. Those books aren't fit for anyone, let alone. . .

MERRILL: Have you read the books, Mr. Monihan. . . any of the books right through?

CLINT: I don't have time for reading. I earn a living for my family. But we taught our kids right from wrong, and Jody showed me some places that I consider pretty strong stuff. Lots of us parents worry about the kind of education our kids get now. . . this family life education is just a cover-up for loose talk about sex. We didn't hire you to teach family life, Miss Adams.

MERRILL: You don't understand, Mr. Monihan. I wasn't teaching Family Life Education. . . but young people at this age are very confused about. . .

CLINT: Way Jody tells it you got sex on your mind.

MERRILL: I think Jody has problems, Mr. Monihan. . . she's very withdrawn, lonely. . .

CLINT: I'm not surprised if she withdraws from all this free talk in your class. Her face was red as fire when she came home today . . . that's how embarrassed she was. Anyway you give my daughter a transfer to Business English tomorrow.

MERRILL: Very well.

CLINT: And if I were you, I'd remove that list from the classroom and the books on that list from the school. If you don't, I think the principal and the school board should be contacted. Are you prepared to back down on that list?

MERRILL: No, Mr. Monihan. I'm not prepared to back down. The books are by reputable authors and are no threat to the morals or innocence of my students.

CLINT: That depends on the point of view, doesn't it? We'll see. You may find you got a grizzly by the tail. I want Josephine transferred tomorrow. Sooner she's out of your class the better. . . Are you some kind of liberated free thinker? What do you think you gain teaching our kids to go against the way their parents believe?

MERRILL: Goodbye, Mr. Monihan.

(MERRILL hangs up telephone as does CLINT who moves off.)

MERRILL: Oh God, what did I read to the class. . . I can't remember . . . Some poems about love, yes. . . I wanted to share. . .

VOICE: *(Cool and dispassionate)* Your own loneliness? You don't have a man now, Miss Adams. You lost him. Were you sublimating, . . . desire? Lust? Were you asking those kids to share your loneliness? What did you read? You can't remember?

MERRILL: What did I read to them that would. . .

(Slowly) "*As the Mist leaves no Scar*". . . that was one.

As the mist leaves no scar
   On the dark green hill
So my body leaves no scar
   On you, nor ever will.

As wind and hawk encounter. . ."

That was one. And I read from *The Catcher in the Rye.*

(The actor playing male parts comes out as DUBRICK, the principal of school to Area B. MERRILL moves down to him. Chairs may be used.)

DUBRICK: That was unwise, Miss Adams. Please come in. You know that one of your students came to me for a transfer from your class?

MERRILL: Yes, Mr. Dubrick. Jody. . . Josephine Monihan. I hoped I could visit her parents. Mr. Monihan hardly gave me a chance to discuss the transfer when he phoned.

DUBRICK: He phoned me too. He claims you gave out a list of questionable books, read aloud from them in class. He doesn't want his daughter exposed to indecent literature.

MERRILL: Jody's over-reacting to the books, Mr. Dubrick. She's a withdrawn, lonely child. Some of her essays seemed. . . well, as if she needed help.

DUBRICK: You didn't send her to a counsellor, Miss Adams?

MERRILL: No.

DUBRICK: About this list of books? Where did you get it?

Gwen Pharis Ringwood

MERRILL: Some of the books were on a list I had at University. Others were my own choice. Poetry and fiction that have to do with human relationships. . . family life, love, death. . .
DUBRICK: We don't offer Family Life Education in this school. You weren't hired to teach it.
MERRILL: I know that. We were discussing television shows, movies, plays the students had seen. We talked about violence, love, hate, passion. . . Some of those young people seemed to need to know more than they know now. . . I thought the books would be helpful, make discussion easier. I brought the list.
DUBRICK: Thank you. Hmm. . . Shaw; Atwood; Salinger; Shakespeare; Lawrence; Purdy; Cohen; Synge; Whitman; O'Neill; Wolfe. You feel these are all suitable at the Secondary Level?
MERRILL: Yes, Mr. Dubrick, I do. Some of the books are outspoken but students are capable of judgment. In a year or two most of these students will be out earning a living. . . some of them will be married.
DUBRICK: So, you're arming them for the battle of life?
MERRILL: (Protesting) I thought they'd find these particular books interesting. Anyway this year may be the last chance for them to get a feeling for literature, for language and poetry. There's nothing wrong with controversy and ideas and imagery.
DUBRICK: I'm not questioning your motives, Miss Adams. Monihan said that you read aloud passages containing obscenities. . . four letter words.
MERRILL: I'm sure they weren't new to my students.
DUBRICK: No. Or to their parents. But the last thing this school needs is a furore about books or sex education or obscenities in poetry. This is probably a tempest in a tea pot but for now I'll ask you to concentrate on the basics. . . grammar, spelling. . . heaven knows they can benefit from that.
MERRILL: I teach those too, Mr. Dubrick.
DUBRICK: Of course. I understand you write yourself?
MERRILL: I try. I haven't written much lately.
DUBRICK: I'd like to read some of your writing.
MERRILL: I'll. . . I'll see what I can find.
DUBRICK: Fine. I find, Miss Adams, that in the classroom one can generate a good deal of discussion on ecology or war or death. And they're a lot safer than love and sex.
MERRILL: You make me feel as if I'd done something wrong. . . been a bad teacher. I suppose I have if I've lost a student. I. . . I'll miss Jody.
DUBRICK: I've been pleased with your work so far, Miss Adams. And you're not losing a scholar in Josephine Monihan. She's probably better off in Business English.
MERRILL: I still feel bad about her. I just couldn't seem to reach her.

DUBRICK: We always fail to reach some of our students. And some parents too. I'll drop into your class soon. . . give you a little support. Thanks for coming, in, Miss Adams.
> (MUSIC *bridge guitar. . .* DUBRICK *moves out with one of the chairs.* MERRILL *moves desk slightly, puts on glasses, sits down as if behind her own desk in school room.* JODY *moves towards her.*)

MERRILL: You weren't in class, Jody.

JODY: I came to get my books, Miss Adams.

MERRILL: We'll miss you. (*No answer*) Tell me, why are you afraid of words or a picture or a piece of sculpture?

JODY: I already told you. . . because it's all phony. Ugly.

MERRILL: I want to help you, Jody. I was brought up very strictly too. I think I understand. . .

JODY: I don't need your help, Miss Adams.
> (PAUL *moves to them.*)

PAUL: Miss Adams, I have to tell you something. Wait, Jody. . . you're in it, too.

MERRILL: In what, Paul?

PAUL: You know my column for the Willamont Courier? High School Rambles? Well yesterday I wrote about that list of books and our right to read them. I didn't mention any names but I told about a student objecting. Anyway it's in the paper this morning and Mr. Harding says there's already been phone calls. I didn't want to make any trouble for you, Miss Adams, or Jody. . .

JODY: Why did you write it then?

PAUL: I told you. Because I don't believe in censorship. That's why!

JODY: I don't care what you wrote. I don't even read that paper. You're supposed to sign my transfer, Miss Adams.

MERRILL: Very well, Jody. There you are.
> (JODY *takes paper and leaves.*)

PAUL: I brought my column, Miss Adams. Shall I read it?

MERRILL: Please.

PAUL: "Yesterday one of our classmates left class because she objected to reading a list of books chosen by our teacher to help us understand the problems we face in modern life. We are very confused about our future and anything that can help us to understand the adult world is good. So I can't understand why any student should object to books and poems dealing with love and sex and family relationships. I will defend to the death my right to read."

I really mean that, Miss Adams.

MERRILL: Some people think books are dangerous, Paul. They burned books in Hitler's Germany.

PAUL: Mr. Harding said they burned books in the southern states just a year or so ago. That wouldn't ever happen here would it?

Gwen Pharis Ringwood

MERRILL: I hope not, Paul. Good night.
(MUSIC. . . MERRILL *moves from center Area to Area A as telephone in Area A rings. . . Male actor as* STEVE HARDING *moves to Area C with telephone.*)
MERRILL: Hello.
STEVE: Miss Adams?
MERRILL: Speaking.
STEVE: Steve Harding here, editor of the Willamont Courier. Have you seen our morning paper?
MERRILL: No.
STEVE: Paul Rae wrote a student column.
MERRILL: Yes. He read it to me, after school.
STEVE: Did a student leave class because of objections to a list of books?
MERRILL: Yes.
STEVE: Have you any comment, Miss Adams?
MERRILL: The books on that list are good books, Mr. Harding.
STEVE: Mrs. Verna Gliddens has just left my office. She's running as candidate for the School Board. Mrs. Gliddens asks me to publish your list in the Courier. Have you any objection?
MERRILL: I. . . I don't know. Perhaps I should talk it over with my principal.
STEVE: He knows about the books, then?
MERRILL: He does now. Yes.
STEVE: Mrs. Gliddens raises some questions about the selections you read aloud to your class. Can you tell me what they were?
MERRILL: Not off hand. I usually read a poem or a piece of prose to . . well, it starts the class off. . . I choose pieces I like. Sometimes I ask a student to read the selection.
STEVE: Of course. Would you grant me a personal interview, Miss Adams? I think it's important to get the facts before the public.
MERRILL: You make it sound as if I'm on trial.
STEVE: Secondary education is a touchy subject around here. Especially with the School Board election coming up. Could I talk to you some time tomorrow?
MERRILL: I suppose so.
STEVE: Thank you. I'll be in touch. Oh, by the way, Mrs. Gliddens is on local television tonight. She will probably bring up the list.
MERRILL: I see. Goodbye, Mr. Harding. (MERRILL *puts down the telephone.*) Why am I frightened? There's nothing wrong with those books or the things I read aloud. What did I read aloud? I can't even remember. What did I read? Some things I wrote. Some poems I'd collected.
(*As she leafs through some papers her own voice and that of* PAUL RAE *and others blend in a kind of collage. . . One selection falling away as another takes over. . . With the occasional ripple of music (guitar or flute) blended with the reading.*)

416

VOICE: What did you read, Miss Adams?
MERRILL: "As the mist leaves no scar
on the dark green hill
So my body leaves no scar
On you, nor ever will
As wind and hawk encounter. . .
VOICE: Yes. Cohen. You read a lot of his poems.
2ND VOICE: What about this one?
IMPOSED VOICE OVER: Go by brooks, love,
where fish stare. . .
Go by brooks, . . .
VOICE: In my craft of sullen art
Exercised in the still night
When only the moon rages
And the lovers lie abed. . .
IMPOSED VOICE: Go by rivers, where eels throng. . .
Rivers, love. . .
VOICE: Galileo, Galilei
Comes to knock and knock again
At a small secluded doorway
In the ordinary brain. . .
MERRILL: Apple trees are bent and breaking
And the heat is not the sun's
And the Minotaur is waking
And the streets are cattle-runs. . .
IMPOSED VOICE: Go by oceans, where whales sail. . .
Oceans love. . .
VOICE: And the orchard which is burning
And the hills which take the light;
PAUL: And she leads you to the river
she is wearing rags and feathers
from Salvation army counters
The sun pours down like honey
VOICE: O Comrades, this instant is the javelin
We hurl through Time's enormous shield
Never wear it silent under the
fingers or pen it raging behind
a walled humility.
MERRILL: Give it life, comrades
VOICE: In this friend's face I know
the grizzly still, and in the mirror.
lay my ear to the radio's conch
and hear the atom's terror.
VOICE: . . . high in space together
The clinching interlocking claws, a living, fierce, gyrating
wheel
Four beating winds, two beaks, a swirling mass

Gwen Pharis Ringwood

PAUL: My father moved through dooms of love
MERRILL: I went out to a hazel wood
             because a fire was in my head. . .
VOICE: From the raging moon I write
         On these spindrift pages
         Not for the towering dead
MERRILL: But for the lovers, their arms
             round the grief of the ages. . .
VOICE: And the orchard which is burning
         And the hills which take the light
         And the candles which have melted
         On the altars of the night

         Galileo, Galilei
         Comes to knock and knock again
         At a small secluded doorway
         In the ordinary brain.
PAUL: His sorrow was as true as bread
         no liar looked him in the head
         and every child was sure that spring
         danced when she heard my father sing. . .
2ND VOICE: And pluck till time and times are done
             The silver apples of the moon, the golden
             apples of the sun.
VOICE: Tomorrow and tomorrow and tomorrow
         Creeps on this petty pace from day to day
         and all our yesterdays have lighted fools
OVER VOICE: to the last syllable of recorded time
             and all our yesterdays have lighted fools
             The way to dusty death. . .
VOICE: And dreaming through the twilight
             that doth not rise or set
         Happily I will remember or happily forget.

         they are not long, the days of wine and roses,
         Love and desire and hate. . .
         Our path emerges for awhile. . .
MERRILL: This instant is the scimitar with which we sever darkness.
         Never wear it silent under the
         fingers or pen it raging behind
         a walled humility.
         Give it life comrades
         Make it freer than ourselves.

         There's nothing wrong with those words. . .
         why am I frightened?
         (*She remains in Area A as the lights come up on Area C.*

The female actor as VERNA GLIDDENS *appears as if making a speech before a television camera.*)

VERNA: My friends, Mrs. Purvis, the chair person, of the School Board denies that any list on family education went out from the School Board office. Nevertheless a list of books was given out in English A at Willamont Secondary. I have it here. I received it from the father of a student who found the discussion generated by these books in English A offensive and embarrassing. I have looked at some of the books on this list. I would not want them in my home. The books will be on display at our next meeting of the Dedicated Parents League, of which I am a member. You will be able to judge for yourself. My friends, I promise that if I am elected to the School Board I will fight to see that we parents decide what reading material is given to our children. Thank you.

   (*As the lights go down on Area C and* MRS. GLIDDENS, *the telephone rings in* MERRILL's *apartment. She answers, holds the phone for a moment and then slowly, fearfully puts it down. The actress who played* JODY *now appears costumed as* MRS. PURVIS, *chairman of the School Board and is joined by* STEVE HARDING.)

MRS. PURVIS: No list of books on Family Life Education went out from the School Board office, Mr. Harding.

STEVE: Where did it come from then?

MRS. PURVIS: One of our teachers put it up in her classroom.

STEVE: Does the Board countenance Family Life Education at the discretion of a teacher?

MRS. PURVIS: The Board is looking into the matter.

STEVE: Did you know a committee of Dedicated Parents has been formed to check into the material used in English classes at Willamont High?

MRS. PURVIS: I've been away.

STEVE: An exhibit and report on such material is to be shown to coincide with your next School Board meeting. Will that meeting concern itself with this matter?

MRS. PURVIS: Yes.

STEVE: Will your meeting be open to the press?

MRS. PURVIS: I don't know yet.

STEVE: This is a democracy, Mrs. Purvis. We've had calls at the paper asserting that our educational policy is being dictated by pointy-headed intellectuals and communists. Are you a communist?

MRS. PURVIS: Oh for heaven's sakes, of course I'm not a communist! I'm an elected member of the School Board that saw fit to make me Chair Person.

STEVE: Mrs. Purvis, there's been controversy about Family Life Education and Language programs in Alberta, California, Ontario, Virginia and in British Columbia. They burned books in Kentucky, Mrs. Purvis.

419

Gwen Pharis Ringwood

MRS. PURVIS: We have not initiated a Family Life Program.

STEVE: Rumor has it that this list was a try-out.

MRS. PURVIS: That is not true.

STEVE: Is it true that a special Board meeting has been called to consider the dismissal of the teacher in question?

MRS. PURVIS: No such meeting has been called.

STEVE: Then you don't intend to fire the teacher?

MRS. PURVIS: I didn't say that. We intend to look into the whole matter.

STEVE: Thanks for talking to me, Mrs. Purvis.

(STEVE *leaves Area B as* MRS. PURVIS *picks up telephone*.)

MRS. PURVIS: Mr. Dubrick. Opal Purvis speaking. I think we'd better get together over this book list business, Mr. Dubrick. . . Miss Adams is it? No, I prefer to talk to you without her being present at this time. This afternoon? Good. Thank you, Mr. Dubrick.

(MUSIC *bridge as* OPAL PURVIS *moves off*.)

(STEVE *and* MERRILL *play this scene in Area A* MERRILL's *apartment. Knock*.)

MERRILL: Yes? Who is it?

STEVE: Steve Harding from the Courier, Miss Adams.

MERRILL: (*Opening the door*) Hello, Mr. Harding.

STEVE: I wanted to talk to you about an editorial I'm writing. . . over your battle of the books. . .

MERRILL: I didn't mean it to be a battle.

STEVE: I'm afraid Paul's defense of his right to read is causing a lot of trouble. For you, especially.

MERRILL: The worst part of it is I'm beginning to feel guilty. Please sit down. What do you want to know?

STEVE: Facts, mostly.

MERRILL: You published the list. You know the books.

STEVE: Look, I'm no witch hunter, Miss Adams. I may even be able to help you. You say you always read poetry or some prose selection to begin your class?

MERRILL: Yes. Until lately. I like to start a class off with something that. . . well, expands their awareness. . .

STEVE: You've read excerpts from Ginsberg, Purdy, Earle Birney, D.H. Lawrence?

MERRILL: Yes. And others.

STEVE: Poems about loneliness and love and sex. . ?

MERRILL: And about bears and cats and sharks and Hiroshima and Dachau and Vietnam and God. I chose things that seem meaningful to me. . . to my students. . . to our times.

STEVE: You know, Miss Adams, many people have been brought up to consider any reference to human sexuality out of bounds? An invasion of privacy.

MERRILL: Yes. I was brought up that way.

420

STEVE: Your own parents would object to some of these selections?
MERRILL: My mother would. My father's dead.
STEVE: So you knew you were on dangerous ground?
MERRILL: No. I didn't. I don't. As I said, the worst thing is I keep wondering if I really have done something wrong.
STEVE: So, you regret the way you have been teaching English A?
MERRILL: No. I want my students to care about the language, to appreciate that words aren't just a string of dried cat-gut. That words don't need to be ads for toothpaste or newspaper reports . . . I'm sorry.
STEVE: That's all right. But why didn't you stick to Shakespeare? He says it all, and you'd be spared all this back-lash?
MERRILL: We do study Shakespeare. But I wanted my class to realize that we have poets who live in their world, their society. Cummings called poetry "a remembrance of miracles". . . the miracle of everything, of being alive. Does that sound dangerous? Immoral?
STEVE: No. (*Pause*) Miss Adams, were you at Kent state in Ohio in May, 1970?
MERRILL: Yes. Yes, I was. Why?
STEVE: You lived in a commune?
MERRILL: I stayed in a big house where a lot of people were staying.
STEVE: Activists?
MERRILL: Some were.
STEVE: You marched with the protesters on the day of the shooting?
MERRILL: Yes. Why do you ask me this?
STEVE: Someone in the town has made it their business to ferret out incidents in your life, Merrill. You were involved with a man named Rick D'Arcy?
MERRILL: That was nearly seven years ago. I wasn't eighteen then. What has that to do with now?
STEVE: Some people want you fired.
MERRILL: I'm a good teacher. I know I am.
STEVE: Paul Rae says you're the best teacher he's ever had. Merrill, some time ago I read a story in Northern Review. . . "Night on Garibaldi". You wrote it?
MERRILL: Yes.
STEVE: The story starts with a ski trip, but it's really about the young woman's thoughts after she's had an abortion. Is that right?
MERRILL: Yes. Only it wasn't meant to be as. . . well, you make it sound different than I meant.
STEVE: I liked the story. You also had another one in the Review. . . "Cover Me with Leaves."
MERRILL: I wrote that five years ago.
STEVE: The rape and death of a stranger in a small town.
MERRILL: It was based on a true story.
STEVE: And the other wasn't? (*Pause*) Tell me about Josephine Monihan.
MERRILL: For the paper?

Gwen Pharis Ringwood

STEVE: No. I'm trying to get a perspective on this affair.
MERRILL: Jody's hard to reach. She seems sullen and doesn't make friends at school. Some of her essays made me feel sad. . . they were very emotional and confused. . . especially about sin and punishment. I kept hoping I would get to know her better, perhaps help her somehow.
STEVE: Her father gave Mrs. Gliddens your book list.
MERRILL: I can't believe all this could result from a class in English literature.
STEVE: The Battle of the Books always makes good copy, Merrill. The city papers have picked up on this one.
MERRILL: Oh no. . . my mother will be so upset.
SOUND: *Telephone rings. . .*
STEVE: Your telephone.
MERRILL: I'm afraid to answer it. I've been getting obscene calls. . .
STEVE: Go on. Answer it.
MERRILL: Hello. Yes, Mr. Dubrick. Tomorrow night? Yes, I'll listen. You'll be on the panel. I see. Thank you.
(*She puts down the receiver.*)
MERRILL: My principal says there's a radio program on Family Life Education in the school. He says I'd better listen.
STEVE: I'm on that panel.
MERRILL: Mr. Dubrick says I've opened "a can of worms." I hate that expression.
STEVE: Yeah. I like "a remembrance of miracles." Hang on to that one. And Merrill, get yourself an unlisted telephone number. Good night now.
MUSIC: *Bridge. . .*
(*Actors as* MONIHAN, PAUL RAE, VERNA GLIDDENS, HARDING *appear with microphones in Area B. . .* MERRILL *listens in Area A.*)
MONIHAN: I'm Clint Monihan. I don't pretend to be a public speaker but I know what I think. Mrs. Monihan and I have brought up our children to respect their teachers, their parents and their religion. We think these Family Life subjects are the affair of the parents and the church, and we don't approve of books that discuss personal matters or show free living. I think we in Willamont should be careful of the kind of teachers we hire to teach our kids.
ANNOUNCER'S VOICE: Thank you, Mr. Monihan. And now, Paul Rae.
PAUL: When I wrote my column three weeks ago I didn't expect to stir up all this argument. We had a meeting at school and 70% of students think that talks about human problems should be part of school. Especially at our age. In one or two years we'll be voting or fighting in a war or getting married and having children. We see a lot of immoral things but it's not because of books. In English A we've been trying to really look at modern

society. I don't believe the censorship of books will make a more moral society. Thank you.

ANNOUNCER'S VOICE: Mrs. Verna Gliddens. School Board Candidate.

VERNA: I believe in old fashioned values — work, morality and the sanctity of the home. I oppose any school or any teacher or educational policy that infringes on our rights as parents. I find most of the books on this infamous list offensive and I resent the fact that parents have no voice in choosing the reading material used in the school or placed in the school library. We pay the piper but we don't get to call the tune. And it is our tax money. They are our children. If elected I promise you. . .

ANNOUNCER: Thank you, Mrs. Gliddens. Mr. Harding, editor of the Courier is our final panelist.

STEVE: I hope the people in Willamont will stay cool on this issue. These students have been brought up with television, movies, magazines and newspapers that are very explicit about aspects of life that used to be taboo. We ask our schools to do many things that once were the province of the home — health, physical fitness, domestic arts, drugs education, student counselling. Do any of you really think that the fiction or poetry on that list can turn your children into delinquents? Gossip, rumor, fear and envy, bigotry are what we have to watch out for. . . not books.

ANNOUNCER'S VOICE: And now we have some time for calls from our listeners. The lines are open for your opinion.

> (*The panelists remain in Area B.* MERRILL *listens in Area A. During the telephone scene which is a kind of collage. . . snips of ads for violent movies, news reports, ads may be flashed on a screen in Area C with very brief musical snatches interrupting. . . The scene could be a nightmare in* MERRILL's *mind. Telephone rings. . .*)

VOICE: What I think is teachers live off the fat of the land and don't care about the kids they teach. They got short hours, long holidays, high pay. And you see teachers sitting in the pubs at all hours. That's what I think.

> (*Telephone*)

VOICE: Mr. Harding's right. This uproar over a list of dirty books so called has turned Willamont into a laughing stock. We've hit every paper in the country.

> (*Telephone*)

VOICE: What we got to face is that these so-called liberals are front troops for a communist take-over. They're boring in. Just like they're behind the movement to make us register all fire-arms. A man's duty is to protect his home.

> (*Telephone*)

VOICE: The beast is in the land. It's Sodom and Gomorrah all over again. Sodom and Gomorrah.

> (*Telephone*)

VOICE: This namby-pamby school board should fire that teacher. . . the sooner she's out the better. Get rid of this school board, get rid of those books, get rid of that teacher. . . it's as simple as that.

(*Telephone*)

VOICE: Those books corrupt our innocent children. I'd like to see those books burned in public. Burn them. Burn them.

(*A long shrill musical sound as lights go down on Area B and* MERRILL *clicks off the radio.*)

MERRILL: Oh I can't listen any more. I can't. What have I done? What have I unleashed?

COOL IMPERSONAL VOICES: Are you a good teacher, Miss Adams. Have you anything to hide?
"Whatsoever things are of good repute". . .
are you of good repute, Miss Adams?
Why did you choose those particular poems?
Out of loneliness? Regret? Desire?
Why? Why?

(PAUL RAE *moves to Area A and knocks.* . .)

MERRILL: Yes. Who is it?

PAUL: It's me. Paul Rae.

MERRILL: Hello, Paul.

PAUL: Did you hear that radio program, Miss Adams?

MERRILL: I heard the first part. I turned it off.

PAUL: Bunch of cranks, mostly.

MERRILL: They don't think they're cranks. They think they're right. And I think I'm right. I hope I am. Did you want something, Paul?

PAUL: No, not really. Except to see if you're all right. If it wasn't for that column I wrote you wouldn't be in this fuss.

MERRILL: I think there would have been complaints anyway, Paul. Mr. Monihan would see to it.

PAUL: And Mrs. Gliddens saw her chance to make it an election issue.

MERRILL: What do your parents think?

PAUL: My Dad says it's hysterical nonsense. My mother. . . well, she joined the Parents' committee. . . she's kind of narrow minded. She only reads Red Book herself.

MERRILL: Oh, I never meant to cause all this trouble. Shouldn't you be at home, Paul?

PAUL: Yeah, I guess so. I wish I could help you, Miss Adams. I really do. I. . . I think you're beautiful.

MERRILL: You'd better go, Paul. I have work to do.

PAUL: Right. I'd better go. Walking over here I was thinking a lot about the poems you read to us. Who wrote that one that starts "I went out to a hazel wood, because a fire was in my head."

MERRILL: Yeats. The Song of Wandering Aengus.

PAUL: There was another one that I memorized. . .
"Galileo, Galilei

Comes to knock and knock again
At a small secluded doorway
In the ordinary brain.

Into light the world is turning
And the clocks are set for six
And the chimney pots are smoking
And the golden candle sticks.

Apple trees are bent. . .

MERRILL: You must go, Paul. Thanks for coming. I did teach you something, didn't I?

PAUL: I wish you'd read poems in class again, Miss Adams.

MERRILL: I will. I promise. Goodnight.

PAUL: (*reluctant to leave*) That poem about Galileo. Who wrote it?

MERRILL: Andrew Smith. An American poet.

PAUL: "Apple trees are bent and breaking
And the heat is not the sun's
And the Minotaur is waking
And the streets are cattle runs. . .

What does it mean?

MERRILL: I'm not sure I know, Paul. But I like it too.

PAUL: At least nobody can complain about that poem. What amazes me is how poets find just the right words. . . the exact right words.

MERRILL: They work at it. They work very hard to find them.

PAUL: Yeah, I guess so. Well, I'd better go. . .

MERRILL: Yes.

PAUL: If I can help you in any way. Well, I really want to. I mean. . . I wish I could. . .

MERRILL: Good night, Paul.

(PAUL *leaves reluctantly.* . . MERRILL, *shaken by* PAUL's *adoration, turns away.*)

MERRILL: Dear Paul. . . I mustn't hurt you. I mustn't.
. . . *Music bridge*

COOL IMPERSONAL VOICES: Isn't that what you want, Miss Adams? That all your students love you. . .
that they think you beautiful and brave and daring. . .
Is that what you want? You want them to love you?

MERRILL: No. No! I wanted to reach out, share with them.

VOICE: Are you sure? How do you feel about teaching?
How do you really feel about your class?
Do you know how you feel, Miss Adams?

MERRILL: I think I know. I look at them, see their faces. . . wary, suspicious. . . I face their unknown faces. I look at them and wonder what shivers the spine, what activates the skull. . .

425

What shudders tremulous flesh?
What dreams or nightmares crouch on the edge of sleep?
VOICE: You'd invade their privacy then? Is that what you want, Miss
Adams?
MERRILL: No. No. Don't you see,
I remember how it was with me when I was that age.
I want to reach out. . . to know them. . .
VOICE: They're not the same as you. How could you know them?
How pretend to know?
MERRILL: There's no way to know them. No way to wholly know.
VOICE: You see? Why not be content to give them the facts, teach them
the basics? You're safe with the three R's, the facts, statistics.
That's what teaching's about. . . purveying facts.
MERRILL: Sometimes my class and I, we look at one another, share
some word, idea. . . some image, we break a word in half and
share it, make a sign in space. . . we look to one another as if
each flashed uncertain signals in the dark. . . one. . . to the
other.
VOICE: Uncertain signals. Really? In the dark?
Tiberius used light signals to keep in touch with Rome. You do
teach facts then?
MERRILL: And when it happens, when we reach one another, I always
wonder if it's enough. . . Can this be light enough for them or
me? I ask myself. And then I think. . . "it must be. . .
It may be all the light there is.
It must be."
(*Music bridge. . .*)
(OPAL PURVIS, VERNA GLIDDENS, CLINT MONIHAN *are in
Area B.*)
VERNA: The League of Dedicated Parents is meeting in the library,
Mrs. Purvis. They ask Mr. Monihan and I to report back to them
about the action the School Board is taking over the book
controversy. Where's the principal?
PURVIS: Mr. Dubrick couldn't be here tonight.
VERNA: I thought he was making a report to your Board.
PURVIS: Next meeting.
VERNA: Rather late, isn't it?
MONIHAN: We want this thing settled.
VERNA: What action is the Board prepared to take?
PURVIS: The Board has instructed that an advisory committee
consisting of seven teachers and seven parents be set up. . . this
committee is to review all books on the curriculum in Willamont
schools.
VERNA: We'd prefer nine parents, seven teachers. . .
MONIHAN: That's right. Teachers come and go. Parents live here. . .
they should have control.
PURVIS: The Board feels neither teachers or parents should have a
majority.

VERNA: Does the committee also have authority to dispose of questionable books in the school libraries?
PURVIS: If the committee votes that to be necessary, the Board has empowered them to review the library books too.
VERNA: Good.
PURVIS: Your group could elect their seven representatives tonight, if you wish. The teachers will choose their delegates next week. . . The Board asks that Mr. Dubrick, the principal of Willamont Secondary be one of the committee.
VERNA: Well, I suppose the League will accept these terms. I'll recommend that we do accept. Now the second question. . .
MONIHAN: Yes. What action are you taking about that teacher, Merrill Adams?
PURVIS: No action will be taken at this time.
MONIHAN: No action! What do you mean by that?
VERNA: You aren't firing this teacher?
PURVIS: We've deferred this matter until we get a report from the local Teachers Association and Mr. Dubrick; we also expect to ask Miss Adams to state her own position to the Board.
MONIHAN: Her position! She's the cause of this uproar. She's the one sponsoring immoral books, delinquent actions, free living.
PURVIS: Mr. Monihan, the School Board refuses to be swayed by the hysteria that is taking over this town. We feel. . .
VERNA: So I'm expected to go back to those parents and tell them you haven't dismissed Merrill Adams. You're making a mistake, Mrs. Purvis.
MONIHAN: As long as she's teaching, you won't get support from us parents. You better think about that.
PURVIS: We did think about it. A young teacher's reputation is at stake, Mr. Monihan.
MONIHAN: That's her fault. She should have thought about her reputation when she. . .
PURVIS: We also think of the possibility of a suit brought against the Board, the possibility of staff members resigning in sympathy. We need time.
MONIHAN: That teacher should have been fired weeks ago!
PURVIS: Look, some one's throwing books out the library window.
VERNA: I told you, people are angry. . .
PURVIS: My God, next thing they'll be burning books in the streets. . . Come on, we must stop this. Now!
   (*Music bridge.* . .)
   (*Lights up on Area A* MERRILL *and* STEVE HARDING. . .)
MERRILL: Mr. Dubrick told me to stay out of that meeting, Steve, but I went anyway. . . I asked to speak and they said I could and I started. I thought I was getting through to them. Then there was some confusion at the back and the next thing was somebody throwing books out the window. Then one of my students ran in

and told me someone had messed up my classroom. My papers were all over the place and some things I'd written were torn in two. And there was something on the board. It said "We don't want your kind in Willamont." I just want to run and hide. . .

STEVE HARDING: You can't run. No place to hide. Did a reporter from the Sun talk to you tonight?

MERRILL: No.

STEVE: He will. He's been interviewing a lot of people. His angle is that Willamont is a sick town, and all its frustrations are being played out over this one issue.

MERRILL: If this gets in the papers at home, my mother will be humiliated. She'll never understand how I got into it. We've never been able to talk.

STEVE: I'm sure she'll survive.

MERRILL: I haven't written anything about this to her. I couldn't. I never told her about being at Kent State or about Rick or. . . I've never told her about anything important.

(*Telephone rings.* DUBRICK *phones from Area B.*)

MERRILL: Yes.

DUBRICK: Nick Dubrick here. Are you all right?

MERRILL: Yes.

DUBRICK: I understand your classroom was messed up. Anything missing?

MERRILL: I don't know for sure. Papers were thrown around and books. . .

DUBRICK: I want you to take a week or so off from your classes, Miss Adams. You've been under a lot of strain. You'll probably be glad of the rest.

MERRILL: You mean I've been fired, Mr. Dubrick?

DUBRICK: No. The School Board asks you to appear at their next meeting. . . that's after the election. I'll be there too.

MERRILL: Wouldn't it be better for everybody if I just resign?

DUBRICK: No.

MERRILL: It would save trouble for you.

DUBRICK: If you resign, I feel I must resign too, Miss Adams. A principal is responsible for the conduct of his school. Could you come in and see me on Friday?

MERRILL: Yes, sir. I'm sorry, Mr. Dubrick.

(DUBRICK *hangs up and* MERRILL *puts down receiver.*)

MERRILL: I'm not to teach for a week or so. . . Somebody else will be teaching my classes. . .

STEVE: You still care, don't you?

MERRILL: Yes, I care. I really care.

(*Music bridge as lights are up on Area C. . .*)

ANNOUNCER: December 18 may go down as a record turn-out for voters in Willamont. Final Results for Town Council should be in within the hour. What we do know is that Mrs. Verna

428

Gliddens has won the vacant school board position by a large
majority. And here she is. . . Verna Gliddens.
VERNA: Thank you for electing me. I pledge myself to the task of
resisting forces that would undermine the education of our most
precious commodity. . . our children.
(*As the lights fade on Area C* MR. DUBRICK *moves into
Area B and sits at desk.* MERRILL *moves to him.*)
DUBRICK: Sit down, Miss Adams. We've missed you in the school.
MERRILL: I've missed my classes. How are they getting on?
DUBRICK: They've been very busy signing petitions to get you back.
Please sit down! One petition has gone to the Courier, one to me.
And one is going to the School Board. In Assembly we've had
speeches about the Dreyfus Case, the trial of Carrie Nation, the
the great evolution controversy. You're a cause célèbre.
MERRILL: What will happen at the Board meeting tomorrow, Mr.
Dubrick?
DUBRICK: They've asked me for a statement. Then I think they'll call
on you to. . . defend yourself. Mrs. Purvis is very anxious that
you get a hearing before the whole Board.
MERRILL: Oh, God help me.
DUBRICK: They're not all out for blood, Miss Adams. And after all
Mrs. Gliddens is the new member. . . she may not be too vocal.
The meeting's in camera. So we'll be spared the press and the
media. A quite informal session. I'm hoping we'll be able to
keep to the facts. It's the rumours and innuendo that are fanning
the flames now.
MERRILL: About me?
DUBRICK: Yes. About your private life. . . before you came to
Willamont. And about the stories you wrote. Someone has taken
the trouble to. . . look into those.
MERRILL: I see. Will they want me to apologize. . . for my whole life?
DUBRICK: I doubt it. Perhaps for teaching outside the curriculum. Do
you feel like apologizing?
MERRILL: For awhile I just wanted to run away. But that would be
admitting that my teaching in English A was wrong. I. . . I've
examined my conscience over and over, Mr. Dubrick. . . I don't
think my teaching was wrong. No. I can't apologize.
DUBRICK: If you had it to do over again would you put up that book
list. . . carry on the same class discussions. . . read the same
selections aloud to the class.
MERRILL: Knowing now how it's upset this town, I'd be a fool if I did.
But in my heart I think I was right.
DUBRICK: I've looked at the books pretty carefully. Some of them
shocked me.
MERRILL: The National news is shocking.
DUBRICK: The news comes into the house and can be turned off. When
we recommend books to our students we have some responsibility

429

as to their value and effect. Take the four letter words. . . one of the main causes for this whole seething uproar. We don't use obscenities in the classroom. Most of us avoid them in ordinary conversation. Of course the students know the words but that doesn't mean we countenance foul language in our schools. I'm not saying writers haven't the right to use such expressions, but I don't want to run a school in which anything goes. And I am running a school. You do see my position?

MERRILL: Yes, I do. But the four letter words aren't the reason the book was written. The books have something to say about the . . . human situation.

DUBRICK: Were you in no way embarrassed when you read those passages from *The Catcher in the Rye* in an English A class?

MERRILL: Perhaps I was. . . a little. But we were talking about Holden's fight against evil, and the passage where he says he couldn't rub off all the. . . obscenities. . . on the walls in the city if he had a million years to do it, is relevant to that fight. That's why I read the passage.

DUBRICK: These stories, Miss Adams. Yours. Someone left them on my desk yesterday. They are very explicit in both subject matter and language. The language in Cover me with Leaves is rough. Perhaps writers travel in freer circles than most of us. Do you think you have failed to understand the customs and values of a small town?

MERRILL: I was brought up in a small town.

DUBRICK: Could it be that you've been pushing your students towards some sort of. . . sophistication. . . above their age group?

MERRILL: You make me sound like a. . . a child seducer. I was very strictly brought up. And I was a very confused adolescent. Young people need to talk about their problems. The books were a way to open up those subjects. I. . . I didn't intend my stories for adolescents. I didn't read them in class.

DUBRICK: We aren't psychiatrists, Miss Adams. We're teachers.

MERRILL: I wasn't trying to be a psychiatrist. I'm teaching English literature and hoping in the subject to show them some. . . well, not answers, but at least some understanding of people, life.

DUBRICK: You're a popular teacher. I think a good one. I want to support you tomorrow, but if I don't do it unreservedly it's because I can't. I must prepare you for censure from me. . . as well as from so many people in this community. I'm sorry.

MERRILL: (*Close to tears.*) So am I. Whatever happens, I really love this school, Mr. Dubrick. Please, may I go now?

DUBRICK: I'll see you tomorrow.

(*Music bridge. . .*)
(MR. DUBRICK *remains in Area B as* MERRILL *moves just outside.* JODY *appears as if waiting outside to see* MR. DUBRICK.)

MERRILL: Jody. You wanted to see me?

DUBRICK: No. I wanted to see Mr. Dubrick.

MERRILL: Can't I help you?

JODY: No. I didn't mean to get you fired, Miss Adams.

MERRILL: I haven't been fired, Jody.

JODY: My Dad says you will be. My Dad says I have to go to that School Board meeting tomorrow. That's why I have to see Mr. Dubrick.

MERRILL: To tell him you're going?

JODY: No. I want him to tell my Dad I don't have to go.

MERRILL: You've changed your mind about the books, Jody?

JODY: No. But I can't go. It's nothing to do with you. It's something else. Something I can't talk about. . . and they might ask me. My Dad says they'll want to know about my character.

MERRILL: They might ask you what, Jody?

JODY: It's none of your business, Miss Adams. Because it was a long time ago, and it wasn't my fault either. It wasn't ever my fault.

MERRILL: Jody, what happened to your wrist?

JODY: Nothing. I. . . I hurt myself.

MERRILL: Jody, no. . .

JODY: Will you tell Mr. Dubrick to tell my Dad I can't go to that meeting, Miss Adams?

MERRILL: Yes. Yes, I will. (*Turning back*) Come with me. Mr. Dubrick. . .

DUBRICK: Yes?

MERRILL: Jody. . . Jody Monihan wants to talk to you. Please help her, Mr. Dubrick. Please.

DUBRICK: Come in, Jody. What can I do for you?

JODY: It's about. . .

MERRILL: Jody hurt her wrist, Mr. Dubrick.

DUBRICK: I see. You go along, Miss Adams. I'll take care of this.

MERRILL: Perhaps I could. . .

DUBRICK: I'll see you tomorrow, Miss Adams.

> *Brief music bridge. . .*

(The lights go down on JODY *and* MR. DUBRICK.)

MERRILL: Jody, what have I done? I wanted to help you. What have I done?. . .

> (MERRILL *moves towards stage right where* STEVE *waits for her.*)

MERRILL: Oh, Steve, I'm glad to see you.

STEVE: I've been waiting for you. Come on, let's go have a drink. You look like you need it.

MERRILL: I just saw Jody Monihan.

STEVE: Well?

MERRILL: Oh, I don't know. . . I'm just upset, that's all.

STEVE: Sit down. Look, Merrill, there are a lot of people around here you can count on. . . I'm one.

(*They sit in Area A*)

MERRILL: I know. I can't tell you how much I appreciate your being around the last few weeks.

STEVE: I think what you're doing is important. I like your courage. I like you.

MERRILL: Will you be at the School Board meeting tomorrow?

STEVE: Cheer up. Don't worry about tomorrow. I've written an editorial and I've sent a special delivery copy to Opal Purvis so she'll have it before she chairs that meeting. It's good. Do you want to hear it?

MERRILL: Right now everything that's been said or happened since October is going round in my head. I keep asking myself questions. . .

STEVE: Stop asking. Listen. Are you listening?

MERRILL: I'm listening.

STEVE: Okay. "Tomorrow the School Board meets in camera to discuss the Battle of the Books which has been raging in Willamont for two months. When a scapegoat is found, the fears and frustrations of a community surface and attach themselves to the victim at hand. In primitive societies, the sacrificial victim was stoned to death. In Willamont many things are being played out that have nothing to do with the teaching of English, a list of books, or four-letter words, or the language employed by poets. Books aren't hurting Willamont. Poetry isn't hurting Willamont. A young teacher of English is no threat to Willamont. But fear and anger and hate can destroy this town."

What do you think of that? Pretty good eh?

MERRILL: Yes. It's. . . it's fine.

STEVE: You don't sound very impressed.

MERRILL: Sorry. It's just that the truth about everything. . . anything . . . is so complex. Nothing's ever simple. (*Pause*) I wonder if I can make a living. . . writing.

STEVE: Oh come on. After tomorrow things will simmer down. . . you'll be back in your classroom. . . all those kids will think their petition saved you from the dragon. I'll think this editorial saved you. Dubrick and the Teachers' Alliance will think. . .

MERRILL: Sure. I'll be queen of the May.

STEVE: I've got to go. I've work to do. Wear a pretty dress tomorrow and smile a lot and when you go in to face the lions, don't let them see you tremble. Good luck.

MERRILL: Thanks, Steve.

(*Music bridge. . .*)
(*In Area A* MERRILL *moves to her desk. Her hair is loose as if she had just washed it. She sits at the desk writing a letter . . . and speaking her thoughts as she does so.*)
MERRILL: Dear Mother: Yes, I did get your letters. I meant to write before but I couldn't. I go before the Board tomorrow.

Outside the snow is falling. White, clean snow. I've taken a shower and I've washed my hair, and now I'm trying to tell you how it really is. I'm sorry you're disappointed and ashamed. I know you had high hopes for me. (*she stops writing.*)

High hopes, high, high. I've taken a shower and I've washed my hair but I don't feel clean. So after all whatever happens tomorrow, they've won. (*she resumes writing.*)

I imagine what happens at the Board meeting tomorrow will be on the news so you'll know the results of the meeting before you get this. No, I haven't resigned and I haven't been officially fired, but I haven't taught my classes for two weeks. I'll write again soon. Love, Merrill. (*she stops writing.*)

Oh Mama, I wish I could tell you how it is. I couldn't tell you about Kent State or about Rick, or how I felt when Rick told me it was over. . . I couldn't tell you that I went through with the abortion, even when I didn't want to. I didn't tell you how frightened I've been when the phone rings even though I changed to a silent number. I'm frightened about tomorrow. . . will they bring up all the rumours and the gossip as if I'm not fit to teach their children? Will they use the stories I wrote to prove I don't belong in the school room? But I couldn't tell you before, Mama, and I can't tell you now. I can't even tell you that I'm in love with Steve Harding, and I keep hoping he'll feel the same way but I don't think he does. I wish I could tell you. I'm sorry.
VOICES — IMPERSONAL — COLD
Time to report, Miss Adams.
Why didn't you stick to the basics?
Why didn't you stay with Shakespeare?
Should writers be given license to undermine our social values?
Are you fit to instruct our children?
The motto of our school is "whatsoever things are of good repute." Are you of good repute, Miss Adams?
(*Music bridge. . .*)
(*In main playing Area B* OPAL PURVIS *is seated as chairman of the Board and speaks to audience as if to the other Board Members,* VERNA GLIDDENS *is seated at the side. . . chairs may be provided for* DUBRICK *and* MERRILL *in the Area.*)

Gwen Pharis Ringwood

PURVIS: I think this Board has discussed pretty well everything we know or think about the list of books in English A, about Family Life education, Teacher's rights and teacher responsibility. I suggest we now ask Mr. Dubrick and Miss Adams to come in. Whatever your opinion, please give them your respectful attention.
(She moves as if to a door. . .)
Come in, Miss Adams, Mr. Dubrick. I'm sorry we've kept you waiting so long. Please sit down. We've made this a very informal meeting so don't feel that you're in any way. . . what I mean is, all the Board wants is to hear what you have to say. And perhaps to ask a few questions. Mr. Dubrick, perhaps you'd start off.

DUBRICK: Madame Chairman, Members of the Board. I regret and I know Miss Adams regrets the trouble caused by a list of books that went to English A in my school. Any criticism of the list must come to me as principal. I should have been aware of how Miss Adams was dealing with the needs of her students, and I should have offered advice and judgment. Miss Adams has taught only three years and is new to our school. The recommendation of some of those books may have been indiscreet. But I know this teacher felt that the books and the selections she read in class would be useful to her students. I've inquired about the reaction in English A to this material and find that only 5 students question the positive value of this prose and poetry. Willamont students have expressed great admiration for Miss Adams as a teacher. The Board has seen their somewhat flamboyant petitions on her behalf. As Principal, I wish to take full responsibility for the action of a young woman who will become a very good teacher.

PURVIS: Mr. Dubrick, did Miss Adams ask your opinion about the discussion of family life, sex, . . . matters of some delicacy. . . in her class?

DUBRICK: No.

PURVIS: Do you approve of such discussion?

DUBRICK: Sometimes they come up out of the regular study. They can't be avoided.

GLIDDENS: I disagree, Mr. Dubrick. They can always be avoided.

PURVIS: Miss Adams, would you tell us whether you foresaw the results of your book list, your class readings and discussion?

MERRILL: No. We had arguments and disagreements in class. I didn't set out to outrage the community.

VERNA GLIDDENS: You know very little then of an average community. I looked at those stories, poems. . . no rhyme or metre in the poetry. Obscenities. No sense that I can find. As for the fiction some of the language is fit only for the gutter. Those books are garbage.

MERRILL: Either you didn't understand the books, Mrs. Gliddens, or you read isolated bits out of context. Synge, Shakespeare, Shaw,

Atwood, Purdy, Birney. . . you call them garbage? That's nonsense.

VERNA: Most of the people in this town agree with me, Miss Adams. You evidently think that teen age children should be allowed to read any and all written material, no matter how shocking or pornographic or immoral. You would supply them with it, under the guise of teaching English.

MERRILL: That's not true.

PURVIS: Please. Miss Adams, could you tell us how you see yourself as a teacher of English, what you hope to accomplish.

MERRILL: I wanted my students to learn to choose between good and bad books. I wanted to show them that good writers work hard to express meaningful experience, to communicate what they know, feel, see around them. Writing is hard work. Honest writing is like pulling something out of yourself, getting rid of clutter, pretense, peeling off the sugar-coating, stripping off the masks we all wear in polite society.

GLIDDENS: I personally prefer to live in a polite society. Perhaps that's what this is all about.

MERRILL: I want my students to realize that language is something more than instructions or how we take our tea, or what kind of car runs best. Language is man's blessing. It can express nuances of thought and feeling. . . it can sing. Poets celebrate life, and even twisted, ugly, or ordinary experience can be the subject. I believe that Art helps us to endure and to accept despair, maybe helps us to change the bad things, change the world. I don't think Art can deal with what is polite and pleasant and easy to swallow. To me and I hope to some of my students fiction can help us find our way, poems are shores of light. E.E. Cumming said that poetry is "a remembrance of miracles". That's what I wanted to teach. It's the only way I know to teach. That's all I have to say.

PURVIS: Thank you for coming in, Miss Adams. You won't need to stay further. We'll be in touch with you this evening.

Music bridge. . .

(As MERRILL *moves away the lights go down on the others.* PAUL RAE *moves towards* MERRILL.)

PAUL: Miss Adams.

MERRILL: Hello, Paul.

PAUL: I was waiting for you.

MERRILL: Oh.

PAUL: Mr. Harding told me you had to appear at the School Board. So I was waiting.

MERRILL: I thought perhaps Steve. . . Mr. Harding. . . would be here. I thought he'd want to know how. . .

PAUL: Oh, he took the plane, Miss Adams.

MERRILL: He's gone away?

PAUL: For two weeks. He had a newspaper conference. He asked me to

Gwen Pharis Ringwood

tell you "good luck". . . He said he thought his editorial made
a big impression on the Board.

MERRILL: I see.

PAUL: Did you see our petition from Willamont Secondary?

MERRILL: No.

PAUL: Oh. I hoped you'd see it. It was about six feet long.

MERRILL: Thank you, Paul. Well, I'd better go home and pack.

PAUL: You mean they fired you?

MERRILL: I don't know. But either way, I'm through here, Paul. I
couldn't teach in Willamont now. I. . . I just want to leave.

PAUL: Please don't leave. I brought you something. . . from our class.
A book of our poems and stories we wrote for you. We put them
all together in a book. Here it is.

MERRILL: Thank you. "Signals in the Dark."

PAUL: We got the title from something you read us.

MERRILL: Thanks. Thank the class for me, please.

PAUL: Don't go, Miss Adams.

MERRILL: I must, Paul. I want to go now. Goodbye.
(PAUL *remains on stage rather in shadow as* MERRILL *moves
to Area A and slowly puts things in a suitcase. Snatches of the
poetry used in the earlier collage mingle with music as she
packs. . . They come from all around her in a kind of
music. . . She closes the suitcase and the poetry begins to fade
into a single voice. . .* PAUL RAE *continuing the Galileo
poem.*)

"Galileo, Galilei
In a flowing scarlet robe
While the stars go down the river
With the turning, turning globe

Kneels before a Black Madonna
And the angels cluster round
With grave uplifted faces
Which reflect the shaken ground

And the orchard which is burning
And the hills which take the light
And the candles which have melted
On the altars of the night.

Galileo, Galilei
Comes to knock and knock again
At a small secluded doorway
In the ordinary brain."
(*As the poem is read* MERRILL *with her suitcase comes down
from Area A across the stage and moves out through the
audience.*)

The End

The Lodge
A Play in Three Scenes

Characters

ALICE HOBBES
EARDLEY HOBBES
SHELLEY HOBBES MARSDEN
ALLAN MARSDEN
MARYBELLE
MAJOR ROLAND ANDERSON
CONNIE ANDERSON
ROBIN DARAVALLEY
JASMINE DARAVALLEY
JIMMY LASHAWAY

THE PLACE: *Wilderness Lodge, an isolated hunting and fishing Resort. Scenes I and III—The living room at the Lodge. Scene II—The Soda Springs.*
THE TIME: *A September afternoon in the early 70s.*

SCENE I: *Arrivals.*

The basic units of an interior set surrounded by looming trees and shadows gives the feeling of Wilderness Lodge, an isolated hunting and fishing resort. A large antlered moose head dominates the room. Furniture is worn and comfortable — two batiks, some sketches, an abstract painting give life to the room. A fireplace and stairway to the bedrooms upstairs may be indicated.

The stairway or entrance to the bedrooms is at Stage Left. Right Centre is a doorway to the kitchen and Down Right an entrance from Outside. A window is indicated Right Centre.

The fir trees shot with some yellow poplar surround and enclose the room.

437

Gwen Pharis Ringwood

The time is September in the early '70s.
ALICE, a substantial matron in her late forties, enters Left. She
moves to the window, looks out, back to the fireplace, looks at the batiks,
sketches, and is obviously ill at ease and unhappy.

ALICE: Oh Shelley, my poor darling Shelley.
  (EARDLEY *enters quietly from outside.*)
EARDLEY: Well, Alice.
ALICE: You startled me!
EARDLEY: Sorry. I thought you were bird-watching with your sister.
ALICE: You know I don't like birds. Where were you?
EARDLEY: Washing the car. It took a beating coming in last night.
ALICE: I hate this place.
EARDLEY: You praised it, at breakfast. Overdid it, I thought.
ALICE: For Shelley's sake. Eardley, why in God's name did you let
  them take on this run-down lodge?
EARDLEY: I wasn't consulted, remember. Your mother's romantic
  memories of Wilderness Lodge triggered their investment.
ALICE: I could cry. Run-down plumbing; flickering light plant; no
  phone; no television; great looming trees everywhere you look. I
  could kill Mother for sending them that ad.
EARDLEY: Where do you think she is? Your *mother.*
ALICE: Why isn't she here? In this letter she said she'd be here when we
  arrived. I'm worried sick.
EARDLEY: She probably postponed her birthday.
ALICE: I didn't sleep a wink. I heard things howling.
EARDLEY: Coyotes.
ALICE: You and Allan talked about a cougar.
EARDLEY: Cheer up, old girl. I won't let a cougar get you.
ALICE: Hmm. I've decided two things. One: We're going to get Allan
  and Shelley out of here.
EARDLEY: How?
ALICE: You offer Allan a place in the drug stores. . . you promise him
  a partnership.
EARDLEY: Good God, Alice. What are you trying to do to me?
ALICE: He's Shelley's husband, Eardley.
EARDLEY: She chose him. I didn't. I've spent my life building an
  image. . . the Family Drug Store. He doesn't project the image.
  I tried to get Shelley to take Pharmacy.
ALICE: Or Home Economics. She could have been a Home Ec teacher.
  I wanted to be a Home Ec teacher. I dreamed of it.
EARDLEY: Why didn't you?
ALICE: I married you, remember. After one summer working in the
  cosmetics department. That's not enough preparation.
EARDLEY: You thought you were pregnant, Alice. I thought you were
  pregnant.

ALICE: I made a mistake. How could you say such a thing to me. . . now. . . when I'm worried sick.

EARDLEY: We've done all right, Alice. (*Pause*) Haven't we?

ALICE: I suppose. (*Pause*) Why isn't my mother here? That's the other thing I decided.

EARDLEY: Oh?

ALICE: Mother has to move into the Silver Threads. It's near us; I'm on the Auxiliary, I could keep an eye on her.

EARDLEY: Your mother hates an eye kept on her. Besides Silver Threads is very expensive.

ALICE: We can't have her in a poor place, Eardley. . . What would our friends think?

EARDLEY: I can't afford Silver Threads. Do you want to give up Palm Beach?

ALICE: If Mother sells us the High Valley ranch, our payments will take care of Silver Threads.

EARDLEY: That makes sense. But I've made three offers for the Alberta ranch and she just ignores them.

ALICE: Her letter sounds sort of—frightened to me—I think she's coming round. I think she needs us.

EARDLEY: Could be. That ranch is worth something, I tell you. Sub-divided that ranch is worth—

ALICE: Did Allan meet the bus?

EARDLEY: He did. No Jasmine.

ALICE: If she isn't here by dinner we'll have to go looking for her.

EARDLEY: If we do, we don't come back. I'm not taking my Cadillac over those roads but once.

ALICE: I think as much of the car as you do, Eardley.

EARDLEY: (*affectionately*) I know that, Alice.

ALICE: My blood pressure's up. I can always tell.

EARDLEY: You worry too much.

ALICE: I hear cougars howling all night. My mother arranges her own birthday party and doesn't show up. My daughter's out here living like a covered wagon. And you tell me not to worry.

(ALICE *goes off to the bedroom area.*)

EARDLEY: Take it easy, old girl, take it easy. . . .

(ALLAN'S *voice is raised from the kitchen.*)

ALLAN: It just makes the difference of the fall payment on this lodge, Shelley. That's what difference it makes.

(*He enters and sees* EARDLEY)

Oh, I didn't know you were in here.

EARDLEY: It's all right. I was just—

ALLAN: Shelley and I were just—

SHELLEY: (*entering*) We were having a fight, Daddy.

ALLAN: We got this letter from New York—

SHELLEY: That's between us, Allan.

ALLAN: Your father might like to know—

SHELLEY: No! I'm sorry, Daddy. It's our business.

EARDLEY: I was just going to take a look around. See what you kids have here. Maybe scare up a grouse.

ALLAN: Sure.

SHELLEY: Our land is posted. You have to hunt outside our fence.

EARDLEY: Maybe a grouse will attack me? What about that? (*His joke falls flat. Donning hunting vest & hat*) Hah. Hah. Hah. Say, Allan, you said last night there was a radio telephone at the reserve.

ALLAN: There is.

EARDLEY: Shelley's mother is worried about the old lady. Could you telephone the airport and the bus. . . see if they have a line on her.

ALLAN: You want me to phone the police?

SHELLEY: No. Grandma would hate us stirring up the police. Her birthday's tomorrow, Daddy. She'll get here.

EARDLEY: Leave the police for now. Just ask the bus and the airport if they've seen a spinny old lady with a paint box.

ALLAN: O.K.

EARDLEY: Thanks. I'm off.

(*He goes out.*)

ALLAN: Why couldn't I tell your father? It might convince him I'm capable of supporting you.

SHELLEY: It's our business. And I don't want those hunters.

ALLAN: Seven hunters at a thousand a week each. That's our payment on the place, Shelley.

SHELLEY: If we start taking big-game trophy hunters, we'll never look back.

ALLAN: When we've paid for this lodge, we could change things.

SHELLEY: You helped write our ad. "Good food, Quiet, Wilderness, and the Seasons." Now you're selling out. That letter's post-marked August 10. It's too late to answer anyway.

ALLAN: I've already answered it. I told them to come.

SHELLEY: And you didn't bother mentioning this to me?

ALLAN: I knew you'd say "No."

SHELLEY: I thought we were so together on this. And all the time you. . . When are they coming?

ALLAN: October 7th.

SHELLEY: Everything's changed. The whole thing's changing.

ALLAN: Come on, Shelley, be reasonable. We can't afford to pass up those hunters.

SHELLEY: I hate that moose head. I don't want to be a part of anything like that, ever.

ALLAN: All right, you take over. Wire them we'd like their money but they can't hunt. They can smell the pine trees. Tell them we're Quaker vegetarians and we fight hunters tooth and claw!

SHELLEY: I will. I am half owner.

ALLAN: You do that. Oh, bloody hell.
SHELLEY: What's the matter?
ALLAN: My socks don't match.
SHELLEY: I'll get you a pair.
ALLAN: No. The radio phone goes off at five. I've got to track down your Grandmother.
SHELLEY: If you find her, be sure to explain that we're turning her sanctuary into a slaughterhouse.
(*Sound of shots off.*)
ALLAN: Hear that? That's your Uncle Roland shooting my ducks. I notice you didn't stop him.
SHELLEY: I tried. He said he was outside our property.
(MARYBELLE *enters with clothes from line and a batik.*)
MARYBELLE: Sorry I'm late for work, Shelley.
ALLAN: Hello, Marybelle. How did the meeting go?
MARYBELLE: Oooh. Stormy. But I'm still a Counsellor. And Granddad's still the Chief.
ALLAN: Good.
MARYBELLE: With Granddad away, I had to talk for him. They figure he's spending too much money building up the herd. Did you see Shelley's new batik? It's for her Grandma's birthday.
ALLAN: Hmm. . . What is it?
MARYBELLE: Wild geese. Can't you see?
ALLAN: Their necks are too long.
SHELLEY: I wanted their necks long.
MARYBELLE: She wanted their necks long.
ALLAN: Shelley doesn't look carefully at things. Like those horses.
SHELLEY: What's wrong with my horses?
ALLAN: Their legs look broken. Horses' legs aren't made that way.
SHELLEY: Maybe I just can't draw horses.
ALLAN: You don't look at things. Who ever saw a horse with front legs like that?
SHELLEY: Enter the Art Critic.
ALLAN: Things should look like they are. That picture of your grandmother's. She calls it *Flight*. There's not a bird or an aeroplane in it.
SHELLEY: It's after four.
ALLAN: I'm going. (*He starts off, then turns.*) You'd better tell your Aunt Connie to wear a red hat when she's out bird-watching. Someone might take her for a Wood Duck.
(*He goes out.*)
SHELLEY: Oh, I hate him, I hate him. I don't care if their legs are broken. I like them. He's awful. He's mean.
MARYBELLE: Don't cry. . . Look, all summer when you two were cleaning up this place you were laughing and joking together.
SHELLEY: Allan doesn't see things my way at all.
MARYBELLE: He's got in-laws buzzing around him. My Uncle took a shot-gun and scared the in-laws right off his place.

SHELLEY: I was nice to his parents.

MARYBELLE: (*folding laundry*) It's harder on men.

SHELLEY: Oh? His mother told me and told me that when Allan lived at home he wore only hand-knit socks. Men just want you to bow down. Knit socks. Fold socks. Mend socks.

MARYBELLE: Match socks? Cheer up, your laundry's all dry. It's Indian summer—

SHELLEY: I'm pregnant.

MARYBELLE: Shelley, that's great. You said you wanted—

SHELLEY: I haven't told Allan. I haven't told anybody.

MARYBELLE: Why?

SHELLEY: I don't know. I might not even have it.

MARYBELLE: You better think a long time about that, Shelley.

ALICE: (*off*) Shelley. Shelley?

SHELLEY: Here, mother.

ALICE: (*entering*) I tidied up the linen cupboard. You'll be able to find things now.

SHELLEY: Thank you.

ALICE: I'm going to burn this book. You don't want it in your library. It's full of obscenities.

SHELLEY: What book?

ALICE: Some person named Lenny.

SHELLEY: Lenny Bruce.

ALICE: I'm burning it.

SHELLEY: No. Give me my book, mother.

ALICE: I will not. This man should be in jail. There.
        (*She throws book into fireplace.*)

SHELLEY: How could you, mother? (*Retrieving book.*) You've no right.

ALICE: I'm sorry. I just can't bring myself to admire dirty words. And nowadays they're everywhere. No escape.

MARYBELLE: (*gently*) They're only words, Mrs. Hobbes.

ALICE: That's your opinion, Marybelle. (*Pause*) Where's Allan?

SHELLEY: He went to the reserve to phone about Grandma.

ALICE: Thank heaven. My poor dear mother. I think she's falling apart. Your father and I feel she mustn't live alone any longer.

SHELLEY: Some people like living alone. Sometimes I. . . .

ALICE: Where is your father?

SHELLEY: Looking around. Planning.

ALICE: I hope he has sense enough to watch out for that cougar. He wishes he'd brought his rifle.

SHELLEY: We don't want the cougar killed. We think it will go away.

ALICE: Nonsense. We can't let carnivorous animals take over.

SHELLEY: I saw a cougar once. Its eyes blazed in the carlights. It was all tawny gold on big soft feet.

MARYBELLE: Their feet look soft but they got terrible claws.

ALICE: Cougars are dangerous. They leap down on one.

MARYBELLE: Somebody's bound to kill this one, Shelley. People get nerve-racked with a big cat around.

SHELLEY: Pretty soon there won't be any animals. I bet if this was the last cougar on earth somebody would shoot it down.

MARYBELLE: They'd have bad dreams. That cry would shiver all around the place.

ALICE: You should have warned your Aunt Connie to stay away from the trees, Shelley. Dear Connie! I don't think she cares a cent about bird watching. It's just a pose.

SHELLEY: Mother, that's mean.

ALICE: Mean? Of course not. I just know my own sister. After all she is a lot like mother. (*To* MARYBELLE:) You're folding that wrong, dear. Let me show you.

SHELLEY: Mother!

ALICE: Marybelle doesn't mind. There's a right way and a wrong way. Listen dear, I've a pair of very good shoes that I can't wear. I think they'd fit you.

MARYBELLE: Thanks, Mrs. Hobbes, but I have a pair of shoes.

ALICE: These were very expensive. I was going to offer them to Connie but. . . well, I thought it might seem—

MARYBELLE: Patronizing?

ALICE: Exactly. You must have had a good education.

SHELLEY: Marybelle's better educated than I am.

ALICE: That's nice. Education's the answer, isn't it? But so many refuse. They prefer welfare. I've always been quite interested in the Indian problem.

MARYBELLE: (*smiling as she takes laundry out right*) So have I, Mrs. Hobbes. So have I.

(MARYBELLE *goes off.*)

SHELLEY: Mom, how can you say such things?

ALICE: (*disarmingly sweet*) There you go, dear—criticizing. Live and let live, remember. I've been so lonesome for you, Shelley. I live for your letters.

SHELLEY: We've been busy, fixing up the place.

ALICE: I'm afraid the work here is too much for you. You don't look well. Sometimes I find it hard to forgive mother for pointing you at this place.

SHELLEY:Grandma didn't point us. She sent the ad. We decided.

ALICE: Why?

SHELLEY: It's ours. I love being outside a lot. Hearing that cougar— the loons. Picking wild berries.

ALICE: Connie and I used to pick berries at High Valley. That is I picked. Connie ate. The world seems to be divided—some people pick; some people eat. I was a picker.

SHELLEY: (*with a rush of affection*) I know you were Mama. I know you were.

ALICE: Mother sacrificed her family life for her painting, Shelley. Painting was never a little hobby with her. It was everything. Now I'm different. I studied the piano but I never let myself get too involved. It was a little hobby—like your batiks.

443

SHELLEY: My batiks are more than a hobby.

ALICE: We all have our dreams, but we settle. I just wish you'd settle in a less primitive place.

SHELLEY: We didn't.

ALICE: I sacrificed my life to my family. I never begrudged it, even though I've lost your brother.

SHELLEY: Mother, Quentin didn't die! He got married!

ALICE: To a divorcee with a child. And he went to Africa. He just escaped. (*Pause*) Shelley, I think your father's going to make an offer to Allan—about the new drug store.

SHELLEY: No.

ALICE: He just might. What is this, Shelley?

SHELLEY: Horses on our prairie.

ALICE: Oh. Oh, I see.

> (MAJOR ROLAND ANDERSON *enters from back—he is wet, muddy, angry*)

SHELLEY: Uncle Roland!

ALICE: You're dripping.

ROLAND: Where's Allan?

SHELLEY: At the reserve.

ROLAND: I want the police. Look at me. Look at my gun.

SHELLEY: Your new jacket.

ROLAND: Who drives an old yellow van with crabs on it?

SHELLEY: I don't know.

ROLAND: I'm waiting for a flight when this van stops at the beach. Some fellow gets out and strips. Just then three big mallards fly in. I stand up in the boat, get my sights ahead of them when the fool starts waving and shouting. I fire—but when he shouts the ducks veer, so I miss. I turn to give him a piece of my mind when your boat tips. There in the mud with my gun. And that fool swims out quacking. I don't take things like this lying down, Shelley.

ALICE: You're dripping all over the floor.

ROLAND: I catch cold easily too. Where's Connie?

ALICE: Bird watching.

ROLAND: Call her. Tell her I need her. I'd better take a hot shower.

SHELLEY: I'm afraid the water heater's gone off again.

ROLAND: Really, Shelley, how can you expect to run a shooting lodge without hot water—or a bar—or a telephone—When I get hold of that ninny hammer I'll. . . . He upset the dogs too.

> (ROLAND *exits right.* ALICE *calls after him.*)

ALICE: Marybelle's up there. If you give her your clothes I'm sure she'd run them through the washer. It was all right to say that, wasn't it?

SHELLEY: Yes, Mother. But Marybelle isn't just a hired worker. She's my friend. Please don't hurt her feelings.

ALICE: Oh, I wouldn't. Why, I love Marybelle. I love Indians. I send the cosmetics samples to the Reserve at home. They must love getting them. Such pretty boxes.

SHELLEY: Why don't we go for a walk?

ALICE: No thank you. Roland's right, dear, if you want people like us you'll have to civilize this place.

(CONNIE *enters with field glasses and her book.*)

CONNIE: Three Canada Jays, a blue bird, two hairy woodpeckers, four Downies. But the Pyliated escaped me. A shy fellow, the Pyliated. Oh, I'm exhausted.

SHELLEY: The kettle's on. I'll make tea.

(*She starts out*)

CONNIE: And a bald headed eagle too, by the lake.

SHELLEY: He nests in the big tree, Aunt Connie.

CONNIE: (*calling to kitchen*) The birds are choosing their winter feeding stations, Shelley. Get out the suet. (*To* ALICE) She can have feathered friends all winter.

ALICE: I hope Shelley won't be here in the winter.

CONNIE: But dear—

ALICE: If you had children, Connie, you'd understand.

CONNIE: Shelley seems like a daughter to me.

ALICE: But she isn't.

(ALICE *continues her needlepoint.*)

CONNIE: I heard Roland firing away at the lake.

ALICE: He fell in. He looked very funny.

CONNIE: Oh. Perhaps I'd better go—

(MARYBELLE *goes through the room.*)

MARYBELLE: I've got the Major's clothes, Mrs. Anderson. I'll wash them.

CONNIE: Thank you. Is he all right?

MARYBELLE: He's really worried. His gun got wet.

(SHELLEY *enters with tea tray*)

SHELLEY: There's tea.

MARYBELLE: Later. I'll get these out.

(SHELLEY *places tray in front of* ALICE *who pours.*)

ALICE: Well, wilderness or not, at least there's tea.

CONNIE: You should have come with me. (*To* SHELLEY) The poplars blaze.

SHELLEY: Like Moses' burning bush.

ALICE: I really don't like Nature very much. It's so wild. Untidy.

CONNIE: Remember how Mother would rush out to paint the fall colour?

ALICE: I do.

CONNIE: No word yet?

ALICE: Nothing.

CONNIE: She probably forgot the date.

ALICE: Yes. Flighty and thoughtless and forgetful. That's our mother, Connie.

CONNIE: Roland thinks she's losing her marbles.

ALICE: How would he know? It's his mother you fuss about.

CONNIE: Roland only meant because she sent us all that money. To come here. For a family reunion. What about the Daravalley children?

SHELLEY: They're not children, Aunt Connie. Cora's at least thirty and Robin's my age.

ALICE: She probably sent them twice as much. How much did she send you?

SHELLEY: Three hundred dollars. But we were going to give it back.

ALICE: Don't be silly. She gave Cora that antique highboy for a wedding present. She always favored James's children.

CONNIE: Only because they lost their parents.

ALICE: We can't all be orphans, Connie.

CONNIE: Mother gave you her diamond ring, Alice. I got the opal. Not that I'm complaining.

ALICE: You shouldn't. You and Roland borrowed money from her to buy that expensive lot on the island.

CONNIE: We paid that back.

ALICE: I'm sure you did, dear.

CONNIE: Roland can show you the receipt.

ALICE: Connie dear, that's not necessary. I just happened to see the note when we visited Mother in the spring. I didn't mean to upset you.

CONNIE: You always manage to upset me. You always have.

ALICE: Shelley, dear, could we have some hot water? The tea's a little strong for my taste.

SHELLEY: (*getting up.*) Please don't quarrel.

ALICE: Darling, why would we quarrel? We're sisters. We're both worried about Mother, that's all. Hot water, dear.

(SHELLEY *goes*)

CONNIE: When Mother comes she'll tell you we paid her back. . .

ALICE: *If* Mother comes. Connie, I've been worried about Mother ever since we were there. . . She's taken to giving away her best things . . . to strangers. We have to take steps.

CONNIE: What steps?

ALICE: Eardley and I are going to buy the Alberta ranch.

CONNIE: But half of High Valley should be mine.

ALICE: We're *buying* it from Mother, Connie. With our payments, Mother can move in to a rest home in the Lower Mainland. You'll be proud to visit her there, Connie. The best people put their parents in Silver Threads.

CONNIE: Mother never liked the best people, Alice.

ALICE: Time she started. Oh, I've gone off my pattern.

(SHELLEY *returns with hot water jug.*) Thank you dear. (*Noise of engine*) Is that Allan?

SHELLEY: No. It's. . . It's Robin. Robin Daravalley. (*She runs out*) Robin! You came.

ALICE: I hoped he wouldn't come.

CONNIE: He and Shelley were very—close, weren't they?

ALICE: Well, they're cousins.

CONNIE: That's what I mean. The Europe trip. People talked. (*Pause*) It's true. There was talk.

> (SHELLEY *and* ROBIN *enter.*)

ROBIN: Hi, Aunt Connie. How's my favorite aunt?

CONNIE: Robin dear. How nice to see you.

ROBIN: Hello, Aunt Alice.

ALICE: You're looking well, Robin. Welcome to Shelley and Allan's home.

ROBIN: I hope I'm welcome.

SHELLEY: Of course you are.

ROBIN: I carved a necklace out of a deer antler. I found this antler so I—Those deer grow antlers and then every spring they just shed them.

SHELLEY: It's beautiful, Robin.

ROBIN: You haven't changed, Shelley. I was afraid you'd change.

ALICE: Tea, Robin?

ROBIN: Sure. Thanks. So this is your Wilderness, Shelley.

SHELLEY: There's still a lot to do.

ROBIN: Where's Grandma?

SHELLEY: We don't know.

ROBIN: She'll be here. She's always late.

CONNIE: Alice, you don't think mother would—hitch hike?

ALICE: No.

ROBIN: She might. But I'd have picked her up in the old van.

SHELLEY: The van. It's yours?

ROBIN: My home, my castle.

SHELLEY: Uncle Roland is planning to kill you.

ROBIN: Uncle Roland. . .

SHELLEY: You quacked at him.

ROBIN: The duck hunter. Oh God. I was. . . I was trying out a Green Peace manoeuvre. Getting between him and the ducks. I'm sorry, Aunt Connie.

CONNIE: And you were right, Robin. Somebody has to stand up for the ducks.

ROBIN: How can you stand it, Shelley? All that banging away? You, of all people running a hunting lodge.

SHELLEY: We. . . we don't plan it to be a hunting lodge, Robin. I mean, we didn't. . . .

ROBIN: Who could shoot down a magnificent animal like that moose?

SHELLEY: The former owner shot that moose.

ROBIN: They should have mounted the former owner. Do you think Allan's going to mind my being here?

SHELLEY: No.

CONNIE: You are cousins, after all.

SHELLEY: Robin and his friends disrupted a resort owner's convention last spring. They want all fire arms registered.
ROBIN: Allan took offence. I didn't know he was your husband, Shelley.
CONNIE: That's right. You weren't at the wedding.
ROBIN: No.
CONNIE: And here you are now. Mother will be pleased.
ROBIN: Do you expect Quentin, Aunt Alice?
ALICE: No.
ROBIN: He's doing fine work in Africa.
ALICE: Yes.
CONNIE: I saw him on television. Did you see him?
ALICE: No.
CONNIE: You missed your own son?
ALICE: We were at Palm Springs.
ROBIN: Quentin really found a purpose for his life.
ALICE: Oh, yes.
ROBIN: Shelley and I admire him very much.
ALICE: Indeed.
ROBIN: When we were in Europe we used to talk a lot about Quentin.
CONNIE: I expect Allan and Shelley talk a lot about Quentin too. Now that they're married.
ROBIN: I suppose.
SHELLEY: Excuse me. I have to see. . . I have to put my bread in the oven. . .
ROBIN: Can I help?
SHELLEY: No, thanks.
CONNIE: Quentin's married too. He has an adopted daughter.
ALICE: I'm sure Robin's aware of that.
CONNIE: She was on television too. She's darling. Very black. White teeth.
ROBIN: Do you have pictures, Aunt Alice?
ALICE: Not here.
ROBIN: I admire Quentin very much. So does Shelley.
ALICE: You said that, Robin.
(ALLAN *enters. He is burdened with a radio telephone.*)
ALICE: What did you find out, Allan?
ALLAN: Nothing. The radio phone's not working. (*To Robin*) Hello.
ROBIN: I'm Robin.
ALLAN: I know. Where's Shelley?
ALICE: That means we're isolated.
ALLAN: Shelley. Shelley.
SHELLEY: (*enters from kitchen*) Did you find out anything?
ALLAN: I couldn't get through to town.
SHELLEY: Allan, the hot water heater's gone off again.
ALLAN: That ties it. What do you do to it?
SHELLEY: I don't do anything to it, except wash sheets and towels and dishes and floors and underwear and jeans and socks. . .

ALICE: Allan dear, your socks don't match.

ALLAN: I know, Mother Hobbes, I know. Your daughter is color blind.

SHELLEY: Please, be civil.

ALLAN: I'm trying, Shelley. Make yourself at home everybody.

(ROLAND *comes in from left*.)

ROLAND: Allan, there's no hot water and your pipes make funny noises.

ALLAN: Yes, Major. Thank you very much.

(*He goes out to kitchen*.)

ROLAND: (*Seeing* ROBIN) You're the one. You tried to drown me!

ROBIN: Oh no, sir.

ROLAND: You made me miss. You upset the boat. You upset me. You upset the dogs.

ROBIN: I. . . I only. . .

ROLAND: I know you all right, even with your clothes on. Nose. Long hair. Voice. Go ahead—quack. I dare you.

CONNIE: Robin's our nephew, Roland.

ROLAND: Yours!

CONNIE: He's already explained. He was protecting the ducks. The ducks should have a chance.

ROLAND: Keep still, Connie. I don't interfere with your bird watching. And let me tell you, you can do a lot of harm prying at unhatched eggs.

CONNIE: We never touch the eggs. That's a rule.

ROLAND: What about terrorizing the parent birds? No hatch. That's what about. No hatch.

ALICE: I agree with Roland. Birds and beasts were put on this earth for our use.

ROLAND: That old Audubon you love so much. How did he get birds to sit still while he painted them? He stuffed them. That's how!

CONNIE: I can't bear it when you speak of Audubon in that voice.

ROLAND: Tooth and claw. That's nature's law.

ROBIN: As a vegetarian. . . .

ROLAND: Hah. You won't go far on lily roots. Dandelions and pig weed never fed an army. It's survival of the fittest and the fittest eat meat.

CONNIE: Remember your blood pressure, Roland.

ROLAND: My gun may never be the same again.

CONNIE: I hope it isn't.

ROLAND: I have a god-given constitutional right to bear arms, Connie. And I still have my rifle. What's more I intend to track down that cougar and mount him on my wall. And every rancher in the country will applaud. (*To* ROBIN) You can put that in your water pipe and smoke it!

(*He goes off back*.)

SHELLEY: Please don't let him kill the cougar, Aunt Connie.

Gwen Pharis Ringwood

CONNIE: His mind's sealed. I gave him a camera. I told him about whales. I bought a record of The Ancient Mariner. I tried to get him to read Johnathan Livingston Seagull, but he wouldn't.
ALICE: Roland likes bridge. You wouldn't learn to play.
CONNIE: I tried, but he said I refused his demands.
ALICE: I'm going upstairs and pack!
SHELLEY: You only got here last night. . .
ALICE: I can't sit here and listen to you talk about whales and sea gulls when my mother is out there wandering confused and lost.
CONNIE: I'll pack too. She's as much my mother—
ALICE: For all you seem to care she could be mugged or high-jacked or doped.
ROBIN: Not Grandma.
ALICE: Anything can happen when you're old—broken legs, bankruptcy, insanity. . .
CONNIE: Roland won't want to leave before dinner. He says an army travels on its stomach.
ALICE: Do as you like, Connie. I'm packing.
  (*She goes upstairs.*)
CONNIE: I'd better tell Roland. He hates sudden decisions.
  (CONNIE *goes out back*)
SHELLEY: If only Grandma would get here.
ROBIN: We could go looking.
SHELLEY: No, Robin, we couldn't.
ROBIN: You never answered my letters.
SHELLEY: When I wrote about Allan and me. . . I told you it was over. I'm married.
ROBIN: But why? You were free, Shelley. You could have—
SHELLEY: I didn't want to stay in Spain forever. You did.
ROBIN: Not after you left. I couldn't believe you'd gone. I read that note over and over and over.
SHELLEY: I'm sorry. I thought you'd stay in Spain.
ROBIN: I went back last summer. Everything's changing. You can't see our beach for the Hiltons.
SHELLEY: What's Mexico like?
ROBIN: Come and see. I'm doing some good work there.
SHELLEY: I'm glad.
ROBIN: I was always happy when I was with you, Shelley. I felt—whole. Quentin used to say that's what it's all about—the search for wholeness.
SHELLEY: I don't think Quentin meant another person, Robin. I think he meant—
  (ALLAN *enters*)
ALLAN: I think the damn heater's working now. Shall I build up the fire, Shelley?
SHELLEY: No. They're going looking for Grandma. Mother's packing.
ALLAN: Look, you and I had better go. They'd probably take the wrong road.

450

ROBIN: We could take the van. I mean, the three of us.

ALLAN: That would be cosy.

ROBIN: I made you a bowl, Shelley. . . I'll get it. I made Grandma one too. You want to share a joint?

ALLAN: No thanks.

ROBIN: Shelley?

SHELLEY: No.

(ROBIN *goes outside.*)

SHELLEY: You're clicking your teeth. What's the matter?

ALLAN: A simple, nervous habit. Your uncle Roland is banging away at my ducks; your parents are in a state of shock because their precious Shelley cooks on a wood stove with no telephone; that potter offers you paradise in a yellow van; and your Aunt Connie wants me to get her an Eagle's nest for show and tell at the bird club. Any man in his right mind would click his teeth.

SHELLEY: Go ahead and say what you're thinking. You hate my family.

ALLAN: I'm hardly overjoyed at the thought of combing the woods from here to Calgary looking for your crazy grandmother.

SHELLEY: She's not crazy. A little impractical. . .

ALLAN: You take after her then. We have a payment to make!

SHELLEY: You go right ahead and have your hunters. Just count me out.

ALLAN: And you ride off into the sunset with cousin Robin.

SHELLEY: What makes you say such things?

ALLAN: I'm not a fool. He's back in the game isn't he? Or maybe he was never out of it.

(MARYBELLE *enters.*)

MARYBELLE: Brr. I feel a chill in here.

SHELLEY: Malicious animal magnetism. It emanates from Allan.

MARYBELLE: This may be a bad time to bring it up but the Council of Indian Bands would like to have their meeting here in October. October 8 to 18th.

SHELLEY: How many people?

MARYBELLE: Twelve—maybe fourteen.

SHELLEY: Meals?

MARYBELLE: Room and meals. Thirty dollars a day?

SHELLEY: We'd almost have our payment, Allan. We could cancel the hunters.

ALLAN: Your Council's supposed to be a pretty militant bunch, Marybelle.

MARYBELLE: We just want the land that belongs to us.

ALLAN: Yeah. Lease land. Every white rancher in the country would be down our necks.

MARYBELLE: We can go to Quesnel. No sweat.

ALLAN: We'll let you know. We'll talk it over.

SHELLEY: I can answer now. I want the Council.

MARYBELLE: Think about it, anyway, Allan.

(*She goes out.*)

451

ALLAN: I don't want to take sides on this lease land issue, Shelley.

SHELLEY: You never want to take sides on anything.

ALLAN: What's the matter with you? You didn't used to be so unreasonable.

SHELLEY: Lots of things are the matter. Right now the thought of those hunters stamping about shooting at everything that moves makes me sick. Physically sick. I just can't talk about it.

ALLAN: Shh. Your Dad's coming.

> (SHELLEY *starts out as* EARDLEY *enters.*)

EARDLEY: Shelley. . .

SHELLEY: Sorry, Daddy, I can't talk now.

> (*She leaves.*)

EARDLEY: Well! What's up?

ALLAN: Nothing. Phone's not working.

EARDLEY: Hmm. Too bad. That will upset Alice.

ALLAN: It did.

EARDLEY: Hmm. I got these just beyond the fence. One ruffled. One pintail. Two shells. I was right on.

ALLAN: Good.

EARDLEY: You know Allan I've been thinking. You got this lodge and the land for a song. You've done some fixing up. But you haven't studied your market. First thing you should do is put in a swimming pool.

ALLAN: We have the lake.

EARDLEY: Too far, too cold, too big. Wilderness makes people feel small—so, you control your wilderness. Pools, tennis courts, a bar—then people feel safe. I've sized up your problem here and I'm beginning to percolate.

ALLAN: I see.

EARDLEY: And when I percolate, it usually means Profit. I seem to have a head for business and a nose for profit. And they're at your service.

ALLAN: Thanks.

EARDLEY: No need to be grateful. After all her mother and I want Shelley to have the best. I'd better hang these. (ROBIN *enters.*) (*Pausing.*) Oh. Who are you?

ROBIN: I'm Robin Daravalley, Uncle Eardley.

EARDLEY: Oh yes. James's son.

ROBIN: I came for Grandma's birthday.

EARDLEY: Oh. You didn't see her anywhere. . . on the way.

ROBIN: No. But she'll show up.

EARDLEY: Good. You know Allan, Shelley's husband?

ROBIN: Yes.

EARDLEY: I was just going to hang these. . . You shoot?

ROBIN: I don't believe in killing birds.

EARDLEY: Harvesting birds. There's a difference.

ROBIN: Not to those grouse, Uncle Eardley.

EARDLEY: What's that?
ROBIN: A piece I made for Shelley.
EARDLEY: Hmm. Dancers.
ALLAN: Spanish dancers.
EARDLEY: Hmmm. Looks Spanish. So you're a potter, Robin? You make any money at potting?
ROBIN: I get by.
EARDLEY: Alice potted one summer. Made a lot of frogs. For the garden. I tried them in the drug store. Whole display case full of frogs. They didn't go. You make any coffee mugs?
ROBIN: No.
EARDLEY: Too bad. Might be able to move some coffee mugs. Well I'll. . .

(*He indicates birds and starts out back.*)

SHELLEY: (*returning*) Sorry. Oh, Daddy, why did you have to shoot them?
EARDLEY: That's what they're for, Shelley. To eat.
SHELLEY: I won't cook them.
EARDLEY: Your mother will.
SHELLEY: She's packing.
EARDLEY: I'm not going traipsing out of here tonight. I just washed the Cadillac.
SHELLEY: Oh, Robin, that's beautiful. (*the sculpture*)
ROBIN: It's for you.
ALLAN: Memories of Spain. I'll gas up the jeep. Are you coming?
SHELLEY: Where?
ALLAN: To look for Grandmother, remember.
ALICE: (*on stairs*) Thank you, Allan. I'm ready.
ALLAN: No need for you to go, Mrs. Hobbes.
ALICE: No need! She's my mother. Connie would just stay here and hope for the best, but I'm different. I worry. I care.
CONNIE: (*entering*) I heard that Alice. I care too.
ALLAN: My jeep can only take three people.
ALICE: You see? Allan, Eardley and me.
ALLAN: What about Shelley?
CONNIE: Mother would want us to wait till morning. People bear up better in the morning. And if anything's happened Mother would want us to bear up bravely.
ROBIN: Grandma isn't helpless, Aunt Alice.
ALICE: How would you know? Eardley and I saw her last spring. She was giving her things away, painting the strangest looking pictures; she'd cut up her oriental rug for Yoga mats. She wants to be a Lotus. Now she sends you all cheques to come here to celebrate what she calls her last birthday. Does that sound like normal behavior?

(EARDLEY *and* ROLAND *enter.*)

Gwen Pharis Ringwood

EARDLEY: Alice, Roland and I are agreed—we'll take his station wagon early in the morning—

ROLAND: And the dogs.

EARDLEY: And we'll find your mother.

ROLAND: Do you happen to have anything that belongs to Granny Daravalley—a glove, a shawl, socks? If the dogs once got her scent. . .

ALICE: Allan will take me in the jeep tonight.

EARDLEY: I forbid it.

ALICE: You see. You don't care.

EARDLEY: After all your mother has lived a full life. The time comes. The hands are still. The clock stops for us all.

SHELLEY: Grandma isn't a clock, Daddy.

ROBIN: And she never knows what time it is.

CONNIE: She always loved Handel's Largo.

(MARYBELLE *enters*.)

MARYBELLE: Allan, my brother was here. He says they found cougar tracks near the corral at the reserve. He says you should keep an eye out and make a noise if you're walking in the woods.

ALICE: You see. I told you about cougars. First they attack the Indians —then us.

MARYBELLE: It could be worse, Mrs. Hobbes.

ALICE: I don't see how.

MARYBELLE: It could be the other way.

ALICE: I know now what's happened. I feel it. Mother started driving out here in that old car. It broke down.

EARDLEY: You don't know that, Alice.

ALICE: The Ouija board always moves for me, Eardley. I sense things. Mother has left the car. She's stumbling along trying to reach us. And that cougar's crouched in a tree waiting for her. Poor Mother. My foolish, selfish Mother. If she gets herself killed by that cougar. I'll. . . I'll never forgive her.

(*Sound of bells outside as door opens.* JASMINE *appears. She is wearing a colorful poncho, carries bells, rug, paint box etc.*)

SHELLEY: Grandma. Oh, Grandma, I'm so glad to see you.

(*They embrace*.)

JASMINE: Shelley. Little Granddaughter. And here's Allan. These bells are for your door.

SHELLEY: Dear Grandma. Everyone was getting worried.

JASMINE: I brought you half of my rug. For Yoga. What a beautiful country this is. I could hardly believe the colour.

ALICE: Mother.

JASMINE: Alice, dear. You look very well.

ALICE: I was worried sick.

CONNIE: I'm here, Mother.

JASMINE: Connie.

CONNIE: I was worried sick too, but I didn't want to upset the others.
JASMINE: I'm sorry.
ALICE: If it's going to be your last birthday, you could at least have got here on time.
JASMINE: I tried. Eardley. And Roland.
ROLAND: I didn't worry. I'm used to people going A.W.O.L.
JASMINE: And Robin.
ROBIN: Good to see you, Grandma. How'd you get here?
JASMINE: Well I. . . I hitch-hiked.
ALICE: Mother.
JASMINE: Not with a stranger, Alice. With Jimmy Lashaway.
ALLAN: The Chief. Has he gone?
JASMINE: I hope not. I wanted to—Is the jeep still there?
ALLAN: I'll get him.
          (ALLAN *goes out*)
ALICE: You hitch-hiked in a jeep with an Indian! Mother, what if he'd. . .
JASMINE: Alice, I knew Jimmy years ago, when your father and I were here. I got lost in Kamloops looking for the bus. So I stopped to watch them load this huge bull into a truck, and there was Jimmy Lashaway. So of course he brought me.
ALICE: I knew you were lost. I felt it.
CONNIE: Alice thought you were doped or murdered or extinct.
          (ALLAN *and* JIMMY LASHAWAY *enter.*)
ALLAN: Chief Jimmy Lashaway, everybody. This is Shelley's family.
JIMMY: Hi. We had a good trip. Shelley, your grandmother's pretty smart for a white woman. (*To* JASMINE) That's Marybelle, my granddaughter. She's pretty smart too.
JASMINE: Hi, Marybelle.
MARYBELLE: Welcome, Mrs. Daravalley.
JIMMY: Am I still Chief?
MARYBELLE: You're still in there. Rough meeting.
JIMMY: (*to* ALLAN) Some of them bastards was on the war path because I was spending band funds to buy a bull. They call this meeting when I'm in Kamloops buying the bull.
ALLAN: Where is the bull?
JIMMY: I had it trucked to Williams Lake. Not much room in the jeep for a bull—with her coming. Well I better get down to the reserve. (To MARYBELLE) You coming?
MARYBELLE: Sure.
JASMINE: Thanks for the ride, Jimmy. I'll be ready when you come.
JIMMY: Don't rush yourself. We got some time yet.
          (JIMMY *and* MARYBELLE *go out.*)
ALICE: You look exhausted, Mother.
JASMINE: I don't feel exhausted, Alice. I did some sketches at the river—the old bridge. Such color. I was full of excitement. . .

ALICE: You stopped to sketch—and I'm out of my mind with worry. Then you breeze in here as if it were a tap dance. You can't do that, Mother.

JASMINE: I know I can't. I won't.

ALICE: You must rest. Not there. Over here. I'll get you a hot water bottle and a cup of tea.

JASMINE: No thanks, dear. Eardley, you and Alice must be happy about Shelley and Allan on their own in this beautiful place.

EARDLEY: Why. . . yes. Yes.

ALICE: We wish it were less—primitive.

EARDLEY: And more profitable, eh, Allan?

ALICE: It's really your fault they're here, Mother.

ALLAN: We chose the place.

ALICE: But Mother sent you the ad.

JASMINE: I remember this lodge so fondly.

ALICE: Allan's been meeting all the buses for three days.

JASMINE: I told you, Alice, I couldn't find the bus, and anyway the next one is tomorrow.

ROBIN: I carved a necklace for you, Grandma. I carved one for you and for Shelley.

JASMINE: Thank you, dear.

CONNIE: Alice was afraid the Cougar would get you. I wasn't.

ALICE: You should have been. A cougar could leap down on an open jeep and. . .

JASMINE: I'd like to paint a cougar.

ALICE: Oh, Mother, act your age. (*Pause*) We were wondering about all those paintings, Mother, when you. . . when. . .

JASMINE: When I die? You mean the A.Y. Jacksons?

ALICE: Oh no. We have room for them. I mean—Well I suppose you call them the Jasmine Daravalleys.

JASMINE: Yes, I do. I don't have many now.

ALICE: Oh, good.

ROBIN: The Jasmine Daravalleys. . . that sounds great.

CONNIE: Mother's real name is Lydia.

JASMINE: But I never did feel like a Lydia. So I changed. Mind you it caused a stir. (*To* ROBIN:) But your grandfather never batted an eye—he liked Jasmine. (*Pause*) This is a pleasant room, Shelley. Your grandfather and I were here in 1953. The telegram came—about James—and finally we just got in the car and headed West with no special destination. This place had some sort of healing atmosphere for us. I've never forgotten Wilderness Lodge.

ALICE: You and father came out here and all the time we had to stay in boarding school. I hated that school.

CONNIE: I liked it. You only hated it because they put you at the diet table.

ROLAND: Well now we have the prodigal in our gates. To Granny Moses Daravalley. You've heard of Granny Moses?

JASMINE: Yes, Roland. I think I have.

SHELLEY: And tomorrow we'll have a great birthday dinner—with presents and cake and everything. Like birthdays at High Valley. We'll all dress up.

CONNIE: You always wore a long dress at our birthdays. And your sapphire brooch.

JASMINE: I still have the long dress, Connie.

ALICE: But you gave the brooch away to a stranger.

JASMINE: No stranger, dear. To John Wilding's daughter.

ALLAN: Who's he?

ALICE: A painter.

CONNIE: He died.

ALICE: He was nothing to us.

ROBIN: He was something to Grandma. She went to Greece with him. Isn't that right? She was there when Shelley and I were in Spain. We wanted to join them. Didn't we, Shelley?

(Pause)

JASMINE: I like that batik. It's good.

SHELLEY: Thank you. Allan doesn't like it.

ALLAN: I didn't say that.

(Pause)

JASMINE: I'm sure you were all upset when you heard about the fire.

EARDLEY: Fire?

ALICE: What fire?

CONNIE: When?

JASMINE: It was on the news. I sent you the insurance money to come here.

ALICE: We heard nothing about a fire. How could you forget to tell us?

EARDLEY: Thank God, your apartment is fire-proof.

JASMINE: No. After you left in the spring I moved to the old Hartley mansion. I'm sure I told you.

EARDLEY: We've been opening a new store, Granny.

JASMINE: Well, the furnace exploded.

EARDLEY: Good God. Why didn't you go with it?

JASMINE: I was at Banff—painting.

ALICE: Did you lose much?

JASMINE: Everything.

ALICE: Mother. So that's why you got us all here. To tell us there's nothing left.

JASMINE: That's partly the reason, Alice.

ALICE: The silver. The cloisonne. The Limoges.

CONNIE: You had priceless books. Some original Audubons. The French doll.

JASMINE: All the fire department could do was keep the fire from the other houses. And nobody died.

457

Gwen Pharis Ringwood

ROLAND: That matched set of dueling pistols?
JASMINE: They went.
ALICE: I feel as if the family never existed. Posterity won't get a thing.
JASMINE: I spent years tidying things for posterity, Alice. When the fire came it tidied the whole thing up. Don't slump, dear. You're quite pretty when you sit up straight.
CONNIE: Your jewelry?
JASMINE: Except my ring.
EARDLEY: I suppose you keep your money in your stocking.
JASMINE: No. The copper kettle. It went too.
ROLAND: The whole shebang.
JASMINE: Yes. Jars of fruit. Scraps of a patchwork quilt. Edward's diary. Forty-two sketch books and all my paintings. And newspaper clippings about the Roosevelts, and Hiroshima and Belsen and the first meeting of the United Nations. King Edward's abdication. Gandhi's salt march. Nehru's death. The odds and ends and scraps and pieces of a life time.
ALICE: No, of generations! You held them in trust.
JASMINE: I meant to send you the Limoges, Alice, and the French doll to Connie. . .
ALICE: But you were too busy painting!
EARDLEY: Too bad you weren't there when the fire broke out.
JASMINE: I feel lucky. . .
EARDLEY: I meant you might have saved something.
JASMINE: That was one choice I didn't have to make. I went back and saw the place gutted, finished—I felt as if I'd been wiped out too. Nothing left, but skin stretched over old bones, and a skull, five dull senses—
SHELLEY: Oh Grandma, why didn't you come here?
JASMINE: I'm here now, Shelley. You know for a lot of my life I've felt like a piece of broken china—the pieces all there but not together. An eye, a flower, a skeleton, some odds and ends and earwinkles—
ROBIN: I know that feeling.
SHELLEY: Yes. Me too.
JASMINE: When your father was killed, Robin, and again when Edward died, I thought maybe I wanted to die too. I didn't feel that way about the fire. . . but I did feel lost. Without my things. Things can be like a cocoon around you. Make you feel safe. Then all of a sudden I realized that I'm free. . . free to find a new shape, or to fill up the one I'm supposed to have. I don't have to live in my things any more. I can just live.
ALICE: You offered me the Princess Alexandria tea set, and I didn't take it. (To EARDLEY) You said we didn't have room in the car.
CONNIE: I wanted that tea set too.
JASMINE: I'm sorry to lose some of my paintings, some old letters and pictures of you children but I remember them. And after the fire

all of you seemed close to me—pins and needles of memory kept
sticking into me. Your pigtails, Alice. Connie in a pinafore. The
two of you putting a doll's dress on a piglet.

CONNIE: I remember that, Alice.

ROBIN: I stole Grandad's harmonica.

JASMINE: He didn't mind. You needed a harmonica. Shelley riding the
pony. Quentin making an Indian shield. And Cora—

ROBIN: There's a cave at High Valley. A deep cave.

SHELLEY: And a well with a pump, and you can always hear the creek.

JASMINE: I waited for your letters but they didn't come. I went back to
Banff and painted, but you all kept walking through my mind. . .
there were things that needed to be said. A snatch of something
Edward used to say kept floating like a feather in my head.
"What am I here or hereafter, O Finn, but the love you give me
and the love I give back to you." So here I am.

(*Pause*)

EARDLEY: You did have insurance?

JASMINE: Oh yes, more than enough to buy the tickets and reserve the
lodge and I sent money to Quentin and Cora too. Nearly five
thousand dollars.

EARDLEY: That's all?

ROLAND: My God, the pistols were worth that.

ALICE: Mother!

CONNIE: Our heritage.

JASMINE: I didn't expect a fire.

ALICE: So here you are, stripped.

JASMINE: Except for my rug and my skin and my paint box.

ALICE: Thank heaven you still have High Valley. And us. I see now
why you wanted us all together here. . .

JASMINE: Do you, Alice?

ALICE: It's perfectly clear. You need us. You don't have a home. You
can't live alone at High Valley. Fortunately Eardley and I—

EARDLEY: Your mother looks tired, Alice. We'll discuss things
tomorrow.

JASMINE: Discussion wasn't quite what I had in mind.

ALICE: What then?

JASMINE: Reaching out? Starting over?

ALICE: You want to change your name again!

JASMINE: Calm yourself dear. You're looking flushed. You should
lose weight.

ALICE: That's mean.

CONNIE: But it's true, Alice. You have beautiful clothes but they're
always too tight.

ALICE: You two always side against me. You always have. I felt like
Cinderella. I still do. Before the ball.

SHELLEY: We all love you, Mama.

ALICE: I'm sorry. I'm just upset. . . over the fire. . . And I worry about you, Mother.

JASMINE: Of course you do, dear.

ALICE: I'm making you a shawl, and I brought the cake, and the turkey
—for your birthday. I thought I was doing everything right.

JASMINE: And you are, dear. Shelley, I am a little tired. If I could—

SHELLEY: Of course, Grandma. Come with me.

(*They start upstairs.*)

JASMINE: That's a good batik.

SHELLEY: Thank you. It's wild horses on our prairie. But their legs
aren't right.

JASMINE: You could try another dye — cover them with mist or long
grasses.

SHELLEY: I'll try that.

JASMINE: Use your mistakes, Shelley. If you don't, you'll never finish
anything. Well, I'll just rest until dinner. Do my yoga.

ALICE: I'll bring your dinner up to you.

JASMINE: Oh no. After the moon rises, Jimmy Lashaway is taking me
up to the Soda Spring. He took Edward and me there when we
were here before.

ALICE: Mother, you can't go chasing off into the night. Don't you
realize you're an old lady?

JASMINE: Oh yes, Alice, I do. You know, I can see you now. . . all of
you. . . as children. I want to run back and kneel down and put
my arms around you. The years go by so fast, Shelley, so fast.

(*They go upstairs.*)

ALICE: You see. She's quite irresponsible. We can't let her go tonight.
She'll catch her death.

ROBIN: But she wants to go, Aunt Alice.

ALICE: She's over-excited. She needs a sedative.

(MARYBELLE *enters*)

MARYBELLE: I hear Mrs. Daravalley's going to the Soda Spring with
the Chief.

CONNIE: Have you been to this spring, Marybelle?

MARYBELLE: I've been there. My Grandad took me when I was twelve.
Last year I went there myself. Most people don't know about the
spring. It's kind of a secret.

ALICE: Why? Why don't people go there?

MARYBELLE: They're scared.

ALICE: Just what is this Soda Spring, Marybelle?

MARYBELLE: You wouldn't think much of it, Mrs. Hobbes. The soda
spring's not like any place else. It's strange. Like hearing that
cougar cry in the night is strange. When I went there alone—
(*Pause*) Yeah, that's it all right. It's—strange.

(*Curtain.*)

SCENE II: *The Soda Spring*

Mist, slabs of rock, an old tree and a clearing. A feeling of mystery. The Soda Spring is right of centre. Moonlight is bright but intermittent. JASMINE and JIMMY come to the edge of the clearing. JIMMY carries a lantern.

JIMMY: That is a big climb; are you all right?
JASMINE: Yes. I'll rest a minute.
JIMMY: You got a bad heart?
JASMINE: I'm supposed to be careful.
JIMMY: You got lots of guts.
JASMINE: No. I just don't want to die before I die, if you know what I mean.
JIMMY: I know.
JASMINE: I'd forgotten how big the rocks are.
JIMMY: They're big all right. Old.
JASMINE: You brought Edward and me up here in the afternoon. We stayed till it was night.
JIMMY: Yeah. I went down and caught some fish. When I come back you were still sitting.
JASMINE: And now I'm here, alone. An old lady.
JIMMY: Not many people know about the soda spring. I don't tell them. Not many Indians come here. They are scared. Of the mist.
JASMINE: It takes strange shapes.
JIMMY: When you were here this was the Government's. Then they sold it. But nobody ever came. (*Pause*) I think nobody should own this place. It is the earth's.
JASMINE: (*after a pause.*) I own this land, Jimmy.
JIMMY: I thought maybe so. It was you offered to sell it to my band five years ago.
JASMINE: Yes.
JIMMY: We didn't have the money. Anyway some said they wouldn't come here. They were scared of bad spirits. What will you do with it when you die?
JASMINE: I don't know.
JIMMY: You will leave it to your kids, I guess.
JASMINE: I don't know. I thought maybe Shelley and Allan—
JIMMY: We might buy it now, if you want to sell.
JASMINE: I can't decide.
JIMMY: How many acres?
JASMINE: 160.
JIMMY: Nobody ever logged it. You can sell the timber. Take the timber, then you sell the land. That's the smart thing.
JASMINE: You sound like Eardley. My family.
JIMMY: That's the way it is now. Turn everything to money.

JASMINE: I don't want the trees cut down. Look over there. Some of those trees must be seven hundred years old.

JIMMY: I think so. When they log now, they cut down everything. Then they plant some little spindles so everything will be the same size. They don't want old trees. Maybe they don't want old people. But they don't cut us down yet.

JASMINE: No. You're still the Chief.

JIMMY: Them bastards tried to get me out. But the people voted for me again. I can still stand up.

JASMINE: Like those trees.

JIMMY: Yeah. A big wind might take them. Or me. Are you all right now?

JASMINE: Yes.

(They move towards the soda spring.)

JIMMY: There it is.

JASMINE: *(kneeling)* It's the same. The very same.

JIMMY: It's not big, is it?

JASMINE: No. Not big.

JIMMY: Just a small hole in the ground with the soda water bubbling up.

JASMINE: It's warm. It's like touching the heart of the earth.

JIMMY: In the old days the Indians used to come here before the fall hunt. They would sing and dance. It was a ceremony.

JASMINE: Yes. A visit to the oracle.

JIMMY: My grandfather came here when he was a boy. He told me he came here a boy but he was a man when he went down to the people. I brought Marybelle here when she was twelve. Three years ago she came here and stayed two nights alone. She never told me how it was. But she was changed.

JASMINE: How?

JIMMY: She was proud again, like when she was little. In the old way. She quit running around. She studied. She knew she was an Indian. She was glad. I think so. You want a drink from the spring now?

JASMINE: We should make a ceremony.

JIMMY: Sing and dance? *(Chuckling)* That old tree would think it's funny, two old people singing and dancing underneath the moon.

JASMINE: We could make a wish.

JIMMY: At our age?

JASMINE: I still have some wishes.

JIMMY: Yeah. I have some too.

JASMINE: So, we'll drink the soda water and we'll make a wish.

JIMMY: I'll dip for you. There.

(He does so.)

JASMINE: *(taking the cup)* I wish not to be helpless. I wish to die before I'm helpless.

JIMMY: I hope you get your wish.

462

JASMINE: I've been afraid of. . . It's your turn. (*She dips the cup into the spring*) I hope you get your wish too.

JIMMY: I wish my granddaughter, Marybelle, will have her children and her grandchildren around her and come here some time. That is my wish.

JASMINE: Your wish wasn't for yourself at all.

JIMMY: I will die before I'm helpless. I know that about myself.
  (*Pause*)

JASMINE: I have another wish. Would it be all right?

JIMMY: Sure. We are playing this game. Here. Do you think the water tastes funny?

JASMINE: A taste of soda and something else—something from deep down inside the earth.

JIMMY: Yah. (*Hands cup.*)

JASMINE: (*intensely*) Please God let me go on painting. Another chance. Another chance to—

JIMMY: Maybe you will paint this place.

JASMINE: Maybe. If I have time.

JIMMY: What time is left we have. Time to see the sun rise and go down. This moon shining. Time to tell the young ones how it was.

JASMINE: They don't listen, Jimmy.

JIMMY: Sometimes they listen. Marybelle says the spirit of the old way is here in this spring. I think the people want her to be Chief after me. I think she listens.

JASMINE: You are lucky then.

JIMMY: Yah. What time is left we have, old woman. (*Softly he sings a snatch of an old Indian song punctuating it with a rattle he produces from his pocket. For a moment the place vibrates with mystery. He breaks off abruptly at the sound of halloos and shouts off stage*). Some people are coming.

JASMINE: Oh, no.

JIMMY: I think your family has followed. (*Chuckling*) They don't trust us.

JASMINE: You didn't want people to come here. I've spoiled it.

JIMMY: Sooner or later they would come. I can't stop them.

JASMINE: But if I hadn't told them. Forgive me.

JIMMY: The spring isn't mine. You say you own it. The spring comes out of the ground. I don't own the ground. I think I will climb up to the top of the cliff.

JASMINE: Shall I come?

JIMMY: It is too steep for you. You couldn't make it.

JASMINE: I'd better wait for them, anyway.
  (JIMMY *goes off up the cliff. Shouts off.* SHELLEY *comes in with a torch.*)

SHELLEY: Grandma. I hurried ahead. I know you didn't want us to follow you. I couldn't stop them. I tried.

JIMMY: It's all right, Shelley.

Gwen Pharis Ringwood

SHELLEY: Where's Jimmy?

JASMINE: Up the cliff. Sit down, Shelley.

SHELLEY: All right.

JASMINE: We don't know each other very well, do we?

SHELLEY: No. I wish we did. I'm sorry I didn't write you, after we bought the Lodge.

JASMINE: Your mother told me you bought it. She blames me.

SHELLEY: I know. (*Pause.*) I've never been up here before. (*Kneels by the spring.*) I see why you wanted to come here. The water comes up and then it's out of sight and then it comes again. . . for a million years.

JASMINE: Jimmy and I drank the soda water and made a wish. A kind of ceremony.

SHELLEY: I'd be afraid. I might make the wrong wish.

JASMINE: What's the matter, Shelley?

SHELLEY: Nothing. Nothing's the matter. But you can't go around making wishes if you don't even know what you want. . . if you don't even know who you are.

JASMINE: You don't know those things?

SHELLEY: I thought I did. When we first came out here I was sure it was the right place for us. But now sometimes I feel trapped. I don't seem to be able to be a wife and a person too. And I think all Allan wants is a wife. It's a silly word—wife. I don't like it. Allan makes fun of my work—my sketches and batiks. He thinks of them the same way he thinks of his mother's crocheted doilies. I just feel. . . trapped, that's all.

JASMINE: And you were free when you were with Robin?

SHELLEY: Yes. No. I wasn't really. I. . . I felt guilty, because we were cousins. And because, well, he depended on me. . . for everything. It was always whatever I wanted to do. Sometimes I felt like a tyrant. Now I feel like a bondswoman. With child. What'll I do, Grandma?

JASMINE: Shelley, dear, I don't know.

SHELLEY: Allan doesn't even know I'm pregnant.

JASMINE: Why, Shelley?

SHELLEY: Because I didn't tell him. I just went ahead. It's my body. There was a woman here with a baby and I envied her because she looked so—so I—Oh, if I could just sort things out.

JASMINE: You will dear, you will.

SHELLEY: Here they come. (*She suddenly reaches down and cupping her her hands drinks from the spring.*) Help me, somebody. Help me.

EARDLEY: Hello, this place. Shelley. Shelley. Grandma.

SHELLEY: It's all right, Daddy. We're here.

EARDLEY: (*Entering with torch*) Well. There you are. What in God's name did you want to come up here for, Granny? That's a steep climb.

JASMINE: You needn't have come, Eardley.

EARDLEY: The girls were worried. So was I. So everybody decided to come. Hey, this is quite a place. Reminds me of Stonehenge.

JASMINE: Yes.

EARDLEY: Shelley kneeling like a high priestess. Well, we brought some refreshments. We'll have a party. . .

ALICE: (*entering*) Mother, If I'd known what that trail is like, I'd have. . . I'd have locked you up.

JASMINE: Wasn't I lucky to escape, dear?

ALICE: Is that your Soda Spring? I expected something more dramatic. You could start the bon fire, Eardley.

JASMINE: Please, not here.

EARDLEY: Why not?

SHELLEY: Not here, Daddy. Leave this place alone. Please.

EARDLEY: All right, ladies, all right. Your wish is my command. I'll build it over there—on that flat ledge.
    (*He moves off.*)

ROLAND: (*off*) Follow me, Connie and you'll be all right. Are you following, Connie?

CONNIE: I'm right behind you, Roland. (*They enter*) Wait Roland. Listen! (*The loons call from the lake.*) Oh, it's the loons. It's been a long time since I heard loons calling.

ALICE: It's a lonely sound.

CONNIE: Wild. Wild and free.

ALICE: You always exaggerate things, Connie.

ROLAND: She gets that from Granny. I'm out of breath. That's rough terrain.

    (MARYBELLE *enters. She pauses. Then moves quietly to* JASMINE)

MARYBELLE: I told them you'd be all right with my Grandad, but they had to come.

JASMINE: I know, Marybelle.

MARYBELLE: Where is Grandad?

JASMINE: He climbed the cliff.

MARYBELLE: You like this place?

JASMINE: I like it.

MARYBELLE: Some of the people are afraid to come here. To me it's a good place. I'll drink from Grandad's cup.
    (*She bends to the spring.*)

JASMINE: We made a wish when we drank.

MARYBELLE: O.K. I make a wish. I wish this place will stay the same. (*She stands up.*) I'm going up the cliff now. (*Turning*) Allan stopped at the Beaver Dam. He'll be along.
    (SHELLEY *acknowledges this with a nod.*)

ROLAND: So, this is your great Soda Spring, Granny. . . that little hole in the ground! What happened? Did it shrink since you were here before?

JASMINE: I think it's always been the same.

465

ROLAND: I expected some sort of big cave. What are you doing, Shelley? Praying?

SHELLEY: (*getting up*) Grandma said we should make a wish when we drink from the spring. I. . . I was making a wish.

CONNIE: A solemn wish? A real wish? I'd be embarrassed.

ROLAND: Silly girl—what secrets have you got? (*He stoops and takes up cup.*) Here, I'll make a wish! I want that cougar. That's what I want. I want that cougar nailed on my wall.

CONNIE: No!

ROLAND: (*holding cup but not drinking.*) Come on, Connie. A man waits for the chance to pit himself against something as cunning and merciless as that cat. The once-in-a lifetime chance. You sight him. You wait for the moment. Is your hand steady? Is your eye sure enough? He's out there now. . .waiting for me. (*Drinks*) I want that cougar.

SHELLEY: Why, Uncle Roland?

ROLAND: You women will never understand. To prove something. To prove I can protect what's mine if I have to. That's why.

CONNIE: (*With a sudden fierce passion she throws herself down beside the spring, pounding on the ground.*) Make him miss! Make him miss! Make him miss!

ALICE: (*Sharply*) Connie!
 (*There is a stunned silence.*)

ROLAND: I won't miss, Connie. I won't miss.
 (CONNIE *remains crouched at the spring, silent, tense as a small animal*)
 Ever since she joined those bird watchers, my wife talks a lot of mealy-mouthed spineless drivel. She doesn't mean half she says.

CONNIE: I mean it. I do mean it.

ROLAND: (*angry*) There's something wrong when a man's own wife betrays him. I've taken good care of you, Connie. You stop to think now. Haven't I taken good care of her, Granny?

CONNIE: For years I followed you from army base to army base, and every fall I followed you and the dogs over hills and coulees, and I hated it. I hated the dogs. I hated the guns. Sometimes I hate you, Roland.

ROLAND: Get up. Get hold of yourself.

CONNIE: All you care about is your dogs and your guns. All you care about is killing.

ROLAND: No!
 (*Pause*)

CONNIE: Between us there's a great gulf, Roland.

ROLAND: She gets upset these days. It's that time of life. (*Very low*) If we'd had children. . . we both wanted a family. . . (*Turning*) Come over by the fire, Connie. I'll fix you a drink.

CONNIE: No. I want to stay here.

ROLAND: Stay then. Stay. But you won't stop me, Connie. My time isn't up. Nobody can stop me. (*Sound of a loon*) Hear that loon? That should do your heart good. Why don't you answer it, Connie? There's no gulf there. Answer that crazy loon!
(ROLAND *goes to fire off stage. There is a silence.*)

CONNIE: Oh God, God, God.

SHELLEY: It'll be all right, Auntie Connie.

ALICE: I hate this place, Mother. Why did you bring us here?

JASMINE: You came.

ALICE: Because of you. That old tree. . . the rocks. . . Mist all over. . . No wonder Connie went to pieces.

CONNIE: I. . . I shouldn't have said that to Roland. . . about a great gulf.

ALICE: I agree.

CONNIE: (*forlorn*) Except. . . it's true.

SHELLEY: But you've stayed together all these years, Aunt Connie.

CONNIE: We have to. Where would I go? We own everything together. We're. . . we're all each other has. I don't know what happened to me.

(ALICE *gets up suddenly and begins peering about*)

JASMINE: What is it, Alice?

ALICE: My purse. I put it down somewhere. I have to find it.

SHELLEY: (*smiling*) Mother, you. . . you brought your purse. . . here?

ALICE: Of course. I always carry it. It's here somewhere. It has to be.

JASMINE: There, dear. . . by the stump.

ALICE: Oh, thank goodness. I'm so relieved. You know, if people get hold of your Chargex card, they can go on a rampage.

JASMINE: Dear Alice.

ALICE: Well, it's true. One thing I hope you'll get from me Shelley is that you'll look after your things. Connie and Mother never have. Remember that doll you gave me when I was eight? Rosalind. I kept her perfect. She was a pretty doll, Shelley. I thought she looked like Mother. Mother was very pretty and Father adored her and they both admired James. And of course everybody loved Connie, the baby. That's true, Shelley. Connie was May Queen three years running.

CONNIE: Was I? I'd forgotten that. Was I really May Queen?

ALICE: I felt such a lump. I hated that diet table. I'd sneak off and eat the other girl's cookies. Mother never sent us cookies.

JASMINE: I think I sent cookies.

ALICE: You didn't.

SHELLEY: What happened to Rosalind?

ALICE: I went to camp and Mother let Connie play with her and Connie wrecked her.

CONNIE: It was an accident. I dropped her. . . accidentally. . .

ALICE: In the toilet.

Gwen Pharis Ringwood

CONNIE: You never could forgive. You hold grudges.
ALICE: I don't. But I take care of nice things. I know where my things
are. I keep a list of birthdays. And a list of all our possessions and
their value. If you'd done that, Mother, you'd have known to get
insurance. How could you give my doll to Connie?
SHELLEY: Oh, Mother, it's so long ago. Forget about it.
ALICE: I try. But I swore then I'd never have three children. . . it's too
hard on the middle one. You just don't get much love.
JASMINE: Alice, we loved all three of you.
ALICE: In all those albums there's dozens of pictures of James and
Connie and hardly any of me.
JASMINE: We loved you.
ALICE: Then why didn't I feel it? It's getting late. I miss the National.
I always listen at home. I don't see why you think this is a good
place, Mother. . . Connie's upset the Major; Allan chooses not to
appear. Probably because you invited Robin, the last person you
should have asked. What are you doing to us, Mother?
SHELLEY: Grandma's trying to have a family reunion. You're spoiling
it.
JASMINE: What should I be doing, Alice?
ALICE: You should give up traipsing around the country and settle
down in a good home near Eardley and me where I can look
after you.
JASMINE: Oh, Alice I can't. I couldn't. I have things to do.
ALICE: At your age? What things? Hitch hiking, dashing off to paint
while your things burn up. That fire upset me very much.
JASMINE: Alice. We must stop this. The past is the past. Nothing can
change it. We must get above it. Go on.
ALICE: You think I should take up painting, don't you?
JASMINE: You need something.
ALICE: I've plenty to do. I. . . I'm lonely. The bridge club only meets
once a month now. Shelley won't let Allan come into the store.
You're a thousand miles away. And Quentin's like you. . . he
thinks only of himself.
JASMINE: (sharply) You should be proud of Quentin. I am.
ALICE: Proud of him? He turned his back on everything we stand for.
If those Africans don't know how to farm it's their fault. Why
should Quentin teach them? What's he trying to do, be a saint?
JASMINE: Don't destroy, Alice!
ALICE: Why did you bring us here, Mother? Why did you come here?
Why?
JASMINE: I. . . I thought it was time. . .
(ROBIN *calls from off stage right.*)
ROBIN: Shelley. Shelley.
SHELLEY: Up here, Robin.
ALICE: I'm cold. I'm going over by the fire.
JASMINE: I'll come with you. Connie?
CONNIE: Yes. What do I say to Roland, mother?

JASMINE: Perhaps you just have a drink with him, Connie. It depends on what you really want, doesn't it?

ALICE: You'd better come, Shelley. Your father's trying to give us pleasure. He's made a fire. He hoped we'd sing, enjoy ourselves.

SHELLEY: Yes, Mother.

(ALICE, CONNIE and JASMINE *move left.* EARDLEY *meets them.*)

EARDLEY: Hey, you girls. We've got the fire going. One match! Alice, you've got to take a look at this place. There's springs all around us. See that mist. That means warm springs under this whole mountain side. If we get hold of this place we can have another Radium. Without that sulphur smell. You follow. Who owns this place, Shelley?

SHELLEY: I don't know.

EARDLEY: This is a hot property, Shelley. And it's right on your doorstep.

ROLAND: (*coming in from left*) I'll just get a thermos of that soda water for the Scotch, Eardley. (*As he does so*) Eardley's really hopped up about this property, Alice.

EARDLEY: We've got to get something going here. (ROBIN *appears*) Hey, Robin, come over here. I want you to taste this water. . .

ROBIN: Thanks.

(*He moves towards* EARDLEY)

ROLAND: Don't make any wishes when you drink it. I made a wish and you'd think the sky is falling.

EARDLEY: Wish. I'll make a wish. I wish I could get hold of this mountain side. I can see it now. Campers and tents down there, Swiss cottages all the way up to the cliff here. Swimming pool. Whirlpool. Club house. Golf course on Allan's place. Why, it's a gold mine. That's my wish—a real recreational property.

ROLAND: I might sell my Jolly Jumper stocks and buy in.

EARDLEY: Wilderness Lodge would be the base complex. Over there where I built the fire I'll have a Solarium. Allan should be here. Come on you girls, let me show you the shape of things to come. Come on, Connie. How would you like a bird sanctuary down there by the dam?

(*They all go except* ROBIN *and* SHELLEY)

ROBIN: Ah yes, the shape of things to come. Change without progress. Shelley—

SHELLEY: Yes?

ROBIN: Just. . . Shelley.

SHELLEY: Did you see Allan?

ROBIN: He stopped to investigate the beavers. They're re-routing his creek.

SHELLEY: We've tried to discourage them but they're stubborn. We broke down their dam and the next day it was all built up again.

ROBIN: They don't want you here. Neither do I.

Gwen Pharis Ringwood

SHELLEY: But we are here, Robin. The beavers will get used to it. So will you.
ROBIN: I didn't come for Grandma's birthday. I came to see you.
SHELLEY: I know.
ROBIN: How could you walk away from everything we had together?
SHELLEY: Spain wasn't real, Robin. The whole Europe thing wasn't real.
ROBIN: Don't tell me that. Laughing and swimming and working together, being together. It was real.
SHELLEY: We were high on pot and wine and the excitement of getting away from home. We didn't really see Spain. We saw each other, and people like us. . . the young travellers.
ROBIN: We planned to go on. . . to join Quentin. To do what he's done —teach, serve, change things.
SHELLEY: We talked a lot. I guess I got tired of talk. I. . . got homesick.
ROBIN: Why didn't you tell me? Instead of just. . . leaving.
SHELLEY: Because I wanted to. That's the way it was supposed to be — no strings—for both of us.
ROBIN: So you end up in a hunting lodge, with someone who doesn't have a clue. You call that freedom?
SHELLEY: I have to find my own way, Robin. I have to fight for who I am. . . with you there was no fight. We were like twins, trapped in one another. We couldn't grow. I can't ever go back with you, Robin.
ROBIN: For two years I waited, thinking you'd come. Now it's like. . . like finding out a missing person is really dead. Only I don't believe it.
SHELLEY: Dear Robin.
ROBIN: I used to imagine us very old, sitting on a beach in the sun, admiring all the things we'd made together. . . like Philemon. . .
SHELLEY: Philemon and Bacchus.
ROBIN: That's it. They gave wine to a stranger and he turned them into two great trees, with their branches mingled together and their leaves murmuring all the things they remembered. That's my wish, Shelley.
(*He dips from the spring.*)
SHELLEY: No. Wish for yourself, Robin.
ROBIN: (*drinking*) You're my wish. Maybe you'll change your mind.
SHELLEY: I'm pregnant, Robin. Next March I'll have a baby.
ROBIN: Congratulations. (*Pause*) Yes—congratulations.
(*Pause*)
SHELLEY: Where will you go, from here?
ROBIN: I don't know. High Valley maybe. There's some good clay there, if I remember right. By the river. Keep in touch, eh?
SHELLEY: I will. You too.
(ALLAN *enters at right.*)
ALLAN: The cousins. Communing with nature.

ROBIN: Right. Did you deploy the beaver?

ALLAN: Bloody chewers. They never know when to quit. Where are the others?

SHELLEY: Dad built a fire over on the ledge.

ALLAN: I suppose we should talk, the three of us. A cosy talk by the old spring. A Pow-wow.

SHELLEY: There's nothing to talk about.

ALLAN: Oh no. I don't share those lovely Spanish memories. Why can't you leave Shelley alone?

SHELLEY: Don't, Allan.

ALLAN: Shelley married me. We're getting along.

ROBIN: I'm sure you are. I'm impressed with the work she's done. Three batiks.

ALLAN: They're good too.

ROBIN: She used to carry a dozen sketch books everywhere we went. She really worked.

SHELLEY: Stop it, Robin.

ROBIN: Maybe I didn't offer you much, Shelley, but I don't stifle you.

ALLAN: If Shelley had needed you, she'd be with you. Isn't that right? Tell him.

ROBIN: An artist can't be chained up. And you've got her chained. . . to a hunting lodge.

ALLAN: Shelley's free to choose. Go on, Shelley. . . choose. . . before I kill the son of a bitch.

SHELLEY: Leave me alone, both of you. Leave me alone.

ROBIN: O.K. Shelley. Sorry.

(*He goes off left. . .*)

ALLAN: I asked you to choose. You couldn't. Where does that leave us?

SHELLEY: Nothing's changed.

ALLAN: No? We're a thousand miles apart, that's all.

SHELLEY: When you could accept those hunters without even consulting me, that's pretty far apart isn't it?

ALLAN: Suppose we do it your way. We take the Band Council. What about next year and the year after? How do we make a living?

SHELLEY: How we planned it in the first place. We hold out for what's here. Without killing everything off.

EARDLEY: (*coming in*) Hey, you kids. The party's starting. Great fire. Food. Scotch and home-grown soda. You better get over there.

SHELLEY: We're coming.

ALLAN: Thanks, Mr. Hobbes.

EARDLEY: Why can't you call me Eardley? I'm approachable.

ALLAN: Thanks, Eardley.

EARDLEY: You kids are sitting on a gold mine. I've been percolating.

SHELLEY: Please, Daddy, don't percolate.

EARDLEY: Don't be foolish. You've a great potential here. . . right under your feet. Alice wanted me to put you in as manager of the

471

new drug store, Allan, but you've a lot better chance to make it right here. Do you want to hear some creative thinking about this place?

SHELLEY: Not now. We'll join you in a minute.

EARDLEY: Sure. Sure. Sorry I interrupted.

(*He goes off.*)

SHELLEY: Daddy thinks we've got another Radium. A spa.

ALLAN: Hmm. And your mother wants me to sell toothpaste and deodorants. And your cousin wants you to take off with him.

SHELLEY: What do you want, Allan?

ALLAN: To keep our place. To make a living for us here. Why can't you go along with that?

SHELLEY: I could, if you'd respect my opinions. You only respect your own opinions.

ALLAN: If I don't respect them, who will? What's the use of having opinions, if you don't. . .

SHELLEY: What about mine? I work here too.

ALLAN: I know that. Your parents won't let me forget how hard you work. Shelley, do you really think being married to me is depriving the world of a great artist?

SHELLEY: I never said that.

ALLAN: Not to me, not in words. But you managed to give Robin the picture. He's out to rescue the chained princess.

SHELLEY: Can't we leave Robin out of this?

ALLAN: How? He's the ghost of Christmas past, isn't he, Shelley? Your past. The change the world people. I never pretended I was going to change the world. After school I worked in a machine shop. My old man worked. My mother worked. We didn't have time to think about changing the world.

SHELLEY: All I ever asked was that we take our own small steps. Refuse to spoil things. Quentin used to tell Robin and me to make our hands gentle when we picked wild berries, so we wouldn't spoil the branches for next year. That's what I meant.

ALLAN: I'm not Robin and I'm not Quentin either. I can't go to Africa and teach farming. I don't speak Swahili. And I can't swim out to stop people shooting whales or polar bears either.

SHELLEY: So, we'll tell our children that there were once bears and wolves and cougars living wild here, but now they can only see them in picture books. Or chained up in some far-off zoo. And they'll ask why, and we'll say "Oh, we got rid of them, dear. We helped to shoot them." And they'll say "Why?" And we'll say "Because we needed them — to hang on our walls."

ALLAN: O.K. You've convinced me. We take the Band Council. We go back to dignified little ads for back-packers. We'll be a sanctuary for wild beasts, a grizzly paradise.

SHELLEY: Our children will thank us, Allan.

ALLAN: I doubt we'll make enough out of the nature-lovers to afford children. Children are expensive.

SHELLEY: Not at first. If the mother eats an extra egg, glass of milk and two slices of bread, she can feed her child. I read that.

ALLAN: Very interesting. What about college?

SHELLEY: They'll get scholarships.

ALLAN: Don't count on it. Thank God for the pill.

SHELLEY: I didn't take any pills for two months, Allan.

ALLAN: Shelley! What do you do?

SHELLEY: Nothing.

ALLAN: You stopped without telling me. Without a word! Why?

SHELLEY: I wanted to stop.

ALLAN: An important decision and you make it without saying a word to me? Shelley!

SHELLEY: Like the hunters. Like you did.

ALLAN: I can wire those hunters not to come. You could be pregnant.

SHELLEY: Yes. I am.

ALLAN: How do you know? You haven't been to a doctor? You couldn't know.

SHELLEY: I know.

ALLAN: Good God. We must be far apart for you to get pregnant without even telling me.

SHELLEY: I didn't feel far apart then. I felt great. When that photographer was here with her baby, I envied her.

ALLAN: You could have asked me.

SHELLEY: Whenever I talked about it, you said no.

ALLAN: I'll be a father.

SHELLEY: Is it such a terrible idea?

ALLAN: Yes. I'm not ready. Anyway, how could I conceive a child and not know? How can something that important happen to you without your knowing?

SHELLEY: It's usually kind of a surprise.

ALLAN: Hmm. I feel like. . . I feel like Joseph. When did it happen?

SHELLEY: Over two months ago, give or take. . .

ALLAN: Give or take. What kind of answer is that? You have no sense of time, Shelley. I'm not ready to have a family. I wanted to get the Lodge paid for and established. I wanted to paint all the boats, install a radio telephone, overhaul the jeep. I've got a big list!

SHELLEY: I won't have an abortion. I'll bring him up by myself.

ALLAN: On batiks?

SHELLEY: Sure.

ALLAN: That dye is toxic. It says so right on the package. You'll have to stop those batiks. You can draw.

SHELLEY: Thank you, Allan.

ALLAN: I suppose I can cope. I'll have to make a new list. Set deadlines. How long have I got?

SHELLEY: Six months, give or take. It takes nine altogether.

ALLAN: I know that. Why does it take so long?

SHELLEY: It just does.

Gwen Pharis Ringwood

ALLAN: I suppose it's nature's way of settling a person down. We'll be settled down by then, won't we?

SHELLEY: I hope so.

ALLAN: (*looking down at the spring.*) We have to be. We must. (*He kneels by the spring.*) You ought to look at this spring, Shelley. It's kind of. . . mysterious. Strange. . . We should come up here often.

SHELLEY: Yes. Are you angry?

ALLAN: I don't know. I feel — left out. Bowled over. I should be angry. I don't know. Everything's changed. We're not free any more. I have to get used to the idea. Of course I'm angry. You would be too if I suddenly announced I was going to have a baby.

SHELLEY: Sh. . . they're coming. Don't tell Mother. She'll be terrified.

ALLAN: So am I. (*Drinking from the spring water in his hand.*) (*Softly*) Worthy. That's the word. A man wants to be. . . worthy.

(EARDLEY *comes in with* ALICE *and* JASMINE *close behind.*)

EARDLEY: Well, you missed the party. Robin's putting out the fire. Everybody wants to go home.

ALICE: I'm tired, Eardley. Besides you want to talk to Allan.

EARDLEY: Allan, we must talk. I've really let the old imagination flicker tonight. I dipped into the future far as human eye could see. . . Saw a vision of the world. . . That's what you need— vision. You know I can't understand my nephew—Robin. He doesn't have an idea what I was getting at. No ambition. Just wants to make pots.

SHELLEY: It's Robin's life, Daddy.

EARDLEY: What kind of a life is that? Making pots. You have to think ahead. Agreed, Allan? Maybe I would have liked to let my hair grow down to my shoulders and go off to Tibet to sit at the feet of the Maharajah. Sure. Why not? Because I'm a responsible person, that's why. Kids like Robin have had it too easy. Time we stopped the hand-outs. Come on, Alice. We'll start down. See you at the Lodge. You better come with us, Grandma.

JASMINE: I'll wait for Jimmy Lashaway.

ALICE: I'd feel a lot happier if you'd come now.

(ROLAND *and* CONNIE *enter*)

ROLAND: Hurry up, Connie. Station wagon's leaving. I want to be up early in the morning. Are you coming?

CONNIE: (*turning*) I'll walk down with Robin. We haven't had a chance for a visit. Is that all right, Robin?

ROBIN: (*coming in*) Certainly. My arm, Madame. Goodbye, you old Soda Spring. Keep right on truckin'.

(*They go out. Sound of the loon. Answering call from above.*)

SHELLEY: That's Marybelle answering. She can make their sound.

JASMINE: She's lucky. I never could.

(*The loons sound again.*)

MARYBELLE: (*entering from above.*) I gave those loons something to think about. Oh, it was great up there. You feel like you can reach out and touch the moon. It's hard to believe people really walked out on that moon. I hope they leave it up there. Granddad's on his way down. He said to wait for him. Good night.

JASMINE: Good night, Marybelle.

(*She moves to the spring as* MARYBELLE *goes out.*)

SHELLEY: (*Struck by the old woman's stillness*) Are you all right, Grandma?

JASMINE: Yes, Shelley. I'm all right. I'd just like to be here alone for a few minutes. Please.

ALLAN: But we ought to. . .

SHELLEY: Come on, Allan. We won't be far ahead.

(*They go.* JASMINE *crouches by the spring. Her hands down into the bubbling water. She rocks a little as she lets the water fall over her hands. Her voice is a whisper.*)

JASMINE: So hard to love. So hard to know how to love. Show me the way. . . "What am I here or hereafter, O Finn.—"

(*She remains crouched by the spring as* JIMMY LASHAWAY *enters.*)

JIMMY: You waited for me to come. I thought you would go with them.

JASMINE: Did you go to the top of the cliff?

JIMMY: Yeah. I did.

JASMINE: Good.

JIMMY: Yeah. I could see a long way. A lot of land. I could see how it was in the old days. Too bad you couldn't climb up there.

JASMINE: I remember it from before.

JIMMY: Yeah.

JASMINE: Are you going to town tomorrow?

JIMMY: Yeah. I have to go.

JASMINE: Would you come by the Lodge before you go?

JIMMY: Sure. I come by about noon.

JASMINE: (*Getting up.*) I'd better take a good look at this place, Jimmy. I won't be here again.

(*Sound of cougar crying*)

JIMMY: You hear that?

JASMINE: Yes.

JIMMY: You know what it is?

JASMINE: It's the cougar, isn't it?

JIMMY: Yeah. Over there. How did you know it was a cougar?

JASMINE: I don't know. I've always known. I think I've always known.

(*They stand listening. After a moment* JIMMY *takes out the rattle and softly at first, then louder sings a strange, eerie Indian chant. . .*)

CURTAIN.

Gwen Pharis Ringwood

SCENE III: *Departures.*

*The living room of Wilderness Lodge. The first light of early morning
seeps into the dark living room.* JASMINE *comes down the stairs, carrying
her prayer rug, paints.*
  *She crosses to the window, looks out, then places rug at left and
assumes across-legged position.*
  *After a moment, Roland comes downstairs. He switches on the light.
He sits to clean his gun, and doesn't see Jasmine until she speaks.*

JASMINE: Good morning, Roland.
ROLAND: (*startled.*) Oh, it's you, Granny. What are you doing down
  here, all scrunched up?
JASMINE: I couldn't sleep. I was going to meditate.
ROLAND: I don't go for that Eastern mystic stuff. What's wrong with
  good old Christianity?
JASMINE: Nothing, Roland.
ROLAND: Connie and I worry about you, Granny. You've taken up
  some pretty outlandish ideas. Lunatic fringe ideas. Lunatic fringe.
  (*Pause*) I couldn't sleep either.
JASMINE: The full moon, I expect.
ROLAND: Did you hear that cougar last night?
JASMINE: I heard it.
ROLAND: I'm going after him. Now.
JASMINE: Why?
ROLAND: If I don't, he'll kill. They kill. Cattle. People. I have to go after
  him. You can't stop me.
JASMINE: I'm not stopping you.
ROLAND: Connie can't stop me. Make him miss, she said. I think she
  was out of her mind for a moment. Make him miss. I didn't even
  know her. Shakes a person. All these years Connie's been a good
  wife and suddenly. . . Women have a lot to learn about men,
  Granny.
JASMINE: I expect that's true.
ROLAND: Connie's taken up that bird watching as if her life depended
  on it. Do you think I should put a stop to it?
JASMINE: No, Roland.
ROLAND: She'll probably get over it. "Make him miss" she yelled, with
  that cougar out there waiting for me. Men have hunted ever
  since—
JASMINE: Cain.
ROLAND: That's right. Well, I'll be back, Granny, and I'll have that big
  cat to hang on my wall. You can paint him.
JASMINE: I'm not sure I'd want to paint a dead cougar.
ROLAND: A magnificent animal. You just can't understand. I'm never
  happier than when I'm out there in the forest waiting for whatever
  turns up. I feel the heart-beat of nature all around me. I'm off.
  You'd better go back to bed. Connie and I worry about you.

(ROLAND *goes out with his gun.* JASMINE *stands at the window watching* ROLAND *go. Then she switches off the light, stands looking at* SHELLEY's *batik.* ROBIN *comes in.*)

ROBIN: Grandma! You're up early. Happy birthday.

JASMINE: Thank you, dear. Did you sleep well?

ROBIN: I didn't go to bed. I was down by the lake. I came here because of Shelley, Grandma.

JASMINE: Yes.

ROBIN: I've loved Shelley all my life, Grandma. Ever since we were children at High Valley. She was the freest person I ever knew. And she's talented. She takes after you, Grandma. So do I.

JASMINE: You and Shelley have a desire and a certain facility, Robin. After that you sweat it out of yourself. Maybe one or both of you will do that.

ROBIN: Shelley will never do it here. She may not need me. But she should be with creative people. She's not doing any work here. You could help me get Shelley out of here, Grandma.

JASMINE: People do what they see to do, Robin. I wouldn't think of interfering in Shelley's life. Or yours.

ROBIN: You helped Quentin. He told me.

JASMINE: Quentin had found his road, Robin. Long before I helped him. He'd have got there without me.

ROBIN: I did a lot of thinking last night. I found a road too. High Valley.

JASMINE: Isn't that a road back, Robin?

ROBIN: I wrote you about High Valley. You didn't answer.

JASMINE: I read the letter many times.

ROBIN: I'd make it a place for people to come and work. . . paint, make pots, write. . . a retreat. . . I know a lot of young artists who need a place like it would be. Shelley could come there for a couple of months even, in the winter. You could paint there, like you used to. We'd be back where we belong, Grandma. Where we have roots.

JASMINE: I can't give you High Valley, Robin.

ROBIN: Why? The others will just sell it. I'd use it. Please think about this, Grandma. It could mean a whole new life to a lot of people.

JASMINE: Go along now, Robin. I came down here to do my Yoga. The floor in the bedroom creaks.

ROBIN: High Valley could be an ashram.

JASMINE: Beautiful young people all doing yoga. . .

ROBIN: And making things. Creating. You'd see the start of it, and if you should die. . .

JASMINE: When I die, Robin.

ROBIN: All right, when. . . a long time from now you'd sit up there in heaven looking down on High Valley and you'd clap your hands.

JASMINE: I can see myself. I'm all in white. . . Do you think there's any sound?

ROBIN: Sound?

JASMINE: Up there. When I clap my hands?

ROBIN: Well, if you let the others have High Valley, you won't be clapping your hands. You'll be turning in your grave.

JASMINE: I'd hate that. So cramped, for turning. Now go along.

ROBIN: I'm going. (*At the door*) You and Grandpa made High Valley a great place for us, a long time ago. That's why. . . . I'll see you.

> (ROBIN *goes out.* JASMINE *takes her rug behind the screen and settles down. The loons cry from the lake. Somewhere the clock strikes the hour.* SHELLEY *comes from upstairs and goes to the kitchen without seeing* JASMINE. *After a moment* ALICE *and* CONNIE *creep down the stairs.*)

ALICE: Sh. . . . Connie. Quiet. Don't creak.

CONNIE: I'm trying not to creak. Why do we have to come down here?

ALICE: So Mother won't hear us. Those walls are like paper.

CONNIE: Why are you shivering?

ALICE: Because I'm cold.

CONNIE: You have cold blood. I have warm blood. You'd think it would be the other way when I'm the slender one.

ALICE: The skinny one. We must decide what to do about Mother, Connie. You can see now that she's becoming very erratic.

CONNIE: What have you decided, Alice?

ALICE: Eardley and I will take Mother home with us in the Cadillac. We'll get power of attorney, control of High Valley, and control of Mother.

CONNIE: What if she won't go with you?

ALICE: Don't talk so loud. She's got ears like a lynx.

CONNIE: (*whispering*) What if she won't go?

ALICE: What else can she do? She's burned up everything except High Valley. She can't live there alone. At the Silver Threads there's people to watch her so she can't get into trouble.

CONNIE: She'd be better off with me, Alice. You always fight with her.

ALICE: She depends on Eardley. She never liked Roland. And you have to think of Roland. He's retired. Your first duty is to him.

CONNIE: What about your first duty?

ALICE: Eardley's not retired. He has a rich and full life in the drug stores. Besides, Mother isn't going to live with us, just near us. So we can take her out on Sundays for little treats.

CONNIE: It doesn't sound like Mother. She'll say "No".

ALICE: Then we'll take steps?

CONNIE: What steps?

ALICE: We'll have her committed to the Loving Care Unit of Silver Threads.

CONNIE: How?

ALICE: Stop yelling.

CONNIE: (*whispering*) How?

ALICE: Two close relatives simply sign that she's confused. Incapable of managing her own affairs.

CONNIE: Two close relatives. That would be you and I.

ALICE: That's why we had to talk this over. Mind you I'm hoping she'll be reasonable and come along willingly.

CONNIE: I wouldn't like to sign away my own mother.

ALICE: Nobody likes it. It's for her own good.

CONNIE: Mother may be erratic, but she's not crazy. I don't want to sign.

ALICE: What do you intend to do? Sit around while James's children get High Valley?

CONNIE: I'm glad you admit I have a share! You always talk as if everything should come to you.

ALICE: You'll get your share. You'll be a partner in the company Eardley's going to form. He's got it all down on paper.

CONNIE: Someone's coming. What if it's mother. . .

ALICE: Oh, it's only you, Eardley.

EARDLEY: Have you talked to Connie? We want your agreement on the plan, Connie. . . so we can wrap everything up. I want to get back to those springs this morning. . . Here's the plan, Connie. Item One. Alice and I buy High Valley from your mother. We slap a mortgage on it or sell it and we plough the money into developing those springs.

CONNIE: You and Alice. What about me?

EARDLEY: You get stocks in the development.

CONNIE: I'm not sure I want to put all my money in hot springs. What if they run cold or dry?

EARDLEY: They've been there a million years, Connie. You can count on them. Picture the whole thing. . . Sasquatch Hot Springs. Huge footprints on the rocks in the Canyon in permanent luminous paint. Sign—Follow the Sasquatch. An outline of a Sasquatch in colored lights right on top of the cliff. Big plastic animals at the gate—bear, moose, cougar, just like real life only four times the size. The springs and swimming pools flooded with changing colored light. Boy, am I on fire!

CONNIE: Mother may refuse to sell you High Valley.

EARDLEY: She can't. We can't allow the old to hold back progress. We've had too much of that. We'll offer her $60,000.

CONNIE: Roland asked a realtor about that property four years ago. He valued it at half a million.

EARDLEY: All right. $80,000. That would keep her in Silver Threads until she's a hundred. What does she need money for except to buy paint?

ALICE: I'm not sure if they'd let her paint at Silver Threads. Painting's so untidy.

EARDLEY: Girls, last night I visualized an empire devoted to recreation, stretching from this lodge right up to that spring. A recreational empire.

479

CONNIE: The birds would stop nesting here, Eardley.

EARDLEY: We'd fence them in, . . . We'd import birds. Come outside. I want to show you my vision. . .

(*Sound of a shot*)

ALICE: Someone's shooting.

EARDLEY: After all, it's the season.

CONNIE: Roland went out early.

EARDLEY: Come on, girls. . . Follow the Sasquatch. I'm going to put this place on the map.

(*They go outside.* JASMINE *peaks out from behind screen to make sure they have gone. She is on her hands and knees behind the screen. She is very upset. . .* ALLAN *comes in from upstairs.*)

ALLAN: Shelley. Shelley are you. . .

JASMINE: Oh, Allan. Help me up. Quickly.

ALLAN: Grandma. What's the matter? Are you all right?

JASMINE: I just want to escape. . .

ALLAN: What were you doing down there?

JASMINE: My yoga. Only. . . I have to get out of here. They mustn't see me. I was trapped. Trapped.

ALLAN: You must have had a nightmare. Walked in your sleep.

JASMINE: They mustn't find me here.

(SHELLEY *comes in from kitchen*)

SHELLEY: I heard a rifle shot, Allan. Grandma!

JASMINE: I'll be all right, Shelley.

ALLAN: She's had a nightmare. You better go up with her.

JASMINE: My rug.

SHELLEY: I'll get it. Come on, you'd better go back to bed for a little while.

JASMINE: I was trapped, Shelley. Hurry, they're coming.

(SHELLEY *and* JASMINE *go upstairs.*)

EARDLEY: (*outside*) A fantastic potential. Fantastic.

(EARDLEY *comes in followed by* ALICE *and* CONNIE)

EARDLEY: Allan, I have to talk to you. With this place and the Soda Springs we're going to make another Kubla Khan. Remember that poem? "In Xanadu did Kubla Khan, a stately pleasure dome decree. . ." That's it. Stately pleasure domes from here to the cliff.

ALLAN: (*to* CONNIE) Did your husband go out shooting?

CONNIE: Yes.

ALLAN: I'd better see what's happening. . .

EARDLEY: Allan, will you take a minute and listen. You tell me you want to get ahead with this place. After all my daughter's happiness means a lot to her mother and me.

ALICE: You see, Allan, you don't seem to realize that Shelley wasn't brought up to rough it.

480

ALLAN: If Shelley wants to go home or anywhere else she'll go. Until she does, I guess her happiness is our affair. We're a couple, remember.

ALICE: All Eardley asks is that you listen to him.

EARDLEY: That's right. You and Shelley could make a mint out of this place. Nobody sneers at a mint, Allan. What I want is. . .

(MARYBELLE *comes in from outside.*)

MARYBELLE: Allan, Major Anderson's at the edge of the woods. He's shouting for you to come.

ALLAN: Oh, God.

MARYBELLE: Granddad's outside in the jeep. He'll take you over.

ALLAN: (*taking his rifle.*) Tell Shelley I'm out tracking down her uncle.

(*He goes off.*)

EARDLEY: You see. He just won't listen!

ALICE: (*Indicating* MARYBELLE) Sh. . . (*To* MARYBELLE) Good morning, Marybelle. I placed those shoes just outside my door. I want you to have them.

MARYBELLE: I'd better start the fire for breakfast.

(*She goes into kitchen*)

ALICE: Well, really. That was rude. It just doesn't pay to be kind.

EARDLEY: Here's Allan, a young man, and yet when it comes to looking ahead, he's as blind as that old lady upstairs. No imagination. They see a piece of land with some good natural features—I see a Canadian Disneyland!

(JASMINE *and* SHELLEY appear)

ALICE: Here's my mother. Good morning, dear. I hope you slept well.

SHELLEY: She didn't. She had a bad dream. She dreamed she was trapped and couldn't get away.

ALICE: Trapped. Imagine. It's because you won't lean on any one. Isn't it, Connie?

CONNIE: Well, it seems easy to be liberated and on your own in the day time. But at night—

(JASMINE *is no longer upset but very calm. Both her clothes and her manner are changed.*)

JASMINE: Alice, Connie, all of you. I want to talk to you. I owe you an explanation. I didn't just call you here to celebrate my birthday or for a reunion. There were other reasons.

ALICE: You realize now how much you need us, don't you, Mother?

JASMINE: I did want to see you all. And I think we must talk about High Valley.

ALICE: We think so too, Mother.

JASMINE: In the last five years I've had letters from all of you concerning the ranch. You all remember it very fondly. I was touched by that.

CONNIE: Alice wouldn't remember it the way I do. . . because she was older when we went there.

Gwen Pharis Ringwood

JASMINE: You not only remember it. You all have made great plans for it. I brought along some letters. In this one Robin suggests that High Valley could be a retreat for creative people.

EARDLEY: A potters' haven eh? Potter's field is more like it.

JASMINE: Cora visualized a centre for women, a place to discuss their problems, to help one another.

ALICE: That sounds like Cora. She's botched up two marriages, what makes her think she could run a Centre for Women?

JASMINE: Toby, my nephew, wanted a wild life compound.

CONNIE: I don't see what right Toby has to. . .

JASMINE: Your letters, Connie. You would turn High Valley into a retirement village. You and Roland would administrate it from the Ranch House and you invite me to live in the cottage by the creek. You make it sound very pleasant.

ALICE: You never consulted me about that, Connie.

CONNIE: Why should I? Eardley will never retire. Why should I consult you?

ALICE: I'm the eldest.

JASMINE: These letters from Eardley and Alice are offers—cash offers—for the ranch.

EARDLEY: I didn't offer enough, Grandma. I'm prepared to offer more now. Land values have gone up.

JASMINE: I believe they've gone up considerably, Eardley.

ALICE: We want you to spend your last years in comfort. There's nothing wrong with that.

JASMINE: Of course not. Shelley and Quentin never asked for the ranch. . . they do say they hope it will stay in the family.

CONNIE: You never answered my letters.

ALICE: Or ours. You ignored our offers.

JASMINE: I couldn't decide what to say. So after the fire I thought if we were all together. . . here. . . in a place that seemed to. . . well, a good place. . . then I could. . .

ROBIN: (coming in) God, Shelley, they've shot that cougar. Allan and Uncle Roland and Jimmy are bringing him in on a pole.

SHELLEY: Oh, no.

ROBIN: Look out there. See for yourself.

SHELLEY: How could they? .

ROBIN: It takes three men to carry him.

EARDLEY: God, he is beautiful.

SHELLEY: Allan promised he wouldn't let Uncle Roland. . .

CONNIE: Shelley, Roland isn't a bad man. He was brought up to think it was all right.

ALICE: He did the right thing. You've read about what cougars can do. . . maul and kill children. . . This place isn't good for you, Shelley. You should come home.

SHELLEY: He's all golden, with big soft paws.

EARDLEY: Where's the camera, Alice? We don't get many chances to see a big cat.

CONNIE: Roland's walking behind. He looks. . . I'd better. . .
   (She goes out, followed by EARDLEY.*)*
ALICE: Here's the camera. I feel safer now that that animal isn't stalking
   the woods.
   *(*EARDLEY *and* ALICE *go out).*
SHELLEY: That's what your dream meant, Grandma. It was the cougar
   that was trapped.
ROBIN: And now they've killed him. Do they really maul and kill
   people?
JASMINE: Some times, yes.
   *(*ALLAN *enters)*
ALLAN: I had to shoot that cougar, Shelley.
SHELLEY: *You* shot him?
ALLAN: Yes. He was. . .
SHELLEY: You pretended you thought he should go free. Last night
   you. . . Now you've killed the only big cat that's been in this
   country for years. . . The only one. That's. . . That's cruel. He
   hadn't hurt anybody. Look at him. He's beautiful.
ALLAN: Shelley, listen. . .
SHELLEY: How can I listen? You say one thing and do another.
ALLAN: *(very angry)* Don't listen, then. Think what you want to think.
   I'm some sort of. . . sadist. I like killing.
   (He goes to kitchen)
SHELLEY: How could he do it? How could he. . .
JASMINE: Allan was trying to tell you something, Shelley.
ROBIN: I want to take a picture. I'd like to try a sculpture some time.
   Come on, Shelley. . . we should look at him close up. We won't
   have another chance.
SHELLEY: No. I don't want to. You go.
   (After a moment's hestitation ROBIN *goes out. He meets*
   ROLAND *at door.)*
ROBIN: Well, you got your wish Uncle. You can hang him on your
   wall.
   *(*ROLAND *just looks at* ROBIN *without speaking and after a*
   moment ROBIN *goes out. . .)*
ROLAND: I missed, Granny. After all my talk, I missed that cat. I
   wounded him but I didn't kill him.
JASMINE: I'm sorry for you, Roland.
ROLAND: *(very distressed.)* I thought I would track him down and
   show you all. He was right in my sights. I should have killed him
   the first shot. But I didn't. I shattered the hip. His back leg was
   dragging. He went for a tree, but he couldn't climb. I came back
   for Allan. We went in the bush after him. There was blood all
   over and we could hear the cougar snarling and sort of crying
   too. Suddenly he was there. . . crouched right in front of us.
   Allan fired. I fired too but it was Allan who put the poor beast
   out of his misery. I had a clean chance and I crippled that
   cougar, Granny. . .

(He stands in despair at the sideboard drinking.)

SHELLEY: I blamed Allan.

JASMINE: You didn't listen, Shelley.

SHELLEY: I know. I don't listen, do I? I don't listen.

ROLAND: He was right in my sights. *(dully)* My gun's down there. I'd better get it.

JASMINE: I'll come out with you, Roland. Robin's right. . . we might not see another big cat.

(As ALLAN *returns from kitchen)*

It's good you shot him, Allan. Roland says the poor thing was suffering.

ALLAN: Yes, he was. So were we. And we were scared too. If I'd missed he'd have got us. One of us anyway. It's a wonder I got him. My hand was shaking.

ROLAND: Allan fired just as he sprang at us. The bad thing was my first shot. . . a clean chance and I crippled him.

(ROLAND *and* JASMINE *go out).*

SHELLEY: I'm sorry. Forgive me.

ALLAN: You really don't know me, do you?

SHELLEY: I want to.

ALLAN: Sure. I have strong opinions. But I can change mine. You go right back to where we were before. . .

SHELLEY: I should have listened.

ALLAN: Yes, you should. You seem to want to push me into some role. . . the destroyer, the killer. . . Not just the cougar. Everything. As if I were out to trap you. I'm not. If you really think of me as some bloody-minded Cain, then you'd better leave me. I may not draw or paint or make pots. . . but I can like those things. I even like those damn Spanish dancers. I like your horses but I can't help seeing that their legs look broken. I'm not out to cripple your talent, trap you. I told you I had no intention of shooting that cat out there unless he became a nuisance. Why couldn't you believe me, trust me? If I really am the man you seem to think I am, you'd better leave me.

SHELLEY: I think I've been afraid of. . . turning into my mother or Aunt Connie. . . that's part of it. I just want to be myself, if I can find out who I am. I had to fight you over the hunters. I really believe we shouldn't take them. . .

ALLAN: And I gave in. You convinced me. Now you. . .

SHELLEY: We just have to hang on, Allan. We're going to be a family.

ALLAN: We've got to do more than just hang on, Shelley. That's not good enough. We have to learn how two people can live and grow together and not cripple one another.

SHELLEY: Sometimes when you hold me, our hearts beat right together. . . the same beat. Then when we get far apart—it seems so hard to get back together again. . . We lose each other.

ALLAN: That's true. You know what we need? Wings.

SHELLEY: Wings? You mean we have be—angels?

ALLAN: No. Something I saw this morning. . . the ospreys flying. They'd soar way apart and then they'd fly back together and fly awhile and then off they'd go, flying far apart again but always they'd come together. They looked so free, flying like that. I envied them. . . for us.

SHELLEY: That's beautiful.

ALLAN: (*Pause*) We're sending that cougar to the taxidermist for the museum. Jimmy's going to take him. Your Uncle Roland feels awful about shattering that hip. He cried.

SHELLEY: He should. The cougar wasn't bothering him. He didn't need a cougar.

ALLAN: True. But I still feel sorry for your Uncle.

(JASMINE *enters.*)

JASMINE: Children, I've asked everyone to come in here for a few minutes. A family meeting. Please stay, Allan.

ALLAN: I'll just give these knives to Jimmy.

(*He goes out*)

SHELLEY: (*smiling at* JASMINE) I'm learning to listen, Grandma. I know I can.

JASMINE: Sometimes that's the best thing to do, Shelley. . . and the hardest, isn't it? It took me most of my life to even begin to listen.

ROBIN: (*entering*) That's a shattering way to start your birthday, Grandma.

ALICE: (*behind him*) Don't talk about it any more, Robin. At least we won't be awake all night listening for that cry. Hurry up, Connie.

CONNIE: Don't be so bossy.

ALICE: Where's Eardley?

EARDLEY: Here, Alice. (*He and* ROLAND *come in.*) Cheer up, Roland, old man. We all miss sometimes.

(ROLAND *remains apart still brooding over his failure.*)

ALICE: Allan. Allan.

ALLAN: (*off*) Here, Mrs. Hobbes. Be right there.

ALICE: Shelley, please insist Allan call me something besides Mrs. Hobbes. Now are we all here? (*She sees* ALLAN *and* MARYBELLE *in the doorway*) Oh, Marybelle, Mother has something to say. . . well, to the family.

MARYBELLE: Oh, excuse me.

JASMINE: Please don't go, Marybelle.

(MARYBELLE *hestitates*)

ALICE: But mother.

JASMINE: It's all right, Alice. Stay, Marybelle.

JASMINE: Now, children, it's time you got your answers about High Valley. As I told you Eardley and Alice offered to buy it from me. . .

ALICE: We're only thinking of your own good, Mother. Silver Threads is an ideal home for senior citizens, but it is expensive.

JASMINE: I'm sure it is. There isn't any High Valley Ranch now. I sold it four years ago.

EARDLEY: You sold it.

ALICE: Mother. Without telling us. You couldn't.

CONNIE: Why? Why?

EARDLEY: Who bought it?

JASMINE: The Government. As a heritage property.

ALICE: Everything burned up, and what you don't burn, you sell. I can't understand you.

EARDLEY: I hope you got a good price.

JASMINE: I did.

EARDLEY: I hope you invested the money wisely.

JASMINE: I think I did.

EARDLEY: Oil? Telephone? Hydro?

JASMINE: No, Eardley.

ALICE: What have you done with the money, Mother?

JASMINE: I endowed a school in East Africa.

CONNIE: So! Quentin got it out of you!

JASMINE: No. The school is in a village where there never had been a school of any kind. It's doing well. It serves a lot of people, children and parents both go.

CONNIE: You gave our inheritance to some Africans you've never even seen?

ALICE: So now you expect us to support you. You squander what's yours, and expect to live on what's ours. You lied to us about High Valley.

JASMINE: I didn't really lie. I evaded the question.

EARDLEY: God knows I offered financial advice. She wouldn't take it.

ALICE: You're out of your mind, Mother.

ROBIN: We were all after it, weren't we, Grandma?

ALLAN: After all, it was your mother's ranch, Mrs. Hobbes.

ALICE: She held it in trust. And she gave it away. Now she'll have to stay with Eardley and me until we find a cheaper place.

JASMINE: Oh Alice, no. I can't. I leave next Thursday.

ALICE: Leave? For where?

JASMINE: That's why I wanted to see you all. . . I wanted to make a clean breast. . . say goodbye. I'm going to Australia. I've been offered a chance to teach, and study Maori Art.

ALICE: You can't. That's selfish.

JASMINE: It's all arranged.

EARDLEY: All arranged. So that you can unleash hundreds of black artists on the world and upset everything! Is that what you want?

JASMINE: Yes, Eardley. I think it is.

EARDLEY: Well, there goes a dream. I was going to let you in on an empire, Granny. Stately pleasure domes. I was going to let you in on the ground floor.

ALICE: I blame you, mother. I blame you for Quentin going to Africa. For Shelley and Allan settling in this wilderness. For deserting Connie and me when we were children to go off painting, and for deserting us now when you ought to need us. And you say you love us. . .

JASMINE: I do. I do.

(ALLAN *gets up suddenly and moves in front of* ALICE.)

ALLAN: Excuse me, Mrs. Hobbes. I just want to. . .

ALICE: To what?

ALLAN: Take down this moose head to send to the museum. I'm sick of him up there staring down at me like the eye of God. *(To* ROBIN*)* Give me a hand.

ROBIN: Sure.

ALLAN: Besides, it gathers dust. Have you got him?

ROBIN: I've got him. You want him in the truck?

(ALLAN *nods and* ROBIN *takes out the moose head.)*

ALICE: I'm numb with shock. Just numb.

CONNIE: I'm number than you, Alice. Roland and I. . .

(She moves to ROLAND*)*

ROLAND: How could I have missed, Connie? I had him right in my sights. I should have. . .

MARYBELLE: Australia. I feel like going with you.

JASMINE: Come along.

ALICE: You'd take her. She's not your family.

MARYBELLE: Don't worry, Mrs. Hobbes. I can't go. I got things to do here. A lot of things to do.

(JIMMY LASHAWAY *enters followed by* ROBIN)

JIMMY: We got him loaded, Allan. Moose head too.

EARDLEY: Hey, Chief, I want to ask you something. Why didn't your band buy those springs when you had the chance?

JIMMY: We didn't have the $24,000.

EARDLEY: Twenty-four thousand — that's peanuts.

JIMMY: We didn't have those peanuts.

EARDLEY: Who approached you?

JIMMY: Real estate fellow. I don't remember.

ALICE: Without High Valley, you can't do anything with the springs, Eardley. Mother's fixed that.

JASMINE: Yes. You see I own the Soda Springs, Eardley.

ALICE: You. Mother.

JASMINE: Edward and I bought that place years ago, after we were here. We were afraid someone would spoil the place. So, we bought it. For very little.

EARDLEY: But that puts a different light on everything. You're a canny old fox. Grandma Daravalley.

487

ALICE: And all the time you pretended. . . .

JASMINE: I came here planning to give the Soda Springs, and the land around it to all of you, together.

ALICE: All of us. That isn't fair. After all—

JASMINE: I've changed my mind.

EARDLEY: Because I've shown you their potential. You think you can cash in on them.

CONNIE: When did you change your mind?

JASMINE: This morning. This morning I realized that it's too late for you to nurture the land, and too late for it to heal you. Sooner or later you'd spoil what's there, defile the mystery. And when the mystery is gone, the land would become your enemy. The Indians owned that land once. I want them to have it back. Jimmy, I am leaving the soda springs to your reserve, providing it is left as it is now for a hundred years. Would you agree to that?

JIMMY: That's a good deal. I agree. You should ask Marybelle. She may be Chief after me.

MARYBELLE: *(moving to* JASMINE*)* Last night I wished the Soda Spring would stay the same. You heard me. I would not spoil that place.

JASMINE: Jimmy and I will draw up the agreement in town.

EARDLEY: That's crazy. It's moving backwards. I wasn't just dreaming for myself. I was thinking of the future, your future, Shelley, your children's future.

SHELLEY: I don't need stately pleasure domes, Daddy. But thank you anyway.

ALICE: You're like that cougar, Mother. You leap down on one!

JASMINE: The cougar had no escape route, Alice. I have. *(Pause)* So the slate's clear. We're all tidied up. I'm going to town with Jimmy. I'd better get my things.

ALICE: You can't. We haven't even forgiven each other. You can't. I don't want you to go. I. . . I need you, mother.

JASMINE: Maybe I'm setting you free, Alice. All of you.

SHELLEY: Not yet, Grandma. Don't go yet. I made your birthday cake. See, it's got a seven minute icing. I got up early and it took me a whole hour to make a seven minute icing.

JASMINE: It's a beautiful cake, Shelley.

SHELLEY: We have to have the cake and light the candles and you make a wish and after the cake, the presents and we sing Happy Birthday and after the presents we all sing and tell stories about when we were children. It's. . . It's. . . like a ceremony, Grandma.

JASMINE: Of course. A ceremony.

SHELLEY: *(lighting the candles)* When they're all lighted, you make a wish and then you blow them out. *(In a small voice)* Happy birthday, Grandma.

JASMINE: I wish. . . . I wish. . . .

(She blows all the candles out. Curtain.)

The End

Mirage
A Play in Two Acts
For Tom Kerr, who made the Mirage a reality.

Characters

DOWSER RINGGO
JOHN RYLAND
RYAN RYLAND
HILT RYLAND

JEANNE WHITE CALF
MARY WHITE CALF   *May be played by one actor*
LAURA RYLAND

WHITE CALF
TOM WHITE CALF   *May be played by one actor*
SAMMY WHITE CALF

JEANNE RYLAND
STELLA BURKHOLT   *May be played by one actor*
CISSIE BURKHOLT RYLAND

FRED BURNS
GARFIELD BURNS   *May be played by one actor*
MARK RYLAND

MARG BLAIR
ROSE MEEKER
CHAIRMAN

SETTING: *Southern Saskatchewan farmland.*
TIME: *1910 to the present.*
COSTUMES: *Must be designed for period, quick changes, contrast.*

Gwen Pharis Ringwood

PROLOGUE

The cast is all on stage in various attitudes of work or play. As the music that brought them on fades, they freeze. DOWSER *moves forward to give the prologue.*

DOWSER: A prairie vision must inform my song.
Much that I count as beautiful or strong
I learned here, long ago,
Here in this central plain where my world began
Stretching out wide and far
Under the high dome of wheeling stars.

What gods I knew
Rose in plumes of dust at high bright noon
Or flattened themselves on the long shadows
Of morning and evening on the prairie.
Phantoms in drifting snow howled with the blizzard,
Etched mandalas on the window pane
In the stillness of late dawn when it seemed
The world would crack apart with cold.

Elusive spirits rose on the breath of patient cattle
Huddled against winter.
Spirits that shimmered in mirage,
Sailed with the high cry of wild geese flying,
And moved across wheat fields in soft undulation.

They were no easy gods,
Nor could they be deployed by easy offering.
They hid in buffalo wallows,
Took feather shape, drifting on air,
Or lynx-eared padded on soft cat feet.
Yet where they trod, the downy crocus pushed up through
Snow in spring-time
And golden rod nodded on autumn roadsides.

No gentle gods were these,
Riding the smoke of camp fire and of tipi,
Howling with wind and coyote, (kyot)
Whirling with dervish dust-cone down the long furrow,
Raging with thunder.

No easy gods, and yet they challenge, crying "hunt us down,
Uncover us from beneath your monuments of wood and stone,
Come, dance and sing with us,
For without us you are homeless.
Hunt us down for without us you are forever homeless."

(There is a swirl of wind music as the cast is caught in a vision of unseen spirits moving across sky and distance, and as they move towards the rear of the stage, DOWSER *joins them.)*

Act I

SCENE 1

The lights come up on forestage as JEANNE WHITE CALF *and* HILT
RYLAND *move foreward. Sound of Meadow Lark.* JEANNE WHITE CALF
comes on stage, she hears the song and stops to listen. HILT RYLAND
enters unaware of JEANNE WHITE CALF. *He turns and calls back. . .*
DOWSER *is not on stage. In the background is an abandoned farmhouse
with one porch railing broken.*

HILT: Are you coming, Dowser?
DOWSER: (*off*) I'll wait for you here, Hilt.
HILT: You're sure? Are you all right?
DOWSER: I'm all right.
JEANNE: Hi.
HILT: Oh. . . I didn't see you. I. . . I was just. . . I brought an old
   man out with me. . . Dowser Ringgo.
JEANNE: I know him. He sure is old. I guess I'm trespassing. I hope
   you don't mind. . .
HILT: I don't mind.
JEANNE: I know you too. Ryland. Hilt Ryland.
HILT: Who are you?
JEANNE: I'm Jeanne White Calf.
HILT: You live across the river?
JEANNE: That's my reserve. I don't stay there much. Not any more.
HILT: Where do you stay?
JEANNE: I move around. I've been up North lately.
HILT: Did you work up there?
JEANNE: I was waiting tables in a cafe. (*Pause*) I got my name from
   your grandmother. My people were friends with her, I guess.
   Sometimes they worked here. Are you going to farm this place?
HILT: I don't know. My Dad's offered it to me, if I want it.
JEANNE: You mean he'd just give it to you?
HILT: No. He has to get something out of it, if he retires. But I could
   buy it from him through a government scheme to keep farms in a
   family. . .
JEANNE: I used to see you at the University.
HILT: I didn't ever see you there.
JEANNE: I only took a few classes. One of them was Cree.
   (*she chuckles ironically*) My own language. I still don't speak it
   very well. (*pause*) I've just come back from a Sun Dance. For
   three days. They danced for three days. The old people said
   everything was like it was before the Whites came. . . except we
   went there in trucks and cars.
HILT: Did you like the Sun Dance? I mean. . . did it mean any thing to
   you?

Gwen Pharis Ringwood

JEANNE: Yes, it meant something. For a little while I felt like I was where I belonged. For a little while. . . I felt changed. But when you leave, it's the same again. . . it's still the same old hassle.

HILT: I know. I used to go to church sometimes. I'd come out feeling I knew the answer. . . do no harm. . . all you need to do is decide whether an action you take is one you'd want other people to take. But it's not that simple. (*Pause*) I didn't know you still had the Sun Dance.

JEANNE: We do. (*Pause*) Why don't your folks want to keep on farming this place?

HILT: This is the first year they didn't put a crop in. My Dad has arthritis. He says it won't hurt to let the land rest for a year or so.

JEANNE: Do you know how to farm?

HILT: I should. I grew up on a tractor. (*Pause*) I got an offer of a job this morning. A high paid job. I graduated in Science. Geology.

JEANNE: If you take the job you could buy the place.

HILT: I couldn't farm it. The job's in the North.

JEANNE: Uranium?

HILT: How do you know?

JEANNE: I've just been North, remember. It's really changing. My uncle works for that French company.

HILT: I have to decide this week whether I'll take this offer. I hate making choices.

JEANNE: My uncle digs uranium ore with a back-hoe. Do you know every time he leaves the job he has to shower and change all his clothes. Every single time he leaves that digger for even five minutes because of the dust from the uranium.

HILT: I'd be looking for new fields.

JEANNE: My uncle says the real danger is in those plants. . . like Three Mile Island. . . you remember that?

HILT: I remember.

JEANNE: My uncle says he wouldn't work in one of those plants because a tiny leak can cause damage to a person or even kill you. He'd rather surface-mine any time.

HILT: There's risk all right. There's risk in everything. Farmers use fertilizers, weed sprays, grasshopper poison. That's risky. What can you do? We have to have food. . . we have to grow food. . .

JEANNE: When the gulls eat the poisoned grasshoppers, I suppose the gulls die too. No more miracles then.

HILT: Miracles?

JEANNE: There was one. My grandfather told me. There was this terrible plague of grasshoppers so that the sun was blotted out. At Wascana Lake, near Regina, when the plague came you couldn't see the sun. Those grasshoppers ate every leaf and blade and they travelled like a cloud. In 1937 in the spring the grasshoppers came like a cloud and everybody was full of madness. Their crops disappeared and their gardens and every living leaf. And then suddenly the sky was full of white gulls, flying and squawking into that cloud of grasshoppers, gobbling them up until they were all gone. It's true! You can read it in a book. My grandfather said things began to get better on the land after the white gulls came. The Miracle of the White Gulls, my grandfather called it.

HILT: (*irritably*) All right. I won't poison the grasshoppers. What am I supposed to do. . . catch them in a sieve?

JEANNE: You're touchy! I was only telling you about the Gulls. I always liked that story.

HILT: I'm sorry. I have to make up my mind what I'm going to do. . . that's all. An American company owns all the land around this place. . . eight sections. Now they want this farm too. Do you know what they'd do with the house here? They'd use it for a granary. They'd store wheat in the house I grew up in!

JEANNE: I always liked this house. I used to wish we had a house like this one.

HILT: My grandfather broke this land. Rylands have lived here since before the first World War.

JEANNE: Hah. White Calfs have lived across the river a lot longer than that. Well, I'd better be going.

HILT: No, please wait.

JEANNE: Look, you came out here to think about the job and the farm and all that stuff.

HILT: I need to talk to someone.

JEANNE: It's your worry. I got my own worries. When we owned the land we didn't have to have power. . . except the sun and the running rivers. We didn't even say we owned the land then. . . we lived on it. A person could carry what he owned on his back or on a horse. At that Sun Dance I almost wished I didn't live now. . . I wished I could have lived before. . .

HILT: I know. Before we came.

JEANNE: That's right. But it's too late for that. . . I've got to find some way to hold myself together now.

HILT: Wait, Jeanne!. . . my grandmother. . . your namesake. . . she sent me out here for something. I want you to see it.

JEANNE: See what?

HILT: Don't laugh. . . it's a medicine bag. An Indian Medicine bag.

JEANNE: Why would I laugh at that? You Whites have a queer sense of humour.

HILT: Now, who's touchy? It just seems strange that an old Scotch lady should have kept this all her life. Here it is. Maybe it belonged to your family.

JEANNE: No. Ours has a wolf tooth on it. I wonder whose it was.

HILT: My grandmother kept it all these years. How did she come to have it?

(*The lights fade and a humming soft sound that is identified with the medicine bag fades too as* HILT RYLAND *and* JEANNE WHITE CALF *retire to join the cast.*)

493

Gwen Pharis Ringwood

SCENE 2

The lights dim and slowly come up to sunrise. Song may be used to make transition between Scene I and II. As JEANNE WHITE CALF *and* HILT RYLAND *retire the hum of the medicine bag blends into the sound of wind rising softly and then louder on the prairie.*

    During the song the cast as CHORUS *moves across the stage as if settlers looking for land. The men are in work clothes, the women in long skirts with shawls or head scarves. A train whistle is heard occasionally.*

SONG: (*If desired the song may be omitted and the transition be made with wind and music.*)

> Prairie magic prairie light
> Grasslands stretching far
> Will we find the dream we follow
> Under prairie stars?
>
> Prairie magic prairie light
> Morning mists arise
> Will we find the home we search for
> Under prairie skies?
>
> Sunrise and the lark ascending
> Fills the air with sound.
> Have we come to journey's ending
> Here on prairie ground?

>   (*Or the following verses may be set to music and used: perhaps only one verse will be needed.*)

> They are not easy gods
> Who ride in the smoke of campfires
> Howl with the wind and shimmer in mirage,
> Dancing with Northern lights, glowing in sun-dogs,
> These gods who challenge us to hunt them down.
>
> They are not gentle gods
> Who hide in the hawk's dawn shadow,
> Cry with wild geese or move with drifting snow.
> They whirl with the dervish dust cone down the furrow
> Eluding us, but will not let us go.
>
> They are not easy gods
> Drifting on air with feathers
> Or moving in waves across the golden plain.
> They bellow with lost bison, rage with thunder,
> Calling, "Come follow and hunt us down again."
>   (*A swirl of music may be used to bring* JOHN RYLAND *and his*

wife, JEANNE *into the main playing area. Their costumes indicates 1911 or 1912.)*
JOHN: Close your eyes, Jeannie MacDonald Ryland. I'm going to carry you across the threshold. (*He lifts her in his arms in a wide arc before putting her down.*) There! You can open your eyes.
JEANNE: What do you mean, John — threshold?
JOHN: Your new home, Jeannie. You're standing on what will be the front verandah.
JEANNE: You didn't tell me last night. I thought we were just camping overnight and then going on.
JOHN: I wanted you to see our place in the sunlight. Here's the stake of our North West corner. John Ryland's homestead. Well, what do you think?
JEANNE: I. . . I have to get used to it. The flatness, The emptiness. I've never lived where there were no trees. Or hills. Or hedges. I have to get used to it.
JOHN: There's light, Jeanne. Lots of sunlight and miles of blue sky. . . miles around you, miles above you. Look over there, see how far it is before the earth and sky come together.
JEANNE: I feel so small, John. Insignificant. Just grass and sky and space. It frightens me.
JOHN: We'll have a house, barn, buildings. You can plant some kind of hedge.
    (*Sound of shot off*)
JEANNE: What was that?
JOHN: Someone shooting.
JEANNE: At us?
JOHN: No. It came from way over there, by the coulee. Someone shooting gophers or grouse. Sound travels a long way here. We'll camp in the tent for now, Jeannie, but by fall we'll have a soddy right here.
JEANNE: John, there's a river down there, and trees!
JOHN: That's the river we crossed yesterday.
JEANNE: We can build down there, John. Near the trees.
JOHN: Afraid not. Our border is a mile this side of the river. Those trees are on Indian land.
JEANNE: You didn't tell me there'd be Indians.
JOHN: I didn't know until I saw the map yesterday.
JEANNE: Will they resent us, the Indians?
JOHN: Why should they? They have a reservation.
JEANNE: If I were Indian, I'd resent us.
JOHN: They signed the treaties. They have to live with it.
JEANNE: I suppose. (*Pause*) What's a soddy?
JOHN: Those houses built out of turf we passed yesterday. They can be warm and snug. You'll see.
JEANNE: Will we start today to build it?
JOHN: No. When I get through breaking the sod and seeding we'll build it. Can you do with the tent until then?

JEANNE: Aye. By then my mother will have sent my things from Scotland. My aunt left me a set of bone china and her silver tea service. If I had them now, I'd serve you a fine cup of tea right here in the middle of the prairie.

JOHN: Your folks won't think much of me when they hear you're living in a tent. They'll wish they kept you home, but, I'll make you a real home here, Jeanne. . . I promise.

JEANNE: Will we have cattle?

JOHN: Only a cow or two. This is wheat land.

JEANNE: You'll plough the grass under?

JOHN: I will. Some of the best wheat in the world comes from this prairie. By fall I'll have wheat rolling out of the separators in a golden stream. As soon as I can I'll get another section of land. This is wheat land.

JEANNE: The farms at home were very small, and the houses were tucked into the hillside, with trees and vines. There was water rushing down the glens. The farms at home were small, cosy.

JOHN: We'll have a big farm, Jeannie. . . this is just the beginning. You'll see.

(WHITE CALF enters)

JEANNE: (startled) John! Someone's here. . .

WHITE CALF: Hello.

JOHN: Hello.

WHITE CALF: I am White Calf.

JOHN: You were shooting over there?

WHITE CALF: Good hunting in that coulee.

JOHN: The coulee belongs to me now. John Ryland. It's part of my farm.

WHITE CALF: Many grouse there. Sometime deer. Antelope.

JOHN: I plan on fencing my land. The coulee too.

WHITE CALF: White man like lots of fences.

JOHN: I hear hunting's very good on the reservation.

WHITE CALF: Sometimes good. Sometimes bad. (to JEANNE) Mrs. that tipi. . . up near sky. . . that's my place.

JEANNE: I see it. Near the ridge. I've never seen a tipi before.

WHITE CALF: (to JOHN) I shot this grouse in the coulee.

JOHN: It's all right this time. But no more hunting on my land. You understand.

WHITE CALF: For you. I shoot this for you.

(WHITE CALF drops the grouse on the ground and turns abruptly starting off)

JEANNE: Oh, thank you. Thank you. . . White Calf. . .

JOHN: Yes, Thanks.

(WHITE CALF leaves without looking back)

JEANNE: Oh John, he came to bring this to us. To be friendly.

JOHN: How could I know that? Anyway, it's just as well he understands that the coulee's mine. We don't want them wandering all over the place. Well, do we?

JEANNE: I suppose not. Only. . .

JOHN: The land agent says Indians hire out as field hands in the fall. I'll probably be able to give him some work, if he wants it.

JEANNE: I felt afraid for a moment. . . you know, all the stories about Indians we heard as children. . . then I knew he meant no harm to us. Perhaps I'll get to know his wife.

JOHN: You're lonesome for another woman, Jeanne. There's a family . . . Burkholt. . . six miles along. You'll have neighbors, Jeanne. A woman to talk to.

JEANNE: They put their tipi in a good place. . . by a glen and sheltered . . . they can see the river and across to here and on. You must take me to see their tipi, John.

(DOWSER *enters whistling a merry tune*)

DOWSER: Hail and good morning to all here. Welcome to your new home, John Ryland. Mrs. Ryland. The name's Ringgo. Dowser Ringgo.

JEANNE: How did you know we were here?

DOWSER: Prairie telegraph. I figured you'd be needing my services so here I am.

JEANNE: You live near here?

DOWSER: I come and go with my old horse, Blackie. I witch wells, sir. And on the side I carry a store of useful items. . . needles, threads, extracts, sweet spices from the Orient. Your Raleigh man. I figure you'd want a well witched so I came this way.

JOHN: We're not settled. As you know we came last night.

JEANNE: We're camping.

DOWSER: You'd be foolish to build a house until you're sure of water.

JOHN: I don't put much stock in witching wells. Of course I hear some people think they have the gift.

DOWSER: I have the gift, John Ryland.

JOHN: How much do you charge?

DOWSER: Three dollars.

JOHN: I figured I'd haul from the river for awhile.

JEANNE: Let him try, John. Three dollars isn't too much to be sure of water. With a well, I can have a garden.

JOHN: All right. We'll take a chance. God knows we'll need a well.

DOWSER: (*showing forked willow branch*) My wand.

JEANNE: That sounds like magic.

DOWSER: A willow stick . . that's all, but when the power's on me, it turns to a wand, you'll see. My grandfather had the power. It's in the blood. (*moving with willow stick in his two hands.*) Now we'll see what lies here underneath the ground. If we're lucky, we'll find some underground stream not too far down.

JEANNE: That forked willow stick is all you need?

DOWSER: That's all. See how loosely I hold it in my hands. No pressure. I just hold it and wait for the willow to find water. Without water there'd be no joy for you in this new holding. Not here. Nor here. (*to* JEANNE) I'm looking to find some pool or running stream not too deep underground. When I was a boy I used to think there was a kingdom beneath the ground with pools and caves and corridors and meadows dotted with flowers. . . in a way, I still believe it. . . In a way that's what it is. . . Hmm. . . something here, perhaps.

JEANNE: John. . . the willow bends. . . it's trembling in his hands.

DOWSER: Yes, the wand bends, twists in my hand. Just here. And here. Now I can't hold it. . . now it takes on its own life and I can't hold the wand. That means water. You're in luck, John Ryland.

JEANNE: Oh, how grand!

JOHN: You're sure?

DOWSER: The willow bends, pulls downward. You may have to dig deep but there's water below this place. Dig here, beside this rock. Put your well down there.

JOHN: If you're right, we're lucky. And obliged.

JEANNE: Do you always find water?

DOWSER: No. Sometimes there's none to find. I've known a man to drill seven dry holes, and finally move away. Sometimes too. . . the power leaves me. . . I don't know why.

(*slight pause*)

JOHN: Here's your money. If we get a good well, I'll have a windmill here. There seems to be wind to spare.

DOWSER: Yes, there's wind. You'll learn to know the arch in the sky that tells you a Chinook is coming.

JEANNE: Chinook?

DOWSER: West wind bringing warm air from the Pacific. For you, Mrs. Ryland. . . a souvenir.

JEANNE: You don't need it?

DOWSER: I'll cut another when I cross the river.

JEANNE: Thank you. There's a fire at the camp. I can make tea.

(*She moves away a little*)

DOWSER: Next time. When you're settled I'll call in my other capacity . . . your travelling Raleigh man. I'm taking some spice today to your neighbor, Stella Burkholt. She'll be glad to have a woman nearby.

JEANNE: I'm glad too. Look, I've found something. . . What is it?

(*She finds medicine pouch*)

DOWSER: That's an Indian medicine bag, Mrs. Ryland.

JEANNE: I found it between these rocks. I bent to pick that little purple flower.

DOWSER: Crocus.

JEANNE: The bag was just there.

JOHN: Probably it belongs to that Indian across the river.

DOWSER: White Calf. I think not.

JOHN: (*taking the pouch*) Well, it will be interesting to see what. . .

JEANNE: Don't open it, John! It's not ours to open!

JOHN: The owner's not here to open it.

JEANNE: Please. (*she takes pouch back*) I wonder who was the owner.

DOWSER: Some long-gone Chief, I expect.

JEANNE: Or a woman. Why not a woman?

DOWSER: I think only men carried the Medicine Bag. But I'm not sure
. . . I never asked.

JEANNE: We aren't alone here then.

JOHN: What do you mean, Jeannie?

JEANNE: Just that this belonged to someone who was here before.

JOHN: Probably someone who died before we were born.

DOWSER: Whoever owned it should rest easy that it's in good hands,
Mrs. Ryland. Good luck to you both.

(DOWSER *starts off then pauses.*)

DOWSER: (*turning*) There were Dinosaurs on this place once. Long ago,
before the Buffalo. Did you know that?

JOHN: No.

DOWSER: I've seen bones. Perhaps this was no plain then. A jungle.
But Dinosaurs roamed the land, bigger than elephants. Don't
plough all your land, John Ryland. Leave a strip here and there
in prairie wool — obeisance to the Dinosaurs.

(DOWSER *goes.* JOHN *and* JEANNE *look after him.*)

JOHN: Obeisance. What does that mean?

JEANNE: In church I think it means kneeling, to kneel down.

JOHN: Kneel down to Dinosaurs? Hmm. He's a strange one. Why
would I want to kneel down to Dinosaurs? I probably threw
away three dollars on the well.

JEANNE: Wait and see, John. You know when I hold this pouch, I feel
as if I hold someone's life in my hands. I'll keep it. The owner
may come for it.

JOHN: Not likely. No more likely than that buffalo skull I hung
by the tent will come to life. I'll call this place the Buffalo Horn.
Is that all right?

JEANNE: Aye. I expect it's foolish, John, but I feel comforted somehow
. . . finding this. . . John. There's something I have to tell you.
I. . . We're going to have a baby.

JOHN: Jeanne! You're sure?

JEANNE: Of course I'm sure.

JOHN: When! When will he come?

JEANNE: October or early November.

JEANNE: Jeannie! Think of it. Our son. Blood and bone of the two of
us and all those wild ancestors that raven around in our veins.
Think of the miracle of it. Oh Jeannie, here I am on my own land
with my own wife — and my son knocking at the door. . .
(*He whirls her around. Suddenly tender, he puts her down gently.*)
Your folks must miss you, Jeannie. . . As soon as I can, I'll take
you back to Scotland for a visit. (*Handing her medicine bag*) You
keep this. You found it.

JEANNE: Yes, I'll keep it. If it had power for its owner it may have
strength for us too, John.
> (*The sigh of the wind again as* JEANNE *moves back.*)

SCENE 3

*The transition may be made with lights and music or wind sound if
desired — or the following song may be used.*

SONG: THE PLOUGHMAN'S SONG.

(*Cast as* CHORUS *may move in mime as if ploughing. . .*)

> Grass turned under in a long straight furrow
> Grass turned under as the horses plod
> Pleating the earth into black straight furrow
> Ploughing the prairie, breaking the sod.
>
> Get up there, Rony . . Pull you, Mackie. . .
> Get up you team. . . move now. . . move along. . .
> Plough the prairie into rich black wheat land.
> Before you know it, the grass land's gone.
>
> Grass turned under into rich black wheat land
> Horses pull and the plough shares gleam
> Grass turned under in long straight furrows
> Sowing the seed for a harvest dream.
>
> (*As the song ends the cast freezes briefly and there is a sound of
> Drums as of distant guns. . . Softly the whisper mounts*)
> > War. . . War. . . War. . .
> > Stop the Kaiser Stop the Kaiser
> > Your country needs you Your country needs you
> > War War War
>
> (*The drums crescendo.*)

PLACE: *There is a well with a pump and an unpainted stoop.* JEANNE
RYLAND *may be on knees as if weeding a garden.* STELLA
BURKHOLT *enters and comes to* JEANNE.
TIME: *1917.*

JEANNE: Stella! Oh, I'm glad to see you. I've been promising Ryan
we'd ride over to your place but I just haven't got round to it.
STELLA: We brought your mail, Jeannie. There's a letter from John.
JEANNE: Thank God for that. The last one was over two weeks ago.
Will you stay awhile and visit?
STELLA: Just for a minute. Ed's anxious to get home. Read your letter,
Jeannie. . .
JEANNE: If you'll excuse me, I will.
STELLA: That letter's post-marked France.
JEANNE: He's been there for months. In the trenches.
STELLA: I don't know how you stand it, Jeanne.
JEANNE: I have to stand it, Stella. It's my duty. John's doing what he
must do. I have to stand it.
STELLA: Ed wanted to join up when John volunteered but they told
him he was too old. I was glad, Jeanne. That may not be patriotic
but I was glad.
JEANNE: (*reading letter*) John says they've had a lot of rain and they
have a time trying to keep dry clothes. . . he got the socks I sent.
He's some place called Vimy. . . Vimy Ridge. He says there's
going to be a push that might be a turning point. . . but some
lines are blocked out. . . censored. . .
STELLA: Time for a turning point. John told Ed he'd be home for
harvest. . . that was three years ago. Three years you've been
alone here, Jeanne. . . you and Ryan. I couldn't bear with that.
Ryan's in bed?
JEANNE: Aye.
STELLA: I'll just take a peek at him, before I go.
(*She moves away.* JEANNE *continues reading the letter. If
desired, as in original production,* JOHN *and two companions
may suddenly appear on a darkened stage as if in trenches.
They freeze and* JOHN *reads letter while writing it.*
JOHN: "Oh, Jeannie, I remember the clean smell of your skin
and your nightgown and the sheets we slept in. . . here where
nothing's clean. If I ever get home to you I'll never leave. I can't
tell you how it is here or how much I miss you. Hug little Ryan
for me. My son won't know his father but I'll make it up to him,
when I get home.*
(*Blackout on* JOHN *and companions.* JEANNE *takes up
reading of letter. Lights change.*)
JEANNE: Home. . . you and Ryan and our own place. That's all that
keeps me going. Yours. John." Oh John. . . How long will the
war go on? How long?

501

STELLA: (*returning*) That's a beautiful little boy you have, Jeanne. Is John all right?

JEANNE: Yes. Lonesome. Oh, Stella. . . sometimes I. . .

(STELLA *puts her arms around* JEANNE *to comfort her.*)

STELLA: I know. I know. John will be proud of you, Jeannie, the way you've managed.

(*Pause*)

CALL OFF: Stella! We've got to get home. Milking time.

STELLA: (*calling*) Coming. We don't need any clocks in our house. We've got those cows. Jeannie, these are a few things my Bert grew out of. They might do for Ryan, if you wouldn't be offended.

JEANNE: Thanks, Stella. I'm not offended.

STELLA: You get over now whenever you can. And if you need anything. . .

JEANNE: Bye. I do appreciate all you've done, Stella.

(STELLA *goes.* JEANNE *looks at the letter. Finally she takes up the medicine bag.*)

JEANNE: Help me. Whoever you are, whose life is in this bag, help me to endure. I've never told John how afraid I am without him here. I'm afraid of the sound of the wind at night. Afraid when the creak of the windmill wakes me or the house cracks as it settles in the cold. How afraid I am when the snow comes and there's no one nearer than five miles away. I never told John but I'm full of fear. Perhaps I should have taken Ryan home to Scotland like John wanted me to. Will I ever feel at home here? Help me to endure.

(FRED BURNS *approaches*)

BURNS: Good evening, Mrs. Ryland.

JEANNE: (*startled*) Good evening. Mr. Burns.

BURNS: Fred.

JEANNE: Is there. . . do you bring bad news? Is John. . .

BURNS: Calm yourself, girl. I dropped by to see if you needed some help. How are you getting along out here, all on your own?

JEANNE: Very well. The Burkholts were just here. They brought a letter from John. He's in France.

BURNS: They tell me those doughboys have a lively time in gay Paree. You know the song "How you gonna keep 'em down on the farm after they've seen Paree."

JEANNE: John hasn't been to Paris, Mr. Burns. He's in the trenches.

BURNS: I brought you a newspaper since I was passing by.

JEANNE: Thank you, Mr. Burns.

BURNS: Fred. And you're Jeannie. . . when I think of you I always think of Jeannie with the light brown hair.

JEANNE: (*taking paper*) Excuse me. . .

BURNS: There's a long list today. Mustard gas casualties.

JEANNE: I always look at the Wounded column first. Then the others . . . the dead.

BURNS: (*touching her*) Rest yourself, girl. John Ryland's name isn't there. I looked before I brought it.

JEANNE: Oh. It was good of you to bring the paper.

BURNS: I'd do a lot more than that for you, Jeannie. Anything I can do for you, I'll be glad to do. . .

JEANNE: We're getting along fine, Mr. Burns.

BURNS: Fred. Please.

JEANNE: Fred.

BURNS: I thought I saw Joe Whipple working your summer fallow.

JEANNE: Yes. He comes after he's finished at the railroad station.

BURNS: Joe Whipple's a Red, Jeannie. That man's a dyed-in-the-wool communist. I.W.W. He's behind all this farm union movement. He's a paid union organizer sent in here to get the farmers all stirred up. Joe Whipple means trouble.

JEANNE: The farmers are uniting to try to get a stable price for our wheat. I went to a meeting with the Burkholts.

BURNS: And Joe Whipple was one of the main speakers.

JEANNE: He had something to say. But so did the farmers.

BURNS: A farmer is his own man, Jeannie. I hate to think you've been taken in by that radical.

JEANNE: I hired Joe to put in our crop, Mr. Burns, and do the field work that has to be done while John's over there trudging through the mud. Joe's been a good help to me. . . to me and John.

BURNS: Look, girlie, I could send you full-time help. All you have to do is ask. I think a lot of you, Jeannie. . . the way you've managed without a man, the way you carry yourself. . .

JEANNE: Please go now. I have things to do. Please.

BURNS: Whatever you say. But I'm around, Jeannie. . . all you have to do is say the word. . . (*he starts off. . . looks out*) Hey, that old Indian from across the river. . . he's coming in your gate. His boy's name is in that paper. Tom White Calf.

JEANNE: Tom. Dead?

BURNS: Wounded.

JEANNE: Oh. . . Oh no. . . Tom's their eldest. I'll have to tell White Calf. He comes here to see if I have the newspaper. He doesn't read.

BURNS: Reckon you'd be happier if I stay around till they go.

JEANNE: No. I'd rather tell them without anyone else here.

BURNS: Just as you like. (*He moves as if to embrace her.*) I really think a lot of you, Jeannie. . .

JEANNE: Go, Mr. Burns. And please don't come back here. I don't want you to come back.

BURNS: Have it your own way. I only. . . (*He starts to leave and as he passes* WHITE CALF *he speaks*) I been waiting for those beaded gloves a long time, White Calf. I paid you for them, remember.

Gwen Pharis Ringwood

WHITE CALF: I remember. My wife wanted to use some porcupine quills. We don't get them yet.
BURNS: Well, try to hurry them up.
 (He goes)
WHITE CALF: Hello, Mrs. You get paper?
JEANNE: Hello White Calf. Mary.
WHITE CALF: That fellow wants her to make buckskin gloves. . . they take long time.
JEANNE: White Calf. . . I have to tell you. . . Tom's been wounded. Hurt.
MARY: Tom killed?
JEANNE: No, Mary, but his name's in the list of the people who've been shot or hurt. See here's his name. . . Tom White Calf.
WHITE CALF: They don't say nothing else.
JEANNE: You'll get a letter.
WHITE CALF: Maybe he dies.
JEANNE: He'll be sent home. Tom might get home soon.
 (WHITE CALF *speaks in Indian.* MARY WHITE CALF *turns away silently looking off, lost in her own pain)*
WHITE CALF: Show me his name again.
JEANNE: There. White Calf. Private Tom White Calf. . . Wounded in the service of his country.
 (Pause)
WHITE CALF: When John Ryland comes home first time in those soldier clothes, then my Tom says he must go and be soldier too. I tell him not to go. I tell him it is the White's war.
JEANNE: I'm sorry.
WHITE CALF: Why should my son fight their war? I tell you something, Mrs. Frog Lake was because white men don't listen. My father tried to tell them they were wrong, but the Whites don't listen. Now my son gets shot in their war. Why?
JEANNE: He wanted to go, White Calf. He and John and all the others were ready to die for their country. That's courage. We should be proud of them. Your boy wanted to go.
WHITE CALF: Once this was Indian land. . . all Indian. The buffalo moved like a brown field. Their hoofs drum loud on the ground. Now that's all gone. The old ways. . . the hunting. . . the Sun Dance. . . all gone.
MARY WHITE CALF: *(to* JEANNE) We go now. *(She indicates the paper).* You give?
JEANNE: Oh yes. I'm sorry, Mary.
 (MARY *moves out of* JEANNE's *touch and away alone)*
WHITE CALF: *(seeing medicine pouch)* Where you get this, Mrs?
JEANNE: I found it here. . . when we first came. Is it yours?
WHITE CALF: No. A wolf's tooth is on my pouch. My father's too. This is Northern Cree, I think. Where you find?
JEANNE: Just over there. . . beside a rock. Do you . . do you want me to give it to you? I. . . I didn't open it.

WHITE CALF: No. You keep, Mrs. It could be good medicine for you
. . . You say maybe my boy comes home?
JEANNE: Often they send the wounded men home as soon as they can
travel, often they send them. . .
    (*She breaks off.* WHITE CALF *moves away after* MARY
    WHITE CALF *and then turns*)
WHITE CALF: From my place we see smoke from your fire, Mrs.
    Winter and summer we see smoke from your fire in the morning.
JEANNE: I can see yours too, White Calf. Thanks.
    (*The transition occurs as the lights go down — while a railing
    and vine are placed around the stoop. There is a roll of drums,
    then silence, followed by whispered "Peace, Peace, It's over.
    The war's over, Peace." Music into Scene 4*)

SCENE 4

TIME: *The mid-twenties.*
PLACE: *Ryland farm — stoop has wood railing, perhaps a vine.*
    JOHN RYLAND *moves down stage and looks off as if at a mirage.*
    DOWSER *enters.*

DOWSER: Well, John Ryland, you're sky watching eh?
JOHN: Dowser! Good to see you. Look — mirage.
DOWSER: Hard to believe those elevators are twenty miles away.
JOHN: I never get used to it. . . they can shimmer on the horizon as
    real as the barn down there. Then suddenly they're gone.
DOWSER: Prairie magic.
JOHN: Magic all right. It's a long time since you came by, three, four
    years?
DOWSER: Yeah. I went out to the Coast in twenty-four. But it never
    seemed confortable somehow. . . Fog, rain, no snow. . . great
    big trees cutting off the view. Something about the prairie.
JOHN: You're right. When I got back from France I felt like getting
    down on my knees and. . .
    (*He breaks off slightly embarrassed*)

Gwen Pharis Ringwood

DOWSER: Your crop looks good. I hear you've bought the Eastern
    section.
JOHN: I've had my eye on it for a long time, Dowser.
DOWSER: You going to run cattle?
JOHN: No. I'll have it all summer-fallowed this year. I've got new
    machinery. . . disc, seed drill. I figure on buying a tractor.
DOWSER: I hate to see that grass ploughed up. Roots can go down six
    feet looking for water. It's tough grass. Has to be.
JOHN: You're no farmer, Dowser. You stick to finding water. . .that's
    wheat land.
DOWSER: There used to be a pile of buffalo bones over near the coulee.
JOHN: A few buffalo bones won't get in my way.
DOWSER: I always wondered how they came to be there. Did the
    buffalo take themselves to the coulee to die some year when there
    wasn't enough water or grass. Or was there a big drive? You
    know I remember this country when there was just a great sea of
    grass stretching out to the sky in every direction. Different from
    any other place I know about. Leave some of that grass, John.
    For the prarie dogs and the gophers and the meadowlarks. And
    me.
JOHN: And for grass fires. Your prairie wool isn't so pretty when a fire
    starts spreading. Anyway, I've Jeanne and Ryan and Mark to
    think about. . . I have to look ahead.
DOWSER: Mark? You've another son then?
JOHN: He's going on four. And you won't know Ryan. He's nearly as
    tall as I am.
    (JEANNE and STELLA move to them)
JEANNE: Dowser. Oh, I'm so glad to see you again. We've all missed
    you.
STELLA: We have, Dowser. Welcome home.
DOWSER: Thank you, Stella. Jeannie, I hear you've a boy I've not seen
    yet.
JEANNE: We do. Mark. Stella's girl, Cissie, took him down to the
    coulee to pick wild flowers. And Ryan's at school. You must wait
    to see them both.
JOHN: I'm driving my car over to the new section, Dowser. Come
    along? We'll probably pick up Cissie and Mark.
DOWSER: Sure. I'll just put Blackie in the shade.
JOHN: You still haven't bought a car?
DOWSER: Oh, I'd be lonesome travelling my route without old Blackie.
    He knows every stop. I bought him back first thing after I got
    back here.
    (JOHN and DOWSER go off. JEANNE and STELLA pull out
    bench and sit, shelling peas or cleaning carrots)
JEANNE: I've missed Dowser, coming along with his spices and herbs
    and remedies for man and beast.
STELLA: He won't have so much business with the stores carrying all
    those things.

JEANNE: He can still witch wells, Stella. And there's thousands of new-comers taking up land.

STELLA: That's true. Ed's against all this immigration from Central Europe. He thinks we should limit immigration. Ed's very set in his mind. He's still against women getting the vote.

JEANNE: But you voted, Stella. I saw you.

STELLA: We had such a row about that, Jeannie! The first time I stood up to Ed was over voting. When he saw I was determined, he wrote down exactly how I was to vote. Every name.

JEANNE: Did you?

STELLA: I went into that little booth and I stood there shaking. Honestly, I was shaking. . . And I marked that ballot and I came out and put it in the box and smiled at Ed. He doesn't know to this day that I didn't vote for one single person he told me to. Not one.

JEANNE: Stella!

STELLA: It was a matter of principle.

> (MARJ BLAIR *and* ROSE MEEKER *enter. They have made themselves outfits that are in style of the twenties.*)

MARJ: Mrs. Ryland, Mrs. Burkholt. . . could you give us a few minutes?

JEANNE: Of course, Mrs. Blair, We're just getting the peas ready for canning.

ROSE: You farm people don't know how lucky you are, all those fresh vegetables.

MARJ: Rose, you'd hate a farm. You'd die of boredom. I heard you tell your husband you wish he'd move to Regina.

ROSE: I get restless all right. I trained in Regina. I'm a nurse, Mrs. Ryland. . . at least I was.

MARJ: Oh, I'm sorry. . . this is Mrs. Meeker. . . our dentist's wife.

JEANNE: Would you ladies care for a cup of tea?

MARJ: Oh no thank you, we couldn't. . . We just came by to ask a little favour.

ROSE: I'd love a cup of tea, Marj.

MARJ: Rose, we don't have time! I have to get the car back. We almost hit a cow coming in here. I forgot about the brakes and that cow seemed to think she had the right of way.

ROSE: Besides, you're a terrible driver, Marj.

MARJ: I am not. Anyway the thing is we have this little social club. . . young married people in town — the Go-Getters.

ROSE: For dancing. I'm crazy about dancing. You know, boop oop a doop—the Charleston,. . . I guess you'd think it pretty wild.

JEANNE: I've always wanted to see someone doing that Charleston. Fancy your knowing how.

ROSE: Oh, Marj doesn't know how. She's got no rhythm. Well, face it, Marj. You never get the beat. It just comes naturally to me. "Roll 'em girls, roll 'em. . . everybody roll 'em. . ."

507

Gwen Pharis Ringwood

MARJ: Rose, we came here for a purpose!
ROSE: Mrs. Ryland asked me to Charleston, Marj!
(*She sits*)
MARJ: We understand you ladies belong to that Farmers Cooperative that meets in the I.O.D.E. hall on Saturday nights.
JEANNE: We do. (*mischievously*) Would you like to join, Mrs. Blair?
MARJ: Oh no, no. . . my husband would have a fit. Mr. Blair thinks its quite amusing the way farmers have begun to dabble in politics.
JEANNE: He may be in for a surprise. After all, this province is built on agriculture.
ROSE: She's right, Marj. Where would we be without Robin Hood flour and all those cows and pigs?
MARJ: What I came for, Mrs. Ryland. . . what we wanted to ask is just a small favour. . . if you could change your meetings to Friday night we'd have the hall for the Saturday night dances. Just that simple change.
STELLA: Farmers go to town on Saturdays. The children go to the motion pictures, and we have our meetings and a social evening.
MARJ: Wouldn't Fridays be the same? What difference?
STELLA: What difference to you?
MARJ: Oh, Saturday nights is best for us. We can sleep in on Sunday.
ROSE: Anyway, I can't stand staying home on a Saturday night. I never could.
STELLA: Neither can I. Fridays wouldn't be the same at all.
JEANNE: I doubt we can see our way to changing, Mrs. Blair.
MARJ: But you have to!
JEANNE: We'll take it up at our meeting but I'm sure the answer will be no.
MARJ: The I.O.D.E. said they didn't object.
JEANNE: The I.O.D.E. may not want to lose us.
MARJ: Mrs. Ryland, the business men in town allow credit until after harvest as a favour to farmers. We're only asking a very little favour in return.
JEANNE: We'll discuss your request, Saturday, Mrs. Blair. Now if you'll excuse me, I really must see to my pressure cooker.
MARJ: I'm sure when you consider everything you'll realize. . .
ROSE: Come on, Marj. For all you know her pressure cooker is blowing up. Look at that cow! She's eating something out of the car.
MARJ: My shawl. My Spanish shawl. Your cow's eating my shawl.
JEANNE: That's a stray cow, Mrs. Blair.
(MARJ *starts running off*)
MARJ: Stop that, you cow! That's the cow that threatened my car! Drop my shawl. Put it down.
ROSE: It's all right, Marj. She's left it on the fence. (*to* JEANNE *and* STELLA) She didn't like it. Goodbye, ladies. Wish me luck. Marj is a terrible driver.
(*They go*)

STELLA: Well! I don't care if that cow did eat her shawl. I think they have their nerve to ask us to. . .

JEANNE: And to threaten us. . . about the credit. I won't be bullied.

STELLA: When we get the Co-op started, it'll be a different story. We won't have to have their credit.

JEANNE: Aye, if we ever get it started. Those two. . . they really put on airs.

STELLA: Its hard to believe that Mrs. Meeker is a trained nurse. Oh well, it takes all kinds.

JEANNE: I envied those women one thing, Stella. I did.

STELLA: The dancing club?

JEANNE: No. The bobbed hair. Stella, would you cut my hair?

STELLA: Jeanne.

JEANNE: I'm tired of my long hair. I want a change. Would you?

STELLA: What will John say?

JEANNE: He won't blame you. Come in now, let's get it done. I wanted to ask you before.

STELLA: You're sure? It's a big step, Jeanne.

JEANNE: I'm sure. It'll be a surprise for John. Hurry, they're coming.

(STELLA *and* JEANNE *go in.* JOHN *and* DOWSER *enter*)

JOHN: (*calling off*) Cissie, don't let Mark tease that old rooster. He's a mean one.

DOWSER: You're moving fast, John. All that land and machinery, you'll be a rich man.

JOHN: Comfortable, I hope. One of these years I want to take Jeannie and the boys to Scotland to see her parents. Next year maybe. . . (TOM WHITE CALF *enters*) Hello, Tom.

TOM: Your mare was running with the Indian horses across the ridge. I brought her in.

JOHN: Thank you, Tom. Where is she?

TOM: I put her in the barn, I think she's going to have a colt pretty soon.

JOHN: How much do I owe you?

TOM: I don't know.

JOHN: Three dollars all right?

TOM: Sure. Thanks.

DOWSER: You remember me?

TOM: Yeah. When I was a kid once you gave me money to see a circus. I remember.

DOWSER: How you getting along?

(TOM *shrugs*)

JOHN: He does fine. He rides. Pitches hay. Everything he did before he lost that leg.

TOM: (*as he moves off*) Not as good as before, but I get along. I'm still kicking. With my good leg, I'm still kicking.

JOHN: (*almost defensively*) He's doing all right, Dowser. I think he is.

Gwen Pharis Ringwood

DOWSER: I hope so. (*slowly*) Tom White Calf was the first man to get home, John. . . long time before you came. The night the news came that the war was over, they had a celebration in town. Victory celebration. Bon Fire. They had this big puppet. . . stuffed with straw, spiked helmet, bayonet. . . supposed to be an effigy of the Kaiser. To celebrate the peace they burned this effigy. Hung it over the bon fire. . . looked real. People howled like wolves. I saw Tom White Calf standing there in uniform on crutches. . . there at the edge of the crowd. He looked like he couldn't believe what he saw. Pretty soon he shook his head and walked away. . . limping home alone. I never forgot that look as he turned away.

JOHN: Well, it's past now, Dowser. Over. We won't get mixed up in any European war again.

DOWSER: Maybe not. I think I'll go along now, John. I'll see Ryan next time.

JOHN: Glad you came by. Good luck, Dowser.
      I better patch this tire. . . first flat I've had.
      (DOWSER *goes off.* JOHN *rolls out tire in mime and begins to fix it.* JEANNE *enters. She is wearing a motoring veil.*)

JEANNE: Did you pick up Mark and Cissie, John?

JOHN: I did. They're getting the eggs.

JEANNE: I thought we could drive Stella and Cissie home if you have the time.

JOHN: Sure. Soon as I fix this tire.

JEANNE: Did you see Mrs. Blair and Mrs. Meeker?

JOHN: We met them at the gate.

JEANNE: They want us to change our meeting time to Friday nights.

JOHN: They can go on wanting. Saturday night's town night for farmers.

JEANNE: I told them that. Did you notice their clothes, John? The new style?

JOHN: How could I help but notice? Rouged up to the eyebrows. Skirts to their knees. And that hair! Where do they think they are, New York city?

JEANNE: I wouldn't wear such short skirts myself. But everybody's getting their hair cut, John.

JOHN: I forbid you to cut your hair, Jeanne. Absolutely forbid it. Good heavens, woman, you're no flapper. You're the mother of two growing boys.

JEANNE: I know I'm no flapper.

JOHN: Mark and Ryan deserve something better than a mother who looks like she's joined the Follies.

JEANNE: But if I did cut my hair. . .

JOHN: I think I'd leave home. I don't intend to sit across the table from someone who looks like a baby magpie.

JEANNE: Oh, John!

JOHN: That's how I feel.

(JEANNE *takes off her scarf. Her hair is shingled*)
JOHN: Jeannie!
JEANNE: Please don't leave home.
JOHN: Your beautiful hair. How could you do this to me?
JEANNE: I'm the same person underneath. Do I look like a baby
    magpie?
JOHN: Worse. I'll never get used to it. You've a wild streak in you,
    Jeanne Ryland. I suppose next thing you'll be smoking cigarettes.
JEANNE: No, I won't. I tried and I hated it. But there's one thing, John,
    and I might as well say it now. . . I do intend to. . . I want. . .
JOHN: You intend to do what?
JEANNE: I want to learn to drive the car.

(*Swirl of twenties music ends the scene.* MRS. MEEKER *may
do Charleston across the stage as part of transition scene. The
music rises becoming somewhat discordant and breaking off
at the top of a crescendo. . . sliding downward music as off a
fall.*)

SCENE 5

*Into wind sound. . . the cast moves into the wind. . . it blows against them
and they move together in a little ragged group as if at a social. Mid-
thirties, bare stage with benches, with violin or piano, or accordion music
behind scene.*)

JEANNE: It's good of you and Ed to get us together, Stella. We need a
    little pleasure these days.
STELLA: Well, when Ed's cousin came with his fiddle, it seemed a good
    time for a social.
JEANNE: John says the whole country seems to be blowing away.
STELLA: We're all in the same fix anyway. Some comfort in that.
    Nobody has a crop.

(*sound of fiddle tuning up*)

JEANNE: Where's Cissie?

STELLA: She's working for her board in Moose Jaw. Going to school. I think Cissie has a crush on your Ryan, Jeannie. She's always asking about him.

JEANNE: Ryan quit school. He thought he had a job in a coal mine but it petered out. I don't know where Ryan is, Stella.

STELLA: Is he riding the rods?

JEANNE: Aye. He is. (*deliberately changing the subject*) I brought my flour sack quilt to show you, Stella (*calling*) Mark, bring in my quilt. It's in the back of the Bennett buggy.

MARK: Sure, Mom.

ED: Gather round, folks. Stella found a jug of chokecherry wine in the root house, so gather round.

STELLA: I better get out some glasses. I hope it's not too strong. It's five years old.

CALLER: Swing your partners, everybody. Fiddler's ready.

> (*He moves among the group who join in the dance as a caller calls the square dance. In the medley of reels the fiddler plays "I Danced With The Dolly With A Hole In Her Stocking". At the end of the first round the music breaks off suddenly.*)

ED: Hey, that's a good song for this year. A hole in her stocking. Most of us have holes in our shoes if we have any shoes.

MAN: How you fixed for seed wheat, John?

JOHN: I saved some, if we don't have to make porridge out of it.

MAN: Jeez, if we don't get more than 20 cents a bushel, we're better to eat it.

ED: What riles me is that R.B. Bennett don't have an idea what we're up against out here.

MAN: You ever hear Tommy Douglas on the radio?

JOHN: We hear him often.

MAN: I heard Douglas speak in Weyburn. He told a good story. It seems there was this country mostly made up of mice. Every four years the mice elected a new government. First they elect the White Cats but White Cats don't do a thing for the mice. So next time round they elect Black Cats. But the Black Cats are even worse. They treat mice terrible. Every four years — White Cats, Black Cats. . . and nothing ever changes. Finally at the meeting a small mouse gets up and says: "Hey, why don't we elect Mice?" "Why don't we elect Mice?" Bet those mice were wearing gum boots and overalls with patches on the seat. Saskatchewan mice.

> (*another round of the dance rises and then breaks off*)

JEANNE: This is the quilt I made from the flour sacks.

STELLA: It's real pretty, Jeannie. I'm wearing a flour sack petticoat. I found enough rick rack to trim it. And I made Cissie a blouse. What ever would we do without flour sacks? We could have a prairie fashion show. . .

JEANNE: The Robin Hood flour sack collection. (*pause*) I'm not sure we'll be able to buy flour much longer. What'll we do for clothes?

512

STELLA: Ah, it will be better next year. . .

(Back into the dance this time the music crescendos and then stops abruptly and the dancers move apart and freeze. It is their thoughts that are spoken:)

WOMAN: Stella poured out the coffee grounds into the stove. There was still good in them. We haven't had coffee in the house for months.

MAN: Tomorrow I have to go in and ask for relief. God, the word goes round in my head. . . Relief, Relief, Relief. I never thought I'd come down to asking for charity.

ANOTHER MAN: Millie's smiling. She doesn't smile often now. Sometimes I feel like walking out on her and the kids so the government will have to take care of them. Sometimes I stay out in the barn, rather than face my family, when I can't do nothing for them.

WOMAN: Our Amy brought home twenty dollars. She said she made it waiting tables. . . tips. But she didn't buy the clothes she was wearing waiting table. She's on the street. I know she is. I hope her Dad never finds out.

MAN: My girl. I took her twenty dollars and let on I believe her about how she got the money. I feel like a pimp. Our Amy.

FIDDLER: Home waltz, everybody. Home waltz.

(as the waltz goes on it becomes very soft and JEANNE and JOHN move downstage with STELLA BURKHOLT.)

JEANNE: Thank you for a wonderful evening, Stella. Give our love to Cissie when you see her.

STELLA: And hers to Ryan. He'll be home again, Jeannie.

JEANNE: I pray he will. Good night.

JOHN: Come on, Mark. Time to head home. Thanks, Ed, Stella.

STELLA: Glad you came. Next year we'll be standing under the horn of plenty.

JOHN: Sure. Next year will be better. . .

(soft fade out on "next year. next year." The wind rises. The people separate and stand isolated. . . chorus of dust-dust-dust may be used behind.)

DOWSER: Four. . . five years. . . on and on. . . the wind raises the dust like smoke. The top soil's drifting. . . drifting.

WOMAN: There's dust up to the windows, it's in the walls.

MAN: It covers the fences and the roads and the barns and the houses. My cattle are dying of starvation.

WOMAN: We had two good cows, Dowser. Today I saw them lie down by a dried up slough and die.

MAN: There's nothing to hunt. No game.

WOMAN: We had such dreams when we broke our land. Now they're gone, buried in dust. Will the wind never stop? The wind and the dust. . . will they never stop?

(the others retire as DOWSER and JEANNE take positions downstage)

Gwen Pharis Ringwood

DOWSER: Your well's dry, Jeannie. I can't pump a drop.

JEANNE: John's taken the Bennett buggy to haul two barrels from the river. Sometimes it seems there's a curse on us Dowser. All of us. All that black soil drifting to God knows where. And the everlasting wind. . .

DOWSER: Children of Job. Seems like that's what we are. Children of Job.

JEANNE: I'm worried about John. He's been working the roads trying to scrape enough together to keep our taxes paid. He comes in so tired, tired. I don't know how long he can go on.

DOWSER: Have you heard from Ryan?

JEANNE: No. I've a feeling he got no work picking berries. I think Ryan stays away so we won't have another mouth to feed.

DOWSER: He ought to write.

JEANNE: John thinks Ryan should have stayed home, worked on the road, too, for the taxes. But they weren't getting on. Ryan got this idea of growing onions, Bermuda onions. John says even if we could grow them, who'd buy bushels of onions? John wanted to get some sheep. Ryan hates sheep. So now he's just riding the freights back and forth across the country looking for jobs that don't exist. Ryan's grown up in a world that's never needed him Dowser. That's what hurts me. It's not so bad for Mark. He's so much younger. Oh, Dowser, if only I knew how it is with Ryan. . .

(*The light fades — shrill police whistle. Ryan and another boy run from police — whistle, scuffle — Ryan thrown down. Whistle — dim light on Ryan*)

RYAN: I can't tell my folks I'm in the Regina jail. They'd never understand. I was so goddamned sick of being pushed around and when that policeman grabbed hold of me I hit him. I couldn't help it, I hit him. I had to. We have a right to go to Ottawa. We were marching peaceful. I couldn't believe it when they fired on us. All I want, all any of us want is a chance to work. A chance at a job with a half decent pay check. Surely to God they'll listen to us. All I want is a chance to work. Is that too much to ask?

(*the lights go down on* RYAN *and are again on* JEANNE *and* DOWSER)

JEANNE: Ryan's a good boy, Dowser. It's not his fault that there's no work.

(MARK *moves to them*)

DOWSER: Hello, Mark

MARK: Hi, Dowser, Mom, I got twenty-seven gopher tails today. With what I got yesterday, I'll have a dollar forty. We can get some soap and some tea.

JEANNE: That will be a help, Mark.

(STELLA BURKHOLT *moves to them*)

JEANNE: Stella! We haven't seen you for weeks. How are you?

STELLA: I came to tell you, Jeannie. We're leaving. We're going to try to make it to the Peace River.

JEANNE: Stella! You're all going?

STELLA: We have to. We've lost the farm. They foreclosed on us. Mr. Burns was out today to list our furniture for auction. They sell everything except what's on a list they gave us. . . a list of essentials you can keep. But everything nice we ever owned has to be sold. My handpainted china, the little clock. . .

JEANNE: How can he do such a thing?

STELLA: He says it's the law.

JEANNE: When do you go?

STELLA: As soon as the auction's over. We have to get some feed for the horses for the trip. Have you heard from Ryan?

JEANNE: No.

STELLA: Cissie wanted me to ask. She was hoping to see Ryan before we left. She doesn't want to go with us, but she's tried everywhere for a job.

JEANNE: I don't even know where Ryan is.

STELLA: You'll be at the auction won't you. . . please. . . Mr. Burns is doing it.

JEANNE: We'll be there.

(STELLA *goes*)

MARK: I don't blame them for leaving, Mom. Sometimes I wish we'd pack up and leave.

JEANNE: Mark! Your father's worked so hard. He's paid our taxes. I couldn't leave my nasturtiums to die. . . Anyway, how could we get there?

MARK: We could walk.

JEANNE: Your father says we'll hang on here. And that's what we must do. . . hang on. Stay for supper, Dowser. I'm making scones.

DOWSER: Thanks. I've a little sugar and tea with me. Can I donate it?

JEANNE: You can.

(JOHN RYLAND *comes in with pails of water*)

MARK: Hi, Dad.

(*He takes pails*)

JOHN: Thanks, son. Hello, Dowser. It's clouding up as usual. . . dust clouds. You were always at me to leave some of the prairie wool on the place, Dowser. Reckon you've been saying "I told you so" these last years.

DOWSER: I didn't foresee anything this bad, John, or this long.

MARK: Do you want me to unload the water barrels, Dad?

JOHN: No, they're too heavy for you. You unhitch the team.

MARK: Sure.

(MARK *leaves*)

JOHN: The river's low, lowest I've ever seen it. Some places you can walk across to the reserve. I brought you this, Jeannie, for your collection.

Gwen Pharis Ringwood

JEANNE: Oh John, it's perfect. Look Dowser, it's a fossil of some little water insect and some ferns. It's just perfect. Thanks, John.
(BURNS *moves to them*)
BURNS: Hello. Ryland? I'd like to talk to you.
JOHN: Talk away.
BURNS: Privately.
JOHN: I've no secrets, Mr. Burns. What do you want?
BURNS: I have an order to take inventory of your household goods for foreclosure sale.
JOHN: What's that? You have what?
BURNS: You're in debt to the machine company and for gas. I've orders to seize your household effects, except for the exempt items on this list. The rest will be sold at auction.
JOHN: I pay my debts. I may be slow but no man can say John Ryland doesn't pay what he owes. You take your list and your closure order and get off my place.
BURNS: No use threatening me. It's the law.
JOHN: I'll sell my seed wheat to pay those bills. I'll shovel it down your throat.
BURNS: You don't have enough seed wheat. We checked. You can't fight this, Ryland. It's the law. And I have to have the list of what can be sold today. The auction's ten days from now.
(BURNS *starts towards the house as he moves past JEANNE. JOHN stops him*)
JOHN: Don't you go into my house. I told you, get off my place. Now. And don't you set foot on my land again as long as you breathe. Get out. Now. Before I kill you.
BURNS: All right. I'll leave! But I'll be back here with the police. Who do you think you are, John Ryland?
(BURNS *goes*)
JOHN: The bastard. I wanted to kill him. The bastard.
JEANNE: But we do have to pay the bills, John, or they will be back. You know it. The Burkholts are losing everything. . . their farm too.
JOHN: Dowser, those buffalo bones. I heard a company in Minnesota will buy them for fertilizer. Is that true?
DOWSER: Yes. They've sold some from up North.
JOHN: I'll load them up and ship them tonight. I might get enough out of them to. . .
(TOM WHITE CALF *limps toward them*)
TOM: Hi
JOHN: (*angrily*) I told you at the river, Tom, I don't have any work for you. I couldn't pay you if I did.
TOM: I know. I brought some beaded gloves and moccasins. We thought you might buy. . .
JOHN: (*breaking in*) We can't buy anything. I'm broke, just like you.
TOM: You?
(*to DOWSER*)

516

DOWSER: I can't buy them, Tom. I wish I could.

TOM: There's no game. I've no food for my kids.

JOHN: Give him some of that flour we had ground at the Mennonite mill.

JEANNE: I will. And I can give you four eggs, Tom.

TOM: Thanks.

JEANNE: Don't sell that beautiful bead work. It took hours to make it. I'll get the flour.

(*She moves away*)

JOHN: (*to* TOM) You come with us. We're loading those buffalo bones by the coulee. . . we think we can sell them. You have a share in those bones. (*calling*) I'll unload the water barrels by the trough, Jeannie. You water the stock. I'll take Mark with me.

DOWSER: I'll go with you.

JOHN: Good. Let's go.

TOM: First I take the flour home. My kids are hungry.

(DOWSER *and* JOHN *move away*)

JEANNE: Here's flour, the eggs, some potatoes. You must go to the Relief Office, Tom. I went there. John doesn't know but I went to the Relief office last month.

TOM: I went there too, Mrs. Ryland. They told me I don't have the right paper. I can't find what paper they meant. They say Indians can hunt. I can't find one grouse most days. I walk holes in my boots and no game.

(MARK *runs in*)

MARK: Mother, come! It's Dad! He was unloading the water barrel. I think it's bad. I think he's. . . hurry, Mom!

JEANNE: Get the doctor, Mark. Ride as fast as you can. Oh John. . . John. . .

(*She runs off. The light go down as* MARK *leaves and* WHITE CALF *moves away. The auction comes up almost immediately. Lights come up on the auction scene which is in progress. The auction is going on off stage in a sort of musical dissonance that rises from time to time behind the scene. A small group is huddled stage left.* DOWSER *moves to them.*)

DOWSER: You're going North with the Burkholts, Jeannie?

JEANNE: Yes. I couldn't stay here without John. I couldn't. Mark and I can travel with Ed and Stella in the Bennett buggy. Oh, Dowser, I haven't heard from Ryan. He doesn't even know his father's dead. That the service is over. Mark thinks the police aren't even trying to find Ryan.

DOWSER: I'll see what I can find out, Jeannie.

JEANNE: Mark's been a great help. We think we'll look for some kind of work up north instead of trying it on the land. I'm a good cook. Maybe I can cook for harvest crews. . .

DOWSER: I can give you eleven dollars for the bay horse, Jeannnie, if that seems reasonable.

Gwen Pharis Ringwood

(MARK *comes in and moves to* JEANNIE *indignantly*)

MARK: Mother, that guy sold Daisy for six dollars. Six dollars for a good cow. We shouldn't let them have her for that, Mother. We should take her with us.

JEANNE: We can't, Mark. She'd never make that long trip.

MARK: I feel like busting that auctioneer. . . him and his stupid jokes. If I ever come back here I'll hunt him up and I'll bust him in the nose.

JEANNE: Dowser's offered us eleven dollars for the bay, Mark. What do you think? We'd know he would get good care.

MARK: We better take it. (*to* DOWSER) Maybe when we're settled up North I can buy him back from you, Dowser.

DOWSER: Sure, Mark. You take care of your mother up there.

MARK: I'll sure try, anyway. Hello, Cissie.

(CISSIE *enters*)

CISSIE: You know what? A Town woman bought my mother's hand-painted tea set for four dollars. Four measly dollars.

MARK: It's awful, Cissie.

JEANNE: I didn't lock the house, Dowser. Would you look in when you're passing? It's still my home.

DOWSER: I will.

JEANNE: I've a few keepsakes in this flour sack. My collection, John called it. And I brought the medicine bag. It's not been much strength to me this last while, but somehow I feel we should take care of it.

(RYAN *appears stage right*)

CISSIE: It's Ryan. Ryan!

JEANNE: Oh Ryan, Son!

(RYAN *embraces her, puts his hand on* MARK's *shoulder*)

RYAN: I came as soon as I heard. I only got word about Dad two days ago. I. . . I can't believe it, Mom.

JEANNE: I know.

RYAN: I got a month's work in a mine in B.C. They said they tried to find me. . .

JEANNE: We knew you'd come if you could, Ryan.

RYAN: They told me in town you're selling our stuff. Leaving.

JEANNE: We're going to try the Peace River, Ryan. If we get work maybe we can come back after a few years.

RYAN: Your family's going North too, Cissie?

CISSIE: That's right.

RYAN: You're going?

CISSIE: I tried for work here but there's nothing.

JEANNE: You could come with us, Ryan. If you want to.

(*auctioneer's voice rises*)

CISSIE: I've got to help my mother check the money from our stuff, Ryan. I'll be back. To say goodbye, I mean. . . unless you decide to come with us.

RYAN: I don't know yet, Cissie. I don't know.

518

(CISSIE *leaves.* RYAN *moves towards auction*)

RYAN: Mom, that's Dad's saddle he's selling. Dad's good saddle. He's selling it.

JEANNE: It's the law, Ryan. They tell you what things you can keep.

RYAN: I was with Dad when he bought it. We took a long time deciding. My Dad's saddle. . . and I don't have the money to bid on it. I can't bid on it.

(*auction sounds rise*)

JEANNE: We have to check the sales too, Ryan. Keep track. We get what money's left above the debts we owe. Come on, Mark.

(*they move away*)

DOWSER: I bought the bay pony from your mother. If you need her, I'll . . . well, you take her.

RYAN: Thanks, Dowser. I don't know what I'm going to do.

(DOWSER *moves away also.* CISSIE *returns.*)

CISSIE: They don't need me. I came back. I guess you've been all over since I seen you last.

RYAN: Yeah. You've sure grown up.

CISSIE: I'm sixteen. Do you think you'll come North?

RYAN: Oh, I'm sick of moving from place to place Cissie. Never belonging anywhere. I kept thinking I'd just come home and help Dad. . . we didn't get along working together though, but I always figured we'd work it out. Now. . .

CISSIE: This is still your farm, Ryan. They sold ours right out from under us for the taxes. But your Dad worked off your taxes. It's still your farm. The wind's got to stop blowing sometime. Your mother asked me to give you this.

RYAN: The medicine bag? Why?

CISSIE: She said she wants you to take care of it for awhile. Keep it with you.

RYAN: When we were kids, we wanted to open it. She never let us open it. We got to thinking there was some kind of magic in it. Sure, I'll keep it. God knows I could use. . . (*turning*) You know, you're right, Cissie.

CISSIE: About what?

RYAN: The wind's got to stop blowing some time. I'm not leaving this place. Even if I have to eat gophers and sow the crop by hand, I'm staying. This is Ryland land. You tell Mom I'll put this back in its old place.

CISSIE: I sort of figured I wouldn't go north, Ryan. I'd only be another mouth to feed. So I. . . Well, if you're going to live off the country, Ryan John, I sort of figured — well, you'd need somebody to do the cooking?

(*They move together as the lights go down.*)

*　　*　　*

Intermission

519

Act II

SCENE 1

(The training planes sound again in the sky above. CISSIE *stands looking up at them as* RYAN *enters. He is in Air Force uniform.)*

RYAN: Surprise, Cissie.

CISSIE: Ryan! No!

RYAN: I enlisted.

RYAN: You didn't warn me. You didn't even talk it over.

RYAN: I know. I'm sorry.

CISSIE: How could you do that?

RYAN: You won't understand. I. . . well I just had to. I wanted to.

CISSIE: You went to see about a loan for a new house.

RYAN: I didn't get a loan. I didn't take out a loan.

CISSIE: The bank turned you down so you got mad and joined up.

RYAN: It wasn't that way. We can borrow money for a house if we slap a big mortgage on the land. A crop failure or two and we lose everything, same as your Dad did. We've been working hard on this place for four years, Cissie. I don't want to chance a mortgage. Not on those terms.

CISSIE: I suppose going to war solves everything.

RYAN: It makes sense for us, Cissie. We'll have a pay check coming every month.

CISSIE: Besides you always did want to fly.

RYAN: I'm lucky to get in the Air Force. Maybe Mark's happy in the Navy, but I figure I'll be more at home in the sky than on the ocean.

CISSIE: Mark doesn't have a wife. I thought we were going to start a family this year.

RYAN: There'll be time for a family after.

CISSIE: Our wheat will be up in two weeks. And you just take off. Don't you care anything about the farm. . . or me.

RYAN: Of course I care. We'll have some money, Cissie, to put this place in shape. God knows it needs money to get it back to where we can make a profit.

CISSIE: What am I supposed to do?

RYAN: You can come with me while I'm training.

CISSIE: Sure. I help put in a crop and then I just turn my back and walk away from it. That's a great idea. While you go off to some sort of holy war in a country you've never even set foot on.

RYAN: Somebody's got to stop Hitler. How would you like it if troops could come in the night and ship you off to God knows where and take your farm? That's what's happening in Europe.

CISSIE: I'm sick of hearing about Europe. What I care about is here . . . this country, this province, this place.

RYAN: I figure I'll ask Al Marshall to harvest the crop. He can farm the place on shares while I'm away.

CISSIE: So! I don't have any say about anything! About what happened?

RYAN: You do. Cissie, I know how you feel about the war. There was no use telling you I wanted to enlist. We'd have just had a row.

CISSIE: What about your mother? We haven't paid her anything.

RYAN: We'll send her something out of my pay check every month. Maybe she can move back to town and take it easy. Maybe you could stay with her and finish school, or get a job.

CISSIE: You really have everything all mapped out, haven't you?

RYAN: When I get back we'll be able to buy modern equipment. A combine. Fertilizer. We can build dug-outs and dams. We'll be farming scientifically instead of hit and miss. I want us to have a good house, a good car, a decent living. (*Pause*) Who's down at the barn?

CISSIE: Dowser. He's letting his route go. He thinks like you do. He thinks it's our war too. If you men had the babies, nursed them, got up at night with them, maybe it would be a different story.

RYAN: Maybe it would.

CISSIE: I don't want a baby if you're going to war, Ryan.

RYAN: When I come back, Cissie.

CISSIE: Sure. (*Pause*)

RYAN: I wanted to talk to you about enlisting, Cissie. I. . . I tried.

CISSIE: I know. I always yelled you down. (*Pause*) You look good in that uniform.

RYAN: You never saw me in a decent suit of clothes.

CISSIE: I finished seeding the North field.

RYAN: That's great.

CISSIE: You better ask Dowser to stay for supper. I'll start up the fire.

RYAN: Don't be mad at me, Cissie. . .

CISSIE: I'm not. It's done. But I'll tell you something. I'm not having Al Marshall harvest the wheat I helped put in. I'm going to run this farm. I'm not sitting around in somebody's basement suite waiting for you to come home, Ryan. I'll get your mother down here with me and together we'll run this place. I'll run this farm somehow.

RYAN: You could, Cissie. I bet you could.

CISSIE: I know I can.

RYAN: And mother would love to come home.

CISSIE: We always got along together. (*Pause*) When do you go?

RYAN: Next week. I have to report for basic training next week.

CISSIE: Oh. What day next week?

RYAN: Thursday. I report on Thursday.

CISSIE: Oh. Oh Ryan. . . (*she moves to him*) Ryan John.

(*Transition: Sound of planes, drums. Music might be used — World War II songs or theme charged with sound of bugles and planes intermingled.*)

SCENE 2

Farmer's meeting hall — a few chairs, turned. Verandah may become speaker's platform.

CISSIE: (*to* JEANNIE *off*) Hi Jeannie. I'm just putting up the flag. Some people try to make out the C.C.F. is out to destroy the flag.

JEANNE: (*entering*) Cissie, Bert Carswell telephoned. He can't make the meeting. He wants you to speak in his place.

CISSIE: Me? I'm not prepared.

JEANNE: He says for you to just outline the party platform.

CISSIE: Oh. . . I don't know. . .

JEANNE: The speech you gave to the Farm Women, it would be fine.

CISSIE: I suppose I can say something.

JEANNE: I brought the mail. A letter for you from Ryan and I got one from Mark. He's had shore leave in London.

CISSIE: How is Mark?

JEANNE: Tired of dried eggs and spam, but he's enjoying the sights and the history. Mark doesn't want to come home to Saskatchewan. He wants to look for a place at the Coast. (*reading*) "All I remember is dust and grasshoppers and forty below with a wind blowing. You selling butter at ten cents a pound and Dad killing himself to keep the farm. We'll find a place where you can have fruit trees and roses and where we can smell the ocean. I've come to love the smell of the sea." That's how he feels, Cissie.

CISSIE: When he sees the trees we've planted, he'll change his mind. I'm afraid to open Ryan's letter.

JEANNE: Afraid?

CISSIE: Ryan's against the C.C.F. He doesn't want me to work for it.

JEANNE: He's afraid you'll change, Cissie.

CISSIE: (*opening letter*) Of course I've changed. I have to change. You can't stay a teen-ager forever. (*reading* RYAN's *letter*) "I had a day with Mark in London, but he shipped out that night. His ship is headed for the Far East. By the time you get this, my little brother may be off the coast of Africa or India or Japan. Imagine! As for me, I'm almost finished my second tour. We've been pounding the Nazis every night for two weeks. I barely got the old Halifax home last night. I'm taking out a new plane tonight. My crew's been great. I hope you don't get too involved with this C.C.F. Cissie. You say the service men's vote may be critical. I have to tell you, I'm voting against the C.C.F." Jesus, he hasn't even listened to my letters. Can't he see what we're trying to do for farmers? The old line parties never did much for Saskatchewan, or for Ryan either.

JEANNE: Ryan's a right to his opinion, Cissie.

CISSIE: I've a right to mine too. (*reading again*) "We think the war may be over soon; the Russian front seems to have crippled Hitler". The rest is sort of personal.

JEANNE: I'm glad my boys got together. I'm glad.

CISSIE: So am I. I only wish Ryan would see what we're trying to do here.

(MARJ BLAIR *and* ROSE MEEKER *enter together. Twenty years has turned them into small town society matrons complete with hat and gloves.* ROSE *is somewhat overdressed.*)

MARJ: Hello, Cissie. Mrs. Ryland. I saw your truck outside. There was something I wanted to talk over.

CISSIE: Can it wait, Mrs. Blair? We're having a meeting.

MARJ: I know that. Rose, I wanted to speak to Cissie — privately.

ROSE: Sure, Marj. Don't mind me. I'm not staying, but I just wanted to see this farmers hall. Say, it's a nice little place.

CISSIE: Thanks.

ROSE: It is. It's really nice. Marj, this is just the place for our party! (*to* CISSIE) You see, we have this social club that was started twenty years ago next month. . .

JEANNE: The Go-Getters.

ROSE: You remember! But we dropped that name. We're just the Country Club Golf and Dance Society now. Anyway for our anniversary party we're having an Arthur Murray dance teacher come out to teach us all the latest dances. You know. . . the cha cha. . . tango. . . You farm ladies could cater for the dinner. I know you do that. I've already planned the menu, roast turkey, scalloped potatoes, broccoli with a French sauce, molded salad, and baked Alaska for dessert. I always think Baked Alaska gives a really gourmet touch, don't you?

MARJ: Rose, I told you I wanted. . .

ROSE: I'm going, Marj. But this is important. . . why is it you never think of anything but yourself? Now where was I? Oh, the Appetizers. I had the most original little idea for them. What I want you to do is grate up a lot of orange cheddar cheese and when its soft enough to handle we shape the cheese into baby carrot shapes, and then we put a little sprig of parsley into the top of each carrot, and there you are, baby carrots made of cheese! To go with the martinis. (*to* JEANNE) That's a special drink. Don't you think that's a cute idea? My mother used to say "Rose you just have a natural born artistic sense." And I have. Why, I can make carrot slices look exactly like. . .

JEANNE: Cheddar cheese?

ROSE: No, Mrs. Ryland. Flowers. Little carrot flowers.

MARJ: Rose. . .

ROSE: I'm going, Marj! I'll be in touch about the catering. So nice to have a visit with you, Mrs. Ryland. . .

(ROSE *goes off*)

MARJ: (*sighing*) Poor Rose. She just can't stop talking. Well, Cissie, my brother Fred Burns tells me you and he are going to fight it out

523

on this platform tonight. We're all agog. (*moving to* JEANNE) Your daughter-in-law is very busy, Mrs. Ryland. She not only runs the farm, works part time in my shop, but has ambitions as a public figure. You could be spreading yourself pretty thin, Cissie.

JEANNE: Cissie, I'm going to take some flowers over to the church. I'll be back for the meeting.

(*she goes*)

MARJ: My brother said he'd come along early so you two can consult. He doesn't want to see you embarrassed.

CISSIE: I'm not embarrassed Mrs. Blair. I'm scared.

MARJ: I don't blame you for being nervous. Fred is a very formidable opponent. And he represents a party that stands for tradition, stability.

CISSIE: We stand for farm security and social justice.

MARJ: Cissie, I think it's time we had a little talk. I understand you need your part-time job in my shop to keep the farm going.

CISSIE: The money helps, yes.

MARJ: Surely you can see that opposing my brother in this election seems pretty ungrateful.

CISSIE: I hadn't thought about it.

MARJ: Do, Cissie. Fred didn't want to run. He was pressed into service by those of us who don't want our way of life destroyed by the hysteria that's sweeping the farm population.

CISSIE: We're not hysterical. We're fighting for a better deal.

MARJ: Co-operative buying? Is that fair competition for small businesses?

CISSIE: The co-op can sell us machinery at lower prices.

MARJ: That's merely a come-on. You're being manipulated. Gullible people taken in by outside interests with a long range plan to destroy free enterprise, initiative, freedom.

CISSIE: You haven't listened to our platform.

MARJ: Don't be naive. Communism is behind this C.C.F. You remember Joe Whipple. He was a key organizer. And everyone knew he was a communist. He even fought side by side with them.

CISSIE: Joe Whipple fought in the International Brigade against Fascism before any of us even knew what Fascism meant. Joe Whipple died in Spain. He really cared about the common people.

MARJ: I wonder how Ryan will feel when he finds out you are involved with the most radical elements in the province. He's over there fighting for freedom. How will he feel when he finds his own wife is being used as a spokesman? They're playing on the farmer's ignorance.

CISSIE: We aren't so ignorant. We read the papers. We listen to the radio. . . to Mr. Coldwell and Mr. Woodsworth. Tommy Douglas.

MARJ: That man!

CISSIE: Tommy Douglas is no communist. He's a Baptist minister.

MARJ: He was. He lost his church when he ran for parliament. Now he's not content with a seat in parliament. Now nothing will do but that he put Saskatchewan in his pocket.

CISSIE: He promises medical insurance, farm security.

MARJ: You give me no choice, Cissie. You either give up these half-baked radical ideas or your job with me. I won't have my money subsidizing communists in Regina. Do I make myself clear?

CISSIE: Very. I won't be in tomorrow, Mrs. Blair.

(FRED BURNS *enters*.)

BURNS: Hello, Marj. Little Cissie Burkholt. Grown up.

CISSIE: My name's Ryland now, Mr. Burns.

BURNS: I know. I remember you as a wild little tomboy running around your Dad's farm.

CISSIE: I remember you too.

BURNS: Cissie and I better have a talk about this meeting, Marj. You don't mind?

MARJ: I doubt Cissie will listen to you, Fred. She certainly won't listen to me. I'll be at the meeting.

(MARJ *leaves*)

BURNS: Don't let Marj scare you, Cissie. She means well. Now, my dear, I hope we can manage a friendly discussion tonight. After all I'm not one to put a pretty young woman on the spot.

CISSIE: We'll have equal time, Mr. Burns.

BURNS: Of course. I want the farmers' vote, Cissie. I own land myself. I live in this constituency. We can offer stable government, new markets, decreased freight rates. Don't go against us. When your husband gets home he'll want the support of the business people in this town. It won't do him any good for you to stand against everything we believe in. . . everything he's fighting for. Don't go out on a limb for this shyster Carswell.

(*rest of cast move into the audience as* CHAIRMAN *enters*)

CHAIRMAN: If you speakers are ready, the hall's filling up. Time to start the meeting.

BURNS: Certainly. Let the little lady speak first.

(*they move to their chairs*)

CHAIRMAN: Ladies and Gentlemen, The Farmers Co-op have sponsored this meeting so you can hear both sides early in the campaign. Fred Burns, Conservative, is contesting the seat with Bert Carswell, C.C.F. Unfortunately Mr. Carswell was unavoidably detained and tonight will be represented by our own local Co-op secretary, Cissie Ryland.

VOICE: Sounds like Carswell! Hiding behind a woman's skirts.

BURNS: He chose a pretty young woman anyway, friend.

VOICE: Give him hell, Cissie.

525

Gwen Pharis Ringwood

CHAIRMAN: Order. Cissie Ryland will speak for the Cooperative Commonwealth Federation first. If, during her talk, you have questions please stand and raise your hand. Cissie Ryland.

CISSIE: Friends. The C.C.F. pledge is to put humanity first in 1944. Voters in Saskatchewan must decide what they want. . . free enterprise and poverty or a commonwealth of social justice. We've seen enough of free enterprise and poverty.

VOICE: You can say that again, Cissie. It's time to take a stand.

CISSIE: The C.C.F. promises a moratorium on farm debt. Rural electricity. Good roads. Education for our young people. Medical care for pensioners. The C.C.F. promises to eventually introduce medical care for every man, woman and child in the province.

BURNS: Dear Cissie, forgive my interrupting. . . but that would mean we'd lose every doctor in Saskatchewan. Think about it, friends.

VOICE: You're right, Fred. State medicine is communism. You go for that and our doctors will pick up and leave.

SECOND VOICE: How the hell will we get along without doctors?

CHAIRMAN: Gentlemen, please. Go ahead, Cissie.

CISSIE: They said at the meeting last week that you are born Liberal or Conservative. You have to think your way into the C.C.F. Well, I've done a lot of thinking and I think farmers are foolish to turn down what we offer. Did you know that one hundred and forty-nine farms were foreclosed in 1943? One hundred and forty-nine farms were lost last year because of debts and taxes during the thirties. The C.C.F. promises Farm Security. We promise you won't lose your farms.

VOICE: You elect the C.C.F., and they'll seize your farms for the government. They're out to make you tenant farmers. Right, Mr. Burns?

BURNS: Right! Our brave boys overseas won't have any farms to come home to if you elect this renegade Baptist minister.

CISSIE: Tommy Douglas promises to save our farms from foreclosure. Vote for him. Vote for the C.C.F. Thank you.

(She sits down. Cheers and boos.)

CHAIRMAN: And now, Fred Burns, Conservative.

BURNS: That was a good speech, Cissie. You almost convinced me, Fred Burns. I reckon we all like to agree with a pretty girl. Unfortunately I can't be convinced. Friends, the C.C.F. offers the most dangerous political philosophy that ever hit this country. If that party should by some fluke get to Regina, every oil company in this province will pull out. There'll be no country, no oil development, no investment. If you vote for the C.C.F. you sound the death knell for Saskatchewan. Goodbye American capital. Goodbye to our doctors. Goodbye progress. This country was pioneered by strong individuals who believe a man has the right to own property and to develop it for the good

526

of himself and his family. We betray those pioneers if we elect a government out to nationalize land, industry, resources. Am I right, friends?

VOICE: No! Tommy Douglas wants to save our farms!

VOICE: You're right, Fred. Every man for himself, that's what I believe in. Every man for himself.

CISSIE: Sure. Do you know Tommy's answer to that? "Every man for himself is what the Elephant said while he danced among the chickens." Think about it. Throw out this old tired government. It's time for a change.

VOICES: Time for a Change. Time for a Change. Time for a Change. Put Humanity First. Time for a Change.

CHAIRMAN: Please. Let Fred finish.

BURNS: Friends, I'm not a smooth speaker like Woodsworth and Douglas. . . they've had a lot of practice in the pulpit but even their churches aren't behind them; and I'm no Bert Carswell who is too busy to come to our small meeting. I live here. I'm in business, yes, but I also farm. I'm a farmer like yourselves. I know our problems. I don't want my land nationalized.

CISSIE: Mr. Burns, a lot of us here know how you got your land. You bought your land at tax sales and evicted people who'd worked that land for years. That's how you got your land.

VOICE: She's right. Fred. We don't forget that.

BURNS: It's a lie! It was the law!

VOICE: Sure. A bad law. I'm for Douglas. He'll save our farms!

VOICES: Douglas. Douglas. Douglas.

>*(They join in singing* Solidarity Forever *and the meeting breaks up in confusion. At the end* CISSIE *is putting on her coat when* BURNS *approaches her)*

BURNS: You made a mistake there, girl. A bad mistake. And I won't forget it. Sure I got some of my land for taxes. Legal sale. You and your husband may find you'll look a long way for credit around this town, Cissie. I can break you, and I will if I have to. Your C.C.F. hasn't the hope of a snowball in hell of getting in power. You made a bad mistake tonight.

>*(*BURNS *leaves* CISSIE *standing alone. She looks apprehensive as she takes up* RYAN'*s letter and re-reads it. A tide of C.C.F. enthusiasm brings the cast back on stage shouting and singing the C.C.F. song. . .* CISSIE *moves away and later unobtrusively joins them. . . At the height of electoral fever an old fashioned radio is brought on stage and the cast groups around it. . .)*

RADIO NEWSCASTER: It's all over Folks. The last vote's been counted. People will remember this 1944 election. The people of Saskatchewan have elected a C.C.F. government with a landslide vote. Forty-seven out of fifty-two seats in the Saskatchewan legislature have gone to the Cooperative Commonwealth

Gwen Pharis Ringwood

Federation. We bring you the Honourable T.C. Douglas, premier of Saskatchewan.
(*Cheers from all assembled but one or two. The voice of Tommy Douglas is heard briefly through the radio.*)
CHAIRMAN: We've won, Cissie. We're in. We've won!
(*Music up on "Solidarity Forever", then drops to soft melody. Curtain.*)

SCENE 3

TIME: *1945.*

JEANNE *is planting bulbs as* CISSIE *comes to her.*

JEANNE: You've hauled the last load of wheat, Cissie.
CISSIE: It's going a fair grade, We'll be able to pay off the machinery.
JEANNE: The people from the University were here to see the crested wheat grass we sowed for them. They were pleased. They took pictures for their 1945 report.
CISSIE: I want Ryan. . . and Mark. . . to be proud of the Ryland farm, when they come home.
JEANNE: Mark may see that Saskatchewan doesn't have to be dust and grasshoppers.
CISSIE: I wonder if Ryan and I will even know each other any more.
JEANNE: Of course you will. It may take a little while. . . it did for John and me.
CISSIE: I got a letter today from the Minister of Agriculture in Regina. They want me to be on an advisory committee.
JEANNE: You worked hard for the C.C.F., Cissie.
CISSIE: It's not a paid job but they pay expenses to the meetings. I'm supposed to present the problems I see here.
JEANNE: You know you can do that, Cissie,

CISSIE: I hope Ryan won't mind. Ryan thinks I just went into the C.C.F. because I'm lonesome. Sure I'm lonesome, but I'm right too! I have to have a mind of my own, Jeannie.

JEANNE: (*smiling*) You do have, Cissie. You do have a mind of your own.

CISSIE: Do you want help with those bulbs?

JEANNE: No. I like to plant them myself. It gives me pleasure to know they're deep in the gound under the snow waiting for the spring. (DOWSER *enters*) Dowser, I'm glad to see you.

(DOWSER *moves to them*)

DOWSER: I. . . I don't bring good news, Jeannie.

JEANNE: One of my boys?

CISSIE: Ryan?

DOWSER: Mark. A torpedo got their ship. This telegram came out of Singapore.

(*He hands* JEANNE *a telegram*)

JEANNE: (*opening it*) Oh. . . Oh. Mark, my Mark.

CISSIE: Jeannie.

(JEANNE *motions her away and moves dazed towards the back of the stage*)

CISSIE: (*bitterly to* DOWSER) It isn't fair! Mark never had any life, any grown-up life, not really. Would you come in the house, Jeannie?

JEANNE: No, Cissie, no. Just leave me alone, please.

CISSIE: (*to* DOWSER) I'll get her a sweater. It's chilly.

(CISSIE *goes into the house*)

JEANNE: (*in a dull voice*) Only two days since they dropped that bomb on Hiroshima, Dowser. They said it would end the war but there's still the war. Mark wrote me that he felt sure his ship would be heading to Vancouver soon, and he'd be home. Now he won't ever come home, not ever. Oh Dowser, I'm hurting so bad.

(SAMMY WHITE CALF *comes in*)

SAMMY: Hi.

DOWSER: Hello.

SAMMY: (*to Jeanne*) You remember me, Mrs. Ryland? Sammy White Calf.

JEANNE: I remember you, Sammy.

SAMMY: You got coffee? I was drinking too much last night I guess. I made some money riding broncs but then I got drinking. They scratched me from riding.

JEANNE: The coffee pot's on the stove.

SAMMY: Thanks. I don't know what happens to me when I'm in town. Every time I go there I feel like I'm lost. That's how I feel. Like I'm lost.

JEANNE: It's late for you to go home. You'd better stay here tonight. You can sleep in the boys' room.

SAMMY: O.K. Mrs. Ryland. That's good. I'll chop you some kindling tomorrow. (*he starts off, turning*) I was doin' real good

529

ridin' those broncs but then I got drinking. That's no good. But I get so mad sometimes. You know? Mad. So goddamned mad! I can't figure out what happens to me.
(*He moves away.* DOWSER *and* JEANNE *remain silent. . . finally* JEANNE *speaks as if her thoughts had to be voiced.*)

JEANNE: Mark, my young son. He'll never be old now. He'll move through my mind always just as he was when he went away in a kind of gleaming brightness with the sun on him.

Would it be easier, Dowser, if he'd been taken by a storm or a fever, instead of a torpedo sent by his own kind? I don't know.

When I was a child in Scotland I heard tales of Highland battles where the men met lance to lance and spear to spear as if they met in some game or sport, and I heard of the proud burials of the heroes with the pipes playing. And when John went to war in 1914 there were drums sounding and flags waving. When he came home, John never spoke of the war. But in dreams he cried out and many a night he woke up screaming. And now this war drags on, but there's no lances or spears and proud burials. There's cities burning under a deadly rain and children that are rubble by the roadside. When will it stop?

DOWSER: I don't know, Jeannie. We plough up our land until it blows away into dust. We hurl bombs on our cities until the children blow away in the dust. I don't know.

JEANNE: Part of me lies in the deep ocean with Mark, but I don't grieve for Mark only. I grieve for the ones like my Ryan who've thrown down the torpedoes and the land mines and the bombs and I grieve for the ones who fell under them. And most of all I grieve for the children, Dowser. As you say, the four winds are heavy with the children that have been blown away, all the wasted children.
(*She moves forward and slowly begins to plant the tulip bulbs. There is a sound of a lament far off. There is the sound of bells ringing and music. . .* JEANNE *moves stage right while the rest of the cast are a group except for* RYAN. RYAN *appears among the crowd, looks for* CISSIE, *sees her. They stand looking at one another. . . one of the cast takes* RYAN'*s air force hat, then jacket (officer's) and gives him overalls over his arm.* RYAN *appears unaware of anything but* CISSIE *as they move slowly together and embrace. Music becomes lighter — evoking optimism and a sense of driving forward into the late 50's. While lights are down, larger shrubs and painted garden bench are placed on stage — place looks more prosperous. A portion of "Change Song", may come here, as transition while* CISSIE *and* RYAN *change for Scene 4.*)

SCENE 4

1958. CISSIE *is near the end of pregnancy.* CISSIE *and* RYAN *together.*)

RYAN: We've a great crop, Cissie. I'm sure that field will go forty
   bushels to the acre. . . maybe higher.
CISSIE: I won't be any help at harvest this year.
RYAN: I was hoping we'd have the new house built before the baby
   arrives.
CISSIE: So was I.
RYAN: They promise they'll pour the foundation next week. I've added
   a sleeping porch to our bedroom, Cissie. In summer we can wake
   up to the sunrise and the meadow larks.
CISSIE: And the baby.
RYAN: How are you feeling?
CISSIE: I've had a few pains but then they fade away.
RYAN: Maybe I should take you to the hospital now.
CISSIE: Not yet. I hate waiting around for hours. I was in that hospital
   two days before Laura came. Anyway I promised Dr. Sherman
   I'd hold off until he'd heard the election results. He's expecting
   1958 to be the greatest Conservative victory in history.
RYAN: Dief's going to get a mandate, Cissie. And I hope he does.
CISSIE: I know, Ryan. If we'll only all follow John Diefenbaker we'll
   have no problems.
RYAN: I didn't say that. Where's Laura?
CISSIE: In town. . . she's staying with Caroline.
RYAN: Why?
CISSIE: Because your daughter is a Brownie, and Caroline offered to
   keep her on Brownie nights.
RYAN: I suppose it's all right.
CISSIE: Of course, its all right. Caroline loves Laura.
RYAN: I know. But Caroline's so damn radical.
CISSIE: Radical? Just because you and Caroline had that argument
   about Universal Medical Insurance. . .
RYAN: Look, we pay for old people and children now. Working adults
   ought to pay for themselves. Every person with a sliver in his
   finger will be running to the doctor.
CISSIE: Better that, than stay home because you can't afford the
   doctor's fee.
RYAN: Ed Sherman says the doctors will strike the moment that plan's
   introduced. If I were you, Cissie, I'd just move out of the C.C.F.
   right now. You'll be busy with the new baby, Laura's going to
   need support at Brownies and that sort of thing, and whatever
   time or money we have for politics would be a lot better spent
   supporting Diefenbaker federally. You watch, medicare will kill
   the C.C.F. deader than a doornail.

Gwen Pharis Ringwood

CISSIE: I've never objected to your politics, Ryan. Why do you get so riled up over mine?

RYAN: Dief doesn't promise to put a silver spoon in everybody's mouth. He doesn't offer cradle to the grave support. Dief's a realist.

CISSIE: Damn it, Ryan, we've had fourteen years of good government here. And I'm going to fight for Medicare for everybody in Saskatchewan if it's the last thing I do. Oh. . .

RYAN: What's the matter?

CISSIE: Nothing. But I think I'll put my things in a suitcase. I might as well be in the hospital as here, when all we can do is fight.

(*She moves away. Before* CISSIE *gets off* DOWSER *enters.*)

CISSIE: Hello, Dowser.

DOWSER: How are you, Cissie?

CISSIE: I'm in a rage. My husband's turning into a bigot.

RYAN: I am not a bigot, Cissie. I'm a realist.

CISSIE: That's what bigots always say. Do you know why we got into this fight, Ryan?

RYAN: Because you're blind to logic.

CISSIE: No. Because you wanted to go to the station to see John Diefenbaker this morning, and I didn't feel good, and you wouldn't go without me. You've been sulking all day. That's why.

(*she goes in*)

RYAN: Women! Did you get to the station?

DOWSER: I was there. They rolled out the red carpet right there on the platform and Dief rolled out the oratory right back. Actually it was a good speech.

RYAN: What did he say?

DOWSER: Chinese market for surplus wheat. Cities on the permafrost. Road to our resources. One Canada.

RYAN: He means it all. And he can make it happen.

DOWSER: He'll try. I'll say that much. He'll try.

RYAN: Will you witch us a new well, Dowser? We're building a house at last, with waterworks.

DOWSER: If the power's on me and the water's there, I'll find you a well.

RYAN: What are you doing these days?

DOWSER: I'm packaging rape seed for the University.

RYAN: I think I'll grow some next year.

DOWSER: The last ten years have seen some changes, Ryan.

RYAN: Yes. Potash turns out to be a bonanza. And they're finding more coal, oil. . .

DOWSER: Secrets under the ground; minerals, oil, fossils, all down there crushed under that oncoming ice. Sometimes I stand and this prairie turns into a tropical jungle; palm trees, ferns, great purple flowers. Dinosaurs roaming the land. Tyrannosaurus Rex.

Brontosaurus. Triceratops. Mastodon. Huge mammals crashing around in the swamp. Oh I can feel them down there. . . Secrets under the ground. Untold secrets.

RYAN: Can you witch anything besides water, Dowser?

DOWSER: Let them lie, Ryan. I don't want to push my luck. I better stick to witching wells. Let them lie.

(ROSE MEEKER *enters*)

ROSE: I saw you at the station, Mr. Ringgo. Wasn't it wonderful? When John Diefenbaker gave that speech about one Canada, I actually wept. I broke right down and wept. One Canada living in harmony in the Commonwealth. He's a great man. You should have been there.

RYAN: I'd have liked to hear him.

ROSE: Of course, your wife's always been one for the socialists. But you, Mr. Ryland, you'd have cheered. We sang the Diefenbaker song, you know (*she sings*). . . "Diefenbaker, Diefenbaker, Diefenbaker, yea. . . John's the man who's ringing, swinging, swinging, back our way." I brought this radio so I can hear the election results. I know 1958 is Diefenbaker's year! What I came by for, Mr. Ryland, was to ask if we could borrow that lovely old buggy again for the parade at the fall fair. I'm in charge of the Nurses' float and thought. . .

JEANNE: (*coming out*) Ryan, I've telephoned for Dr. Sherman. I don't think Cissie can make it to the hospital. I think the baby's on its way. Oh, Mrs. Meeker, what a godsend! Please come in.

RYAN: My God, did you get Ed on the phone?

JEANNE: I left a message.

ROSE: Don't you worry, Mr. Ryland. I'm a whiz in maternity, I'll cope. Here, take this radio and listen to the election returns and leave the rest to me and Cissie.

RYAN: You mean she's going to have the baby here?

ROSE: Be calm now. My mother used to say, if there's one thing Rose can do it's cope with an emergency. So calm yourself. Relax. (*turning*) I almost drove by, Mr. Ryland, but something told me today was the day I should ask about that buggy. Something told me this was the day, and I just followed my instinct. It's just as if I was led here to. . .

RYAN: Please Mrs. Meeker, see to Cissie. Please.

ROSE: Don't panic, Mr. Ryland. You've done your part. It's up to us women now.

(*She goes in*)

RYAN: I've waited around all day to take Cissie to the hospital and kept putting it off. All the time we were arguing she could have been in the hospital having the baby. Why would she put off something as important as that?

DOWSER: She'll be all right, Ryan. Cissie had Laura without any trouble.

RYAN: There was a doctor to help her when she had Laura. And she was in a hospital. You didn't have any children, Dowser. You don't know whether it'll be all right. Hey, Mrs. Meeker, I want to come in there and help Cissie. Do you hear? I'm coming in. I'm the father, you know.

JEANNE: (*appearing*) Cissie doesn't want you in there, Ryan.

RYAN: Why not?

JEANNE: She's afraid you'll faint. She's coming along very well, son.
   (*yell off*)

RYAN: That's Cissie, yelling!

JEANNE: We told her to yell if she feels like it. We said "Yell your head off. . . nobody minds."
   (JEANNE *goes off*)

RYAN: "Yell your head off." What kind of medicine is that? I better go looking for Ed Sherman. (*calling*) Hey, Cissie, I'm going for the doctor. You just hold off, and I'll be right back. . . If you just take your time, and hold off. . .

JEANNE: Ryan, the doctor's on his way. Here's a cup of tea.

RYAN: Did you tell Cissie he's coming? Did you tell her to wait?

JEANNE: I know what you could do, Son. It would be a big help.

RYAN: What? What could I do?

JEANNE: You could bring in the clothes from the line. I must go now.
   (*She goes*)

RYAN: Bring in the clothes! What good would that do Cissie? (*drinking tea*) What are you doing, Dowser?

DOWSER: I was just trying to see if I could make this thing work.

RYAN: We can't listen to an election now. Can we?

DOWSER: I just thought I'd see what's happening. Cissie may be a few hours, you know.

RYAN: All this about not letting fathers be present when their own children are getting born, there's something wrong about that! It's like the women wanted to keep everything a secret. That's not right. . . not right at all! I got a right to be in on. . .

DOWSER: Hey, you know something? Dief's got a landslide! Greatest election victory in history. Whole country votes for Diefenbaker! A landslide.

RYAN: That's good. I'm in favour of that. Why isn't Cissie yelling?

DOWSER: Listen "the greatest election victory in history of Canada gives solid power to. . ."
   (*Sound of baby's cry*)

RYAN: What's that? Does that sound like. . .? Oh my God, it is. It must be. Listen!

DOWSER: I hear! Congratulations, Ryan.

RYAN: Yeah. Yeah. Thanks.
   (JEANNE *enters*)

JEANNE: You've a son, Ryan. A little boy. They're both fine.

RYAN: A son? You're sure?
JEANNE: Quite sure.
RYAN: Hilton John Ryland. Hey, Dowser, hear that? That's my son!
He's here! Hilton John Ryland has arrived!
DOWSER: Hilton John, good name, Ryan.
RYAN: Sure. For old Dief and for my Dad and for me. You know
something Dowser? We got one Saskatchewan prime minister in
Ottawa and another one upstairs. I better tell my wife!
(*Up on baby crying. Radio election results may be used as
transition if desired.*) *Radio*: "The election saw John
Diefenbaker sweep the country with 248 of 252 seats. We
bring you the Prime Minister of Canada the Honourable
John Diefenbaker."

(*Transition: into music of the late 60's — a Bob Dylan song or similar
music could be used. New porch — garden furniture on stage while lights
are down.*)

SCENE 5

1970: JEANNE *is knitting.*

DOWSER: (*entering*) Well, Jeannie. You're looking good.
JEANNE: You too. It's Sammy White Calf with you. You've been away
Sammy?
SAMMY: I been working up North, Mrs. Ryland. Building roads. Lots
of things happening up North now.
JEANNE: You live up there?
SAMMY: We come home in the winter. I just came out to see my folks.
I've got a good job up there.
JEANNE: I'm so pleased for you, Sammy.
SAMMY: My car broke down by the river. I had to go to town to get a
new battery. Dowser's taking me now to get my car going again.
I see Ryan's on the combine. I guess he missed me this year.

JEANNE: He missed you, Sammy.

DOWSER: I brought you this paper for your souvenirs, Jeannie. They walked on the moon. Do you believe it?

JEANNE: I have to. I saw it happening.

DOWSER: This is a picture of the earth they took from out there in the sky.

JEANNE: Oh, it looks so small.

DOWSER: Small and fragile. A giant step for mankind. I guess it is. It must be.

JEANNE: Imagine. Someone out there taking a picture of our earth. . .

SAMMY: I sure was surprised. Those men in space-suits floating around like dandelion pods in the wind. I didn't think I'd ever see a thing like that.

JEANNE: Things are happening so fast now, I can't keep up. People moving from place to place, everything happening so fast.

DOWSER: Like a whirlwind sweeping everybody up, everything we knew. A whirlwind catching us all up and spinning us round and round. Well, we better get along, Sammy if you want to start North tonight.

JEANNE: Come back for supper, Dowser.

DOWSER: Thanks, Jeannie. I will. Here's Laura!

    (LAURA *enters*)

LAURA: Hello.

JEANNE: We didn't expect you today, Laura.

LAURA: I know.

DOWSER: See you later then.

    (*he and Sammy leave*)

LAURA: Where's everybody, Grandma?

JEANNE: Your father's in the field and your mother's on the phone to Caroline.

LAURA: Is Hilt home yet?

JEANNE: He'll be late tonight. 4H meeting.

LAURA: Grandma, is Mother really going to run in the next election?

JEANNE: She's been nominated, Laura.

LAURA: I think that's selfish. What does Dad think?

JEANNE: You know they don't agree on politics, Laura. But Ryan says it's her decision.

LAURA: What if she gets elected? They'll have to move to Regina.

JEANNE: Your Dad says No. Hilt wants to stay in school here. He couldn't have a 4H Calf in an apartment in Regina.

LAURA: It's not fair. My earliest memory of my mother is waiting in the car while she canvassed for the N.D.P. Oh, I know they've done some good things, but mother seems to think they're perfect. We've lost a lot of doctors in this province and one of them was Dad's best friend. Who does Dad play chess with now?

JEANNE: Your Dad misses Dr. Sherman.

LAURA: I know. So does everybody.

JEANNE: He didn't have to leave, Laura.

LAURA: He wanted to. Maybe he was tired of Saskatchewan. I am.

JEANNE: You're young and restless, Laura. When I was first here and I got restless, John used to get me to walk out to the coulee with him and we'd watch the sunset. I never got tired of the sunset. Look at it now.

(CISSIE *comes out*)

CISSIE: Laura! I thought you had classes today. I hope you don't go to class in that outfit.

LAURA: I hear you got the nomination.

CISSIE: Yes. (*pause*) You don't want me to run.

LAURA: It's your business, Mother. After all Hilt's nearly twelve years old, and he always has Dad and Grandma.

CISSIE: I'll only be away a few months of the year. Laura, I've turned down the chance to run twice in the last ten years.

LAURA: Because of us?

CISSIE: Yes. Now I want to be a part of what's happening. And great things are going to happen here, Laura.

LAURA: Sure.

CISSIE: I didn't have your chances, Laura. I didn't get through High School. But I've worked for a government that made those things possible for you and Hilt. Some day you'll appreciate that.

LAURA: I do.

CISSIE: Your father and I want you to have the chance we didn't have.

LAURA: I'm not going to University now, Mother. I withdrew two weeks ago.

JEANNE: Laura!

LAURA: You'll get a refund. You'll get your money back.

CISSIE: Laura, you've only started your second year. You can't stop now.

LAURA: I have stopped.

CISSIE: Why? Why?

LAURA: I want to travel. I want to get out of Saskatchewan.

CISSIE: Once you start teaching, you can do that.

LAURA: That's the trouble. I don't want to teach school.

CISSIE: What do you intend to do?

LAURA: I'm going to Europe.

CISSIE: How? We aren't going to finance a grand tour for you, Laura!

LAURA: I sold my old car and I've saved my allowance and I've been waiting tables over a month. I've bought a ticket to Athens and a European railway pass.

CISSIE: You can just send it back. (RYAN *enters*) Ryan, your daughter has stopped University and bought a ticket to Athens. Tell her she can't go.

RYAN: Why, Laura? Why?

LAURA: There's so much I want to see, Daddy. Find out about. At first I was going to go without telling you, and phone you from the ship after we sailed. But I can't do that.

Gwen Pharis Ringwood

RYAN: We?

LAURA: Maria Galvani and Wilson Roberts are going too. I won't be alone.

CISSIE: Wilson? The American boy we met?

LAURA: Yes. Maria has relatives in Assizi. And Wilson was in Greece with his parents before. . .

RYAN: Before he burned his draft card.

LAURA: Daddy, please listen. All last summer when I was working in that restaurant in the park, I spent all my free time in the studio of a woman who works in clay.

CISSIE: Karen somebody, a potter.

LAURA: Yes. She also does sculpture in clay, and in stone too. She encouraged me. I think I could do some good work with clay.

CISSIE: You can pot here, Laura. There are lots of people potting here. What about your poetry? Last year you were going to be a poet.

LAURA: My poems are just ways of trying to find out what I feel, mother. But I believe that maybe I can do something with my hands, honestly I really think I have a feeling for clay and stone and. . .

CISSIE: You could never make a living at it, Laura. Nobody does.

LAURA: Maybe not here. Not yet. Right now I know what I want to do . . . I want to see great paintings and sculpture and small perfect pieces of pottery. I want to wake up in a town where for hundreds of years people have made beautiful things. I want to see hand made carpets and cave paintings and stained glass windows. I want to walk through a park where there's sculpture by Brancusi and Henry Moore and. . .

CISSIE: You brought home that book of Henry Moore's sculpture. Great bodies with holes in them. . . they don't seem beautiful to me.

LAURA: I know they don't. And if you're in the government you'd vote against buying something like that. Sure we've got good social services and farm improvements and well lighted schools but that's not what civilized countries leave behind. They leave behind great buildings and music and art and poetry. We're. . . we're such a flat province, Mother, and I don't see your government doing much about it. I have to go, Daddy. I just have to get away and see other places. Until I get away from all the flatness and all the sheltering, I won't know what I can do.

RYAN: All right, Laura.

LAURA: I can go?

RYAN: Your mother and I will talk about it.

LAURA: I want your permission, but I'm going anyway. I've a few things I want to take.

(*she goes into the house*)

CISSIE: You're going to let her go, Ryan? You can't. She's too young. Tell him he's got to stop her, Jeannie.

JEANNE: She's eighteen, Cissie. Older than you were when you stayed
here with Ryan. Older than I was when I came here with John.
CISSIE: You approve?
JEANNE: You have to keep the way open. You can't close the door.
And Laura will go anyway. In your heart, you know she will.
CISSIE: Oh Ryan, I can't stand it. I hardly know her any more. I don't
want to lose her, not yet. You and I didn't have to go traipsing off
across the world looking for ourselves. If I said I wouldn't run for
the legislature, maybe she'd decide to stay.
RYAN: No, Cissie. What we'd better do is deposit enough for a return
ticket and a small allowance each month. I wouldn't want my
daughter broke in some country where she can't even speak the
language.
CISSIE: I can't understand it. Why would she want to spend her life
making things out of clay? Why would she want to do that?
RYAN: It's the earth, Cissie. I suppose it feels good under your hand,
shaping it. . . Maybe she has a talent. If she does she's lucky. She
has to find out.

> (LAURA *comes out. There is a pause. For a moment* LAURA
> *takes up the medicine bag and holds it silently*)

RYAN: When do you sail?
LAURA: Two weeks. I'll be back before we leave. Tell Hilt I'll be back
to say goodbye. Don't cry, Mother. I'll be all right. Honestly I
will. Daddy, I always remember the owl we raised and the baby
coyote and how you wouldn't let them dam the coulee. And those
big rocks that you spent all day pushing up by the pond. . . I'll
remember those forever. Grandma, maybe I'll get to see where
you grew up in Scotland. Oh, I want to see it all! The whole
world!

> (DOWSER *enters*)

DOWSER: You're off again so soon, Laura?
LAURA: Yes. Dowser, do you know what's happening? I'm going to
stand on the steps of the Parthenon and I'm going down in a cave
where people painted those animals you told me about. . .
DOWSER: Wild bulls? Mastodons?
LAURA: That's right. I'm going to wind my way through the labyrinth
in Crete and see Scylla and Charybdis. And who knows. . .
perhaps I'll cut a willow wand and find an underground river
that's been there since time began.
DOWSER: You have the power, Laura. Like I told you, you have the
power.
LAURA: I wrote this poem for you, Grandma, for your birthday. . . I
better give it to you now. It's called *Circle Song.*

> (*she starts to go, turning*)

Don't mind what I said. . . It's the rest of Saskatchewan that's
flat. Not this place. This place is hardly flat at all.

Gwen Pharis Ringwood

(Transition: "Circle Song". Verses 1, 4. and 5 of the song were used in the 1980 production as set to music by Rick Fox.)

CIRCLE SONG

1. Through sun, moon, star, rain
   The small earth turns and turns again
   While summer, autumn, winter, spring
   To wind and sky their banners fling.

2. Day and dark take turn about —
   Tide's in — Tide's out.
   Water, rock and salt and fire
   Merge in motion, form, desire.

3. Beast and flower, bird and tree
   Forsake the star-fish and the sea,
   While man with hand and memory blest
   Begins his restless, hungry quest.

4. And birth and death their changes ring
   To summer, autumn, winter, spring.
   And the small earth turns and turns again
   Through sun, moon, star, rain.

5. Sun and moon and star and rain
   Sun and moon and star and rain.

*   *   *

(While lights are down, slight changes are made to bring setting up to 1978 — a modern, well kept farm — garden scene — wicker table and chair etc. RYAN is looking off, standing at stage left. All have aged.)

SCENE 6

1978: DOWSER *enters and approaches* RYAN.

DOWSER: Ryan.

RYAN: Dowser! Good to see you. How did you get here?

DOWSER: Cissie picked me up in town.

RYAN: Of course. For mother's birthday. She's eighty-three.

DOWSER: She was eighteen when she came here with your Dad. I was twenty. Your Dad just a few years older. I remember John standing in this same place. . . looking out across the land.

RYAN: It's the light. . . the changing light. I never stop wondering at it. If I were an artist, I think I could spend my life trying to catch that light.

DOWSER: Your place looks good. Your Dad would be proud of the Ryland farm.

RYAN: We've worked at it. Not always in the right way, but we've worked at it. Sure, I've grown good wheat, but if I had it to do over again I'd try it another way. I wouldn't depend on fertilizers and sprays. The Saskatoon bushes in the coulee don't bear fruit like they once did. And there aren't as many wild flowers as there used to be. I had the great idea that I was farming scientifically. Now I wonder if I've just been mining the land.

DOWSER: The top soil blew away before you took over. Once it's gone. . .

RYAN: There are ways to replenish. . . rebuild the soil. I've been ploughing alfalfa under in that south field. It'll raise a great crop in a couple of years. I only began to look for other ways lately . . . Before that I just poured on the commercial fertilizer. And I suppose that's what will happen from now on. . . whoever buys the place.

DOWSER: You're selling?

RYAN: We've got an offer. It's hard to turn it down.

DOWSER: I can't imagine anyone else here.

RYAN: We used to think of this as a big farm. Not any more. Now they say you need three, four sections of land. If I sell this place, I can make more on the interest in the bank than I make farming it, growing food.

DOWSER: That doesn't seem fair. Raising food's important.

RYAN: I always thought it was. After thirty years of working this place an accountant with his computer tells me I'd be ahead to sell out and invest the money. The outfit that wants this place has nine sections under cultivation. Conglomerate farm. My land would be a part of that.

DOWSER: I thought you'd want Laura or Hilt to have the place. Rylands.

RYAN: Laura and Wilson have a place in the Qu'Appelle Valley. Wilson manages a machine shop that services heavy equipment. Laura has a studio on the river bank. She's working on some big pieces of sculpture. One of them was commissioned by the Alberta government. They've found their place. I had a great time with the two grandchildren. I bought them a pony.

DOWSER: What about Hilt?

RYAN: He's in graduate school. Two more years.

DOWSER: Agriculture?

RYAN: Science. Geology. Oh, the logical thing to do is sell the place, bank the money. . . go to Florida in the winters. . . California. . . Live in one of those trailer parks or carry your house around with you like a turtle. Cissie's practically packing already.

DOWSER: And Jeannie?

RYAN: She says she'll live in that lodge in town. She claims she wants to. I've been putting off signing the deed of sale. I suppose I keep hoping some miracle will happen and I'll feel young again and my arthritis will go away and I'll refuse the offer.

(BURNS *enters*)

BURNS: Mr. Ryland?

RYAN: That's right.

BURNS: I'm Garfield Burns. Acme Real Estate. We wrote you a letter outlining our client's offer.

RYAN: I got it.

BURNS: We hadn't heard from you. Our client's anxious to close the deal. Your wife sent me down here to see you.

RYAN: We haven't decided.

BURNS: Oh, Mrs. Ryland seemed to think it was just a matter of a few details. I don't want to pressure you, but since you are thinking of retiring, I think I can offer you a few extras, above what we said in the letter. . .

RYAN: Extras?

BURNS: Well, we can put a bit higher value on the house. Not that my client needs the house. . . but your wife seemed to feel — well let's face it — houses have a sentimental value. Anyway, I hope you'll be in tomorrow.

RYAN: You're mighty anxious to get hold of my place, aren't you?

BURNS: Not me. My client would like to add this place to his holdings, but it's your decision. You deserve to retire, Mr. Ryland. You've worked a long time. My Dad went to Arizona years ago. Still plays golf and he's close to ninety. You knew him. Fred Burns.

RYAN: I knew him. He foreclosed on my father.

BURNS: Those were rough times. Terrible. Lot of difference now. Here we are talking about three hundred and fifty thousand dollars give or take for your place and the machinery.

RYAN: Well, you've said your piece. I'll let you know.

BURNS: Good, I know you'll be satisfied with our deal. If you sell, you'll never have to depend on the old age pension to keep you comfortable. Do you mind if I look over the place?

RYAN: I see no reason for it.

BURNS: Whatever you say. I just wish I had your chance to get out from under. These small farms don't pay wages any more. They've had their day. Well, take it easy. I'll be in touch tomorrow.

(he goes)

RYAN: I couldn't stand his father. I can't stand him. The Indians are right, Dowser. A man doesn't own the land. The land owns him. A man just holds it, in trust. You always felt that way. Yet you never worked the land.

DOWSER: No, but when I was witching a well I'd feel that willow stick tremble in my hand. After that a man can't feel separate any more.

RYAN: I planted some apple trees over by the coulee. I hope they make it through the winter.

(CISSIE enters)

CISSIE: Jeannie says there's time to beat you at crib before supper, Dowser.

DOWSER: She beat me last time. My turn.

(He goes)

CISSIE: Did Garfield Burns come out here?

RYAN: He did.

CISSIE: He's offering us a lot of money.

RYAN: Yeah.

CISSIE: Like you said last night, we'd be foolish to turn it down.

RYAN: Do you really want that job in Regina?

CISSIE: It's a challenge. I'd be setting up Farmer's markets, advising small producers. I've liked the part-time job here.

RYAN: I can't see myself sitting around an apartment.

CISSIE: You said we'd buy a house. . . you'd fix it up. . . houses are good investments. You were the one who decided we should sell, Ryan.

RYAN: What about Hilt? What if he wants it?

CISSIE: Hilt chose Science, not Agriculture. He's a good future in Geology. He's already had an offer from that Uranium company.

RYAN: I'm not convinced that Uranium is such a windfall. I'm not convinced at all.

CISSIE: It's bringing money and investment into this province, Ryan.

RYAN: I'm sick of rushing into new things. I suppose I'm as out-dated as the dodo bird. The other day I had a notion of rebuilding Dad's old windmill. Twenty years since that windmill fell down and I still miss it.

You don't have any doubts about selling, Cissie?

CISSIE: Some, but I can't see you go on working the way you've always worked. Sure I have some doubts. Last night I woke up and I tried to imagine us leaving. Do you know what I kept worrying around in my mind? The Medicine Bag. . . Jeanne's medicine bag. . . What do we do with it? Does it go with her or with us or do we leave it here where she found it? Who does it belong to?

RYAN: Jeannie always says it belongs where she found it.

CISSIE: It would be different if we were selling to a person. But we're selling to a company.

RYAN: And the Ryland Farm won't exist any more. It'll be swallowed up. You don't think there's a chance Hilt will want it?

CISSIE: He's two years more before he finishes, Ryan.

RYAN: You're right. I wonder why a man wants to pass on something he's worked at, toiled for. . . something of himself to the ones who come after. Hilt won't know how I feel when I plant a crop year after year, watch it grow, wait for the rain to come, hope the frost will hold off and the snow won't come till after harvest. Hilt won't know how our hearts lifted when we saw that the shelter belts were holding the soil from blowing away or how we welcomed the bluebirds and meadow larks that nested there, the ducks swimming on that pond. Hilt won't know how I feel when I hold a full golden head of wheat in my hand and see wheat standing as high as my waist around me and feel that I'm feeding people a thousand miles away. The map of this farm's inside me, Cissie, the contours, the places that need work, the clean rich fields, the ponds we built to hold water, the coulee. Those who come after won't know a man can carry a map of every acre of his farm inside himself. How could Hilt or anyone who comes new to the place know how thirty years has imprinted that place on the man who worked it? Why should I care who takes it on after me? But I do care, Cissie. God help me, I do care. I'd like Hilt to at least have the chance to take over. I want to keep on farming until he's through University. Another two, three years. . .

CISSIE: Then all we have to do is tell Burns "No."

RYAN: You'll go along with me on this?

CISSIE: Ryan. You went along with me when I ran for the legislature. You comforted me when I lost. Sure I'll go along.

RYAN: What about that government job?

CISSIE: We'll say No to that too. Come on, I've got to get Jeannie's birthday supper on the table.

*   *   *

(*Transition "Which Way, What Way" song or other music*)

WHICH WAY WHAT WAY

Which way, what way, where do we go?
This way, that way, how do we know
   Where do we go from here?
(*rather like a carillon*)
   CHANGE CHANGE CHANGE CHANGE
   CHANGE CHANGE CHANGE
Which road, what road, where do we find
Something to last for time out of mind?
   Where do we go from here?
(CHANGE CHANGE ETC. . .)
This road, that road, where do we start?
Find something to challenge the mind and the heart?
   Where do we go from here?
(CHANGE CHANGE ETC. . .)
Which way, what way, where do we go?
This way, that way, how do we know?
   Where do we go from here.

> (*While lights are down garden furniture is taken off — one railing of porch is broken — slight deterioration shows after some absence — Scene is as in Act I, Scene 1.*)

SCENE 7

(*1980:* RYAN *and* CISSIE *move back to join the company and the actor playing* RYAN *makes quick change necessary for the role of* HILT RYLAND *as in Scene 1. The music fades and is replaced by the sound of wild geese in the distance. The cast stands looking upward turned away from the audience. . . the sound of the geese at first distant, then directly above and fades off again. The company watch the flight.*

JEANNE WHITE CALF *moves down stage into position as at the end of Scene 1. She is holding the medicine bag.* HILT RYLAND *takes up position as at end of Scene 1 also.*)

Gwen Pharis Ringwood

HILT: My grandmother kept this all those years. How did she come to
have it?

JEANNE: Perhaps she wants you to keep it now.

HILT: Maybe. She told me I was to get something else too. . . a flour
sack in the bottom drawer of her dresser. I'll get that now. You
don't go away?

JEANNE: I can stay ten minutes or so. Then I have to go.

HILT: I'll be right back. You look good sitting on that rock.

JEANNE: It's a comfortable rock.

(HILT *goes off right.* JEANNE *sits quietly as* DOWSER *(old)*
moves to her)

DOWSER: Hello.

JEANNE: Hi.

DOWSER: You're a White Calf.

JEANNE: Yes, I'm Jeanne. You're the water finder. . . Dowser.

DOWSER: That's right. You know something. . . I knew your great
grandfather. . . He was a good man. You're Sammy's girl?

JEANNE: I'm his youngest. Hilt Ryland's in the house. He's looking for
his roots. . . you know.

DOWSER: I know. What about you?

JEANNE: I'm drifting right now. Drifting.

DOWSER: You know the saying "when the teacher's needed, the
teacher will appear."

JEANNE: How about that? Are you the teacher?

DOWSER: No. I gave that up.

(HILT *returns carrying (in mime) a sack that might have*
contained twenty pounds of flour)

HILT: I found it. Dowser, this is Jeanne Whitecalf.

DOWSER: We know each other, Hilt. Look over there.

HILT: A mirage. The elevators.

DOWSER: Prairie magic.

HILT: That's what it is all right.

JEANNE: I'm always surprised, every time it happens. A mirage doesn't
usually last as long as a rainbow but it's. . . it's even more. . .
surprising. I never saw a mirage up north.

HILT: Grandma told me to open this.

DOWSER: I went to see her yesterday. She's frail.

HILT: (*to* JEANNE) She's in the hospital. . . extended care.

DOWSER: Yes. She said "this is only temporary, Dowser. . . only
temporary."

HILT: Look at this flour sack. . . it's all embroidered. But you can still
see the print: Robin Hood Flour, Moose Jaw, Saskatchewan.
Why would anybody embroider a flour sack? Why would
Grandma keep her souvenirs in a Flour Sack?

DOWSER: It's a long story, Hilt.

HILT: Well, here goes. The deed for the homestead. . . the Ryland
farm. . . Honourable discharge World War One. . . Sgt. John

Ryland. . . a medal. More medals. Navy. . . they'd be Uncle
Mark's. And here's my Dad's. . . Air Force. Some fossils. A
willowstick. . . yours, Dowser? (DOWSER *nods*) Gold certificates
for Number one hard wheat 1913 Toronto. Notice of auction.
And here's a gopher tail. . . why would she keep that? Oh, I can't
look any more. Not now. I. . . I want to look at the rest with
Grandma. Now you open the medicine bag.
> (*He starts to give it to her.*)
JEANNE: No. Oh no. (*Pause*) You don't understand. It's not to be
opened. . .the medicine bag is. . . well, it's sacred. We mustn't
open it. (*She takes it in her hand*) Look, whoever owned it carved
something in the leather.
HILT: It's a man looking up at a star. He's holding a bow.
JEANNE: I guess he's waiting for a vision.
HILT: A vision. God help us, a vision.
> (*Pause*)
JEANNE: I have to go now.
HILT: Wait. Where are you going?
JEANNE: To a meeting. (*ironic smile*) Indian Rights.
HILT: I'll see you again, won't I?
JEANNE: I imagine. My reserve's right across the river. (*giving him
medicine bag*) Your Grandmother kept this all her life. (*sternly*)
You keep it. Maybe it will help you make up your mind. You
know, about the job or the farm. . .
HILT: I'll keep it.
JEANNE: Well, see you
> (*She goes*)
HILT: She's beautiful.
DOWSER: Yes.
HILT: Dowser. . . was it all. . . just a mirage? Like those elevators?
DOWSER: All what, Hilt?
HILT: All the living that was in these. (*he indicates the bags*) All those
lives ploughed into this land? You know. . . hopes, plans, work,
. . . everything. . . Is it just a mirage?
DOWSER: Well, if it is, what about it? Mirage? Vision? Without it, we're
just like the other animals. Not that I think that's bad. . . A lot
of animals are nicer than some people I know. Still, it's the one
thing we have that the animals don't seem to have. Maybe it is a
mirage. That's all right. (*Pause*) It's all up to you now, Hilt
Ryland. . . All up to you.
> (HILT *moves to place medicine bag in its old position. For a*
> *moment we hear that strange hum. Then* HILT *moves into*
> *company and* DOWSER *speaks the epilogue with music or*
> *Wind Song behind if desired. The company all move in as*
> *quietly as if they too were a mirage. They freeze for Epilogue.*)

Gwen Pharis Ringwood

EPILOGUE

They are no easy gods
Who ride in the smoke of campfires
Howl with the wind and shimmer in mirage
Dancing with Northern lights, glowing in sundogs
These gods who challenge us to hunt them down.

They are not gentle gods
Who hide in the hawk's dawn shadow,
Cry with wild geese or move with drifting snow
They whirl with the dervish dust-cone down the furrow
Eluding us, they will not let us go.

They are no easy gods,
Drifting on air with feathers,
Or moving in waves across the golden plain,
They bellow with lost bison, rage with thunder,
Calling "come follow and hunt us down again."

The End

Garage Sale

for Barney

First performance presented by
The New Play Centre
at the Waterfront Theatre, Vancouver
April 14-25, 1981
in the Du Maurier Festival of One Act Plays
directed by Jace van der Veen

Characters

RACHEL: *Dorothy Davies*
REUBEN: *Peter Jaenicke*

PLACE: *The Back Yard.*
TIME: *The Present.*

The verandah and a portion of the small garden of an old fashioned little house on a city street. A door to the house opens on to the porch. Two old fashioned chairs are placed on the verandah. There is a bench in the garden as well as a bird bath and a bird feeder.
    In the original production the plum tree, the old fence, the lane were imagined to be in the audience area and were not shown.
    The time is April and there is spring in the air.
A home-made tool box or small bench on the porch may be useful.

A crocheted afghan covers one of the chairs and a crocheted cushion in the same pattern is on the other chair.
RACHEL comes out the door carrying a basket of wool and a partially completed Afghan (probably Granny squares pattern.) In the basket too is a container carrying Sunflower seeds and she also has a jug of water for the bird bath. She closes the screen door carefully, places the basket of wool and afghan on the chair at right, moves to the bird feeder. She is humming softly to the tune of "Lulla lulla Lulla Bye Bye".

RACHEL: "Lulla lulla lulla lulla bye bye
Do you want the moon to play with?
A star to run away with . . ?"
(She breaks off to talk to her familiar visitors that hover just out of sight.)
There. That's all you get today. You'll eat us out of house and home if we don't watch out. Is that how you get to the feeder, you naughty thing? We'll have to cut the branch back. Oh, you silly squirrel. Come on down. I won't hurt you. Who do you think puts these sunflower seeds out every day? Mind you leave some for the chickadees. Don't be greedy.
(She moves to the plum tree.)
So! You're all in bud this morning. Good for you. Mind you, you're a little slow. The tree across the lane burst all its buds out yesterday. Of course it gets more sun. But they neglect it. They've never pruned it once. I want you to be in full blossom when Daphne comes home next week. Like a bride in a wedding veil. Daphne looked so beautiful walking down that aisle. Radiant. But somehow that all fell apart. I don't know why. I never did know why. *(Indignant, as if tree had replied.)* Of course I asked. *(Moving away)* You hurry up now. The tree across the lane is in full bloom. *(She moves to stage right to look out at the tree across the lane.)* For goodness sakes! Would you look at that now? They must be going to. . .Oh, that's sad. Those poor young people. Hmmm. That's very sad. *(She turns away, moving towards chair left on porch.)* Mind you, I'm not surprised. But still, it makes me feel—sad. *(Bemused, she sits down and begins crocheting.)* Poor people. *(Pause.)* Poor Everybody.
(REUBEN comes out the door, closes it, moves onto porch.)
REUBEN: Well, Rachel. You're out here. I wondered. Who were you talking to?
RACHEL: Oh, just the squirrel. The plum tree.
REUBEN: Hmm. Well, they say it makes them grow.
RACHEL: That's right.
REUBEN: I wish you'd stop talking to that jade tree in the house though. It's threatening us. Taking over.

RACHEL: The jade tree is a horticultural triumph, Reuben.
REUBEN: Who says so?
RACHEL: The Avon lady. She called once.
REUBEN: Oh yes.
RACHEL: Those were her very words—a horticultural triumph.
REUBEN: Whatever she said, you shouldn't go on encouraging that jade tree. Couldn't you. . .
RACHEL: Couldn't I what?
REUBEN: Well, couldn't you. . . just bow?
       (*He bows elaborately.* RACHEL *ignores this sally.*)
RACHEL: I put your bran flakes out.
REUBEN: I ate them. And the avocado.
RACHEL: For breakfast? (*Crossly*) I was saving it, for a salad.
REUBEN: I've always wanted to eat an avocado for breakfast and today I did. It's going to be a nice day.
RACHEL: Occasional showers. Sunny periods.
REUBEN: Sun's burning through now. I'll get my journal and write it up out here. I've got behind on my journal what with all that pruning and painting and refurbishing.
RACHEL: Well, we're doing it for Daphne.
REUBEN: (*Moving to the door*) All on the chance she's coming.
RACHEL: This time she'll come. The end of April, she said. And that's next week. Don't hold the screen door open, Reuben. We don't want mice in the house.
REUBEN: If there was a mouse around I'd see it.
RACHEL: You might not see it. Mice move fast.
REUBEN: We've lived in this house for five years, Rachel, and every time I open this door you tell me to watch out for mice.
RACHEL: There was one. . .
REUBEN: You've blown mice up out of all proportion. Mice are not the enemy.
RACHEL: They are to me.
REUBEN: Do you know what's the enemy? Oxen.
RACHEL: Oh, you and your black oxen.
REUBEN: "The years like great black oxen tread the world, And I am trampled by their passing feet." There's your enemy.
RACHEL: Maybe I feel trampled by mice. Can I help that?
REUBEN: Yes, you can. You can refuse to allow yourself to be trampled.
RACHEL: It's not that simple. Not for everybody.
REUBEN: You have to fight back. I fight back. (*He turns to go into the house*) What was it I was going to get?
RACHEL: Your journal.
REUBEN: Oh, right.
       (*He goes in.* RACHEL *moves down stage and looks across.*)
RACHEL: Not that simple.

Gwen Pharis Ringwood

(*She returns to her crocheting.* REUBEN *returns with journal, carefully closing the door behind him. He sits on the edge of the porch and begins entries in journal.*)

REUBEN: Let's see. April 25th. Up at 7.30; shaved; dressed. Ate bran flakes, and a whole avocado. (*He glances at* RACHEL *who ignores this.*) Rae in garden. . . singing. (*Looking at her*) Well, how's it coming?

RACHEL: How's what coming?

REUBEN: The Work. The Ultimate. Definitive. The Afghan.

RACHEL: It doesn't come. I fabricate it. Hand and eye.

REUBEN: What about the wool? You don't fabricate it. That's the sheep's job.

RACHEL: This wool's acrylic.

REUBEN: Oh.

RACHEL: Sheep's wool shrinks. Who wants that?

REUBEN: I do. I hate acrylic.

RACHEL: It's my afghan. I'm the one crocheting.

REUBEN: I used to think that word was pronounced "crotchet" to rhyme with "watch it". (*Writing*) Rae's crotcheting an afghan, square by square, breath other breath, each square identical to the one before, same pattern, color, size. On to infinity she spreads the crotchet afghan.

RACHEL: You said you'd hook a rug. You promised.

REUBEN: I will. I'm going to.

RACHEL: Five years now. No rug.

REUBEN: You'll see. I'll get around to it.

RACHEL: I bought you a rug kit when you—when you had that little —warning.

REUBEN: The heart attack.

RACHEL: Yes. An expensive rug kit.

REUBEN: It's a poodle pattern. If I make a rug, I'm not spending my time hooking poodles.

RACHEL: I thought you liked dogs.

REUBEN: I like dogs all right. I just don't like dogs on rugs. Besides, I plan to make my own pattern.

RACHEL: For a first rug? That's dangerous.

REUBEN: So? I'll take my chances. I'll teeter on the edge. Now I'll get this journal up to date. Remember yesterday, note down today. What's happening. Where I'm at. Who called. Did anybody call?

RACHEL: Not yet.

REUBEN: I thought I heard—

RACHEL: Heard what?

REUBEN: Heard someone calling. Would we answer?

RACHEL: We always answer. (*Pause*) Reb, did anybody call? Did anyone really call?

REUBEN: Oh yes, Rachel.

RACHEL: When?

REUBEN: At Christmas. The children. If they can get through, they always call at Christmas.

RACHEL: Sometimes when the phone rings I think it might be Doris calling. I know it couldn't be, Reb, but just for a moment I. . .

REUBEN: I know the feeling.

RACHEL: Do you? (*He nods.*) Doris was always so thoughtful.

REUBEN: (*Getting up to show her*) See, here's the Christmas entry. John and Daphne called. Rae's brother George dropped in, having strong drink taken. Aunt Selina phoned. And we saw Mary. . . looks like Poppins. Who's she?

RACHEL: Someone on the television.

REUBEN: There, you see. It pays to keep a journal.

RACHEL: I suppose they called. Lately all I seem to hear is that buzz saw. All day yesterday. . .

REUBEN: I told you, it's not a buzz saw, Rachel. It's a bull dozer.

RACHEL: Oh.

REUBEN: The're bulldozing down the old church to make way for a high rise.

RACHEL: The old church falling. One wouldn't expect it to be so loud.

REUBEN: It was a strong old church, well built. Besides, the sound reverberates against that old fence, the same as a bullet ricochets.

RACHEL: That fence is not so old. I think the Longs put it up. Then the Prentergasts painted it. And now it's the. . . the. . .

REUBEN: The Crangs.

RACHEL: Oh yes, he's Crang. She's Simla. They're on their way out now.

REUBEN: Moving?

RACHEL: Not just moving. They're terminating the relationship.

REUBEN: How do you know that?

RACHEL: Look across the lane. Through the gap in the Virginia Creeper. Everything's out there.

REUBEN: You're right. It could be they're house cleaning. It's spring.

RACHEL: They're not house cleaning, Reb. They're having their garage sale.

REUBEN: Don't jump to conclusions, Rachel. If it were a garage sale there'd be customers.

RACHEL: If you'd wear your glasses you could see the sign. Garage Sale, 10 o'clock.

REUBEN: Those glasses hurt my ears. Besides I like the way things look without them. Soft around the edges.

RACHEL: Blurry!

REUBEN: All right. I like things blurry. No one's come yet. So far there's just odds and ends piled helter skelter. Chain saw, Sofa. . . or is that a hideabed. . . or what? I'll get the field glasses.

RACHEL: Reuben.

Gwen Pharis Ringwood

REUBEN: They won't know. I'm interested. I might want to pick
    something up.
        (*Telephone rings*)
RACHEL: Listen.
REUBEN: The telephone. I'll get it. Coming. Hold on, I'm coming.
        (*He rushes into the house.*)
RACHEL: If it's John or Daphne I'll come so keep them on the line, Reb.
    (*looking at watch*) It must be John or Daphne. Who else could
    phone so early? I'm coming! (*She becomes tangled in the
    afghan*) Oh damn it. Don't hang up, Reb. I'll be right in. (*The
    sound of a trail bike starting next door is heard.*) Do you hear me,
    Reuben? I just have to. . . Oh, that noisy trail bike. I'll be glad to
    hear the last of it.
        (RACHEL *starts towards the door.* REUBEN *comes out. He
        has the field glasses with him.*)
RACHEL: What was it, Reb?
REUBEN: Daphne. Daphne was on the phone.
RACHEL: And you didn't call me? Is she all right?
REUBEN: She's fine. Just fine.
RACHEL: You know I wanted to speak to her. I was just coming.
REUBEN: She had no time, Rae. She was waiting to board a plane.
RACHEL: Oh, she's on her way then? She's leaving London now. . .
    today!
REUBEN: Yes, Rae but. . .
RACHEL: But what?
REUBEN: Rae, the plane was going to Italy. To Milan.
RACHEL: Oh. So she's not coming home.
REUBEN: Well, no. She's got this good offer. She's doing the costumes
    for a film they're making in northern Italy. She couldn't refuse
    such a good offer, Rae.
RACHEL: I see.
REUBEN: She hopes we'll come visit her when she gets back to
    London.
RACHEL: She knows we won't do that.
REUBEN: Why not?
RACHEL: With your heart condition we can hardly go trapping off. . .
REUBEN: Excuses. Excuses. You know the doctor said—
RACHEL: How did she sound?
REUBEN: Fine. Happy. She sends her love. She couldn't stay while I
    called you. . . her flight was waiting. . .
RACHEL: Well, that's that. John won't be coming. Daphne won't be
    coming.
REUBEN: John can't come Rae. He's bound by contract.
RACHEL: We might as well not have children. Oh, Reb.
REUBEN: (*moving to her, comforting her*) It's all right, Rae. They're
    grown up. My God, John's forty years old.

RACHEL: Forty-one. Why did he have to go to Nigeria? And Daphne's
never even seen this house. Now if we'd stayed in the old house
where they grew up, like I wanted to. If we hadn't moved. . .
REUBEN: We went back, remember. Everything was changed.
RACHEL: Where in Italy? Where will Daphne be?
REUBEN: Lake Gardona. That's where they make the pirate films. I
read about it in the Geographic. I'll bring out the Globe. We'll
find it on the Globe. You wait here.
   (*He moves to the house*)
RACHEL: That Globe's all out of date.
REUBEN: (*as he goes in, carefully closing the door behind him*) I
don't thing Italy has changed that much.
RACHEL: (*At bench, gazes forlornly at the plum tree*) You don't have
to hurry. She's not coming. You might as well take your time.
   (REUBEN *returns with large globe.*)
REUBEN: Well, here we are. . . our turning Globe.
RACHEL: Don't leave the. . .
REUBEN: I know. Watch out! Mice!
   (*He closes the door elaborately.*)
RACHEL: How did she sound, Reb? How did Daphne sound?
REUBEN: Fine. Excited. Remember when you gave me this Globe?
Our 10th anniversary.
RACHEL: Fifth. Our fifth.
REUBEN: Here it is. Right here, near Milan. Now if I could find that
Geographic, we'd have the whole picture. We can pretend we're
there.
RACHEL: All last night I was thinking of the children. Especially Doris.
She seems so alive to me, Reb. Sometimes it's as if she's closer
than the others. Finally I got up and looked through all the
photographs.
REUBEN: You were asleep at five. I was up at five and when I came
back to bed, you were asleep, all warm and cosy.
RACHEL: I was awake. I felt your cold feet on me.
REUBEN: We could manage a trip to Italy, Rae, if you want to.
RACHEL: How?
REUBEN: Encroach on capital. We'd get a room at Lake Gardona. . .
RACHEL: No. We'd be in the way.
REUBEN: We wouldn't need to stay long. We could take Daphne out
to dinner. Hail and Farewell. Then go on to Rome or Alexandria
—traverse the turning globe.
RACHEL: We'd have to get used to a new globe, Reuben. And I warn
you, everything's changed.
REUBEN: You don't suppose they'd be getting rid of a Globe? Crangs,
I mean. Theirs would be recent. I'll take a look. (*using glasses*)
Chain saw, cross country skis, pressure cooker, blender, pair of
skates—those would be his.
RACHEL: The dressing table's hers. Pretty, isn't it?

Gwen Pharis Ringwood

REUBEN: I don't see any Globe out there. (*sound of trail bike off*) Hey, here he comes back. I hope he's not selling his trail bike. He'll need that. Hmm. He is selling it. Leaving it out with all the rest. He's just walking away from it into the house. That's terrible! I wonder how much he'd want for. . .

RACHEL: (*Moving to him in indignation*) Reuben, what on earth would you do with a trail bike?

REUBEN: (*Angrily*) I'd. . . I'd. . . What does anybody do? I'd explore! (*Turning it into a joke*) It rides two. We'd hit the trail together.

RACHEL: (*Sitting to crochet*) We'd hit the ditch together and end up in jail.

REUBEN: He looked gloomy. Poor kids. I can see them now.
   (*He moves to other chair and sits down.*)

RACHEL: How can you see them if they're in the house?

REUBEN: In my mind. I see them in my mind. Don't you?

RACHEL: No. No, I don't.

REUBEN: He'll be at the stereo, fingering all those records they collected. She's standing on a chair reaching the back of cupboards, pulling down the unused wedding gifts.

RACHEL: I don't think they were married. Twice the postman left letters here addressed to Ms. Rosanne Simla. I returned them.

REUBEN: To her?

RACHEL: Of course not. To the Postman. He's the one responsible.

REUBEN: We could go over. We might pick up a few things. We bought the bird bath at the Long's garage sale.

RACHEL: At least the Longs nodded to us.

REUBEN: Crang ducked his head at me. Twice. When I was mowing.

RACHEL: I took mint jelly over.

REUBEN: You did?

RACHEL: I went across the lane right into their back yard and offered her the jelly.

REUBEN: She refused it?

RACHEL: She thanked me but she said she already had mint jelly.

REUBEN: You never told me.

RACHEL: I was embarrassed. I felt like a fool.

REUBEN: She was just being honest. Rae. After all, a person can only use so much mint jelly. We know that.

RACHEL: She's very wasteful. She only uses the tips of the asparagus. The stalks go in the garbage. A lot of good in them just wasted.

REUBEN: (*looking across the lane*) Hey, here they come. She's carrying the baby. He's putting out a laundry basket. She's just putting the baby down in the basket. Rae, you don't suppose. . .

RACHEL: Of course not.

REUBEN: Last year I heard a radio program. All about a black market. . . in babies.

REUBEN: Oh, Reuben (*Unbelieving*)

REUBEN: A true program. Documented.

RACHEL: Not in Canada.
REUBEN: This was in Canada. A flourishing black market.
RACHEL: That's awful. How could anybody. . .
REUBEN: Have you seen their baby?
RACHEL: Just from here. I made some bootees for it, but I never took
then over.
REUBEN: Why not? You should have.
RACHEL: After the mint jelly?
REUBEN: Pink blanket. The baby must be a girl.
RACHEL: They don't make that distinction any more. They often use
yellow. They call it Unisex. Is there a tag on that basket?
REUBEN: I can't see. The snowmobile's in the way. Oh dear, you're
right, Rachel. They're breaking up. They've brought out the
waterbed.
(RACHEL *moves to him to look across.*)
RACHEL: So that's what they're like. It doesn't even look comfortable.
REUBEN: They've drained it, Rachel.
RACHEL: Oh, Reuben.
REUBEN: It's collapsed like a burst balloon. They're breaking up all
right.
RACHEL: (*returning to her chair*) I didn't think it would last. I said to
myself: "Rae that young couple is headed for the rocks."
REUBEN: I thought just the opposite. All that singing around the
barbecue. And the smell of those steaks, sizzling over charcoal.
I thought they'd make it.
RACHEL: The barbecues were a last stand. New-found friends. A raise
in pay. Of course they put on a front during the barbecues. But
every time I heard their singing I could foresee today.
REUBEN: How?
RACHEL: She had that gaunt look. Woman against the wall.
REUBEN: He left the good car for her. He drove the old jalopy.
(*Hopefully*) Maybe they're just tired of their things. Want to start
over—with new things.
RACHEL: No. They had a row. A lot of rows. He failed an exam. He
said it was her fault he failed. He said she was too demanding.
REUBEN: Poor kid. He was trying to better himself.
RACHEL: She wanted to sing in the Civic Opera. He didn't like the
way those people carry on—always kissing each other.
REUBEN: He was the one who sang at all the barbecues. I never heard
her sing.
REUBEN: She used to sing. When they first moved in she sang like a
fallen angle.
REUBEN: (*Irritated*) Why fallen? Why not like an angel?
RACHEL: Her song had a falling sound. They weren't angelic songs.
The opposite. A falling sound.
REUBEN: Where was I when she was singing?
RACHEL: Cleaning your fish tank or down at the corner hobnobbing
with old Ginger and his cronies.

REUBEN: Ginger's in hospital. Extended care.

RACHEL: His asthma?

REUBEN: Emphysema. No breath left.

RACHEL: Too bad. I wondered why you haven't been going down to get the paper.

REUBEN: I'll go tomorrow. I just have to adjust. Anyway, what have I missed? Wars, kidnappings, Murders.

RACHEL: All those obituaries you read.

REUBEN: So? I have to keep up. After all, it's better to know than to ask about someone after that someone's dead. Remember you wrote that sympathy letter to Arnold Burns and his wife hadn't died at all. You listen to gossip. I wait for the obituary.

RACHEL: If you can trust the papers.

REUBEN: You can trust them when it comes to the obituary. They can't afford to misrepresent a person's death. In fact, I understand they have them all ready, waiting for you.

RACHEL: Only if you're important. (*Slight pause*) I expect they have yours ready.

REUBEN: (*Shyly pleased*) Do you think so? Well, I suppose. . . . head of repairs for the Telephone Company. . .

RACHEL: Vice chairman of the Kinsman Park committee. . .

REUBEN: So I was. I'd forgot that, Rachel. I suppose I could go down to that newspaper office and read what they have to say about me.

RACHEL: Better not, Reb. What's happening now?

REUBEN: Crang's setting up the coffee urn. They're going to serve refreshments to the customers. You know I saw him in the store last week he was buying light bulbs—5 year warranty. (*Pause*) He must have felt secure then. She's bringing out some sort of harp.

RACHEL: (*Moving to him*) Her auto harp. Oh, I hate to see her selling that. She used to play the auto harp and sing. . . She'd sit out by the electric fountain and play and sing and her hair hung down in ringlets, like that song.

REUBEN: One of the roving kind.

RACHEL: He was the rover. Her singing drove him mad. He'd say "For God's sake, can't you sing something cheerful."

REUBEN: "Roll out the Barrel." Around the barbecue they sang "Roll out the barrel."

RACHEL: I wonder how much she wants for that auto harp?

REUBEN: Why would you want an auto harp, Rae? We've more stuff now than we need, cluttering up the place.

RACHEL: There you go again, disparaging my afghans.
> (*She turns from him and goes back to take up the jug of water and in next sequence moves towards the bird bath with it.*)

REUBEN: Well, face it. We've no room for any more. (*back to glasses*) He's looking at the bird cage. It's empty! They've lost the bird.

RACHEL: She was cleaning the cage. The budgie slipped through her fingers. She tried to catch it.

REUBEN: Where would it go?

RACHEL: Away. It blew away.

REUBEN: (*Cross*) You mean it flew. It flew away.

RACHEL: I meant what I said, Reuben. The budgie blew away.

REUBEN: Oh, I don't like that.

(*Pause.*)

RACHEL: (*At bird bath*) Reuben, suppose we had one. . .

REUBEN: A budgie?

RACHEL: Just supposing. What would we sell?

REUBEN: Oh. You want a garage sale?

RACHEL: Well, it would get rid of clutter.

REUBEN: We'd be in the stream of things. We'd be keeping up.

RACHEL: What would we give over?

REUBEN: What would we keep? That's the ultimate, definitive decision?

RACHEL: Ultimate. Definitive. You're always harping on that these days. There's time enough for that.

REUBEN: The mounted deer head. I'd sell that.

RACHEL: You were proud of that six pointer. Boasted. There'd be a light place on the wall where it was hanging. They always leave a shadow on the wall.

REUBEN: I wouldn't shoot the deer now. That was my hunting stage.

RACHEL: I doubt you could shoot it now.

REUBEN: Why not? (*holding out hand*) Well, perhaps a tremor. Nothing to worry about. We'd sell those partridge feathers.

RACHEL: I always meant to do something with them. Make something.

REUBEN: A nest?

RACHEL: A fan to stir the wind. It gets close here.

REUBEN: There's a perambulator in the basement. Antique perambulators are worth a lot today.

RACHEL: No. Daphne might need that. Those years you went to war, I put John and the twins in and wheeled them all down to post those blue air mail letters. I was so afraid something would happen to the children while you were away.

REUBEN: I knew you'd manage. Hey, that China dog Aunt Connie gave me when I was on leave.

RACHEL: That China dog was a present, a good door stop.

REUBEN: I always hated it. Mean eyes, staring at me.

RACHEL: Well, if you're selling presents, what about the gold watch the telephone company gave you? You never use it.

REUBEN: I might use it. For ceremonies. It's my ceremonial watch.

RACHEL: The cowboy boots and hat John didn't want. Why have we still got them?

REUBEN: Maybe.

RACHEL: The shot gun!

Gwen Pharis Ringwood

REUBEN: No. Not the shot gun. A man never knows when he may
have to stand up and be counted. I notice the things you want to
sell are all mine. You can't play fast and loose with other
people's things!

RACHEL: You make the list then.

REUBEN: The Afghans. I'd get rid of them all—lock, stock and barrel.

RACHEL: I thought so.

REUBEN: We'd see the furniture again. The clean lines of the Morris
chair, the sofa, the oak table, the piano.

RACHEL: We'd see the holes and scars and dints and dents.

REUBEN: You'd have your hands free. You could use your hands
for—other things.

RACHEL: What?

REUBEN: Well, kneading bread. Dialing the telephone. You never
use the telephone any more.

RACHEL: The lines are always busy.
        (*Brief pause*)

REUBEN: Patting. You could use your hands for patting.

RACHEL: What would I pat? The China dog? You've sold it.

REUBEN: Me? You used to pat me. You never pat me any more. Too
busy crotcheting.

RACHEL: That's a silly word. Childish.

REUBEN: I pat you.

RACHEL: You slap me on the bottom. "How are you, old girl" you say
and you slap me on the bottom.

REUBEN: I won't do it again. Mark my words. Not again. Not ever.

RACHEL: Good.

REUBEN: You'll see! (*pause*) Well, what else do we get rid of?

RACHEL: My old fur coat.

REUBEN: You'd sell that? I bought you that coat when the twins were
born. The daughters. I went in debt to buy that coat.

RACHEL: It's muskrat. I wanted Hudson seal.

REUBEN: Why didn't you say so?

RACHEL: You never asked. You brought the muskrat home and I was
too young to tell you, but inside I was crying.

REUBEN: For Hudson seal? That's *dyed* muskrat, Rachel.

RACHEL: So? Now you know.

REUBEN: Sell it. By all means. Sell it. Don't think of my feelings in the
matter.

RACHEL: The National Geographics. Forty years of them. They're
probably worth a fortune now. It's not as if we ever traveled
much.

REUBEN: That's why we had the Goegraphics. Our minds were free
to travel.

RACHEL: We'd sell that Globe. It still shows Persia, Siam, Macedonia.
They're gone long ago. All gone.

560

REUBEN: (*Upset*) Where? Where did they go? They couldn't drop into the bottom of the sea like lost Atlantis. I ask you, where did they go, Rachel?

RACHEL: They were swallowed up. Changed. Re-christened. I would have liked a coat of Persian lamb.

REUBEN: I couldn't sell the National Geographics or the Globe. It would be like selling dreams.

RACHEL: Dreams aren't worth much—not mine, anyway.

REUBEN: Day dreams, Rachel. The things you dream when you're awake. You know.

RACHEL: I'm not sure I do.

REUBEN: "A rose red city twice as old as time. . ." or was it "dawn". I'm there at the gates about to enter as the sun's rays touch the highest minaret. "My name is Ozymandias, king of kings, Look on my works, ye Mighty, and despair." I'm in the desert now— Sand everywhere you look, Sand and sky and a fallen obelisk.

RACHEL: (*Softly*) You always were one for the poetry.

REUBEN: Yes. Yes, I was.

RACHEL: In my sleep, I dream the same thing often.

REUBEN: A recurrent dream. They call that a recurrent dream.

RACHEL: I dream of the missed appointment.

REUBEN: Oh?

RACHEL: It's very important that I reach this place. . . this meeting place on time. I've promised, said I'd be there, checked my watch, turned all the right corners but each time something. . . someone. . . delays me. I begin to hurry, try harder, explain I mustn't tarry. The clock's hands move on and frantically I strain to get there. Too late. Too late. I wake up trying to explain why I wasn't there for. . . that important appointment.

REUBEN: Who with? Why were you going, Rachel?

RACHEL: I don't know. It's just that I want to keep my promise. . . try. Something. . . someone delays me.

REUBEN: (*Tenderly*) You can't hurry any faster than you can, Rachel. You do your best.

RACHEL: One's best is never good enough.

REUBEN: Don't say that.

RACHEL: Well, is it?

REUBEN: I used to think it was. I think it is. I hope so. (*Pause. He touches her.*) You seemed to think it was. Isn't it.

RACHEL: Oh, that. Yes, it was. Is.

REUBEN: You're blushing.

RACHEL: Who wouldn't? The way you go on.

REUBEN: I could go and price that waterbed. Would you like me to?

RACHEL: Don't be licentious, Reuben.

REUBEN: Rabelaisian. That's a nicer word. Rabelaisian.

RACHEL: Men. One thing on their minds.

Gwen Pharis Ringwood

REUBEN: You wouldn't want me different. (*Pause. He moves away from her towards front.*) Was the missed appointment—did that have to do with us, Rachel. With me?

RACHEL: Are they still outside? Has anybody come?

REUBEN: (*Demanding*) Answer me, Rachel. Did it?

RACHEL: No. No, it was something else. Nothing to do with you, Reuben—with us. The children, perhaps. The world outside.

REUBEN: (*Moving to her.*) Remember that fall picnic and the muskrat coat? You put it down, spread it out, and we lay on it together. I never forgot that picnic. It was the best picnic we ever went on together.

RACHEL: (*Sharply*) All right. We'll keep the muskrat coat.

REUBEN: And the National Geographics. They're our life line. What about the books?

RACHEL: Those high school years' books. No one will ever look at them. And all those "how to do and how to eat and how to live". . . let's get rid of them. We're beyond them. It's come down to that.

REUBEN: Come down to what?

RACHEL: To us and it.

REUBEN: It?

RACHEL: Whatever's outside the skin. Outside the casing. You know.

REUBEN: Yes, I know. The Whatever.
          (*Pause.*)

RACHEL: We'll put the books out then.

REUBEN: The jade tree. I see they've put their tree out.

RACHEL: Yes. He should never have brought home that tree without consulting her.

REUBEN: A very exotic tree. What kind?

RACHEL: He called it a Yucca tree.

REUBEN: A touch of the tropics in his living room.

RACHEL: She hated it. She wanted something softer, not so spiny.

REUBEN: It's spiny all right. Spiny as an aardvaark. More suitable for the lobby of a zoo.

RACHEL: Those were almost her exact words, Reuben. Fancy you're saying that. Has anybody come?

REUBEN: No. But it's only a quarter to. . . Rachel, do you suppose if we put some music on the phonograph, opened the windows wide, so they had to listen. . .?

RACHEL: What kind of music?

REUBEN: You know. Music to stir the heart. Scheherezade. The Surry with the Fringe on Top. Going my Way. That might give them pause. They'd remember all their days and nights and cancel the whole operation.

RACHEL: The music might wake the baby. They both get upset when the baby cries. (*Moving*) There's one dead branch on the plum tree.

REUBEN: I'll prune it.

RACHEL: Not now. After it blooms.

REUBEN: He's brought the mugs out. We might go over and have a cup of coffee.

RACHEL: They'd think we're prying.

REUBEN: We'll say we plan to have a garage sale of our own, want to find out how to go about it. We'll buy some little thing and we'll get talking. I'll just happen to mention the time you left me and went to Minneapolis to visit your cousin Opal. I thought I'd lost you, Rachel.

RACHEL: I was lost myself that fall. Nothing seemed right between us. The house was never tidy. Measles, mumps. John fell off the swing and broke his arm.

REUBEN: That was my fault. I didn't put the swing up right.

RACHEL: That old stove with the oven that wouldn't heat. My cakes always fell. And you. . . you didn't seem to have any time for us—for me.

REUBEN: (*Outraged*) It was the other way. You shut me out. All your time went to the children. You were so pretty, and you'd turn away. . . Then one day I came home and you'd gone. You and the children.

RACHEL: You knew Opal sent the tickets, Reb.

REUBEN: I didn't think you'd use them. I didn't think you'd go.

RACHEL: I wouldn't have, but you started to help those Legion women paint the hall.

REUBEN: Rae!

RACHEL: Well, it was inconsiderate. Out every night painting away with Jane and Sophy while I'm home cleaning and washing and taking care of. . . How could you do that, Reb? That's awful.

REUBEN: Rae, Jane was old enough to be my mother. And as for Sophy. . . Oh, you're impossible. Taking off on a flimsy excuse like that!

RACHEL: It wasn't flimsy. Not to me! I wanted you to know how it feels to sit home alone.

REUBEN: You managed that all right!

(*Pause*)

RACHEL: I only meant to be gone a week, but then I found out the return ticket couldn't be used until a month was up.

REUBEN: You could have written. I would have sent money for tickets.

RACHEL: I was too proud to ask. It seems foolish now.

REUBEN: I'd come home and play the music loud so I wouldn't hear my own feet walking in an empty house.

RACHEL: I thought that month would never end.

REUBEN: You and the children came through that gate, and it was raining.

RACHEL: The door was locked. We never locked the door. I thought you'd gone.

Gwen Pharis Ringwood

REUBEN: I locked it. To gain time.

RACHEL: To gain time?

REUBEN: I was crying, Rachel. Men weren't allowed to cry.

RACHEL: So that was it. I always wondered. We couldn't tell them about Minneapolis, Reb. That's too personal.

REUBEN: I suppose we couldn't. What about the books? You know, that book on marriage—Ideal Marriage. I always thought it did *you* good. And there's another one about mirroring the anger, softening the blow. I could just casually toss them over the fence. They might help.

RACHEL: I think not, Reuben. Best not to interfere. Let things take their course.

REUBEN: They're both out now. She's fed the baby.

RACHEL: Bottle?

REUBEN: Breast.

RACHEL: That's nice.

REUBEN: Yes, she's pretty. Too thin, but pretty.

RACHEL: The baby keeps her thin.

REUBEN: Rachel, if they're breaking up, you don't think. . . They wouldn't give up the baby. Would they?

RACHEL: The Longs did. The minute their garage sale was over, they farmed out all five children, hit and miss. Couldn't get rid of them fast enough.

REUBEN: The baby's back in the laundry basket. These two keep their faces turned away from each other. Their faces are like masks. Did we do that?

RACHEL: We did. Do.

REUBEN: Punishing?

RACHEL: Protecting.

REUBEN: From each other?

RACHEL: From. . . Whatever.
    (*Pause.*)
    I could finish off this Afghan. Take it over. I'd say "this is for your baby to keep it warm." No. I'd say "this is for you to keep your baby warm."

REUBEN: To protect it from Whatever. Poor baby! They haven't any right to give it up. None at all.

RACHEL: It's their garage sale, Reuben.

REUBEN: Well, if they're looking for a foster home. . . Couldn't we. . .?

RACHEL: At our age? Social services would never allow such a thing.

REUBEN: We could lie. Say we'd found it somewhere. . . among the asparagus stalks. We could say we're the grandparents. That we're holding it in trust.

RACHEL: We'd get a puppy for it.

REUBEN: Puppy?

RACHEL: A cocker spaniel. They're the best. Remember Foxy. The twins grew up with Foxy. She protected them. Oh Reb, wouldn't it be wonderful? I'd learn to play the auto harp. I'd sing to it.

REUBEN: I'd teach it all that poetry from the Golden Treasury. "They are not long, the weeping and the laughter, Love and desire and hate. . ."

RACHEL: We'd paint the spare bedroom with flowers and little rabbits, and I'd put up a mobile. We never had one.

REUBEN: "And dreaming through the twilight
That doth not rise or set
Haply I may remember, or haply forget."
No, that's too sad. I'd have to brush up on Father William.

RACHEL: There's a high chair in the basement.

REUBEN: He's chain smoking. She's on her knees.

RACHEL: Oh, no. Begging?

REUBEN: Not her. She'd die before she'd beg. She's sorting something.

RACHEL: What?

REUBEN: I can't see. Is it important?

RACHEL: It could be.

REUBEN: Oh, it's nothing. A pile of towels marked *His* and *Hers*.

RACHEL: That used to be the style.

REUBEN: She's looking up this way.

RACHEL: Perhaps she hopes the budgie will come back. Such a beautiful blue it was. . . like a saphire, flying. Get back!

REUBEN: She can't see me. Classical, her face I mean. Oval, with dark eyes.

RACHEL: Hmm. I hadn't noticed. (*She is jealous*)

REUBEN: (*Oblivious to Rachel's reaction*) "Is this the face that launched a thousand ships And burnt the topless towers of Ilium?" He's handing her a drink. They lift their glasses as if they're toasting one another. Hail and farewell. Ave atque Vale. "I have been faithful to thee, Cynara, in my fashion."
(*Sound of cars arriving next door.*)
Oh dear, the rummagers are arriving! We haven't much time left!

RACHEL: Time?

REUBEN: To save them from themselves. Rachel! Suppose I bring out The Golden Treasury and pretend I'm reading that poem out loud to you, but louder so they'll hear. Do you suppose that would make a dent?

RACHEL: The one about being faithful?

REUBEN: It's worth a try. It might make them see that they're sitting among the best days of their lives. I'll get that book.
(*He starts towards door*)

RACHEL: (*Getting up to look across*) I think it's too late, Reb. The sale's begun. It's no time for poetry.

Gwen Pharis Ringwood

REUBEN: (*Returning*) You're right. They'd never hear me. The rummaging, the twisting and the turning, the hunting down the bargains. It's all begun! There's tags on everything. Oh, oh, there goes the waterbed!

RACHEL: (*Moving away from him in agitation*) I'd better finish this off, in case—you don't think it's too gaudy?

REUBEN: What.

RACHEL: This Afghan. For the baby.

REUBEN: No—it's the best one you've fabricated. Far the best. It looks like they've sold the barbecue. Oh, I don't like that.

RACHEL: What!

REUBEN: Someone's taking away the crib.

RACHEL: Where's the baby?

REUBEN: Still in the laundry basket. Crang's putting a record on the stereo.

RACHEL: Is there a tag on the basket?

REUBEN: Yes. Yes, there is. They'll probably sell the basket right out from under the baby. Put the baby in a cardboard box. There goes the Yucca tree, thank heaven. She looks pleased.
        (*Sound of music*)

RACHEL: Why do they play their music so loud?

REUBEN: To fill the emptiness. Oh no, no! Hold on there! Hold on.

RACHEL: What's happening?

REUBEN: Someone's looking at the baby. Measuring it. Weighing it. I feel like going over there and. . .

RACHEL: She can't give up that baby. It's not weaned! You can't wean a baby without notice!

REUBEN: They are, There's a bottle in that basket. It's true, Rae. I think it's true. They're giving up that child. A girl not more than seventeen has the baby in one arm and the basket in the other. Money's exchanging hands.

RACHEL: She's much too young. How can they be so irresponsible? Maybe we're much too old. May we're not legal, but we've had experience. We know what babies need.

REUBEN: I'm going over there. I'll tell them what I think of parents who don't live up to their responsibilities.

RACHEL: We'll take it. . . if they have to give it up.

REUBEN: Right.
        (*He starts off*)

RACHEL: Tell them they don't have to pay us.

REUBEN: We'll pay them.
        (*He goes again*)

RACHEL: Right. Have you got your check book? In case they want a deposit?

REUBEN: I've got it.

RACHEL: Throw in the jade Tree and the National Geographics, Reuben. The China dog. (*To plum tree*) Well, Tree, something

566

important is happening, so forget what I said about not hurrying! (*Indignantly*) Of course we can look after that baby- We'll guard and protect it for them—at least until they come to their senses. There goes Reb! He's so excited. He shouldn't tear off like that, though. It can't be good for his heart. Calm down, Reb. Take it easy. Please. Take your time. He's doing it. He's making an offer!

(*She looks through the field glasses.*)

Waving his cheque book—telling them about the perambulator and the high chair, ready—waiting. I hope he remembers the puppy. The puppy, Reb. The puppy. Oh dear, they're. . . why, they're. . . How could they? Dear Reb, I should never have let him go and face that loud music all alone. He's looking up this way. I'll pretend I didn't see. (*She puts field glasses down.*) He looks all right, I think. Well, Tree, you can forget what I said about forgetting what I said about. . . better just stand by till I. . . I'll go to meet him. No, he wouldn't want me to. I'd better just stand by too. I'll pretend I'm. . . (*She moves to crocheting, trying to hide her agitation.* (REUBEN *returns*) Oh, Reb. You're back! I'm just finishing this off. Are you all right?

REUBEN: Fine. I'm fine.

RACHEL: Oh, I'm glad.

REUBEN: It's not what we thought though. Over there. That girl's just a sitter they hired for the day. Until the sale is over.

RACHEL: Oh.

REUBEN: It's not your ordinary garage sale.

RACHEL: Oh.

REUBEN: Young Crang's been transferred. To Thailand.

RACHEL: I see.

REUBEN: They're both going. Taking the baby too. Divesting themselves of everything else, but taking the baby. It's a girl. Good thing I. . . Good thing we. . .

RACHEL: Found out.

REUBEN: Yes. Crang said they wouldn't dream of leaving her behind.

RACHEL: Oh, that's good. But we were standing by—in case—No reason to blame ourselves.

REUBEN: They laughed at me, Rae. When I offered to. . . They all laughed. (*He tries to hide his agitation.*)

RACHEL: That's rude. I hope you. . .

REUBEN: Oh, I carried it off. Pretended I was joking. Said I really came about the trail bike.

RACHEL: Well, you did think about buying that trail bike.

REUBEN: Rae, I went charging in there, shouting about responsibility, waving my cheque book, offering a home for a baby they never thought of giving up. I wanted to sink into the ground.

Gwen Pharis Ringwood

RACHEL: You couldn't know it wasn't like the Longs.
REUBEN: (*He is very upset*) I offered them money. Just like those pirates in that baby market on the radio. Old fool—meddling in other peoples's lives. That's what I am. An old fool.
RACHEL: (*Striving to give him back his self-esteem*) You did it for me. I got carried away.
REUBEN: She. . . she felt sorry for me, I think. She asked us to come to see the baby—after the sale. But I couldn't face them again—
RACHEL: (*Resolutely*) Why not? We'll go, Reb. We'll show them we're glad they're a family. We'll take them this afghan.. . . (*Wistfully*) I'd like to see that baby.
REUBEN: Hm. A Hail and Farewell Afghan. Suitable. Oriental word.
RACHEL: It's my last one. My last Afghan.
REUBEN: No?
RACHEL: It is. It's time I have my hands free for other things.
REUBEN: Patting?
RACHEL: Men! But I wouldn't want you different, Reb. Where's Thailand?
REUBEN: It's the old Siam. It's on the globe.
RACHEL: You envy them going there.
REUBEN: Oh no. Face it, I'm too old to go traipsing off. . .
RACHEL: Not you. I'm the one. I've been sitting around waiting for a child to come home ever since. . . ever since Doris died. I'm the one, Reb.
REUBEN: You know we could go to Italy, to see Daphne, if you want to.
RACHEL: No. She's busy. But we could go somewhere else.
REUBEN: Nigeria?
RACHEL: John doesn't need us either.
REUBEN: Where then?
RACHEL: Oh, Macedonia. Peru. Wherever. You choose the first step and we'll go on from there.
REUBEN: (*Thinking she's not serious*) You really had your hopes set on that baby, didn't you.
RACHEL: Hah! I forgot about walking the floor at night, croup, measles. Go on, Reb, choose.
REUBEN: You don't think it's too late?
RACHEL: Too late?
REUBEN: Your dream. The missed appointment?
RACHEL: But we'll be together. Go on, Reb, choose.
(*She spins the globe.*)
REUBEN: Here goes then. Samothrace! Hah. The isles of Greece. "The Isles of Greece, where burning Sapho loved and sang." Let's go!

568

RACHEL: Well, we. . . we can't go tomorrow, Reb.
REUBEN: Oh.
RACHEL: First we have to. . . you know. . . get rid of the clutter.
REUBEN: Oh.
RACHEL: Don't we?
REUBEN: I suppose so. Right. But when?
RACHEL: What about—Saturday?
REUBEN: Next Saturday? Why not? We'll have it. We'll put up a sign.
   "Saturday. Ten o'clock. The Ultimate, Definitive Garage Sale."

The End

The Furies
A Tragedy in One Scene.

Characters

MARTHA, *between 50 and 60 years old*
CELESTINE, *about 50 years old*
SELINA, *a strong old woman of 84 years*
ANNE MARIE, *about 17*
ELLEN, *also 17*
JOSEPHINE, *18 years of age*
ROSE, *16*
SELINA, *(as a young girl of 14)*

TIME: *Somewhere near the present and seventy years in the past.*
SETTING: *The stage indicates a rocky, uneven space with a looming platform like a high rock back stage left. The trunk of a huge fir tree grows from the rock and its unseen branches cast shadows on the stage. Front stage there may be a rock and a large log for sitting on.*
SOUND: *The sound of wind—eerie, musical is needed at times. Music may be substituted.*
COSTUMES: *The old women are dressed in heavy skirts, worn wool sweaters, heavy shoes. The young women wear soft straight dresses, beaded belts, necklaces and moccasins. These costumes are neither strongly Indian or white. A kind of 1910 compromise that does not call attention to the design, but is youthful and attractive.*
PLAYING TIME: *about one half hour.*

MARTHA: That's a cold wind, Celestine. I'm shivering.
CELESTINE: Build up the fire then.

571

Gwen Pharis Ringwood

MARTHA: There is no wood here. This is barren ground.
CELESTINE: That dead branch under the old fir would burn.
MARTHA: I'm afraid to go up there.
CELESTINE: These juniper roots will burn for a long time, Martha.
MARTHA: There is no heat in them.
CELESTINE: I brought them to keep away bad spirits. And they smell nice burning.
MARTHA: You are shivering too.
CELESTINE: It's cold all right—for spring.
MARTHA: My grandmother told me that once the lightning burned all around this place. Lightning cracked the high rock and burned up everything alive, except the old fir up there.
CELESTINE: I have seen the scars the lightning made.
MARTHA: My grandmother said the tree was not touched because the spirits guard it. Because of what happened here.
CELESTINE: The old ones make up stories, Martha, to keep the young girls close. I made up such stories for my girls.
MARTHA: I think it was no story of what happened here.
CELESTINE: It was so long ago. After so long it's hard to tell what's true and what's made up.
MARTHA: There is blood in this ground, and voices in the air.
CELESTINE: The wind in the fir tree, Martha.
MARTHA: You don't believe that. Listen. (*a sound of wind, like music*) Don't you hear voices crying?
CELESTINE: I hear the wind.
MARTHA: (*moving left*) I want to go back down. I think old Selina put a spell on us, or we would not be here.
CELESTINE: We gave our word to meet her, Martha.
MARTHA: Why can't we meet her down there, where the road turns?
CELESTINE: She told us to wait here.
MARTHA: The road used to go under the tree. The people moved it away from here. For years the road has gone around this place. I'm afraid of that old woman with her songs and spells.
CELESTINE: If we don't keep our word, she could put a spell on us.
MARTHA: She can mimic the voice of the loon and raven. They say she can leave her body and mingle with the spirits. Do you believe that?
CELESTINE: Perhaps.
MARTHA: Now she brings us here. Why, Celestine, why?
CELESTINE: I think it has to do with Lucy Johnny's death. I think Selina heard something yesterday about her grandchild's dying.
MARTHA: Lucy was not Selina's grandchild. You know that.
CELESTINE: Lucy called Selina "grandma". Selina raised Lucy from a baby.
MARTHA: That old cabin across the river was no place for a child. No wonder Lucy ran away. Selina was too old to raise a child.
CELESTINE: Yes, but when Lucy ran away, I think the sun's light went out for old Selina.

MARTHA: Lucy Johnny died on the edge of the town. Not here. And she is buried by that cabin across the river—not up here, with them.

CELESTINE: Since Lucy's death, Selina comes here often. As if she waited for some message.

MARTHA: Let's get out of here. Go home. Why should we shiver up here at the wish of a crazy woman?

CELESTINE: (*pushing* MARTHA *down to sit on a rock near the fire.*) Sit down, Martha. Get hold of yourself. It is not crazy to mourn a loved one's death. A loved one's murder.

MARTHA: They did not call it murder in the courts.

CELESTINE: It was murder.

MARTHA: In the court they said Lucy Johnny died because she fell down and was too drunk to get up again. She ran out of the car, stripped off her clothes, and ran off to that gravel pit. It was the cold that killed her.

CELESTINE: Yes, they said that.

MARTHA: The three young men all swore they looked for Lucy Johnny and couldn't find her; and thought she'd got a ride with someone back to town. They swore that in the court.

CELESTINE: I was sitting in the court beside Selina and I think there were lies told in that room, before that judge. Lies.

MARTHA: I heard that Lucy went wild in town, crazy.

CELESTINE: Ayeyah. And in the court they said she went with men for money, and when these three had none she made them stop the car, ran away screaming curses at them. But there were bruises on her arms. . .

MARTHA: Where she fell down.

CELESTINE: Her shoes and clothes were found a long way from where she died, Martha. It's an old story. A young girl's rape and murder—and no one pays.

MARTHA: The young men went to jail.

CELESTINE: (*contemptuously*) Yes. For two years. Selina is right. What is two years for a young girl's life?

MARTHA: The old woman won't be alive to see them out of jail. And if she thinks I'm going to get mixed up in. . .

CELESTINE: Hush! She's coming.

(*They turn towards Stage Left where* SELINA *enters.*)

SELINA: Martha. Celestine. You keep your word.

CELESTINE: That is a steep climb for you, Selina.

SELINA: My feet remember the old road, where it came.

MARTHA: The people call this a forbidden place, Selina. They stay away from here. Why did you bring us here?

SELINA: From here we can watch the road down there each way, and see who comes.

CELESTINE: Some one else is coming?

SELINA: In an hour a wagon will come along the road and turn on the old trail and stop just below here. In an hour the wagon will come.

Gwen Pharis Ringwood

MARTHA: Who's coming?
SELINA: You must wait to know that.
MARTHA: Let's wait below then.
SELINA: No! It is here we wait. Stay, Martha. I will not die with secrets
    pressing down on me. You two will be witness of what I say here
    and what I do.
MARTHA: Selina, you are alone too much. You are sick with grieving
    over Lucy Johnny, crazy with your grief. Lucy is dead, Selina.
    Nothing can change that. . . tell her, Celestine, tell her she can't
    change things. Make her come home with us.
CELESTINE: We keep our word, Selina. What do you want of us?
SELINA: Swear you will be witness to what I say here and what I do.
CELESTINE: I swear.
SELINA: And you, Martha?
MARTHA: I. . . don't know.
CELESTINE: If you would sleep at night, I tell you, swear.
MARTHA: I swear then.
SELINA: I will need your help. I was young with your mothers and I
    knew your grandmothers and I know your children and their
    children. I have told the Chief you are to share what things I have
    in my cabin. You will find my things and Lucy's there. . . what
    we had. They will be yours. Not much, but what we lived with
    before Lucy left me. Except for this. . . this doll.
CELESTINE: This dress is fine velvet. . . with pearl beads.
SELINA: (turning the doll in her hand) And it had a white China face.
    You see.
MARTHA: Oh, her face. Someone's smashed her face. No, I don't want
    to touch it. Oh, I don't like this place. There is something that
    trembles in the air. . .
SELINA: Their voices, Martha. Young girls' voices. I hear them often.
    For more than seventy years I have heard their voices.
CELESTINE: You believe the legend?
SELINA: No legend, Celestine. Oh the story has been told here and
    there by this person and that person and always I kept silent. But
    I know what happened here. What happened here split my life in
    two as clean as an axe splits a young birch tree. Sit down,
    Celestine. Seventy years ago and I was young, young and alive as
    Lucy was before she left me. Our bloody tribute to the moon
    came on me at thirteen. Soon after I ran to a lover's arms,
    heedless of tomorrow. The old women's warnings fell on deaf
    ears as I ran with a high heart in that sweet, short summer. I
    burned with a woman's longing but I was still child enough to
    delight in the doll he gave me. . . this doll. . .
MARTHA: But its face. . .
SELINA: Smashed. With a rock. I smashed it.
    (SELINA *goes back to her story, standing like some ancient
    priestess recalling the past.*)

The salmon run was good and there was a celebration with music and drums and singing and dancing. The people came from all the neighboring reserves and from the ranches. I saw my man ride down the hill, tether his horse, join in the dancing, and my heart soared like a young eagle flying. I waited, waited for him to dance with me, and my eyes followed him as if he were a young god dancing. Then I got a message, and I came here to this rock, this old tree, thinking to meet my lover. And what happened here split my life in two as clean as the axe splits a young birch tree.

(*Music and drums and wind rise in crescendo as the lights change. The old women become shadows on the edge of the stage as Selina's story is played out.* ANNE MARIE *eyes blazing, runs in, stands looking up at the great tree.* ELLEN *follows her in.*)

ELLEN: Where is he, Anne-Marie? Where is Jacques LaRange?

ANNE MARIE: He'll come here. I promise.

ELLEN: You said he'd meet me here. Now I've left the dance and he's not here. You're playing some joke on me.

ANNE MARIE: I play no joke, Ellen.

(JOSEPHINE *enters*)

JOSEPHINE: What kind of game is this? You said LaRange would come here. What are you doing here then? I thought you were my friend.

ANNE MARIE: There is something I must tell you, Josephina. And you too, Ellen.

ELLEN: Keep your secrets. I'm going back to the dance.

ANNE MARIE: No, wait. When the others are here, I'll tell you. Then you can go back, if that is what you want.

(YOUNG SELINA *and* ROSE *enter Left.*)

ROSE: So, Anne Marie. Is this a trick? Why are these others here? Selina says you told her the same story you told me. You said I was to wait up here for Jacques LaRange.

JOSEPHINE: Why would you wait for him, Rose? LaRange is my man.

ROSE: That's not true.

JOSEPHINE: The priest will marry us in the spring. Then we leave this place and go back to his own country.

ELLEN: I don't believe you.

JOSEPHINE: Tell her, Anne Marie. LaRange asked you to bring me here so we can make plans together.

ELLEN: This bracelet. I showed it to Anne Marie. It was his gift to me.

ANNE MARIE: Rose has a ring. Is that not so, Rose? Show them.

JOSEPHINE: How did you get his ring?

ROSE: He gave it to me.

ANNE MARIE: I have a ring too. And what gift did he give you, Selina? Tell them.

SELINA: No.

ANNE MARIE: Tell them.

SELINA: It was a doll. This doll.

ANNE MARIE: You see.

ELLEN: So. He gave you presents. To me he gave his word. You are jealous, Anne Marie. I saw you dancing with my man and whispering. I saw you leave the dance with him. Now I'm going back down there and tell him how you lie.

ANNE MARIE: You know I speak truth, Ellen. You all know now. . . and why we are here, all five. I too have seen pictures of the house that's like a palace, Josephina. And I wear this locket that he gave me the first night we were together at the meadow. Look at me, all of you. Tonight at the dance he was boasting about his nights of love with us. Boasting as a hunter boasts when he has brought down many deer. We were a kind of sport for Jacques LaRange. He named us all by name. And so I pried into your secrets, found out what trinkets he offered, promises. Oh he makes a fool of each of us. You saw him drinking and laughing with his friends. It was at us they laughed.

SELINA: You would not lie to me, Anne Marie?

ANNE MARIE: I don't lie, Selina. We have no secrets now. By tomorrow every one will know.

ELLEN: He told me we would marry. And now you say he laughs?

ANNE MARIE: He pointed out each one of us by name to the strangers who came with him from up the river. To him we were easy targets, like fool hens sitting in a tree to be picked off one by one.

JOSEPHINE: My mother told me it would be this way. She said I should keep to my own kind. Blood is blood, she said.

ELLEN: Yes, they told us. Keep to your tribe that has been made small by strangers' gifts. Replenish the tribe now small from the small pox and lung sickness and whiskey. I wouldn't listen.

ANNE MARIE: Right now our names are made ugly to the young men of our tribe. Tonight our young men feel ashamed for us.

ELLEN: You say he laughed at us?

ANNE MARIE: My face burned when I heard my name. And yours. All of you. Yes, he laughed.

ROSE: Our people will be ashamed.

ANNE MARIE: Now do you believe me, Ellen?

ELLEN: I believe you. And hate burns inside me like a fire.

SELINA: I can't believe he'd laugh. He was gentle. His mouth was like a flower on my mouth. He said he'd take me to live in a house lit with a thousand candles, and I'd wear velvet dresses like this doll. I think I have his child inside me.

ANNE MARIE: Selina! You, a child yourself.

SELINA: I'm fourteen. I was going to tell him tonight so we would be married and everyone would honor me and the child I carry. But I had no chance to tell him.

JOSEPHINE: You think they would honor you, Selina? Oh no. When I went with him I knew I risked dishonor in the tribe. I've seen our people, look at these strangers, look with masked faces, their eyes burning with anger. They would not honor you or any of us. We have been stripped naked and thrown down like toys.

ELLEN: Did he tell you of the room in that house where all his ancestors are painted on the walls and that you too would be painted and look down from those walls. Did he tell you that?

SELINA: He told me.

ROSE: And me. I hate him now.

ANNE MARIE: You see, he told the same story to each one of us and each of us believed him.

ELLEN: He'll pay. I'll make him pay. For sixteen years I was happy here, fished the dark river, hunted with my father for moose in winter, gathered sweet berries with my sisters in the coulee, and the old songs drummed in my blood. I thought to marry into the Canoe Creek tribe, a Chief's son. Then LaRange rode by, stopped beside a silent pool where I fished for trout, and my blood turned to water. I forgot my family, my tribe, the Chief's son. I thought to follow him half way across the world.

SELINA: He seemed like a young prince out of a story book I saw once, or some god come down to earth.

JOSEPHINE: Some god—who lies and cheats and promises false dreams —who spills his seed as careless as weeds in summer. I feel now that I knew he was lying, but I was too blind to see. And now we are shamed before the people. (*to* ELLEN) You said LaRange will pay. How will he pay?

ELLEN: I have a knife. It is not a big knife but it is sharp—

SELINA: You'd kill him? No.

ELLEN: With this knife.

ANNE MARIE: And you would hang for it.

ELLEN: A knife can be used more than once.

SELINA: I couldn't kill him. No.

JOSEPHINE: You are soft, Selina. How can you care what happens to someone who promises all of us, says the same words, tells the same lies to all of us, all five? You, with his child inside you. Of all of us, you should think of killing.

ELLEN: We are fools to stand here arguing. Let us go back down and Anne Marie will call him outside, bring him out to where we stand waiting, and then. . .

JOSEPHINE: We'll use the knife. Bring him to the ground.

ELLEN: Stab him. Each one of us. . .

JOSEPHINE: Until his blood flows and bathes our mouths and hands.

ELLEN: We'll wrench him from life into the shadow country. Then run with his corpse under the full moon.

ROSE: There will be thorns in his eyes and cactus in his mouth that told us lies.

JOSEPHINE: We can drink from his skull, and wash ourselves in his blood and our own tears.

ELLEN: We'll watch his life slip slowly, drained by our woman's rage and thirst for vengeance. And when he dies, we'll run together across the hills, crying like ravens, howling like wind song. We'll rage as the spirits rage, when the Shaman sets them loose, and dance like the ghost lights of the northern sky.

JOSEPHINE: I have a knife too.

ROSE: And I. Shall we go now, Ellen?

ANNE MARIE: Wait!

JOSEPHINE: Where is your knife, Anne Marie? Why do you hang back?

ANNE MARIE: I brought you here.

ELLEN: Come then. Join with us.

ANNE MARIE: I have a better plan than killing. We can do worse than kill him—worse and better. . .

ELLEN: How?

ANNE MARIE: Think for a moment. We are here now by the trail LaRange takes when the dawn breaks. He'll ride here flushed with his drinking and his own high words, come singing along this trail, and as he mounts the rise with the sun rising and the moon still in the sky, what will he see?

ELLEN: The old tree. The rock up there. What else?

ANNE MARIE: Oh, my plan is beautiful. Do what I say, and I promise you that from this morning he'll never know a single night without the riding nightmare of what he sees here. He'll be afraid to go to sleep because of mocking dreams. He can flee across the world but his bad dreams will follow him. . .

JOSEPHINE: You'd let him go free! No! No!

ELLEN: To run away to his own country? No!

ANNE MARIE: Where he goes won't matter. Always the five of us will prick at his eyeballs, tear at his breast, stab at his brain until his lips foam with madness.

JOSEPHINE: She'd let him live. Not me. Come, Ellen, let us go down now.

ANNE MARIE: You came to meet with LaRange. It can be that way if you do what you must do.

ELLEN: Stop telling riddles, Anne Marie. What would you have us do?

ANNE MARIE: Together, the five of us—with our belts and necklaces and the rawhide laces that we wear—together he finds us hanging from that tree.

ELLEN: You want us to. . . .

ANNE MARIE: Together.

ROSE: Oh no, no.

ANNE MARIE: Oh, you are children if you think only of killing him. Then we are thrown into a strange jail, stand in court, sent to be hanged by a strange judge. Or if we live, we live on and our people tell and tell over how we listened to a stranger's lies and believed him and thought to end up in a palace wearing jewels. The people will scorn us and tell the story again and then again and the years will tramp us down. It is our people's way to choose death before shame. You know that. Think how it will be. He rides here, looks up to the big fir and sees us, all hanging down our black hair waving, our dresses dancing, our feet stepping on air, our empty reaching arms, our eyes staring at the nothing we have made of him.

SELINA: We will be a testimony, like when the priest comes.

ANNE MARIE: Yes, Selina. Like that. . . a testimony. We won't grow old or wrinkled with clawing hands and eyes red with sores. We won't weep over dead sons or lost daughters or unkept promises. They'll talk of us by campfires. Winter, summer they'll whisper our story as they net the great salmon, play LaHel, drum for us at Easter, whisper our names in the streets of cities, cry out for us—come back, come back. They'll say that on this dawn in a spring of the budding trees and running sap, here at this place we gave up the spring of our beginnings. They'll remember the sweet flesh of our breasts and thighs, the fever of our blood. Remember us forever as we hang here, warning betrayal, crying against false words and promises. We'll live as long as the memory of our people lives.

SELINA: You make it sound beautiful, Anne Marie.

ANNE MARIE: Oh, it will be beautiful. We gave love and it was spat out, but we become legend here.

SELINA: And they'd sing our names.

ANNE MARIE: Do any of you choose to die this sweet death with me?

JOSEPHINE: I choose. It is not the first time I have thought of dying. Often I think why not get over all the pain and join the shadow people. Let my blood water the trees, let flesh turn into grass, leave bones for coyotes, my brain with its big dreams be food for worms. It is not the first time I have thought of dying.

ROSE: The priest won't bury us.

ANNE MARIE: The people will bury us. Here. Our voices will sigh on the wind morning and evening and our tongues cry out and our laughter ripple along the river. And like you say, little one, the people will sing our names.

ELLEN: I don't know. I still thirst to kill. . .

ANNE MARIE: And end up with a rope around your neck in a strange cell far away? Think, Ellen.

ELLEN: I won't have them judge me. I would kill myself first. I choose your way.

ROSE: I'm a coward, Anne Marie. Afraid.

ANNE MARIE: Go back down then. Back to where he and his friends shake with laughter and drink to the ways we give ourselves in love.

ROSE: I won't go first.

ANNE MARIE: We go together. We climb to that rock above the fir tree and jump then into the waiting branches. The tree's arms won't betray us.

ROSE: We will be buried here, together?

JOSEPHINE: I think our people will bring us down and bury us here together.

SELINA: And in the spring the sun flowers will spread down across this hillside.

JOSEPHINE: And the roots of the old tree will find us and the tree will send out new branches to the next spring and the next. And we'll be free of living, free of shame.

ELLEN: We'll move in the swaying birch trees and the thunder.

ANNE MARIE: Our spirits will warn against false promises. Cry out for honor. Oh, it will be beautiful. He'll come at dawn and see us and nothing will ever be the same. By this death we change things. . . We change the way things are.

JOSEPHINE: Our spirits will race over the hills and follow all false lovers until they're lost in madness and dark dreams.

ELLEN: Until they stand with no breath, frozen in fear.

SELINA: And the people will sing our names.

ANNE MARIE: (*Moving stage left and swaying with the sound from below in a kind of hypnotic trance. The others follow her. A sound of chanting and drums increases. The five maidens join in, chanting and moving gradually up the high slope. They move on until they are out of sight.*) Listen! They're singing now. The drums are sounding and the people singing. They sing the old songs, sound the old drum words. Soon he'll be coming. Listen!

(*Their faces become like masks as they take up the chant.*)

ANNE MARIE: Now. Now. We go up together. You first, Josephina and I will be at the last. Come, Selina. Give me your hand. It is now time.

(*The drums and chant grow louder as they move upward. They move out of sight. There is a sound as of a wild wind music screaming down and then a silence. SELINA runs in from above and kneels rocking below. She still has the doll.*)

SELINA: I can't. I can't go with them. God help me. I can't go. What do I do? What happens to me now? Jacques. Jacques LaRange.

(SELINA *moves off stage in despair, the doll hanging from her hand. The lights change and the three old women take the stage again.*)

SELINA: (*old*) And so I failed. I couldn't follow them. I ran back down thinking to find LaRange to warn him not to come this way, thinking to beg him to take me away where I could bear his child, but when I tried to speak he turned away. I was left shamed. And so he rode here in the dawn to see them hanging like ripe fruit, like dolls. They say he ran across the hills pursued by demons, fell into madness until one day he died. They say too he went back to his own country but I don't know what happened. (*Drums and wind music come in behind* SELINA'S *speech and the young* SELINA *appears from time to time playing out some of her life as if it were a dream or shadow dance.*) My child was born dead and when I buried it I thought to bury this doll too, but something held me back. Instead I took a rock and smashed its face. And I lived on and on. But some part of me stayed here watching me live my life out.

YOUNG SELINA: I stayed on and watched you.

SELINA: Watched me turn from the scorn in the people's eyes.

YOUNG SELINA: Watched when you moved to town.

SELINA: I lived a bad life in town. And when my youth was gone

YOUNG SELINA: I watched you creep back to the old cabin across the river

SELINA: I dug for roots, fished, found the old medicine and spells. They called me. . .

YOUNG SELINA: Crazy Selina. Part of me stayed here. . . with them.

SELINA: Watched these hands become twisted, listened to the words and curses.

YOUNG SELINA: And the dreams.

SELINA: And the dreams.

YOUNG SELINA: It was I who dreamed.

SELINA: Then I got Lucy. I was an old woman when my niece died but the Chief let me take her child to raise because he owed me for curing his son of a sickness. I was alive in Lucy. I, an old woman, was alive in Lucy. And the part of me that stayed here with them became dim as a drift of smoke. (*The* YOUNG SELINA *freezes*) Lucy was small and wild, swift-footed, graceful as a willow, warm as sunlight. We lived there in a cabin by the river and the voices here grew softer and the part of me that stayed here was dim as a drift of smoke or mist. But one day in winter Lucy slipped away, went to the town to hunt for something else, a locket, a life. She was fifteen. One morning her bed was empty and she was gone and though I begged her, she wouldn't come back again. And then they killed her. And now I hear her voice crying with their voices on every wind that blows. (*Once more the* YOUNG SELINA *moves forward as if beckoning and calling, watching.*) And once more one part of me stands outside this skeleton, this dried flesh and watches while I—

YOUNG SELINA: Live out day after day.

SELINA: Until tonight! Tonight I come back to this ground and I will be paid back until the very hills whisper the story. (*There is a wail of wind song and the* YOUNG SELINA *moves part way up towards the high rock and freezes.*) And you will be witness. Listen. Do you hear a wagon creaking along the old road, Celestine?

CELESTINE: I hear it.

SELINA: The wagon will stop just below here. Soon my nephew's son and his friend will leave the wagon and slip away from here.

Gwen Pharis Ringwood

MARTHA: What do you do, Selina?
SELINA: Two of the men who killed Lucy Johnny are tied down in the wagon.
CELESTINE: No, old woman. They are in jail for a long time yet.
SELINA: These two came back last week. Our young men saw them, heard them talking as if nothing had happened. My nephew's son saw and heard them and he came and told me and swore he'd kill them, but I said "No. . . we have had enough of courts and judges. Bring them here and I will do the rest." And now he and his friend bring the two tied and bound in that wagon.
MARTHA: You will bring the police on us, Selina.
SELINA: No.
CELESTINE: You will take their lives for Lucy Johnny's life?
MARTHA: You are mad, Selina. I'll have no part in this. I'm going out of here, away.
MARTHA: You will stay, Martha. You will help me. Swear you will tell my story. Celestine.
CELESTINE: I'll tell it.
SELINA: And you.
MARTHA: Why do you not tell your own story as you told us?
SELINA: I do not go back down to the reserve with you. I have lived with the spirits for too many years and tonight I join them here. Tonight I will no longer be a life that's split in two. Swear, Martha, if you would sleep at night.
MARTHA: I swear.
          (*There is a low call off stage.*)
SELINA: So, they have come. My nephew's son and his friend will leave now. No one must know they brought the wagon here. The friend is your grandson, Martha. Now we go down and do what we must do.
CELESTINE: I will not kill for you or Lucy Johnny.
SELINA: No killing. The two are sleeping. . . I saw to that. When they wake, they will be less than men. Gelded. They will be free to watch themselves live out their empty lives. Then I am paid back for Lucy's dying. This is Ellen's knife. You will whisper what you have heard tonight, and what we do. Swear you will make it known among the people.
          (*The* YOUNG SELINA *moves to the top of the rise, and stands immobile.*)
YOUNG SELINA: And the people will sing our names.
          (*The drums and chant rise and fall away as the lights go down and the wind music rises and fades.* SELINA *raises the knife, then deliberately throws down the doll. It is the last thing shown on stage. Curtain.*)

The End

Bibliography

Primary Works

Typescripts of plays and some other materials mentioned in the bibliography, and the Ringwood correspondence, 1936-81, are held in the Special Collections Division, University of Calgary Library, Calgary, Alberta.

"Afterwords," *Atlantis: a Women's Study Journal/Journal d'études sur la femme*, v. 4, no. 1, Fall 1978, pp. 164-165. Prose poem.

"Anchor to Northwards," Typescript, 1955. Radio play. Not produced. The voyage of Captain Cook.

The Bells of England, Typescript, 1953. Radio play. Produced CBC Radio National Network, May 7, 1953. To commemorate the coronation of Queen Elizabeth II.

Books Alive, Typescript, 1951. School script. Produced CBC Radio, Edmonton, Dec. 1951. For young audience.

"Carrie," Typescript, circa 1977. Short story. Never submitted.

Chris Axelson, Blacksmith 1938. *Collected Plays*. Stage play. Produced Chapel Hill, N.C., by Carolina Playmakers, May 26, 1938.

"Christmas, 1943," Typescript, 1943. Long verse read at Edmonton University Women's Club, 1943.

"Clock Time," Typescript. Never submitted. Tribute to Einstein, written soon after his death.

Coffee House Sketches. Typescript and *Collected Plays*. Various short sketches and plays produced in Williams Lake. Latest produced in 1970 under title *Encounters* and included *Wail, Winds Wail* and *Compensation Will Be Paid*.

Compensation Will Be Paid, 1970. *Collected Plays* Coffee House sketch.

The Courting of Marie Jenvrin; a comedy of the far North, 1941. *Carolina Playbook*, Dec. 1941; Mayorga, M. ed., *Best One Act Plays of 1942*, N.Y.: Dodd, Mead, 1943; Jones, E.M., ed., *Canadian School Plays*, series one, Toronto: Ryerson, 1948; Selden, S., ed., *International Folk Plays*, Chapel

Hill, N.C.: Univ. of N. Carolina Pr., 1949; [Edition], N.Y.: S. French, 1951; Ross, J.M. [et al] eds., *Adventures in Reading*, N.Y.: Harcourt, Brace, 1952; Richards, Stanley, ed., *Canada on Stage; a collection of one-act plays*, Toronto: Clarke, Irwin, 1960, pp. 90-125; *Collected Plays*. One act stage, family. First produced Banff School of Fine Arts, Aug. 25, 1941.

Dark Harvest; a tragedy of the Canadian prairie, Written Chapel Hill, N.C., 1939. Brodersen, George, ed., *[Title]*, Toronto: Thos. Nelson, 1945; *Canadian Theatre Review*, v. 5, Winter, 1975, pp. 70-128 (rev. version); *Collected Plays*.
Three act stage, full length treatment of some elements in *Pasque Flower*. Rev. 1945 after first production, University of Manitoba Dramatic Society, Jan. 17, 1945. Produced CBC Radio, Wednesday Night, Sept. 12, 1951.

"The Day the Loons Came Back," Typescript. Never submitted. Children's story.

The Days May Be Long, 1940. *Collected Plays*. One act, stage.

The Deep Has Many Voices, 1969. *Canadian Drama*, Fall, 1980; *Collected Plays*. One act. First production CBC Shoestring Theatre, 1969. Rev. version for the opening of Centennial Park and Gwen Ringwood Theatre, Williams Lake, B.C., 1971.
Earlier title: *The Edge of the Forest*.

The Dragons of Kent, Typescript, Edmonton, University of Alberta, Dept. of Extension, 1935.
One act stage, for young audience. First produced Banff School of Fine Arts, 1935. Rev. 1980.

The Edge of the Forest, see *The Deep Has Many Voices*.

"Encounters," Typescript, 1970. *Coffee House Sketches*, written in Williams Lake, includes *Wail, Winds, Wail*.

"Elizabeth Haynes and the prairie theatre." Typescript. Essay.

"Excursions" or "Think of it as a challenge." Ms. Essay.

The Face in the Mirror, see *Widger's Way*.

The Fight Against the Invisible, Typescript, 1945. Produced CBC Radio, Western School Network, Science Series Script, 1945.

A Fine Coloured Easter Egg (The Drowning of Wasyl Nemitchuk), 1949. ed., *Prairie Performance*, ed., Diane Bessai. Edmonton: Newest, 1980; *Collected Plays*.
One act stage, first produced Banff School of Fine Arts, August 11, 1950. Radio version produced CBC Radio, Edmonton.

Frontier to Farmland, Typescript, 1952. Radio play. Western school network, CBC, 1952.

The Furies, 1981. *Collected Plays*. One act stage. Prod. June 1982, Univ. of Victoria.

"A gallery of faces." Typescript. Essay.

"Generra." Typescript. Essay.

"Get Along Little Dogie," *Wide Open Windows*, Toronto: Copp Clark, 1947. Short story.

The Garage Sale, 1981. *Collected Plays*: One act stage. First produced at the New Play Centre at the Waterfront Theatre, Vancouver, April 21-25, 1981, Du Maurier Festival of One Act Plays, directed by Jace Van der Steen.
Radio version produced CBC Vancouver for Saturday matinee, May 24, 1981, directed by Ron Solway, National Network.

584

The Golden Goose, 1973. In: [Title], Toronto: Playwright's Co-op, 1979. One act stage, for young audience.

Hatfield, see *The Rainmaker*.

Health Highway Series, Typescript, 1952. Produced CBC Radio Vancouver 1952. Includes *Rhymes and Fables for a Wise Child*. School network scripts about health.

Heidi, Typescript, 1959. Adaptation of novel, *Heidi*, in thirteen episodes. Broadcast CBC Toronto 1959.

"Home Base," Family Herald, 33, 27 Sept. 1962, pp. 62-63. Short story.

Indian trilogy. Includes: *The Stranger*, 1971; *Lament for Harmonica*, 1959; and *The Furies*, 1981. Prod. June 1982 Univ. of Victoria.

The Jack and the Joker, 1943. *Collected Plays*. One act stage. Produced Banff School of Fine Arts, 1944. Radio version CBC Winnipeg.

Jana, see *The Stranger*.

Lament for Harmonica (Maya), 1959. *Ten Canadian Short Plays*, ed. John Stevens. New York: Dell, 1975; *Collected Plays*.
One act stage. First prize in 21st annual playwrighting competition sponsored by Ottawa Little Theatre, 1958/59. First produced by Ottawa Little Theatre, 1959.
Television production CBC TV Shoestring Theatre, Montreal, Feb. 14, 1960. CBC radio production directed by Tom Kerr, 1979.

"The Last Fifteen Minutes," *Stories with John Drainie*, ed. John Drainie, Toronto: Ryerson, 1963, pp. 36-41. Short story.

"The Lion and the Mouse," Typescript, 1964, rev. 1980. Stage play, one act, for a young audience.

"The Little Ghost," Short story.

"Weary," *Canadian Short Stories*, Oxford.

"Little Joe and the Mounties," Family Herald, n.d. Children's story.

The Lodge, 1977, rev. 1978, 1979. *Collected Plays*. One act stage. First produced West Vancouver Little Theatre, 1977. Placed third in Smile Theatre Competition, 1980.

Look beyond You, Neighbour, Typescript, 1961. Musical play. Commissioned as a celebration of 50th anniversary of Edson, Alberta, railway town. First produced Edson High School Auditorium, Nov. 2-5, 1961. Produced at Studio Theatre, Edson, May 31, 1962 for meeting of Commonwealth Education delegates, 1962. Music by Prof. Chet Lambertson, Victoria, B.C.

"Ludmilla's Odyssey (Scenes from a country life)," Typescript. Begun as *Report to Kazantzaklos*, a collection of short pieces, myth, memory, humour. Includes *An Appetite for People*; *A State of Grace*; *The Ne'er Do Wells*; *The Bells*; *Red Light District*; *Venus Arising*; *The Columbines*; and others. Begun 1976, in progress.

The Magic Carpets of Antonio Angelini, 1976. *Kids' Plays*, Toronto: Playwright's Press, 1980. One act comedy for young audiences. First production, Winnipeg Multicultural Festival, June-July, 1976, directed by Jean Louis Hébert, St. Boniface. First place Multicultural National Theatre Competition, 1976.

Maya, see *Lament for Harmonica*.

Mirage, 1979, rev. 1980. *New Canadian Drama-2*, ed. Patrick O'Neill. Ottawa: Borealis Pr., 1981; *Collected Plays*.
Long play, one act. First produced May-June, 1979, Greystone Theatre, University of Saskatchewan, commissioned by Tom Kerr, for Learned Societies' meetings. Revived in new version for tour of Saskatchewan's 75th anniversary celebration, 1980. Performed at Canadian Multicultural Theatre Festival in Edmonton, July 17 and 18, 1980, with direction for the tour and Edmonton performance by Tom Kerr for the University of Saskatchewan Summer Stock Theatre.
Music for the 1979 production by Gary Walsh and Alvin Cairns, for 1980 by Rick Fox. Music by Rick Fox may be obtained for a fee from the composer, Canadian Equity Association.

"Mr. Finburley and the Nesting Swallow," Typescript, never submitted. Short story.

"Mr. Gunderson and the President of the Republic," Typescript, circa 1952. Never submitted. Short story. Harry Truman incident.

New Lamps for Old. Ms burned. Twenty play series for CKUA Radio 1936-37. Ten by Mrs. Ringwood, ten by Elsie Park Gowan.
Titles: "Beethoven, the Man who Freed Music;" "Christopher Columbus;" "Florence Nightingale;" "Galileo, Father of Science;" "Henry, The Navigator;" "Nansen of the North;" "Oliver Cromwell;" "Socrates, Citizen of Athens;" "Threat to Planet Earth;" "Valley of Ignorance."

"Niobe House," Typescript. Radio play.

"Oh Canada, my country." Typescript. Poem.

Father of Science;" "Henry, The

One Man's House, 1937. *Collected Plays*. One act stage. First produced Univ. of North Carolina, Dec., 1937, and April 20, 1938.

Pageant for Young Canadians. School pageant produced in Edmonton in late forties. Included poem *Oh Canada, My Country*.

"Pascal," Typescript, 1968-70. Alternate title: *You Walk a Narrow Bridge*. Novel.

Pasque Flower; A Play of the Canadian Prairie, 1939. Koch, Fred H., ed., *The Carolina Playbook*, Chapel Hill, N.C.: Univ. of N. Carolina Pr., v. 12, no. 1, 1939; *Women Pioneers*, ed. Anton Wagner. Toronto: CTR Publications, 1980, pp. 184-204 (Canada's Lost Plays, v. 2); *Collected Plays*.
One act stage. Predecessor of *Dark Harvest*. First production at North Carolina Playmaker's Theatre, Chapel Hill, N.C., March 2, 1939.

"The Percolator," Typescript, 1976-77. Never published. Short story.

"Plans for a light-hearted novel." Typescript. Essay.

"Portrait of a Woman (Miriam at the Window)," Typescript, mid-1950s. Never submitted. Some material from *Portrait* used in *The Deep Has Many Voices*.

"A polished performance." *Creative writing*, CBC Vancouver, 1954. Children's play.

"The potato puppet twins." Ms. A Children's play.

"Questions (Lines written for my granddaughter soon to be 13)," *Atlantis; a Women's Study Journal/Journal d'études sur la femme*, v. 6, no. 2, Spring, 1981. pp. 134-135.

The Rainmaker, 1944. [*Title*], Toronto: Playwright's Co-op, 1975, 30p.; *The Developing Mosaic*, ed. Anton Wagner. Toronto: *Canadian Theatre Review Publications*, 1980, (*Canada's Lost Plays*, v. 3); *Collected Plays*.
One act stage. Story of Hatfield of Medicine Hat, commissioned under the Alberta Folklore and History Project. First produced Banff School of Fine Arts, Aug. 22, 1945.

Red flag at Evening, 1939-40, Rev. 1980. *Collected Plays*. Short sketch for use as acting material in classes and variety productions. First produced Youth Training Schools, Edmonton, 1939.

A Remembrance of Miracles, 1975-79. *Collected Plays*. Long play. Produced CBC radio, 1979. Also stage version extant.

"*Restez, Michelle, Don't Go*," 1977. Short story. Read by Dorothy Davies, early 1977. CBC.

Rhymes and Fables for the Wise Child, see *Health Highway Series*.

Right on Our Doorstep, Typescript, 1952. Radio play. Broadcast Western Canadian school broadcasts, 1952.

"*The road.*" *Tribune*. (Williams Lake, B.C.) 1958 Centennial edition. Poem.

The Road Runs North, Typescript, 1967. Full length musical play, music by Art Rosoman. Commissioned for Centennial celebration in Williams Lake, B.C. First produced Williams Lake Junior High School, June 7, 1967, through week-ends to July 2, 1967.

Rundle Pageant, 1940. Outdoor show produced spring 1940, commemorating Rundle's missionary service in Edmonton area, at request and with collaboration of Rev. Berry, Edmonton.

"Salute to Stalingrad," Typescript. Verse. Allied Arts' Council program read on radio.

"Sammy Joe and the Moose; a Chilcotin Tale," [Title]. Drawings by Joe Poole. [n.p.], c1973. Alternate title: *Some People's Grandfathers*.

"Sandy," 1937. *Carolina Playbook*, Fall 1937. Poem.

"Saturday Night," 1940. Typescript, Edmonton: Univ. of Alberta, Dept. of Extension 1940; *Collected Plays*.
Short sketch for stage for use as acting material in class and variety productions.

The Sleeping Beauty, 1965. *My Heart is Glad*, Book II, Williams Lake: 1965; [Title], Toronto: Playwrights' Co-op, 1979.
First produced Cariboo Indian School, Williams Lake Festival, 1965.

"*So Gracious the Time*," Typescript. Williams Lake, 1954. Short Christmas story. Radio version read by Claire Drainie on C.B.C. National network, Christmas, 1954.

"Some People's Grandfathers (Give them cigarettes to smoke)," *Family herald*, no. 3, 31 Jan. 1963, p. 44. Children's story.

"Some memories of the theatre in Alberta." Typescript. Essay.

"Some tall tales from the Alberta hills." Typescript. Essay.

Stampede, 1945. *Collected Plays*. Three act stage. First produced by University of Alberta Drama Society, March, 1946, directed by Sidney Risk. Produced Banff School of Fine Arts 1946, directed by Sidney Risk, and Banff School 25th anniversary directed by Esther Nelson.

Still Stands the House, 1938, Chapel Hill, N.C. *The Carolina Playbook*, v. 11, no. 2, June, 1938; *American Folk Plays*, ed. F.H. Koch, N.Y.: Appleton-Century, 1939; *Argosy to Adventure*, ed. C.L. Bennett, Toronto: Ryerson, 1950; [Title], Toronto: S. French, 1955; *Eight One-act Plays*, Toronto: Dent, 1966; *Encounter: Canadian Drama in Four Media*, ed. Eugene Benson. Toronto: Methuen, 1973; *The Prairie Experience*, ed. Terry Angus. Toronto: Macmillan, 1975; *Transitions I: Short plays*, ed. Edward Peak. Vancouver: Commcept Publishing, 1978; *Literature in Canada*, eds. Douglas Daymond, *et* al. v. 2, Toronto: Gage, 1978; Ford, Theresa M., ed., *Panorama*. Edmonton: Alberta Education, 1979; *Collected Plays*.
One act, adult, stage and radio. First produced Carolina Playmakers, Chapel Hill, N.C., March 3, 1938. First prize for native Canadian play, Dominion Drama Festival, 1939.

The Stranger, 1971. *Canadian Drama*, v. 5, no. 2, Fall, 1979; *Collected Plays*. One act stage. First produced Gwen Ringwood Theatre, Williams Lake, June 19, 1971.

"Supermarket," Typescript, circa 1950. Never submitted. Short story.

The Three Wishes, Typescript, 1965. One act children's, stage. First produced Williams Lake, Christmas, 1965.

"Tree House," Typescript. Never submitted. Short story.

"The Truth about the Ten-Gallon Hat," Typescript, late 40s. Written with Elsie Park Gowan.

"Upland Game," Typescript, 1976/77. Never submitted. Short story.

"The Voyages of Captain Cook," Typescript, 1955. One act, radio.

"Wail, Winds, Wail," 1970. *Collected Plays*. One act, stage.

The Wall, 1950. *Collected Plays*. One act radio, musical play. Music by Bruce Haak. Produced CBC Radio, Winnipeg, and Edmonton, 1953.

"The well adjusted parent." Typescript. Essay.

Widger's Way, 1952. [Title], Toronto: Playwrights' Co-op, 1976; *Collected Plays*. Full length stage, comedy. Commissioned and produced by Robert (Imbert) Orchard. First produced University of Alberta, Studio Theatre, Edmonton, Alberta, March, 1952 and toured for Maytime Tours. Produced Dec. 3, 1959, by Williams Lake Players' Club, Williams Lake, B.C., under title *The Face in the Mirror*. Produced Kawartha Festival, Summer 1976.

Younger Brother, N.Y.: Longman's Green, 1959. 213p. Novel for young reader. Radio version by George Salverson, ten episodes, CBC, 1960.

Secondary Works

"Alberta writers," *Alberta Folklore Quarterly*, v. 1, no. 1, March 1945, pp. 27-28.

Anthony Geraldine. *Gwen Pharis Ringwood*. Boston: G.K. Hall 1981. (Twayne World Authors series). Notes, references, secondary sources, pp. 171-185.

―――. "Gwen Pharis Ringwood," *Stage voices: twelve Canadian writers talk about their lives and work*, ed. Geraldine Anthony. Toronto: Doubleday Canada, 1978. pp. 86-89, 105-107.

―――. "Gwen Pharis Ringwood," *Newsletter of the Association for Canadian Theatre History*, v. 3, no. 1, Sept. 1979. p.12.

―――. "The Magic Carpets of Gwen Pharis Ringwood," *Canadian Children's Literature*, nos. 8/9, 1977.

―――. "The Plays of Gwen Pharis Ringwood: an appraisal," *Atlantis: a Woman's Studies Journal/Journal d'études sur la femme*, v. 4, no. 1, Fall, 1978. pp. 132-141.

―――. "The Ringwood Plays of Social Protest," *Canadian Drama*, v. 5, no. 2, Fall, 1977.

Benazon, Michael. "Ringwood's Saskatchewan mirage," *Canadian Theatre Review*, no. 24, Fall, 1979, pp. 122-123.

Bessai, Diane. "Prairie Playwrights and the Theatre," *Prairie Performance*, ed Diane Bessai, Edmonton, NeWest Press, 1980. (Prairie Play Series, no. 3), pp. 176-191.

Brodersen, George L. "Gwen Pharis — Canadian dramatist," *Manitoba Arts Review*, v. 3, no. 5, Spring, 1944.

Conference across a continent. Toronto: Macmillan, 1963.

Gowan, Elsie Park. "History into theatre." *Canadian Author and Bookman* 51:1, Fall 1975, 7,8.

"Gwen Pharis Ringwood: Alberta graduate", *Gateway* (University of Alberta) 35:17, 15 Feb. 1945.

Hinchcliffe, Judith. "Still Stands the House: the Failure of the Pastoral Drama," *Canadian Drama*, v. 3, no. 2, Fall, 1977.

Jones, Emrys. "Courting of Marie Jenvrin,"*Winnipeg Tribune*, 1941.

Kerr, Tom. [Talk] *Newsletter of the Association for Canadian Theatre History*, v. 3, no. 1, Sept., 1979. p. 13.

Koch, Frederick H., ed. *American Folk Plays*. New York: Appleton-Century, 1939, p. xvi.

―――. "Canadian frontier theatre: the fourth summer of playmaking at Banff," *Carolina Playbook*, v. 13, no. 4, Dec. 1940.

―――. "Folk Drama Defined," *Carolina Playbook*, v. 12, no. 3, Sept. 1939, p. 68.

―――. "From farthest North," *Carolina Playbook*, v. 14, no. 4, Dec. 1941.

―――. "Playmaking at Banff," *Carolina Playbook*, v. 10, no. 3, Sept. 1937.

―――. "Western Canada: a new playmaker from the Alberta prairie," *Carolina Playbook*, v. 11, no. 2, June 1938.

Noonan, James. "A review of Stage Voices," *Queen's Quarterly* 86:2, 1979, pp. 362-64.

Orchard, Imbert. "Widger's Way," *Edmonton Journal*, 12 March 1952.

Pasque Flower, [Review] *The Daily Tar Heel*, v. 47, no. 123, March 3, 1939, p. 2.

Peck, Edward, ed. "On Still Stands the House," *Transitions 1: Short Plays*, Vancouver: Commcept Pub., 1978.

Ringwood, Gwen Pharis, [Article] Stage voices: twelve Canadian writers talk about their work, ed. Geraldine Anthony. Toronto: Doubleday Canada, 1978, pp. 90-105.

_____. "The adjuticator says," *Gateway*, 35, no. 17, 15 Feb. 1945, pp. 4-5.

_____. "She demanded greatness," *Remember Elizabeth*. Edmonton: University of Alberta Pr., 1974, pp. 5-6.

_____. [Talk]. *Newsletter of the Association for Canadian Theatre History*, v. 3, no. 1, Sept. 1979, pp. 11-12.

_____. "Theatre rededicated." *Carolina Playbook*, 11, no. 4, 1938, pp. 111-14.

_____. "Women and the theatrical tradition," *Atlantis,* v. 4, no. 1, 1978, pp. 154-158.

Thompson, Bruce. [Review], *Williams Lake Tribune*, 23 June 1971.

Tovell, Vincent M. "Drama," *University of Toronto Quarterly*, xvi, April, 1947, pp. 264-268.

Ursell, Geoffrey Barry. *A triple mirror: the plays of Merrill Denison, Gwen Pharis Ringwood and Robertson Davies*. Winnipeg: University of Manitoba, 1966. (Canadian theses on microfilm: TC722).

Wagner, Anton, ed. [Bibliography] *The Brock Bibliography of Published Canadian Plays in English*, 1766-1978. Toronto: Playwright's Press, 1980, pp. 267-269.

_____. [Bibliography] "The developing mosaic: English Canadian drama to mid-century," *Canadian Theatre Review Publications*, Toronto, 1980. pp. 196-197. (*Canada's Lost Plays*, v. 3).

_____. [*Introduction*] "Women pioneers," Toronto: *Canadian Theatre Review Publications*, ed. Anton Wagner, Toronto, 1979, pp. 184-185. (*Canada's Lost Plays*, v. 2).

_____. "Gwen Pharis Ringwood Rediscovered." *Canadian Theatre Review*, no. 5, Winter, 1975, pp. 66-123. Includes note by Mrs. Ringwood, script of *Dark Harvest* and Bibliography by A.W., pp. 68-69.

Date Due